W9-BUO-624

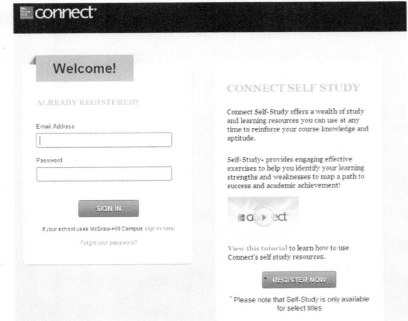

connect

Welcome!

CONNECT SELF STUDY

Connect Self-Study offers a wealth of study and learning resources you can use at any time to reinforce your course knowledge and aptitude.

Self-Study• provides engaging effective exercises to help you identify your learning strengths and weaknesses to map a path to success and academic achievement!

connect

View this tutorial to learn how to use Connect's self study resources.

REGISTER NOW

* Please note that Self-Study is only available for select titles

Help   Exit

connect

Student Registration

Tell us your email address

We'll check to see if you already have a McGraw-Hill Education account and show you your registration options. ⊠ Our Privacy Policy

Email Address:

Example: jcoe@email.com

Cancel   Submit

Help   Exit

Student Registration

Have a registration code?

Enter your registration code below. You'll find your code on a card that either came with your textbook or that you purchased separately.

Registration Code:

☐ - ☐ - ☐ - ☐ - ☐   Submit

Examples: 6RFU-BYHA-6MYJ-FGMK-F9XA

How to register with a registration code | View sample registration card

Don't have a code?

Buy access online

No registration code, no problem. You can buy access to Student Self Study right now. All you need is a credit card.

VISA MasterCard   Buy Online

NORTHERN ARIZONA UNIVERSITY

Department of English

University Writing Program

Northern Arizona University
PO Box 6032
Flagstaff, AZ 86011-6032

928-523-4911
928-523-7074 fax
www.nau.edu/english

Dear Student,

Welcome to ENG 105!

As you may know, ENG 105 is the class that most students take to fulfill NAU's first-year writing requirement.

We've designed the course to help you learn about and to construct *academic* writing, the kinds of writing you will do in your other NAU classes (and which you'll also do once you graduate). The classroom activities you'll do, the writing assignments you'll construct, and the textbook you'll use in ENG 105 are all designed to help you *after* you graduate, too, in your personal, professional and civic lives. After all, while you'll be at NAU for four or five years, you'll spend the next 40 or 50 years of your life involved with — and writing in — the professional, personal, and civic aspects of your life.

Those of us who teach in NAU's Writing Program believe that writers learn to write effectively by receiving rhetorical instruction about audience, purpose, process, and so on, and then by drafting, getting useful, thoughtful feedback from a range of readers on their writing, and then by revising (often several times) their initial drafts, working to more effectively accomplish a specific rhetorical purpose for a specific audience, in a particular context.

In your ENG 105 class, you'll read effective examples of the kind of writing we'll ask you to construct, and to spend some time analyzing how those models "work" to accomplish their own rhetorical goals—that will help you understand how writing functions to accomplish a specific task for a particular audience, within a specific context.

We also want you to become a proficient reader of your own writing (putting yourself into your audience's place, so to speak), so you can learn how to effectively revise your own texts (both in ENG 105 and in your other classes). And we want you to learn how to accept and effectively use feedback from others as well as practicing writing in a range of genres.

And of course, we want to help you to learn how to find, evaluate, and integrate the thoughts and ideas of others into your own writing (and to cite those ideas appropriately and correctly).

We've designed ENG 105 to help you learn about—and more importantly, to **do**—all of the above. And please note that ENG 105 is a **four credit-hour class**—so you can expect to do more work than you would in a three credit-hour class.

Sincerely,

Gregory R. Glau, PhD
Associate Professor and Director, University Writing Program
Northern Arizona University
Department of English - PO 6032
Flagstaff, AZ 86011-6032
Office: 928 523 6713   Fax: 928 523 7074

1A

Students please note: the information below includes parts of our standard ENG 105 syllabus, writing prompts, etc. Your instructor will give you a handout showing all due dates, etc. – a daily schedule of what is expected and when it is due. And, if your teacher modifies any of the information below, he or she will give you a handout reflecting those changes.

FYLi First Year Learning Initiative	**English 105, Section _____** **Critical Reading and Writing in the Academic Community** Semester: _____ Instructor: _____ Meeting Times: MTWTh _____ Office: _____ Student Consultation Hours: _____ and by appointment
	→ ALL SUBJECT TO CHANGE ←

Course Description

English 105 is a four-credit-hour survey course that introduces you to critical reading and writing in the academic community. Throughout the semester we practice the *reading process*: generating questions or deriving answers from texts; summarizing texts; identifying examples, drawing inferences, and making logical or comparative connections; organizing information in a variety of ways; seeing and learning rhetorical skills used by effective writers; and evaluating the merits of what we read. At the same time, we practice the *writing process*: identifying audience and purpose; gathering or finding ideas; organizing and interrelating those ideas for readers; drafting in order to develop, support, and illustrate ideas; revising from trial-and-error and in light of peer input; editing for clarity and accuracy.

Course Goals

- To introduce fundamental writing principles used in academic settings
- To understand the connections between critical reading and writing skills through close attention to the production and interpretation of texts
- To apply critical reading and writing skills to formal writing tasks, including an extended writing project
- To develop technological literacy skills to rhetorically analyze online resources based on the audience addressed, the purpose explored, and the language used

To help achieve these broad course goals, the Writing Program at NAU subscribes to the "Outcomes Statement" produced by the national Council of Writing Program Administrators. This statement describes the common knowledge, skills, and attitudes sought by first-year composition programs in American postsecondary education.

We believe that learning to write is a complex process, one that is both individual and social, and something that takes place over time with continued practice and informed guidance.

At the end of this semester, you will be asked to submit a complete writing portfolio—electronic copies of final drafts of all of the major writing projects that you construct in ENG 105. Along with those copies, we will ask that you construct a reflective letter about your work in ENG 105—an analysis and summary of that work in which you will provide specific details and examples about your writing over the semester. In effect, this reflective letter will be an argument: here is what I learned about writing, and here are some examples I can point to, in my portfolio, that exemplify and show what I mean.

The "Outcomes Statement" includes five broad categories, so your reflective letter will be read based on how you demonstrate your knowledge about:

2A

Rhetorical Knowledge
Possible questions for you to focus on, in your reflective letter:
- What examples in your portfolio demonstrate that you can focus on a purpose?
- What in your portfolio demonstrates that you can respond to the needs of different audiences and rhetorical situations (including using conventions of format and structure appropriate to the rhetorical situation)?
- What can you point to that demonstrates your use of appropriate voice, tone, and level of formality?

Critical Thinking, Reading, and Writing
Possible questions for you to focus on, in your reflective letter:
- What in your portfolio demonstrates that you can use writing and reading for inquiry, learning, thinking, and communicating?
- What can you point to that shows how you understand a writing assignment as a series of tasks, including finding, evaluating, analyzing, and synthesizing appropriate primary and secondary sources?
- What examples can you cite where you integrate your own ideas with those of others?

Processes
Possible questions for you to focus on, in your reflective letter:
- How can you demonstrate that it usually takes multiple drafts to create and complete a successful text?
- How can you show that you are able to develop and use flexible strategies for generating, revising, editing, and proofreading?
- What examples can you point to and/or cite to show that you've learned to effectively critique your own and others' work?

Knowledge of Conventions
Possible questions for you to focus on, in your reflective letter:
- What can you point to where to demonstrate the appropriate means of documenting your work, as well as controlling such surface features as syntax, grammar, punctuation, and spelling?

Composing in Electronic Environments
Possible questions for you to focus on, in your reflective letter:
- How can you demonstrate that you can effectively use electronic environments for drafting, reviewing, revising, editing, and sharing texts?
- What can you point to in your work that demonstrates that you can effectively locate, evaluate, organize, and use research material collected from electronic sources, including scholarly library databases; other official databases (e.g., federal government databases); and informal electronic networks and internet sources?
- What can you cite that shows your effective use of visuals in your texts?

Textbook for ENG 105
Roen, Duane, Gregory R. Glau and Barry M. Maid. *The McGraw-Hill Guide: Writing for College, Writing For Life* (Special Edition for NAU). McGraw-Hill, 2013. Note that your book will include a code for the online handbook, *Writing Matters*. This handbook will be available to you for **four years** from the date when you register it.

Assignments
- **Reading:** During the semester we will read a variety of texts. You, as an individual, will also research and read sources to support an extended argument paper. Reading assignments may involve various response activities--for instance, summaries, critiques, self-evaluations, quizzes, reaction writing about specific questions, and so on.

- **Writing:** During the semester expect to write both in and out of class.

Grading breakdown:

**Class work, reflection papers, participation in class discussions and group
activities, peer editing, Research Logs, etc.**   **25% (of total grade)**

> *Out-of-Class Writing* will involve drafting and revision to produce the following:

- **Writing Project # 1:** a short, polished essay that shows your skill in **rhetorical analysis** writing (approximately three to five typed, double-spaced pages). You also will reflect on your writing following this project.   **10%**

- **Writing Project # 2:** a short, polished essay that shows your skill in **evaluative** writing (approximately three to five typed, double-spaced pages). You also will reflect on your writing following this project.   **10%**

- **Writing Project # 3:** a short **informational argument** that shows your understanding of an issue or question or problem: **what are the various "sides" to the topic?** (three to five typed, double-spaced pages). While you may or may not be "neutral" in this paper (you can argue a side), you **must cover** the various "sides" to the issue you're focusing on. This gives you the chance to kind of "examine the conversation" that is going on, about the issue or problem, and you need a minimum of six (6) sources for this project. You also will reflect on your writing following this project.   **15%**

- **Writing Project # 4:** a **prospectus** and **annotated bibliography** that shows your research and preparation for your extended argument paper: "here is what I've read (annotated bibliography) and what I plan to argue (prospectus) for my extended argument paper"
                                                                 5%

- **Writing Project # 5:** Your prospectus and annotated bibliography lead into the **extended argument** paper **(20%)**, where you pick a side and construct an effective argument involving library research that showcases your understanding of critical reading, writing, and argumentation skills (eight to ten typed double-spaced pages + individual presentation/discussion) **(5%)**. You also will reflect on your writing following this project.   **25%**

- **Writing Project # 6:** a polished essay that shows your skill in **reflecting** on your experiences in English 105 (approximately four to six typed, double-spaced pages).
                                                                 10%

Grading
Assignments in English 105 will be evaluated according to the following criteria:
- "A" work is excellent work that fulfills assignment criteria with exceptional skill, quality, style, persuasiveness, or sophistication
- "B" work is good work that meets assignment criteria
- "C" work is acceptable work that meets assignment criteria but contains notable flaws you should have remedied in planning, drafting, revising, or conferring with your instructor
- "D" work is poor work that does not meet assignment criteria
- "F" work is poor work filled with numerous severe flaws

Calculate your grade on the familiar 100-point scale:
90-100 is A, 80-89 is B, 70-79 is C, 60-69 is D, 59 and lower is F.

The first version of each essay will be discussed in small group workshops and your teacher will comment on your writing in conference. You then will revise this essay into a final draft, often working through several workshop versions, using the suggestions you received as a starting point for the final version. Remember: writing is never "done" the first time; (re) vision means (re)seeing . . . (re)cognizing . . .

4A

Portfolio: At the end of the semester you are required to submit a portfolio (your essay assignments) in **electronic copy** to your instructor. **Make sure that you save all your work on disk in case you lose your hard copies.** *Please note:* To pass English 105, you must also submit a completed writing portfolio, which will be kept in the University Writing Program office. Your electronic portfolio must include final copies of

- Writing Project # 1 – Rhetorical Analysis
- Writing Project #2 -- Evaluation
- Writing Project # 3 – Informational Argument
- Writing Project # 4 – Prospectus, Annotated Bibliography
- Writing Project # 5 -- Extended Argument
- Writing Project # 6 – Final Reflection
- The permission form, electronically signed by filling in your name and checking a box on the form

Technological Literacy: English 105 incorporates computer literacy as an integral part of teaching critical thinking, reading, and writing skills. Our work with Blackboard Learn and other forms of technology are not intended to teach you computer skills, but are intended to teach you to look more critically at how technology influences our understanding of the writing process and our thinking about reading and writing in a technology-supported environment. Just about everyone works in a technologically-rich environment and your work in ENG 105 will help you prepare not only for the rest of your college career, but for the rest of your life. A research instruction module developed by Cline Library is available in our BB Learn shell, which will help you make the most of the depth of research materials Cline provides to NAU students.

Attendance
English 105 heavily depends on classroom activities--workshops, discussions and brainstorming sessions, impromptu writing, group preparation for writing assignments -- so your attendance is very important. When you miss class, you not only miss information important to your success, but you jeopardize the collaborations among students that this course depends on: part of the class goes missing with you. Therefore, if you miss too many class sessions, your grade will be lowered or you will fail the class.

You are allowed **four absences** without penalty: save those for the unexpected or unavoidable.

*Each unexcused absence beyond those four will cost you **three percent** of your overall course average.* While 3% doesn't seem like much, missing only few extra class days over the semester can easily drop you a whole letter grade – **missing a week's worth of class will drop your final grade by 12%.**

While class attendance is required as noted, please be cautious about attending class if you are feeling ill. Please inform your teacher by phone or email if you are feeling unwell; if you are experiencing flu-like symptoms, you should not attend class; please take precautions not to infect others, and seek medical attention if your symptoms worsen.

Please note that you need a doctor's note to verify any absence that you want to be excused: **Doctor's notes must be approved by the Director of the University Writing Program. The student must meet with the Director and teacher and submit the doctor's note for verification as soon as possible after any absence for which you want to be excused. Bringing in doctor's notes after classes have ended for the semester will not excuse your absences.**

You will not be penalized for missing class is you have an **institutional excuse** (this means you are attending an event as a representative of the university. There are three types of institutional excuses.

- The Academic institutional excuse is approved by the Dean of the College and is for students participating in a scheduled class activity outside of normal class meeting times and similar kind of events.
- The Extracurricular institutional excuse is approved by the Dean of Students and is for students participating in sanctioned and approved events of student organizations and non-NCAA athletic competitions.

- The Athletic institutional excuse is approved by the Vice Provost for Undergraduate Studies and is for students participating in NCAA sanctioned events.

<u>Students are responsible</u> for notifying class instructors and showing them a copy of the institutional excuse at least 5 working days (or one class period if the class meets less frequently than every five days) prior to start of the time period it covers. Class instructors are not required to honor institutional excuses presented to them less than the stipulated time period stated in the previous sentence. It is recommended that athletes, at the beginning of the semester, provide their faculty a schedule of all events in which the team will be participating for which an institutional excuse will be granted. <http://www.cefns.nau.edu/faculty/documents/StudentInstitutionalExcuses.doc>

To accommodate students who participate in university-sanctioned activities, we offer sections of this course at various times of the day and week. We have asked advisors across campus to help students enroll in appropriate sections. If you think that this course may conflict with a university-sanctioned activity in which you are involved—athletics or the debate team or whatever--please see me after class today.

Note: If you are more than 15 minutes late to class, your teacher will count you absent for this class session. If you are 5-15 minutes late to class, your teacher will count this as being tardy. Being tardy four times will count as an absence.

Always, and this holds true for all of your classes, if you know that you'll be absent, contact your teacher and ask about making-up any missed work and assignments.

Office Hours/Conferences
Your teacher will have open office hours and will let you know when those are. He or she will also make an appointment with you if you cannot stop by during office hours. The office hours are posted on your teacher's office door. If your teacher's office is located in Peterson Hall, note that Peterson Hall does not have elevators. If you are unable to walk up stairs, please let your instructor know so you can arrange an alternate meeting place.

Late Writing Projects
Do not turn your Writing Projects in late, unless you negotiate with your teacher BEFORE the due date-- NEVER on the same day a Writing Project is due. Writing Projects that are late will be marked down **10 points** for each <u>day</u> they are late. As with the attendance policy, your teacher will not vary on deducting for late Writing Projects, no matter what "excuse" you might have.

Topic selection: Please note that your teacher can restrict what topics you might write about (some of us get tired reading papers on this or that topic). Please also note that you cannot change your paper topics without your teacher's approval. **If you do change topics without your teacher's approval you will receive an F for the paper.**

If your teacher is absent: If your instructor needs to cancel class because his or her car broke down, or if he or she is ill, etc., your teacher will try to get someone to post a sign. He or she also will try to email you all, before class. However, if you come to class and your teacher is not here by the time 15 minutes has elapsed (from when class is to start), please assume that class is cancelled.

Manuscript preparation: Please consider <u>every</u> piece of writing you do for this class to be "public property." We will discuss your writing in both large and small groups. Several times during the semester, you will be asked to duplicate your Writing Project for your writing groups (approximately four copies). If you do not have hard copies of your papers on the day when those papers are due so your workshop group members can get them in class, **you will lose one letter grade from the final grade for that paper**. Even if you post copies on BB Learn later that day, or send them through email later to your group members, <u>if you don't have the hard copies in class, your final grade for the paper will be lowered by one letter grade</u>.

ALL VERSIONS of ALL Writing Projects, **except research logs**, must be typed, double-spaced. Please do not use cover sheets (let's save trees) or binders.

The public nature of class writing and discussions: Part of becoming a good writer is learning to appreciate the ideas and criticisms of others, and in this course our purpose is to come together as a writing community. Remember that you will often be expected to share your writing with others, so avoid writing about things that you may not be prepared to subject to public scrutiny, or things you feel so strongly about that you are unwilling to listen to perspectives other than your own. This does not mean that you are not entitled to an opinion but that you adopt positions responsibly, contemplating the possible effect on others.

Class Procedures: For every class period, there will be reading assignments. We will discuss and/or write about these texts in detail, so be sure to read them and annotate carefully, so please remember to bring your textbook to class each day.

For most class periods, you will have a **Research Log (RL)** entry. Each entry in your Research Log should be dated and be about 200 words long (1 typed or 2 handwritten pages). Most often, you will annotate and respond to the readings in your Research Logs. Research Logs will be graded on a √+, √, and √- basis. Generally, research logs will move you up or down about half a letter grade. That is, if most of your Research Logs are √+, then they'll help you if you're close to the next higher grade. If many are √, and you're "between grades," you'd probably receive the lower grade for the class. Average research logs, marked with a √, will keep you about the same. Your teacher strongly, <u>strongly</u> recommends that you put a lot of time and effort into your Research Logs--and in the end, it will help you construct better Writing Projects. <u>RESEARCH LOGS MUST BE TURNED IN THE DAY THEY ARE DUE.</u>

Please also keep a copy of any Writing Project you turn in, for your own files. You'll need them for the final portfolios in ENG 105 and also if you want to file a grade appeal. Please also note: when you turn in the final version of any Writing Project, you must also <u>turn in all earlier versions</u>, including notes, peer review comments, outlines, etc.

Plagiarism
Plagiarism is a form of theft. It is grounds for failing the course. Plagiarism occurs when a writer uses someone else's phrasing, sentences, or distinctive insights without giving proper credit. Be sure to acknowledge your sources! In this age of downloadable papers, remember that turning in work that, in whole or in part, is not your own is also plagiarism. When in doubt about quotation, citation, or acknowledgment of sources, see me. Note that we will implement a system through BB Learn called *SafeAssign*, which will allow you to check your papers for phrases, sentences, etc. that come from another source, <u>before</u> you turn in the final version. Therefore, all of your papers should be cited accurately and completely.

Other notes:
Please feel free to say anything you wish in class; your teacher will. At the same time, your teacher will respect you as adults and will expect you to treat the others in the class the same way. This might seem a minor point, but you will be doing a lot of commenting on your classmate's Writing Projects, and it's important to always be considerate as well as honest. Your instructor will call on everyone equally, whether you raise your hand or not, so know in advance that you will be expected to talk in class. Finally, remember the 6 Ps.

<u>Connecting to the rest of the university</u>

ENG 105 is a foundation requirement of NAU's Liberal Studies Program

As an NAU student, you need to know how to produce effectively written, thoughtful texts if you are to succeed in your NAU classes and beyond, in your professional, personal, and civic lives.

The Mission of NAU'S Liberal Studies Program is to prepare students to live responsible, productive, and creative lives as citizens of a dramatically changing world. To accomplish this mission Northern Arizona University provides a Liberal Studies Program that challenges students to gain a deeper understanding of the natural environment and the world's peoples, to explore the traditions and legacies that have created the dynamics and tensions that shape the world, to examine their potential contributions to society, and thus to better determine their own places in that world.

The Principles to Guide the Development of Student Learning Outcomes are:

- To understand natural processes and the fragility of the earth's environment (you may, with your teacher's approval, chose to focus on, research, and write about environmental issues in ENG 105)
- To understand the world's peoples and their diversity (the readings in the ENG 105 textbook, along with other readings your ENG 105 teacher may ask you to read, will give you a sense of cultural diversity)
- To understand the traditions and legacies that have created the dynamics and tensions that shape the world (as with issues affecting the environment, you may chose to research and write about large, world-shaping issues)
- To understand the potential for and limitations of technology to enhance human and other life (again, another useful and interesting subject to write about. In addition, you will use technology in many forms in ENG 105)
- To act upon the individual's responsibilities and connections to local, national, and global communities and environments (part of any writing task are the ethical aspects of any discourse, including correct and proper attribution of source materials)
- To practice the habits of an examined or self-reflective life to facilitate ethical and responsible living (a large part of ENG 105 is the reflective aspect, where your teacher will ask you to think about and reflect on all major writing assignments, as well as to construct an individual large-scale reflection about the class and your work in it)

ENG 105 is part of NAU's First Year Learning Initiative

 The First Year Learning Initiative (FYLI is grounded in the following three key areas:

- **Socializing students for excellence**
  FYLI courses establish the attitudes, skills, and behaviors that enable students to succeed in the first year and beyond. Critical aspects include increased rigor and excellence and providing effective scaffolding for students to succeed.
- **Design**
  FYLI courses maximize student engagement through critical design features. These include requiring substantial student engagement beginning in the first week, setting high standards, and effectively using the learning opportunities in both the classroom and in the co-curriculum.
- **Alignment**
  In FYLI courses, learning outcomes will clearly connect with the course's learning activities and assessments.

Campus Resources: There are many resources available at NAU, including

- The **University Writing Center** provides valuable resources for NAU students. Using proven techniques, The Writing Center (located in the North Student Learning Center, University Union, building 30, room 254) will empower students to become an effective, insightful communicator — a skill that's in high demand no matter what their field.

- **ENG 100:** The University Writing Program also offers a one-credit, one-on-one tutoring course, ENG 100, offered in the fall and spring semesters and available to any student, regardless of their major—ask your ENG 105 teacher for more information about ENG 100.

- **The Grade Performance Status (GPS) system:** GPS allows your professors to contact you (with a copy to your advisor) about any issues with your classroom performance. If you do get a GPS email, read and pay attention to it—it is your professor reaching out to help you succeed in his or her course.

- **Supplemental Instruction (SI)** is offered in some classes—ask your professor. SI provides group discussions that help students better understand course material, led by an SI Peer Leader, who is a student who has been previously successful in the course, attends the course again and holds weekly office hours and study sessions for that course and for that professor. They also work with the professor to better understand what concepts are being emphasized at a given time and what patterns of difficulty the students have had with the course material. This allows the SI leader to develop course-specific and instructor-specific study guides, quizzes, practice tests, etc. to share with students who attend the SI sessions. SI attendance is completely voluntary, as the emphasis is on helping students to become independent learners.

- **The Student Learning Centers (SLC)** are comprised of three different programs: the tutoring program, Supplemental Instruction and the Peer Jacks Mentoring program. The SLC's tutoring program has two different locations for individual appointments and several satellite locations for drop-in tutoring, including online tutoring. We serve students in a variety of subjects, but focus a great deal on Biology, Chemistry, Math, Engineering and Business courses. Tutors work with students on content, but also assist students in identifying various study skills that will strengthen their ability to be successful in the course. The SLC also offer a variety of skill based services such as study skills appointments and workshops that address things like test taking strategies, time management, writing at the university, as well as others. Our mission for the tutoring program is to help students become independent learners by working with them to meet the various needs they have. For more information and for a full listing of our study skills workshops, please visit http://home.nau.edu/edsup/slc/

- **LEADS Center** Leadership | Engagement | Achievement | Diversity | Service combines three campus departments to bring you the best in advising, mentoring, and cultural celebrations: **Leadership** - Peer mentors and staff to provide guidance and to encourage the development of talents; **Engagement** - Opportunities for active involvement in community; **Achievement** - Tools and resources to help students become responsible and independent learners; **Diversity** - An environment that values and supports students with different perspectives, experiences, and backgrounds; **Service** - Personal attention to individual needs - http://home.nau.edu/leads/

  - **Multicultural Student Center (MSC)** The **Multicultural Student Center (MSC)** serves a broad array of university students. Relevant transition services and support are provided for many first generation students including a growing number of historically underrepresented students. The MSC promotes student success through academic, personal, and cultural growth; provides an access point into the campus community; and develops leaders that enrich our diverse society. Services: Academic support, financial aid guidance, Peer advising, Cultural events and programs, Cultural and personal guidance, Career exploration, Social events and connections Service referrals. 523-5656. http://nau.edu/ims/

  - **Native American Student Services (NASS)** NASS provides support services to undergraduate and graduate students to help ease the transition to college and connect students to resources that help ensure academic and personal success. Services: Academic support;

Financial aid and tribal aid guidance; Cultural and personal guidance; Career exploration and preparation; Social connection and events; Peer mentorship and leadership opportunities 523-8086 http://nau.edu/nass/

- ○ **Student Support Services (SSS)** SSS provides one-on-one academic support and educational services to help assist students in adjusting to college life and the rigors of academic study. Services: Academic support; Tutoring and study skills building; Career/personal guidance; Financial aid assistance; Cultural and educational events. **To be eligible for SSS, students must be either:** low-income (Pell Grant eligible), first-generation to college, or registered with the office of Disability Resources. SSS, 523-6980 http://nau.edu/student-support-services/

- **Disabilities Resources** Section 504 of the Rehabilitation Act and the Americans with Disabilities Act requires that all NAU programs, services and facilities be accessible to individuals with disabilities, except where the action necessary to achieve accessibility would result in a fundamental alteration of the program or service or would impose an undue burden. Northern Arizona University is proactive in its dealings with students who have disabilities. Services are available for all NAU students who provide the required documentation and meet the eligibility standards set by Disability Resources in accordance with Section 504 and the A.D.A as amended. Services are designed to provide access to all programs, services and facilities in the most integrated setting appropriate to the needs of the qualified student with a disability. Accommodations are established on an individual basis, and are tailored to the needs of each student. http://www4.nau.edu/dr/

- **Gateway Student Success Center.** The Gateway Student Success Center is one of very few advising centers where advisors are cross-trained in both career and academic advising. Through this Gateway works to empower individuals to discover their passion and potential as well as pursue lives of purpose. The Gateway provides academic advising for undeclared students as well as all first year and transfer students with less than 24 units. Also available at the Gateway are Prelaw and Premedical assistance for all undergraduates, and career/employment advising for all current students, graduates, and alumni. http://www4.nau.edu/gateway/

(Thanks to Linda Shadiow for this list of resources and to Yvette Schmelzle for help with this project.)

Resource listing for lower division syllabi from University College

Resources for Student Success

Successful university students take advantage of services and resources designed to boost learning and achievement. NAU recommends that you begin with:

- **Supplemental Instruction**- attend these course-specific review sessions whenever offered; proven to reduce D's and F's
- **Student Learning Centers**- free drop-in, online, and individual tutoring appointments for math, writing, and over 100 courses; available Monday through Friday
- **ResourceConnect**- your online central navigation point for all NAU student resources

For a full listing of University College services visit: http://nau.edu/University-College/

FYLI
First Year Learning Initiative

Writing Sample: Finding out where you are as a writer

The essay your instructor may ask you to write for our "Writing Sample" is intended to show us where you are as a student writer.

Your teacher may have you respond to one or more of the brief statements in *This I Believe*, the book used by NAU Reads, or may ask you to respond to one of these prompts:

- **Academic Achievement vs. Age (Persuasive)**
  "School children should be grouped according to their levels of academic achievement rather than by their ages." Discuss the extent to which you agree or disagree with this opinion. Support your views with specific reasons and examples from your own experiences, observations or reading.

- **Achievements vs. Talents (Persuasive)**
  "Parents, teachers and employers should reward achievements rather than talents."
  Discuss the extent to which you agree or disagree with this opinion. Support your views with specific reasons and examples from your own experiences, observations or reading.

- **An A for Effort (Persuasive)**
  "Although some people argue that grades should be based entirely on students' level of mastery, rewarding effort will teach students the importance of hard work."

  Discuss the extent to which you agree or disagree with this opinion. Support your views with specific reasons and examples from your own experiences, observations or reading.

- **Cell Phone Jammers (Persuasive)**
  The use of mobile phones is discouraged in many public spaces, with varying degrees of success. If the technology were legal and available, should "jammers" be used?

If you would like help with your writing throughout the semester – whether you consider yourself a brilliant writer or a writer who is in the process of learning the tricks of the trade – ask your teacher about English 100, a one credit course that allows you to work with a writing consultant on a one-on-one basis.

Writing Project #1:
Rhetorical Analysis

The objective of this assignment is to enable you to write a well-constructed rhetorical analysis that makes a claim regarding the rhetorical tools exhibited in a text. Your instructor will provide you with information on what specific text(s) you will use for your analysis.

In a rhetorical analysis, you need to focus on some of the following aspects:
- Contextualize a piece of writing (author, audience, and purpose)
- Identify the structure of a piece of writing (chronological, cause/effect problem/solution, topical, etc)
- Identify the rhetorical appeals of a piece of writing (logos, ethos, pathos)

Research Focus
Crafting an effective text calls for a clear understanding of the research process. For each unit over the course of the semester, we will have a focus on various aspects of research, such as identifying sources, citing them, and incorporating quotes or paraphrases into your text, among many other things. For the rhetorical analysis, we will focus on becoming familiar with the following areas of research:
- General library introduction
- Specific information resources and retrieval tools
- Introduction to using information responsibly while appropriately citing research
- Knowledge of the detriments of plagiarism

Your essay should include the following parts:
- Introduction: this is where you introduce the text you will analyze and let your readers know what your standpoint on this text will be. Be sure to include an explicitly stated thesis.
- Body:
  - Contextualize: who is the author, who is the audience, what is the purpose?
  - Identify the rhetorical appeals, and/or
  - Discuss the structure of the argument
  - Provide examples from the text that support your thesis
  - Remember to keep your analysis as objective and rational as possible
- Conclusion: this is where you restate the claim you have made about the text and explain why your analysis supports that claim.

Length: three-five typed double-spaced pages.

Peer Review: all major writing assignments for ENG 105 are peer-reviewed, which means your classmates and teacher will give you comments and suggestions on how to improve your work—and you also will provide them with your comments and suggestions for improving their papers. Part of your grade for each writing project depends on the peer review suggestions you provide, as well as how effectively you use the suggestions you receive as you revise your own work.

Reflection: Your instructor may ask you to complete a series of reflective questions, once you're done with this assignment.

Writing Project #2:
Evaluation

The objective of this assignment is to construct a brief evaluation of a product, concept, performance, or service. As with any evaluation, the **criteria** on which you'll base your evaluation is critical, for in essence you are "matching-up" some item to a set of specific criteria—so the criteria you select and define is critical. Any criteria must be appropriate to the item you're evaluating (you will evaluate a backpack differently than you would evaluate, say, a bicycle).

Research Focus
Crafting an effective text calls for a clear understanding of the research process. For each unit over the course of the semester, we will have a focus on various aspects of research, such as identifying sources, citing them, and incorporating quotes or paraphrases into your text, among many other things. For the evaluation essay, we will focus on becoming familiar with the following areas of research:
- Exploring sources of information with an interdisciplinary mindset
- Incorporating multiple perspectives, drawing on and recognizing relationships among local, regional, and global perspectives
- Generating multiple options for search terms

Your essay should include the following parts:
- Introduction:
  - This is where you introduce the subject of your evaluation; generally, the more complex the subject, the more detailed and interesting your evaluation will be. This is where you also should at least list your criteria
- Body: This is where you will explain your criteria in detail, so readers can clearly understand on what basis you are evaluating your subject. Then you will explain how well (or not) the subject of your evaluation matches-up with your criteria. For example, you probably evaluated several colleges or universities before you decided to attend NAU. On what basis did you make your decision? That is, how did NAU "match up" in terms of criteria you may have used:
    - Tuition cost
    - Financial aid received
    - Living aspects
      - Dorm availability / quality / cost
      - Food availability / quality / cost
    - Location (how far from home)
    - Reputation
      - Class size
      - Class availability
      - Your major . . . And so on . . .
- Conclusion:
  - This is where you explain your conclusion for your evaluation: how the item/concept/performance, etc. "matches-up" with the criteria you decided on

Length: three-five typed double-spaced pages.

Peer Review: all major writing assignments for ENG 105 are peer-reviewed, which means your classmates and teacher will give you comments and suggestions on how to improve your work—and you also will provide them with your comments and suggestions for improving their papers. Part of your grade for each writing project depends on the peer review suggestions you provide, as well as how effectively you use the suggestions you receive as you revise your own work.

Reflection: There are reflection questions on pages 324-325 that your instructor may ask you to complete.

Writing Project #3:
Informational Argument

The objective of this assignment is to construct a short **informational argument** that shows your understanding of an issue or question or problem: **what are the various "sides" to the topic?** While you may or may not be "neutral" in this paper (you can argue a side), you **must cover** the various "sides" to the issue or problem or topic that you're focusing on. This gives you the chance to kind of "examine the conversation" that is going on, about the issue or problem. The more in-depth you can examine your topic, the better prepared you will be to construct an **extended argument**, should you choose to remain with the same topic.

Research Focus

Crafting an effective text calls for a clear understanding of the research process. For each unit over the course of the semester, we will have a focus on various aspects of research, such as identifying sources, citing them, and incorporating quotes or paraphrases into your text, among many other things. For the informational argument essay, we will focus on becoming familiar with the following areas of research:

- Developing and refining strategies to create and modify keywords lists for the research process.
- Selecting appropriate search engines such as Academic Search Complete, WorldCat, and subject specific databases.
- Evaluating sources individually, implementing criteria such as the currency, relevance, accuracy, authority, and purpose of the source in order to determine if it is appropriate to use for this project
- Properly citing and creating a Works Cited/References page using the MLA or APA styles of citation

Your essay should include the following parts:

- Introduction:
  - This is where you introduce the topic (problem or issue or question). If you want to present your information in a neutral manner (so your readers don't know which "side" you are on), that's fine. If you want to let your readers know what your stand is on this issue or problem is, that's fine, too. But be sure to examine all the sides, all the arguments, about your topic. You'll need at least **six (6) sources for** this project. Note that **visual aids** are critical to this assignment, so you will want to select, use, and discuss **at least two (2) visuals**: charts, photographs, maps, drawings, cartoons, graphs, etc. Be sure to explain and discuss them in your own text, so they connect to one or more of the various arguments you are discussing.
- Body:
  - This is where you discuss and write about and examine all the "conversation" that is going on about your topic. It's your opportunity to examine something that you are interested in, in depth, to really think about and consider all of the "arguments" that swirl around any controversial issue or topic. Remember that whatever "side" you come down on, you always want to present all arguments accurately and as completely as you can. For example, if you wanted to write about rising tuition costs, you'd want to consider
    - Are rising tuition costs really a problem? Why? For who?
    - How can you demonstrate or show the problem?
    - Does the problem exist elsewhere?
    - How do tuition costs here compare to tuition costs elsewhere? Are costs at community colleges increasing at the same rate as at the universities? Why or why not?
    - Who determines tuition costs?
    - How does the rate of change for tuition costs here compare to tuition costs elsewhere?
    - What does tuition pay for, anyway?
    - What do some of your friends have to say?

14A

- (and so on) (Note that the same kinds of questions could be asked for, say, textbook costs, or class fees, or housing costs, etc.)
- Conclusion:
    o This is where you briefly outline the topic and the arguments and conversations about it.

Length: three-five typed double-spaced pages.

Peer Review: all major writing assignments for ENG 105 are peer-reviewed, which means your classmates and teacher will give you comments and suggestions on how to improve your work—and you also will provide them with your comments and suggestions for improving their papers. Part of your grade for each writing project depends on the peer review suggestions you provide, as well as how effectively you use the suggestions you receive as you revise your own work.

There are peer review questions for the informational aspect of this paper on page 187.

There are peer review questions for the argumentative part of this assignment on page 271.

Reflection: There are reflection questions on pages 194-195 and on 278-279 that your instructor may ask you to complete.

Writing Project #4:
Prospectus and Annotated Bibliography

1. WHAT IS A PROSPECTUS?

A prospectus is a formal proposal for your final argument paper (250 words) in which you define the proposed topic for your final paper, explain why you chose the topic, discuss what you expect to find out by researching the topic, and, state your position on the argument, if you have one.

Topic selection
- You will need to choose a specific topic that will fit into the confines of the final research paper (8 – 10 pages). Try to pick a topic you are passionate about, but not so much that you cannot approach the topic even-handedly; remember you will be working with this topic for the remainder of the semester, so choose something that you won't lose interest in over the next few weeks. Ideally, you will work with what you already have some information about, from WP#3 that you just completed.
- You will need to ensure that your topic has at least two distinct, arguable sides.
- You will need to ensure that you will be able to find enough information (ten sources) about your topic.
- You will need to ensure that your topic is not overdone (like abortion, prayer in school, etc.)

Requirement for the prospectus
- You need to introduce your topic and while doing this try to answer: Why is this issue important? What is an ongoing argument about the topic? What can you add to the ongoing discussion? Why will it be worthwhile for you in particular to research this controversy?
- You need to outline your position if you have one (which side will you argue and what points, aspects will you focus on?) and provide the general reasoning behind your argument.

2. WHAT IS AN ANNOTATED BIBLIOGRAPHY?

An annotated bibliography is a list of citations of books, articles, and documents. Each citation is followed by a brief (usually about 150 words) descriptive and evaluative paragraph, the annotation. The purpose of the annotation is to inform the reader of the relevance, accuracy, and quality of the sources cited. Your annotated bibliography should include at least ten (10) sources. No more than four (4) of these may be web sources (web sources are those that exist solely on the Internet—like a web page with content that does not appear elsewhere in print. If you find a source that was originally printed (like an essay) but you download it from the web (through a library database, for example), then that is NOT a "web source").

Research Focus
Crafting an effective text calls for a clear understanding of the research process. For each unit over the course of the semester, we will have a focus on various aspects of research, such as identifying sources, citing them, and incorporating quotes or paraphrases into your text, among many other things. For the annotated bibliography and prospectus, we will focus on becoming familiar with the following areas of research:
- Identifying research needs in order to develop a research question.
- Understanding that there are specific resources for different information needs.
- Understand research and how different sources shape and support the components of a text.
- Integrating excerpts (quotes, paraphrases, visual aids, etc.) into texts appropriately.

THE PROCESS

Creating an annotated bibliography calls for the application of a variety of intellectual skills: concise exposition, succinct analysis, and informed library research.

1. Locate and record citations to books, periodicals, and documents that may contain useful information and ideas on your topic.
2. Briefly examine and review the actual items.
3. Choose those works that provide a variety of perspectives on your topic.
4. Cite the book, article, or document using **MLA or APA style**.
5. After the citation, write an annotation that includes information from each of the following four categories:

   - **Summarize**: Summaries should be at least 3 sentences. Address the main arguments. What is the point of this book or article? What topics are covered? If someone asked what this article/book is about, what would you say? The length of this summary will vary depending on the source.
   - **Assess/evaluate**: After summarizing a source, assess it. Is it a useful source? How does it compare with other sources in your bibliography? Ask how it fits into your research. How might it help you shape your argument? How does this work contribute to your understanding of your topic? Has it changed how you think about your topic and if so, in what way(s)?
   - **Evaluate credibility**: It is useful to mention why this particular author/organization is credible and applicable to the research you are doing. Is the information reliable? Is this source biased or objective? What is the goal of this source, do you suppose? Be sure to mention why you have decided to use the information from this source to add to your ethos.
   - **Excerpts**: List at least two excerpts from this source (e.g., photos, quotes, paraphrased material, graphs, charts, visuals) to include in your annotation. With each excerpt, please include an accurate in-text citation/parenthetical citation.

Peer Review: all major writing assignments for ENG 105 are peer-reviewed, which means your classmates and teacher will give you comments and suggestions on how to improve your work—and you also will provide them with your comments and suggestions for improving their papers. Part of your grade for each writing project depends on the peer review suggestions you provide, as well as how effectively you use the suggestions you receive as you revise your own work.

Part of Writing Project #5:
Extended argument in-class presentation

I'd like you to "present" in an informal way to your classmates, for about <u>five (5) minutes</u>, including class discussion time, about your topic and the research you've been conducting. This presentation will come after you've written an **informational argument**, which may have helped you decide what to focus on as you conduct research for your **annotated bibliography** and your **prospectus**, where you outline what you think your final paper will be about. The object of this assignment is to give a presentation that explains the issue that you are writing about, provides a context for that issue for your classmates, articulates what action you are arguing should take place and explains the support and counterarguments for that action.

One easy way to think about this presentation is in terms of your prospectus—you have already detailed many of these areas in your prospectus, so it may be good to start from that in preparing your presentation. Some areas that you may focus on are:

- Introduce your issue and provide an explanation of the issue, as well as a bit of context for the issue's importance in our society or an international society if that applies.
  - Why is it a problem?
  - Why should we care about it?
  - What aspects are there to it?
  - How complex is it?

  Examine whether your issue is a commonly known one, and consider providing an appropriate amount of context so that your classmates can fully understand your presentation.
- Present your call to action—what are you arguing should take place? How do you support this call to action? You may include quotes or statistics in this area to further strengthen the case that you are building.
- Present multiple perspectives on the argument: What are the benefits of each? The problems with each? The costs of each?
- For the discussion, make sure that you have a few questions for the class to consider in order to encourage lively debate. You are responsible for leading a good discussion, so having numerous questions ready will help to ensure a strong discussion session. Also, you are expected to participate in other people's discussion sessions, and not doing so will negatively affect your grade, so make sure that you note down interesting points or questions that you have during your classmate's presentations.

We'll spend several class days asking each of you to tell your classmates what your focus is, what your general argument is, and how the evidence that you've collected helps to support that argument. Your classmates will be encouraged to ask questions and to make suggestions.

You may consider using a form of technology (a PowerPoint presentation, digital story, etc.) to aid in your presentation, but it is not required.

Writing Project #5:
Extended Argument

The objective of this assignment is to construct an extended **argument** that (ideally) builds on the work you've done for Writing Project #3 (informational argument) and Writing Project # 4 (proposal and annotated bibliography). You also will "present" briefly in class, as part of this assignment.

The informational argument asked you to examine the various perspectives and arguments about some issue or problem. Writing Project #5 asks you to now **pick a side** and argue for that position. It also is critical to take "the other sides" into account (and refute them), as that will make your own argument more effective.

In an argumentative paper, you need to
- Make a specific claim with your thesis about what you are arguing **should happen** concerning the topic.
- Do research on who your audience is to help you determine the most effective way to convince that audience
- Choose a specific structure for your argument.
- Find **convincing reasons** to support your claim.
- **Adequately inform** your audience about the issue you are analyzing.
- Do research in order to justify your reasons, **read/evaluate** the material critically, and provide **sufficient evidence** for each reason.
- **Analyze** the opposing views and deal with them **honestly and fairly.**

Research Focus
Crafting an effective text calls for a clear understanding of the research process. For each unit over the course of the semester, we will have a focus on various aspects of research, such as identifying sources, citing them, and incorporating quotes or paraphrases into your text, among many other things. For this assignment, we will focus on using the information we find, in our own writing:
- Using and manipulating various information retrieval tools to select credible and appropriate sources.
- Integrating those quotations and paraphrases appropriately to support the writer's argument, with accurate MLA or APA citation throughout text and in Works Cited or References page.
- Note that **visual aids** are critical to this assignment, so you will want to select, use, and discuss at least two (4) visuals: charts, photographs, maps, drawings, cartoons, graphs, etc. Be sure to explain and discuss them in your own text, so they connect to one or more of the various arguments you are discussing, and be sure to cite them appropriately and accurately.

Your essay should include the following parts:
- Introduction: this is where you tell your readers what the essay is about. This is also where you need to make sure that you capture your readers' attention, provide background information, describe existing arguments and counterarguments, etc. *For this paper, your introduction need not be limited to a single paragraph.*
  - Thesis: this is where you establish your debatable claim. Make sure that your claim is very specific. Your thesis should include a brief outline of your whole paper and may appear somewhere within the first two pages of the essay, towards the end of your introduction.

- Body:
  - Each paragraph in the body of your paper needs to have a main point that you can support with specific evidence. That evidence must be cited appropriately and correctly. You should include appeals to ethos, pathos, and logos.
  - This is also where you outline opposing points of view—at least acknowledging them and, as appropriate, refuting those other claims.
- Conclusion: this is where you close your essay by briefly recapping your essay, describing its connection with similar issues, and stating the significance of your paper with future directions and implications of your research.
- Works Cited: The Works Cited page is not your annotated bibliography – it should follow proper MLA format for a Works Cited page and reference only the sources that you include in your essay. For this essay, you will need to include at least ten sources, at least five of which should be print sources. (Remember that web sources are those that exist solely on the Internet—like a web page with content that does not appear elsewhere in print. If you find a source that was originally printed (like an essay) but you download it from the web (through a library database, for example), then that is NOT a "web source" but rather a print source).

Length: eight to ten typed double-spaced pages.

Peer Review: all major writing assignments for ENG 105 are peer-reviewed, which means your classmates and teacher will give you comments and suggestions on how to improve your work—and you also will provide them with your comments and suggestions for improving their papers. Part of your grade for each writing project depends on the peer review suggestions you provide, as well as how effectively you use the suggestions you receive as you revise your own work.

Reflection: There are reflection questions on pages 420-421 that your instructor may ask you to complete.

Writing Project #6:
End-of-Semester Reflection

This assignment is intended to help you reflect *in very specific detail* on how your writing, critical thinking, critical reading, and visual literacy skills have developed over the course of the semester. Your audience for this project is your classmates, the NAU community, and me.

For this assignment, please both *inform* your audience on what you have learned and also *demonstrate* your learning by providing specific examples—in other words, cite your own work. The evidence for your thesis (main idea) comes from these experiences and the writing you constructed. Your argument needs to support or reveal your experiences to your readers—which you do by citing your own work, or pointing to specific examples in the papers you wrote for the class.

Remember that you can draw on the in-class reflections that you wrote.

In effect, this reflective letter will be an <u>argument</u>: here is what I learned about writing, and here are some examples I can point to, in my portfolio, that exemplify and show what I mean.

The "Outcomes Statement" (at the start of your ENG 105 syllabus) includes five broad categories, so your reflective letter will be read based on how you demonstrate your knowledge about:

Rhetorical Knowledge
Possible questions for you to focus on, in your reflective letter:
- What examples in your portfolio demonstrate that you can focus on a purpose?
- What in your portfolio demonstrates that you can respond to the needs of different audiences and rhetorical situations (including using conventions of format and structure appropriate to the rhetorical situation)?
- What can you point to that demonstrates your use of appropriate voice, tone, and level of formality?

Critical Thinking, Reading, and Writing
Possible questions for you to focus on, in your reflective letter:
- What in your portfolio demonstrates that you can use writing and reading for inquiry, learning, thinking, and communicating?
- What can you point to that shows how you understand a writing assignment as a series of tasks, including finding, evaluating, analyzing, and synthesizing appropriate primary and secondary sources?
- What examples can you cite where you integrate your own ideas with those of others?

Processes
Possible questions for you to focus on, in your reflective letter:
- How can you demonstrate that it usually takes multiple drafts to create and complete a successful text?
- How can you show that you are able to develop and use flexible strategies for generating, revising, editing, and proofreading?
- What examples can you point to and/or cite to show that you've learned to effectively critique your own and others' work?

Knowledge of Conventions
Possible questions for you to focus on, in your reflective letter:
- What can you point to where to demonstrate the appropriate means of documenting your work, as well as controlling such surface features as syntax, grammar, punctuation, and spelling?

Composing in Electronic Environments
Possible questions for you to focus on, in your reflective letter:

- How can you demonstrate that you can effectively use electronic environments for drafting, reviewing, revising, editing, and sharing texts?
- What can you point to in your work that demonstrates that you can effectively locate, evaluate, organize, and use research material collected from electronic sources, including scholarly library databases; other official databases (e.g., federal government databases); and informal electronic networks and internet sources?
- What can you cite that shows your effective use of visuals in your texts?

Your project should include the following parts:
- Introductory information: this is where you tell your readers what the reflection/argument is about. Provide a space that focuses your reader on the specific aspects you will discuss. In essence, you are going to create a statement of central focus (thesis) that tells your readers why you are going to discuss this specific aspect of your English 105 experience.
- Body: this is where you provide specific detail to illustrate the importance of your educational experience. You can write (visually enhanced) about a specific reading, an essay, a collaboration, a lesson, an exercise you did in class, using BB Learn, peer review comments (and what you did with them), etc. Make sure that each of your main ideas in this reflection is supported by examples (written and/or visual) or descriptive detail. For each skill or piece of knowledge that you include in your assertions, provide evidence that you have learned what you claim to have learned. The "evidence" that you provide will, of course, comes from the writing and other activities that you do this semester; use examples from those texts and activities to show what you learned.
- Conclusion: this is where you round up your reflection and make connections to the larger world. With this, you give your readers a sense of completion.

Length: 4-6 well-developed pages.

Peer Review: all major writing assignments for ENG 105 are peer-reviewed, which means your classmates and teacher will give you comments and suggestions on how to improve your work—and you also will provide them with your comments and suggestions for improving their papers. Part of your grade for each writing project depends on the peer review suggestions you provide, as well as how effectively you use the suggestions you receive as you revise your own work.

Peer Review
(courtesy of Erica Jones)

Lesson Objectives:

The objectives of this lecture are
- To gain an understanding of the most effective approaches to the peer review process
- To become familiar with the various tools available to aid in the peer review process

Peer Review
There are a few things to think about before beginning the peer review process. First, it is extremely important to be as specific as possible when responding to your peers' work. It is not helpful to give comments such as "It was good" or "I was confused." For every question that you answer in peer review, you should point to specific moments in the text. If you liked a specific paragraph, identify the paragraph and then describe what you liked about it. If you are confused by something in the text, identify the moment that confused you and then tell the author why you are confused. The more specific your feedback is, the more helpful it will be to the author of the essay.

Second, it can be awkward to give your peers feedback. Sometimes, if we are not confident in our own writing, it is difficult to give feedback to other people. We sometimes question whether our insights or suggestions are correct or even helpful. However, as a peer, you have a unique perspective to offer the author of the essay. You have read the same lectures, completed the same assignments, and are responding to the same prompt. Your insights and opinions are valid. You may even consider offering advice by relating some of your own experiences. For instance, if you notice that your peer is struggling with complete sentences, you may consider giving them information about how you make sure your sentences are complete—the more we learn about how other people approach the writing process, the more tools we have to choose from in our own writing process.

Third, there may be instances when you identify a moment in your peer's essay that seems awkward or wrong, but you're not sure what the problem is. Don't feel like you have to have all of the answers in peer review—it can be helpful just to point to a sentence and say "this doesn't seem right, but I'm not sure why." When you are able to offer suggestions or advice, by all means do. But please don't refrain from commenting on an area of text because you don't know how to improve it. Sometimes it's just helpful to have these moments identified.

Using Feedback
As if simply giving feedback wasn't enough work, once you get your responses from your peers, you have to decide what feedback you would like to incorporate into your revision, and what feedback you don't want to use. The first thing that I want to emphasize here is that the essay is, in the end, your essay. You need to take ownership of the revision process, and this means reading your responses with a critical eye. Don't just blindly accept every suggestion or response.

For all of the feedback that you get, you should first decide whether you understand what the reviewer was trying to say, and then decide whether you think it is helpful to the essay that you are trying to create. Maybe they're giving good advice, but they didn't understand what you were trying to say or do with a certain moment of your text. If this is the case, even if you don't take their specific advice, you should look at that moment and see how you can make your ideas more clear. Maybe you disagree with what the reviewer is saying, and that is fine. Or maybe the reviewer has given you great advice that you will incorporate into your revision process.

23A

If you don't understand a comment or suggestion that a reviewer made, feel free to ask them for more information, either through email or your group's discussion board.

One Last Thought About Peer Review
Sharing your work with other people can be an extremely intimidating thing. Because of this, it is extremely important that we are all respectful of each other's work as we go through the peer review process. Please keep all of your comments constructive and specific. You should never say something like "I don't like this," but instead should stay focused on *why* a specific moment is working. Is it confusing, or does it need more explanation? And always, when you have ideas, make suggestions for ways the author could improve the text.

Also, don't hesitate to point out what is working well. We can learn as much from hearing about moments that are clear, concise and interesting as we can by hearing about moments that are confusing. When we know what type of writing if most effective for our readers, we can gear the rest of our writing to more closely reflect those moments. Plus, it's always nice to hear positive feedback.

Sample Questions for Peer Review, Problem/Solution Essay

Author's Name: _____   Reviewer's Name: _____

How effectively does the introduction draw you into the paper? Why? Does it present all of the main ideas addressed in the essay? How might the introduction be improved?

Comment on the writer's focus. That is, how well does the writer stay on track or how much does the paper wander off course? If the paper loses focus, indicate where.

In the main part of the paper, are words or sentences that are confusing? Please highlight them in the author's essay and if possible, explain why they are confusing. Can you offer suggestions for improvement?

Are there any parts of the paper that could use more explanation or definitions?

Reread the conclusion. What could be added or changed to make it more effective? How well does it tie everything together? To what extent does it make you want to learn more about this topic?

Tools for using WORD for peer review (courtesy of Erica Jones)

Whenever we do peer review in this class, I will provide you with a series of questions to answer for each of your peers' essays. In addition to answering the questions, I will ask that you give your peers comments and suggestions throughout their essay. To do this, you will need to utilize two tools in Microsoft Word—the "Track Changes" function and the "New Comment" function.

Track Changes

Track Changes is a tool that highlights any changes that you make to the body of a text. To turn this tool on, you should first open your peer's essay. Then, you should click on the "Review" tab, which is towards the middle at the top of your screen. Almost immediately under the word "Review" you should see the words "Track Changes." If you click on this once, it will turn on. Then, you should just click on it again when you want to turn it off.

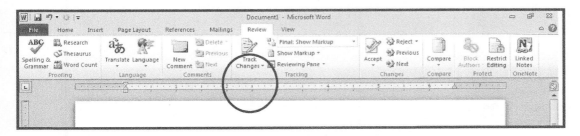

Once you turn this tool on, anything that you type or delete will be highlighted in red and underlined. If you change anything to the format of the paper, it will add a comment in the margin to describe the change that has been made. It will look something like this:

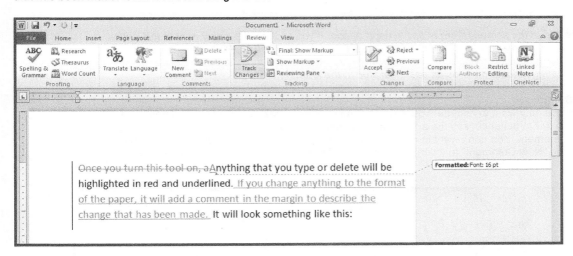

Also, notice that a line appears in the left side of your essay whenever a change is made. You will need to accept or reject every change in order to make the lines disappear. You should NEVER submit a final draft that still has any lines in the left margin.

25A

Accepting or Rejecting Format Changes (or, Getting Rid of all that Red)

Once you receive your essay back from your peers, you can either take their suggestions and manually make the changes in your own draft, or you can choose to use one of the drafts that your peers returned to you. If you have a response from a peer who has offered very helpful feedback, you may choose to simply accept or reject their changes and then continue your revision in that version of your essay. Accepting and rejecting changes is very easy. Simply move your mouse so that it is somewhere over the highlighted area, and then right-click. You'll be given a menu box with the options to either accept or reject the change. If you accept the change, your peer's suggestion will stay, but the font color will be changed to black and the underlining will be removed. If you reject the change, the text will revert back to your original text, the font color will be returned to black, and the underlining will be removed.

Note: At the top of the screen, there is an "Accept" option. If you click on the arrow next to this option, it will offer you the opportunity to "Accept All." PLEASE DO NOT USE THIS OPTION. An essential part of the peer review process is trying to understand why specific moments need to be revised. Blindly accepting all suggestions removes an essential step in the learning process.

Inserting Comments

Sometimes you may want to comment on a specific moment in the text without actually changing the body of the text. For instance, say the author says something really well, and you want to tell them that you like that moment. You don't want to change the text, so you should add a comment. To do this, you should use the "New Comment" function, which is located in the "Review" tab to the left of "Track Changes."

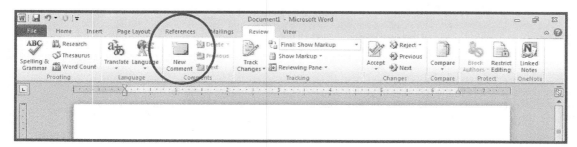

To begin, you'll highlight the section of text that you want to comment on. To do this, click your mouse at the beginning and then continue to hold the mouse button down as you drag your mouse across all of the text that you want to highlight. When you get to the end, release the mouse button and don't click anywhere else in the body of your text. Scroll your mouse to the review tab and click on it, then click on "New Comment." This will highlight all of the text you've selected and link it to a comment box. Then, just type your comment in the comment box.

If you need to delete a comment, simply right click over the comment box and the select "delete comment."

Note: There is a keyboard shortcut to adding a comment. Once you've highlighted the text, if you hit the control, alt, and "M" key all at the same time, it will add a comment to your highlighted text.

SAFE ENVIRONMENT POLICY

NAU's Safe Working and Learning Environment Policy prohibits sexual harassment and assault, and discrimination and harassment on the basis of sex, race, color, age, national origin, religion, sexual orientation, gender identity, disability, or veteran status by anyone at this university. Retaliation of any kind as a result of making a complaint under the policy or participating in an investigation is also prohibited. The Director of the Office of Affirmative Action & Equal Opportunity (AA/EO) serves as the university's compliance officer for affirmative action, civil rights, and Title IX, and is the ADA/504 Coordinator. AA/EO also assists with religious accommodations. You may obtain a copy of this policy from the college dean's office or from the NAU's Affirmative Action website nau.edu/diversity/. If you have questions or concerns about this policy, it is important that you contact the departmental chair, dean's office, the Office of Student Life (928-523-5181), or NAU's Office of Affirmative Action (928) 523-3312 (voice), (928) 523-9977 (fax), (928) 523-1006 (TTD) or aaeo@nau.edu.

STUDENTS WITH DISABILITIES

If you have a documented disability, you can arrange for accommodations by contacting Disability Resources (DR) at 523-8773 (voice) or 523-6906 (TTY), dr@nau.edu (e-mail) or 928-523-8747 (fax). Students needing academic accommodations are required to register with DR and provide required disability related documentation. Although you may request an accommodation at any time, in order for DR to best meet your individual needs, you are urged to register and submit necessary documentation (www.nau.edu/dr) 8 weeks prior to the time you wish to receive accommodations. DR is strongly committed to the needs of student with disabilities and the promotion of Universal Design. Concerns or questions related to the accessibility of programs and facilities at NAU may be brought to the attention of DR or the Office of Affirmative Action and Equal Opportunity (523-3312).

ACADEMIC CONTACT HOUR POLICY

Based on the Arizona Board of Regents Academic Contact Hour Policy (ABOR Handbook, 2-224), for every unit of credit, a student should expect, on average, to do a minimum of three hours of work per week, including but not limited to class time, preparation, homework, studying.

ACADEMIC INTEGRITY

Integrity is expected of every member of the NAU community in all academic undertakings. Integrity entails a firm adherence to a set of values, and the values most essential to an academic community are grounded in honesty with respect to all intellectual efforts of oneself and others. Academic integrity is expected not only in formal coursework situations, but in all University relationships and interactions connected to the educational process, including the use of University resources. An NAU student's submission of work is an implicit declaration that the work is the student's own. All outside assistance should be acknowledged, and the student's academic contribution truthfully reported at all times. In addition, NAU students have a right to expect academic integrity from each of their peers.

Individual students and faculty members are responsible for identifying potential violations of the university's academic integrity policy. Instances of potential violations are adjudicated using the process found in the university Academic Integrity Policy. The complete policy is in Appendix G of NAU's Student Handbook http://www4.nau.edu/stulife/handbookdishonesty.htm

RESEARCH INTEGRITY

The Responsible Conduct of Research policy is intended to insure that NAU personnel including NAU students engaged in research are adequately trained in the basic principles of ethics in research. Additionally, this policy assists NAU in meeting the RCR training and compliance requirements of the National Science Foundation (NSF)-The America COMPETES Act (Creating Opportunities to Meaningfully Promote Excellence in Technology, Education and Science); 42 U.S.C 18620-1, Section 7009, and the National Institutes of Health (NIH) policy on the instruction of the RCR (NOT-OD-10-019; "Update on the Requirement for Instruction in the Responsible Conduct of Research"). For more information on the policy and the training activities required for personnel and students conducting research, at NAU, visit: http://nau.edu/Research/Compliance/Research-Integrity/

SENSITIVE COURSE MATERIALS
University education aims to expand student understanding and awareness. Thus, it necessarily involves engagement with a wide range of information, ideas, and creative representations. In the course of college studies, students can expect to encounter—and critically appraise—materials that may differ from and perhaps challenge familiar understandings, ideas, and beliefs. Students are encouraged to discuss these matters with faculty.

CLASSROOM DISRUPTION POLICY
Membership in the academic community places a special obligation on all participants to preserve an atmosphere conducive to a safe and positive learning environment. Part of that obligation implies the responsibility of each member of the NAU community to maintain an environment in which the behavior of any individual is not disruptive. Instructors have the authority and the responsibility to manage their classes in accordance with University regulations. Instructors have the right and obligation to confront disruptive behavior thereby promoting and enforcing standards of behavior necessary for maintaining an atmosphere conducive to teaching and learning. Instructors are responsible for establishing, communicating, and enforcing reasonable expectations and rules of classroom behavior.

These expectations are to be communicated to students in the syllabus and in class discussions and activities at the outset of the course. Each student is responsible for behaving in a manner that supports a positive learning environment and that does not interrupt nor disrupt the delivery of education by instructors or receipt of education by students, within or outside a class. The complete classroom disruption policy is in Appendices of NAU's Student Handbook http://nau.edu/Student-Life/Student-Handbook/.

Effective Summer 2014
Approved UCC – 1/28/14
Approved UGC – 2/12/14

Where to find help in *The McGraw-Hill Guide:*

In the table of contents for Chapters 3 and 5–12, identify the chapter that corresponds to your writing assignment.

To set your writing goals, consider the guidelines that appear in the **Setting Your Goals** section of each chapter.

Where to find help in *The McGraw-Hill Guide:*

Chapters 3 and 5–12 are organized around four general writing goals:

1. To demonstrate **rhetorical knowledge**
2. To practice **critical thinking, reading, and writing**
3. To work through **writing processes**
4. To follow **conventions**

Successful writers adapt these goals to the particular needs of their situation. In Chapters 3 and 5–12 you will find clear guidance on how to think about the four goals and how to achieve them in relation to your specific assignment.

Where to find help in *The McGraw-Hill Guide:*

Chapters 3 and 5–12 all conclude with a guided **self-assessment** that will help you gauge how effectively your writing meets your goals.

THE McGraw-Hill
GUIDE

Writing for College, Writing for Life

With Additional Materials

THIRD EDITION

Duane Roen
Arizona State University

Gregory R. Glau
Northern Arizona University

Barry M. Maid
Arizona State University

Northern Arizona University

Mc
Graw
Hill
Education

2 3 4 5 6 7 8 9 0 QVS QVS 17 16 15 14

ISBN-13: 978-1-259-32823-7
ISBN-10: 1-259-32823-6

Learning Solutions Consultant: Adam Poston
Project Manager: Vanessa Arnold

Brief Contents

Contents

PART TWO   Using What You Have Learned to Share Information   74

PART FOUR | **Strategies for Effective Communication   422**

*"When I think about **achieving my goals,** I think about invention strategies to use, where I can find good ideas, whether I will need to conduct research, how I should organize my ideas, how my peers can help me improve my writing, and which writing conventions I need to check in my writing."*

"When I think about **assessing my goals**, I think about whether I attained the outcomes I hoped for and how my audience responded to my writing."

21 Writing about Visual Texts

SETTING YOUR LEARNING GOALS FOR WRITING ABOUT VISUAL TEXTS

 Rhetorical Knowledge

Writing about Visual Texts

Writing Assignment Options

 Critical Thinking, Reading, and Writing

Qualities of Effective Writing to Analyze Visuals

Reading to Learn about Analyzing Visual Texts

    WILL STOREY, REVISITING THE DAISY AD REVOLUTION (Visual Analysis)

    SEBASTIAN SMEE, FROM CHAOS, A SUSPENDED BEAUTY (Visual Analysis)

 Writing Processes

Invention: Getting Started • Organizing Your Ideas and Details • Constructing a Complete Draft • Revising

 Knowledge of Conventions

Editing • Genres, Documentation, and Format

 A Writer Achieves Her Goal: Ashley TenBrink's Visual Analysis

    ASHLEY TENBRINK, A RIDER FROZEN IN MOTION (Visual Analysis)

 Self-Assessment: Reflecting on Your Goals

22   Writing about Creative Works

SETTING YOUR LEARNING GOALS FOR WRITING ABOUT CREATIVE WORKS

 Rhetorical Knowledge

Writing about Creative Works

 Critical Thinking, Reading, and Writing

Writing to Learn about Literary Works

    JAMAICA KINCAID, GIRL (Short Story)

    AMY TAN, ALIEN RELATIVE (Short Story)

 Writing Processes

Selecting a Creative Work to Write About • Recording Your
Initial Responses • Finding a Feature to Analyze • Integrating
Visuals When Writing about Creative Works • Organizing
Your Ideas • Constructing a Full Draft • Revising

 Knowledge of Conventions

Editing • Genres, Documentation, and Format

 A Writer Achieves Her Goal: Katrina Montgomery's Final Draft

    KATRINA MONTGOMERY, INDIRECT CHARACTERIZATION IN JAMAICA
    KINCAID'S "GIRL" (Literary Analysis)

 Self-Assessment: Reflecting on Your Goals

Handbook

About the Authors

Duane Roen is Professor of English and Head of Interdisciplinary and Liberal Studies in the School of Letters and Sciences at Arizona State University, where he has also served as Director of Composition and Director of the Center for Learning and Teaching Excellence. Prior to that, he directed the Writing Program at Syracuse University, as well as the graduate program in Rhetoric, Composition, and the Teaching of English at the University of Arizona. Early in his career, he taught high school English in New Richmond, Wisconsin, before completing a doctorate at the University of Minnesota. In addition to more than 200 articles, chapters, and conference papers, Duane has published numerous books including *Composing Our Lives in Rhetoric and Composition: Stories about the Growth of a Discipline* (with Theresa Enos and Stuart Brown), *A Sense of Audience in Written Discourse* (with Gesa Kirsch), and *Views from the Center: The CCCC Chairs' Addresses, 1977–2005,* among others. Duane has served as Secretary of the Conference on College Composition and Communication (CCCC) and President of the Council of Writing Program Administrators (WPA). Duane's interest in family history has motivated him to construct a database that lists more than 32,000 of his ancestors and to collaborate with his wife, Maureen, to write more than 15,000 pages of journal entries about their two children, Nick and Hanna.

Gregory R. Glau is Director of the University Writing Program at Northern Arizona University. Previously, he was Director of Writing Programs at Arizona State University. Greg received his MA in Rhetoric and Composition from Northern Arizona University, and his PhD in Rhetoric, Composition, and the Teaching of English from the University of Arizona. With Linda Adler-Kassner of University of California—Santa Barbara, Greg is co-editor of the *Bedford Bibliography for Teachers of Basic Writing* (2001; 2nd ed., 2005); third edition 2010 (co-edited with Chitralekha Duttagupta of Utah Valley University). Greg also is co-author of *Scenarios for Writing* (Mayfield/McGraw-Hill, 2001). Greg has published in the *Journal of Basic Writing, WPA: Writing Program Administration, Rhetoric Review, English Journal, The Writing Instructor, IDEAS Plus,* and *Arizona English Bulletin.* Greg regularly presents at CCCC and has presented at WPA, MLA, RMMLA, the Western States Composition Conference, NCTE, and others. He (with Duane Roen and Barry Maid) is past managing editor of *WPA: Writing Program Administration.*

Barry M. Maid is Professor of Technical Communication at Arizona State University, where he led the development of a new program in Multimedia Writing and Technical Communication. He has spent most of his career in some form of writing program administration. Before coming to ASU, he taught at the University of Arkansas at Little Rock where, among other duties, he directed the Writing Center and the First Year Composition Program, chaired the Department of English, and helped create the Department of Rhetoric and Writing. He has written or co-authored chapters for more than a dozen books. His work has also appeared in *Kairos, Computers and Composition,* and the *Writing Lab Newsletter,* among other technology-oriented publications. More recently, Barry has co-authored articles on information literacy for library journals. His professional interests remain primarily in computers and writing, writing program administration (especially program assessment), and partnerships between academia and industry. Barry enjoys long road trips. Over the past several years, he has driven along the Pacific Coast Highway from Los Angeles to Oregon, through national parks in Utah, Arizona, Montana, and Wyoming, and through much of the Carolinas and Tennessee.

A Letter from the Authors

Becoming a writer is a lifelong journey. While this journey often begins in the classroom, it continues and changes throughout an individual's professional, civic, and personal life.

With *The McGraw-Hill Guide* students learn to apply a goals-oriented approach to any writing situation, making effective choices by asking three questions:

- How do I **set** my goals?
- How do I **achieve** my goals?
- How do I **assess** my goals?

Why a Goal-Setting Approach?

In our lengthy careers as writing program administrators and instructors, we have discovered that students are most successful when they have a clear idea about their writing goals. Consequently, we structured *The McGraw-Hill Guide* to help students set goals for their writing, use effective composing strategies to achieve those goals, and assess their progress toward achieving them. By understanding these goals, and the processes by which they can accomplish them, students are empowered to take ownership of their writing and their development as writers. In the short term, once they understand the underlying principles on which their writing is assessed—by assessing it themselves—the grades they receive from their instructors no longer seem arbitrary or mystifying. In the long term, students develop the strategies they need to support their writing development when they leave the classroom.

Goals Based on the WPA Learning Outcomes

The student writing goals in *The McGraw-Hill Guide* are drawn from the learning outcomes established by the Council of Writing Program Administrators because we know how important they have been in shaping discussions about writing curricula in the United States and other countries. These learning outcomes demonstrate the value of the full range of skills and knowledge that writers need to develop: rhetorical knowledge; critical thinking, reading, and writing; composing processes; knowledge of conventions; and composing in electronic environments.

The McGraw-Hill Guide Works

Two groundbreaking multi-institutional research studies illustrate the efficacy of *The McGraw-Hill Guide*.

- The MARC (McGraw-Hill Assessment Research in Composition) study showed that students who focused on the goal-setting approach of the *Guide* performed better across all outcomes than those who did not. These students outperformed their peers on average by the equivalent of a full grade point.
- The SCORE (Southern California Outcomes Research in English) study showed that students who used *Connect* also performed better across all outcomes and had superior gains in holistic scores than their peers!

We are proud of the fact that *The McGraw-Hill Guide* is the only product of its kind to have a research-proven track record of success. To review the evidence yourself, please visit **www.mhhe.com/hssl/roen**.

We hope you enjoy the time you spend with *The McGraw-Hill Guide*.

Sincerely,
Duane Roen
Gregory R. Glau
Barry M. Maid

How do I *set* my goals?

Research has shown that effective writers set goals that address the particular situation—the purpose, audience, and context—in which they are writing. With *The McGraw-Hill Guide*, instructors can help students understand and set their writing goals using the assignment chapters in Parts Two and Three (Chapters 5–12). Every chapter of the guide can be assigned and customized online—using only the material needed for any particular assignment. By following the unique structure of *The Guide*, students will be encouraged to:

SET	**How do I set my goals?** Setting Your Goals (p. 240)
ACHIEVE	**How do I achieve my goals?** Rhetorical Knowledge: Understanding the rhetorical situation for your project (p. 242) Critical Thinking, Reading, and Writing: Thinking critically about this type of writing (p. 246) Writing Processes: Establishing a process for composing your project (p. 260) Knowledge of Conventions: Polishing your work (p. 272)
ASSESS	**How do I assess my goals?** Self-Assessment: Reflecting on Your Goals (p. 278)

Preview each chapter.

Assignment chapters begin with newly expanded outlines that show students how that chapter will help them to set, achieve, and assess their writing goals.

Consider their writing goals.

The *Setting Your Goals* feature, located near the beginning of Chapters 3 and 5–12, introduces the foundational concepts that will guide students' writing—rhetorical knowledge, critical thinking, writing processes, and knowledge of conventions. Based on the WPA outcomes, these goals encourage students to create a framework for their writing assignments grounded in sound rhetorical principles.

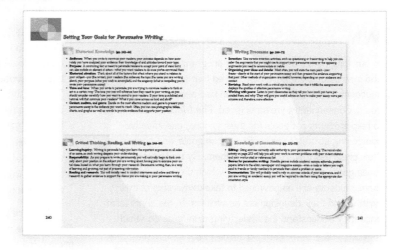

Scenarios for Writing | Assignment Options

Your instructor may ask you to complete one or more of the following assignments that call for persuasive writing. Each of these assignments is a *scenario*.

Writing for College

SCENARIO 1   **Academic Argument about a Controversial Issue**

What controversial issues have you learned about in other college classes? Here are some possibilities:

Writing for Life

SCENARIO 3   **Civic Writing: An Editorial about a Campus—Community Problem**

Every college campus has problems, ranging from scarce parking, to overcrowded computer labs, to under-age drinking, to too little community involve-

Consider contexts.

Recognizing that writing is a lifelong journey, *The McGraw-Hill Guide* gives students and instructors the option—and the flexibility—of responding to writing scenarios based on academic, professional, civic, and personal contexts. Customizable assessment rubrics are available online for each assignment, giving instructors the ability to show students how writing in different contexts can have an impact on their goals.

Let *CONNECT COMPOSITION* Help Your Students Set Their Goals:

McGraw-Hill's solutions are proven to improve student performance. Powered by a four-year student subscription to *Connect Composition 2.0, The McGraw-Hill Guide* incorporates groundbreaking adaptive diagnostic technology and a personal learning plan (PLP) that truly individualizes grammar instruction and helps improve student writing. *Connect* equips instructors and students with tools for practicing, sharing, posting, and assessing student writing and other composition coursework.

The *CONNECT COMPOSITION PLUS 2.0* eBook for *The McGraw-Hill Guide*, 3e

The *Connect Composition Plus 2.0* eBook provides *The McGraw-Hill Guide* content in a digital format that is accessible from within *Connect* and *Blackboard*. Students can link directly to activities and assignments within *Connect* from the eBook, giving them all the resources from *The McGraw-Hill Guide* right on their computer's desktop!

With digital tools developed by composition experts, *Connect Composition Plus 2.0* enables you to create a state-of-the-art teaching and learning environment that engages your students with their course assignments, including:

- Group assignments
- Discussion board assignments
- Blog assignments
- Writing assignments

Connect's Personal Learning Plan (PLP)

Through an intuitive, adaptive diagnostic that assesses proficiencies in five core areas of grammar and mechanics, students generate a personalized learning plan tailored to address their needs in the study time available to the student. The personalized program includes contextualized grammar and writing lessons, videos, animations, and interactive exercises, and it provides immediate feedback on students' work and progress.

Based on metacognitive learning theories, the Personal Learning Plan continually adapts with each interaction, while built-in time-management tools keep students on track to ensure they achieve their course goals. The Personal Learning Plan is designed to improve student writing while allowing instructors to focus on critical writing processes in the classroom. The Plan supports writing program goals with reports that present data related to student progress and achievement.

How do I *achieve* my goals?

After presenting the qualities of effective writing related to a particular purpose, each assignment chapter (3 and 5–12) then illustrates the steps of the writing process with clear examples of a student writer adapting to a specific writing situation. Designed to emphasize their goals as writers, each assignment chapter helps students to:

Emphasize critical thinking and synthesize information.

A new chapter (Chapter 3) on Writing to Understand and Synthesize Texts helps students develop the strong reading skills and ability to synthesize ideas from different sources they will need to achieve their writing goals. A section on "Synthesizing and Integrating Sources into Your Draft" appears in Chapters 6–12.

INTEGRATING SOURCES

Including Others' Perspectives in Narratives (p. 97)
Quoting Sources (p. 139)
Paraphrasing Sources (p. 181)
Incorporating Numerical Data (p. 224)
Incorporating Partial Quotes (p. 266)
Creating Visuals to Show Your Data (p. 311)
Summarizing Information from Sources (p. 356)
Including Research Information (p. 401)

Synthesizing and Integrating Sources: Incorporating Partial Quotes in Your Sentences

Often, your research will provide you with lots of quotations, which means you have to determine how to incorporate the quotations you want to use into your text. One way to use quotations, whether they come from a source you interviewed or from source you read, is to incorporate them into your sentences, a using a phrase such as "she said" or "Johnson comments":

> I interviewed Joy Watson and she said, "The recycling program is working."

Another method of incorporating a quotation is to integrate it into the structure of your sentence. For instance, in the following example, Santi DeRosa quotes Joe Watson from an article in the campus newspaper by integrating the quotation within his own sentence, and then he repeats part of the quotation that he wants to emphasize in his next sentence:

Strategies FOR Success: Openness

Successful writers are open to new ideas and a wide range of perspectives. In writing to convince, openness is especially important because readers are more likely to accept your ideas if they think that you are open-minded. As you consider other perspectives, think about how they compare and contrast with your own ways of looking at the world. How does viewing an issue from another perspective enable you to see the world in new ways? If you find a new idea easy to accept, why is that the case? If you find a new idea difficult to accept, why is that so? If a perspective differs from yours, what distinguishes the two? What are the points of agreement? How can the two perspectives be combined to form yet another way of looking at the world?

Develop strategies for success.

Based on the eight "habits of mind" that have been developed by the WPA, the National Council of Teachers of English (NCTE), and the National Writing Project and identified by the WPA as "essential for success in college writing," this feature offers students tips on how to develop their curiosity, openness, engagement, self-reflection, flexibility, creativity, persistence, and responsibility.

Choose the appropriate genre.

Ways of Writing tables present examples of different genres relevant to the chapter topic and describe their advantages and limitations. "Genres Up Close" provides a closer look at one genre relevant to the chapter's writing purpose. Genres covered include a literacy narrative, a profile, and a poster. An example of the genre follows each of these sections.

Ways of Writing to Analyze

Genres for Your College Classes	Sample Situation	Advantages of the Genre	Limitations of the Genre
Behavioral analysis	In your social psychology class, you are asked to construct a statistical analysis of the behavior in specific situations of male college students in groups, as compared to how they act individually in those same situations.	Your research and statistical analysis will provide your readers with useful information about behavior.	It is difficult to find enough reliable statistics for such an analysis; there sometimes are time constraints that limit your research.
Rhetorical analysis	Your writing professor asks you to analyze the rhetorical appeals on a Web site.	This analysis will help you to understand how a Web site appeals to its readers.	This is only one way to examine a Web site.
Nutrition analysis	In your health and nutrition class, your professor asks you to analyze several new diets.	You can provide useful information to readers.	Your analysis is not an evaluation of a diet, which often is what readers want.
Letter to your campus newspaper	Your ethics professor asks you to draft a letter to your college newspaper analyzing a campus problem.	Your college newspaper is a useful forum in which to publicize your analysis of the campus problem to the right audience.	A letter to the editor allows only limited space for your analysis. It might not be published.
Chemical analysis report	Your biology teacher asks you to construct a report on the toxicity of a specific group of chemicals when they are combined.	This report helps readers understand the interaction between chemicals. Such knowledge is critical whenever medicine is dispensed.	A chemical analysis report might not provide everything needed for your biology class.
Visual analysis	Your writing teacher asks you to analyze the visual features of advertisements for	A visual analysis will help you to understand that visuals can have as much impact on	A focus on visual elements can divert attention from verbal content.

Let CREATE's customizable resources help you achieve your program goals.

Your courses evolve over time, shouldn't your course material? With McGraw-Hill Create™, you can easily arrange and rearrange material from a variety of sources, including your own. You can select content by discipline or collection, including 4,000 textbooks, 5,500 articles, 25,000 cases, and 11,000 readings. When you build a Create book, you'll receive a complimentary print review copy in 3 to 5 business days or a complimentary electronic review copy (eComp) via e-mail in about one hour.

Go to www.mcgrawhillcreate.com and register today.

With Create you can:

. . . choose what you want from:

- *The McGraw-Hill Guide*'s print text chapters
- Two additional chapters (also available online through CONNECT)
- Any of the selections currently in the text
- A range of additional selections designed for the *Guide*

. . . choose which resources you want from:

- other McGraw-Hill collections such as *The Ideal Reader* (800 readings by author, genre, mode, theme, and discipline), *Annual Editions* (5,500 articles from journals and periodicals), *Traditions* (readings in the humanities), *Sustainability* (readings with an environment focus), *American History and World Civilization Documents* (primary sources including maps, charters, letters, memoirs, and essays)
- your own works, such as syllabi, institutional information, study guides, assignments, diagrams, artwork, student writing, art, and photos

. . . choose which format you want:

- Print
- Electronic

How do I *assess* my goals?

The McGraw-Hill Guide gives students experience evaluating the work of their peers and responding to others' evaluations of their own work through Writer's Workshop activities and online peer-reviewing tools. Then, by reflecting on the writing process, students assess themselves. To help students assess whether they have achieved their goals, *The McGraw-Hill Guide* encourages students to:

Learn effective strategies for assessing writing.

Throughout *The McGraw-Hill Guide,* students are shown how to assess writing critically and rhetorically—whether written by a professional, another student, or themselves. Framed in the context of the core outcomes of the course, this skill has been shown to improve student performance. A compelling assortment of both professional selections and student samples—60 percent of which are new to this edition—features authors such as Sherman Alexie, Marian Wright Edelman, Susan Cain, Andrew Sullivan, Maureen Dowd, and Jonathan Liu, with additional selections available online.

WRITER'S *Workshop*	Responding to Full Drafts

Working with one or two classmates, read each paper, and offer comments and questions that will help each of you see your papers' strengths and weaknesses. Consider the following questions as you do:

- What is your first impression of this draft? How effective is the title at drawing you in? Why? What are your overall suggestions for improvement? What part(s) of the text are especially persuasive? What reasons could use more support? Indicate what you like about the draft, and provide positive and encouraging feedback to the writer.

- How tight is the writer's focus? Does the paper wander a bit? If so, where?

- How accurate and appropriate is the supporting evidence? How clearly does the author indicate the sources of statistics and other supporting evidence?

- Might visuals such as charts, tables, photographs, or cartoons make the text more convincing?

- How clearly and effectively does the writer present any opposing points of view? How effectively does the writer answer opposing viewpoints? How might the writer acknowledge, concede, and/or refute them more effectively?

- How well has the writer demonstrated an awareness of readers' knowledge, needs, and/or expectations? How might the writer

Collaborate with peers.

Online, *The Guide* provides several powerful tools that help students to improve their writing skills, better understand their readers, assess the impact of their writing, and revise to address the needs of their audience. With *The Guide*'s digital peer-review system, not only can students see and consider the comments of others, but they can also reflect on their work and create a road map for revision based on the feedback they receive. Instructors can use the technology to arrange peer groups and improve the peer group experience.

Let *CONNECT COMPOSITION* help you assess your goals.

Outcomes-based assessment tools

The McGraw-Hill Guide's powerful, customizable assessment tools in *Connect* provide instructors with a way to communicate assessment criteria for each class or across the entire writing program so that students clearly understand the outcomes of the course as well as the grading rubrics used to assess their writing. These tools allow instructors to define learning outcomes for the course and create rubrics to assess students' writing holistically or in the context of outcomes for each writing assignment. Powerful reporting tools give instructors opportunities to generate assessment data for individual students, one or more sections of the course, or all sections to evaluate the success of their entire writing program.

Blackboard and MH Campus

All the content of *The McGraw-Hill Guide*—writing instruction, readings, assignments, documentation flowcharts—can be integrated with your program's course management system to offer single sign-on, seamless use of all *Connect Composition* 2.0 assets, and synchronization for all assignment and grade book utilities.

Tegrity

TEGRITY CAMPUS is a service that makes class time available all the time. By automatically capturing every lecture in a searchable format, students can review course material when they study and complete assignments. With a simple one-click start-and-stop process, you can capture all computer screens and corresponding audio. Students replay any part of any class with easy-to-use browser-based viewing on a PC or Mac.

Go Digital with McGraw-Hill's Best-in-Class Support Team

- **Digital Success Academy**—The Digital Success Academy offers a wealth of online training resources and course creation tips for instructors. Broken down into easy-to-navigate sections, the Digital Success Academy offers Connect 100 and 200 level video clips, PowerPoint documents, and Clickthrough Guides that explain how to navigate the Connect platform and how to use course-specific features. **http://create.mcgraw-hill.com/wordpress-mu/success-academy/**

- **Digital Success Team**—The Digital Success Team is a group of dedicated McGraw-Hill professionals available to work online with instructors—one-on-one—to demonstrate how the *Connect* platform works and recommend the best ways to incorporate *Connect* with your syllabus. You can request a Digital Success Team personal consultation through your McGraw-Hill sales representative (**http://catalogs.mhhe.com/mhhe/findRep.do**) or by visiting our Digital Products Support Center at **http://mpss.mhhe.com/orientation.php**.

- **Digital Learning Consultants**—Digital Learning Consultants are local resources who work closely with your McGraw-Hill sales representative and can provide face-to-face instructor support and training. To request a Digital Learning Consultant to speak with you, please e-mail your McGraw-Hill sales representative.

- **National training webinar schedule**—join us online at **http://fd7.formdesk.com/mh/ Connect_Composition_2.0_webinar** to learn more about what Connect has to offer and how you can incorporate into your course!

- **Customer Experience Group (CXG)**—McGraw-Hill is dedicated to making sure that instructors and students can reach out and receive help for any of our digital products. To contact our customer support team, please call us at 800-331-5094, or visit us online at **http://mpss.mhhe.com/contact.php**.

New to This Edition!

* Indicates a new chapter.

Chapter 1: Writing Goals and Objectives for College and for Life

- Coverage of composing in electronic environments has been updated.
- A new section that introduces the "Strategies for Success" feature has been added.

Chapter 2: Reading Critically for College and for Life

- "Genres Up Close: Writing a Rhetorical Analysis" and the Writing Activity that goes with it have been moved to the chapter's end so that students can apply the instruction on reading critically to this assignment.

*Chapter 3: Writing to Understand and Synthesize Texts

- Two professional readings on the issue of protecting intellectual property on the Internet, "Kill the Internet—and Other Anti-SOPA Myths" by Danny Goldberg and "We Are the Media, and So Are You" by Jimmy Wales and Kat Walsh, serve as the texts the student writer responds to and synthesizes.
- Two new student papers and assignment options are included: a critical response and a synthesis.

Chapter 4: Writing to Discover and to Learn

- Minor updates and adjustments.

In Chapters 6 through 12:

- **Visual Thinking:** This new element shows the student writer selecting an appropriate visual for his or her paper and ends with critical-thinking questions that get students to reflect on how a visual or visuals will work within the context of the student essay.
- **Strategies for Success:** New feature shows students how successful habits of mind in areas such as persistence, creativity, openness, and engagement will help them as writers.

Chapter 5: Writing to Share Experiences

- This is now a briefer assignment chapter, with fewer selections and streamlined process coverage.
- New selections include "Superman and Me" by Sherman Alexie and "Augustinian Influences" by Brad Whetstine (eBook). "Facing Poverty with a Rich Girl's Habits" by Suki Kim appears in the eBook.

Chapter 6: Writing to Explore

- New selections include "Why I Blog" by Andrew Sullivan, "The Tuskegee Airmen Plane's Last Flight" by Owen Edwards, "World's Best Blogger?" by Jesse Kornbluth (eBook), and a new Web site (*Kiva*, a nonprofit organization that facilitates microloans).

Chapter 7: Writing to Inform

- New selection: "A Brief History of Wikipedia" by Dan Fletcher.
- A new "Genres Up Close" that focuses entirely on writing an annotated bibliography, with a sample annotated bibliography tied to the student paper for this chapter, replaces the example of a review of the literature by Pamela Brandes.

Chapter 8: Writing to Analyze

- New selection: "The Power of Introverts" by Susan Cain.

Chapter 9: Writing to Convince

- New selection: "Still Hungry in America" by Marian Wright Edelman.

Chapter 10: Writing to Evaluate

- New selections include "The 5 Best Toys of All Time" by Jonathan H. Liu and two reviews of *Harry Potter and the Deathly Hallows: Part 2* by Roger Ebert and Andrew O'Hehir.
- A revised section on "Synthesizing and Integrating Sources into Your Draft: Creating Visuals to Show Your Data" discusses how to present data as a table.

Chapter 11: Writing to Explain Causes and Effects

- New selections include "How Urban Myths Reveal Society's Fears" by Neal Gabler, a new student essay "Brothers, Brethren, and Kin: The Role of Family in the Lives of Harriet Jacobs and Black Hawk" by Hanna Lake, and a new anti-smoking poster. "The Real Reason Why Highway Deaths Are Down" by Robert Reich appears in the eBook.

Chapter 12: Writing to Solve Problems

- New selections include "The Case for Girls" by Anya Kamenetz, "Education Needs a Digital-Era Upgrade" by Virginia Heffernan, and a new student essay "Staying Ahead of Skimming Scams" by Susan DeMedeiros.

Chapter 13: Using Strategies That Guide Readers

- An updated box on "Electronic Environments" and an updated food diagram in Figure 13.3.

Chapter 14: Using Strategies for Argument

- An updated box on "Electronic Environments."
- New selection: "The Myth of Energy Independence: Why We Can't Drill Our Way to Oil Autonomy" by Jordan Weissman.

Chapter 15: Using Strategies for Collaboration

- Minor updates and adjustments.

Chapter 16: Making Effective Oral Presentations

- A new section on online presentations has been added.

Chapter 17: Choosing a Medium, Genre, and Technology for Your Communication

- The sections on synchronous chat, wikis, peer-review applications, and graphics software have been revised and updated, with a new example of a digitally manipulated image.

Chapter 18: Communicating with Design and Visuals

- Updates include a new example of a poster using cool colors, updated examples of common typefaces, and a new example of a table.
- The section on "Designing New Media" has been moved to the end of the "Principles of Document Design" section.

Chapter 19: Finding and Evaluating Information

- New screen images showing the results of searches of an academic database (JStor) and Google.
- New or updated examples of a book, a popular magazine, a public affairs magazine, the Web site of a government agency, a blog, and *Wikipedia*.

Chapter 20: Synthesizing and Documenting Sources

- The section on "Plagiarism" has been revised to make it more concise and focused.
- New examples have been added to the section on "Quotations," and new examples of faulty and acceptable paraphrases have been added to the section on "Paraphrases."
- A new "Electronic Environments" box on managing research notes has been added.
- New examples of unacceptable and acceptable summaries have been added to the section on "Summaries."
- For "MLA Style: In-Text Citation," there is a new example for a Work with One Author (replacing the previous example).
- For "MLA Style: Constructing a List of Works Cited," pairs of entries that show the difference between the MLA and APA styles have been updated (replacing previous examples).
- A new example of a title page and copyright page from a book has been added (Figure 20.2): *The Classical Tradition*, replacing *Unpaid Professionals*.
- For "MLA Style: Constructing a List of Works Cited": 14 new examples

- A new "Electronic Environments" box on "Using Microsoft Word to Develop Citations" has been added.
- For "APA Style: In-Text Citation": 4 new examples
- For "APA Style: Constructing a References List": 10 new model entries

*Chapter 21: Writing about Visual Texts (eBook Chapter)

- Two professional readings that analyze visual texts, "Revisiting the Daisy Revolution" by Will Storey (an analysis of a famous political advertisement) and "From Chaos, a Suspended Beauty" by Sebastian Smee (an analysis of a sculpture), are included.
- Seven assignment options, with visuals, offer students a wide range of ideas to choose from.
- A student visual analysis of an advertisement is provided, with examples of the student's writing process and first draft in the "Writing Processes" section of the chapter.

Chapter 22: Writing about Creative Works (eBook Chapter)

- Chapter now includes the Set-Achieve-Assess framework to make it consistent with the other assignment chapters, providing a "Setting Your Goals" box at the beginning of the chapter and a "Self-Assessment: Reflecting on Your Goals" section at the end.
- Chapter now includes sections on Rhetorical Knowledge; Critical Thinking, Reading, and Writing; Writing Processes; and Knowledge of Conventions—making it consistent with other assignment chapters.
- "Girl" by Jamaica Kincaid replaces "Ascent by Balloon from the Yard of Walnut Street Jail" by John Edgar Wideman. The book review, "Haiku for Cats" by Joanna Rudge Long," has been cut.
- Chapter now includes a student analysis of "Girl": "Indirect Characterization in Jamaica Kincaid's 'Girl'" by Katrina Montgomery.

Appendix A: Constructing a Writing Portfolio

- Minor updates.

Appendix B: Writing Effective Essay Examinations

- Minor updates and adjustments.

Appendix C: Standard Document Forms

- Updates and adjustments
- New sample memo
- New sample Listserv posting
- New sample newsletter
- New sample Web site

Acknowledgments

On a personal level, we'd like to thank our colleagues at Arizona State University and at Northern Arizona University, who've heard us talking about the project (probably more than they'd wished to!), offered constant support, and gave us good advice: Shealyn Campbell, Fred Corey, Barbara D'Angelo, Chitralekha Duttagupta, Scott Guenthner, Shari Gustafson, Barbara Hanks, Ashley Hopf, Claire Lauer, Keith Miller, Margaret Munson, Camille Newton, Cynthia Villegas, Brooke Wonders, and Allen Woodman. Duane would like especially to thank Hanna, Maureen, and Harley Roen.

A number of people have made important contributions to this text and its media components. Sherry Rankins-Robertson of the University of Arkansas at Little Rock updated the Electronic Environments boxes and provided valuable insights and suggestions for Chapter 17 and 18 and the Visual Thinking boxes, for which we thank her. Video producers Peter Berkow and Bruce Coykendahl prepared the videos that are part of the *McGraw-Hill Guide Online* and the Faculty Development Web site. Whitney Olson wrote the learning objectives for *Connect* and provided helpful guidelines for using *Connect* in the Instructor's Manual.

At McGraw-Hill, we were fortunate to have some of the best in the business helping us with this project, including Mike Ryan, vice-president and general manager, Humanities, Social Science, and Language group; David Patterson, Managing Director, Skills group; Kevin Colleary, our tireless and creative marketing manager; Nanette Giles, executive market development manager; and Ray Kelley, our terrific field publisher. Sherree D'Amico, our senior sales representative, and Mina Mathies, our regional manager, have both provided us with valuable advice. Preston Thomas oversaw the beautiful design of the text, Jan Fehler copy edited the text, Margaret Marco and Ann Janette handled the photo research, and Jolynn Kilburg and Danielle Clement were responsible for seeing the text and *Connect* through production. We owe special thanks to Lisa Moore, who originally helped us develop the concept and signed the project, and to Chris Bennem, executive sponsoring editor, who has guided us "editorially" in a thoughtful and kind manner. We also owe a special thanks to Carla Samodulski, senior development editor, who is quite simply the best developmental editor in the business—and to Cara Labell and Judith Kromm, who served cheerfully and professionally as the developmental editors for the second edition. Thanks Lisa, Chris, Carla, Cara, and Judith.

Finally, we are indebted to all our fellow First-Year Composition instructors whose valuable advice helped shape the third edition.

McGraw-Hill Assessment Research in Composition (MARC) Partners

McGraw-Hill is honored to partner with these five higher education institutions to conduct research on the ways in which pedagogical tools can constructively impact student performance in writing.

Collin College

Martha Tolleson

Sonja Andrus

Lauryn Angel-Cann

Betty Battacchi

Tammy Brightwell

Cathy Cloud

David Flanagin

Margaret Gonzalez

Susan Grimland

Lisa Kirby

Sarah Moore

Dana Moran

Beth Morley

Gordon O'Neal

Ray Slavens

Clay Stevens

John Wu

Johnson & Wales University—Providence

Donna Thomsen

Eileen Medeiros

Terry Novak

Northern Arizona University

Jacquelyn Belknap
Valerie Robin
Nicholas Tambakeras

Richland College

Paula Eschliman
Anthony Armstrong
Suzie Baker
Sarah Bowman
Debra Frazier

University of Texas—El Paso

Beth Brunk-Chavez
Christie Daniels
Judith Fourzan
Maggie Smith
Adam Webb
Judika Webb

Reviewers

This edition of *The McGraw-Hill Guide* was developed with the guidance of the following instructors.

Abraham Baldwin Agricultural College Bonnie Asselin, Erin Campbell, Sandra Giles, Wendy Harrison, Jeff Newberry

Arizona State University Regina Clemens Fox, Nicole Khoury

Atlanta Metropolitan College Hristina Keranova, Kokila Ravi

Bakersfield College David Moton

Bellarmine University Olga-Maria Cruz

Chesapeake College Eleanor Welsh

Cleveland Community College Tajsha Eaves

College of DuPage Jacqueline McGrath, Sheryl Mylan, Beverly Reed, Helen Szymanski

College of Saint Rose Megan Fulwiler,

Jennifer Marlow

Community College of Aurora Susan Achziger

Cowley County Community College Marlys Cervantes, Julie Kratt

Dixie State College Tim Bywater, Cheri Crenshaw, Randy Jasmine

Drexel University Scott Warnock

El Paso Community College Gloria Estrada

Front Range Community College Donna Craine

Glendale Community College Alisa Cooper

Grand Rapids Community College Mursalata Muhammad

Guilford Technical Community College Jo Ann Buck, Carolyn Schneider

Harrisburg Area Community College Valerie Gray

Hawaii Pacific University-Honolulu Rob Wilson

Henderson Community College William Gary

Indiana University–Purdue University Indianapolis Steve Fox, Scott Weeden, Anne Williams

Iowa State University Sheryl McGough

Ivy Tech Community College Sandy Hackemann, Susan Howard, Dodie Marie Miller, John D. Miller, Carol Schuck

James A. Rhodes State College Sally Angel, James Fallon

Johnson and Wales University Eileen Medeiros, James Anderson, Terry Novak

Kansas City Kansas Community College James Krajewski

Lake-Sumter Community College Jacklyn Pierce, Melanie K. Wagner, Patricia Campbell

Lee College David Hainline, Gordon Lee,

Loyola Marymount University K. J. Peters

Madisonville Community College Gregory Dennis Hagan, Lawrence Roy, Jr.

Maryville University Jesse Kavadlo

MCC-Longview Community College Dawnielle Walker

McLennan Community College Arvis Scott, Jim McKeown

Mississippi College Kerri Jordan, Jonathan Randle

Northern Arizona University Jacquelyn Belknap, Valerie Robin, Nicholas Tambakeras

Northern Carolina State Susan Miller-Cochran

Northern Kentucky University Kristi Brock

Oklahoma City Community College Angela Cotner, Michael Franco, Jon Inglett, Kim Jameson, Chris Verschage

Owens Community College Brenna Dugan, Jen Hazel, Deborah Richey, Ellen Sorg

Pittsburg State Universty John Franklin

Prince Georges Community College Leela Kapai, Odeana Kramer, Wendy Perkins,

Pueblo Community College Deborah Borchers

Purdue University–Calumet Karen Bishop Morris

Riverside City College Jason Spangler

Seminole State College of Florida Karen L. Feldman, Chrishawn Speller

Shawnee State University Neil Catpathios, Deborah S. Knutson

South Suburban College Laura Baltuska

Southeast Community College Kimberly Ann Fangman, Janet Kirchner

State Fair Community College Anneliese Homan

Texas Christian University Charlotte Hogg

Triton College Bill Nedrow, William Nedrow

University of Alabama at Birmingham Peggy Jolly, Cynthia Ryan, Rita Treutel

University of Alabama–Tuscaloosa Karen Gardiner, Steffen Guenzel, Jessica Fordham Kidd, Maryann Whitaker

University of Arkansas Sherry Rankins-Robertson

University of California–Irvine Lynda Haas

University of Central Florida Lindee Owens

University of Findlay Terri LaRocco, Ronald J. Tulley

University of Georgia Brandy James

University of Montana Amy Ratto Parks

University of Southern Indiana Jill Kinkade

University of Texas–El Paso Beth Brunk-Chavez, Christie Daniels, Judith Fourzan, Cira Montoya, Maggie Smith, Adam Webb, Judika Webb

University of Wisconsin–River Falls Jenny Brantley, Kathleen Hunzer, Lissa Schneider-Rebozo

Wilkes Community College Lisa Muir, Julie Mullis

Symposium Attendees

As part of its ongoing research in composition and in the design and administration of writing programs, McGraw-Hill conducts several symposia annually for instructors from across the country. These events offer a forum for instructors to exchange ideas and experiences with colleagues they might not have met otherwise. The feedback McGraw-Hill has received has been invaluable and has contributed directly to the development of *The McGraw-Hill Guide.*

Abraham Baldwin Agricultural College Jeff Newberry

Angelina College Diana Throckmorton

Arapahoe Community College Sallie Wolf

Brevard Community College Heather Elko

Brigham Young University Brett McInnelly

Broome Community College David Chirico

Broward Community College Sandra Stollman

Chattanooga State Technical Community College Joel Henderson

Clayton State University Mary Lamb

Coastal Bend College Anna Green

College of the Canyons Jia-Yi Cheng-Levine

Dutchess Community College Angela Batchelor

Ferrum College Katherine Grimes

Florida A&M University Nandi Riley

Glendale Community College Alisa Cooper

Heartland Community College Jennifer Cherry

Ithaca College Susan Adams Delaney

Indiana University-Purdue University Indianapolis Mel Wininger

Kapiolani Community College Georganne Nordstrom

Lake Sumter Community College Patricia Campbell

Lehigh Carbon Community College Douglas Rigby

Lindenwood University Ana Schnellmann

Loyola Marymount University K. J. Peters

Mercer County Community College Noreen Duncan

Michigan State University Bill Hart-Davidson

Montgomery County Community College Diane McDonald

Naugatuck Valley Community College Anne Mattrella

North Central Texas College Rochelle Gregory

North Idaho College Lloyd Duman

Northern Illinois University Eric Hoffman

Oakland Community College Subashini Subbarao

Old Dominion University Matt Oliver

Oregon State University Susan Meyers

Pearl River Community College Greg Underwood

Pima Community College-Downtown Kristina Beckman-Brito

Quinnipiac University Glenda Pritchett

Seminole State College Ruth Reis-Palatiere

Spokane Community College Angela Rasmussen

Salt Lake Community College Brittany Stephenson

Sacramento City College Jeff Knorr

Santa Ana College Gary Bennett

Savannah State University Gwendolyn Hale

Sinclair Community College Kate Geiselman

Southeastern Louisiana University Jeff Wiemelt

Southern Illinois University-Carbondale Ronda Dively

Southwestern Illinois College Winnie Kinney

Southwestern Oklahoma State University Jill Jones

St. Louis Community College-Florissant Valley James Sodon

St. Louis University Janice McIntire-Strasburg

Sussex County College James Rawlins

Tarrant County College Jim Schrantz

Tidewater Community College Joe Antinarella

Truman State University Monica Barron

University of California-Irvine Lynda Haas

University of the District of Columbia LaTanya Reese Rogers

University of Florida Creed Greer

University of Idaho Jodie Nicotra

University of Missouri-St. Louis Suellynn Duffey

University of Nevada-Las Vegas Ruby Fowler

University of Rhode Island Libby Miles

University of Texas-El Paso Beth Brunk-Chavez

University of Wisconsin-Eau Claire Shevaun Watson

University of Wisconsin-Stout Andrea Deacon

Wilbur Wright College Phillip Virgen

WPA Outcomes Statement for First-Year Composition

Adopted by the Council of Writing Program Administrators (WPA), April 2000; amended July 2008

For further information about the development of the Outcomes Statement, please see

http://comppile.tamucc.edu/WPAoutcomes/continue.html

For further information about the Council of Writing Program Administrators, please see

http://www.wpacouncil.org

A version of this statement was published in *WPA: Writing Program Administration* 23.1/2 (fall/winter 1999): 59–66.

Introduction

This statement describes the common knowledge, skills, and attitudes sought by first-year composition programs in American postsecondary education. To some extent, we seek to regularize what can be expected to be taught in first-year composition; to this end the document is not merely a compilation or summary of what currently takes place. Rather, the following statement articulates what composition teachers nationwide have learned from practice, research, and theory. This document intentionally defines only "outcomes," or types of results, and not "standards," or precise levels of achievement. The setting of standards should be left to specific institutions or specific groups of institutions.

Learning to write is a complex process, both individual and social, that takes place over time with continued practice and informed guidance. Therefore, it is important that teachers, administrators, and a concerned public do not imagine that these outcomes can be taught in reduced or simple ways. Helping students demonstrate these outcomes requires expert understanding of how students actually learn to write. For this reason we expect the primary audience for this document to be well-prepared college writing teachers and college writing program administrators. In some places, we have chosen to write in their professional language. Among such readers, terms such as "rhetorical" and "genre" convey a rich meaning that is not easily simplified. While we have also aimed at writing a document that the general public can understand, in limited cases we have aimed first at communicating effectively with expert writing teachers and writing program administrators.

These statements describe only what we expect to find at the end of first-year composition, at most schools a required general education course or sequence of courses. As writers move beyond first-year composition, their writing abilities do not merely improve. Rather, students' abilities not only diversify along disciplinary and professional lines but also move into whole new levels where expected outcomes expand, multiply, and diverge. For this reason, each statement of outcomes for first-year composition is followed by suggestions for further work that builds on these outcomes.

 RHETORICAL KNOWLEDGE

By the end of first-year composition, students should

- Focus on a purpose
- Respond to the needs of different audiences
- Respond appropriately to different kinds of rhetorical situations
- Use conventions of format and structure appropriate to the rhetorical situation
- Adopt appropriate voice, tone, and level of formality
- Understand how genres shape reading and writing
- Write in several genres

Faculty in all programs and departments can build on this preparation by helping students learn

- The main features of writing in their fields
- The main uses of writing in their fields
- The expectations of readers in their fields

 CRITICAL THINKING, READING, AND WRITING

By the end of first-year composition, students should

- Use writing and reading for inquiry, learning, thinking, and communicating
- Understand a writing assignment as a series of tasks, including finding, evaluating, analyzing, and synthesizing appropriate primary and secondary sources

- Integrate their own ideas with those of others
- Understand the relationships among language, knowledge, and power

Faculty in all programs and departments can build on this preparation by helping students learn

- The uses of writing as a critical thinking method
- The interactions among critical thinking, critical reading, and writing
- The relationships among language, knowledge, and power in their fields

 PROCESSES

By the end of first-year composition, students should

- Be aware that it usually takes multiple drafts to create and complete a successful text
- Develop flexible strategies for generating, revising, editing, and proofreading
- Understand writing as an open process that permits writers to use later invention and re-thinking to revise their work
- Understand the collaborative and social aspects of writing processes
- Learn to critique their own and others' works
- Learn to balance the advantages of relying on others with the responsibility of doing their part
- Use a variety of technologies to address a range of audiences

Faculty in all programs and departments can build on this preparation by helping students learn

- To build final results in stages
- To review work-in-progress in collaborative peer groups for purposes other than editing
- To save extensive editing for later parts of the writing process
- To apply the technologies commonly used to research and communicate within their fields

 KNOWLEDGE OF CONVENTIONS

By the end of first-year composition, students should

- Learn common formats for different kinds of texts

- Develop knowledge of genre conventions ranging from structure and paragraphing to tone and mechanics
- Practice appropriate means of documenting their work
- Control such surface features as syntax, grammar, punctuation, and spelling

Faculty in all programs and departments can build on this preparation by helping students learn

- The conventions of usage, specialized vocabulary, format, and documentation in their fields
- Strategies through which better control of conventions can be achieved

Composing in Electronic Environments

As has become clear over the last twenty years, writing in the twenty-first century involves the use of digital technologies for several purposes, from drafting to peer reviewing to editing. Therefore, although the *kinds* of composing processes and texts expected from students vary across programs and institutions, there are nonetheless common expectations.

By the end of first-year composition, students should

- Use electronic environments for drafting, reviewing, revising, editing, and sharing texts
- Locate, evaluate, organize, and use research material collected from electronic sources, including scholarly library databases, other official databases (for example, federal government databases), and informal electronic networks and Internet sources
- Understand and exploit the differences in the rhetorical strategies and in the affordances available for both print and electronic composing processes and texts

Faculty in all programs and departments can build on this preparation by helping students learn

- How to engage in the electronic research and composing processes common in their fields
- How to disseminate texts in both print and electronic forms in their fields

Writing Goals and Objectives for College and for Life

Whenever you write, you strive to fulfill a goal. In school, you write papers and essay exam answers to demonstrate what you have learned and to communicate your ideas to others. Outside of school, you use writing to perform your duties in the workplace, to make your voice heard in your community, and to communicate with friends and family. Most discourse has a goal or **purpose:** to explain, to inform, to persuade, and so on.

Whatever the purpose, effective writers achieve their objectives. **Rhetoric** is the use of words—either spoken or written—as well as visuals to achieve some goal. Each chapter in this book has a *rhetorical* focus on what you as a writer want your writing to *accomplish.*

The first decision a writer makes is rhetorical: What would you like this writing to *do* for a particular group of readers—your **audience**—at a particular place and time? Once you have determined your goals, you are

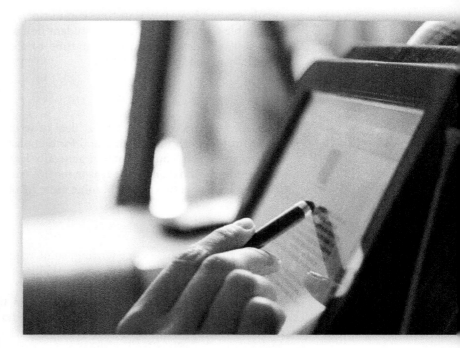

prepared to decide how much and what kinds of information your audience needs to know and what will be convincing to this audience. You also decide how to collect this information and how to present it in an appropriate format. This rhetorical approach applies to writing that you do in various settings—not just in the classroom.

This chapter provides the context for the exploration of writing in subsequent chapters. Here we look at writing in the four areas of life, the course learning goals, the concept of becoming a self-reflective writer, and strategies for success.

Writing in the Four Areas of Your Life

Improving your ability to write effective college papers is an important goal of this course and this text. However, Writing skills are vital not only in college but also in the professional, civic, and personal parts of your life.

Consider how you plan to spend the twenty-four hours in each day for the next week, the next month, the next year, the next four years, the next decade, and the next six decades. If you are like most students, during the next few years, you will devote much of your time to your academic studies. When you finish your academic studies, however, your time commitments will probably change. Although it is possible that you may still be a student half a decade from now, it is more likely that you will devote most of your time to the other three parts of your life—especially to your professional life.

Writing as a College Student

See Chapter 4 for writing-to-learn strategies.

You will be expected to do a great deal of writing in college because writing is a powerful tool both for learning and for demonstrating learning. Students who use writing to explore course material generally learn more—and get higher grades—than students who do not. The reason for this enhanced performance is fairly simple: Writing is an effective way to become more involved with your course material.

Writing as a Professional

Almost all jobs require some writing; some require a great deal of it. Furthermore, employers frequently list strong writing skills as one of the most important qualifications they seek in job candidates.

Surveys of employers consistently confirm the importance of writing in the work world: Employers want to hire people who can write and speak clearly and effectively, think critically, solve problems efficiently, work well in teams, and use technology thoughtfully. The most competitive job seekers are those who begin honing these skills early.

Writing as a Citizen

As Thomas Jefferson frequently noted, democracies—and societies in general—work most effectively when citizens are well educated and involved. If you have strong feelings about certain issues and want to have a voice in how your society functions, you need to participate in your community. One important way to make your voice heard in a representative democracy is to write. You can write to elected officials at the local, state, and federal levels to let them know what you think about an issue and why you think the way that you do. In the civic part of your life, you often will work with others to solve problems—neighbors or other citizens who are involved and interested in issues that affect them, their neighborhood, and their community.

Writing Activity

Balancing the Four Areas of Life

W orking with two or three of your classmates, answer the following questions about the bar graph shown in Figure 1.1. Compare and discuss your responses. Your instructor may ask your group to share its findings with the rest of the class.

- Which group of bars (1, 2, 3, or 4) comes closest to representing the current balance in your life?
- Which group of bars comes closest to representing what you consider the ideal balance for someone enrolled full-time in college? For someone enrolled part-time? For a student with family responsibilities and/or a part-time or full-time job?
- Which group of bars best represents the balance that you would like to achieve a decade from now? Two decades from now? Five decades from now?

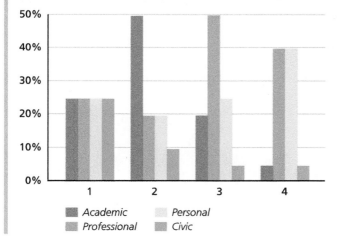

FIGURE 1.1
Balancing the Four
Areas of Life

Writing as a Family Member or Friend

Even though writing in the academic, professional, and civic areas of life is important, the writing that you do in your personal life at times can be the most important of all. We write—whether on paper or in cyberspace—to the people who are significant to us to accomplish life's daily tasks and to fulfill our needs.

Writing in the Four Areas in This Course

Because the academic, professional, civic, and personal parts of our lives are all important, this book offers numerous opportunities to write in all four areas. In each chapter in Parts 2 and 3, you have the option of writing in response to an academic or other type of situation. In addition, the writing assignments in these chapters are built around **scenarios**—simulated but realistic writing situations. Each scenario assignment provides a specific purpose for writing and a specific audience.

Learning Goals in This Course

Whether you are writing for an academic, a professional, a civic, or a personal audience and purpose, you will draw on the same set of writing skills. Your work in this course will help you to learn and to apply these skills to specific writing situations. To achieve this end, throughout the text we have incorporated the learning goals developed by the Council of Writing Program Administrators (WPA), a national organization of instructors who direct composition courses. The goals are organized into five broad areas: rhetorical knowledge and analysis; critical thinking, reading, and writing; writing processes; knowledge of conventions; and composing in electronic environments.

Rhetorical Knowledge

Rhetorical knowledge includes an understanding of these aspects of the writing situation:

- Audience
- Purpose
- Rhetorical situation
- Writer's voice and tone
- Context, medium, and genre

AUDIENCE

To write for others successfully, you need to tailor your writing to their expectations and needs. You need to focus on where there is a meeting of minds—yours and theirs—and where there is not. For example, if you were to write the following grocery list and take it to the store, you would probably know precisely what you had in mind.

Grocery List
cereal
milk
coffee
bread
paper

If you were sick, however, and had to rely on a close family member to do your grocery shopping for you, you might have to revise the list by adding a few more details.

Version of the Grocery List for a Family Member
Cereal
1% milk
Coffee beans
Multigrain bread
Sunday paper

If you handed the list to a neighbor, though, you would probably have to add much more specific information.

Version of the Grocery List for a Neighbor
Grape Nuts Flakes
1% milk (half gallon)
whole-bean Starbuck's Sumatra extra-bold coffee
Grandma Sycamore's multigrain bread
the New York Times

In each case, you would adjust your list for the person who needs to act on the information. When you share a great deal of experience with your reader, you can leave gaps in information without causing serious problems. The fewer experiences you have in common with your audience, however, the more you need to fill in those gaps as you draft and revise, rather than after you have finished writing.

PURPOSE

In this book chapters 3–12 focus on common rhetorical purposes for writing: to understand and synthesize texts, to learn, to share experiences, to explore, to inform, to analyze, to convince, to evaluate, to examine causes and effects, and to solve problems. In Chapter 3 you will learn to respond critically to a text and to synthesize texts. In Chapter 4 you will have opportunities to experiment with many forms of writing to learn, which will serve you in this course, as well as your other courses. In chapters 5–12, you will have opportunities to engage with those purposes in some detail.

RHETORICAL SITUATION

When writers compose for a particular purpose, in response to the needs of a particular audience, they are responding to a **rhetorical situation.** A rhetorical situation consists of the following elements:

- Writer
- Purpose
- Audience
- Topic
- Context/occasion

Although each rhetorical situation is unique, there are general types of situations that require writers to use the appropriate conventions of format and structure.

For example, if you are writing a lab report for a biology course, your instructor will expect you to structure your report in a certain way and to use a neutral, informative tone. If you are proposing a solution to a problem in your community, your readers will expect you first to describe the problem and then to explain how your solution can be implemented, using a reasonable, even-handed tone and giving some attention to possible objections to your proposal.

WRITER'S VOICE AND TONE

A writer's **voice** is the personality or image that is revealed in the writer's text—the impression made on the reader. To establish a distinctive voice, a writer thoughtfully and consistently makes decisions about such elements as diction (word choice), syntax (sentence structure), and punctuation. For instance, think about a close friend whose use of a particular word or phrase clearly identifies that friend.

Tone is the writer's attitude toward the topic, the audience, and other people. Tone can reveal the extent to which a writer is respectful/disrespectful, patient/impatient, supportive/unsupportive, angry, happy, irritated, accommodating/unaccommodating, and the like. For example, Jay Leno, host of *The Tonight Show*, sometimes comments on the attire of individual members of the audience. Leno will say something like, "I see that you took extra time getting dressed for the show," to an audience member wearing cutoff blue jeans, a torn T-shirt, and flip-flops. Everyone knows that his tone is ironic; he clearly means the opposite of what he is saying.

CONTEXT, MEDIUM, AND GENRE

The context for writing affects the writer's choice of medium and genre. For example, an executive who needs to announce a company's plan for furloughs (required time off without pay) to thousands of employees in several cities will probably

How would your writing change if you were writing to (a) a friend who is still in high school about your new roommate, and (b) a housing administrator to request a housing change?

choose to send a memo (the genre) via e-mail (the medium). This genre and this medium make sense in this context because companies often use memos for such announcements. Further, the medium of e-mail is cost effective.

Context: Throughout this book you will have opportunities to write in a variety of **contexts,** or the circumstances that surround your writing, in all four arenas of life—the academic, the professional, the civic, and the personal. These opportunities appear in scenarios describing various rhetorical situations that give rise to writing. Consider what you would write if you were in the following rhetorical situations:

1. You want to convince the financial aid officer at your college that you need a scholarship to stay in school next semester.
2. After a disagreement with your spouse/fiancé/girlfriend/boyfriend, you want to write a letter to apologize for having said something that you regret.
3. After a disagreement with your supervisor at work, you want to write a letter to apologize for having said something that you regret.

As you contemplate these rhetorical situations, consider how the purpose, audience, topic, and context/occasion might alter what you will write. For instance, how does writing an apology to a love interest (no. 2 above) differ from writing an apology to your supervisor (no. 3 above)? In this case the purpose is the same, but the audiences differ.

Medium: A medium is a physical or an electronic means of communication. **Media** include books, pamphlets, newspapers, magazines, CDs, DVDs, and the World Wide Web. As you develop projects for chapters 5–12, you will be encouraged to use various media to communicate with your audience. Although you may want to use what feels most comfortable, you may also want to try forms of media that you have not used before.

Genre: *Genre* is a French word meaning "kind" or "type." Although people frequently use the word **genre** to refer to kinds of texts, such as a letter, a formal paper, a report, or a memo, people use this word in a wide variety of ways. You may have heard *genre* used to refer to the **content** of texts. For example, Shakespearean plays are labeled tragedies, comedies, or histories. If a friend tells you that she saw a film version of a Shakespearean tragedy last night, you could guess fairly accurately that she saw characters die as a result of foul deeds. Likewise, if another friend said that she had read résumés all morning, you would know that she was reading about people's educational and work backgrounds.

Genre also refers to different **forms** of texts. For example, think again about the friend who said that she had read résumés all morning. Résumés have not only standard content (educational and work background) but also a generally standard, easily recognized format.

From a rhetorical standpoint, you select the format or overall structure of the piece of writing you are constructing. A letter will have a salutation, a body, and a signature, although the structure of the body of that letter could vary widely—it could be organized in paragraphs or as a list, for instance. The point is that content can come in many kinds of packages. For example, in writing to convince people to wear seat belts, you could use any of the following: an academic paper, a flyer, a poster, or a Web site in which you present an argument in support of wearing seat belts; a poem, short story, play, or song about someone who died because he neglected to use a seat belt; an obituary; or a newspaper story.

You may choose from a wide variety of genres for writing projects in chapters 5–12. In each of these assigned chapters, you will find information about genres that are commonly used for that rhetorical purpose. For example, in Chapter 9, "Writing to Convince," you will find information about editorials, position papers, job references, and advertisements. In writing, *genre* means that you follow the conventions of a kind of writing and provide, generally, what readers expect from that genre. A paper for one of your college classes will usually be more formal and detailed than an e-mail you might write to your classmates asking them to vote in an upcoming election.

Rhetorical Analysis

For more information on rhetorical analysis, see Chapter 2.

A **rhetorical analysis** is an examination of the relative effectiveness of a particular text written for a particular audience for a particular purpose. It can include any of the previously mentioned features of rhetorical situations: audience, purpose, voice and tone, context, format, and genre. The average person does many rhetorical analyses each day. When someone says, "I don't think so," "yeah, right," or, "whatever," in response to a statement, that person is questioning the credibility of the speaker or the accuracy of the information. Although formal rhetorical analyses are more elaborate than this example suggests, the principle is the same.

Throughout this book, you will have opportunities to engage in rhetorical analysis. For example, at the end of each reading in chapters 5–12, you will have an opportunity to write brief rhetorical analyses of those texts.

Critical Thinking, Reading, and Writing

To get the most out of your reading and to accomplish your goals as a writer, you need to develop and use critical thinking skills. In Chapter 2 we offer some informal reading and writing activities that promote critical thinking. Although these activities will help you read more thoughtfully, many of them are also tools for generating ideas and material for the more formal writing tasks you will do in all four parts of your life.

In general, you engage in **critical thinking** when you examine an idea from many perspectives—seeing it in new ways. For example, when you write a formal argument, you will need to address others' objections to your ideas if you hope to persuade your audience to accept your point. As noted in Chapter 3, when you respond to texts or when you synthesize the ideas in several texts, you are thinking critically. You can also apply critical thinking to understand the relationships among language, knowledge, and power. That is, language often has a greater impact when it is used by people in positions of social, political, or economic power. When used effectively, language is often far more powerful than physical weapons. Many modern governments have written constitutions and written laws derived from those constitutions. The most politically and economically powerful people in societies tend to be those who use critical thinking and language most effectively to present their ideas.

Writing Processes

Although writing processes vary from writer to writer and from situation to situation, effective writers generally go through the following activities:

- Generating initial ideas
- Relating those ideas to the writing situation or assignment
- Conducting research to find support for their ideas
- Organizing ideas and support and writing an initial draft
- Revising and shaping the paper, frequently with the advice of other readers
- Editing and polishing the paper

The order of these processes can vary, and often you will need to return to a previous step. For example, while drafting you may discover that you need to find more support for one of your ideas; while revising you may find a better way to organize your ideas.

When writers revise, they add or delete words, phrases, sentences, or even whole paragraphs, and they often modify their ideas. After they have revised multiple times, they then edit, attending to word choice, punctuation, grammar, usage, and spelling—the "surface features" of written texts. Writers also revise and edit texts to meet the needs of particular readers.

Effective writers also ask others to help them generate and refine their ideas and polish their prose. Published writers in academic, civic, and professional fields rely heavily on others as they work, often showing one another drafts of their writing before submitting a manuscript to publishers.

Because effective writers get help from others, this book provides many opportunities for you and your classmates—your **peers**—to help one another. One key to working productively with others is to understand that they bring different backgrounds, experiences, knowledge, and perspectives to the writing task, so it is critical to treat what others think and say with respect, no matter how much you agree or disagree with them. You should also remember when working with others that the suggestions and comments they make are about your *text*, not about you.

Knowledge of Conventions

Conventions are the table manners of writing. Sometimes they matter; other times they do not. Writing notes to help yourself learn course material is like eating breakfast alone at home. In this situation, table manners are not very important.

When you are having dinner with your employer or the president of your college, though, table manners do matter. The same principle applies when you write for readers. Effective writers know which writing conventions to use in particular settings.

To make their writing more appealing to readers, writers need to master many conventions: spelling, punctuation, sentence structure, and word choice. While some conventions are considered signs of the writer's respect for readers (correctly spelling someone's name, for instance), other conventions, such as punctuation, organization, tone, the use of headers and white space, and documentation style, help your readers understand what you are saying and where your information comes from.

Composing in Electronic Environments

Initially you might wonder, "Why is composing in electronic environments a learning goal for a writing course?" In fact, most writers use some kind of electronic environment for parts of their composing process. Although many students choose to use pen and paper for note-taking or for the initial parts of their writing process, others write exclusively in a digital environment, taking notes on a laptop or tablet or even on a smartphone. At some point in the process, however, most students are likely to use a word-processing program.

Although you are likely aware that you will be using some kind of digital technology to produce your final drafts for your college assignments, digital writing will be a major part of the writing you do in all aspects of your life, whether you are sending an e-mail to a professor or supervisor, composing a text message to a friend, or updating your *Facebook* status. Part of what it means to compose in electronic environments is to understand the rhetorical strategies that are necessary in each different situation. You won't use the same strategies when you send a text message to a friend that you would when you e-mail an instructor. Likewise, the rhetorical strategies you use when updating your *Facebook* status are very different from the ones you employ when writing a paper for a course.

Further, using electronic environments strategically can help you throughout the process of composing. It is clearly easier to revise and edit using the functions of a word processor. However, a variety of technologies also make it extremely easy to share your work and review the work of others. You can share files simply by e-mailing them or sharing a flash drive, or you might choose to use a collaborative writing environment such as *Google Docs* or a wiki.

Finally, because research is often done electronically, it is essential to understand how to find credible online sources. To locate these sources, you need to understand how to use your college library's Web site as a portal to a wide range of scholarly databases and credible Web sites.

Writing Activity

Assessing Your Strengths and Weaknesses

In no more than two pages, assess your current strengths and weaknesses in each of the five goal areas: rhetorical knowledge and analysis; critical thinking, reading, and writing; writing processes; knowledge of conventions; and composing in electronic environments. Share your self-assessment with two or three classmates.

┌───┐
ELECTRONIC ENVIRONMENTS) **Sharing Digital Literacy**

You and your classmates can help each other get more out of the writing technologies that are available on your campus. Offer to show your friends or the members of your study group shortcuts and tools in programs you are familiar with. Don't be shy about asking friends and classmates for tips and tricks they've picked up while developing their projects. You can use your own computing knowledge as "social collateral" in classes because some students will be more comfortable than others with various programs. For example, you might show your classmates how to use some of the formatting tools in the word processor and ask others to show you how to use slide show presentation, spreadsheet, or sound file–mixing software.
└───┘

Writing Activity

Assessing Your Uses of Technology

Think about the ways in which you have used digital technologies in the past year. In the grid below, list a few tasks that you have done with technology. Compare your list with those of several classmates.

Technological Tool	Academic Situation	Professional, Civic, or Personal Situation
• E-mail		
• Word-processing software		
• Web browser (e.g., Mozilla Firefox, Internet Explorer)		
• Web site composing tools (e.g., *Dreamweaver*)		
• Presentation software (e.g., *PowerPoint, Prezi*)		
• Other		

Becoming a Self-Reflective Writer

By evaluating your strengths and weaknesses in each of the five learning outcomes, you have taken a step toward becoming a more reflective—and therefore a more successful—writer. Throughout this course, you will continue to build on this foundation. Toward the end of each chapter in Parts 2 and 3, you will be asked to reflect on the work you did for that chapter. Reflecting—in writing—on your own writing activities helps you learn what worked (and perhaps what did not work). That kind of activity will help you remember the most useful aspects of your process the next time you face a similar writing task.

GENRES *Up Close* **Writing a Reflection**

An important form of thinking and writing, **reflection** is an opportunity to consider carefully the importance, value, or applicability of something. Reflection may improve your ability to learn a skill or acquire knowledge. A reflection includes two components:

- A description of what is being reflected on. For example, if you reflect on a lab experiment, you first need to describe the experiment. If you reflect on what you learned from reading a novel, you first need to summarize the novel. When you describe or summarize the subject of your reflection, you make it easier for your readers to understand it. In addition, the action of describing or summarizing helps you to focus your attention on the subject of your reflection.

- A thoughtful consideration of the subject of your reflection. For example, you could ask the following kinds of questions:

  - Why is the subject of my reflection important? How can I apply it?
  - What have I learned from this experience?
  - What do I know about _____? What do I still need to learn about _____?
  - What do my readers know about _____? What do they not know about _____? What do they need to know about _____?
  - Why am I engaged in this activity?

In this book you will be asked to engage in many forms of reflection. The following example is an excerpt from a reflection by student writer Santi DeRosa, whose paper appears in Chapter 9. Notice how DeRosa addresses his knowledge and skills, as well as connections between the academic and personal arenas of his life:

> I could be more passionate about this paper than the previous paper I wrote. Then, I wanted to kind of distance myself from the topics that were assigned to us, but this time, I was really involved. This topic made me upset (and my readers can probably tell!).
>
> When I started defining the issue, I was more involved in the topic. However, this paper was more difficult to organize than the first one. When I read the article about what happens during recruiting at my school, I was surprised and angry. Having these emotions made it easier to write the paper—I guess that they'd add to what my teacher called an "emotional appeal." During my research, I found that there are many ways in which women are objectified, and there are many ways to define "objectification."
>
> I enjoyed writing this paper because it allowed me to explore my own feelings as well. Each time I revised the paper, I found that I had more to say. Because of peer review and input—as well as input from my wife (who is my best critic), I was able to organize the paper and develop the ideas more fully. I hope that it reads well.
>
> My skills are getting better, but I feel that I still have much to do. Writing this paper also allowed me to consider the women in my life and get a better understanding of what makes them the way they are.
>
> I also think that this persuasive essay might make a real difference to people, at colleges, if they read it and understand my point and then see if their school has a similar program. . . .

Strategies for Success

Successful people use strategies that are effective in most areas of life. Recognizing this, several professional organizations—the Council of Writing Program Administrators, the National Council of Teachers of English, and the National Writing Project—have identified eight strategies that can help writers achieve their goals:

- **Curiosity:** the desire to know more about the world
- **Openness:** the willingness to consider new ways of thinking and being
- **Engagement:** a sense of being involved in and committed to learning
- **Creativity:** the ability to use new and unusual approaches for generating, investigating, and representing ideas
- **Persistence:** the ability to remain interested in and involved with your projects, regardless of their length
- **Responsibility:** the ability to take ownership of your actions and understand the consequences of those actions for yourself and others
- **Flexibility:** the ability to adapt to situations, expectations, or demands
- **Metacognition:** the ability to reflect on your own thinking, as well as on the way that people in your culture tend to think

In chapters 5–12 in this book, you will find suggestions for using these eight strategies to help you become a more effective writer. As you use these strategies, however, think about how they can help you to become more successful in anything that you attempt to do in life.

2 Reading Critically for College and for Life

In Chapter 1, we considered how writing skills will serve you in the academic, professional, civic, and personal areas of your life. This chapter focuses on an activity that reinforces and helps you improve your writing skills: **reading.** When we read, we make meaning out of words on a page or computer screen. We also "read" photographs and other visual images. Actually, then, reading is the active process of constructing meaning.

In this chapter, we ask you to consider how you currently read different kinds of material and give you some helpful reading strategies. Specifically, the chapter presents prereading strategies, strategies for reading actively, and postreading strategies. All of these strategies will help you better understand what you read and use that information to make your own writing more effective.

In your college classes, you will be asked to read (and write) about all kinds of print and digital texts for all kinds of purposes. More often than not, you will use some of what you read in the papers that you write for your college classes. The connection between what you read and how

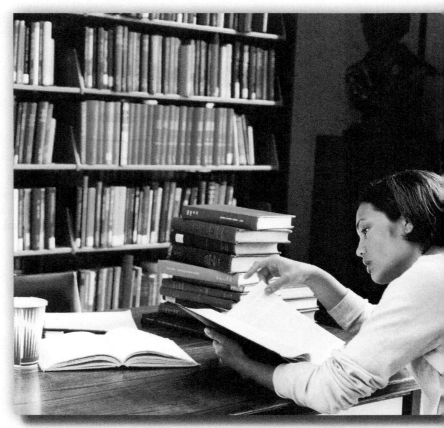

you use that material in your writing requires you to read *critically.*

What does it mean to *read critically?* One thing reading critically does not mean is to be "nit-picky" or negative. Rather, when you read a text *critically,* you question what you read, make connections to other texts you have read and to your own

experiences, and think about how the information in the text might help you as you develop your own writing. To read critically means to read *thoughtfully,* to keep in mind what you already know, and to interact *actively* with the text. Critical readers underline, make notes, and ask questions as they read.

Why Read Critically? Integrating Sources into Your Own Writing

Why do you suppose that your instructor asks you to read critically and thoughtfully? In addition to reading to understand the information, a key reason to read critically and thoughtfully is so that you will be able to put the information and concepts you read about into your own writing, to support your own ideas.

Reading critically also has an added bonus: It helps you understand how the writing you read "works"—what makes that writing effective (or not) or how that writing connects to and affects (or doesn't affect) readers. As you read and learn to understand how the writing your instructors ask you to read *functions*, you will be able to construct more effective texts.

In your college classes, you will be asked to read *a lot*. Understanding what you read and relating what you read to what you already know is, to a large extent, what college is about. As you read for your college classes, consider how you might use that information in your own class papers or examinations. For example, if you know your philosophy instructor will ask you to construct a paper in which you outline and explain "philosophy of the mind," you should look for both of those terms and anything that connects them as you read. Ask yourself:

- What is the main point, the thesis? How does it relate to what I already know? To what I'm reading for this class?

- How are important terms defined? How do the author's definitions compare to what I think the terms mean? What terms or concepts are not explained (and so I'll need to look them up)?

- How effective is the supporting evidence the author supplies?

- What did the author leave out? How does that omission affect his or her argument?

- What information in this text will help me construct my own paper?

You *use* what you learned from your reading by integrating those ideas into your own writing, by citing and paraphrasing the concepts you glean from your reading. You can read about using quotations in your own writing in Chapter 6. Chapter 20 discusses how to paraphrase and attribute those ideas correctly.

Writing Activity

How Do You Read?

Take a few minutes to answer the following questions:

- What kinds of books or magazines do you like to read? Newspapers? Web sites? Blogs?

- How does the way you read a text online differ from the way you read an article from a print magazine or newspaper?

- How do you read your college textbooks? How do the strategies you use to read a text for one course differ from those you use to read texts for another course?

- What strategies do you use to read long, complex nonfiction texts?

- What strategies do you use to help you understand and remember what you have read?

Share your answers with several classmates. How do your responses compare with theirs? What strategies do they use that might be helpful to you?

Using Prereading Strategies

When you write, you have a purpose in mind. As we noted in Chapter 1, the reason for writing is your **rhetorical purpose**—what you hope to accomplish. Likewise, before you read, think about your rhetorical purpose: What are you trying to accomplish by reading? Are you reading to be entertained, to learn new information, to understand a complex subject in more detail, or for some other reason? If you consciously think about *why* you are reading, as well as *how* you plan to read a particular piece of writing, you will have a strategy you can follow as you begin reading.

Before you start to read any written work, take a few minutes to preview its content and design. Look for the following elements:

- The title of the work, or of the particular section you are about to read
- Headings that serve as an outline of the text
- Boxes that highlight certain kinds of information
- Charts, maps, photographs, or drawings
- Numbered or bulleted lists (such as this one) that set off certain information

Think about what you bring to your reading task: In what ways does the text seem similar to or different from others of this type or on this topic that you have already read? What can you bring to the new reading that you have learned from your past experiences? If you are actively involved in the reading process and if you think of reading rhetorically—that is, if you think about what you want to get from the reading—then you will start with a useful map for any text you read.

Next, skim the text by reading the first and last sections or paragraphs, as well as any elements that are highlighted in some way, such as boxes, section titles, headings, or terms or phrases in bold or italic type. Sometimes a box or highlighted section at the beginning of an article—often called an **abstract**—will give you a quick summary of what lies ahead.

As a final step before you start to read, consider again what you hope to accomplish by reading this particular text. Ask yourself:

- What information have I noticed that might help me with my writing task?
- How have I reacted so far to what I have seen in the text?
- What questions do I have?
- What in this text seems to relate to other texts that I have read?

Reading Actively

Now that previewing has given you a sense of what the text is about, you are ready to read actively. Here are some questions to ask yourself as you read:

- What is the writer's thesis or main point? What evidence does the writer provide to support that point? Does the writer offer statistics, facts, expert opinion, or anecdotes (stories)?

- How reliable is the information in this text? How conscientiously does the writer indicate the sources of his or her data, facts, or examples? How credible do these sources seem?
- What else do you know about this topic? How can you relate your previous knowledge to what this writer is saying? In what ways do you agree or disagree with the point the writer is making?
- Has the writer included examples that clarify the text? Are there photographs, drawings, or diagrams that help you understand the writer's main points? Graphs or charts that illustrate data or other statistical information? In what way(s) do the examples and visuals help you better understand the text? What information do they give you that the written text does not provide? What is the emotional impact of the photographs or other visuals?
- What information or evidence is not in this text? (Your past experience and reading will help you here.) Why do you think that the author might have left it out?
- If you are reading an argument, how effectively does the writer acknowledge or outline other points of view on the issue at hand?

For more on strategies for argument, including dealing with opposing views, see Chapter 14.

By asking questions like these, and annotating as you read, you can read all kinds of texts critically, including visuals and Web pages.

Annotating Effectively

When you **annotate,** you interact actively with the text as you read. To annotate a reading, make the following kinds of notes (Figure 2.1 on page 18):

- Underline the main point or thesis of the reading, or otherwise mark it as the key point.
- Underline key supporting points, and indicate in the margins next to the corresponding paragraphs why you think each point is important.
- List any questions you have.
- Respond to the text with your own remarks.
- Jot down key terms and their definitions.
- Mark sections that summarize material as "summary."

Reading Visuals

As a college student, you will most often be asked to read words on paper, but you can usually apply the same strategies you use to read sentences and paragraphs critically to other types of texts as well. You might think that

Writing Activity

Annotating "The Ethics of 'Stealing' a WiFi Connection"

"The Ethics of 'Stealing' a WiFi Connection" discusses a growing issue: Who "owns" the right to Internet access that comes from a person's or business's network? Annotate the rest of Eric Bangeman's comments (see Figure 2.1). As you work, keep in mind your own responses to his comments.

Your instructor may want you to share your annotations with several of your classmates, noting places where your responses are similar and where they may differ.

Margin annotations (handwritten):

> Wonder what this is—guess it's just a network designation and not something I really need to understand.

> Wow—more than half "steal" Internet access. Well, I know some people who do, too.

> My friend Nick has this kind of network—wonder if he is helping people "steal" the Internet? Is someone who has an open network complicit in other people using that network?

> Cool story! I can imagine doing that.

> But is it really silly to use something someone else is paying for and didn't give you permission to use?

> Not sure this analogy works here.

> Neat to be able to use your phone to surf the Web.

> So he is saying that this is a victimless crime?

> I didn't know there was such a thing—have to do some research on what this means.

The ethics of "stealing" a WiFi connection - Ars Technica

http://arstechnica.com/security/news/2008/03/the-ethics-of-stealing-a-wifi-connection.ars

The ethics of "stealing" a WiFi connection

A recently released study by a security firm says that using an open WiFi network without permission is stealing. Ars looks at the ethics of open WiFi

By Eric Bangeman | Last updated January 3, 2008 9:12 PM CT

Network security firm Sophos recently published a study on what it terms WiFi "piggybacking," or logging on to someone's open 802.11b/g/n network without their knowledge or permission. According to the company's study, which was carried out on behalf of The Times, 54 percent of the respondents have gone WiFi freeloading, or as Sophos put it, "admitted breaking the law [in the UK]."

Amazingly, accessing an unsecured, wide-open WiFi network without permission is illegal in some places, and not just in the UK. An Illinois man was arrested and fined $250 in 2006 for using an open network without permission, while a Michigan man who parked his car in front of a café and snarfed its free WiFi was charged this past May with "Fraudulent access to computers, computer systems, and computer networks." On top of that, it's common to read stories about WiFi "stealing" in the mainstream media.

It's time to put an end to this silliness. Using an open WiFi network is no more "stealing" than is listening to the radio or watching TV using the old rabbit ears. If the WiFi waves come to you and can be accessed without hacking, there should be no question that such access is legal and morally OK. If your neighbor runs his sprinkler and accidentally waters your yard, do you owe him money? Have you done something wrong? Have you ripped off the water company? Of course not. So why is it that when it comes to WiFi, people start talking about theft?

The issue is going to come to a head soon because more and more consumer electronics devices are WiFi-enabled, and many of them, including Apple's iPhone and most Skype phones we've used, come ready out of the box to auto-connect to open WiFi networks. Furthermore, as laptop sales continue to grow even beyond desktops, the use of open WiFi is only going to grow along with it.

Steal this WiFi connection!

When you steal something, there's typically a victim. With WiFi, Sophos thinks the ISPs are the victims. "Stealing WiFi Internet access may feel like a victimless crime, but it deprives ISPs of revenue," according to Sophos' senior technology consultant Graham Cluley. Furthermore, "if you've hopped onto your next door neighbors' wireless broadband connection to illegally download movies and music from the 'Net, chances are that you are also slowing down their Internet access and impacting on their download limit." In Sophos' view, then, both ISPs and everyday subscribers can be victims.

In one fell swoop, "stealing WiFi" gets mentioned in the same breath as "illegally" downloading movies and music. The fact is, people join open WiFis for all manner of reasons: to check e-mail, surf the web, look up directions to some place, etc. Those don't sound like nefarious activities, however, and certainly not activities which are likely to get someone in trouble. Of course if you run an open WAP (wireless access point) and it is heavily used for just e-mail, you could still hit your bandwidth cap (if you even have one), but that has to happen only once for that user to figure out what's up, and fix the problem. And let's be honest: it is their problem. No one forced that user to install an open WAP or to leave it wide open. We'll get back to this in a minute.

The argument that using open WiFi networks deprives ISPs of significant revenue is also a red herring. Take the case of public WiFi hotspots: official hotspots aren't that difficult to find in major cities—every public library in Chicago has open WiFi, for instance. Are the public libraries and the countless other free hotspot providers helping defraud ISPs? No, they're not. There's no law that using the Internet requires payment of a fee to an ISP, and the myriad public hotspots prove this.

Really, there's only one time when you could argue that an ISP is being gypped, and that's when someone is repeatedly using his neighbor's open WiFi in lieu of paying for his own service. Is this really wrong? Let's consider some parallel examples. If the man in question were given a key and told that he could enter his neighbor's house whenever he wanted to use a PC to access the Internet, would this be wrong? Of course not. They key here (pun intended) is the "permission" given by the owner of the home. Our leeching friend would clearly be in the wrong if he were breaking into the house, of course, because he would be sidestepping something clearly set up to keep him out. If he has permission, I suppose one could argue that it's still not right, but you won't find a court that will punish such a person, nor will you find too many people thrilled at the idea that someone else can tell them who they can and can't allow into their homes for what purposes.

Some people leave their wireless access points wide open deliberately. A friend of mine and recent seminary graduate lived in a campus-owned apartment building. In addition to being a man of the cloth, Peter is a longtime Linux user and open-source advocate. While living here in Chicago, he got his DSL from Speakeasy and shared the connection with others in his building...and anyone else who needed a quick Internet fix (Speakeasy even encouraged this). He even positioned his router so that anyone in the church across the street could pick up a signal. Obviously, not everyone is like Peter. But despite easy-to-read instructions and a plethora of warnings about the need to secure your WAP, some people just can't be bothered to enable the most basic security settings.

To the person with a laptop and a sudden need to check e-mail or surf the web, it's not possible to tell who is leaving their access points open deliberately and who just plain doesn't care. The access point is there and the virtual doors are unlocked, so why not take advantage of it if you're in need?

A couple of caveats: be familiar with the law of the land. As the examples at the beginning of this story show, it's illegal to access a WAP without permission—even if it's wide open—in some places. Also, you should never use an open point for anything illegal or even unneighborly. Don't log onto the first "linksys" WAP you see and fire up a torrent for your favorite, just-released Linux distro.

And as always, don't leave your own 802.11b/g/n router wide open unless you're comfortable with random surfers using your 'Net access for their own purposes.

Open WiFi is clearly here to stay.

FIGURE 2.1   Example of Annotations on a Page

ELECTRONIC ENVIRONMENTS **Using the Internet to Find Definitions**

Are you faced with a college reading assignment that contains unfamiliar language? When the glossary in the book just isn't enough, try searching for definitions online. A number of good dictionaries and thesauruses are available online. One research strategy is to use a Web search engine to find definitions of complex terms. For example, if you're looking for a working definition of *existentialism*, type "define: existentialism" (without quotation marks) into a search engine's search box. Often the results at the top of the list will include dictionary sites, academic Web sites, and technical sites that have developed working glossaries for students, experts, and professionals.

visuals are easier to read than written text, but this assumption is not accurate. In fact, you often have to pay more attention to visual images, not only because they are sometimes subtler than written text but also because you may not be accustomed to reading them critically.

Although the process of understanding photographs, bar and line graphs, diagrams, and other visuals may seem different from that of reading and understanding textual information, you are essentially doing the same kind of work. When you read a text, you translate letters, words, and sentences into concepts and ideas; when you read a visual image, you do the same kind of translation. Just as you read a local newspaper or other printed text for information, you also read the photographs in the newspaper or the images on your television or computer screen to be informed.

As you read visuals, here are some questions to consider:

- How can you use words to tell what the visual shows?
- If the visual is combined with written text, what does the visual add to the verbal text? What would be lost if the visual were not there?
- Why do you think that the writer chose this particular format—photo, line drawing, chart, graph—for the visual?
- If you were choosing or designing a visual to illustrate this point, what would it look like?
- How accurately does the visual illustrate the point?
- What emotions does the visual evoke?

Reading Web Sites

Today many of us read Web sites, which can include not only text, with type in different colors and various sizes, but also photographs or other visual elements, videos that we can click on to view, and music. To read Web sites actively and critically, you need to examine the information on your screen just as carefully as you would a page of printed text or a visual in a magazine or newspaper. Because there are more aspects of the text to examine and consider, however, and also because it is often more difficult to establish where a text on the Web comes from, active

Writing Activity

Reading Text and Visuals in an Advertisement

Select a full-page advertisement from a newspaper or magazine, and read both the written text and the visual elements carefully, keeping in mind that nothing in an advertisement is left to chance. Each element, from the kind and size of the typeface, to the colors, to the illustrations or photographs, has been discussed and modified many times as the advertisement was developed and tested. On a separate piece of paper, jot down answers to the following questions:

- What is this advertiser trying to sell?
- What kinds of evidence does the advertisement use to convince you to buy the product or service?
- Does the advertiser appeal to your beliefs and sense of fairness (the rhetorical appeal of *ethos*—see page 27), and if so, how?
- Does the advertiser use factual data, statistics, or quotations from experts (the rhetorical appeal of *logos*—see page 27), and if so, in what way?
- In what ways does the advertisement appeal to your emotions (the rhetorical appeal of *pathos*—see page 27)?
- What strategies does the advertiser employ to convince you of the credibility of the ad's message?
- How effective is this advertisement? Why?
- How might the various elements of the advertisement—colors, photos or other visuals, background, text—be changed to make the ad more, or less, effective?
- How much does the advertisement help potential buyers make in formed decisions about this product?

If your instructor asks you to do so, share your advertisements and notes with several of your classmates. What similarities did you find in the advertisements that you selected? In what ways did the advertisements make use of visuals? What were the most effective elements of the advertisements?

reading becomes even more important. Consider the following additional questions when you are reading a Web page:

- The uniform resource locator (URL) of a site, its address, can give you clues about its origin and purpose. For any page you visit, consider what the URL tells you about the page, especially the last three letters—*edu* (educational), *gov* (U.S. government), *org* (nonprofit organization), or *com* (commercial). What difference does it make who sponsors the site?
- How reputable is the person or agency that is providing the information on this page? You can check the person's or agency's reputation by doing a Web search (using *Google, Bing,* or *Yahoo!,* for instance).

Writing Activity

Reading Web Pages: What You Can See

Using the questions on pages 20 and 22, read the following Web page. Respond in writing to as many of the questions as you can. Compare your responses with those of your classmates.

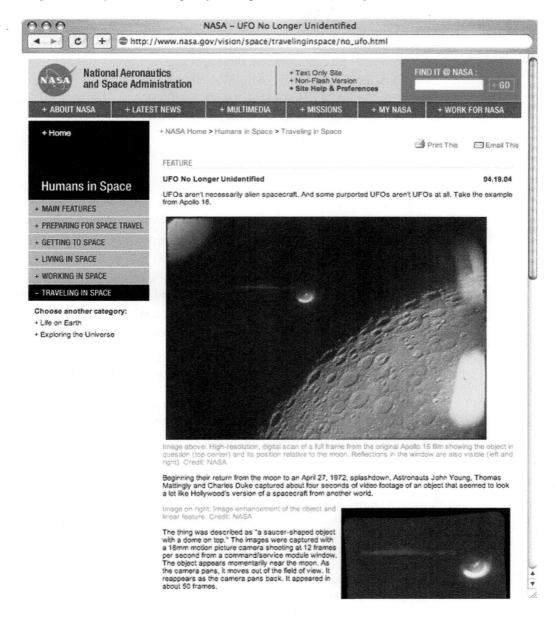

- What clues do you see as to the motives of the person or agency that is providing this information? Is there a link to an explanation of the purpose of the site? Usually, such explanations are labeled something like "About [name of organization or person]."
- How current is the information on this page? Can you find a date that indicates when the page was last updated?
- Does the site make use of facts and statistics from credible sources (*logos*)? Is the site's author a recognized authority, and has he or she linked to other credible sites (*ethos*)? Does the site appeal to readers' emotions (*pathos*)? (See p. 27 for more on these three appeals).
- How does the structure of the Web site affect its message?
- If there are links on the page, how helpful is the description of each link? Are the links working, or do they lead to dead ends?

For further details about evaluating information on the Web, see Chapter 19, "Finding and Evaluating Sources."

Using Postreading Strategies

After you have read an essay or other text actively and annotated it, spend a bit of time thinking about what you have learned from it and even writing in response to it. Review your annotations and answer the following questions:

- What is the main point or idea you learned from working through this text?
- What did you learn that surprises or interests you?
- How does the information in this text agree with or contradict information on this topic you have already read or learned from your own experience?
- What questions do you still have about this text?
- Where can you find answers to those questions?
- What in this reading might be useful in your own writing?

One useful method for storing and keeping track of what you have learned from your reading is to keep a writer's journal. A journal is a handy and accessible place to write down the information and ideas you gather, as well as your reactions to and insights about the texts you read. Other effective postreading strategies include writing summaries, synthesizing information, and using your reading in your writing. Finally, you might be assigned to write a rhetorical analysis of a text you have read.

Starting Your Writer's/Research Journal

A writer's journal is a place where you keep track of the notes, annotations, and summaries that you make from your reading. Because any writing project longer than a page or two demands more information than you can usually store in your memory, it is vital to keep a written record of information that you discover. You can use the entries in your journal as the basis for group discussions as well as for writing tasks.

The information that you include in your journal can vary based on the needs of the project you are working on. The format and design will also vary to suit your purpose. In other words, your rhetorical situation will have an impact not only on the material you collect, the notes that you take, and the summaries and syntheses that you write (see pages 23–26 and Chapter 3), but also on the physical makeup of your journal. If you are working on a project that requires a large number of illustrations, for example, you will need to include space in your journal to store them.

It is usually a good idea to keep a journal of some sort for *each* writing project you are working on. Consider the following questions for each journal:

- What kinds of information (data, charts, anecdotes, photos, illustrations, and so on) should you collect for this project?
- What information will help you get your message across to your intended audience?
- What information might you jot down that may lead to more complex ideas? Why would more complexity be desirable?
- What questions do you have, and how might you go about finding answers to those questions?
- What kinds of illustrations might help you *show* what you mean?

As you write in your journal, you should note where ideas or quotations come from in the original texts so that you will be able to properly cite them in your own writing. Get in the habit of noting the information you will need to cite your source, including the page number an idea or quotation comes from.

For more on taking notes from and properly citing sources, see Chapter 20.

Writing Effective Summaries

After they have read and annotated a text, many readers find that summarizing it also helps them to understand it better. A **summary** is a concise restatement of the most important information in a text—its main point and major supporting points.

Writing Activity

Reading a Text Critically

Assume that for your business ethics class, you have been asked to read the column "Downloading Music: Harmful to the Artist, the Recording Company, or Neither?" by Carlton Vogt, which appears on page 24. Vogt wrote the piece for *InfoWorld*. Based on what you have learned in this chapter, consider how you should go about reading this text. Use the critical reading skills you have learned to do the following:

- Explain what you already knew about this topic just from the title.
- In a brief paragraph, explain what you did before you read this text. Did you skim it?
- Annotate the first paragraph.
- Jot down your answers to the following postreading questions, using no more than two sentences for each response.
  - What was your initial reaction and response to this text?
  - What is the main idea you learned from working through this text?
  - Did you learn anything that surprises or interests you?
  - In what ways does the information in this text reinforce or contradict other texts you have read or what you know from your own experience?
  - What questions do you still have about this text?

(continued)

Reading a Text Critically (*continued*)

InfoWorld

http://www.infoworld.com/articles/op/xml/01/05/04/010504opethics.html

---

Ethics Matters by Carlton Vogt

Downloading music: harmful to the artist, the recording company, or neither?

I may be the best person to talk about Napster—or the worst. You can see where this is going already. I don't buy a lot of CDs. In fact, I can't remember the last time I bought one. I don't download music from the Internet. And I don't write or perform music. So I'm either completely neutral or totally out of the loop.

That's the nice way of putting it. Some readers, responding to recent columns, put it less charitably. Their verdict: I haven't thought about it enough, I'm totally clueless, or I'm an idiot. All of these were comments about my position on Napster, which is puzzling, because I haven't taken one. However, these readers pointed out to me that the situation is perfectly clear:

1. Downloading music is not stealing.
2. Downloading music is definitely stealing.
3. Downloading music is wrong, but not stealing.
4. Downloading music is neither wrong nor stealing.

How could I be so dense? There were several variations on these themes. Some thought you could rip music off a purchased CD to use on other devices. Others thought you could share certain tracks—but not the whole CD—with intimate friends (although they didn't say what level of intimacy you need to have achieved first). A few argued that the music industry was so evil that anything you can do to use music for free is totally justified.

And, in typical fashion, many were convinced that their opinions were not only correct, but also self-evident. So I'm glad we've cleared that up.

A few argued the fine points of copyright law, but the connection between law and ethics is, at best, tenuous—and the subject of a future column—so I usually hesitate to look to the law for the proper ethical answer.

But let's take my CD-buying experience as an entry point. What sometimes happens is that I go to the store, look at a CD that strikes my fancy, find four out of 12 tracks that I find appealing, and put the CD back. Is the recording company better off or worse off that I've not bought the album? I suppose you could say it's worse off, although I could argue that it's neither, because its position hasn't changed from before I looked at the album. However, it has lost a potential customer. Have I done anything wrong? No. I have no obligation to make the company better off by buying the album.

How about the artist? Again worse off—and on two counts. Not only has the artist not gotten whatever royalty would come from the sale of the CD, but also I haven't heard the music. And isn't the whole point of performing so that people will hear what you do?

I'm a writer, and I get paid for it. InfoWorld puts my column on its Web site. On one level I'm satisfied; I've got my money. However, if the Web site traffic maven were to come and tell me that my column got only two page hits, I would be devastated. I would be more devastated if InfoWorld didn't come through with the paycheck, but not having anyone read the column hurts a lot too.

Getting back to music, suppose I download the four CD tracks I like from the Internet? Is the record company better or worse off? It's not worse off, because I wasn't going to buy the CD anyway. It may be better off, because I just may buy the next CD the artist puts out if I like this one. Or I may tell someone about it, who might then go out and buy the CD.

How about the artist? The artist is definitely not worse off, because I wasn't going to buy the CD anyway. So he or she isn't losing anything. But, in the sense of having someone appreciate the performance, the artist is definitely better off. There may be some artists who don't care at all about audience appreciation, but if all a performer is interested in is the money, I suspect I wouldn't even be downloading the music.

So putting aside legal considerations, the ethical question at hand is, "Have I harmed anyone?" That is, have I set back any of their important interests without justification? Because I have no obligation to buy a CD, if I don't want one, it's hard to say that I have harmed either the artist or the recording company by not buying the CD. And in downloading the music, I may have advanced at least one of the artist's interests because I am listening to the music.

On the other hand, if I am downloading or sharing the music to avoid otherwise buying the CD, then you could say that I was harming both the artist and the recording company because I was depriving them of income they otherwise would have had—my money. And that makes all the difference.

The fly in the ointment lies in who determines whether or not I would have bought the CD. You certainly don't know and neither does the recording company. I may think I know, but we have a remarkable ability to deceive ourselves, especially when self interest is involved.

Carlton Vogt is a former InfoWorld editor.

Done

Writing a Summary: To write an effective summary, start by listing the main points of the text, in effect outlining what you are reading. Remember, however, that a summary is more than just a list; a summary provides a brief narrative structure that connects these main ideas.

STEPS FOR WRITING A SUMMARY

1. Read the text relatively quickly to get a general sense of what it is saying.

2. Read the text again. Mark or highlight a sentence that expresses the main point of each paragraph, and paraphrase that point—put it entirely into your own words—in the margin.

3. For a longer text, label the major sections. If the writer has provided subheadings, use them as they are or paraphrase them. If not, write subheadings.

4. After considering what you have done in the first three steps, write a statement that captures the writer's main point or thesis.

5. Working backward from step 4, craft a paragraph—in your own words—that captures the gist of what the writer is saying.

Synthesizing Information in Readings

Synthesis calls for the thoughtful combination or integration of ideas and information with your point of view.

Suppose that you would like to see a particular movie this Saturday. You hope to persuade a group of your friends to accompany you. You have read several reviews of the film, you know other work by the director, and you have even read the novel on which this movie is based. At the same time, simply sending your friends all the information you have about the film might overwhelm them. Unless you effectively structure what you have to say, one piece of information may contradict some other point that you want to make.

To organize your information, you could focus on what you see as the most compelling reasons your friends should see the film: the novel the film is based on, along with the director of the movie. You would then provide information to support your points:

- Specific examples to show how interesting the novel is
- Reviews or other information about the film to show how effectively the novel has been translated to film
- Other films by the same director that you know your friends like

For more help with writing a synthesis, see Chapter 3.

Writing Activity

Summarizing "Downloading Music: Harmful to the Artist, the Recording Company, or Neither?"

In no more than one page, summarize "Downloading Music: Harmful to the Artist, the Recording Company, or Neither?" (page 24). If your instructor asks you to, share your summary with several of your classmates.

For more on avoiding
plagiarism, see
Chapter 20.

When you synthesize effectively, you take the jumble of facts, data, information, and other knowledge you have on hand and put it into an understandable format that fulfills the purpose you want to accomplish. And, of course, when you cite reviewers' opinions (in the hope of convincing your friends which movie to see), you will need to indicate where the comments came from—to properly attribute what the reviewers had to say and to lend their authority to your argument. Failure to properly attribute ideas to original sources constitutes plagiarism.

As we have noted, to fully understand information and then be able to synthesize it effectively, you must read critically, questioning, challenging, and engaging the text as you work through it. One strategy that will help you improve your critical thinking and reading is to work with others. When you work with your classmates, you hear their perspectives and ideas and have the opportunity to consider various points of view. Working with others also helps you learn to construct the most effective questions to ask, to help you become an active reader.

Writing Activity

Synthesizing Information

Using what you have learned from this chapter on critical reading and synthesizing information, reread "The Ethics of 'Stealing' a WiFi Connection" (page 18) and "Downloading Music: Harmful to the Artist, the Recording Company, or Neither?" (page 24). Both readings involve ethical issues: Synthesize the issues outlined in these readings in no more than two pages. Remember that a synthesis is a thoughtful integration of your readings with your own point of view. Where do you stand on these ethical dilemmas? What else have you read in your college classes that relates to these ethical situations?

Using Your Reading in Your Writing

Information that you find in your reading can be used in many ways in your writing. If you have annotated the texts that your instructor asked you to read for a writing project in this course or another course, you can often use those annotations in your own writing. Likewise, if you have summarized sources for a research project, you can refer to and use those summaries to spot the important points of each text you have read, and then use relevant information as evidence to support your main idea. If you have found statistical information in graphical form, or photographs, drawings, maps, or other illustrations, these too can become part of your text. Of course, it is always important to indicate where you found information, whose ideas you use in your text, and where statistical information came from in order to establish your credibility and avoid *plagiarizing*—representing the words or ideas of others as your own ideas or words.

In the chapters in Parts 2 and 3 of this book, you will read various selections. As you read these texts or conduct research in the library and on the Web to find support for your writing, you will find it helpful to use the reading strategies described in this chapter.

Constructing a Rhetorical Analysis

When you *analyze* something, you mentally "take it apart" to determine how the various parts or aspects function and relate to the whole. If you were to analyze, say, the winning team in last year's Super Bowl or World Series, you would examine the coaching, the players, the game plan, or perhaps all of these elements to determine how the parts of that team work together to make it the best. (For more on analysis, see Chapter 8.)

A rhetorical analysis is a way of looking at something, often a text, from a *rhetorical standpoint*. The purpose of examining a text from a rhetorical perspective and then constructing a rhetorical analysis of that text is to help you understand how it functions: how each aspect works to fulfill its purpose. If a text is trying to persuade you of something, you should examine how the various parts of that text work to *persuade*. If a text is intended to be informational (a newspaper article, for example), then you should look for evidence of how that text informs.

A rhetorical analysis includes a search for and identification of *rhetorical appeals:* the aspects of a piece of writing that influence the reader because of the credibility of the author (*ethos*), an appeal to logic (*logos*), an appeal to the emotions of the audience (*pathos*), or all three. The relationships among *ethos, logos,* and *pathos* can be represented as a triangle in which the author is related to an appeal to *ethos*, the audience or reader to the appeal of *pathos*, and the purpose of the text to the appeal of *logos:*

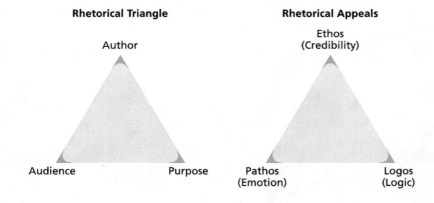

Rhetorical Triangle

Author

Audience   Purpose

Rhetorical Appeals

Ethos
(Credibility)

Pathos   Logos
(Emotion)   (Logic)

(For more on the rhetorical triangle, see Chapter 14.)

GENRES *Up Close*   **Writing a Rhetorical Analysis**

The purpose of a rhetorical analysis is to examine an item—most often a text—to determine how the parts or aspects of the text function together to accomplish the author's purpose. Rhetorical analysis, then, is really a critical reading.

One way to understand how to use a rhetorical approach is to consider an advertisement. How does a specific advertisement work to convince the audience? Most often, an

FIGURE 2.2
Advertisement for
Levi's Copper
Jeans

advertisement is intended to convince a reader to buy a product. Consider the advertisement for Levi's Copper Jeans shown in Figure 2.2. Do you notice the shiny white areas in the ad? The words "original" and "reconstructed"? The coppercolored background, which reinforces the name of the product? Could the ad be suggesting that the copper rivets used in the manufacturing of Levi's Copper Jeans are strong, like the metal used to surgically reconstruct (there is that word again) a broken arm? If so, what kind of rhetorical appeal is the ad making?

How do you interpret the use of the word "original" in this advertisement? Is the ad suggesting that only "original" people wear Levi jeans? That these jeans make you, somehow, original? If so, what kind of rhetorical appeal is the ad making?

Could the skeletal figure have been used to suggest that real "original" people wear these jeans, especially those engaged in dangerous activities (like extreme sports, which might account for the figure's broken arm)? If so, what kind of rhetorical appeal is the ad making?

In a rhetorical analysis, you will usually do the following:

- Identify the context of a piece of writing or a visual text (author, audience, and purpose).
- Identify the structure of the piece (chronological, cause/effect, problem/solution, topical, and so on).
- Identify the rhetorical appeals of the piece (*ethos, logos, pathos*).

Ethos appeals to a reader's beliefs, sense of ethics, and credibility, and to the trustworthiness of the speaker/author. When you read a text to identify the writer's *ethos,* look for the following characteristics:

- Language appropriate to the audience and subject
- A sincere, fair presentation of the argument
- Grammatical sentences
- A level of vocabulary appropriate for the purpose and level of formality

When you read a text to identify the rhetorical appeal of *logos,* look for the following characteristics:

- Literal (dictionary) meanings of terms or reasons, rather than metaphorical or connotative meanings
- Factual data and statistics
- Quotations from authorities and experts, properly cited

When you read a text to identify the rhetorical appeal of *pathos,* look for the following characteristics:

- Vivid, concrete language
- Emotionally loaded language. (For example, calling your friend Ben "pig-headed" has a more negative connotation than calling him "stubborn." Likewise, describing your friend Jane as a "sheep" has a more emotional connotation than describing her as "meek.")
- Examples that evoke an emotional response

- Narratives of events that have an emotional impact
- Figurative language (when you describe one thing by comparing it with something else: "Courtney is as quiet as a sigh").

(For more on rhetorical appeals, see Chapter 14.)

Here are some questions that will help you pinpoint the rhetorical appeals in a text:

- Who is the intended audience? How do you identify the audience?
- What do you see as the writer's purpose? To explain? Inform? Anger? Persuade? Amuse? Motivate? Sadden? Ridicule? Is there more than one purpose? Does the purpose shift at some point within the text?
- Can you identify the rhetorical appeals in this piece of writing (*ethos, logos, pathos*)? What would you add to or omit from it to make the rhetorical appeals more effective?
- How does the writer develop his or her ideas? Narration? Description? Definition? Comparison? Cause and effect? Examples?
- What is the tone of the text? Do you react at an emotional level to the text? Does this reaction change at all throughout the text?
- How does the writer arrange his or her ideas? What are the patterns of arrangement?
- Does the writer use dialogue? Quotations? To what effect?
- How does the writer use diction? Is it formal? Informal? Technical? Does the writer use jargon? Slang? Is the language connotative? Denotative? Is the language emotionally evocative? Does the language change throughout the piece? How does the language contribute to the writer's aim?

For more on these strategies, see Chapter 13.

Writing Activity

Writing a Rhetorical Analysis

Apply the first three questions to the advertisement for Levi's Copper Jeans on page 28. Share your responses with several of your classmates. How are those responses similar? How are they different?

Writing to Understand and Synthesize Texts

Martin is a student in his first semester of college. As soon as he bought his books and examined the course syllabi for his classes, he knew that he would have a lot of reading to do. As part of his first-year composition class, Martin is learning about the process of critical reading. As noted in Chapter 2 (page 14), he found it especially useful to learn that "to read critically means to read *thoughtfully,* to keep in mind what you already know, and to *actively* interact with the text. Critical readers underline, make notes, and ask questions as they read."

Martin has taken this advice, becoming an active reader of the texts assigned in his classes. However, as he skims the assignments for the papers he will be asked to write this semester, Martin can see that he also will have a good deal of outside research to do for assigned course papers. An assignment for his political science class looks especially interesting but also worrisome. It asks students to read three articles and parts of a book and then to relate the information in these reading selections to one another. Martin realizes that he will not only need

to understand everything he reads in these selections, but he will also need to use that information in his own writing: He will need to *synthesize* it.

Reading this chapter carefully and thoroughly (and actively) will help you handle assignments such as the one Martin confronts: It will help you understand the information you read, form a critical response to it, and then synthesize the ideas from more than one source in your own college writing.

31

Setting Your Goals

- **Rhetorical Knowledge:** Because this chapter focuses on "understanding and synthesizing texts," your immediate goal is both to understand the information you will read in your classes and then to use that information effectively by synthesizing it in your own papers, using the instruction this chapter provides. As you read any text you will use as a source, you need to consider the purpose of the assignment you are responding to. (You can find this out by reading the assignments for your various classes.) How do those assignments ask you to explain and then synthesize the information in the essays and books you are required to read for your classes?

- **Critical Thinking, Reading, and Writing:** As you read critically and actively (see Chapter 2), think about how that reading relates to other texts you have read and other information you have learned. Think about what reading strategies you can use to discover the main areas of agreement. By making marginal notes and by annotating the texts as you read them, you will find it much easier to connect information and synthesize it in your own papers.

- **Writing Processes:** If your instructor assigns one of the writing assignment options on pages 33–34, think critically about your own writing process as you work on it: What kinds of invention activities do you find most useful? What organizational approaches help you best achieve your purpose? What kind of feedback helps you revise most effectively? Thinking critically about the answers to those kinds of questions will help you in the future, when you face a similar writing situation.

- **Knowledge of Conventions:** As you edit your work, think critically about how you used sources (your research), and be sure to cite them using the appropriate documentation style.

RHETORICAL KNOWLEDGE

In most of your college classes, much of what you will do involves reading, understanding, and working with texts. In these classes, you will read to glean information as well as to understand concepts. You will be asked to demonstrate that you know the information in your class texts, and often you will be asked to write about how the concepts you have learned relate to one another.

As noted in the opening to this chapter, there is useful advice on how to read critically and effectively all through this textbook, beginning with Chapter 2. As you may recall from that chapter, it can be useful to think about how you read various kinds of materials. Different reading strategies, such as annotating and keeping a writer's journal, can help you to read print texts as well as the texts and images in an advertisement or on a Web site. Finally, when you learn how to read a text critically, you will be able to summarize and synthesize the material you learn from it effectively.

"Ways of Writing to Understand and Synthesize Texts" on page 35 provides examples of genres you may use in your writing, both for college classes and for other areas of your life. The genres of writing you will be assigned will vary depending on the texts you are reading and the audience you are addressing.

Writing to Understand and Synthesize Texts

In this chapter, you will put into practice what you have learned about effective critical reading. We ask that you focus on the two terms in the title of this chapter:

- When someone asks you whether you **understand** a text, what does that question mean to you? How might you demonstrate that you have read and understood a piece of writing?
- When you are asked to **synthesize** texts, what does that term mean? How might you show that you can synthesize two or more texts?

Writing Assignment Options

The most effective way to demonstrate your knowledge is to put that knowledge into practice. The two assignments that follow ask for brief pieces of writing that demonstrate your ability to respond critically to a text and to synthesize two texts.

OPTION 1

As you know, reading *critically* does not necessarily mean that you criticize a text or look at it in a negative way, but rather that you read actively, questioning as you read and making connections to other texts you have read. In other words, you work at reading to help you better understand—and then be able to use—the information.

Write a critical response to a brief reading selection, either one of the selections in this chapter (pages 38–42) or a selection chosen by you or your instructor. In your response, explain

- What new information you learned from the text
- How the information relates to what you knew about the subject before you read the text
- What questions you still have after reading this text

OPTION 2

In addition to writing responses to texts for your various college classes, you often will be asked to synthesize the ideas in two or more texts. When you synthesize, you show that you not only understand the texts you read, but that you can explain how the ideas and concepts in the two selections relate to one another. Find two reading selections on a similar topic and read and annotate them, or set up a table comparing the points the authors of the two readings make. Focus on several points each reading makes about the same concept or idea. The goal is to write an essay that provides a fair representation of both points of view on the issue, along with your own perspective. Some questions to consider and answer in your essay include the following:

- What information in the texts is similar, and in what ways?
- What information is different, and in what ways?
- What evidence in each text supports the assertions its author makes? What evidence in the other text supports other assertions or claims?

Rhetorical Considerations in Writing to Understand and Synthesize Texts

Before you begin writing in response to either of the options above, consider the various aspects of your writing situation:

Audience: Who is your primary audience? Who else might be interested in the subject that you are focusing on? Why?

Purpose: Your writing can have various purposes. For example, if you are writing in response to Option 2, your purpose is to inform readers of how the texts you read make similar or differing *claims* (arguable statements requiring support), how the evidence they use to back those claims is the same or different, and so on. That information will help your own readers become more informed about the issues or concepts those texts discuss.

Voice, tone, and point of view: Your instructor will advise you on whether you should use the pronoun *I* in your text, or whether you should write in the third person (avoiding *I*) as you write your critical response (Option 1) or synthesize the information in two texts (Option 2). In either case, your tone should be neutral.

For more on choosing a medium and genre, see Chapter 17 and Appendix C.

Context, medium, and genre: You will need to understand the situation that establishes the occasion to write. How will your writing be used? If you are writing for an audience beyond the classroom, consider what will be the most effective way to present your information to this audience.

Ways of Writing to Understand and Synthesize Texts

Genres for Your College Classes	Sample Situation	Advantages of the Genre	Limitations of the Genre
Review of the Literature	Your psychology professor asks you to read several articles on a topic and then write a review in which you analyze each of them and finally present a synthesis.	This project should give you a better understanding of the subject of these articles.	This project is limited in scope. Since in fields like psychology the most current information is usually preferred, you'll need to make sure your review contains the most recent articles on this topic.
Essay Exam	In your political science class, you have to take an in-class essay exam in which you are asked to synthesize several political trends you have studied.	This kind of assignment allows you to show your instructor that you understand the course material.	A timed essay often limits your ability to show what you really know about a subject.
Academic Essay	Your sociology professor asks you to write an essay that synthesizes several of the theories of social behavior you have studied.	An academic essay will allow you to demonstrate your grasp of these theories.	Academic essays are often written in technical language, making it difficult for those outside of that particular field to understand them.
Critique	Your business instructor asks you to do a critical response to a business plan for a bike-repair shop near the campus.	Since you or people you know may be customers of the proposed business, your critical response may help the new business better understand their potential customer base.	You may not have enough information to completely understand the financial needs of the new business.
Critical Response	Your First-Year Experience instructor asks you to write a critical response to an article you've read about social media.	Looking at an article on social media critically may help you make better decisions about your own use of social media.	Since social media is now everywhere and rapidly evolving, and anyone can participate, you need to make sure of the accuracy and currency of the comments you're critiquing.
Genres for Life	**Sample Situation**	**Advantages of the Genre**	**Limitations of the Genre**
Recommendation Report	You are asked to analyze the phone needs of each department in your workplace. You must then synthesize your findings and recommend the best new phone system.	By looking at each department's needs, you are likely to come up with a global plan.	It's possible that one department has unique needs that you will miss in your search for a global solution.
Memo	After a reorganization at your company, you need to write a memo synthesizing the real effects of the change.	By providing your staff with a synthesis of recent changes, you provide them with truly useful information.	By presenting your staff merely with the basic facts, you may be ignoring some "human effects" of the recent changes.
Consumer Blog	You decide to create a blog for people in your neighborhood. In your blog you will synthesize reviews of local businesses offering consumer services.	By synthesizing the content of multiple reviews, you save your neighbors time.	Blogs need to be updated and maintained regularly.
Review of a competitor's product	Your boss asks you to use a product produced by a competitor and critique it.	By actually using a competitor's product, you will know how it really compares with yours.	You need to be careful that you don't have an internal bias toward your own product.
Response to a proposal to change the storm drainage in your neighborhood.	A group of your neighbors are concerned that a new plan from the city to alter the drainage in your area will damage the streets in your neighborhood and cause flooding.	You will let the city know that you are concerned that their proposal will have a negative impact on the quality of life in your neighborhood.	To be taken seriously, such responses to municipal projects need to be backed up by evidence—in this case, a report from a civil engineer would probably be required.

CRITICAL THINKING, READING, AND WRITING

Often, writing to understand texts takes place informally, in a classroom situation. You write a critical response to a text as a means of learning or to explain the ideas from a single text. In a synthesis you explain to readers how the information in a text is similar to or different from the information in the other text(s) you are synthesizing, or how the information in one text agrees or disagrees with (and thus supports or refutes) the claims made in other texts. The student examples that appear in the following sections will illustrate both forms of writing.

Qualities of Effective Writing to Understand and Synthesize Texts

Effective writing that responds to a text or synthesizes two or more texts engages your readers because the information you present is offered in a compelling way and, in a synthesis, is combined with your own carefully considered point of view.

Readers expect the following qualities in writing that demonstrates understanding of texts or that synthesizes two or more reading selections:

- Clear, complete explanations of the main points of the text or texts. So that your reader will be able to understand your response or synthesis, you need to make sure that the main ideas in the text or texts you are considering are clearly and completely explained. Look for terms that readers might not know and define them. Explain concepts that are difficult to understand.

- An informative thesis and evidence to support it. Your critical response to the text or texts should be clearly articulated in a *thesis statement*—a statement of your main point—and backed by evidence such as examples or quotations.

- Similarities and differences clearly explained in a synthesis. You can, of course, emphasize the areas you consider most important. For example, perhaps the texts present a similar point of view or argument, but differ in these areas:

  - *The kinds of evidence they present.* One text, for example, might use data (numbers, statistics) while the other might use anecdotes or expert testimony.

  - *The emphasis placed on certain ideas or concepts.* Determining which ideas each author is emphasizing gives you a sense of what each author thinks are the most important aspects of the subject being discussed.

*For more on
comparison and
contrast, see Chapter 13.*

- Relationships clearly outlined and explained. The relationships between ideas and concepts and information in the texts you synthesize need to be clearly explained so your readers can see those relationships and connections in the same way that you see them. Explain in detail in what ways the texts agree and disagree with each other.

Reading to Learn about Understanding and Synthesizing Texts

On January 17, 2012, *Wikipedia,* Google, and Craigslist protested pending federal legislation in the House of Representatives, titled the Stop Online Piracy Act (SOPA), and similar legislation in the Senate, titled the Protect Intellectual Property Act (PIPA). Both bills were intended to address a serious problem in the media: foreign Web sites that offer copyrighted content such as music or films without paying for it. Under SOPA, for example, people holding rights to the content would be able to seek legal remedies, including court orders requiring other sites, such as search engines, to cease doing business with an offending site. In protest, *Wikipedia* was blacked out for its English-speaking users. Although Google and Craigslist were not blacked out, the two sites did post language urging members of Congress to vote against the legislation. The following reading selections present some of the issues surrounding this proposed legislation, which was not enacted.

DANNY GOLDBERG

Kill the Internet—and Other Anti-SOPA Myths

Danny Goldberg began his career as a music journalist, writing for *Rolling Stone, Billboard,* and *Village Voice.* He has also written several books: *How the Left Lost Teen Spirit* and *Bumping into Geniuses: My Life inside the Rock and Roll Business.* He is president of Gold Village Entertainment, which manages musical artists and makes their work available to the public via the Internet. Goldberg has served as president of several other music companies. During his career his companies have managed clients such as Nirvana, Bonnie Raitt, Hole, Sonic Youth, The Allman Brothers, Rickie Lee Jones, Allanah Myles, Tom Cochrane, and the Beastie Boys.

This editorial originally appeared in *The Nation,* the oldest continuously published weekly magazine in the country, in January 2012. Founded by abolitionists in 1865, just months after the Civil War ended, *The Nation,* which labels itself as "the flagship of the left," focuses primarily on politics and culture.

1   The House's Stop Online Piracy Act (SOPA), and the Senate's companion Protect Intellectual Property Act (PIPA), were shelved last week in the wake of protests by dozens of websites and large numbers of their users, as well as a virtually unanimous chorus of criticism from leading progressive voices and outlets, including Michael Moore, Cenk Uygur, Keith Olbermann, Alternet, Daily Kos, MoveOn and many people associated with Occupy Wall Street. Judging by the fervor of the anti-SOPA/PIPA protests, a casual observer might think the advocates of the anti-piracy bills were in the same moral league as the torturers at Abu Ghraib.

2   To be sure, the legislators who crafted the ill-fated bills and the film industry lobbyists who supported them have little to be proud of. As someone who makes my living in the music business representing artists who are hurt by piracy, I was frustrated by the failure of the bills' proponents to explain their rationale in language I could understand. This may have been because the bills themselves were so flawed, but it also reflects the delusion that this issue could be settled in the corridors of Washington without public debate. (This presumption was exemplified by the statements of MPAA Chairman and CEO Chris Dodd, who petulantly threatened that the Obama administration's defection to the anti-SOPA/PIPA camp would imperil Hollywood contributions to Democrats.)

3   But before we celebrate this "populist" victory, it's worth remembering that the defeat of SOPA and PIPA was also a victory for the enormously powerful tech industry, which almost always beats the far smaller creative businesses in legislative disputes. (Google alone generated more than $37 billion in 2011, more than double the revenue of all record companies, major and indie combined.)

4   It is also worth contemplating the moral compass of Megaupload.com's Kim Dotcom, who was arrested in New Zealand last week in his 25,000-square-foot

compound surrounded by a fleet of Mercedes and Ferraris, all allegedly made possible by selling content stolen from artists (and yes, entertainment companies) around the world. As film producer (*Mean Streets, The Last Waltz*) and author Jon Taplin wrote on his blog, putting the accused pirate's riches in perspective, "A bunch of the musicians I worked with in the 1960's and 1970's, who made wonderful records that are still on iPod have seen their royalties cut by 80 percent."

One example of anti-SOPA rhetorical over-reach was a tendency by some   5 to invent sinister motives for the sponsors. On his usually brilliant show *The Young Turks*, Uygur said that SOPA's sponsors were "pushing for a monopoly for the MPAA and to kill their competition on the Internet." This is untrue. They wanted to kill those entities that steal their movies and make money off them, either directly or indirectly. There really is a difference.

In a widely viewed anti-SOPA/PIPA speech on Ted.com, Internet philosopher Clay Shirky similarly attributed dark motives to the studios. The targets are   6 not Google and Yahoo!, he said, "They're us, we're the people getting policed." This is accurate only if by "us" he means the people who illegally watched *Hugo* from the likes of Megaupload. If he means a friend sharing Marianne Faithfull's version of "Visions of Johanna" with me on Facebook, then the accusation is absurd.

Shirky's remarks begin with a poignant anecdote about a bakery that   7 stopped allowing children to put up their own drawings of characters like Mickey Mouse because of fear of copyright lawsuits. Examples such as this, or of a theoretical risk of parents being charged for the right to have kids sing "Happy Birthday," are demagogic. The underlying issue is scale. There is a profound moral difference between loaning a friend a book and posting, without permission, the content of bestsellers for commercial gain—and people and legislators ought to take that distinction into account.

SOPA and PIPA bashers were also a little loose with the word "censorship". To me, that word should be reserved for government power that restricts   8 ideas—like the U.S. government locking up Eugene Debs for opposing World War I, or prosecuting City Lights Books for selling *Howl*.[1] This kind of repression is common now in China, where most computers and cell phones are made by oppressed labor. Real censorship is dreadful enough that there ought to be a different word for laws that would try to prevent websites from illegally posting the latest *Mission Impossible* movies or making ancillary income from the eyeballs such transactions attract.

One of Shirky's acolytes wrote on the comments page, "We're talking about   9 *digital* content here. When I copy digital information, no one loses anything. The creator of the content doesn't lose profit, because I haven't taken anything

---

[1] Eugene Debs was a labor leader and five-time Socialist Party candidate for President; *Howl* is a poem by Allen Ginsberg, a famous member of the Beat Generation.

physical from them. It does not cost anything to copy digital information. It isn't stealing to copy a digital something." Umm . . . what about the cost of *creating* the content worth copying?

As Robert Levine describes in his book *Free Ride,* down this road lies a 10 barren culture with lots of dancing kittens on YouTube but no infrastructure that can nurture future artists. Piracy enablers stress the need to maintain incentives for investment in tech companies. But maybe business models that depend on using copyrighted material for free should not attract investment in the first place. iTunes pays artists, record companies and songwriters and is doing just fine. Meanwhile, the degradation of the value of intellectual property elsewhere online has caused a dramatic reduction of investment in businesses that fund the creation of journalism, literature, music and films.

For years, there have been Internet philosophers who claimed that adver- 11 tising revenue would replace copyright revenue and those of us in the "old media" simply needed to get up to date. It's simply not true.

Some argue that, since iTunes and Amazon are surviving, Napster's origi- 12 nal model was legally killed and Kim Dotcom was apprehended, no new laws are needed. The status quo may be what we end up with, but that doesn't make it inevitable or right. Human beings have created the piracy problem and although, like any kind of crime, society can't eliminate it entirely, we can decide whether or not to seriously try.

In a way, this is a fight between Godzilla and King Kong. Consumers may 13 like Godzilla because they don't want any interruption in the full use of their gadgets. And I prefer King Kong because I've never seen an Internet company give advances to writers, musicians or filmmakers that allow them to concentrate on creativity. But let's be real—we should look at all of these companies with a jaundiced eye and question their talking points at least as rigorously as we scrutinize politicians. What is good for Google and Facebook is not always going to be what's best for the 99 percent. (And of course Microsoft and Apple et al. are extremely aggressive when it comes to protecting *their* intellectual property rights).

I hope that in future weeks, some of the anti-SOPA/PIPA progressives will 14 reflect on the content of some of the Kool-Aid that has recently been served and help swing the pendulum back, if only a little, in a direction in which intellectual property can be nourished. Otherwise, we will be complicit in accelerating the trend of the last decade, in which those who write code get richly rewarded, while those who write the music, poetry, drama and journalism that are being encoded have to get day jobs.

JIMMY WALES AND KAT WALSH

We Are the Media, and So Are You

It's easy to frame the fight over SOPA and PIPA as   1
Hollywood vs. Silicon Valley—two huge industries
clashing over whose voice should dictate the future of
Internet policy—but it's absolutely wrong. The bills are
dead, thanks to widespread protest. But the real architects of the bills' defeat don't have a catchy label or a
recognized lobbying group. They don't have the glamour or the deep pockets of the studios. Yet they are the
largest, most powerful and most important voice in the
debate—and, until recently, they've been all but invisible
to Congress.

They are you. And if not you personally, then your   2
neighbors, your colleagues, your friends and even your
children. The millions of people who called and wrote
their congressional representatives in protest of the
Stop Online Piracy Act and the Protect Intellectual Property Act were "organized" only around the desire to
protect the Web sites that have become central to their
daily lives.

Change like this needed a fresh set of voices. The   3
established tech giants may have newfound political
influence, but their fights are still the same closed-door
tussles over minor details. They have been at the table,
and they have too much invested in the process to
change it. More important, they are constrained by obligations to their shareholders and investors, as well as
by the need to maintain relationships with their advertisers, partners and customers.

Wikipedia, its users and its contributors don't have   4
the same constraints. We don't rely on advertising dollars or content partnerships. The billions of words and
millions of images in our projects come from the same
place as our financial support: the voluntary contribution of millions of individuals. The result is free knowledge, available for anyone to read and reuse.

Wikipedia is not opposed to the rights of creators—we have the largest col-   5
lection of creators in human history. The effort that went into building *Wikipedia*
could have created shelves full of albums or near-endless nights of movies.
Instead it's providing unrestricted access to the world's knowledge. Protecting

Jimmy Wales has
degrees from
Auburn Univer-
sity and the
University of
Alabama. He is
a co-founder
of *Wikipedia,*
the online, open-
source encyclopedia
that was launched in
2001. He serves as a member of
the Wikimedia Foundation Board
of Trustees. He is also a fellow of
the Berkman Center for Internet
and Society in the Harvard Law
School. Kat Walsh, a
graduate of Stetson
University and
George Mason
University, is an
attorney special-
izing in technol-
ogy policy,
patents, and copy-
right law. Her inter-
ests include freedom of
speech, licenses for free content,
and access to knowledge. She is
also a member of the Wikimedia
Foundation Board of Trustees. The
following article was originally
published in the *Washington Post*
in February 2012.

our rights as creators means ensuring that we can build our encyclopedias, photographs, videos, Web sites, charities and businesses without the fear that they all will be taken away from us without due process. It means protecting our ability to speak freely, without being vulnerable to poorly drafted laws that leave our fate to a law enforcement body that has no oversight and no appeal process. It means protecting the legal infrastructure that allowed our sharing of knowledge and creativity to flourish, and protecting our ability to do so on technical infrastructure that allows for security and privacy for all Internet users.

6   We are not interested in becoming full-time advocates; protests like the *Wikipedia* blackout are a last resort. Our core mission is to make knowledge freely available, and making the Web site inaccessible interrupts what we exist to do. The one-day blackout, though, was just a speed bump. Breaking the legal infrastructure that makes it possible to operate Wikipedia, and sites like ours, would be a much greater disruption.

7   Two weeks ago we recognized a threat to that infrastructure and did something we've never done before: We acknowledged that our existence is itself political, and we spoke up to protect it. It turned out to be the largest Internet protest ever.

8   The full-time advocates of freedom of information, such as the Electronic Frontier Foundation and Public Knowledge, have been fighting for decades to help create the legal environment that makes our work possible. We cannot waste that effort by failing to speak in our own defense when that environment is threatened.

9   It's absolutely right that Congress cares about the content industry, recognizing its ability to innovate, to create wealth and to improve lives. But existing copyright enforcement laws were written in a world in which the information we had access to on a broad scale came from a few established media outlets. The players were easy to identify. They organized into groups with common interests and fought to protect those interests. The "content industry" is no longer limited to those few influential channels.

10   The laws we need now must recognize the more broadly distributed and broadly valuable power of free and open knowledge. They must come from an understanding of that power and recognition that the voices flooding the phone lines and in-boxes of Congress on Jan. 18 represented the source of that power. These laws must not simply be rammed through to appease narrow lobbies without sufficient review or consideration of the consequences.

11   Because we are the media industry. We are the creators. We are the innovators. The whole world benefits from our work. That work, and our ability to do it, is worth protecting for everyone.

UNDERSTANDING A WRITER'S GOALS: QUESTIONS TO CONSIDER AND DISCUSS

Rhetorical Knowledge: The Writer's Situation and Rhetoric

1. **Audience:** How have Goldberg and Wales and Walsh considered their audiences?

2. **Purpose:** Why did these authors write these two editorials? What did they hope to accomplish?

3. **Voice and Tone:** What are the writers' attitudes toward various stakeholders—those who produce content (for example, musicians, actors, and writers), those who market content (for example, publishers, music companies, film companies), and those who consume content (the general public)?

4. **Responsibility:** How responsibly have these authors represented the interests of all the stakeholders in this controversy? Why do you think that?

5. **Context, format, and genre:** How do the authors of each of these two editorials synthesize others' ideas?

Critical Thinking: The Writer's Ideas and Your Personal Response

6. Which editorial is more closely aligned with your own values? Your own view? Why?

7. How do these editorials challenge you to think about copyright and access in new ways?

Composing Processes and Knowledge of Conventions: The Writer's Strategies

8. After writing the full names of the two pieces of legislation, the writers use their abbreviations (SOPA, PIPA)? Why do they do that?

9. Why does Goldberg cite the story about the bakery that stopped posting children's drawings of cartoon characters?

Inquiry and Research: Ideas for Further Exploration

10. If you were to use these two readings to advise members of Congress on how to craft legislation that protects the rights of all interested stakeholders, what would you say to them?

GENRES *Up Close*   **Writing a Critical Response**

Critical responses are common in all four areas of life. In academic contexts, students are frequently expected to respond to assigned readings. In professional situations, workers respond critically to reports, memos, and proposals. In civic settings, voters respond critically to candidates' stump speeches and debate sound bites. In the personal area of life, people respond to a wide range of texts—product reviews, restaurant menus, labels on boxes and cans, and many others.

An effective critical response will encourage readers to think critically about the text under consideration. An effective response generally includes the following features:

- Enough details about the text so that readers can understand what it is about.

- An accurate and fair representation of the text's main point.

- A clear indication of the writer's perspective on the text.

As you read the following critical response, consider how student writer Margaret Munson has incorporated these features.

MARGARET MUNSON

CRITICAL RESPONSE   **Critical Response to "We Are the Media, and So Are You" by Jimmy Wales and Kat Walsh**

The title of this editorial—on the still controversial Stop Online Piracy Act (SOPA) and Protect Intellectual Property Act (PIPA)—draws upon two key ideas that the article is trying to emphasize. First of all, the catchy phrasing suggests a personal association between the readers and the issue, thus encouraging support for the article and its purpose. Secondly, the authors focus on a major resource that they would like to draw upon in the fight to stop these acts from being passed by Congress: the importance of the individual voter.   1

Munson provides details about the article.

After initially reading through this text, I found I needed to skim it twice   2 before attempting to dissect the rather weighted language. This particular article makes points similar to those I've read and heard throughout various Web sites and the news media; however, this discussion—from the viewpoint of *Wikipedia*—definitely adds an additional perspective. The beginning of the article does not focus heavily on *Wikipedia*, instead explaining how individual voters expressed their views about the bills. After mentioning the idea of Hollywood versus Silicon Valley, in which Hollywood is interested in the continuance of strict copyright rules, while Silicon Valley is more invested in the technological advances of current Internet culture, Wales and Walsh are quick to establish—much like most of the writers who have dealt with this controversy—that it is not the tech giants (Google and so on) nor the Hollywood stars that altered the fate of these two bills, but the individual voter, the "we" and the "you," who actually stopped the copyright laws from being enacted. While this battle is far from over, Wales and Walsh seem to want to make it clear that "we" are the creators and "we" are the only ones who can stop bills like these from becoming law, now and in the future.

As mentioned previously, it would seem that the importance of the individ- 3 ual voter was not the only significant factor in the defeat of these bills, however, but also the relevance and importance of sites like *Wikipedia*, where information is free, and creators are many. Since SOPA and PIPA are bills that address the copyright infringement of Internet spaces like Napster, where individuals often use and/or sell creative property that they did not produce, it is an intriguing perspective to consider the effect this legislation may have on a site like *Wikipedia*, where most text is individually produced. According to this article, the passage of PIPA and SOPA would not only have damaged sites that break the law by selling copyrighted material such as videos and downloadable songs, but it could also greatly hurt the individual posting on a site such as Wikipedia. As this article claims, Wikipedia and other sites encourage "us" to be the producers; these bills, if they were to become law, would affect "us," and therefore the authors encourage "we the people" to do something about future bills that may be introduced. The lingering question I have is simply this: are the people behind sites like Wikipedia really interested in the "we," or are they just invested in the "I"? While *Wikipedia* is nonprofit, other sites to which many people contribute content, such as *YouTube*, are not nonprofit. The issue of who the media is, therefore, is probably more complex than this article indicates.

Munson indicates the main point of the article.

Munson indicates her perspective on the article.

Work Cited

Wales, Jimmy, and Kat Walsh. "We Are the Media, and So Are You." *Washington Post.* Washington Post, 9 Feb. 2012. Web. 27 Feb. 2012.

UNDERSTANDING A WRITER'S GOALS: QUESTIONS TO CONSIDER AND DISCUSS

Rhetorical Knowledge: The Writer's Situation and Rhetoric

1. **Audience:** What does Munson do to appeal to a wide audience?

2. **Purpose:** What has Munson accomplished by writing this response?

3. **Voice and tone:** What is Munson's attitude toward Wales and Walsh? Toward their editorial?

4. **Responsibility:** How accurately has Munson represented the position that Wales and Walsh take in their editorial?

5. **Context, format, and genre:** At the beginning of the second paragraph, Munson reflects on her own reading process. Why would a writer do that in a critical response?

Critical Thinking: The Writer's Ideas and Your Personal Response

6. How does Munson's critical response help you to think critically about Wales and Walsh's editorial?

7. How does Munson's critical response affect your understanding of SOPA and PIPA?

Composing Processes and Knowledge of Conventions: The Writer's Strategies

8. How effectively has Munson paraphrased and summarized material from the editorial? Why does Munson begin her response by commenting on the title of the editorial?

Inquiry and Research: Ideas for Further Exploration

9. Write your own response to Wales and Walsh's editorial, focusing on the ideas that interest you most. How does your response differ from Munson's?

WRITING PROCESSES

You may already recognize that you will engage in many writing processes as you invent and develop your ideas, draft, revise, and edit your writing to understand and synthesize texts. These processes are recursive. In other words, effective writers rarely work in a lock-step fashion but instead move back and forth among the different parts of the process. As you work on the assignment option that you have chosen (see pages 33-34), keep these processes in mind, as well as the qualities of effective writing to understand and synthesize texts (pages 36-37).

 ## Invention: Getting Started

When you are writing to respond critically to a text or to synthesize information you have read in two or more texts, there are a few questions to keep in mind as you read the text or texts for the first few times and begin to develop your ideas. In addition, as you start your critical reading process, asking yourself questions like the following will help you as you read and analyze the text or texts and then produce your critical response or synthesis.

FOR A CRITICAL RESPONSE OR A SYNTHESIS:

- What is the purpose of the text or texts you are responding to critically?
- How solid is the author's argument?
- Do you have any issues with any of the author's assumptions?
- What is the author's main point?
- Does the author appeal more to facts or to emotions?
- To what extent do you believe the author?

FOR A SYNTHESIS:

- What is your purpose in synthesizing information from these texts? For example, are you simply trying to understand complex ideas, or are you trying to convince an audience of a particular point of view?
- Do the different texts you are synthesizing offer multiple perspectives on an issue or a topic or just different versions of the same perspective?
- What have you learned by reading, analyzing, and synthesizing these different texts?
- How similar or different are the thesis statements of the texts you are synthesizing?
- How similar or different are the examples each author uses to make his or her case?
- How do the various perspectives in the different texts you have read and analyzed help you to understand the subject?

Kill the Internet—and Other Anti-SOPA Myths ← Perspective

Danny Goldberg | January 24, 2012

The House's Stop Online Piracy Act (SOPA), and the Senate's companion Protect Intellectual Property Act (PIPA), were shelved last week in the wake of protests by dozens of websites and large numbers of their users, as well as a virtually unanimous chorus of criticism from leading progressive voices and outlets, including Michael Moore, Cenk Uygur, Keith Olbermann, Alternet, Daily Kos, MoveOn and many people associated with Occupy Wall Street. Judging by the fervor of the anti-SOPA/PIPA protests, a casual observer might think the advocates of the anti-piracy bills were in the same moral league as the torturers at Abu Ghraib.

To be sure, the legislators who crafted the ill-fated bills and the film industry lobbyists who supported them have little to be proud of. As someone who makes my living in the music business representing artists who are hurt by piracy, I was frustrated by the failure of the bills' proponents to explain their rationale in language I could understand. This may have been because the bills themselves were so flawed, but it also reflects the delusion that this issue could be settled in the corridors of Washington without public debate. (This presumption was exemplified by the statements of MPAA Chairman and CEO Chris Dodd, who petulantly threatened that the Obama administration's defection to the anti-SOPA/PIPA camp would imperil Hollywood contributions to Democrats.)

But before we celebrate this "populist" victory, it's worth remembering that the defeat of SOPA and PIPA was also a victory for the enormously powerful tech industry, which almost always beats the far smaller creative businesses in legislative disputes. (Google alone generated more than $37 billion in 2011, more than double the revenue of all record companies, major and indie combined.)

It is also worth contemplating the moral compass of Megaupload.com's Kim Dotcom, who was arrested in New Zealand last week in his 25,000-square-foot compound surrounded by a fleet of Mercedes and Ferraris, all allegedly made possible by selling content stolen from artists (and yes, entertainment companies) around the world. As film producer (*Mean Streets, The Last Waltz*) and author Jon Taplin wrote on his blog, putting the accused pirate's riches in perspective, "A bunch of the musicians I worked with in the 1960's and 1970's, who made wonderful records that are still on iPod have seen their royalties cut by 80 percent."

Margin annotations:
- *If creativity is produced in a multitude of ways, how can we harness this with one over-arching bill?*
- *Check out some of these names, esp. the less familiar ones.*
- *Blame on wording rather than on purpose?*
- *Look up*
- *From theft?*

FIGURE 3.1 Margaret Munson's Annotations on the First Part of "Kill the Internet—and Other Anti-SOPA Myths"

- What is the purpose of your synthesis? For example, are you simply trying to understand complex ideas, or are you trying to convince an audience of a particular point of view.

For help with critical reading, see Chapter 2. For more on strategies for argument, see Chapter 14.

For her synthesis assignment, student writer Margaret Munson chose two articles about legislation that aimed to deal with the problem of the unauthorized use of copyrighted material on the Internet. You can read both articles on pages 38-42. (Munson's critical response to one of the articles is on page 44.) She began by reading the two articles critically, taking notes, and annotating them. In her notes and annotations she included reactions to and questions about the articles based on her own knowledge and experience. You can see her annotations on a portion of "Kill the Internet—and Other Anti-SOPA Myths" in Figure 3.1. She then created a table to help her compare the writers' major points.

Munson's Initial Thoughts/Questions

Both articles seem to show (not necessarily believe) that though the individual will not be affected directly, the sites they utilize daily, will be. Kill the Internet seems to think the individual won't be affected unless they utilize sites like megaupload,

Napster, etc. However, what of posted YouTube videos that are "copyrighted," or reworking someone's video and not giving them credit, Facebook posting of song lyrics or "covering" a song—how many artists begin their work that way? Will this become a match with the individual, rather than the mega-corporations? Who loses out with these bills? Should copyright laws be adapted to fit the times, or are we truly thieving intellectual property with our daily posts, thoughts, comments, and videos? When does intellectual property end—is it a quote, a whole song, a commercial entity, or is it merely a large corporation making excessive funds off of individuals? Is this a fight with the individual or the corporation?

We are the Media—view of bills	Kill the Internet—view of bills
About the individual	About the majors (megaupload etc.)
Will affect the individual online spaces	Is geared towards bigger companies
Focus on personal	Focus on politics
Appeal to emotions	Appeal to logic
Individual voters—reason it didn't pass—it affected them personally	Wording of the bill—issue with passing
Supporting sites like Wikipedia—shows side	Countering TED Talks video—shows side
Creativity—to share, created by all, shared by all, funded by advertisers, individuals, corporations	Creativity—physical product, created by few, shared through purchase by individual

Notes on both:

- Agree bills couldn't be settled in Washington w/o public debate—different opinions on why this is so
- Two perspectives, based on completely different systems . . .
- If creativity is produced in a multitude of ways, how can we harness this with one or two overarching bills? Can they account for both perspectives?
- Based around two different infrastructures. Both valid points. The question remains—who is morally correct?

Writing Activity

Reading Critically and Taking Notes

Using the guidelines in Chapter 2 on reading critically, read the article or articles you have chosen, and take notes on your reactions and responses to the questions on page 47. You might annotate the article or articles, using the guidelines in Chapter 2. If you are writing a synthesis of two articles, you might create a table to help you compare the writers' main points.

Organizing Your Ideas and Details

Once you have generated ideas about the text you are responding to or the texts you are synthesizing, you might choose to organize your paper in a variety of ways. The organization for a critical response essay can be relatively straightforward. One possible way to organize your paper is to focus first on the title to see how that leads into the piece, as Margaret Munson did in her critical response to Jimmy Wales and Kat Walsh's article (pp. 44-45). Munson then goes on to analyze and comment on the individual points Wales and Walsh make in the article. She comments both on the effectiveness of the points the authors make as well as some of their shortcomings.

In an academic essay where you have been asked to develop a synthesis of several texts, you will probably start with a description of what you are synthesizing.

You might include a thesis statement in your introduction that articulates the main idea of your synthesis. You can then provide details from the texts you have read that support your thesis.

You might also organize a synthesis by briefly summarizing and analyzing each of the texts you have read in turn, leading up to your synthesis, which you would present at the end. This organization might be effective for a review of the literature on a particular topic.

For help with quoting and paraphrasing sources, see Chapter 20.

Constructing a Complete Draft

Writing Activity

Using your notes from your critical reading of the article or articles you have chosen and the organizational pattern you have decided on, write a complete first draft of your critical response or your synthesis. Remember that your ideas will likely change as you draft your paper.

Once you have decided on the organizational pattern that you think will be most effective, go back over the notes you made during your invention process and see which points you want to include in your draft. Of course, you will need to make sure you can clearly articulate your critical response to the text you have chosen or your synthesis of two texts.

As you write your first draft, you will need to consider whether it will be most effective to paraphrase parts of the text or texts you have read or whether using a direct quotation might be a better way to support a particular point.

Margaret Munson's First Draft

After organizing her details, Margaret Munson wrote a first draft of her synthesis essay. Notice that she has chosen to give her perspective in the two sentences, framed as questions, at the end of the first paragraph. She then contrasts the two articles by paraphrasing some of their points. As she wrote, Munson concentrated on getting her ideas down; in later drafts she edited for style, grammar, and punctuation. (The numbers in circles refer to peer comments—see page 53.)

"Kill the Internet—and Other Anti-SOPA Myths"
by Danny Goldberg and "We Are the Media, and So Are You"
by Jimmy Wales and Kat Walsh ❶

The perspectives these authors associate with are made clear in the rather intensely phrased titles they allot to their individual pieces. What is not clarified, however, is the reasoning for such opposing views, nor the importance of both sides. ❷ The problem, not really addressed in either of these pieces, lies in the infrastructure that each is working within; Wales and Walsh exist in the creative, free-knowledge space of the Internet, while Goldberg resides in the long-established world where physical innovation is purchased by individuals.

Neither of these perspectives is really "old" or "out-dated." It's just the fact that these major sources of creativity and innovation are very different.❸ If creativity is produced in a multitude of ways, how can we harness all under one or two over-arching copyright laws? Can we account for both of these perspectives when they are built within such opposing infrastructures?

Despite the authors' abilities to note the opposing creative worlds they're coming from, they both have relevant notes to offer the reader about their own viewpoints. Goldberg appeals to the audience from a more logical perspective, utilizing politics and the economy to support his points. He states at the start of his piece that the reason that SOPA and PIPA did not pass did not lay in the purpose behind the bills, but in the phrasing of the bills themselves. Wales and Walsh seem to have a different view on how to approach the intended audience. They appeal to the reader's emotions and focus on the personal effect the bills could have on individuals. Wales and Walsh depict that the reason the bills did not succeed actually lay in the individuals' personal associations with these online spaces and their one by one calls to representatives to halt the bills' passing. Personally, I think they're both right. As Wales and Walsh draw upon, and as was seen strewn about the Internet,❹ the *people* of America were simply outraged. But why were they so upset? It would seem according to both of these pieces, people were so enraged because from their perspective, the bills were targeting them and their Internet way of life. The disagreement here lies in whether or not this viewpoint is accurate or not.

As mentioned prior, in "We Are the Media, and So Are You" by Jimmy Wales and Kat Walsh, the authors heavily discuss the influence of these bills on the individual and their everyday Internet spaces. Walsh and Wales support most of their claims with information on how the bills came to be silenced by individual voters. They also discuss the perspective of *Wikipedia* and how on a site such as this, while information is generally produced individually, they will still be heavily affected by bills like SOPA and PIPA, because copyright infringement laws may limit the sharing of certain information, texts, photos, etc. *Wikipedia*❺ is not commercial, it does not stream or sell movies/songs like some sites, they simply share information created by individuals for their company. However, with new copyright infringement laws, this could all change—a comment, or post by one individual could negatively affect the entire structure and ability of sites like *Wikipedia* to function. Wales and Walsh claim, while it's important that Congress cares about the content industry, the times and systems have changed, and so must copyright laws.

From a somewhat opposing viewpoint, Goldberg approaches the issue of copyright laws from the perspective of the major company, rather than the individual. His piece, "Kill the Internet—and Other Anti-SOPA Myths," counters a TED Talks video that portrays a parallel perspective to that of Walsh and Wales. Goldberg believes that the bills were poorly constructed, but that the purpose of these laws was to deal with Internet piracy—major companies that are gaining profit for creative works they did not produce, sites like Megaupload and Napster. The TED Talks' perspective, much like that of Walsh and Wales, claims that sites like Facebook and YouTube (sites we individuals utilize daily) could crash and burn because of their lack of funding and man-power to police individual comments, videos, status updates, posts, etc. They claim that people wish to produce, and not just consume, that individuals should still be allowed to create, and that bills like SOPA and PIPA will prevent that from happening. Goldberg calls out this TED Talks video and claims that sharing videos or text on Facebook is completely different than illegally viewing new movies on an Internet site like Megaupload. He claims that remarks about copyrighting Mickey Mouse or the Happy Birthday song (referencing points in the TED video) is "demagogic." I find the final point intriguing, mainly because Wales and Walsh appealed emotively in their piece, preying on the individual's need to maintain their rights. The question still remains though, who is right and who is wrong? ⑥

Goldberg makes the intriguing claim that people and legislators need to take into account the difference between using others' works for commercial gain, versus, sharing a book, text or song for the sake of sharing. If this were considered for new bills, would copyright laws attempting to kill piracy seem more appropriate? What is the real difference between these two articles—does it lie in the actual argument or just the perspective? Personally I think both these authors are looking for a compromise on the original SOPA/PIPA proposals. It simply comes down to whether or not authorities could (or are willing to) create a bill that can cater to differing infrastructures. Wales and Walsh are coming from a world where innovative ideas are created by all, shared by all, and funded by individuals, corporations, advertising; while Goldberg is coming from a perspective of a creative physical product, created by few and purchased by individuals. Until these two worlds can come together, it does not seem possible that legislators could create a bill that would address copyright issues in both structures that would appeal to the individual, the creator, and the more major companies. ⑦

Student Comments on [Student Writer's] First Draft

1. "Do you think you might come up with a more engaging title?"
2. "Can you mention the specific legislation early on?"
3. "I think I can see they're different, but can you tell me how?"
4. "Can you be a bit more specific here?"
5. "Is this just about Wikipedia? Does it impact other things as well?"
6. "Is this just 'right or wrong'? Can you explain a little more?"
7. "I think you're just repeating yourself here. Can you make this a little more specific?"

Revising

Revising means redoing your work after re-thinking it. After you have finished your first full draft, you are likely to be too caught up in the ideas and language you have just written to be prepared to make real changes. It helps to put the draft of your critical response or synthesis aside for a day or so before coming back to it for revision. For example, you may think of another point to make about the text or texts you are responding to or synthesizing. However, because even experienced writers often find it hard to read their own work with fresh eyes, it also pays to have others look at your draft and provide you with comments. Classmates, friends, or family members can offer suggestions you might not have seen on your own. As you reread your critical response or synthesis draft, here are some questions to ask yourself:

- How effectively have I developed a response or synthesis of the ideas expressed in the text or texts I have read? Have I explained my response or synthesis by using specific examples from the original texts?

- How well do I know the audience I'm writing for? What have I done to make certain that my audience will understand my point of view?

- Are there any terms I use that my audience might not understand? Do I need to define or explain any of them?

- Would using some visuals help my readers understand my points better? Why?

Technology can help you revise and edit your writing. For example, you can use the track-changes function of your word processor to try out your revisions and edits. After seeing what those changes might look like, you can choose to "accept" or "reject" those changes.

WRITER'S *Workshop* | **Responding to Full Drafts**

As you read and respond to your classmates' papers (and as they comment on yours), focus on the nature of critical response or synthesis in this assignment from a reader's perspective. Ask questions about their writing and respond to their ideas by exploring your reactions to their thoughts.

Working in pairs or groups of three, read each other's drafts, and then offer your classmates comments that will help them see both their papers' strengths as well as places where their ideas need further development. Use the following questions to guide your responses to each writer's draft:

- What is your first impression of this draft? Do you think the title is effective?
- What do you like about this draft? Provide positive and negative feedback to the writer.
- What is the writer's focus? How effectively does the writer maintain the focus throughout the paper?

- How effective is the critical response or synthesis? Where is the writer particularly effective? What suggestions could help the writer?
- How does the introduction help the reader understand the topic? What suggestions can you make to strengthen the introduction?
- How effectively has the writer analyzed the text or texts that are being used to develop the critical response or synthesis? Why?
- How effectively does the conclusion bring the critical response or synthesis to a close? How effectively does it sum everything up? What suggestions could strengthen the conclusion?
- Do you see any weaknesses in the paper? What suggestions could strengthen the paper as a whole?

Responding to Readers' Comments

After receiving feedback on their writing from peers, instructors, friends, and others, writers need to decide how to respond. Although you should take seriously all comments from people who have read your work, you are not obligated to use all of them as you revise. Make sure you understand why your readers have made their comments and then, using your best judgment, incorporate their suggestions or answer their questions in your revisions as you see fit.

In the final version of Margaret Munson's paper on pages 56-58, you can see how she responded to her peers' comments.

KNOWLEDGE OF CONVENTIONS

When effective writers edit their work, they attend to the conventions that will help their readers move through their writing effortlessly. These include genre conventions, documentation, format, usage, grammar, punctuation, and mechanics. By paying attention to these conventions in your writing, you make reading a more pleasant experience.

 ## Editing

In college classes, you may respond to or synthesize texts in response to essay examination questions asking you to—for example—find common threads in two or more readings. Editing a response to an in-class essay question can be challenging because time is limited, and you may not be allowed to consult any sources, including the course textbook. Because of these limitations, ask your instructor how carefully you will be expected to edit your essay during the examination. If your instructor expects you to edit a timed essay response, set aside a few minutes to do that task.

Of course, if your assignment is to write an out-of-class critical response to a text or a synthesis of texts, you will have time to edit your essay carefully. Put your writing aside for a day or two so that you can read it with fresh eyes. Also, ask classmates, friends, or tutors to read your paper and note areas that need further editing.

At this point in the process, you need to make sure everything in your paper follows the conventions of grammar, usage, punctuation, and spelling. You can use the spell-check function of your word processing program to help, but be careful. If you've turned off the spell-check function while you've been writing, make sure you run it before your final edit. Remember, the spell-check function will not flag words that are spelled correctly but used incorrectly, such as *there* instead of *their*.

 ## Genres, Documentation, and Format

If you are writing an academic paper, follow the conventions for the discipline in which you are writing and the requirements of your instructor. If you have used material from outside sources, give credit to those sources, using the documentation style required by the discipline you are working in and by your instructor. If you are synthesizing two or more texts, you will need to document any quotations that you use from the texts.

For advice on writing in different genres, see Appendix C. For guidelines for formatting and documenting papers in MLA or APA style, see Chapter 20.

A Writer Achieves Her Goal: Margaret Munson's Synthesis

As you read the final version of Margaret Munson's synthesis, consider what makes it effective. Following the reading, you will find some questions to help you consider Munson's writing.

MARGARET MUNSON

SYNTHESIS   **Protecting Creativity in a Wired World: Two Perspectives**

A peer reviewer asked this question:

Do you think you might come up with a more engaging title? Munson changed the title.

Another reviewer asked this question:

Can you mention the specific legislation early on? Munson added this information.

One of Munson's readers wrote the following comment:

I think I can see they're different, but can you tell me how?

Munson added detail about different ways of exchanging payment.

The titles of these two articles, which hint at the perspectives of the authors   1
on the Stop Online Piracy Act (SOPA) and the Protect Intellectual Piracy Act (PIPA), indicate the strength of their opposing views. The problem, not really addressed directly in either of these editorials, lies in the infrastructures that these authors are working within and writing from: Wales and Walsh work within the creative, free-knowledge space of the Internet, while Goldberg resides in the long-established world where creative products are purchased by individuals. Neither of these perspectives is really old or out-dated or even unnecessary when you consider that both are still extremely prevalent in our society. It's just that within these major sources of creativity and innovation, writers, artists, and other producers exchange their work for payment in completely different ways. If creativity is produced in a multitude of ways, how can we harness it all under one or two overarching copyright laws? Can we account for both of these perspectives when they come from such different infrastructures?

Both Wales and Walsh in their article and Goldberg in his have relevant   2
notes to offer the reader about their own viewpoints on these two pieces of legislation. Goldberg appeals to the audience from a logical perspective, drawing on politics and the economy to support his points. He states at the beginning of his piece that the reason that SOPA and PIPA did not pass did not lie in the purpose behind the bills, but rather in the way the bills were explained to the public. Wales and Walsh, by contrast, appeal to the reader's emotions by focusing on the effect the bills could have on individuals. According to them, it's important to protect "the legal infrastructure that allowed our sharing of knowledge and creativity to flourish." Both viewpoints have merit. As Wales and Walsh evoke, and as could be seen throughout the Internet in January 2012—at the time of the protest of SOPA and PIPA—through Facebook photos, status updates,

Tweets, and even Tumblr pictures, the *people* of America were simply outraged by these bills. But why were they so upset? According to both of these articles, it would seem that people were so enraged because the bills appeared to target them and their daily online interactions. However, from Goldberg's point of view, perhaps it was simply the bills' wording that gave Americans the impression that their lives would be affected. The disagreement here lies in the interpretation of the bills.

In "We Are the Media, and So Are You," the authors discuss the influence   3
these two bills could have on individuals and their everyday Internet spaces. The authors focus a great deal on fear for individual users because their site, *Wikipedia*—while it is a major Internet space—relies heavily on the work of individual authors. Currently, the main concern about SOPA and PIPA is that personal web pages like *Google+* could be flagged simply because of a comment, post, or *sharing* among "friends." If this outcome were indeed the purpose of these new laws, regulating these sites would become next to impossible, which could negatively affect the entire structure and function of individually driven sites like *Wikipedia*. Considering how online spaces have evolved in the past decade, laws like these could cause complete turmoil. Wales and Walsh claim that while it's important for Congress to be concerned about the content industry, the times and systems have changed, and so must copyright laws: "The laws we need now must recognize the more broadly distributed and broadly valuable power of free and open knowledge."

Goldberg, by contrast, approaches the issue of copyright laws from the   4
perspective of the major company, rather than the individual. In his piece, "Kill the Internet—and Other Anti-SOPA Myths," he responds to a TED Talks video of writer Clay Shirky giving a talk about SOPA and PIPA in which Shirky offers a perspective similar to that of Walsh and Wales. Goldberg believes that the bills were poorly constructed, but that the purpose of these laws was to deal with Internet piracy—sites like *Megaupload* and *Napster* that are profiting from the sale of creative works they did not produce. Much like Walsh and Wales, Shirky claims that sites like *Facebook* and *YouTube* (sites we individuals visit daily) could crash and burn because they lack the funding and manpower to police individual comments, videos, status updates, posts, and so on. They claim that people wish to produce, and not just consume, that individuals should still be allowed to create, and that SOPA and PIPA will prevent that creativity from happening. Goldberg, however, claims that sharing videos or text on *Facebook* is completely different from illegally viewing new movies on an Internet site like *Megaupload*. He claims that warnings about illegal drawings of Mickey Mouse or singing the Happy Birthday song at children's parties (points made by Shirky in the video) are "demagogic." He notes that "[t]here is a profound moral difference between loaning a friend a book and posting, without permission, the content of bestsellers for commercial gain." I find the final point intriguing, mainly

A peer asked this question:

Can you be a bit more specific here?

In response, Munson explained why people were angry.

In response to a peer who asked whether the impact of the legislation went beyond *Wikipedia*, Munson acknowledged that *Wikipedia* is only one of the sites that would be affected.

Another peer asked this question:

Is this just 'right or wrong'? Can you explain a little more?

Munson responded by focusing on what the competing interests are.

because Wales and Walsh appeal to readers' emotions so intensely in their piece, calling to mind the individual's need to maintain his or her rights. Is this issue, as Goldberg claims, a question of scale; are we as individual Internet users simply overreacting? Or is the government really attempting to rebuild the entirety of current and past Internet protocol?

Goldberg makes the intriguing claim that people and legislators need to take   5 into account the difference between using others' works for commercial gain versus sharing a book, text, or song for the sake of sharing. If this distinction is taken into account when new bills are drafted, will copyright laws attempting to stop Internet piracy seem more appropriate? What is the real difference between these two articles—does it lie in the actual argument or just the perspective? Personally I think both these authors are looking for a compromise on the original SOPA/PIPA proposals. It simply comes down to whether or not authorities could (or are willing to) create a copyright bill that can work within different infrastructures.

One reader noted that the final paragraph was repetitious. Munson subsequently cut some of it.

Works Cited

Goldberg, Danny. "Kill the Internet—and Other Anti-SOPA Myths." *The Nation.* The Nation. 24 Jan. 2012. Web. 27 Feb. 2012.
Wales, Jimmy, and Kat Walsh. "We Are the Media, and So Are You." *Washington Post.* Washington Post, 9 Feb. 2012. Web. 27 Feb. 2012.

UNDERSTANDING A WRITER'S GOALS: QUESTIONS TO CONSIDER AND DISCUSS

Rhetorical Knowledge: The Writer's Situation and Rhetoric

1. **Audience:** What knowledge does Munson assume that her readers have or do not have? Why do you think that?

2. **Purpose:** What was Munson's purpose in synthesizing the two readings as she did?

3. **Voice and tone:** How does Munson reveal her attitude toward Goldberg, toward Wales and Walsh, and toward all of them?

4. **Responsibility:** How responsibly has Munson presented the ideas from the two readings?

5. **Context, format, and genre:** Munson wrote this synthesis for one of her classes. How has that context affected her synthesis?

Critical Thinking: The Writer's Ideas and Your Personal Response

6. How has Munson helped you to understand the issues that Goldberg and Wales and Walsh are addressing?

7. To what extent do your perspectives on the issues align with Munson's perspectives? Why? Where do you disagree with her?

Composing Processes and Knowledge of Conventions: The Writer's Strategies

8. In places, Munson directly compares Goldberg's views with Wales and Walsh's views. Why do you think that she does that?

9. In some places, Munson quotes directly from the readings. In other places, though, she paraphrases or summarizes ideas in the readings. Why does she use a mix of strategies for presenting ideas from the readings?

Inquiry and Research: Ideas for Further Exploration

10. Conduct a library or Web search to find more details about SOPA and PIPA legislation. If you were to advise Munson on how to include some of those details in her synthesis, what would you suggest?

Self-Assessment: Reflecting on Your Goals

Now that you have considered how to respond critically to and synthesize readings, think further about your learning goals by contemplating the following questions. If you are constructing a course portfolio, your responses to these questions can also serve as invention work for the portfolio.

 ## Rhetorical Knowledge

- *Audience:* How did the audience influence your approach to your critical response or to synthesizing texts?
- *Purpose:* How did your purpose influence your approach?
- *Rhetorical Situation:* How did the rhetorical situation affect your approach?
- *Voice and tone:* How important was your voice in your critical response or in synthesizing the texts you chose? Why? What factors influenced your tone?
- *Context, medium, and genre:* How did the context affect the medium and genre you chose?

 ## Critical Thinking, Reading, and Writing

- *Learning/Inquiry:* What did you need to know about the topic of the article or articles you were responding to or synthesizing in order to write your critical response or synthesis effectively?
- *Responsibility:* What was your responsibility to readers when critically responding to a text or synthesizing two or more texts?
- *Reading and research:* What were some effective critical reading strategies that you used in developing ideas for your critical response or synthesis?
- *Skills:* How did critically responding or synthesizing help you to develop your skills in critical thinking, reading, and writing?

Writing Processes

- *Invention:* What invention strategies were helpful as you approached this project? If you wrote a synthesis, what strategies helped you to compare texts?
- *Organizing your ideas and details:* What have you learned about organizing ideas when you respond to a text or synthesize several texts?
- *Revising:* What tools were useful in revising your critical response or synthesis to meet the needs of readers?
- *Working with peers:* How did peers help you to respond critically to a text or synthesize texts more effectively?
- *Visuals:* How did you use visuals to strengthen your critical response or synthesis? If you did not use visuals, why did you choose not to use them?
- *Writing habits:* What "writerly habits" did you find helpful when completing this project? Why?

 ## Knowledge of Conventions

- *Editing:* As you worked on this project, which editing skills served you well? What editing skills do you still need to develop further?
- *Genre:* What conventions of genre did you find most important in critically responding to or synthesizing the texts you chose?
- *Documentation:* What documentation style did you use to cite sources in your critical response or synthesis?

Refer to Chapter 1 (pages 12–13) to see a sample reflection.

4 Writing to Discover and to Learn

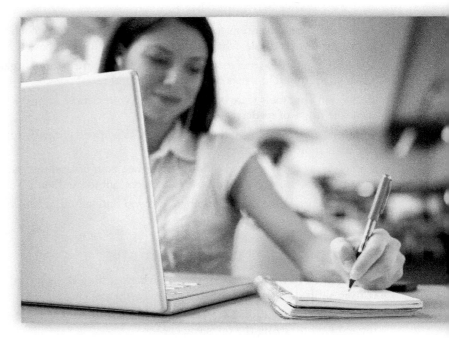

Most of the chapters in this book focus on learning to write for an audience—to accomplish a purpose involving other people. This chapter, though, provides some tried-and-true strategies for using writing to discover ideas and to learn—to accomplish a purpose for yourself. As you do more writing, you are probably noticing that it is a way of learning, of figuring out what you know and understand about a subject. The process of writing is also a way of coming to know and understand a subject better.

This chapter introduces strategies to help you to learn and to prepare for writing assignments. These tools can be used in academic, professional, civic, or personal settings. As discussed in Chapter 2, writing about what you read for your classes can help you learn that information better, not just by rewriting to summarize your notes, but by jotting down your questions and comments, reflecting on what you have read, and noting how any new ideas and information relate to other ideas and information. Relating ideas in a text to ideas in other texts, as you know from Chapter 3, is called

synthesizing, and it is a strategy you will use in most of your college writing. In your professional life, consider how writing about what was useful in a recent business meeting, what problems came up, and what issues did not get solved might help you conduct more effective and efficient meetings in the future.

In almost any situation, writing (immediately afterward) about what you *learned* from an

experience will prepare you for similar situations you might face in the future. If you get into the habit of writing about the events and issues in your life, you likely will come to a more thoughtful and thorough understanding of those events and issues.

The strategies that follow are tools that writers have used to figure out what they have learned and what they still need to know.

Using Invention Strategies to Discover Ideas

As you begin to explore your subject, it is a good idea to use more than one invention activity to generate ideas. No matter what your purpose is for writing, you will need to generate information and knowledge about your topic through invention activities. Whichever of these strategies you use, a helpful accompanying activity is creating an audience profile. The "Genres Up Close" feature on page 65 walks you through the steps of this process.

Listing

Listing involves jotting down keywords that will remind you of ideas as you write more later. You might find it effective to establish categories within your lists to jog your memory. If you wanted to propose a solution to a problem, for example, you might organize keywords under "history of the problem," "how the problem affects my readers," "possible solutions," "failed solutions," and "objections to a solution."

Freewriting

When you freewrite, you simply write for a set time—perhaps five or ten minutes. You jot down, or type, everything that comes to mind, even if you cannot think of anything (in that case, you might write, "I can't think of anything to write," until your ideas start to flow).

Questioning

One way to generate information and ideas is to ask questions about your topic, audience, and purpose:

- What am I trying to accomplish in this paper?
- What do I already know about my topic?
- What might my readers already know?
- What would readers need to know to understand my point?
- What kind(s) of information (for example, graphs, tables, or lists) might be useful to *show* my readers (rather than just to tell them)?
- What kinds of details and explanations can I provide?
- Where might I learn more about this subject (in the library, on the Internet, by interviewing people)?

Answering the Questions *Who? What? Where? When? Why?* and *How?*

You can expand the questioning approach (above) by spending a few minutes jotting down answers to the reporter's questions: *who, what, where, when, why,* and *how.* You may find that your answers lead to still more questions:

- Whom does this subject affect? In what ways?

- Who is involved in making a decision about this subject?
- Who is my audience?
- What am I trying to get my audience to do?
- What can't I ask my readers to do?
- What is important here?
- What are the historical aspects of this topic?
- Where does all of this take place?
- When might something happen to affect this situation?
- When would I like something to happen?
- Why should my readers care about my paper?
- Why is this topic important?
- Why will _____ happen?
- How does the context—the "where"—affect the situation?
- How might _____ happen?
- How might _____ react to the topic I am writing about?

Brainstorming

When you brainstorm, you record on paper or on-screen the information you already know about the topic you are exploring. Once you have written down several possible topics or ideas or possible ways to focus your paper, you may have an easier time finding the one that seems most promising.

Clustering

Clustering is especially useful for figuring out possible cause-and-effect relationships. For more on clustering and an example, see page 71.

Keeping Notebooks and Journals

Writers and learners frequently maintain notebooks and journals because these forms of informal writing are useful places for recording and exploring ideas. Leonardo da Vinci, for example, kept notebooks for years, compiling 1,566 pages of ideas in words and images.

Double-Entry Notebook

One useful type of notebook is what composition scholar Anne Berthoff calls a **dialectical notebook** or **journal.** In a dialectical notebook, you write notes on one page and then write your questions and comments about those notes on the facing page. The **double-entry notebook,** which is a type of dialectical notebook, can be

GENRES *Up Close*   **Writing an Audience Profile**

An *audience profile* is a genre that helps writers understand their audience's needs. While understanding an audience's needs is only one part of the rhetorical situation, the more writers know about their audience, the better they are positioned to achieve their purpose and to present their information effectively. In fact, one of the first things experienced writers do when they start a writing project is to identify and analyze their audience. For example, determining whether the audience is knowledgeable about the topic can help writers choose the appropriate level of detail and decide how technical their language should be. The more writers know about their target audience, the more they can tailor the argument for the maximum impact on that audience. An informative pamphlet on the needs of children with autism in schools might provide different information, depending on its primary audience: parents and relatives of children with autism, parents of children attending classes with children who have autism, or school personnel.

When profiling their audience, writers need to ask themselves the following questions:

- Who is my audience?
- Does this writing task have only one audience, or are there multiple audiences?
- If there is more than one audience, how does each one differ from the others?
- What does my audience already know?
  - Are they experts in the field?
  - Are they knowledgeable laypeople?
  - Will I need to adjust my language and level of detail to meet my audience's needs?
- What does my audience need to know?
- Why is this information important to this audience?
- How do I expect my audience to use this information?

Here is a sample format you might use for an audience profile.

Main Audience

- What are their defining characteristics?

Secondary Audiences

- What are their defining characteristics?
- How do they differ from the main audience?

Audience's Knowledge of the Field

- What background (experience/education) do the audience members have?
- What are their assumptions about the information?
- Does their cultural context affect their view of the information? How?

What the Audience Needs to Know

- Why is this information important to my audience?
- How should I expect my audience to use this information?

Whether your instructor asks you to write an audience profile as a formal writing assignment or not, being able to profile an audience informally for every writing assignment you do is a valuable skill.

easily adapted to many contexts. The double-entry notebook has two columns. The left column is used to present whatever kind of information is appropriate to the context. Thus, in this column, you might record lecture, lab, field, or reading notes; list the steps in a math problem; construct a timeline; or list events in chronological order. The right column is used to respond to, comment on, question, and apply the information in the left column.

For instance, Judy Bowden was enrolled in an art history course. To understand some of the artwork that she was studying in the course, Bowden frequently used the double-entry notebook. Because her journal was electronic, she could download public-domain artwork from the Web and paste it into the left column of her notebook. In the right column, she wrote about the work. Here is an example from Bowden's notebook.

Artwork	My Thoughts
	This is the *Black Bull cave* painting from Lascaux, France. It's amazing that this and other paintings in the cave are 10,000 to 30,000 years old. It's also amazing that 2,000 paintings and drawings in the cave have survived for so long. The details seem very sophisticated for such an old piece of art. I wonder what the four teenagers thought when they discovered the cave on September 12, 1940. If I were in an anthropology course instead of an art history course, I wonder what other things we'd learn about this painting and the others.

Field Notebook

For more on field research, see Chapter 19.

Field notebooks are useful for students who are doing field research. A field notebook can take many forms, depending on the observations that you are making. For instance, Lindsay Hanson was enrolled in a summer session biology course for nonmajors. One of the requirements of the course was to pick a natural habitat and observe some life-forms in that habitat. Lindsay chose to do some bird-watching in a marsh near her campus. She decided to set up her field notebook in columns with headings.

Date and Time	Location	Common Name	Scientific Name	Sex	Comments
6/6/12 6:20 p.m.	west shore of Widespread	red-winged blackbird	Agelaius phoeniceus	♂	The bird was sitting on the top of a weed, which was swaying in the breeze. Partly cloudy, 61°, windy
6/6/12 6:35 p.m.	south shore of Widespread	yellow-shafted flicker	Colaptes auratus	♀	The bird took off from some 8"–10" grass. Partly cloudy, 61°

Writing Activity

Writing Your Own Field Notebook

If you have a class that requires fieldwork, construct a field notebook that includes drawings or other images and your notes on your field research. If you do not have a class that requires field research, spend an hour at some location on your campus, observing and making notes on what you see in a field notebook. Use these reporter's questions to guide you:

- Who is there? What are they doing? How are they dressed? What are they carrying or working with?
- What does the place look like? Can you take photos or make drawings? What sounds and smells are in this place?
- Where is this place? How does it connect or relate to other places on campus?
- When did you visit? Why? What makes that time different from another time when you might observe this place?
- Why did you select this particular spot? What other locations did you consider? Why?

Rewriting Your Class Notes

Whether you use a double-entry notebook or some other method, make rewriting your class notes part of your own "homework" assignment each day:

- Put them into a readable and organized form.
- Think of questions about the information that had not occurred to you when you were taking the notes during class.
- Discover areas of interest that you want to find out more about.

Think of the "re" in the word *rewriting* and what it means: to resee, to reenvision, to reconsider, perhaps even to reorganize. When you rewrite your in-class notes, use the writing as a way to help you learn, not just by transcribing your notes, but by reconsidering them and asking questions, by reseeing what you wrote (and jotting down connections you make with other ideas and texts), and by reorganizing them so they make more sense than they might have made in class.

ELECTRONIC ENVIRONMENTS | **Communicating with Study Groups and Partners**

When you take a college class, remember that your classmates can be a valuable resource. Create communication spaces online for you and your study partners. Exchange contact information with classmates, and use it. If your class has a course management system, like Blackboard, you can access your classmates through the e-mail link. Additionally, you will find collaboration space within the course shell. If you are taking a class at a location that does not have a learning management system,

you may want to use a chat space like *Google Chat, FaceTime,* or *Skype.*

As you begin exchanging ideas and information within your group, make sure you cite sources if you or your group members are posting text or images from reference or online materials. With copyrighted work, you must obtain permission from the source before posting that person's intellectual property on a public site.

After each college class meeting, convert your in-class notes to e-notes in a computer document. Doing so encourages you to reread your notes and put them into a more readable form. Just reading them over again helps cement the ideas in your memory—and writing them down again helps you remember them, too. Also, your notes will be easier to read when exam time comes around. Finally, your notes will be searchable, and you can copy and paste them, as needed, into your college papers.

Minute Paper

A minute paper is a quick, useful way to reflect on a class lecture or discussion, a chance to jot down—in a minute or two—your answers to two questions:

For more on e-mail, instant messaging, and blogs, see Chapter 17.

- What is the most important thing that I learned in class today?
- What is the most important question that I have about today's class lecture/discussion?

For example, Conner Ames, who was enrolled in a general studies course in sociology, responded at the end of a particular class as follows:

1. Today we learned that group behavior often is different from individual behavior: people will act differently in groups than they might act alone. This is especially true for male adolescents when a group interacts with other male adolescent groups.

2. What are more of the real-life implications of group behavior (and I also want to know more about *why* young males like me act as they do when they're in a group)?

Muddiest Point

As its name suggests, the muddiest-point strategy involves jotting down a concept or idea that is unclear or confusing and, if possible, exploring it through writing. This does not mean looking up the definition of a concept, but instead writing about it to clarify your thinking.

Your muddiest point may come from a paragraph in a textbook that you are reading for a course, or it may come from a class lecture or discussion. In many instances, you may be able to work through your confusion by writing. At the very least, you will crystallize the issue and provide yourself with a reminder to raise a question during the next class meeting, in an office-hour visit, in an e-mail to the professor, or on the online discussion board for the course.

Preconception Check

A *preconception* is something you think you know about a subject before you learn more about it in class, through your reading, and from other sources of information. One strategy for overcoming preconceptions is to become aware of them. For instance, Tom Ambrose was enrolled in an astronomy course. As he read a chapter about the solar system, he encountered a subsection titled "Why Are There Seasons on Earth?" Before he read the subsection, he realized that he had some preconceptions about why the seasons occur. He wrote the following in his learning journal for that course:

> I think that Earth has the four seasons because of the elliptical path of the planet as it orbits the Sun. When that path takes us farthest from the Sun (December–March), we have winter. When the path takes us closest to the Sun (June–August), we have summer.

This short explanation may seem trivial, but it served to make Ambrose more attuned to the explanation in his astronomy textbook. When he read that the seasons are caused by Earth's tilt on its axis, he was better prepared to process that information. He noted:

> When I read the chapter, I realized the problem with my preconception. If the elliptical path of Earth's orbit were the cause of the seasons, then the whole planet would have summer in June–August. I forgot that when it's summer in the northern hemisphere it's winter in the southern hemisphere.

Paraphrasing

One strategy you can use to make the material you are studying more understandable is to **paraphrase** it—to restate it in your own words. If you have ever tried to teach something to someone, you know that the act of teaching—explaining, demonstrating, answering questions—often aids your understanding of the subject or concept. This is the rationale behind paraphrasing—by explaining something in your own words, you come to understand it better.

Jack Johnson was taking an introductory physics course for nonmajors. Early in the course, the instructor mentioned "Ockham's razor" but did not define it. Using a popular search engine to investigate the term, Johnson found that it is defined as the principle of economy or of parsimony. After reading several Web sites, Johnson felt he understood the term and wrote the following in his course journal:

> In a nutshell, Ockham's razor means this: if two theories have equal explanatory power, choose the simpler one. That is, keep it simple, Stupid—K.I.S.S. In my geology class we discussed the Grand Canyon, and I kind of now see how the simplest answer to its formation—a river and other natural weather conditions, acting over a long period of time—actually makes the most sense. If I try to get too complicated about something, I need to remember Ockham's razor: if two or more ideas seem to explain something, the simpler is probably the better answer.

For more on paraphrasing, see Chapter 20.

Organizing and Synthesizing Information

Finding and collecting information is part of learning, but effective learners need to organize and synthesize information to make it usable. As you conduct research and locate information that might be useful for your writing, do the following:

- Organize what you learn in a logical manner. Often an effective way to organize your notes is to put them into a digital document; you can then use its search function to locate particular words or phrases.
- Organize your notes by putting them into a spreadsheet like Excel. If you format the spreadsheet cells to "wrap text," you create a database of notes.

For more on summary and synthesis, see Chapters 2 and 3.

- As you take notes, synthesize the information: Condense it into a brief form, where the important aspects are listed, along with the reference, so you can easily locate the complete information.

Invented Interview/Unsent Letter

In an invented interview, you are the interviewer. The interviewee could be a person or a character whom you are studying or a person associated with a concept that you are studying. If you *really* could interview someone for a college class, what would you ask that person? What issues or concepts would you focus on? It is often useful to put your questions into an unsent-letter format so that you have a specific audience you are writing to as you generate interview questions.

Here are some sample questions:

- In a geometry course, you might interview Pythagoras to ask him about the process that led to his development of the Pythagorean theorem.
- In an entrepreneurship course, you might interview Bill Gates to ask him what drove him to found Microsoft.

- In an anthropology course, you might interview a group of Cro-Magnons to ask about their interactions with Neanderthals.
- In a United States history course, you might ask President Harry Truman why he decided to drop atomic bombs on two Japanese cities in 1945.

Taking this concept of an invented interview further, you can conduct research to determine how your questions might have been answered if you had been able to conduct such an interview.

The key to writing such interviews is that you need to move beyond the limits of your initial response to an event or a person. Use the interview as an opportunity to explore a topic from an intellectual as well as an emotional perspective.

Using Charts and Visuals to Discover and to Learn

Just as charts, graphs, tables, photographs, and other visuals help readers understand what you write about, using visuals is often a way for writers to explore ideas and really see and understand what they are writing about.

Clustering and Concept Mapping

Concept maps, or *clustering*, can help us to visualize abstract ideas and also to understand relationships among ideas. Figure 4.1 shows how student writer Santi DeRosa might have developed a cluster map to help him get started with his paper about how female students help recruit male athletes for his school. According to an article in the campus newspaper, women serve as campus guides when potential athletes visit the school. When he read the article, DeRosa had concerns about the ethics of this practice, so he decided to respond by writing an essay on the issue (you can read his complete essay in Chapter 9).

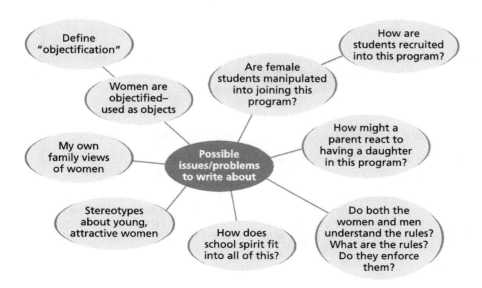

FIGURE 4.1
A Possible Cluster Map on the Topic of Recruiting Practices

Process Flowchart

A process flowchart is another visually useful tool for converting information from verbal to visual form. A flowchart allows you to translate several paragraphs of information into a clear, succinct visual that can make difficult concepts easier to understand. Rather than focusing on relationships in a system (how ideas or concepts might connect to one another), a flowchart indicates how things *move* through a system.

In his political science course, Brian Flores studied the process by which a bill moves through the U.S. House of Representatives. After reading a few pages on the process, Brian converted the material into the flowchart shown in Figure 4.2.

FIGURE 4.2   Following a Bill through the U.S. House of Representatives

Studying for Exams

If you study for tests strategically, you can usually anticipate the questions that will be asked and review the course material more efficiently.

Test Questions

One way to prepare for tests is to write questions that you think your instructor may pose on them. Anticipating test questions also gives you the opportunity to anticipate your answers, thus simulating the test itself.

ELECTRONIC ENVIRONMENTS   **Teaching Yourself by Teaching Others**

Developing documents in electronic spaces enhances your digital literacy skills. One way to learn material more thoroughly is to help someone else learn about it. Create a Web site about yourself or a club or organization to which you belong). Use your knowledge to create links, add visuals, and make connections that will help others learn more about the topic. If you are new to Web design, play around with Web site platforms like *Google Sites*, *WordPress*, or *Weebly*, which can help you get started. If you have some experience, think about using Dreamweaver, Adobe Illustrator, or Photoshop to enhance your design options.

If you are writing questions to prepare for a test, the first step is to ask the instructor about the kinds of questions that you should anticipate. Your instructor will probably indicate the formats that the questions will be in—for example, whether they will be multiple-choice, true/false, matching, short answer, and/or essay questions—and might also indicate the levels of thinking they will require: comprehension, application, analysis, synthesis, and/or evaluation.

One of the most effective strategies for writing test questions is to go through your class notes and reading notes, marking sections that you think are likely to be covered on the test. Then, as soon as possible after class or after reading the textbook, write a few questions and think about the answers. If you write some questions each week, you will learn much more than if you wait until just before the test, and you will cover the material more thoroughly.

For advice on creating an effective Web site, see Appendix C.

Mnemonic Play

Although in many courses you will learn course material without having to memorize facts, there may be times when you need to develop memory aids for some material. Here is an example that may already be familiar to you. Erin Wilson was enrolled in a general science course for nonmajors. To help her remember the order of the planets in the solar system (before Pluto's status as a planet was changed), she used the sentence "<u>M</u>y <u>v</u>ery <u>e</u>ducated <u>m</u>other just <u>s</u>erved <u>u</u>s <u>n</u>ine pizzas." That is, the order, beginning with the planet closest to the sun, is Mercury, Venus, Earth, Mars, Jupiter, Saturn, Uranus, Neptune, Pluto.

For advice on taking essay examinations, see Appendix B.

Writing to Share Experiences

In "A Priceless Lesson in Humility," a story that appears on the Web site for This I Believe (www.thisibelieve.org), Felipe Morales, a network engineer, shares an experience that caused him to learn something about himself:

> A few years ago, I took a sightseeing trip to Washington D.C. I saw many of our nation's treasures, and I also saw a lot of our fellow citizens on the street—unfortunate ones, like panhandlers and homeless folks.
>
> Standing outside the Ronald Reagan Center, I heard a voice say,

"Can you help me?" When I turned around, I saw an elderly blind woman with her hand extended. In a natural reflex, I reached in to my pocket, pulled out all my loose change and placed it on her hand without even looking at her. I was annoyed at being bothered by a beggar.

> But the blind woman smiled and said, "I don't want your money. I just need help finding the post office."
>
> In an instant, I realized what I had done. I acted with prejudice—

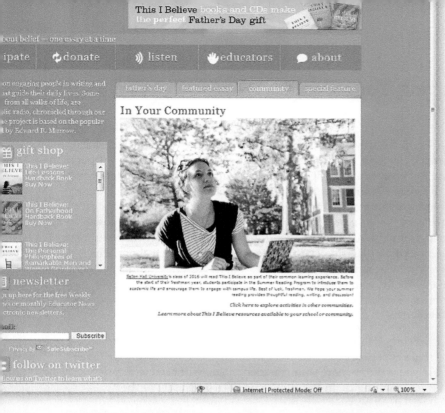

I judged another person simply for what I assumed she had to be.

I hated what I saw in myself. This incident reawakened my core belief. It reaffirmed that I believe in humility, even though I'd lost it for a moment.

The thing I had forgotten about myself is that I am an immigrant. I left Honduras and arrived in the U.S. at the age of 15. I started my new life with two suitcases, my brother and sister, and a strong no-nonsense mother. Through the years, I have been a dishwasher, roofer, cashier, mechanic, pizza delivery driver among many other humble jobs, and eventually I became a network engineer.

In my own life, I have experienced many open acts of prejudice. I remember a time at age 17, I was a busboy and I heard a father tell his little boy that if he did not do well in school, he would end up like me. I have also witnessed the same treatment of family and friends, so I know what it's like, and I should have known better.

But now, living in my American middle-class lifestyle, it is too easy to forget my past, to forget who I am, where I have been, and lose sight of where I want to be going. That blind woman on the streets of Washington, D.C., cured me of my self-induced blindness. She reminded me of my belief in humility and to always keep my eyes and heart open.

By the way, I helped that lady to the post office. And in writing this essay, I hope to thank her for the priceless lesson.

In telling this story on the Web, Felipe Morales was engaging in a common activity—sharing a meaningful experience with other people. On any given day, you share your experiences in a variety of ways. Writing about your experiences helps you as a writer because the act of writing requires reflection, which is a powerful tool for gaining insight into and understanding about life. Also, when you share your experiences with others, you are offering others insight into what has worked well—and not so well— in your life.

Setting Your Goals

- **Rhetorical Knowledge** As you write, you'll need to consider the constellation of factors that make up your *rhetorical situation:* you (the writer), your readers (the audience), the topic (the experience that you're writing about), your purpose (what you wish to accomplish), and the exigency (what is compelling you to write). Readers—your *audience*—may or may not know you or the people you are writing about personally, but you will want to make your experience relevant to them. Your *purpose* may be to entertain your readers and possibly to inform and/or persuade them. You will have a *stance*—or attitude—toward the experience you are sharing and the people you are writing about. Your *voice* and *tone* may be amused, sarcastic, neutral, or regretful, among other possibilities. Finally, your writing *context*, the *medium* you are writing in (whether print or electronic), and the *genre* you have chosen all affect your writing decisions.

- **Critical Thinking, Reading, and Writing** You will need to learn features of writing to share experiences so that you can do so effectively in any writing situation. As you write to share your experience, you will need to do so responsibly, representing them accurately and with sensitivity to the needs of others. You will draw on your own memories, memories of relatives and friends, photographs and documents, and ideas you develop from your reading and research.

- **Writing Processes** It is best to choose invention strategies that will help you recall details about your experience or experiences. Generally, you will need to organize your ideas and details as a series of events. When you revise, you will read your work with a critical eye to make certain that it fulfills the assignment and displays the qualities of this kind of writing. At the revising stage, it often helps to work with peers, classmates and others who can offer you comments on and questions about your work.

- **Knowledge of Conventions** When writers share experiences, they tend to use dialogue to report what they said and what others said to them. When editing, you need to check to be sure you have followed the conventions for punctuating dialogue. If you have relied on sources outside of your experience, cite them using the appropriate documentation style. Finally, choose an appropriate genre; genres for sharing your experience include personal essay, memoir, autobiography, literacy narrative, magazine or newspaper essay, blog, letter, and accident report.

RHETORICAL KNOWLEDGE

When you write about your experiences in a private journal, you can write whatever and however you wish. When you write for other people, though, you need to make conscious choices about your audience; purpose; voice and tone; and context, medium, and genre.

 ## Writing to Share Experiences

Throughout your college career, you will be called on to share your experiences in writing. Such writing can help you learn more effectively because it encourages you to reflect on your academic experiences. Further, much academic writing takes the form of **narratives**—stories about the physical or human world. For example, one of the best-known philosophers in history, Plato, used stories as powerful teaching tools. In the *Republic*, Plato tells "The Allegory of the Cave" to illustrate what it's like to think like a philosopher.

In your own academic life—your life in college—you may be asked to share experiences in the following ways:

- A math instructor may ask you to write about some experience in which you used a math principle or procedure to solve a problem in your everyday life.

- A music instructor may ask you to attend a concert and then write about the experience.

- An education instructor might assign you to observe a classroom and write about your observations.

As humans we tend to organize our lives as ongoing narratives. While your life is one long narrative, within it are thousands of shorter narratives. Those are the kinds of events you will most likely focus on when you write to record and share experiences in the professional, civic, and personal parts of your life.

Star quarterback Peyton Manning is a professional athlete with a reputation for paying attention to detail. Sportswriter Peter King notes that when Manning was searching for a new team to join in 2011, he managed to remember, and acknowledge by name, every coach and assistant coach on every team he visited. This attention to detail helped him to make his final choice. While we don't know if Manning kept notes or has an extraordinary memory, for most of us, using writing to take notes and record details allows us to remember better. You can follow Manning's example of attention to details by using writing to record and analyze your **professional** experiences so that you can learn from them.

To participate effectively in **civic** life, writers also need to share their experiences. For democratic institutions to function effectively, citizens need to be involved with their government, especially at the local level.

In **personal** settings, you have many opportunities to record and share experiences every day. For example, at the wedding of two friends, you may be asked to tell the story of how you introduced them in high school.

"Ways of Writing to Share Experiences" on page 79 provides examples of genres you may use in your writing. The genres of writing you will be assigned will vary by the experiences you are sharing and your specific audience for those experiences.

Scenarios for Writing | Assignment Options

Your instructor may ask you to complete one or both of the following assignments, which call for you to write about your experiences. Each assignment is in the form of a *scenario*, a brief story that provides some context for your writing. The scenario gives you a sense of who your audience is and what you need to accomplish with your writing.

Starting on page 93, you will find guidelines for completing the assignment. Additional scenarios for college and life may be found online.

Writing for College

SCENARIO 1   A Memoir about the Impact of a Teacher

Throughout your formal education, you have studied with dozens of teachers. Some of them have been especially influential in helping you learn to succeed in academic settings—and, of course, their influence may have spilled over into the other parts of your life. You may have chosen your future profession because of a specific teacher's influence.

Writing Assignment: The word *memoir* comes from the French word *mémoire,* which in turn comes from from the Latin word *memoria,* meaning "memory" or "reminiscence." A memoir focuses on how a person remembers his or her life. Although the terms *memoir* and *autobiography* are sometimes used interchangeably, the genre of memoir is usually considered to be a subclass of autobiography. While an autobiography usually encompasses an entire life, a memoir is more likely to focus on memorable moments and episodes from a person's life.

Keeping in mind the qualities of a memoir, write about a teacher who was especially influential in your academic life. Your memoir can be designed for a general academic audience, or it can be designed for a specific course in a specific discipline. As you remember and discuss in writing how this teacher influenced you as a student, include examples that show that influence.

SCENARIO 2   A Literacy Narrative about an Influential Situation

This scenario asks you to construct a *literacy narrative.* Quite often, a literacy narrative is an account of a situation that helped

Ways of Writing to Share Experiences

Genres for Your College Classes	Sample Situation	Advantages of the Genre	Limitations of the Genre
Academic essay	Your sociology professor asks you to construct an academic essay in which you share your family's holiday traditions.	This essay will help you understand how your traditions are unique and/or part of a larger culture	It may be difficult to identify how your traditions are the same as or different from as those practiced by others in a short paper.
I-Search essay	In your technology and society class, you are asked to relate how you use the Internet to connect with friends and family.	An I-Search essay allows you to examine and explain your experiences with technology.	Because you are focusing on your experiences, it may be difficult to present that personal search in a formal assignment.
Academic reflection	After writing an extended argument for your economics class, you are asked to reflect on your writing process and explain what you might do differently next time.	This essay will help you understand your writing process and determine how to improve future performance.	You may have to provide evidence from your own writing and research, which may feel awkward.
Oral/visual presentation	Your humanities professor asks you to profile, in an oral and visual presentation, a period of art that is meaningful to you and explain why.	Perhaps each member of the class will present on a different topic. This gives you the chance to teach the class what you learned.	Because presentation time is limited, you will need to be selective and brief.
Project report	Your business professor asks you to write about your experience of working in a group on a marketing project.	This assignment will help you reflect on the group experience as well as your strengths and weaknesses as a collaborator.	You may feel you can't be honest about the group members who didn't work well with others.
Literacy narrative	Your writing teacher asks you to write about your earliest memories of learning to write.	A literacy narrative can provide insights into your current writing practices.	You may have only vague recollections of early writing experiences.
Genres for Life	**Sample Situation**	**Advantages of the Genre**	**Limitations of the Genre**
Letter to the editor	You want to construct a letter to the editor of your local paper, outlining your experiences with a local nonprofit agency.	A letter to the editor allows you to encourage others in your community to become involved with the agency.	Space is limited, and not everyone reads the local paper or all parts of it. It might not be selected for publication.
Memo	You want to let the president of your firm know of a recent experience you had with a training company that your business uses.	A memo allows you to convey information quickly and professionally.	A memo forces you to write concisely and specifically about your experiences; however, you might need more space.
Blog	You want to construct a blog about being a student at your university.	A blog is an easy and simple way for you to convey information to a wide audience.	Someone will need to monitor the blog for inappropriate comments.
Web page	You want to construct a Web page to describe your experience hiking a local nature trail.	Your Web page will give all readers the same information at the same time; you can update it when necessary.	You may not have the technical skills to construct an interactive Web site.
Poster	You want to construct a poster for a self-help fitness program, focusing on the notion that "I did it—so can you!"	A poster allows you to share your experience with the program clearly and concisely, yet with sufficient detail. The poster's visual impact should engage your audience.	If what your poster presents is too concise, readers will not believe that "they can do it too."

you develop as a writer. One such situation would be how the actions of a parent or a teacher had a significant effect on how you approach writing today.

Writing Assignment: For your college newspaper or an alumni magazine, write a narrative account of a particular situation that you now understand had an influence on how you view writing, language use, or reading. Be sure to tell the story in detail, and then explain how you now understand how that particular occurrence changed you. Unlike a rhetorical analysis (see pages 27–30), in which you explain how the various aspects of a text worked together, a literacy narrative is about your own writing process and how it has developed over time.

Rhetorical Considerations in Sharing Your Experiences

Before you begin the process of writing in response to one of the scenarios presented above, take a few minutes to consider the following aspects of your writing situation.

Audience: Who is your primary audience? Who else might be interested in this subject? Why?

Purpose: Your narrative could have several interrelated purposes. For example, if you are writing in response to Scenario 1, your narrative can serve both to entertain your audience by sharing your experience with them and to thank or honor others who contributed to your academic development.

Voice, tone, and point of view: Depending on the assignment, you may or may not be a major character in your narrative. If you are relating a story in which you are a participant, you have two roles: You are its writer, and you are also a major character in it. If you are not a participant, you will use the third-person point of view. Your attitude toward your characters will help determine the tone of your narrative. For example, your tone could be informal, such as in "Superman and Me" by Sherman Alexie (pages 89–91), or more straightforward and serious. What other attitudes could influence your tone?

Context, medium, and genre: You will need to understand the situation that creates the occasion to write. Keeping the context of the assignment in mind, decide on a medium and a genre for your writing. How will your writing be used? If you are writing for an audience beyond the classroom, consider what will be the most effective way to present your information to this audience.

CRITICAL THINKING, READING, AND WRITING

Before you begin writing to share your own experiences, read one or more examples to get a feel for writing about experiences. You might also consider how visuals could enhance your writing, as well as the kinds of sources you might consult.

Writing about experiences has several qualities—a clear sense of purpose, a significant point, a lively narrative, and an honest representation. The writer also has a responsibility to respect the privacy of anyone who appears in a narrative. The reading selections that appear in this section exemplify these qualities. Further, they may serve to stimulate your own inquiry and writing.

Qualities of Effective Writing about Experiences

Successful writing about experiences—often called *narrative writing*—engages your readers and keeps them interested. One of the best ways to engage readers when narrating your experiences is to incorporate real dialogue. Other strategies include providing telling details and description. The old advice to "show, don't tell" is especially important when writing about experiences.

Even when you are sharing experiences that seem self-evidently fascinating, you need to have a reason for writing about those experiences. In other words, you need to make a point.

Readers expect the following qualities in writing that shares experience:

- A clear sense of purpose. When you write about your experiences, provide readers with clues that will help them understand why you are sharing this narrative. Your tone is one important clue. The explanation and reflection that you include is another clue. If you are simply recording the event so that others can experience it vicariously, for example, you might include very little explanation or reflection. If, however, you want readers to learn something from your experience, or you are trying to convince them of something, you will probably use part of your paper to reflect on the significance of your experience.

- A significant point. Just as you need to have a clear purpose for what you are writing, you also need to use the experience to say something significant. Writers sometimes use their experiences to make a sweeping, clichéd point, such as "if I had known then what I know now," which usually leads to boring, obvious writing. Points have significance for readers when they are fresh and—often—unexpected.

   One way to show significance is to explain—with examples—how the event you are telling about affected you. You may or may not express your point in a thesis statement, however. Many writers who share their experiences use language, tone, and details to make their points implicitly.

- A lively narrative. Although your writing may include other elements, such as reflection, the foundation for writing about experience is a lively narrative. A narrative must answer the following questions: *Who? What? Where? When? Why?* and *How?* To answer these questions, you can use the following conventions of narrative writing:

   - *Dialogue:* Natural-sounding dialogue helps make a piece of writing immediate and lively. Dialogue—what people have to say—brings a narrative to life. Dialogue also can reveal something about the character of the people in your narrative.

For more on narration and description, see Chapter 13.

- *Vivid description:* Detailed descriptions of the people, or *characters*, mentioned in the narrative, the place where it occurs, and the actions that take place all help involve the reader in your story. Describing people, places, actions, and objects so that your readers can relate to them will help make your narrative memorable.

- *Point of view:* Although you will most often relate personal stories from your own point of view (first-person perspective, usually told using the pronouns *I* and *me*), it may be more interesting or effective to tell the story from a third-person perspective—perhaps from the point of view of another participant in the event (called the "third-person limited perspective") or from the point of view of an observer who knows what each participant is doing and thinking (called the "third-person omniscient perspective").

- *A climax or crisis:* Effective narrative *leads* to something: a point the writer wants to make or a concept the writer wants the reader to understand. By constructing your narrative to lead readers to your main idea or point, you keep them interested throughout your narrative. Sometimes, to build suspense, your narrative can lead up to a crisis, which may or may not have already been resolved.

- **An honest representation.** As you share your experiences, it's important to represent them to readers as accurately as possible. Although you can present your own perspective on any situation, it is usually important to present events without unnecessary embellishments, unless you are exaggerating for an obviously humorous purpose. Usually, you are not trying to convince readers to change their ways with this kind of writing, but to honestly relate your experiences so readers can understand their significance.

Reading to Learn about Writing That Shares Experiences

The selections that follow are examples of writing that shares experiences. As you go through each of the selections your instructor asks you to read, consider the following questions:

- How does the author make his or her experiences understandable and indicate their significance?
- What qualities of writing that shares experiences does each selection exemplify?
- How can you use the techniques of sharing experiences exemplified in the selection in your writing?

TANYA BARRIENTOS

Se Habla Español

MEMOIR

The man on the other end of the phone line is telling me the classes I've called about are first-rate: native speakers in charge, no more than six students per group. 1

"Conbersaychunal," he says, allowing the fat vowels of his accented English to collide with the sawed-off consonants. 2

I tell him that will be fine, that I'm familiar with the conversational setup, and yes, I've studied a bit of Spanish in the past. He asks for my name and I supply it, rolling the double *r* in Barrientos like a pro. That's when I hear the silent snag, the momentary hesitation I've come to expect at this part of the exchange. Should I go into it again? Should I explain, the way I have to half a dozen others, that I am Guatemalan by birth but pura gringa by circumstance? Do I add the humble little laugh I usually attach to the end of my sentence to let him know that of course I see the irony in the situation? 3

This will be the sixth time I've signed up to learn the language my parents speak to each other. It will be the sixth time I've bought workbooks and notebooks and textbooks listing 501 conjugated verbs in alphabetical order, with the hope that the subjunctive tense will finally take root in my mind. 4

In class, I will sit across a table from the "native speaker," who won't question why the Irish-American lawyer, or the ad executive of Polish descent, has enrolled but, with a telling glance, will wonder what to make of me. 5

Look, I'll want to say (but never do). Forget the dark skin. Ignore the obsidian eyes. Pretend I'm a pink-cheeked, blue-eyed blonde whose name tag says Shannon. Because that is what a person who doesn't innately know the difference between corre, corra, and corrí is supposed to look like, isn't it? She certainly isn't supposed to be earth-toned or be from my kind of background. If she happens to be named García or López, it's probably through marriage, or because an ancestor at the very root of her family trekked across the American line three or four generations ago. 6

I, on the other hand, came to the United States at age three, in 1963, with my family and stopped speaking Spanish immediately. 7

Tanya Maria Barrientos has written for the *Philadelphia Inquirer* for more than twenty years. Barrientos was born in Guatemala and raised in El Paso, Texas. Her first novel, *Frontera Street,* was published in 2002, and her second, *Family Resemblance,* was published in 2003. Her column "Unconventional Wisdom" runs every week in the *Inquirer.* This essay originally appeared in the collection *Border-Line Personalities: A New Generation of Latinas Dish on Sex, Sass & Cultural Shifting.* We selected this reading because we see an increasing number of students with linguistic backgrounds similar to Barrientos's. As you read her essay, compare your language background to hers.

College-educated and seamlessly bilingual when they settled in West Texas, 8
my parents (a psychology professor and an artist) embraced the notion of the
American melting pot wholeheartedly. They declared that their two children would
speak nothing but inglés. They'd read in English, write in English, and fit into
Anglo society beautifully. If they could speak the red, white, and blue without a hint
of an accent, my mother and father believed, people would be forced to look beyond
the obvious and see the all-American kids hidden inside the ethnic wrapping.

It sounds politically incorrect now. But America was not a hyphenated 9
nation back then. People who called themselves Mexican-Americans or
Afro-Americans were considered dangerous radicals, while law-abiding citizens were expected to drop their cultural baggage at the border and erase any
lingering ethnic traits. Role models like Vikki Carr, Linda Ronstadt, and Raquel
Welch[1] had done it and become stars. So why shouldn't we?

To be honest, for most of my childhood I liked being the brown girl who 10
defied expectations. When I was seven, my mother returned my older brother
and me to elementary school one week after the school year had already begun.
We'd been on vacation in Washington, D.C., visiting the Smithsonian, the Capitol,
and the home of Edgar Allan Poe. In the Volkswagen, on the way home, I'd
memorized "The Raven," and I'd recite it with melodramatic flair to any poor soul
duped into sitting through my performance. At the school's office, the registrar
frowned when we arrived.

"You people. Your children are always behind, and you have the nerve to 11
bring them in late?"

"My children," my mother answered in a clear, curt tone, "will be at the top 12
of their classes in two weeks."

The registrar filed our cards, shaking her head. 13

I did not live in a neighborhood with other Latinos, and the public school I 14
attended attracted very few. I saw the world through the clear, cruel vision of a
child. To me, speaking Spanish translated into being poor. It meant waiting tables
and cleaning hotel rooms. It meant being left off the cheerleading squad and receiving a condescending smile from the guidance counselor when you said you planned
on becoming a lawyer or a doctor. My best friends' names were Heidi and Leslie
and Kim. They told me I didn't seem "Mexican" to them, and I took it as a compliment.
I enjoyed looking into the faces of Latino store clerks and waitresses and, yes, even
our maid, and saying "yo no hablo español." It made me feel superior. It made me feel
American. It made me feel white.

It didn't matter that my parents spoke Spanish and were successful. They 15
came from a different country, where everyone looked alike. In America, fitting
in with the gringos was key. I didn't want to be a Latina anything. I thought that
if I stayed away from Spanish, the label would stay away from me.

---

[1]Three popular entertainers of Hispanic orgin.

When I was sixteen, I told my father how much I hated being called   16
Mexican—not only because I wasn't, but also because the word was hurled as
an insult. He cringed and then he made a radical plan. That summer, instead of
sending me to the dance camp in Aspen that I wanted to attend, he pointed me
toward Mexico City and the Ballet Nacional.

"I want you to see how beautiful Mexico is," he said. "That way when any-   17
body calls you Mexican, you will hold your head up."

I went, reluctantly, and found out he was right. I loved the music, the art, the   18
architecture. He'd planted the seed of pride, but it would take years for me to
figure out how to nurture it.

Back at home, my parents continued to speak only English to their kids   19
while speaking Spanish to each other.

My father enjoyed listening to the nightly Mexican newscast on television,   20
so I came to understand lots of the Spanish I heard. Not by design, but by osmo-
sis. So, by the time I graduated from college, I'd become an odd Hispanic hybrid—
an English-only Latina who could comprehend Spanish spoken at any speed but
was reluctant to utter a word of it. Then came the backlash. In the two decades
I'd worked hard to isolate myself from the stereotype I'd constructed in my own
head, society shifted. The nation had changed its views on ethnic identity.

College professors had started teaching history through African-American   21
and Native American eyes. Children were being told to forget about the melting
pot and picture America as a multicolored quilt instead.

Hyphens suddenly had muscle, and I was left wondering where I fit in. The   22
Spanish language was supposedly the glue that held the new Latino-American
community together. But in my case it was what kept me apart. I felt awkward
among groups whose conversations flowed in and out of Spanish. I'd be asked a
question in Spanish and I'd have to answer in English, knowing that raised a
mountain of questions. I wanted to call myself Latina, to finally take pride, but it felt
like a lie. So I set out to learn the language that people assumed I already knew.

After my first set of lessons, which I took in a class provided by the news-   23
paper where I worked in Dallas, I could function in the present tense. "Hola
Paco, ¿qué tal? ¿Qué color es tu cuaderno? El mío es azul."[2] My vocabulary built
quickly, but when I spoke my tongue felt thick inside my mouth, and if I needed
to deal with anything in the future or the past I was sunk. I suggested to my
parents that when I telephoned we should converse only in Spanish, so I could
practice. But that only lasted a few short weeks. Our relationship was built in
English and the essence of it got lost in the translation.

By my mid-twenties I had finally come around to understanding that being   24
a proud Latina meant showing the world how diverse the culture can be. As a
newspaper reporter, I met Cubans and Puerto Ricans and brown-skinned New
Mexicans who could trace their families all the way back to the conquistadores.

---

[2] Hello Paco. What's happening? What color is your notebook? Mine is blue.

I interviewed writers and teachers and migrant workers, and I convinced editors to put their stories into print. Not just for the readers' sake, but for my own. I wanted to know what other Latinos had to say about their assimilation into American culture, and whether speaking Spanish somehow defined them. What I learned was that they considered Spanish their common denominator, linking them to one another as well as to their pasts. With that in mind, I traveled to Guatemala to see the place where I was born, and basked in the comfort of recognizing my own features in the faces of strangers. I felt connected, but I still wondered if without flawless Spanish I could ever fill the Latino bill.

I enrolled in a three-month submersion program in Mexico and emerged   25
able to speak like a sixth-grader with a solid C average. I could read Gabriel García Márquez with a Spanish-English dictionary at my elbow, and I could follow ninety percent of the melodrama on any given telenovela.

But I still didn't feel genuine. My childhood experiences were different from   26
most of the Latinos I met. I had no quinceañera, no abuelita teaching me to cook tamales, no radio in the house playing rancheras. I had ballet lessons, a high school trip to Europe, and a tight circle of Jewish friends. I'd never met another Latina like me, and I began to doubt that they existed.

Since then, I've hired tutors and bought tapes to improve my Spanish. Now   27
I can recite Lorca. I can handle the past as well as the future tenses. But the irregular verbs and the subjunctive tense continue to elude me.

My Anglo friends call me bilingual because I can help them make hotel   28
reservations over the telephone or pose a simple question to the women taking care of their children. But true speakers discover my limitations the moment I stumble over a difficult construction, and that is when I get the look. The one that raises the wall between us. The one that makes me think I'll never really belong. Spanish has become a pedigree, a litmus test showing how far from your roots you've strayed. Of course, the same people who would hold my bad Spanish grammar against me wouldn't blink at an Anglo tripping over a Spanish phrase. In fact, they'd probably be flattered that the white man or woman was giving their language a shot. They'd embrace the effort. But when I fumble, I immediately lose the privilege of calling myself a full-fledged Latina. Broken Spanish doesn't count, except to set me apart from "authentic" Latinas forever.

My bilingual friends say I make too much of it. They tell me that my Guate-   29
malan heritage and unmistakable Mayan features are enough to legitimize my membership in the Latino-American club. After all, not all Poles speak Polish. Not all Italians speak Italian. And as this nation grows more and more Hispanic, not all Latinos will share one language. But I don't believe them. I think they say those things to spare my feelings.

There must be other Latinas like me. But I haven't met any. Or, I should say,   30
I haven't met any who have fessed up. Maybe they are secretly struggling to fit in, the same way I am. Maybe they are hiring tutors and listening to tapes

behind the locked doors of their living rooms, just like me. I wish we all had the courage to come out of our hiding places and claim our rightful spot in the broad Latino spectrum. Without being called hopeless gringas. Without having to offer apologies or show remorse.

    If it will help, I will go first.   31

    Aquí estoy.[3]   32

    Spanish-challenged and pura Latina.   33

------

[3] I am here.

UNDERSTANDING A WRITER'S GOALS: QUESTIONS TO CONSIDER AND DISCUSS

Rhetorical Knowledge: The Writer's Situation and Rhetoric

1. **Audience:** For whom do you suppose Barrientos is writing about these experiences?

2. **Purpose:** What do you see as Barrientos's purpose in writing this essay?

3. **Voice and tone:** Barrientos has specific attitudes toward her subject matter. What parts of her essay can you cite to show what her attitudes are?

4. **Responsibility:** How reliable does Barrientos seem in the way that she presents factual information? What specific details in her essay seem most credible? Why?

5. **Context, format, and genre:** Although Barrientos presents her experiences as true, she still relates them almost in the form of a story. How effective is this strategy for writing about such experiences? How does Barrientos use dialogue in her autobiographical narrative to represent the views of participants?

Critical Thinking: The Writer's Ideas and Your Personal Response

6. Barrientos says that her parents "declared that their two children will speak nothing but inglés." What were their motives for saying that? What do you think about that declaration?

7. In many ways, this essay is about how Barrientos is trying to fit into American culture and society. Where have you tried to fit in, and what have your struggles been?

Composing Processes and Knowledge of Conventions: The Writer's Strategies

8. Barrientos tells of her experiences in the first person. How would it alter the effectiveness and interest of this essay if it had been written in the third person? Why?

9. Barrientos now and then writes in Spanish. How do the Spanish sentences affect her essay?

Inquiry and Research: Ideas for Further Exploration

10. Interview several family members about their language background and experiences. In a brief paper, explain how their experiences compare to those related by Barrientos.

As illustrated by "Ways of Writing to Share Experiences" (page 79), experiences can be shared through many genres. The "Genres Up Close" feature explores doing so through a literacy narrative.

GENRES *Up Close*   Writing a Literacy Narrative

The literacy narrative has been a popular genre for decades, but it has become increasingly so in recent years. Readers are curious about how others, especially famous writers, have developed their writing and reading skills. When reporters and talk-show hosts interview well-known writers, they frequently ask about the writers' experiences with reading and writing, particularly early in life.

When writers craft literacy narratives, they often do the following:

- **Narrate their experiences with using language—reading and writing in particular situations.** As you craft a literacy narrative, think about those moments when you were most aware that you were using language as a reader, as a writer, or both.

- **Critically reflect on their experiences with using language.** As you craft a literacy narrative, think about the effects of particular experiences you have had with reading and writing. For example, if your first-grade teacher congratulated you for reading a book when you were six years old, how did that positive reinforcement affect your reading after that moment?

- **Think about how they developed ability and confidence as readers and writers.** That is, what has reading and writing allowed them to do in life? As you craft a literacy narrative, think about the ways that reading and writing have helped you to achieve certain goals. Think about how reading and writing have helped you to make a difference in the world.

- **Define "literacy" broadly.** As you consider your literacy experiences, be inclusive. In addition to reading and writing with words, how have you developed other similar or related skills? For example, what are your experiences with visual images? What are your experiences with information literacy (finding, evaluating, and using information)?

To explain how they became literate people, writers may use anecdotes to tell part of their literacy narratives. They also tend to tell stories about people who helped their development as writers and readers. A compelling story can help readers understand the impact of a particular event. Of course, strong positive role models can also motivate someone to keep reading or writing. In the selection by Sherman Alexie, "Superman and Me," notice how Alexie uses both of these conventions to convey how he developed his lifelong commitment to reading and writing.

SHERMAN ALEXIE

Superman and Me

I learned to read with a Superman comic book. Simple enough, I suppose. I cannot recall which particular Superman comic book I read, nor can I remember which villain he fought in that issue. I cannot remember the plot, nor the means by which I obtained the comic book. What I can remember is this: I was 3 years old, a Spokane Indian boy living with his family on the Spokane Indian Reservation in eastern Washington state. We were poor by most standards, but one of my parents usually managed to find some minimum-wage job or another, which made us middle-class by reservation standards. I had a brother and three sisters. We lived on a combination of irregular paychecks, hope, fear, and government surplus food.

My father, who is one of the few Indians who went to Catholic school on purpose, was an avid reader of westerns, spy thrillers, murder mysteries, gangster epics, basketball player biographies and anything else he could find. He bought his books by the pound at Dutch's Pawn Shop, Goodwill, Salvation Army and Value Village. When he had extra money, he bought new novels at supermarkets, convenience stores and hospital gift shops. Our house was filled with books. They were stacked in crazy piles in the bathroom, bedrooms and living room. In a fit of unemployment-inspired creative energy, my father built a set of bookshelves and soon filled them with a random assortment of books about the Kennedy assassination, Watergate, the Vietnam War and the entire 23-book series of the Apache westerns. My father loved books, and since I loved my father with an aching devotion, I decided to love books as well.

I can remember picking up my father's books before I could read. The words themselves were mostly foreign, but I still remember the exact moment when I first understood, with a sudden clarity, the purpose of a paragraph. I didn't have the vocabulary to say "paragraph," but I realized that a paragraph was a fence that held words. The words inside a paragraph worked together for a common purpose. They had some specific reason for being inside the same fence. This knowledge delighted me. I began to think of everything in terms of paragraphs. Our reservation was a small paragraph within the United States.

1

2

3

Sherman Alexie was born on the Spokane Indian Reservation, near Spokane, Washington, and was educated at Gonzaga University and Washington State University, where he graduated in 1991. An acclaimed poet, novelist, and short story writer, he has published a number of works, including a collection of short stories, *The Lone Ranger and Tonto Fistfight in Heaven* (1993), and the novel *Reservation Blues* (1995). He is also the author of the young adult novel *The Absolutely True Diary of a Part-Time Indian* (2007). The following piece first appeared in the *Los Angeles Times* in 1998 as part of the series "The Joys of Reading and Writing." We chose it because we felt Alexie's literacy narrative shows that, even when attained unconventionally, literacy has the power to change lives.

My family's house was a paragraph, distinct from the other paragraphs of the LeBrets to the north, the Fords to our south and the Tribal School to the west. Inside our house, each family member existed as a separate paragraph but still had genetics and common experiences to link us. Now, using this logic, I can see my changed family as an essay of seven paragraphs: mother, father, older brother, the deceased sister, my younger twin sisters and our adopted little brother.

At the same time I was seeing the world in paragraphs, I also picked up that Superman comic book. Each panel, complete with picture, dialogue and narrative was a three-dimensional paragraph. In one panel, Superman breaks through a door. His suit is red, blue and yellow. The brown door shatters into many pieces. I look at the narrative above the picture. I cannot read the words, but I assume it tells me that "Superman is breaking down the door." Aloud, I pretend to read the words and say, "Superman is breaking down the door." Words, dialogue, also float out of Superman's mouth. Because he is breaking down the door, I assume he says, "I am breaking down the door." Once again, I pretend to read the words and say aloud, "I am breaking down the door." In this way, I learned to read. 4

This might be an interesting story all by itself. A little Indian boy teaches himself to read at an early age and advances quickly. He reads "Grapes of Wrath" in kindergarten when other children are struggling through "Dick and Jane." If he'd been anything but an Indian boy living on the reservation, he might have been called a prodigy. But he is an Indian boy living on the reservation and is simply an oddity. He grows into a man who often speaks of his childhood in the third-person, as if it will somehow dull the pain and make him sound more modest about his talents. 5

A smart Indian is a dangerous person, widely feared and ridiculed by Indians and non-Indians alike. I fought with my classmates on a daily basis. They wanted me to stay quiet when the non-Indian teacher asked for answers, for volunteers, for help. We were Indian children who were expected to be stupid. Most lived up to those expectations inside the classroom but subverted them on the outside. They struggled with basic reading in school but could remember how to sing a few dozen powwow songs. They were monosyllabic in front of their non-Indian teachers but could tell complicated stories and jokes at the dinner table. They submissively ducked their heads when confronted by a non-Indian adult but would slug it out with the Indian bully who was 10 years older. As Indian children, we were expected to fail in the non-Indian world. Those who failed were ceremonially accepted by other Indians and appropriately pitied by non-Indians. 6

I refused to fail. I was smart. I was arrogant. I was lucky. I read books late 7 into the night, until I could barely keep my eyes open. I read books at recess, then during lunch, and in the few minutes left after I had finished my classroom assignments. I read books in the car when my family traveled to powwows or basketball games. In shopping malls, I ran to the bookstores and read bits and pieces of as many books as I could. I read the books my father brought home from the pawnshops and secondhand. I read the books I borrowed from the library. I read the backs of cereal boxes. I read the newspaper. I read the bulletins posted on the walls of the school, the clinic, the tribal offices, the post office. I read junk mail. I read auto-repair manuals. I read magazines. I read anything that had words and paragraphs. I read with equal parts joy and desperation. I loved those books, but I also knew that love had only one purpose. I was trying to save my life.

Despite all the books I read, I am still surprised I became a writer. I was 8 going to be a pediatrician. These days, I write novels, short stories, and poems. I visit schools and teach creative writing to Indian kids. In all my years in the reservation school system, I was never taught how to write poetry, short stories or novels. I was certainly never taught that Indians wrote poetry, short stories and novels. Writing was something beyond Indians. I cannot recall a single time that a guest teacher visited the reservation. There must have been visiting teachers. Who were they? Where are they now? Do they exist? I visit the schools as often as possible. The Indian kids crowd the classroom. Many are writing their own poems, short stories and novels. They have read my books. They have read many other books. They look at me with bright eyes and arrogant wonder. They are trying to save their lives. Then there are the sullen and already defeated Indian kids who sit in the back rows and ignore me with theatrical precision. The pages of their notebooks are empty. They carry neither pencil nor pen. They stare out the window. They refuse and resist. "Books," I say to them. "Books," I say. I throw my weight against their locked doors. The door holds. I am smart. I am arrogant. I am lucky. I am trying to save our lives.

By sharing his emotions, Alexie helps readers understand the impact that his reading had on him. With the sentence "I read with equal parts joy and desperation," he indicates how much he valued—and still values—this activity.

In this paragraph Alexie connects his childhood reading to his career choice.

UNDERSTANDING A WRITER'S GOALS: QUESTIONS TO CONSIDER AND DISCUSS

Rhetorical Knowledge: The Writer's Situation and Rhetoric

1. **Audience:** Alexie is writing about some of the childhood experiences that influenced his later life. Who do you think he is writing to? A general audience? The Native American students whom he visits in their schools?

2. **Purpose:** It is clear that books and reading have played an important role in Alexie's life. Do you think he wrote this essay to inspire other Native American children? Do you think he wrote this essay to break down misperceptions non-Native Americans may have about those who grow up on reservations?

3. **Voice and tone:** Alexie tells his story in a conversational tone—almost as though the reader is sitting right next to him, and he is merely recounting a story. Do you feel more comfortable with the "everyday language" Alexie uses than you would if he had written with more formal language? What effect does Alexie's use of language have on you?

4. **Responsibility:** Often when people write an essay about a personal event, they feel their main responsibility is to retell the event accurately as they remember it. Do you think that is the case with Alexie? If you think his essay exhibits a different sense of responsibility, what might that be? Why do you think so?

5. **Context, format, and genre:** Alexie's essay is an example of a "literacy narrative." A "literacy narrative" tells a personal story of an event or events that had an impact on the development of the writer's language, reading, or writing skills. How did Alexie's essay help you understand how reading became important in his development as a person?

Critical Thinking: The Writer's Ideas and Your Personal Response

6. Alexie relates that learning to read became an early passion for him. He used that passion to help frame his entire life. Do you have a passion that you developed in your childhood that still helps shape your life? What is it? How do you use it?

7. Alexie finishes his essay by telling us that he now goes back to the reservations as a guest creative writing teacher. His final sentence is "I am trying to save lives." Specifically, how do you think he is accomplishing that goal?

Composing Processes and Knowledge of Conventions: The Writer's Strategies

8. Alexie says that when he was very young he started seeing the world "in terms of paragraphs." By doing so, Alexie uses "paragraphs" as a metaphor. Do you understand what he means? Do you think using "paragraphs" as a metaphor works? Why or why not?

9. Most of this essay is told in the first person. In paragraph 5, however, Alexie switches to the third person and even notes that he now refers to his childhood experiences in the third person. Do you think this switch in point of view is effective? Why or why not?

Inquiry and Research: Ideas for Further Exploration

10. Either in your school library or online, search for three or four other "literacy narratives." Do they focus only on reading and writing, or, like Alexie, do they place reading and writing in a broader context? If there is a broader context, can you generalize about it? If so, what generalizations can you make? Or does each narrative seem to be unique? If so, how?

ELECTRONIC ENVIRONMENTS | **Organizing Your Files**

Are your files stored in folders (directories) on your computer? If so, have you ever lost track of where you've stored a song, video, project, or paper? Before it happens again, take some time to organize your folders and files.

Start by looking at the names of all the folders you've already created. Did you use some principle for naming and organizing them? Are they named according to project or media type (such as music or video)? Or are the names more or less random? See if you can find relationships among the names of your documents, and look for ways to group documents into folders and files and store them together. Establish a separate folder for the different aspects of your life. For example, you might want a folder titled "School" and another titled "Music" or "Photos." Within those folders you might want to have a separate folder for each course or separate folders for different types of music or locations where photos were taken.

Taking a little time to organize your files and folders now can save you time and prevent confusion when you need to locate specific documents later. Once you have your files organized, you may want to consider backing up the folders to an external source such as a flash drive, an external hard drive, or a Cloud account like DropBox.

WRITING PROCESSES

In the pages that follow, you will engage in various writing processes to help you generate ideas and draft, revise, and edit your writing. As you work on the assignment scenario that you have chosen, keep these processes and the qualities of effective writing about experiences in mind (pages 81–82).

Invention: Getting Started

As you begin to explore your subject, it is helpful to use more than one invention activity to come up with ideas. Especially when you are writing to share experiences, the more detail that you generate about the experience through invention, the better you will be able to convey the experience and its meaning to your readers. As you begin the process, consider the following questions:

- What do I already know about the experience that I am writing about?
- What feelings, attitudes, or notions do I already have about this experience?
- What questions can I ask about the experience? That is, what gaps do I have in my memory of it or knowledge about it that might help me understand what information a reader might need?
- Who would know about my experience (a relative or friend)? What questions might I ask that person in an interview?
- What do I know about my audience? What don't I know that I should know? Why might they be interested in reading my text?
- What might my audience already know about my subject? Why might they care about it?

For more on descriptive writing, see Chapter 13.

- To what extent will sensory details—color, shape, smell, taste—help my reader understand my topic? Why?
- What visuals might I use to help my readers understand my experience?

For help with strategies for discovery and learning, see Chapter 4.

Completing invention activities such as the ones suggested in the first writing activity should yield a wealth of information that you can draw on for your first draft. Consider sharing your invention work with several classmates or friends in order to understand your rhetorical situation more clearly and to generate more useful information.

Writing Activity

Listing, Questioning, and Freewriting

Get started with your paper by using listing, questioning, and freewriting. First, list key words that will remind you of ideas and organize them in related categories, such as location, images, and sounds. Second, generate basic details of the event using the five questions commonly asked by reporters:

- *Who* are the participants in this event, and what information about those participants will help me share my experience?
- *What* are the participants doing and what are they saying?
- *Where* did the event occur?
- *When* did the event occur, and what is the significance of when it happened?
- *Why* did the participants do what they did? What motivated their actions?

Use freewriting (see page 63) to get your ideas down on paper. (For an example of freewriting, see page 135.)

Finally, if you already keep a journal, you might skim through it to find ideas for your writing. If you don't already keep a journal, you might do so while you are getting started on this writing project.

ELECTRONIC ENVIRONMENTS | **Using Technology to Unjam Writer's Block**

You can use technology to "unjam" writer's block! Some writers find it hard to get started when faced with a new task. You can download images related to your topic, play a video from a popular Web site, or even use Twitter® or texting to brainstorm with friends and classmates while you're getting started.

One helpful tip is to use the recorder on your phone or a digital voice recorder to talk out your ideas. State the information that you already know and your ideas about that information, and then as you listen back, take notes on what you said. This can help you get started.

JESSICA HEMAUER'S LISTING

For a memoir about her experience growing up on a farm, Jessica Hemauer, a student in a first-year composition course, generated the following list:

For help with listing, questioning, and freewriting, as well as other strategies for discovery and learning, see Chapter 4.

small town	Blinds
farm chores—endless	Navy blue, understuffed, corduroy sofa
Dad worked hard; we did too	that has one cushion burnt b/c it was
coffee	too close to the woodstove
siblings	White, clean carpet
Orange, multi-stained carpet	Clean table set for 2
Oversized, cluttered table	Neatly lined bookshelves
Stuffed, pine shelves	Round staircase with a wood banister
Steep, creaky stairs	
Bathroom	
Basement	
Loud, plastic runners covering the multi-stained orange carpet	
Warm, rustic steel woodstove	

STUDENT WRITING EXAMPLES

Brainstorming
(pp. 176, 350)

Freewriting
(pp. 48, 135, 261, 396)

Criteria (p. 307)

Listing (p. 95)

Table (p. 49)

Answers to Reporter's
Questions (p. 261)

Organization
(pp. 96, 181)

Clustering (pp. 135, 305)

Interviewing (p. 220)

Research (pp. 137, 177,
222, 263, 308, 398)

Reflection (p. 12)

Strategies FOR Success Creativity

Successful writers are creative. However, being creative doesn't necessarily mean writing fiction or making up details about your experiences. It does mean that when you are writing a narrative, for example, you will need to discover a fresh new perspective on the story in order to be successful. When writing to share experiences, successful writers find ways to use specific details of the story to engage their readers, often taking a rather ordinary event such as a family dinner, or in Tanya Barrientos's case, a phone call about a Spanish class, and presenting it in a new, creative way that makes a powerful statement.

For more on conducting interviews, see Chapter 19.

Organizing Your Ideas and Details

Once you have generated ideas and details about your subject using invention activities, consider how you might organize this material. The questions that you need to ask yourself when deciding on your organization are all rhetorical:

- Who is your audience?
- Why might they be interested in your narrative—and how can you make them interested?
- What is your purpose for writing—that is, what do you want your readers to understand about you or the event you are narrating?

The answers to these questions can help you decide what to emphasize, which in turn will help you choose an organizational strategy.

It is usually helpful to try *several* organizational strategies in early drafts because seeing your words on paper—in various ways—will help you decide what strategy will work best for you. Most often, writing about experiences is sequential: The writer starts at some specific point in the past and then moves to a later time or to the present.

An alternative would be to use the narrative technique known as **flashback**. In a flashback, commonly used in film, something that happened in the past is shown "just the way it happened," and then the narrator returns to the present to reflect on the event's significance.

Jessica Hemauer's Organization

Jessica Hemauer looked over her invention material and then put together a rough outline for her draft. She decided to begin her narrative at a crisis point:

STUDENT WRITING
EXAMPLES

Brainstorming
  (pp. 176, 350)
Freewriting (pp. 48, 135,
  261, 396)
Criteria (p. 307)
Listing (p. 95)
Answers to Reporter's
  Questions (p. 261)
Organization
  (pp. 96, 181)   ➚
Clustering (pp. 135, 305)
Interviewing (p. 220)
Research (pp. 137, 177,
  222, 263, 308, 398)
Reflection (p. 12)

> **Begin as a 10-year-old girl—waking up to feed calves**
> Describe daily family routine
> Good feelings about being in charge when feeding calves
> Describe parents
>   Impact of their relationship on me
> School WAS social life
>   Being a farm girl made me different
>   How I didn't fit in
> Playing basketball in 8th grade
>   Started to feel included—but worked harder than others
>   Falling asleep in class
> THE FAMILY MEETING
> Freed from farmwork and being involved
> Why I'm still different and that's ok.

Constructing a Complete Draft

Once you have chosen the organizational approach that works most effectively for your audience and purpose, you are ready to construct the rest of your draft. Before you begin your draft, review all your invention material to see what needs to be included and what might be left out. To make these decisions, consider your purpose for sharing this experience with others: What is the significance of the experience? How can you help readers see the significance?

Synthesizing and Integrating Sources into Your Draft: Including Others' Perspectives in Narratives

When writers share experiences in first-person narratives, they primarily offer their own perspectives on events because they often are the leading characters in the narratives.

However, most narratives also include other individuals who interact with the narrator. Writers can reconstruct interactions with other people by describing actions and by including dialogue. Although describing actions helps readers see what happened, those descriptions limit the perspective to that of the writer/narrator. Because multiple perspectives help readers see the story from several vantage points, effective writers often include dialogue—either by quoting it or by summarizing it.

In "Farm Girl," which appears on pages 102–6 of this chapter, Jessica Hemauer includes dialogue with some of the other people in her story. For example, in paragraph 17, Hemauer reconstructs the conversation with Ms. Cain, her teacher:

> One time my teacher, Ms. Cain, comes over to my wooden desk, where my head is resting on top of a math textbook. She taps her knuckles on the hollow wood and says, "Jessica, are you okay? Do you need to go to the health room?" Raising my head, embarrassed that she caught me sleeping, I say quickly, "No, Ms. Cain, I'm fine. I'm sorry for being rude and causing a disruption. I promise to be more attentive."

Although Hemauer could have described the dialogue by writing that her teacher asked if she was okay, she instead makes the teacher's concern more concrete by quoting the teacher's words.

Parts of a Complete Draft

Introduction: One of the qualities of a successful narrative is that it grabs and holds readers' attention. A number of strategies for beginning your narrative can help get your readers interested, including the following:

- **Start your narrative with a surprising event or piece of dialogue.** Tanya Barrientos (her essay appears on pages 83–87) starts her essay by telling of a phone conversation and then adds a word readers may not know or expect: "*Conbersaychunal.*"
- **Start with interesting details** to draw the reader in through sensual, descriptive words and phrases.
- **Start with a comment that might startle your readers.** For example, Sherman Alexie begins his essay with the comment "I learned to read with a Superman comic book" (page 89).

Body: The main part, or body, of your narrative is the place to tell your story. Use dialogue and descriptive details to develop the story and reveal the character of the people in your narrative. To hold your readers' interest, build your narrative to a crisis or climax, unless you are writing for an informative purpose and are required to maintain a neutral tone (or unless you are beginning at the crisis point of the narrative). Choose the verb tense that will best serve the purpose of your narrative. If you use past-tense verbs to narrate the experience, you remind readers that the event happened in the past and that you have had time to reflect on it. If you use present-tense verbs, you make the story seem as if it is happening now,

For more on introductions, see Chapter 13.

INTEGRATING SOURCES

Including Others' Perspectives in Narratives (p. 97)

Quoting Sources (p. 139)

Paraphrasing Sources (p. 181)

Incorporating Numerical Data (p. 224)

Incorporating Partial Quotes (p. 266)

Creating Visuals to Show Your Data (p. 311)

Summarizing Information from Sources (p. 356)

Including Research Information (p. 401)

and you will seem to reveal its significance to yourself and to your readers at the same time. Also, you might consider using photographs to complement your words.

Conclusion: Your conclusion should tie things together for your readers by explaining or suggesting the significance of the experience or experiences you have shared. Here are some strategies for concluding a paper in which you have shared experiences:

For more on conclusions, see Chapter 13.

- Review the subject's most important aspects.
- Explain the subject's significance.
- Suggest avenues for a reader's further inquiry.
- Refer back to the introduction of your narrative.

Title: Rather than thinking of a title before you start writing, it is often more useful to construct a first draft and then consider possible titles. As with the introduction, an effective title for a narrative intrigues readers and makes them want to read the text.

Writing Activity

Constructing a Full Draft

Using the writing you did when selecting an organizational approach, write a complete draft of your paper that shares an experience.

Excerpts from Jessica Hemauer's First Draft

After deciding on her organizational approach, Jessica Hemauer wrote the first draft of her essay about growing up on a farm. The following excerpts are from her first draft. Like all first drafts, Hemauer's draft included problems with grammar, spelling, and punctuation. (The numbers in circles refer to peer comments—see pages 99–100.)

Farm Girl
Jessica Hemauer

BEEP! BEEP! BEEP! It's 5:00 a.m. My eyes are heavy with sleep and struggle to open. I think to myself, "A typical ten-year-old child does not have to wake up at five in the morning to do chores!" I hit the snooze button with disappointment, hoping desperately that the cows would for once, feed and milk themselves. Seconds away from falling back into a deep sleep, I hear the heavy footsteps of what could only be my father coming near my bedroom door. They stop and my door opens with a creak. "Jessica, are you awake yet?" my father asks. Without a word, knowing from the past that an argument doesn't get me anywhere, I stagger out of my warm twin bed, trudging dejectedly past the figure at the narrow doorway. I continue down the hall toward the small bathroom to find my sisters, Angie and Melissa, and my brother Nick already awake. ❶

We all proceed with our usual morning routine, which consists of washing our faces, brushing our teeth and taking turns on the white porcelain throne. In the lower level of the old farmhouse our outside clothes await. My mother made it a rule to keep them there so that they wouldn't stink up the rest of the house. As soon as you opened the door to the basement, you can smell the putrid aroma of cows that has seeped from our clothing into the damp cool air.❷ We took our turns going down the steep, narrow steps, using the walls on either side for extra guidance. As we dressed not a single word was spoken because we all felt the same way, "I hate this!" Although most of the time our choice of vocabulary was much more creative. . . .

While Melissa and my father milked the 100 cows, Nick and Angie fed the cows, and I went to feed the newborn calves.❸ Being the youngest in the family, this was my favorite chore because I rarely had the chance to look after someone or feel like I was taking care of them. I have always had older siblings who looked after me, watching every step I took, being sure that I didn't get into trouble. When feeding the calves, I was finally the one in charge. It was a nice feeling, being on the opposite end of the spectrum. They were my responsibility. I was in charge of them and caring for them during feeding time every morning and evening. Little did I know at that time, this was the beginning of a lifetime of responsibilities. . . .

. . . Typically, we would finish with the chores and return to the house around 7:30 in the morning.

When we made our way back to the farmhouse, we draped our clothes on a folding chair next to the washing machine in the basement and crawled up the stairs. The delicious smell of smoked bacon and cheese omelets grew more intense with each step. As our stomachs ached with hunger, we took turns in the shower, cleaning ourselves as fast as possible in order to get to the breakfast table. My brother would be the first to the table because as we all know, girls take longer to get ready than boys. My father would eat and be back outside on the farm by the time my sisters or I would run by the kitchen grabbing a glass of fresh squeezed orange juice and a piece of toast as we yelled frantically at the bus, "Wait!" It seemed our daily lives operated in shifts, not like a real family.❹ . . .

When I finally arrived at school I had already been up for four hours doing chores on the farm in the bitter cold. The other kids in my private grade school just rolled out of their beds inside their subdivision homes an hour before the bell rang. The school day always went by fast.❺ While my other classmates were thinking about what television show they were going to watch after school, I was thinking about the chores that await me once I get off the yellow school bus. . . .

Student Comments on Jessica Hemauer's Draft

❶ "I really liked the description of you getting up early and getting ready. I could almost feel the cold and smell the farm smells."

❷ "I like how the real details (like all of the smells) help me 'be there' with you."

③ "I think you're writing this because you want to tell people that all those awful farm chores really helped you."

④ "I think your point was that all the time you wanted to fit in, and then when you could do things normal kids do, you found out you were different anyway."

⑤ "I'd like to hear more about school and the people there."

As with the comments you will receive from your instructor and classmates, Hemauer had to determine which comments and suggestions made sense—and then to revise her paper accordingly.

Revising

Finishing a complete draft may give you a justified sense of accomplishment. However, you still need to revise and then edit the draft. It is helpful to let your draft sit for a while after you have finished it. When you return to it, you are

---

WRITER'S *Workshop* | **Responding to Full Drafts**

Working with one or two classmates, read each other's paper and offer comments and questions that will help each of you see your paper's strengths and weaknesses. Consider the following questions as you do:

- What is your first impression of this draft? How effectively does the title draw you into the narrative? What do you like about the draft?

- How well does the introduction work? What is effective about it? What suggestions can you make on how to improve the introduction?

- What significant point is the writer making about the experience he or she is relating? How might the writer be able to make that point more clearly?

- Why is the writer relating this experience? What in this piece of writing helps you see why the experience was important to the writer?

- How lively is the narrative? Where has the writer gone beyond simply telling readers about the experience to showing it? How might the writer use more dialogue?

- How has the writer used description to make people, places, and scenes vivid for readers? Where is more description needed?

- How effectively does the story build in terms of reaching a climax and holding the readers' attention throughout? Are there any problems with logic in the way one action follows another? If so, where?

- Has the writer honestly explained the experience? If not, why do you question it?

- What could be added or changed to make the conclusion more effective? How well does it bring the narrative to a satisfying conclusion?

much more likely to find sections that need to be revised: places where details need to be added, other places where details may need to be removed, and still others where some of your words or sentences need to be shifted from one place to another. Classmates may also offer feedback on your draft, and friends or family members might also be willing to read your draft and offer useful suggestions.

Responding to Readers' Comments

After receiving feedback from peers, teachers, writing tutors, and others, writers have to determine what to do with that feedback.

Consider carefully what your readers tell you. Some might not understand your point, or they may misunderstand something you wrote. It is up to you either to accept or to ignore their comments and suggestions. Others may offer perspectives that you may not have thought of. You may find that comments from more than one reader contradict each other. In that case, use your own judgment to decide which reader's comments are on the right track.

Jessica Hemauer's readers had the following reactions:

- Two readers liked some of the descriptive passages in the paper. Hemauer needed to consider whether more description could be added because this strategy had been effective.

- One reader outlined what seemed to be the point, or thesis, of Hemauer's paper. When you get such feedback on your papers, make sure that the reader does understand and reiterate your point. If the reader does not get your point, then perhaps you are not being clear and explicit enough.

In the final version of her paper, on pages 102–6, you can see how Jessica Hemauer responded to these comments, as well as to her own review of her first draft.

 # KNOWLEDGE OF CONVENTIONS

When effective writers edit their work, they attend to the conventions that will help readers understand their ideas. These include genre conventions, documentation, format, usage, grammar, punctuation, and mechanics. By attending to these conventions in your writing, you make reading a more pleasant experience for readers.

 ## Editing

After you revise, you need to go through one more important step: editing and polishing. When you edit and polish your writing, you make changes to your sentence structures and word choices to improve your style and to make your writing clearer and more concise. You also check your work to make sure it adheres to conventions of grammar, usage, punctuation, mechanics, and spelling.

Because it is sometimes difficult to identify small problems in a piece of writing you have been mulling over for some time, it often helps to distance yourself from the text before your last reading so you can approach the draft with fresh eyes. Some people like to put the text aside for a day or so; others try reading aloud; and some even read from the last sentence to the first so that the content, and their familiarity with it, does not cause them to overlook an error. Because checking conventions is easier said than done, though, we strongly recommend that you ask classmates, friends, and tutors to read your work to find sentence problems that you do not see.

Genres, Documentation, and Format

If you are writing an academic paper, follow the conventions for the discipline in which you are writing and the requirements of your instructor. If you have chosen to write a letter to a prospective employer, you should also follow the conventions of a business letter.

A Writer Achieves Her Goal: Jessica Hemauer's Final Draft

The final draft of Jessica Hemauer's essay "Farm Girl" follows. As you read Hemauer's essay, think about what makes it an effective example of writing about experiences. Following the essay, you'll find some specific questions to consider.

JESSICA HEMAUER

MEMOIR   **Farm Girl**

BEEP! BEEP! BEEP! It's 5:00 a.m. My eyes are heavy with sleep and struggle to open. I think to myself, "A typical ten-year-old child does not have to wake up at five in the morning to do chores!"   1

I hit the snooze button, hoping desperately that the cows will, for once, feed   2
and milk themselves. Seconds away from falling back into a deep sleep, I hear
my father's heavy footsteps outside my bedroom door. They stop and my door
opens with a creak. "Jessica, are you awake yet?" my father asks. Without a
word, knowing from past experience that an argument won't get me anywhere,
I stagger out of my warm twin bed, trudging dejectedly past the figure at the
narrow doorway. I continue down the hall toward the small bathroom to find my
sisters, Angie and Melissa, and my brother, Nick, already awake.

We all proceed with our usual morning routine, which consists of washing   3
our faces, brushing our teeth, and taking turns on the white porcelain throne. In
the lower level of the old farmhouse, our outside clothes await. My mother
makes it a rule to keep them there so that they won't stink up the rest of the
house. As soon as we open the door to the basement, we can smell the putrid
aroma of cows that has seeped from our clothing into the damp cool air. We take
our turns going down the steep, narrow steps, using the walls on either side for
extra guidance. As we dress, not a single word is spoken because we all feel
the same way, "I hate this!" However, most of the time our choice of vocabulary
is much more creative.

Nick opens the basement door leading outside to the barn. There is a brisk   4
and bitter wind accompanied by icy snowflakes that feel like needles digging into
our faces. We don't turn back. We desperately want to, but we know my father
is patiently waiting for us to help him milk and feed the cows before school
starts at 8:30 a.m. We lift our scarves and pull down our hats so only our
squinted eyes show. We lower our bodies to dodge the fierce winds and trudge
a half mile to the red barn, which is somehow standing sturdily in the dreadful
blizzard.

When we finally reach the barn, Nick, leading the pack, grabs the handle of   5
the heavy wooden door and props it open for my sisters and me to pass through.
Nick goes immediately to help my father herd the cows and get them into their
proper stalls to be milked. Meanwhile, my sisters and I go to the milk house to
sanitize the milking machines, prepare all the milking equipment, and set up a
station with towels and charts of the cows that are being medicated.

While Melissa and my father milk the one hundred cows, Nick and Angie   6
feed them, and I feed the newborn calves. Because I am the youngest in the family, this is my favorite chore because I rarely have the chance to look after
someone or feel like I am taking care of him or her. I have always had older
siblings who look after me, watching every step I take, making sure that I don't
get into trouble. We all work together—that's critical. When I feed the calves, I
am finally the one in charge. It is a nice feeling, being on the opposite end of the
spectrum. They are my responsibility. Little do I realize it, but this is the beginning of a lifetime of responsibilities.

One of Hemauer's
peer readers wrote
the following
comment:

**I like how the real
details (like all of
the smells) help me
"be there" with
you.**

Notice the sensory
details in this
paragraph.

Again, note the sensory details in Hemauer's paper: the smells, being hungry, fresh OJ, and so on.

After the calves are fed, other chores have to be done. Cleaning out various huts and pens and laying down fresh straw are a part of our daily duties. This is the worst of the jobs I have to do. It is so dusty that I can hardly breathe at times, but we all know it has to be done so there is no sense complaining. My brother, sisters, and I work together to get the chores done as quickly as possible. Typically, we finish with the chores and return to the house around 7:30 in the morning. 7

We make our way back to the farmhouse, drape our clothes on a folding chair next to the washing machine in the basement, and crawl up the stairs. The delicious smell of smoked bacon and cheese omelets grows more intense with each step. Our stomachs aching with hunger, we take turns in the shower, cleaning ourselves as fast as possible in order to get to the breakfast table. My father eats quickly and is back outside on the farm by the time my sisters or I run by the kitchen, grabbing a glass of fresh squeezed orange juice and a piece of toast as we yell frantically at the bus, "Wait!" It seems our daily lives operate in shifts, not like a real family. 8

When I finally arrive at school, I have already been up for four hours doing chores on the farm in the bitter cold. The other kids in my private grade school have just rolled out of their beds inside their subdivision homes an hour before the bell rang. The school day always goes by fast. While my other classmates are thinking about what television show they are going to watch after school, I am thinking about the chores that await me once I get off the yellow school bus. 9

Hemauer uses dialogue to engage her readers in the human interaction of her experience. Dialogue is an effective tool for making the experience more concrete.

One peer reviewer made this suggestion:

I'd like to hear more about school and the people there.

School has always been my social life. I want to join teams or different clubs, but I always have to consider how my chores on the farm will get done, which makes it difficult for me to get involved. If I join a team that practices after school, I can't participate. If I join a club that meets before school, I can't attend the meetings. Being a farm girl means that I can't be like the other kids in my class. Not being able to participate in school activities like my friends makes me feel left out and depressed. The topic of conversation at the lunch table never involves me. 10

"Hey, Carrie, how was basketball practice last night?" Susan asks as she pulls out a chair from the lunch table and sets her plastic tray down next to the tall, broad, blond-haired girl. 11

"It was terrible! Coach was in such a bad mood!" Carrie shoves a handful of French fries into her mouth, spilling catsup down the front of her white tee shirt without noticing. "He made us run sprints for every shot we missed. And Kelly was missing all her shots last night. I'm so sore today." 12

Carrie starts rubbing her legs when she notices the streak of catsup on her shirt. She begins to wipe it off with one of her napkins, with little success. 13

"Hey, Carrie, how was the student council meeting this morning? Did you decide if we're going to have a formal dance this winter?" 14

"Yeah, we're having it on the Saturday before Christmas. Are you going to come?" [15]

I sit listening in silence. The twenty-minute lunch period always feels like eternity. While everyone around me continues talking and laughing, I sit there next to them silently eating my French fries, listening carefully, trying to laugh at the right times. [16]

In eighth grade I really want to play basketball, and after I beg and plead with my parents, they finally say I can join the team as long as I continue to help with chores in the morning before school and after practice. I quickly agree. I become the basketball team's starting point guard. I am thrilled to be on a team, and I finally feel like I am starting to have a life like the other kids. Now I am included in the conversations at lunch, and I feel like a part of the group. I never tell anyone that I have to go home after practice and work on the farm, or that I wake up every morning at five to help with chores. None of my friends, teachers, or coaches know. I don't think they would care and I don't want them to know that I am different. [17]

In high school I become more involved with the school. Coincidently, my father's farm continues to grow. We are now up to two hundred cows, and my dad still wants to expand the farm. During my freshman year I continue to work on the farm before and after school, making sure that I can still play on the basketball team. A few times a teacher catches me with my eyes closed during class. One time my teacher, Ms. Cain, comes over to my wooden desk, where my head is resting on top of a math textbook. She taps her knuckles on the hollow wood and says, "Jessica, are you okay? Do you need to go to the health room?" Raising my head, embarrassed that she caught me sleeping, I say quickly, "No, Ms. Cain, I'm fine. I'm sorry for being rude and causing a disruption. I promise to be more attentive." [18]

Shortly after freshman year, my father arranges a meeting with my entire family. He explains that he wants our farm to continue to grow, and this means that he needs more help on the farm than his children can provide. In fact, he says that he would rather not have us work on the farm anymore, unless we want to. He would rather have us be more involved in school and go on to college. After this meeting, I feel happy and relieved, and I can tell my father is relieved too. He knows that my siblings and I have sacrificed our school activities and social lives to help with the family business, and I know that this is his way of saying thank you. [19]

From this moment on, I become more involved with my school. I join the homecoming club, audition for musicals and plays, serve as the president of the student council as well as president of my class. I also become more social with my friends. I even take on a waitressing job at a resort in a neighboring town. During all these activities, I always notice that I stick out from the group. In school people come up to me and ask how I manage my time so well, without [20]

Note the details and specific examples that Hemauer provides to really show what she means (rather than just telling).

getting stressed out. When I'm with a group of my friends, I always seem to be more mature than they are, leading the group while others try to follow in my footsteps. When it comes to my job, I am always on time, never calling in sick and never complaining about a task I have been asked to do.

One night after work, I sit down in front of the full-length mirror in my bed-room and start thinking about the past years. I had believed that joining various clubs and social activities would make me fit in with my peers. But in fact, it has not. I still stick out. And the more I think about it, the more I realize why. My life growing up has been much different from the lives of my peers. From an early age, I had to learn how to manage my time so that I could do my chores and attend school. When I started to play basketball, I had to manage my time even more carefully. I have always had a challenging amount of responsibility, and I have learned to complete tasks in a timely fashion. The work that I had to do on the farm was far from glamorous. I have done some of the worst jobs conceiv-able, so I have a higher tolerance for work than most people. Though I hated it growing up, working on the farm has taught me many lessons about life, and it has shaped me into the individual I am today. [21]

Each day of my life there are times when I reflect back to working on the farm. And every day people notice that I am different from the rest of my peers. At school, teachers and organization leaders are impressed by my time man-agement skills and the amount of responsibility I take on. At work, my boss continues to ask me where he can find some more hard working people. I sim-ply tell him, "Try hiring some farm girls. I hear they turn out pretty good." [22]

UNDERSTANDING A WRITER'S GOALS: QUESTIONS TO CONSIDER AND DISCUSS

Rhetorical Knowledge: The Writer's Situation and Rhetoric

1. **Purpose:** Why did Hemauer write this essay? How might different audiences see different purposes?

2. **Audience:** Who do you see as Hemauer's audience? What can you point to in the text that supports your claim?

3. **Voice and tone:** How does Hemauer establish her *ethos*—her credibility—in this essay?

4. **Responsibility:** What is Hemauer's responsibility to her readers? To the members of her family? How does she fulfill those responsibilities?

5. **Context, format, and genre:** Hemauer has written a personal essay. When writing in this genre, writers try to relate their own personal experiences to much broader, more general human experiences. How has Hemauer used her personal remembrances of growing up on a dairy farm to help her readers, whose own lives may have been very different from that of a midwestern farm girl, relate to the essay?

Critical Thinking: The Writer's Ideas and Your Personal Response

6. Even though you may have had a much different childhood from Hemauer's, can you relate

to some of her experiences? What does she do to develop interest in the subject of her essay?

7. What do you see as the significance of Hemauer's story?

Composing Processes and Knowledge of Conventions: The Writer's Strategies

8. How do descriptive and narrative details function in the essay? Point to several places where Hemauer "shows" instead of "tells."

9. How does Hemauer use dialogue in the essay? What other methods does she use to show readers what her life as a farm girl was like?

Inquiry and Research: Ideas for Further Exploration

10. Search the Web to find other narratives—even blog entries—in which college students reflect on their life and work experiences. How do they compare to Hemauer's narrative about her farm-life experience?

Self-Assessment: Reflecting on Your Goals

Now that you have constructed a piece of writing to share experiences, revisit your learning goals, which you and your classmates may have considered at the beginning of this chapter (see page 76). Here are some questions to help you focus on what you have learned from this assignment. Respond to the questions in writing, and discuss your responses with classmates. If you are constructing a course portfolio, your responses to these questions can also serve as invention work for the portfolio.

 ### Rhetorical Knowledge

- *Audience:* What did you learn about your audience as you wrote about your experience or experiences?
- *Purpose:* How successfully do you feel you fulfilled your purpose? Why?
- *Rhetorical situation:* What was your rhetorical situation? How have you responded to the rhetorical situation?
- *Voice and tone:* How did you reveal your personality? What tone did you use?
- *Context, medium, and genre:* What context were you writing in? What medium and genre did you choose, and how did those decisions affect your writing?

 ### Critical Thinking, Reading, and Writing

- *Learning/inquiry:* What did you discover about writing about experiences while you were working on this assignment? What did you discover about yourself? About your experiences?
- *Responsibility:* How did you fulfill your responsibility to your readers? To the people you wrote about?
- *Reading and research:* Did you rely on your memories, or did you conduct additional research for this assignment? If so, what sources did you consult? How did you use them?

Writing Processes for Sharing Experiences

- *Invention:* What invention strategies were most useful to you?
- *Organizing your ideas and details:* What organization did you use? How successful was it?
- *Revising:* What one revision did you make that you are most satisfied with? What are the strongest and the weakest parts of the paper you wrote for this chapter? Why?
- *Working with peers:* How did your instructor or peer readers help you by making comments and suggestions about your writing? List some examples of useful comments that you received. How could you have made better use of the comments and suggestions you received?
- *Visuals:* Did you use photographs or other visuals to help you describe your experience or experiences? If so, what did you learn about incorporating these elements?
- *Writing habits:* What "writerly habits" have you developed, modified, or improved on as you constructed the writing assignment for this chapter?

 ## Knowledge of Conventions

- *Editing:* What sentence problem did you find most frequently in your writing? How will you avoid that problem in future assignments?
- *Genre:* What conventions of the genre you were using, if any, gave you problems?
- *Documentation:* Did you use sources for your paper? If so, what documentation style did you use? What problems, if any, did you have with it?

Refer to Chapter 1 (pages 12–13) for a sample reflection by a student.

6

Writing to Explore

When you hear the word *exploration,* you may envision astronauts or explorers of earlier centuries, people who physically ventured to previously uncharted territory. When astronauts Neil Armstrong and Edwin E. "Buzz" Aldrin went to the moon in 1969, they were looking for answers to questions that humans have asked for thousands of years: What is the moon like? What is it composed of? What does Earth look like from the moon? More recently, the Hubble Space Telescope has enabled explorers to view remote parts of the universe, and today's space explorers are often not astronauts but robots—like the Mars Rover.

Although we commonly associate exploration with physical travel, there are many other kinds of explorations. Indeed, some of the most valuable explorations are those that take place in your own mind. Often, through the act of writing, you can discover new ideas or new perspectives.

Playwright Edward Albee once noted, "I write to find out what I'm talking about." In addition to exploring what you already know, exploratory writing gives you

Photo taken on July 20, 1969, by Neil A. Armstrong of Edwin E. "Buzz" Aldrin during the Apollo 11 mission to the moon.

the chance to ask questions and to consider what else you would like to find out.

In any exploration, whether in college or in the professional, civic, and personal areas of your life, you investigate a particular subject closely. You will often need to explore an idea or a concept—or a decision you need to make—in detail, from various perspectives, before you can really see and understand the overall situation.

111

Setting Your Goals for *Exploratory Writing*

Rhetorical Knowledge (pp. 114–18)

- **Audience:** Because you are learning as you write, you will often be the main audience. Who else can you visualize reading your work? What will that person or those people expect to find in it? How can you appeal to those readers as well?
- **Purpose:** Your purpose might be simply to learn more about the topic, but often exploratory writing leads to the unexpected and unfamiliar, so you need to be prepared to be surprised.
- **Rhetorical situation:** Consider the many factors that affect what you write—you (the writer), your readers (the audience), the topic (the subject you are exploring), your purpose (what you wish to accomplish), and the exigency (what is compelling you to write). In an exploratory essay, you are writing to raise questions and to let them guide your inquiry; your readers are reading your text so that they can grapple with those same questions.
- **Voice and tone:** Generally, exploratory writing has an inquisitive tone. Of course, sometimes an exploratory essay can have a humorous tone.
- **Context, medium, and genre:** The genre you use to present your thinking is determined by your purpose: to explore. You will need to decide on the best medium and genre to use to present your exploration to the audience you want to reach.

Critical Thinking, Reading, and Writing (pp. 119–33)

- **Learning/inquiry:** By reading and writing as an explorer, you gain a deeper understanding of diverse and complex perspectives.
- **Responsibility:** You have a responsibility to represent diverse perspectives honestly and accurately.
- **Reading and research:** Your research must be accurate and as complete as possible to allow you to consider the widest possible array of perspectives.

Writing Processes (pp. 134–45)

- **Invention:** Choose invention strategies that will help you thoughtfully contemplate diverse perspectives.
- **Organizing your ideas and details:** Find the most effective way to present perspectives to your readers, so they can easily understand them.
- **Revising:** Read your work with a critical eye to make certain that it fulfills the assignment and displays the qualities of effective exploratory writing.
- **Working with peers:** Your classmates will make suggestions that indicate parts of your text they find difficult to understand so you can clarify.

 Knowledge of Conventions (pp. 146–47)

- **Editing:** When you explore, you might tend to leave your thoughts—and sentences—incomplete. To help you avoid this pitfall, the round-robin activity in this chapter (on page 146) deals with sentence fragments.
- **Genres for exploratory writing:** Possible genres include exploratory essays, profiles, and more informal types of exploratory writing such as blogs, journals, and diaries.
- **Documentation:** If you have relied on sources outside of your own experience, you will need to cite them using the appropriate documentation style.

RHETORICAL KNOWLEDGE

When you write to explore, consider how your exploration will help you gain some greater understanding, how you can help your readers understand your topic in a new way, and why you want them to gain this understanding. Also, decide what medium and genre will help you communicate your exploration most effectively to your audience.

Writing to Explore in Your College Classes

Your college classes give you wonderful opportunities to explore your current interests and discover new ones. Taking a college class in almost any field allows you to begin exploring that field, reading its literature, and listening to and interacting with people who are experts in the field. Each class you take also gives you the opportunity to explore the subject area via writing. During your college career, you may write the following kinds of papers:

- In a history class, your instructor may encourage you to explore several perspectives on the Cuban Missile Crisis in 1962. Such an exploration might then lead to a writing project in which you argue that certain events and factors were the actual causes of this crisis.

- In a nutrition class, your instructor may ask you to explore several perspectives on vegetarian diets. Here, too, your exploration could lead to a paper in which you demonstrate specific effects of vegetarianism or in which you argue for or against such a diet.

- For a communication course, your instructor may ask you to explore whether there is evidence that men and women have different communication styles.

For information on writing a cause-and-effect analysis, see Chapter 11. For information on writing to convince, see Chapter 9.

For all of these writing situations, think about what you might need to do to communicate your ideas effectively: what information you might need to include, how you would describe your exploration, what visuals or examples you might use, and so on.

Writing to Explore for Life

Just as you will undoubtedly write to explore in your academic life, you are likely to use different kinds of exploratory writing in other areas of your life. In much of the exploratory writing you will do in your *professional* life, you will find yourself exploring various options. A manager might ask to what extent hiring Ms. X instead of Mr. Y will make a difference to the business. A teacher might ask what effect one lesson plan would have on a group of students compared to a different lesson plan.

(**ELECTRONIC ENVIRONMENTS**) **Writing a Blog**

The ultimate form of writing to explore might be a personal or professional online journal, or *blog*. A blog (a shortening of "Web *log*") can be a fun place to explore issues and events of the day while developing your voice, style, and expressive self. As you explore your topic and begin conducting research, use a blog to organize and to keep track of your research.

Take a look at one writer's blog about her research on her grandfather's life at http:// www.bookerwright.com/. The blog started as a space to explore her ideas and research and evolved into a documentary about her grandfather. She is now writing a book based on the blog.

People working for the good of a community often deal with *best options*—solutions to problems for which there may not be a single perfect result but rather many possible outcomes. Therefore, those involved in *civic* life can find exploratory writing especially useful.

Your *personal* life offers many opportunities for exploratory writing. You may respond regularly to e-mails or notes from friends, family members, and classmates in which you explore the possibilities for a group gift for someone important to all of you, propose convenient times for getting together, or consider a new wireless carrier. You may keep a journal, where you can explore your thoughts, ideas, responses, and feelings privately.

The "Ways of Writing" feature (page 116) presents different genres that can be used when writing to explore.

For more on blogs, see Chapter 17.

Scenarios for Writing | Assignment Options

Your instructor may ask you to complete one of the following assignments that call for exploratory writing. Each assignment is in the form of a *scenario,* a brief story that provides some context for writing. The scenario gives you a sense of who your audience is and what you need to accomplish with your writing.

Starting on page 134, you will find guidelines for completing whatever assignment option you choose. Additional scenarios for college and life may be found online.

Writing for College

SCENARIO 1 An Academic Paper Exploring a Career

For this scenario, assume you are taking a "career and life planning" class—a class devoted to helping college students decide what discipline they might like to major in. This class gives you the opportunity to explore different career paths, to learn what the educational requirements are for various majors, and to find out what job opportunities will be available and what salaries and other forms of compensation different jobs might offer.

Ways of Writing to Explore

Genres for Your College Classes	Sample Situation	Advantages of the Genre	Limitations of the Genre
Academic essay	For your creative nonfiction class, you are asked to construct an essay exploring the writing styles of several authors you have read and studied.	Your exploration, using the conventions of an academic essay, will help you better understand the details of the writing styles of the authors you've studied.	An exploration often leads to more questions, which can be unsettling to a writer.
Internet exploration	Your writing professor has asked you to explore the Internet for reliable and relevant Web sites pertaining to your research topic and then post links to them with a summary of each on a discussion board for the class.	This activity will help you understand what electronic resources are available, as well as the range of quality.	Depending on your topic, there may be too much information to search through.
Exploratory paper	Your computer science instructor asks you to write an exploratory paper that proposes at least three viable solutions to a networking problem.	This activity will require that you envision multiple solutions rather than just one.	It can be difficult to write fairly about solutions you don't think will work.
Letter	You want to write a letter to your school newspaper that explores the ramifications of a proposed change in campus parking and encourages involvement in the decision.	The school newspaper will allow you to engage the appropriate audience about an issue that matters to them.	A letter to the editor allows only limited space, and you cannot use visuals to show what you mean. It might not be published.
Oral presentation	For your art class, you are asked to construct an oral and visual presentation exploring the "local art scene" by showing and discussing works from local artists.	The visuals in your presentation will allow your audience to see some of the art you are discussing.	Sometimes it is hard to get really good photographs of sculptures and other works of art. Aspiring artists may also not grant you permission to photograph their work.
Genres for Life	**Sample Situation**	**Advantages of the Genre**	**Limitations of the Genre**
Poster	You decide to construct a poster titled "Exploring ____ " to help viewers understand what a specific nonprofit organization does.	Your poster is a visual way to help readers explore the purpose of your nonprofit organization.	A poster restricts the amount of space you can use; illustrations are needed to catch the eye of passing viewers.
Blog	You and two neighbors want to construct a blog to help everyone in your neighborhood explore possible ways to improve the area.	A blog lets your neighborhood interact and share community information.	A blog must be monitored for potentially offensive comments; not everyone will feel comfortable blogging.
Wiki	For your employer, you construct a wiki asking everyone in your organization to explore ways to serve the public more efficiently.	A wiki is an easy and uncomplicated way for everyone in your business to contribute their ideas while building on the ideas of others.	Someone will need to monitor the wiki for inappropriate entries and to collect suggestions.
Web page	You want to construct a Web page allowing members of your community to explore various options for raising tax revenue to benefit the community.	Your Web page can provide text, graphs, charts, and links to related areas.	Readers cannot interact with a static Web page.
E-mail profile	Your family is planning a large family reunion; you construct an e-mail profile of some possible locations.	Your e-mail lets you explore potential locations with a large number of people, with links to relevant Web pages.	An e-mail can get lengthy as family members respond; not everyone will feel comfortable using e-mail.

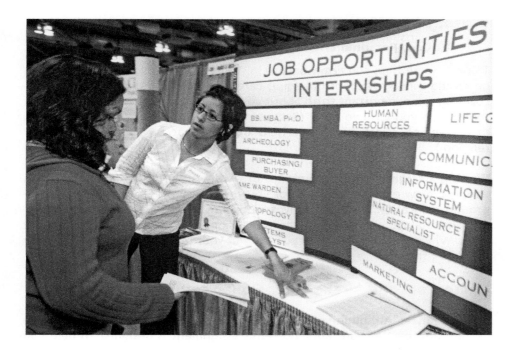

Writing Assignment: Select one college major or career that you may be interested in pursuing, and construct an exploratory paper in which you consider the various aspects of that major or career from many angles, including the preparation you would need for it and the rewards and pitfalls you might encounter if you decide to pursue it. Asking and answering questions about the major or career you are considering will form the heart of your exploratory paper.

SCENARIO 2 A Profile Exploring a Personal Interest

In this writing option, you will explore a subject that interests you personally and write a profile of it. This assignment gives you the chance to explore something or someone you are interested in and would like to know more about.

Writing Assignment: Think of a subject that you would like to know more about—perhaps a type of music or musician, a sport, a popular singer or actor, a local hangout, a community center, or something completely different. This assignment offers you the opportunity to research and write about a topic you are interested in. Use this opportunity not only to learn about the subject but also to examine your perceptions of and reactions to it.

Writing for Life

SCENARIO 3   Personal Writing: An Exploration in a Letter to a Friend

Think of something you firmly believe in. You might want to discuss your views on raising children, supporting aging parents, choosing a simpler lifestyle, discovering some important truth about yourself, or some other quality or belief that makes you who you are. (Because religious beliefs are so personal, you may want to select a strongly held opinion that does not involve your religion.)

Writing Assignment: In a sentence or two, write something you believe in strongly. Now explore the basis for your belief. Consider what in your background, education, history, family, friendships, upbringing, and work experience has helped you come to the conclusions you have reached about the topic. Why do you believe what you do? Put your text into the form of a letter to a good friend.

Rhetorical Considerations for Exploratory Writing

Audience: Although your instructor is one audience for this paper, you are also part of your audience—this assignment is designed to help you think through some possible educational and career choices, to explore an interest, or to explore some of your personal beliefs. Your classmates are also your audience, because some of them may also be considering these issues and ideas. They will learn from your research and perhaps ask questions and think of ideas they had not yet considered. Who else might be part of your audience?

Purpose: Your purpose is to explore the various aspects of your topic in enough detail and depth to lead you to a greater understanding of it and what you believe about it.

Voice, tone, and point of view: As you explore your topic, you will step back to consider whether any preconceptions you may have about it are accurate. Your stance should be objective, and you should be open to the different possibilities you will discover. The point of view you take should be one of questioning—what can you learn by exploring your topic?—but the tone you use can range from humorous to serious.

For more on choosing a medium and genre, see Chapter 17 and Appendix C. For more on writing a causal analysis, see Chapter 11. For more on writing a proposal paper, see Chapter 12.

Context, medium, and genre: Because you will be exploring an area you are already interested in, you will have the incentive to learn more as you research and write. The knowledge you gain may benefit you later. For example, you may be able to use the information you have acquired from this assignment to write a causal analysis or a proposal paper. If you are writing for an audience beyond the classroom, what will be the most effective way to present your information to this audience? You might write a letter to a friend, prepare a formal report for colleagues at work, or construct a Web site.

CRITICAL THINKING, READING, AND WRITING

Before you begin to write your exploratory paper, consider the qualities of successful exploratory writing. It also helps to read one or more examples of this type of writing. Finally, you might consider how visuals could enhance your exploratory writing, as well as the kinds of sources you will need to consult.

Unlike many other kinds of writing, where writers have a clear idea of their intent, exploratory writing frees writers to take intellectual chances and to see where different possibilities may lead. Although effective exploratory writing involves taking intellectual risks and finding alternatives that you may not have thought of before, your writing will not be successful if you simply write anything you please. Effective exploratory writing is based on reasonable options and uses information culled from solid research.

Learning the Qualities of Effective Exploratory Writing

As you think about how you might construct an exploratory paper, consider that readers probably expect the unexpected from this kind of text. Effective exploratory writing will include the following qualities:

- **A focus on a concept or question.** Rather than focusing on a specific, narrowly provable thesis, exploratory writing is more open-ended. Writers are more than likely trying to answer a question, to lay the groundwork for a solution to a problem, or to redefine a concept. For instance, a writer might pose a question such as this: "We had a large number of traffic fatalities in my city last year. What possible solutions might I explore?" In his exploratory essay, Andrew Sullivan seems to answer the question "Why do you blog?"

- **An inquisitive spirit.** Any explorer begins with an interest in finding out more about the subject. Ask questions that you want to answer, and let the answers lead you to further questions. Although you want to ground your queries in reality, you should not feel constrained by conventional thinking. Albert Einstein used "thought experiments" to explore time and space in ways conventional experiments could not. As a result, he developed his revolutionary theory of relativity.

- **A consideration of the range of perspectives in a subject.** As you explore your subject, be willing to see it from different vantage points and to consider its positive and negative aspects. Effective exploratory writing looks at a topic from as many angles as possible. This can be difficult to do sometimes, as we often get locked into our own ways of thinking.

In exploratory writing, however, it is vital to look at alternative views and to understand that others may have a different perspective from yours.

- **Expansive coverage of a subject.** Effective exploratory writing does not try to make a case or attempt to persuade you as writer or your reader of something. Rather, it examines many aspects of the topic, often developing a **profile** of its subject. Look at as much information about your subject as possible, while realizing that not all information is useful or relevant. Use your critical reading and thinking skills to help determine the reliability and relevance of the information you have gathered. Because exploratory writing is often inductive in nature, you might find it useful to organize your details in categories, using a cluster chart or listing.

For more on inductive thinking, see Chapter 14. For more on cluster charts and listing as strategies, see Chapter 4.

Reading, Inquiry, and Research: Learning from Texts That Explore

The following readings are examples of exploratory writing. Each offers perspectives on a subject. As you read each one, consider the following questions:

- What makes this reading an interesting and a useful exploration?
- After reading the selection what else do you want to learn about the subject? Why?
- How can you use the writer's techniques of exploratory writing in your own writing?

ANDREW SULLIVAN

Excerpt from "Why I Blog"

EXPLORATORY ESSAY

To blog is . . . to let go of your writing in a way, to hold it at arm's length, open it to scrutiny, allow it to float in the ether for a while, and to let others, as Montaigne[1] did, pivot you toward relative truth. A blogger will notice this almost immediately upon starting. Some e-mailers, unsurprisingly, know more about a subject than the blogger does. They will send links, stories, and facts, challenging the blogger's view of the world, sometimes outright refuting it, but more frequently adding context and nuance and complexity to an idea. The role of a blogger is not to defend against this but to embrace it. He is similar in this way to the host of a dinner party. He can provoke discussion or take a position, even passionately, but he also must create an atmosphere in which others want to participate.

Andrew Sullivan, a graduate of Oxford and Harvard universities, is a former editor at *The New Republic* and has also written for *The New York Times Magazine.* Best known for his blog, called *The Dish,* Sullivan writes about political issues in the United States. He has published numerous books, including *The Conservative Soul: How We Lost It, How to Get It Back* and *Intimations Pursued: The Voice of Practice in the Conversation of Michael Oakeshott.* This essay originally appeared in *The Atlantic* magazine in November 2008. In it Sullivan provides keen insights into the life of a blogger.

That atmosphere will inevitably be formed by the blogger's personality. The blogosphere may, in fact, be the least veiled of any forum in which a writer dares to express himself. Even the most careful and self-aware blogger will reveal more about himself than he wants to in a few unguarded sentences and publish them before he has the sense to hit Delete. The wise panic that can paralyze a writer—the fear that he will be exposed, undone, humiliated—is not available to a blogger. You can't have blogger's block. You have to express yourself now, while your emotions roil, while your temper flares, while your humor lasts. You can try to hide yourself from real scrutiny, and the exposure it demands, but it's hard. And that's what makes blogging as a form stand out: it is rich in personality. The faux intimacy of the Web experience, the closeness of the e-mail and the instant message, seeps through. You feel as if you know bloggers as they go through their lives, experience the same things you are experiencing, and share the moment. When readers of my blog bump into me in person, they invariably address me as Andrew. Print readers don't do that. It's Mr. Sullivan to them.

On my blog, my readers and I experienced 9/11 together, in real time. I can look back and see not just how I responded to the event, but how I responded to it at 3:47 that afternoon. And at 9:46 that night. There is a vividness to this immediacy that cannot be rivaled by print. The same goes for the 2000 recount,

---

[1]French essayist who lived in the sixteenth century.

the Iraq War, the revelations of Abu Ghraib, the death of John Paul II, or any of the other history-making events of the past decade. There is simply no way to write about them in real time without revealing a huge amount about yourself. And the intimate bond this creates with readers is unlike the bond that the *Times*, say, develops with its readers through the same events. Alone in front of a computer, at any moment, are two people: a blogger and a reader. The proximity is palpable, the moment human—whatever authority a blogger has is derived not from the institution he works for but from the humanness he conveys. This is writing with emotion not just under but always breaking through the surface. It renders a writer and a reader not just connected but linked in a visceral, personal way. The only term that really describes this is *friendship*. And it is a relatively new thing to write for thousands and thousands of friends.

These friends, moreover, are an integral part of the blog itself—sources of   4
solace, company, provocation, hurt, and correction. If I were to do an inventory of the material that appears on my blog, I'd estimate that a good third of it is reader-generated, and a good third of my time is spent absorbing readers' views, comments, and tips. Readers tell me of breaking stories, new perspectives, and counterarguments to prevailing assumptions. And this is what blogging, in turn, does to reporting. The traditional method involves a journalist searching for key sources, nurturing them, and sequestering them from his rivals. A blogger splashes gamely into a subject and dares the sources to come to him.

Some of this material—e-mails from soldiers on the front lines, from scien-   5
tists explaining new research, from dissident Washington writers too scared to say what they think in their own partisan redoubts—might never have seen the light of day before the blogosphere. And some of it, of course, is dubious stuff. Bloggers can be spun and misled as easily as traditional writers—and the rigorous source assessment that good reporters do can't be done by e-mail. But you'd be surprised by what comes unsolicited into the in-box, and how helpful it often is.

Not all of it is mere information. Much of it is also opinion and scholarship,   6
a knowledge base that exceeds the research department of any newspaper. A good blog is your own private *Wikipedia*. Indeed, the most pleasant surprise of blogging has been the number of people working in law or government or academia or rearing kids at home who have real literary talent and real knowledge, and who had no outlet—until now. There is a distinction here, of course, between the edited use of e-mailed sources by a careful blogger and the often mercurial cacophony on an unmediated comments section. But the truth is out there—and the miracle of e-mail allows it to come to you.

Fellow bloggers are always expanding this knowledge base. Eight years   7
ago, the blogosphere felt like a handful of individual cranks fighting with one another. Today, it feels like a universe of cranks, with vast, pulsating readerships, fighting with one another. To the neophyte reader, or blogger, it can seem

overwhelming. But there is a connection between the intimacy of the early years and the industry it has become today. And the connection is human individuality.

The pioneers of online journalism—*Slate* and *Salon*—are still very popular, 8 and successful. But the more memorable stars of the Internet—even within those two sites—are all personally branded. *Daily Kos*, for example, is written by hundreds of bloggers, and amended by thousands of commenters. But it is named after Markos Moulitsas, who started it, and his own prose still provides a backbone to the front-page blog. The biggest news-aggregator site in the world, the *Drudge Report*, is named after its founder, Matt Drudge, who somehow conveys a unified sensibility through his selection of links, images, and stories. The vast, expanding universe of *The Huffington Post* still finds some semblance of coherence in the Cambridge-Greek twang of Arianna; the entire world of online celebrity gossip circles the drain of Perez Hilton; and the investigative journalism, reviewing, and commentary of *Talking Points Memo* is still tied together by the tone of Josh Marshall. Even *Slate* is unimaginable without Mickey Kaus's voice.

What endures is a human brand. Readers have encountered this phenom- 9 enon before—*I.F. Stone's Weekly*[2] comes to mind—but not to this extent. It stems, I think, from the conversational style that blogging rewards. What you want in a conversationalist is as much character as authority. And if you think of blogging as more like talk radio or cable news than opinion magazines or daily newspapers, then this personalized emphasis is less surprising. People have a voice for radio and a face for television. For blogging, they have a sensibility.

But writing in this new form is a collective enterprise as much as it is an 10 individual one—and the connections between bloggers are as important as the content on the blogs. The links not only drive conversation, they drive readers. The more you link, the more others will link to you, and the more traffic and readers you will get. The zero-sum game of old media—in which *Time* benefits from *Newsweek's* decline and vice versa—becomes win-win. It's great for *Time* to be linked to by *Newsweek* and the other way round. One of the most prized statistics in the blogosphere is therefore not the total number of readers or page views, but the "authority" you get by being linked to by other blogs. It's an indication of how central you are to the online conversation of humankind.

The reason this open-source market of thinking and writing has such 11 potential is that the always adjusting and evolving collective mind can rapidly filter out bad arguments and bad ideas. The flip side, of course, is that bloggers are also human beings. Reason is not the only fuel in the tank. In a world where no distinction is made between good traffic and bad traffic, and where emotion often rules, some will always raise their voice to dominate the conversation; others will pander shamelessly to their readers' prejudices; others will start online brawls for the fun of it. Sensationalism, dirt, and the ease of formulaic

---

[2] A highly regarded newsletter published by investigative journalist I.F. Stone (1907–1989).

talking points always beckon. You can disappear into the partisan blogosphere and never stumble onto a site you disagree with.

But linkage mitigates this. A Democratic blog will, for example, be forced to link to Republican ones, if only to attack and mock. And it's in the interests of both camps to generate shared traffic. This encourages polarized slugfests. But online, at least you see both sides. Reading *The Nation* or *National Review* before the Internet existed allowed for more cocooning than the wide-open online sluice gates do now. If there's more incivility, there's also more fluidity. Rudeness, in any case, isn't the worst thing that can happen to a blogger. Being ignored is. Perhaps the nastiest thing one can do to a fellow blogger is to rip him apart and fail to provide a link.

A successful blog therefore has to balance itself between a writer's own take on the world and others. Some bloggers collect, or "aggregate," other bloggers' posts with dozens of quick links and minimalist opinion topspin: Glenn Reynolds at *Instapundit* does this for the right-of-center; Duncan Black at *Eschaton* does it for the left. Others are more eclectic, or aggregate links in a particular niche, or cater to a settled and knowledgeable reader base. A "blogroll" is an indicator of whom you respect enough to keep in your galaxy. For many years, I kept my reading and linking habits to a relatively small coterie of fellow political bloggers. In today's blogosphere, to do this is to embrace marginality. I've since added links to religious blogs and literary ones and scientific ones and just plain weird ones. As the blogosphere has expanded beyond anyone's capacity to absorb it, I've needed an assistant and interns to scour the Web for links and stories and photographs to respond to and think about. It's a difficult balance, between your own interests and obsessions, and the knowledge, insight, and wit of others—but an immensely rich one. There are times, in fact, when a blogger feels less like a writer than an online disc jockey, mixing samples of tunes and generating new melodies through mashups while also making his own music. He is both artist and producer—and the beat always goes on.

If all this sounds postmodern, that's because it is. And blogging suffers from the same flaws as postmodernism: a failure to provide stable truth or a permanent perspective. A traditional writer is valued by readers precisely because they trust him to have thought long and hard about a subject, given it time to evolve in his head, and composed a piece of writing that is worth their time to read at length and to ponder. Bloggers don't do this and cannot do this—and that limits them far more than it does traditional long-form writing.

A blogger will air a variety of thoughts or facts on any subject in no particular order other than that dictated by the passing of time. A writer will instead use time, synthesizing these thoughts, ordering them, weighing which points count more than others, seeing how his views evolved in the writing process itself, and responding to an editor's perusal of a draft or two. The result is almost always more measured, more satisfying, and more enduring than a blizzard of posts.

The triumphalist notion that blogging should somehow replace traditional writing is as foolish as it is pernicious. In some ways, blogging's gifts to our discourse make the skills of a good traditional writer much more valuable, not less. The torrent of blogospheric insights, ideas, and arguments places a greater premium on the person who can finally make sense of it all, turning it into something more solid, and lasting, and rewarding.

The points of this essay, for example, have appeared in shards and frag- 16 ments on my blog for years. But being forced to order them in my head and think about them for a longer stretch has helped me understand them better, and perhaps express them more clearly. Each week, after a few hundred posts, I also write an actual newspaper column. It invariably turns out to be more considered, balanced, and evenhanded than the blog. But the blog will always inform and enrich the column, and often serve as a kind of free-form, free-associative research. And an essay like this will spawn discussion best handled on a blog. The conversation, in other words, is the point, and the different idioms used by the conversationalists all contribute something of value to it. And so, if the defenders of the old media once viscerally regarded blogging as some kind of threat, they are starting to see it more as a portal, and a spur.

There is, after all, something simply irreplaceable about reading a piece of 17 writing at length on paper, in a chair or on a couch or in bed. To use an obvious analogy, jazz entered our civilization much later than composed, formal music. But it hasn't replaced it; and no jazz musician would ever claim that it could. Jazz merely demands a different way of playing and listening, just as blogging requires a different mode of writing and reading. Jazz and blogging are intimate, improvisational, and individual—but also inherently collective. And the audience talks over both.

The reason they talk while listening, and comment or link while reading, is 18 that they understand that this is a kind of music that needs to be engaged rather than merely absorbed. To listen to jazz as one would listen to an aria is to miss the point. Reading at a monitor, at a desk, or on an iPhone provokes a querulous, impatient, distracted attitude, a demand for instant, usable information, that is simply not conducive to opening a novel or a favorite magazine on the couch. Reading on paper evokes a more relaxed and meditative response. The message dictates the medium. And each medium has its place—as long as one is not mistaken for the other.

In fact, for all the intense gloom surrounding the newspaper and magazine 19 business, this is actually a golden era for journalism. The blogosphere has added a whole new idiom to the act of writing and has introduced an entirely new generation to nonfiction. It has enabled writers to write out loud in ways never seen or understood before. And yet it has exposed a hunger and need for traditional writing that, in the age of television's dominance, had seemed on the wane.

Words, of all sorts, have never seemed so now. 20

UNDERSTANDING A WRITER'S GOALS: QUESTIONS TO CONSIDER AND DISCUSS

Rhetorical Knowledge: The Writer's Situation and Rhetoric

1. **Audience:** How does Sullivan's relationship with his blog readers differ from his relationship with the readers of this essay?

2. **Purpose:** Why does Sullivan explain his blogging process in such detail?

3. **Voice and Tone:** What is Sullivan's attitude toward fellow bloggers—both those who share his political views and those who do not? How does he express that attitude in this essay?

4. **Responsibility:** How responsibly has Sullivan represented blogs and bloggers? What makes you think that?

5. **Context, format, and genre:** Sullivan chose the genre of the essay to explain his reasons for blogging. Why do you think he chose that genre instead of a blog to write about his blogging?

Critical Thinking: The Writer's Ideas and Your Personal Response

6. What does Sullivan mean when he writes, "A good blog is your own private Wikipedia"?

7. How does Sullivan's essay affect your own desire to blog? Why?

Composing Process and Knowledge of Conventions: The Writer's Strategies

8. How effective is Sullivan's analogy in which he compares blogging to jazz (paragraph 17)? Why?

9. Although Sullivan comments on the ideas of other people, including bloggers, he does not quote anyone. Why do you think this is so? What might quotations have added to his essay?

Inquiry and Research: Ideas for Further Research

10. Read some of Andrew Sullivan's blog entries. How do they illustrate some of the points that Sullivan makes in his essay?

GENRES *Up Close*

Because people are so curious about other people, they love to write and talk about them. To satisfy that craving, readers can find plenty of venues that offer profiles. Profiles of famous and not-so-famous people appear in magazines such as *People* and *Rolling Stone,* on radio news shows such as *All Things Considered* or *Weekend Edition* on National Public Radio, on television shows such as *E! News,* and especially on social networking sites such as Facebook. Social networking sites are especially popular because they allow ordinary people to read profiles of other ordinary people. A recent Web search using the term "Facebook," for example, yielded more 20.6 billion sites. In fact, Facebook has more than 800 million users. That number is astounding, considering that Earth's population is approximately 7 billion.

Although profiles often focus on people, they also can describe places and events. Profiles have distinctive features. They usually do the following:

- **Provide some insight into the subject.** A profile takes readers behind the scenes to reveal details that are not widely known.

- **Include key details.** A profile describes its subject, offering details that appeal to the senses as well as dialogue and expert opinion.

- **Are logically organized.** Whether the organization is chronological or spatial, an effective profile holds readers' interest as it informs them about its subject.

As you consider the following profile of the last flight of an historic biplane, think about how it exemplifies the features of a profile.

OWEN EDWARDS

PROFILE OF AN EVENT

The Tuskegee Airmen Plane's Last Flight

Parked on the tarmac at Lincoln, California's municipal airport, the open-cockpit biplane looked as if it had just rolled off the assembly line, circa 1944. This past July, the World War II–era two-seater's pilot and owner, Air Force Capt. Matt Quy (pronounced Kwai), took off from Lincoln in the PT-13D U.S. Army Air Corps Stearman, bound for Washington, D.C. and, ultimately, the Smithsonian's National Museum of African American History and Culture (NMAAHC), whose new home is slated to open in 2015.

The Stearman was standard issue for training fledgling pilots during the war. But what makes this particular plane—with its Air Corps blue, yellow, red and white color scheme—an important addition to the new museum's holdings is its backstory. It was used to ready America's first African-American military pilots, the Tuskegee Airmen, for aerial combat.

Owen Edwards is a columnist for *Smithsonian* magazine. He frequently writes about photography and design. He co-authored *Quintessence: The Quality of Having "It"* and the sequel, *Elegant Solutions: Quintessential Technology for a User-Friendly World.* In this profile, which was published in *Smithsonian* magazine in November 2011, he describes the last flight of a plane used by the famous Tuskegee Airmen, a group of African-American pilots who flew in World War II.

Restored PT-13D U.S. Army Air Corps Stearman Biplane

Edwards provides key details about the plane and its history.

Edwards includes telling quotations from the owner of the plane.

Primary training took place at Moton Field in Tuskegee, Alabama, which is where Quy's Stearman was originally based. The first class of five Tuskegee pilots graduated in March 1942, three months after Pearl Harbor.   3

The Airmen manned both fighter planes and bombers. Their 332nd Fighter Group was commanded by West Point graduate Lt. Col. Ben Davis Jr., the son of America's first African-American general. The 332nd was deployed in April 1943 and flew more than 1,500 missions over Italy and the Mediterranean from various bases in North Africa.   4

Quy's love affair with the PT-13D seems almost fated. "I grew up in Apple Valley, Minnesota," Quy recalled as he and I prepared to board the plane for a flight over California farmland. "When I was 7 or 8, my family lived at the end of a grass runway. There was a guy with a Stearman who dragged advertising signs. He'd come right over our house pulling those banners, and I was hooked." After graduating from Minnesota State University in Mankato, Quy became a pilot for Sun Country Airlines. In 2002, he reversed the typical pilot's career path and joined the Air Force. He bought the Stearman, which had been wrecked in a crash, in 2005, sight unseen, by telephone.   5

A Poster from the 2012 Film *Red Tails*, Which Tells the Story of the Tuskegee Airmen

In Houston, Quy, along with his wife, Tina, a pharmaceutical rep, and an aircraft-mechanic friend, Robbie Vajdos, began a three-year effort to make   6 the plane as good as new. "Luckily for me, after the war many of these planes became crop-dusters," he said, "so there are still parts available." And, in Texas, there was ample space available too. "We had three garages for all the stuff," Tina told me. In 2008, Quy and Vajdos finally got the plane aloft, taking it out for a 40-minute spin. "That first flight," says Quy, "was pretty emotional."

Not long after buying the plane, Quy discovered through research that it 7 had been used by the Tuskegee pilots at Moton. Once restoration was complete and the Lycoming engine was back in working order, Quy—who flew a tour of duty in Afghanistan during this period—began taking the plane to air shows and meeting Tuskegee Airmen. Today, the underside of a fuselage compartment door contains the signatures of 45 Airmen. In 2008, an article in the U.S. Air Force Journal brought the story of Quy and his aircraft to the attention of Smithsonian National Air and Space Museum curator Dik Daso; he alerted NMAAHC curator Paul Gardullo.

Gardullo and Daso attended an air show at Edwards Air Force Base in 8 Southern California in 2009, where they met Quy, his wife and two Airmen, Lt. Cols. Alexander Jefferson and Bill Holloman. The Quys agreed that their plane belonged at the Smithsonian, where it would symbolize the Tuskegee Airmen's story for millions of visitors.

On August 2, after a transcontinental journey that included stops at the Air 9 Force Academy in Colorado, air shows in Minnesota and—most significantly—at Moton Field, Quy and his plane touched down on August 5 at Dulles International Airport outside Washington for the official hand over. The landing was timed to coincide with a national convention of Tuskegee Airmen in nearby Oxon Hill, Maryland.

The profile has a chronological organization, ending with the arrival of the plane in Washington.

Gardullo witnessed the landings at Moton and at Dulles. "It was a power- 10 ful experience seeing that plane brought back to its original home," he says of the Stearman's arrival at Moton. And of the plane's final touchdown, he told me, "When this tiny airplane came in among all the big airliners, for several minutes everything was just quiet. That was when the impact of this story really hit me."

UNDERSTANDING A WRITER'S GOALS: QUESTIONS TO CONSIDER AND DISCUSS

Rhetorical Knowledge: The Writer's Situation and Rhetoric

1. **Audience:** Why is this profile suitable for a publication such as *Smithsonian* magazine?

2. **Purpose:** What is Edwards's purpose for narrating this event?

3. **Voice and Tone:** What is Edwards's attitude toward the last flight of the restored PT-13D U.S. Army Air Corps Stearman? How does he convey that attitude?

4. **Responsibility:** What in the essay suggests that Edwards feels a responsibility to honor the service of the Tuskegee Airmen?

5. **Context, format, and genre:** What are the advantages of publishing this kind of profile in an online magazine, as well as in the print magazine?

Critical Thinking: The Writer's Ideas and Your Personal Response

6. Why does Edwards focus on both the restoration of the biplane and its last flight?

7. Given what Edwards says about the Tuskegee Airmen, what else would you like to know about the group? Why?

Composing Process and Knowledge of Conventions: The Writer's Strategies

8. Why does Edwards quote Matt Quy in the profile rather than paraphrasing or summarizing what Quy said?

9. Given that this is a profile of an event, why does Edwards provide biographical information about Matt Quy? What does this information add to the profile?

Inquiry and Research: Ideas for Further Research

10. Conduct a Web search on the Tuskegee Airmen. What do you find most interesting about what they accomplished?

Kiva Web Site http://www.kiva.org

Kiva is a nonprofit microfinance organization that provides loans to poor people around the world so that they can operate small businesses. Almost all of the loans are repaid to lenders, who often then provide loans to others. As you explore Kiva's Web site, consider what the writers have done to make it inviting to readers.

About Us
  Team
  Volunteers
  Board
  Finances
  History
  Statistics

How Kiva Works

About Microfinance

Social Performance

Support Us

Field Partners

How to become a
Field Partner

Kiva Fellows

App Gallery

Do More

Risk and Due
Diligence

Press Center

Help Center

About Us

The people behind Kiva include volunteers, Kiva Fellows, Field Partners, our board, and a team of employees (shown above) and contractors. The Kiva headquarters are located in San Francisco, California.

We are a non-profit organization with a mission to connect people through lending to alleviate poverty. Leveraging the internet and a worldwide network of microfinance institutions, Kiva lets individuals lend as little as $25 to help create opportunity around the world. Learn more about how it works.

Since Kiva was founded in 2005:

776,718 Kiva lenders

$321 million in loans

98.97% Repayment rate

We work with:

152 Field Partners

450 volunteers around the world

61 different countries

More metrics and stats >

Why we do what we do

UNDERSTANDING THE WRITERS' GOALS: QUESTIONS TO CONSIDER AND DISCUSS

Rhetorical Knowledge: The Writers' Situation and Rhetoric

1. **Audience:** How large is the audience for Kiva's Web site? Why do you think the audience is that size?

2. **Purpose:** What are the major purposes of Kiva's site?

3. **Voice and Tone:** Although the authors of this Web site are anonymous, what attitude toward viewers does the site convey?

4. **Responsibility:** How does this Web site encourage responsible behavior?

5. **Context, format, and genre:** What features of the Web site's home page encourage readers to explore Kiva? How would you describe the links on the home page?

Critical Thinking: The Writers' Ideas and Your Personal Response

6. Visit the Web site for Kiva (http://www.kiva.org) and click on some of the links to pages that provide information about the organization. What information is most interesting?

7. What information is most useful to readers who want to learn more about Kiva?

Composing Process and Knowledge of Conventions: The Writers' Strategies

8. Why do you think that the Kiva logo includes an image of a heart?

9. Why do you think that the Kiva home page includes so many photos of people, as well as information about each person featured on the page?

Inquiry and Research: Ideas for Further Research

10. Conduct a Web search with the terms "microfinance" and "microloan." Visit sites for several other organizations that offer such loans to see how they portray themselves. How do they differ from Kiva?

WRITING PROCESSES

As you work on the assignment you have chosen, remember the qualities of an effective exploratory paper, which are listed on pages 119–20. Also remember that writing is recursive—you might start with an invention activity or two and then conduct some research, which leads to more invention work and then a first draft. But then you might need to do more invention work to flesh out your draft and conduct more research to answer questions that come up as you explore your ideas further. And then you'll revise your draft and possibly find another gap or two. So while the activities listed below imply that writers proceed step-by-step, the actual process of writing is usually messier.

As you work on your project, save your computer files frequently because any work that you don't save could be lost. Savvy writers back up their computer files in two or more places—on an internal or external hard drive of the computer, on a USB flash drive, and on a rewritable CD or DVD, for example.

Invention: Getting Started

The invention activities below are strategies that you can use to get some sense of what you already know about a subject. Whatever invention method(s) you use (or that your instructor asks you to employ), try to answer questions such as these:

- What do I already know about my subject?
- What preconceptions—positive, negative, neutral—do I have?
- Why am I interested in exploring this subject?
- What questions about the subject would I most like answers to? Who might I be able to talk to about this subject?
- What do I know about my audience? What can I say to interest them in my subject?
- What might my audience already know about my subject? What questions might they have?
- What is my purpose in exploring this subject? What would I like the end result of my research and writing to be? More knowledge? Information that I might use to pursue some goal?

If you do your invention work in electronic form, rather than on paper, you can incorporate this early writing more easily as you construct a draft.

As with any kind of writing, invention activities improve with peer feedback and suggestions. Consider sharing the invention work you have done so far with several classmates or friends in order to understand your rhetorical situation more clearly and to generate more useful information.

Rick Mohler's Freewriting and Clustering

Rick Mohler was taking a "career and life planning" class at his local community college, so he decided to respond to Scenario 1 on page 115. Rick was interested in a lot of areas—especially sports—but he was not quite sure what he might want to pursue as a career. Here is a portion of his freewriting, which reflects his questions and concerns about finding a career that he will enjoy:

> I think what I like most is sports—playing them, thinking about them, learning new rules and games. Football is my game! But I know I probably won't have a professional career—not many people make it to the NFL. I'm not a very fast runner. I can work at it and try, but I need some fallback position, if I'm not good enough. I can't think of anything, maybe an analyst? Sportswriter? Coach? Sports medicine? Photographer? Trainer? Do something with the physical aspect of football?
>
> But if I can't be an NFL player, what can I do? Do I want to stay with sports? What other careers besides being an athlete goes with sports, especially football? Careers in sports, jobs in sports, jobs about sports. Are there college classes I can take to lead me there?

Rick Mohler also used listing to explore his ideas about a career. (See Chapter 5, page 95, for an example of this strategy.) Then he combined ideas from his freewriting and list into a cluster.

Writing Activity

Freewriting, Listing, and Clustering

Using the questions on page 134, freewrite for ten minutes, writing down everything you can think of about your subject. Even if you cannot think of anything to say, keep writing. Or list your ideas about the subject. Develop categories for your list to help you brainstorm.

Once you have gathered your ideas using one of the above methods, cluster them to determine how they relate to one another.

STUDENT WRITING EXAMPLES

Brainstorming (pp. 176, 350)

Freewriting (pp. 48, 135, 261, 396)

Criteria (p. 307)

Listing (p. 95)

Answers to Reporter's Questions (p. 261)

Organization (pp. 96, 181)

Clustering (pp. 135, 305)

Interviewing (p. 220)

Research (pp. 137, 177, 222, 263, 308, 398)

Reflection (p. 12)

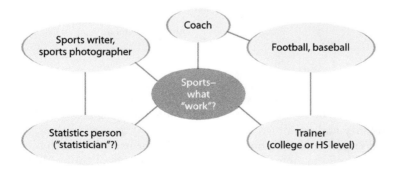

Exploring Your Ideas with Research

Although your opinions and ideas—and especially your questions—are central to any exploratory writing that you do, answer the questions you raise as you explore your subject. Getting those answers usually requires research, which can include reading

For help with locating sources of information, see Chapter 19; for help with taking notes and documenting your sources, see Chapter 20.

books and periodical articles at the library, reading articles in your local newspaper, interviewing people who know more than you do about your subject, and conducting searches online, among other means. The information that you discover through your research can help you respond to the questions that prompted your exploration.

Before you start your research, review your invention work to remind yourself of all that you know about your subject and the questions you have about it. Use the reporter's questions—*who, what, where, when, why,* and *how*—to get started. After you have decided what information you need, determine what kind of research will help you to gather that information. Then conduct research in the library and on the Internet.

You could conduct several kinds of research in response to the scenarios on pages 115–18. For Scenario 1, for example, in which you explore potential majors, you might visit the Web sites of various departments at your school to gather information about degree programs, courses offered, and careers of alumni. You might also visit the Web sites of companies that hire graduates in the fields that you are exploring. You could even search newspapers and the Internet to find job advertisements in those fields. You might interview graduating seniors to ask them about their experiences in the majors that you are exploring or people who hold the kinds of jobs that require those majors. Finally, you could search for and read blogs maintained by people who write about their professional fields and careers.

ELECTRONIC ENVIRONMENTS   **Using the Internet to Gain an International Perspective**

Writing to explore involves the hard work of experiencing and understanding *different perspectives.* A good way to learn about new perspectives is to read news reports from around the world, including those published in foreign newspapers and newsmagazines. Most major publications are now available in English translation. The following are some examples of Web sites maintained by foreign news organizations:

ABYZ News Links (A List of Links to Foreign News Sites)
http://www.abyznewslinks.com
French News
http://www.france24.com/en/
Japan Times
http://www.japantimes.co.jp/
Pravda (Russia)
http://english.pravda.ru/
London Times (UK)
http://www.timesonline.co.uk/tol/news/

Rick Mohler's Research

Student writer Rick Mohler wanted to explore possible careers in the world of sports other than being an athlete. In addition to browsing the Web, he went to his college library and examined recent issues of his school newspaper, some magazines, and several books. To find helpful articles, he used the search term "sports—careers." He used the same search term to search his school's online library indexes. Based on what he read, he made some notes to himself in order to try to find some direction. Here are some of Mohler's notes:

1. Read through back issues of the campus newspaper—*College Press*— there were some interviews with several coaches, all from different sports. Interview them to find out more?

2. Also lots of photos of athletes. That might be an interesting career choice: sports photographer. Probably gets into the games free, too.
3. Someone has to write all those articles in *Sports Illustrated*. I wonder: How do you become a big-time sportswriter?

Writing Activity

Conducting Research

As you generate questions about your topic, consider where you might find the answers—books, journals, databases, the Internet, interviews, and so on. Begin to gather, read, or contact your sources. Manage your research by setting time (for example, two weeks) or quantity (say, ten sources) parameters to ensure that you meet your writing deadlines. Your instructor may specify the number and kinds of resources to focus on.

Reviewing Your Invention and Research

After you have conducted your research, review your invention work and notes. At this point, you may be tempted to decide on a **thesis statement**—a statement that summarizes the main point of your exploration. Even though you might already have a general idea of the conclusion your research is leading you to, it is often hard to know for certain what your thesis will be. Your thesis should come *from* your exploration. It is best to decide on your thesis after you have done a lot of invention

For more on developing a thesis, see Chapter 13.

Strategies FOR Success · Curiosity

Successful writers are curious. Like good reporters, they ask questions, ask follow-up questions, and generally try to find out why things are the way they are and how things work. They like to explore ideas, problems, and various perspectives. Although curiosity is a powerful tool for approaching any kind of writing, it is especially helpful when you are writing to explore. To use your curiosity as you write to explore, pose the following kinds of questions and then consider many possible responses to them: How does the content of any of my courses relate to what I hope to accomplish in this writing project? Why do some people's views on my topic differ from those of others? What kinds of research will help me find answers to my questions? Who else has asked the kinds of questions I'm asking? Who has the answers to these questions?

As you seek answers to these and other questions, work with classmates to discuss possible approaches and answers. Curiosity can be contagious. When you and peers share your curiosity with one another, it can become more intense, driving everyone to ask more questions.

work (listing, brainstorming, clustering, and so on) and research, or even after you construct your first draft.

 ## Organizing Your Ideas and Details

Because the purpose of writing an exploratory text is to examine an idea or concept from various perspectives, you will need to organize your thoughts in a useful manner. The questions that you need to ask yourself when deciding on your organization are all rhetorical:

- Who is your audience?
- Why might they be interested in your exploratory writing, or how can you make them interested in it? One way to emphasize the importance of your exploration to your audience is to show them why your subject is interesting to you.
- What is your purpose for writing—that is, why should your readers explore this topic with you?

Here is a brief outline of three possible organizational approaches to writing an exploratory paper:

Options FOR Organization
Options for Organizing an Exploratory Paper

Classify Ideas	Compare and Contrast Ideas	Relate Details Chronologically
Begin with your questions, perhaps from the least to the most important.	Note how many possible perspectives there may be on your subject and how they relate to one another.	Start from what happens first and move to later events.
Explain each question in detail and then provide possible answers.	Explore each perspective in detail.	Highlight events that were especially important to the subject and that will help readers get a better understanding of it.
Look at each question in detail. You may find that classifying both questions and answers is a useful method of organization.	Recognize that, because you began by noting multiple perspectives, comparison and contrast might be a useful method of organization.	Explore and explain various possible causes or effects, where they apply.
Offer follow-up questions that may lead to further exploration.	Explore your topic through various lenses to come to a better understanding of your subject, especially in relation to the different points of view on it.	End your paper at the present time, or with what seems like the final effect, if appropriate.
Perhaps conclude by suggesting that your exploration does not answer all the questions and that other, specified, questions now need to be asked.	Having presented multiple perspectives on your topic, indicate which conclusion your exploration has led you to.	

Constructing a Complete Draft

Once you know your subject, have recorded your ideas on paper or stored them in a computer file, and have conducted research, you are ready to construct your initial draft. It is possible that you will find a suitable organizational approach before you begin drafting, but you may also find it—or decide to change it— as you are drafting or even after you have constructed a draft. Also, as you write the first version of your exploratory paper, do not worry about editing your work.

Synthesizing and Integrating Sources into Your Draft: Quoting Information from Sources

INTEGRATING SOURCES

Including Others' Perspectives in Narratives (p. 97)

Quoting Sources (p. 139)

Paraphrasing Sources (p. 181)

Incorporating Numerical Data (p. 224)

Incorporating Partial Quotes (p. 266)

Creating Visuals to Show Your Data (p. 311)

Summarizing Information from Sources (p. 356)

Including Research Information (p. 401)

Because effective writers use research, it is important to learn how to integrate sources in your own text. One way writers integrate sources is by incorporating direct quotations.

As mentioned in Chapter 20, there are a number of situations when using a direct quotation is most appropriate—for example, when you are quoting a primary source such as an expert you have interviewed. Generally, you should include a direct quotation—exactly what someone told you—when the comments are concise and support your own assertions. When someone you interview gives you an abundance of information, or if you interview a number of people, you may want to summarize their comments instead of using an exact quotation (for more on *summarizing,* see page 356; for more on *paraphrasing* someone's comments, see page 181).

Whether you are quoting a source directly or paraphrasing or summarizing the information, you should help readers by introducing the information so that they will understand why it is there and how it relates to the point you are making. You will also need to document your source. For example, student writer Rick Mohler lets his readers know who John Wilson is when he introduces his quotation from Wilson (See Mohler's final paper on pages 147–50.) Note also that Mohler tells his reader what questions he asked Wilson:

> John Wilson, the spring workouts *College Press* writer, was kind enough to give me an interview. I asked him what kind of background an aspiring sportswriter needs. "It's not as easy as it sounds," Wilson told me. "I'm an English major, which really helps, and while that combined with my interest in and knowledge of sports is good, what's hard for me is the process of writing." (paragraph 7)
>
> I asked Wilson what he meant about writing and effort . . . (paragraph 8)

Once he completes his interview with Wilson, Mohler relates Wilson's comments to the purpose of his paper, writing that Mohler could see sportswriting "appealing to my competitive nature" (paragraph 9).

When you need to cite research, remember to do the following:

- Introduce the quotation (never just plop it into your text).
- Accurately report and document the source of the quotation.
- Explain how the quotation relates to your thesis.

If you have conducted research by interviewing numerous people, or if one person told you too much to quote directly, you probably need to summarize what you learned. Mohler summarizes his interview with Brad Taylor in paragraphs 11–14. Summarizing allows Mohler to give the reader a great deal of interesting information, including Taylor's football background, the writing he did in college, how that experience developed into newspaper work, and how he eventually became high school sports editor for a newspaper.

Parts of a Complete Draft

Introduction: One of the qualities of successful exploratory writing is that it grabs and holds readers' attention. There are a number of strategies for beginning your paper that will help you hook your readers:

- **Take your readers on the journey.** Let your readers know from the beginning that this is an exploration. Let them be your travel companions. The excerpt from "Why I Blog" by Andrew Sullivan begins with a description of blogging as a process of letting go, "to let others . . . pivot you toward relative truth."
- **Ask one or more questions.** By asking questions, you present options and directions. Your exploratory writing will help you and your reader find solutions.
- **Set the stage by explaining the significance of your subject,** as Owen Edwards does in the first two paragraphs of "The Tuskegee Airmen Plane's Last Flight."

Writing Activity

Constructing a Complete Draft

After selecting an organizational approach, write a complete draft of your paper that explores your topic. In exploratory writing, your thesis statement may not become apparent until after you have completed a first draft. Use as much detail as possible—the more you get down on paper initially, the easier it will be to flesh out and revise your paper later. Your first draft will likely lead to additional questions and answers you will want to include in your revision(s).

Body: The body of your paper will lead you and your readers through your exploration process. You may choose one or several different kinds of organization. You might try classification, for example, where by grouping ideas in like categories, you discover similarities. However, comparison and contrast, where you discover both similarities and differences, might be more helpful. Or you might discover that cause and effect is the most powerful kind of organization for your paper.

Conclusion: Following your exploration, your conclusion should leave your readers feeling satisfied.

- If in your exploration you discover that there will be consequences if certain events occur, you may choose to present these final consequences.

- If you discover that your exploration has led to even more questions, you may simply state the new questions that need to be researched.

- If your exploration does lead you to a reasonable conclusion, state that conclusion, explaining to readers how you reached it. Andrew Sullivan, for example, concludes that both old and new forms of media can coexist and provides examples to prove his point. He concludes by noting that "Words, of all sorts, have never seemed so now."

Title: You might think that you need to craft a title before you start writing, but often it is more useful to get a first draft down on paper or into a computer file and then consider possible titles. For an exploratory paper, your title should indicate your subject and give your reader a reason to want to explore it with you. The title "Why I Blog," for example, indicates that its author has a personal approach to his subject.

Rick Mohler's First Draft: A Sporting Career?

After doing research and deciding on an organizational approach, Rick Mohler was ready to begin his first draft. As he wrote, he did not concern himself with grammar, punctuation, or mechanics, but instead tried to get his questions and answers and ideas on paper. Note that Mohler started his paper with a series of questions—one of the organizational methods described above. Note also that Mohler incorporated some of his research information into his paper. (The numbers in circles refer to peer comments—see page 144.)

A Sporting Career?
Rick Mohler

If you ask most people about a career in sports, they'll usually say, "professional athlete," as that is the most visible (and well-paid) career option. But what about those of us who will never make a professional team? We may have enough desire, but what if we're not big enough, or fast enough, or have enough talent to "make the pros"? Are there other career options available to us and if so, what are they? How can we learn about them? What are some of the good things about those careers, and what are some of the bad things? What might their work entail? What are the opportunities for promotion? ❶

Those are just a few of the questions that I will explore in this paper, as I'm one of the people described above—I'll never be big enough or fast enough to "make the pros," but I also want to pursue a career in sports. ❷

My favorite sport is football—and it's also America's choice, especially NFL football. In addition to the players, what other careers might be associated with the

VISUAL *Thinking* | Going Beyond Words to Achieve Your Goals

FIGURE 6.1   A Photo of a High School Team Making a Play

For his assignment, student writer Rick Mohler decided to explore his interests in sports and how he might find a career in that area. Sports, of course, is a topic that lends itself to illustration, particularly with vivid, dramatic photographs. Because he loves football, "especially NFL football," Mohler decided to add a photo of some action on the field to his project to show readers the excitement that he experiences at a game (Figure 6.1).

In the final draft of his project (pages 147–50), Mohler notes that sportswriter Grantland Rice wrote a particularly inspiring description of the Notre Dame football team—a description that mentions the famous Four Horsemen and the historic Polo Grounds. To illustrate this stirring quotation, Mohler decided to include a photo of the four well-known Notre Dame players. This black-and-white photo would enhance the sense of history that seems to drive his interest in sports writing and bring that history to life for readers.

FIGURE 6.2   Four Horsemen of Notre Dame

Of course, Mohler would need to document the sources for any photos he uses, and if he intends to make his project available online, he would need to determine if the photos are protected by copyright and, if so, seek permission to publish them from the copyright holders.

• What other visuals might Mohler have considered?

NFL? A few come to mind, including coach, weight-trainer/conditioning coach, publicity folks, and others. I want to explore two that interest me:

- Sportswriter
- Sports photographer ❸

One important part of either of these careers is that they are everywhere. Local newspapers as well as national television companies need them, so there are plenty of employment opportunities.

Since I've always been a pretty good writer, the idea of becoming a sports-writer strikes me as an interesting career. Last week's *College Press,* for example, carried seven sports-related articles, all written by student writers. Two touched on football, and perhaps the most interesting article was about spring workouts for our football players.

John Wilson, the spring workouts *College Press* writer, was kind enough to give me an interview. I asked him what kind of background you needed. "It's not as easy as it sounds," Wilson told me. "I'm an English major, which really helps, and while that combined with my interest and knowledge of sports is good, what's hard for me is the process of writing."

I asked John what he meant, and he said "it's just a lot of work. You have to go to the game and take notes. Then you interview some of the people involved—the coaches, the players, etc. Then you figure out some angle or slant that you want to focus on—one big play, or how a coach made a great call, or whatever. Then, finally, you have to write it all into a coherent form." I told John that the process he described was just what I was learning in my college writing class. He also told me that much of the writing has hard deadlines. You have to write fast as well as accurately. John said that he likes the challenge. I can see that appealing to my competitive nature.

Since I wanted to find out what a professional sportswriter might do John also suggested I email Brad Taylor, the high school sports editor of a large local newspaper.

My email correspondence and subsequent phone conversation with Brad Taylor proved even more interesting. Taylor explained to me the path he took to become a sportswriter. Like me, he had played football in high school but wasn't big enough or good enough to play in college. He was a history major in college but also wrote for the *College Press,* being sports editor his senior year. As much as he enjoyed working on the newspaper, he didn't think it was a real career. He expected to either go to law school or graduate school in history and become a history professor.

I was amazed to hear that he had been accepted by some really good law schools and grad schools but chose to start work on a masters degree instead. For a number of reasons, school wasn't as exciting as he thought it would be. On a whim, he went to the sports department of the large local paper. They asked if he had clippings. He brought them some of his college articles. They offered him a job as a stringer covering high school football.

Taylor told me that something clicked when he started covering high schools. He got a real thrill talking to the coaches and the players. Eventually, he dropped out of grad school when offered a full-time reporting job. Over time he became editor for all of high school sports. I could hear the excitement in his voice. It reminded me of the times in my old high school locker room. ④

Student Comments on Rick Mohler's First Draft

1. "The above are really useful questions, but maybe you should kind of build up to the most important ones and leave the rest for the body of the paper. Another question I thought of is about how many possible careers in sports are there?"

2. "That's a really interesting point. Most sports fans think it's either the pros or nothing, so I like the way you're trying to be realistic and still come up with a career that lets you do what you like most."

3. "Why are you interested in these two careers? What about them attracts you? I really do not know what a person in either position does all day long. Maybe to focus the paper a little more, you ought to focus on just one career?"

4. "This is a good story, but I'd like to see more in your conclusion. What's so good about your old locker room?"

Revising

Revising means re-seeing and re-thinking your exploratory text. The most effective way to revise your work is to read it as if you are reading it for the first time. Reading your work in this way is difficult to do, of course—which is why writers often put their work aside for a time. The more you can see your writing as if for the first time, the more you will respond to it as your real readers might, questioning and exploring it. As you reread the first draft of your exploratory writing, here are some questions to ask yourself:

- What are the most important questions, the ones I would really like to have answered? How well have I answered them?

- How well have I answered the questions that will help me understand every facet of my subject?

- How well do I understand the draft? What parts are confusing or need more information? What research might I need to conduct to clarify my ideas further?

- What information, if any, might I provide as a visual?

Technology can help you revise and, later, edit your writing more easily. Use your word processor's track-changes tool to try out revisions and editing changes. After you've had time to think about the possible changes, you can "accept" or "reject" them. Also, you can use your word processor's comment tool to write reminders to yourself when you get stuck with a revision or some editing task.

Because it is so difficult even for experienced writers to see their emerging writing with a fresh eye, it is almost always useful to ask classmates, friends, or family members to read and comment on drafts.

WRITER'S *Workshop* | Responding to Full Drafts

As you read and respond to your classmates' papers (and as they comment on yours), focus on the exploratory nature of this assignment, but from a reader's perspective. Be sure to ask questions of their writing and to respond to their ideas by exploring your reactions and responses to their thoughts.

Working in pairs or groups of three, read each others' papers, and then offer your classmates comments that will help them see both their papers' strengths and places where they need to develop their ideas further. Use the following questions to guide your responses to the writer's draft:

- What is your first impression? How interested are you in reading beyond the first paragraph? Why? Do you have any suggestions for improving the title?

- What do you like about the draft? Provide positive and encouraging feedback to the writer. How interesting, educational, or useful did you find this exploration? Why?

- What is the focus of the paper? How does the focus emerge as you read? How well do you understand how the writer comes to her or his conclusion?

- How easily can you follow the writer's thought process? Comment on how the writer's exploratory writing helps you better understand the questions or problems posed in the introduction.

- How thoroughly does the writer explore the subject? How might the writer explore it more fully?

- How viable are the differing perspectives? How appropriate are the writer's sources?

- Reread the conclusion: How logically does it follow from the rest of the paper? Were you surprised by the conclusion? What are other possible conclusions based on the information the writer has presented?

- What do you see as the main weaknesses of this paper? How might the writer improve the text?

Responding to Readers' Comments

Once they have received feedback on their writing from peers, teachers, friends, and others, writers have to figure out what to do with that feedback. You may decide to reject some comments, of course. Other comments, though, deserve your attention, as they are the words of real readers speaking to you about how to improve your text. You may find that comments from more than one reader contradict each other. In that case, use your own judgment to decide which reader's comments are on the right track.

In the final version of Rick Mohler's paper, on pages 147–50, you can see how he responded to his peers' comments, as well as to his own review of his first draft.

KNOWLEDGE OF CONVENTIONS

When effective writers edit their work, they attend to the conventions that will help readers move through their writing effortlessly. By paying attention to these conventions in your writing, you make reading a more pleasant experience for readers.

■ Editing

The last task in any writing project is editing—the final polishing of your document. When you edit and polish your writing, you make changes to your sentence structure and word choice to improve your style and to make your writing clearer and more concise. You also check your work to make sure it adheres to conventions of grammar, usage, punctuation, mechanics, and spelling, as well as genre conventions. Use the spell-check function of your wordprocessing program, but be sure to double-check your spelling personally. If you have used sources in your paper, make sure you are following the documentation style your instructor requires.

See Chapter 20 for more on documenting sources using MLA or APA style.

As with overall revision of your work, this final editing and polishing is most effective if you can put your text aside for a few days and come back to it with

ROUND-ROBIN EDITING WITH A FOCUS ON

Fragments (p. 146)
Modifiers (p. 189)
Wordiness (p. 232)
Citing Sources (p. 273)
Careful Word Choice (p. 319)
Subordinate Clauses (p. 363)
Inclusive Language (p. 411)

WRITER'S *Workshop* | **Round-Robin Editing with a Focus on Fragments**

Because exploratory writing often includes incomplete thoughts, writers sometimes inadvertently use sentence fragments to express their thinking. A sentence fragment is missing one or more of the following elements: a subject, a verb, or a complete thought.

Some fragments lack a subject, a verb, or both:

FRAGMENT   College sports are popular. *Generating lots of money for schools with successful teams.*

SENTENCE   College sports are popular. They generate lots of money for schools with successful teams.

Other fragments have subjects and verbs, but they begin with a subordinating word like *because* or *although* and so are not complete thoughts:

FRAGMENT   *Although I have played football in high school and college.* I'm not good enough to play on a professional team.

SENTENCE   Although I have played foot-ball in high school and college, I'm not good enough to play on a professional team.

Work with two peers to look for sentence fragments. For each fragment, decide whether to connect it to a nearby sentence or to recast it into a complete sentence.

fresh eyes. Because checking conventions is easier said than done, though, we strongly recommend that you ask classmates, friends, and tutors to read your work to find sentence problems that you do not see.

To assist you with editing, we offer here a round-robin editing activity focused on sentence fragments, a common concern in all writing.

Genres, Documentation, and Format

If you are writing an academic paper, follow the conventions for the discipline in which you are writing and the requirements of your instructor. However, if you are exploring potential majors (Scenario 1), you might choose to write a letter or an e-mail message to family members. If you are doing a personal exploration (Scenario 2), you might want to write a journal entry. If you have chosen to do a personal exploration, you might avoid writing a blog entry, because blogs can have thousands of readers—including potential employers.

For advice on writing in different genres, see Appendix C. For guidelines for formatting and documenting papers in MLA or APA style, see Chapter 20.

If you have used material from outside sources, including visuals, give credit to those sources, using the documentation style required by the discipline you are working in and by your instructor.

 # A Writer Achieves His Goal: Rick Mohler's Final Draft

As you read the final version of Rick Mohler's exploratory paper, consider what makes it effective. Following the reading you will find some questions to help you conduct an exploration of this paper.

RICK MOHLER

A Sporting Career?

EXPLORATORY ESSAY

If you ask most people to name a career in sports, they'll usually say, "professional athlete," because that is the most visible (and well-paid) career option. But what about those of us who have the desire, but not the size, speed, or talent? Are there other career options available to us, and if so, what are they?   1

One of Mohler's classmates made this comment on his paper:

Another question I thought of is about how many possible careers in sports are there?

Notice how he provides information to answer this peer review question.

One of Mohler's classmates wrote this comment on an early draft:

Why are you interested in these two careers (sportswriter and sports photographer)? What about them attracts you? I really do not know what a person in either position does all day long. Maybe to focus the paper a little more, you ought to focus on just one career.

Notice how Mohler does what his classmate suggested, focusing on one specific career path.

Mohler uses direct quotations from his interviews to bring other people's perspectives into his work.

I'm one of those people. I doubt that I have the size or speed to make the pros, but I want a career in sports, as do many others. Perhaps my "wonderings" here can help others as they try to decide what career path they may want to follow. 2

My favorite sport is football—and it's also America's choice. While the players have the faces and names that fans recognize, they are only one part of the big picture that is NFL football. Many other people make the games happen, keep the players in good condition, and tell the rest of America all about the sport. Coaches, weight trainers and conditioning coaches, publicists, writers, and photographers all have a part to play in the game of football. (see Fig. 1). 3

The career path that excites me most is being a sportswriter. The job has an artistic element that appeals to me. As a sportswriter, I wouldn't just describe what took place at a game or event—I would really try to paint a picture. Maybe someday I'll even be able to write something as famous as Grantland Rice's description of the 1924 Notre Dame football team: 4

> Outlined against a blue-gray October sky, the Four Horsemen rode again. In dramatic lore they are known as Famine, Pestilence, Destruction and Death. These are only aliases. Their real names are Stuhldreher, Miller, Crowley and Layden. They formed the crest of the South Bend cyclone before which another fighting Army football team was swept over the precipice at the Polo Grounds yesterday afternoon as 55,000 spectators peered down on the bewildering panorama spread on the green plain below.

Though not all sportswriters become as famous as Rice (see Fig. 2), they are everywhere. Local newspapers as well as national television networks need them, so there are plenty of employment opportunities. Just as most sports have both amateur and professional athletes, a sportswriter can start as an amateur and advance to the pros. It seems to make sense to begin working for a student newspaper, especially since I've always been a fairly good writer. 5

Last week's *College Press,* for example, included seven sports-related articles, all written by student writers. Two touched on football, and perhaps the most interesting article was about spring workouts for our football players. 6

John Wilson, the spring workouts *College Press* writer, was kind enough to give me an interview. I asked him what kind of background an aspiring sportswriter needs. "It's not as easy as it sounds," Wilson told me. "I'm an English major, which really helps, and while that combined with my interest in and knowledge of sports is good, what's hard for me is the process of writing." 7

I asked Wilson what he meant about writing and effort, and he gave me a description of how he typically covers a game: 8

Fig. 1   A high school football team, caught in action by a **sports** photographer.

Source: The Plain Dealer/Landov

Fig. 2   The famous "Four Horsemen" of the 1924 Notre Dame football team: Jim Crowley, Elmer Layden, Don Miller, and Harry Stuhldreyer.

Source: Hulton Archive/Stringer/Getty Images

It's just a lot of work. You have to go to the game and take notes. Then you interview some of the people involved—the coaches, the players, etc. Then you figure out some angle or slant that you want to focus on—one big play, or how a coach made a great call, or whatever. Then, finally, you have to write it all into a coherent form.

I told Wilson that the process he described was just what I was learning in my college writing class. "You have to write fast as well as accurately," Wilson said. He also told me that he likes the challenge. I can see that appealing to my competitive nature.

Because I wanted to find out what a professional sportswriter might do,   9
Wilson also suggested I contact Brad Taylor, the high school sports editor of a large newspaper in my hometown.

My communications with Brad Taylor proved even more interesting. Tay-   10
lor explained the path he took to become a sportswriter. Like me, he had played football in high school but wasn't good enough to play in college. He was a history major in college but also wrote for the *College Press,* becoming sports editor his senior year. As much as he enjoyed sportswriting, he didn't think it was

Mohler ended his first version with the words "locker room," and a peer reviewer asked about his ending:

This is a good story, but I'd like to see more in your conclusion. What's so good about your old locker room?

Notice how Mohler has now added some information to answer his classmate's question.

a real career. He expected to go either to law school or graduate school in history and become a history professor.

Despite being accepted by some really good law schools and graduate   11
schools, he chose to start work on a master's degree at a local college. For a number of reasons, school wasn't as exciting as he thought it would be. On a whim, he went to the sports department of the large local paper. They asked if he had clippings, and he brought some of his college articles. They offered him a job as a stringer covering high school football.

Taylor told me that something clicked when he started covering high   12
schools. He got a real thrill talking to the coaches and the players.

Eventually, he dropped out of graduate school when offered a full-time   13
reporting job. Over time he became editor for all of high school sports. I could hear the excitement in his voice. It reminded me of the times in my old high school locker room—the joy after winning and the disappointment after losing, the camaraderie among teammates, the team meetings to discuss strategy. I wouldn't mind reliving that again—even if it's a vicarious experience.

Work Cited

Rice, Grantland. "The Four Horsemen." *University of Notre Dame Archives.* Web. 5 May 2012. <http://lamb.archives.nd.edu/rockne/rice.html>.

Taylor, Brad. Personal E-mail. 7 May 2012.

———. Personal Interview. 9 May 2012.

Wilson, John. Personal Interview. 30 Apr. 2012.

This paper follows MLA guidelines for in-text citations and works cited. Note that URLs are optional.

UNDERSTANDING A WRITER'S GOALS: QUESTIONS TO CONSIDER AND DISCUSS

Rhetorical Knowledge: The Writer's Situation and Rhetoric

1. **Audience:** Who is the intended audience for Mohler's essay? What in the essay makes you think so?

2. **Purpose:** What does Mohler hope will happen when people read his essay?

3. **Voice and tone:** How would you describe Mohler's tone in his essay?

4. **Responsibility:** How responsibly has Mohler reported information about being a sportswriter to you? To himself? Why do you think so?

5. **Context, format, and genre:** Mohler wrote this paper for a college course. If you were an editor for your local newspaper, would you consider hiring Mohler as a sportswriter? Why or why not? In an exploratory essay, the writer starts with a premise and then follows one or more lines of inquiry to discover something new. Do you think Mohler has adequately explored the possibility of a career in sportswriting? Why or why not?

Critical Thinking: The Writer's Ideas and Your Personal Response

6. What is the main point of Mohler's essay? How well does he focus the essay? How does he support his main idea? What questions do you still have about his subject?

7. How easily can you relate to what Mohler writes about? Why?

Composing Processes and Knowledge of Conventions: The Writer's Strategies

8. In what ways does Mohler establish his *ethos*, or his credibility, in this exploratory essay?

9. How effective are Mohler's introduction and conclusion? Why?

10. What do the two photographs add to Mohler's essay? What other visuals might he have used?

Inquiry and Research: Ideas for Further Exploration

11. In what other ways might Mohler have researched his choice? What sources might he have investigated?

Self-Assessment: Reflecting on Your Goals

Now that you have constructed a piece of exploratory writing, go back and consider the goals at the beginning of this chapter (see pages 112–13). Reflecting on your writing process and the exploratory text you have constructed—and putting such reflections *in writing*—is another kind of exploration: You are exploring, thinking about, and commenting on your own work as a writer. Answering the following questions will help you reflect on what you have learned from this assignment:

Rhetorical Knowledge

- *Audience:* What have you learned about addressing an audience in exploratory writing?
- *Purpose:* What have you learned about the purposes of exploratory writing?
- *Rhetorical situation:* How did the writing context affect your exploratory text?
- *Voice and tone:* How would you describe your voice in this project? Your tone? How do they contribute to the effectiveness of your exploratory essay?
- *Context, medium, and genre:* How did your context determine the medium and genre you chose, and how did those decisions affect your writing?

Critical Thinking, Reading, and Writing

- *Learning/inquiry:* How did you decide what to focus on in your exploratory writing? How did you judge what was most and least important?
- *Responsibility:* How did you fulfill your responsibility to your readers?
- *Reading and research:* What did you learn about exploratory writing from the reading selections you read for this chapter? What research did you conduct? How sufficient was the research you did?
- *Skills:* As a result of writing this exploration, how have you become a more critical thinker, reader, and writer? What critical thinking, reading, and writing skills do you hope to develop further in your next writing project? How will you work on them?

Writing Processes for Exploration

- *Invention:* What invention strategies were most useful to you? Why?
- *Organizing your ideas and details:* What organization did you use? How successful was it?
- *Revising:* What one revision did you make that you are most satisfied with? What are the strongest and the weakest parts of the paper or other piece of writing you wrote for this chapter? Why?
- *Working with peers:* How did your instructor or peer readers help you by making comments and suggestions about your writing? How could you have made better use of the comments and suggestions you received? How could your peer readers help you more on your next assignment? How might you help them more, in the future, with the comments and suggestions you make on their texts?
- *Visuals:* If you used photographs or other visuals to help present your exploration to readers, what did you learn about incorporating these elements?
- *Writing habits:* What "writerly habits" have you developed, modified, or improved on as you completed the writing assignment for this chapter?

For help with freewriting and clustering, as well as other strategies for discovery and learning, see Chapter 4.

Knowledge of Conventions

- *Editing:* What sentence problem did you find most frequently in your writing? How will you avoid that problem in future assignments?
- *Genre:* What conventions of the genre you were using, if any, gave you problems?
- *Documentation:* If you used sources for your paper, what documentation style did you use? What problems, if any, did you have with it?

Refer to Chapter 1 (pages 12–13) for a sample reflection by a student.

CHAPTER 7

Writing to Inform

We all deal with *information* every day of our lives. We learn about facts, ideas, and ways of doing things, and then communicate that information to others through spoken or written words and, at times, graphic or other visual means.

Many newspaper articles are examples of informative writing. The headlines from the *New York Times* Online demonstrate that the primary goal of headline writers is simply to provide information. Readers don't expect headlines to contain elements of persuasion, argumentation, or evaluation. We could argue, of course, that any type of writing has elements of persuasion, and by selecting certain words and emphasizing particular facts, a writer will influence a reader's response. However, the goal of most informative writing, especially the informative writing you will do in college, *is* to be as neutral as possible, so it is the writer's responsibility to present information impartially.

As a college student, you read informative writing in your textbooks and other assigned reading and are expected to write informative responses on tests and to provide information in the papers your instructors assign. While you may think that you encounter informative writing only in your textbooks and in newspapers or magazines, you can easily find examples of such reading and writing in each area of your life. In your professional life, for example, you may need to read (or construct) a training manual, while in your civic life, you may be called on to write a voter guide about two candidates, presenting their positions without revealing your personal views.

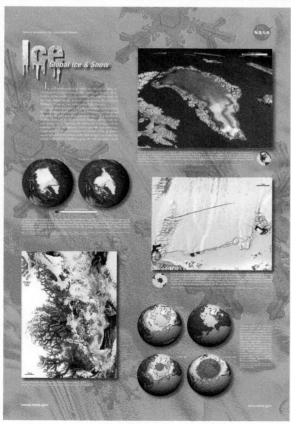

Setting Your Goals for *Informative Writing*

Rhetorical Knowledge (pp. 158–62)

- **Audience:** Consider what your readers need to know—and how you can interest them in that information. What about your subject might your audience be *most* interested in? What information might readers consider unusual?
- **Purpose:** You want readers to understand the information you are sharing, so your writing must be clear. Considering what your audience might *do* with the information that you provide will help you decide how best to share it with them.
- **Rhetorical situation:** In an informational essay, you are writing to share information; your readers are reading your text to learn about (and—you hope—to understand) that information.
- **Voice and tone:** Generally, informational writing has a neutral tone. Sometimes, depending on the situation, an informational essay can have a humorous tone.
- **Context, medium, and genre:** The genre you use to present your information is determined by your purpose: to inform. Decide on the best medium and genre to use to present your information to the audience you want to reach.

Critical Thinking, Reading, and Writing (pp. 162–74)

- **Learning/inquiry:** Because you are helping your readers learn about the subject of your text, decide on the most important aspects of your topic and explain them in a clear, focused way.
- **Responsibility:** You have a responsibility to represent your information honestly and accurately.
- **Reading and research:** Your research must be accurate and as complete as possible, to allow you to present thoughtful, reliable information about your subject.

Writing Processes (pp. 175–88)

- **Invention:** Choose invention strategies that will help you generate and locate information about your topic.
- **Organizing your ideas and details:** Find the most effective way to present your information to your readers so they can easily understand it.
- **Revising:** Read your work with a critical eye, to make certain that it fulfills the assignment and displays the qualities of good informative writing.
- **Working with peers:** Your classmates will make suggestions that indicate the parts of your text they found difficult to understand so you can work to clarify.

Knowledge of Conventions (pp. 188–89)

- **Editing:** Informative writing benefits from the correct use of modifiers, so the round-robin activity on page 189 focuses on avoiding misplaced or dangling modifiers.
- **Genres for informative writing:** Possible genres include newspaper or magazine articles, informative letters, informative essays, and Web documents.
- **Documentation:** If you have relied on sources outside of your experience, cite them using the appropriate documentation style.

RHETORICAL KNOWLEDGE

When you provide information to readers, you need to consider what your readers might already know about your topic. You should also ask yourself, "What other information have I learned about through my research that would interest them and be helpful for them to know." You will also need to decide what medium and genre will help you communicate that information to your audience most effectively.

Writing to Inform in Your College Classes

Much of the writing you will do for your college classes will be informative, as will much of the reading you will do. College textbooks are, almost by definition, informative. You would expect your American history textbook to provide accurate information about the Civil War, for example. The purpose of most of the reading you will do in college is to learn new information—and many writing assignments will require you to relate new facts and concepts to other facts and concepts you have already read and learned about, as in the following examples:

- Your psychology instructor may ask you to read several essays or books about recovered memory and to *synthesize* the information they contain— to explain to a reader the most important points made in each text and how the information in one text agrees or disagrees with the information in the others.

- Your art instructor may ask that you trace the development of a specific approach to art, providing examples and details that show its evolution over time.

- Your political science instructor may ask you to examine "presidential bloopers"—where presidential candidates did or said something awkward—and explain in writing how those instances affected the outcome of the election.

The "Ways of Writing" feature presents different genres that can be used when writing to inform in your college classes.

Writing to Inform for Life

In addition to your academic work, you will also construct informative texts for the other areas of your life, including your professional career, your civic life, and your personal life.

Much of the writing done in professional settings is designed to inform and often to teach. If you have or have had a job, for example, consider how you would explain the details of your job to someone who is going to take it over: What information would that person need to know to do your job effectively? How could you best relay that information to your replacement? What you have just considered are the details that make up a training manual, a type of informative writing that most businesses have in one form or another.

Likewise, much civic writing is designed to provide information to the residents of a certain area to help them decide issues or take advantage of community resources and programs. Perhaps people who live in a neighborhood are being encouraged to participate in a community program such as a citizen's watch campaign, a civic event that would almost certainly require informative writing.

You will also do a great deal of informative writing in your personal life, ranging from notes to family members to Facebook conversations with relatives and friends. While you may feel more comfortable jotting down information for your friends and family than you do for other audiences, you probably feel especially obligated to provide accurate and useful information because you care about your personal relationships.

The "Ways of Writing" feature presents different genres that can be used when writing to inform for life.

Scenarios for Writing | Assignment Options

The following writing assignments call for you to construct informative texts. Each is in the form of a *scenario,* a brief story that provides some context for your writing. The scenario gives you a sense of who your audience is and what you need to accomplish. Starting on page 175, you will find guidelines for completing whatever assignment option you choose or that is assigned to you.

Writing for College

SCENARIO 1 Informative Essay on Littering

Your sociology class has been focusing on student behavior. Just last week a classmate mentioned the problem of trash on campus: "Our campus is a big mess because students just don't care," she said. "They ignore the trash cans and recycling boxes and just toss their garbage everywhere!"

Although this scenario focuses on littering, if you prefer you may write about some other issue on your campus. Your task is not to propose a solution for the issue; rather, your task is to inform other members of the campus community that a problem exists.

(**ELECTRONIC ENVIRONMENTS**) **Using a Camera When Making Observations**

A digital camera or your cell phone camera can be an ideal tool for any assignment that asks you to make observations. Once you have transferred the photographs of your subject to your computer, it is easy to add them to your text. Be sure, though, to get written permission from anyone you photograph before using images of that person in your work. If your instructor allows you to submit your work electronically, you may wish to incorporate video and sound as well into your final project. You can do so by using a screen capture program such as Snagit, Jing, or QuickTime Player.

Ways of Writing to Inform

Genres for Your College Classes	Sample Situation	Advantages of the Genre	Limitations of the Genre
Academic essay	Your sociology professor asks you to make observations about the group behavior of a campus organization (the volleyball team, the debating club, and so on).	This project enables you to engage in primary research that you design; your readers can learn from your research findings.	It is difficult to be objective and present information in a neutral tone; you need to take lots of detailed notes to have sufficient research information.
Review of literature	Your economics teacher asks you to review the current literature on the causes of the Great Depression.	This project gives your reader a better understanding of the economic issues of the time period.	A limited number of texts can be examined, so your focus will be narrow. In many fields, the most current literature is seen as the most important.
Letter to your college newspaper	You want to write a letter to your school newspaper that informs students about an upcoming campus event sponsored by several student organizations.	Your letter will allow you to reach your intended audience and encourage them to attend.	In only a limited amount of space, you must provide all of the details so others will know what the event is, where it will be held, and when. It might not be published.
Profile	Your English professor asks you to make observations and construct a profile—a neutral description—about a place on your campus (the campus recreation center, for example).	You observe and take notes with lots of description, so your readers can "see" what the place looks like, who inhabits this place, what happens there, what the location is like, and so on.	The writer generally does not analyze why things happen in this place, so there is a limited understanding of why the place is as it is.
Narrated timeline	Your philosophy professor asks you to create a timeline of influential philosophers, showing when they lived and outlining their main ideas.	A timeline is a useful way to provide information, and is supplemented with text about the philosophers and their major ideas.	There is lots of ground to cover; it shouldn't be just a timeline showing when the philosophers lived. It will be difficult to describe complex thoughts and ideas and show relationships in limited space.
Genres for Life	**Sample Situation**	**Advantages of the Genre**	**Limitations of the Genre**
Brochure	You need to explain what a nonprofit organization does, what services it provides, and so on.	A brochure can provide readers with a brief overview of the agency's mission and services.	There is limited space for presenting information about the agency's specific services.
Information-sharing blog	You would like to share information about candidates in a local election.	A blog can be an easy way to update and share information with a wide audience.	Someone will need to monitor the comments for inappropriate posts. It should be updated often.
Fact sheet	You want to provide facts about a proposed tax increase for your neighbors, most of whom have children in the same school district as you.	A fact sheet allows you to present the details objectively so that your neighbors can make up their own minds.	It may be hard to remain neutral if you feel strongly one way or the other about the tax proposal.
Business comparison	The company you work for asks you to compare several locations for a possible expansion of the business.	By comparing and contrasting the details about each location, not advocating for one or the other, you let your readers make up their own minds.	With a vested interest in the decision, it is difficult to present information without making a recommendation.
Instructions	To help train new employees, you are asked to prepare a set of instructions for a specific task you do at work.	Step-by-step instructions will give enough detail for someone to understand and to complete the task.	It may be difficult to provide the right kind of detail—not too much and not too little.

Writing Assignment: Construct an informative paper, based on two sets of information: (1) your observations of the problem on campus, and (2) interviews you conduct with at least two of your classmates, asking them what their thoughts are on why some students don't use trash cans as they should, or on the alternate problem you have chosen to write about.

SCENARIO 2   **A Review of Literature**

This scenario asks you to examine and then construct a "review of literature"—basically, what others have said and written about a particular topic. In most of your college classes, it is critical to know what others have said about any topic you might want to write on so that you will not have to "reinvent the wheel," so to speak. The only way to know what others have said is to read their work and see how it relates to other ideas on the same subject. Of course, once you know what others have written about a topic, you can then add your own ideas and thoughts to the continuing discussion.

Writing Assignment: Select a topic that you would like to gather more information about, and construct an informative text that outlines what others have written about it. You will not be able to read everything, of course, so your instructor may outline how many items to read, what kind (such as essays, books, e-mail lists, and blogs), and so on. Your text should outline the most important aspects of each item you are asked to read—essentially reviewing the literature for your readers, in a clear and accurate manner.

Writing for Life

SCENARIO 3   **Civic Writing: Brochure for a Local Service Organization**

Many colleges and universities have a service-learning class or classes that incorporate service-learning activities, such as volunteer work, into a class project. "Service-learning" opportunities include tutoring young children, helping with food banks, volunteering at rest homes, and other ways of serving the community in some manner. As the National Youth Leadership Council notes, service-learning can be conceptualized in this way:

> Picking up trash on a riverbank is _service_.
>
> Studying water samples under a microscope is _learning_.
>
> When science students collect and analyze water samples, document their results, and present findings to a local pollution control agency . . . that is _service-learning._ (www.nlc.org)

Writing Assignment: Select a local nonprofit service agency, and learn about services they provide to your community. Your research might include looking at the Web page for the agency, interviewing people who work there, examining any literature they provide, and volunteering with the agency (probably the best way to learn about it). Then construct a brochure for the agency

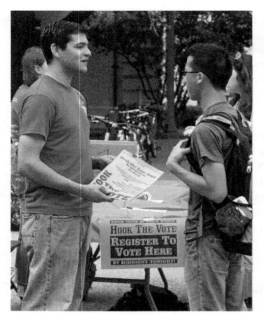

that outlines the work it performs for the community. Think of this brochure as one the agency would actually provide and use. In other words, construct a brochure as if you actually worked for the agency and were asked to develop such a handout.

As with any writing assignment, consider who your audience might be and what they might already know about the agency. What else would you like them to know? What kind(s) of information would be useful to your audience? Are there photos or tables that might show what the agency does, how it spends any donations it receives, or something about the people who work there and the people the agency serves?

Rhetorical Considerations in Informative Writing

Audience: Who is your primary audience? Who else might be interested in your subject? Why?

Purpose: As noted in Chapter 3, writing can be a powerful tool for learning, so use the information you collect and write about as a way to increase your knowledge of your subject, as well as the knowledge of your readers. Bear in mind as you write that your purpose is not to convince readers to agree with an opinion you hold about your subject, but rather to inform them about it in neutral terms.

Voice, tone, and point of view: If you have a limited knowledge of your topic, your stance, or attitude, will be that of an interested investigator, and your tone will usually be neutral. If you are writing about a topic that you know well, take care to keep any biases out of your writing. If you are writing about a problem, present all opinions about the problem fairly, including those you disagree with. Your point of view will usually be third person.

For more on choosing a medium and genre, see Chapter 17 and Appendix C.

Context, medium, and genre: Keeping the context of the assignment in mind, decide on a medium and genre for your writing. How will your writing be used? If you are writing for an audience beyond the classroom, consider what will be the most effective way to present your information to this audience.

 # CRITICAL THINKING, READING, AND WRITING

Before you begin to write your informative paper, read examples of informative writing. You might also consider how visuals can inform readers, as well as the kinds of sources you will need to consult.

Writing to provide information has several qualities—a strong focus; relevant, useful information that is provided in an efficient manner; and clear, accurate explanations that enable readers to understand the information easily. The reading selections and the visual text that appear in the next sections will stimulate your inquiry and writing. Finally, informative writing almost always requires that you go beyond your current knowledge of a topic and conduct careful research.

Learning the Qualities of Effective Informative Writing

As you think about how you might compose an informative paper, consider what readers expect and need from an informative text. As a reader, you probably look for the following qualities in informative writing:

- **A focused subject.** In *The Elements of Style,* his classic book of advice to writers, author and humorist E. B. White suggests, "When you say something, make sure you have said it. The chances of your having said it are only fair." White's comment is especially applicable to informative writing. The best way to "make sure you have said" what you want to say is to have a clear focus. What information about your subject is the most important? If you could boil down your information into one sentence, what would it be? Condensing the important aspects of your information into a single sentence forces you to craft a thesis statement, which in turn helps you connect all your details and examples back to that main point.

  For more on thesis statements, see Chapter 13.

- **Useful and relevant information.** People often read to gain information: They want to check on how their favorite sports team is doing, to find the best way to travel from one place to another, or to learn why high blood pressure is a health concern. How can you present your information so that readers understand what they might *do* with it and how it relates to their lives? Perhaps there is an unusual or a humorous angle on your subject that you can write about. And if you *synthesize* the information you have—explain the most important points made in each source you have consulted and how the information in one source agrees or disagrees with that in the other sources you have read—you will provide readers with a more thorough understanding of your subject.

  For more on synthesis, see Chapter 3.

- **Clear explanations and accurate information.** Information needs to be presented clearly and accurately so it is understandable to readers who do not have background knowledge about your subject. Consider your information as if you knew nothing about the subject. Examples are almost always a useful way to help explain ideas and define terms. Comparison and contrast can be useful when you need to explain an unfamiliar subject—tell the reader what a subject is like and what it is not like. One strategy that will help you write clear, accurate papers is to take careful notes when you conduct research.

  For more on using examples and comparison and contrast, see Chapter 13. For more on conducting research and taking notes, see Chapters 19 and 20.

For more on the use of visuals to enhance your explanations, see Chapter 18.

- **Efficiency.** Information should usually be presented concisely. To help readers grasp the information, you might want to provide them with a "road map," an outline of what you have in mind, at the beginning of the paper so they will know what to expect. Another way to present data efficiently is to "chunk" your writing—put it into sections, each dealing with a different aspect of the subject, making it easier for readers to understand. As you plan your paper, you should also consider whether it would be helpful to present your information in a table, graph, chart, or map. Consider how the title of your informative text not only will help readers understand your focus but also will help to draw them in, motivating them to read your paper.

Reading, Inquiry, and Research: Learning from Texts That Inform

The following reading selections are examples of informative writing. As you read, consider these questions:

- What makes this reading selection useful and interesting? What strategies does its author use to make the information understandable for readers?
- What parts of the reading could be improved by the use of charts, photographs, or tables? Why? How?
- How can you use the techniques of informative writing exemplified here in your writing?

CAROL EZZELL

Clocking Cultures

Show up an hour late in Brazil, and no one bats an eyelash. But keep someone in New York City waiting for five or 10 minutes, and you have some explaining to do. Time is elastic in many cultures but snaps taut in others. Indeed, the way members of a culture perceive and use time reflects their society's priorities and even their own worldview.

Social scientists have recorded wide differences in the pace of life in various countries and in how societies view time—whether as an arrow piercing the future or as a revolving wheel in which past, present and future cycle endlessly. Some cultures conflate time and space: the Australian Aborigines' concept of the "Dreamtime" encompasses not only a creation myth but a method of finding their way around the countryside. Interestingly, however, some views of time—such as the idea that it is acceptable for a more powerful person to keep someone of lower status waiting—cut across cultural differences and seem to be found universally.

The study of time and society can be divided into the pragmatic and the cosmological. On the practical side, in the 1950s anthropologist Edward T. Hall, Jr., wrote that the rules of social time constitute a "silent language" for a given culture. The rules might not always be made explicit, he stated, but they "exist in the air. . . . They are either familiar and comfortable or unfamiliar and wrong."

Carol Ezzell has been a science writer since the early 1990s and currently works as a writer and an editor at *Scientific American,* specializing in biology and biomedicine. She has also worked for *Nature, Science News, Bio/World,* and the *Journal of NIH Research.* An award-winning writer, Ezzell has been recognized for her science journalism by the National Association of Science Writers and the Pan American Health Organization. In 2000, she won a Science in Society Journalism award for her article "Care for a Dying Continent," about how AIDS has affected women and girls in Zimbabwe. This article was originally published in the September 2002 issue of *Scientific American.* We find that our students enjoy and learn from Ezzell's essay, and are sometimes surprised by the information it contains.

In 1955 he described in *Scientific American* how differing perceptions of time can lead to misunderstandings between people from separate cultures. "An ambassador who has been kept waiting for more than half an hour by a foreign visitor needs to understand that if his visitor 'just mutters an apology' this is not necessarily an insult," Hall wrote. The time system in the foreign country may be composed of different basic units, so that the visitor is not as late as he may appear to us. You must know the time system of the country to know at what point apologies are really due. . . . Different cultures simply place different values on the time units.

Most cultures around the world now have watches and calendars, uniting the majority of the globe in the same general rhythm of time. But that doesn't mean we all march to the same beat. "One of the beauties of studying time is that it's a wonderful window on culture," says Robert V. Levine, a social psychologist at California State University at Fresno. "You get answers on what cultures value and believe in. You get a really good idea of what's important to people." Levine and his colleagues have conducted so-called pace-of-life studies in 31 countries. In *A Geography of Time*, published in 1997, Levine describes how he ranked the countries by using three measures: walking speed on urban sidewalks, how quickly postal clerks could fulfill a request for a common stamp, and the accuracy of public clocks. Based on these variables, he concluded that the five fastest paced countries are Switzerland, Ireland, Germany, Japan and Italy; the five slowest are Syria, El Salvador, Brazil, Indonesia and Mexico. The U.S., at 16th, ranks near the middle. Kevin K. Birth, an anthropologist at Queens College, has examined time perceptions in Trinidad. Birth's 1999 book, *Any Time Is Trinidad Time: Social Meanings and Temporal Consciousness*, refers to a commonly used phrase to excuse lateness. In that country, Birth observes, "if you have a meeting at 6:00 at night, people show up at 6:45 or 7:00 and say, 'Any time is Trinidad time.'" When it comes to business, however, that loose approach to timeliness works only for the people with power. A boss can show up late and toss off "any time is Trinidad time," but underlings are expected to be more punctual. For them, the saying goes, "time is time." Birth adds that the tie between power and waiting time is true for many other cultures as well.

The nebulous nature of time makes it hard for anthropologists and social   6
psychologists to study. "You can't simply go into a society, walk up to some poor soul and say, 'Tell me about your notions of time,'" Birth says. "People don't really have an answer to that. You have to come up with other ways to find out."

Birth attempted to get at how Trinidadians value time by exploring how   7
closely their society links time and money. He surveyed rural residents and found that farmers—whose days are dictated by natural events, such as sunrise—did not recognize the phrases "time is money," "budget your time" or "time management," even though they had satellite TV and were familiar with Western popular culture. But tailors in the same areas were aware of such notions. Birth concluded that wage work altered the tailors' views of time. "The ideas of associating time with money are not found globally," he says, "but are attached to your job and the people you work with."

How people deal with time on a day-to-day basis often has nothing to do   8
with how they conceive of time as an abstract entity. "There's often a disjunction between how a culture views the mythology of time and how they think about time in their daily lives," Birth asserts. "We don't think of Stephen Hawking's theories as we go about our daily lives."

Some cultures do not draw neat distinctions between the past, present and   9
future. Australian Aborigines, for instance, believe that their ancestors crawled out of the earth during the Dreamtime. The ancestors "sang" the world into

existence as they moved about naming each feature and living thing, which brought them into being. Even today, an entity does not exist unless an Aborigine "sings" it.

Ziauddin Sardar, a British Muslim author and critic, has written about time 10 and Islamic cultures, particularly the fundamentalist sect Wahhabism. Muslims "always carry the past with them," claims Sardar, who is editor of the journal *Futures* and visiting professor of postcolonial studies at City University, London. "In Islam, time is a tapestry incorporating the past, present and future. The past is ever present." The followers of Wahhabism, which is practiced in Saudi Arabia and by Osama bin Laden, seek to re-create the idyllic days of the prophet Muhammad's life. "The worldly future dimension has been suppressed" by them, Sardar says. "They have romanticized a particular vision of the past. All they are doing is trying to replicate that past."

Sardar asserts that the West has "colonized" time by spreading the expec- 11 tation that life should become better as time passes: "If you colonize time, you also colonize the future. If you think of time as an arrow, of course you think of the future as progress, going in one direction. But different people may desire different futures."

UNDERSTANDING A WRITER'S GOALS: QUESTIONS TO CONSIDER AND DISCUSS

Rhetorical Knowledge: The Writer's Situation and Rhetoric

1. **Audience:** Who is the audience for Ezzell's essay? How can you tell?

2. **Purpose:** What realm (academic, professional, civic, or personal) does Ezzell's essay best fit into? Why?

3. **Voice and tone:** How would you describe Ezzell's tone in this essay? How does her tone contribute to her believability?

4. **Responsibility:** Ezzell discusses the notions of time across different cultures in her essay. How respectful of those cultures is she? Why do you think that?

5. **Context, format, and genre:** This essay was published during a time of worldwide fear of terrorism. How does that context affect your reading of this essay? The essay genre was developed to allow writers to discover other ways of seeing the world. How does Ezzell's essay display this feature of the genre?

Critical Thinking: The Writer's Ideas and Your Personal Response

6. What is the most interesting piece of information in Ezzell's article? Why? The least interesting? Why?

7. What is the main idea—or thesis—in Ezzell's essay? How well does Ezzell provide support for this idea? Why do you think that?

Composing Processes and Knowledge of Conventions: The Writer's Strategies

8. Ezzell uses information and quotations from experts throughout her essay. How does she present this information? What does the presence of these experts add to the essay?

9. Prepare a quick outline of this essay. What does this outline reveal about the way Ezzell has organized her information for readers?

Inquiry and Research: Ideas for Further Exploration

10. Prepare a list of questions that you still have about time and cultures. Interview several of your friends, asking them the questions that you have listed, and then explain, in no more than two pages, their answers to your questions.

DAN FLETCHER

A Brief History of Wikipedia

A R T I C L E

L ike it or loathe it, *Wikipedia* is a force. When contributors penned its new entry on Norwegian actress Beate Eriksen on Aug. 17, the English-language version of the controversial user-generated encyclopedia reached 3 million entries. More impressive still: more than 10 million users contributed to that milestone. Not bad for a service originally conceived as an afterthought to *Nupedia*, a failed first attempt by Internet entrepreneur Jimmy Wales and philosopher Lawrence Sanger at creating a free online encyclopedia.

1

Dan Fletcher studied journalism at Northwestern University and is a self-described "Web nerd." Fletcher's writing generally has focused on social media, including (of course) *Facebook*, and he was recently hired to be *Facebook*'s managing editor. This article originally appeared on *Time.com* in August 2009.

When *Nupedia* was created in 2000, the plan was for it to feature expert-written, peer-reviewed content. But it suffered from a major problem: a lack of speed. In its first six months, only two articles made it through the process. To spur better production, Sanger suggested creating a counterpart that anyone could contribute to without editorial review. *Wikipedia.com* went live on Jan. 15, 2001, and the new model quickly eclipsed its older sibling. By the end of the first year, *Wikipedia* contained more than 20,000 articles in 18 languages. Since then, the site has grown rapidly, swelling to 250,000 articles by 2004 and a million by 2006.

2

Often, we do not realize how widespread *Wikipedia* is, so the illustration at the start of Fletcher's essay is both eye-opening and instructive. In addition, the historical background in Fletcher's essay helps all of us better understand *Wikipedia*.

Even in its earliest days, *Wikipedia* had to reckon with a slew of problems. Among them were vandalism and the lack of a fixed formula for determining what should and shouldn't be included in an encyclopedia unconstrained by physical limitations. The emerging community included a

3

volunteer army of editors, who helped to keep the content aligned with *Wikipedia*'s rules, the first version of which Sanger created in 2002. As the project grew, vandalization and dilution of the encyclopedia's content became more difficult to address. The site's software keeps a log of every modification to every page, and this tracking system has been

WIKIPEDIA

English
The Free Encyclopedia
3 907 000+ articles

日本語
フリー百科事典
799 000+ 記事

Español
La enciclopedia libre
879 000+ artículos

Deutsch
Die freie Enzyklopädie
1 383 000+ Artikel

Русский
Свободная энциклопедия
838 000+ статей

Français
L'encyclopédie libre
1 230 000+ articles

Italiano
L'enciclopedia libera
905 000+ voci

Polski
Wolna encyklopedia
887 000+ hasel

Português
A enciclopédia livre
718 000+ artigos

中文
自由的百科全書
429 000+ 條目

used to bust some high-profile offenders. In May, *Wikipedia* banned IP addresses owned by the Church of Scientology on the grounds that Scientologists were making edits that didn't suggest a "neutral point of view"—the encyclopedia's golden rule.

But since its inception, the biggest issue dogging *Wikipedia* has been concerns about its accuracy. Sanger himself left *Wikipedia* in 2002 over questions about the legitimacy of the project's entries; he later established a competing encyclopedia, *Citizendium,* with more rigorous contribution criteria. While a 2005 study by *Nature* found that *Wikipedia's* science entries came close to matching the *Encyclopaedia Britannica's* in terms of accuracy—with 2.92 mistakes per article for *Britannica* and 3.86 for *Wikipedia*—no one argues that *Wikipedia's* content is flawless. Critics say the writing is clunky or prone to bias and that the authors focus on pet projects. Indeed, the site's list of *Star Wars* creatures totals more than 15,000 words, while the entire entry on World War II has just 10,000.

Running an organization as influential as *Wikipedia* isn't inexpensive. The company's costs reach nearly $6 million per year, and though it recorded more than 100 billion page views last year, the site has no advertisements. With that level of traffic, even a single text advertisement per page would net *Wikipedia* millions of dollars, but Wales is insistent that the service, which is supported by private donations, remains ad-free.

As impressive a milestone as 3 million articles is, it simply makes the English *Wikipedia* the largest component of a massive international enterprise. *Wikipedia* now contains more than 13 million articles in 271 different languages. The German-language version is the next largest, with more than 900,000 entries, but there's something for readers of every language. Even Cheyenne, which is spoken by only 1,700 Native Americans, has its own version of *Wikipedia,* although it boasts just 62 articles. Wales, who remains the "spiritual head" of the movement, says he wants *Wikipedia* to one day contain the sum of human knowledge. It has a way to go, but in just a few years the site has come closer to reaching that lofty goal than anything else.

UNDERSTANDING A WRITER'S GOALS: QUESTIONS TO CONSIDER AND DISCUSS

Rhetorical Knowledge: The Writer's Situation and Rhetoric

1. **Audience:** How would you describe the audience that Fletcher had in mind when he wrote this article? Do you think the illustration near the beginning of the article will help this particular audience? Why?

2. **Purpose:** What purpose(s) would someone have for reading Fletcher's article? In addition to its informative purpose, how is Fletcher's writing also persuasive? How might it alter readers' perceptions of *Wikipedia*?

3. **Voice and tone:** How does Fletcher establish his authority to write about *Wikipedia*? To what extent do you believe what Fletcher has to say? How does his tone contribute to his credibility? Why?

4. **Responsibility:** One important quality of any successful informative text is *clarity*, especially when the author is dealing with a complex subject. How does Fletcher meet his obligation to his readers to be clear? Where might he have been clearer?

5. **Context, format, and genre:** Given Fletcher's topic, it seems natural that his piece originally appeared in an online format (on *Time.com*), with hyperlinks. When you read such an online article, do you ever click on its hyperlinks? Why?

Critical Thinking: The Writer's Ideas and Your Personal Response

6. What in Fletcher's text do you want to learn more about? Does the information in the illustration near the beginning of the essay surprise you? What questions do you still have?

7. Fletcher notes that *Wikipedia* is funded through donations and carries no advertising. Would you ever donate to *Wikipedia*? Why?

Composing Processes and Knowledge of Conventions: The Writer's Strategies

8. Fletcher covers a good deal of ground in this reading selection, yet he has a central idea. What is his central idea, or focus? How does he maintain it?

9. Because this is an article for a magazine, Fletcher does not document the sources from which he collected information. Does this lack of documentation on where he got his information weaken his essay? Why? How could he have indicated his sources?

Inquiry and Research: Ideas for Further Exploration

10. Research a concept or issue on the Web. Make a list of the information you collect that seems contradictory (which is, as Fletcher notes, a problem with some *Wikipedia* entries). How might you reconcile those inconsistencies, to determine what *is* accurate?

11. Read Fletcher's essay at *Time.com* at http://www.time.com/time/business/article/0,8599,1917002,00.html. Click on several of the hyperlinks. How did they help you understand Fletcher's informational essay?

GENRES *Up Close*   **Writing an Annotated Bibliography**

As illustrated in "Ways of Writing to Inform" (page 160), information can be shared through many genres. Many instructors ask their students to construct annotated bibliographies as a means of helping them (1) understand what they are asked to read and (2) relate the information and ideas in an essay to information and ideas from other essays.

An **annotated bibliography** provides the citation for each work and a brief summary, or synopsis, describing what you learned from that specific text about your topic and, often, how that information relates to other information you read about. Annotated bibliographies are a research tool. You may be asked to develop an annotated bibliography as part of a research paper or even as the first step in writing a research paper.

Becoming proficient at writing annotated bibliographies will help you to use the information you learn from your college reading in your own writing.

When constructing an annotated bibliography, a writer should do the following:

- List the appropriate citation information for each work.
- Briefly summarize the cited work.

Below is a typical annotated bibliography entry, by student writer Craig Broadbent (his other invention work, draft, and final paper appear later in this chapter). Note that Broadbent also comments on how he might be able to use the information that he is annotating in his own writing.

"How Long Does Litter Last?" National Park Service. 9 Sept 2011. Web. 16 Jan 2012. <http://www.nps.gov/tuma/forkids/upload/HowLongDoesLitterLast.pdf>.

This article by the National Park Service covers two things. The first is something of a game where students are asked to click on a link that will bring up drawings of a lot of different trash items. Other students are then asked to guess at how long that item will last before it decomposes. The second part of the article lists a number of products and how long they will survive before they decompose. I think I might be able to use these data in my own paper on recycling, but I will only be able to use the more interesting items, as there is a lot of information here.

Student writer Craig Broadbent crafted an annotated bibliography for his informative paper, and it formed the basis for the research he included in his writing (for some of Broadbent's invention work and research, see pages 176–78; an early draft of his paper appears on page 185 and the final draft of his informative paper is on pages 190–93). Note how Broadbent also includes some quotations. He is thinking ahead to what he will want to include in his paper, and jotting down actual quotations now will come in handy as he drafts.

"Buy Recycled." Environmental Protection Agency. 26 July 2011. Web. 16 Jan 2012. <http://www.epa.gov/osw/conserve/rrr/buyrecycled.htm>.

Information from this government Web site includes several definitions I may be able to use in my paper. One definition is of "Recycled-content products" (products made from "materials that would otherwise have been discarded" such as aluminum cans and laser toner cartridges. Another definition is of "Postconsumer content," which is material from products that most often would be called "waste" items. The EPA also notes that things marked as "recycled content" can also refer to material that could have come "from excess or damaged items generated during normal manufacturing processes"—materials "not collected through a local recycling program." A third definition is of "Recyclable products," which are those typically that people put into recycle bins (aluminum cans, most types of plastic bottles, etc.).

> Broadbent includes appropriate citation information for each entry.
>
> Broadbent briefly summarizes the information in each source that might be useful in his paper.

Roberts, Jim. Personal Interview. 15 March 2012.

Jim Roberts is a student I know from my math class. I interviewed him and asked what he knew, if anything, about our college recycling program. "I've never heard of it," he said. "No one mentioned it during orientation. At least I don't recall anyone mentioning it." This information might be useful in my own paper, as it may indicate that the school is doing a poor job of promoting our recycling program.

"Welcome to the RecycleMania Website." Environmental Protection Agency. Web. 16 Jan 2012. <http://www.recyclemaniacs.org/Index.htm>.

This Web site outlines what could be a useful suggestion for our college, something they call "RecycleMania." They claim that it is a "friendly competition among college and university recycling programs in North America and Canada. During 8 weeks each spring, schools compete to reduce waste, increase recycling and raise awareness of conservation issues across campus." This sounds like useful and interesting information I may be able to use in my paper.

The work that Broadbent did in constructing his annotated bibliography (only three of his entries are shown above) helped him as he crafted his informative paper, which focused on recycling on his own college campus.

As an example, note how Broadbent used some of the material about "Recy-cleMania" in paragraph 11 in his own paper (see page 192):

> The EPA provides what might be a useful suggestion for our college, in that they sponsor what they call "RecycleMania." It is a "friendly competition among college and university recycling programs in North America and Canada. During 8 weeks each spring, schools compete to reduce waste, increase recycling and raise awareness of conservation issues across campus" ("Welcome"). Perhaps if we could get our own college involved we could make a huge difference in the environmental awareness of our own students.

UNDERSTANDING A WRITER'S GOALS: QUESTIONS TO CONSIDER AND DISCUSS

Rhetorical Knowledge: The Writer's Situation and Rhetoric

1. **Audience:** What might Broadbent have done to make his annotated bibliography helpful to a wider audience (for classmates, for example, who were writing on the same topic)?

2. **Purpose:** What is Broadbent trying to accomplish in this annotated bibliography?

3. **Voice and tone:** How has Broadbent established his credibility in this excerpt from his annotated bibliography?

4. **Responsibility:** What evidence do you have that Broadbent accurately reported on what he learned from his research?

5. **Context, Format, and Genre:** How does the format Broadbent uses match your understanding of the proper format for an annotated bibliography?

Critical Thinking: The Writer's Ideas and Your Personal Response

6. Broadbent quotes a classmate he interviewed, who claimed to know little or nothing about the campus recycling programs. What do you know about your own campus recycling efforts? How might you learn more?

7. In his annotation on "Buy Recycled," Broadbent writes that, "Information from this government Web site includes several definitions I may be able to use in my paper." When is it useful, do you think, to include detailed definitions in your own papers?

Composing Processes and Knowledge of Conventions: The Writer's Strategies

8. Consult Chapter 20, "Synthesizing and Documenting Sources," to determine which style guide—MLA or APA—Broadbent is using. What evidence supports your conclusion?

9. In Paragraph 9 of his final essay, Broadbent cites interviews he conducted with Jim Roberts and also Tracy Worsam, paraphrasing one and citing the other. Using the guidelines for quoting, paraphrasing, and summarizing (see pages 550–53 in Chapter 20, "Synthesizing and Documenting Sources"), explain why Broadbent may have chosen to paraphrase Roberts and quote Worsam.

Inquiry and Research: Ideas for Further Exploration

10. Do a Web search using the terms "recycling" and "EPA." In addition to what Broadbent cites in his annotated bibliography, what other government information about recycling can you find?

WRITING PROCESSES

As you work on the assignment scenario you have chosen, keep in mind the qualities of an effective informative paper (see pages 163–64). Also remember that writing is more a recursive than a linear process. You will keep coming back to your earlier work as you go through the activities listed below, adding to it and modifying the information to be more accurate as you conduct more research and become more familiar with your topic.

As you work on your project, make certain that you save your data frequently, backing up your computer files in two or more places.

Invention: Getting Started

Use invention activities to explore the information that you want to include in your first draft. It is useful to keep a journal as you work on any writing project, for your journal is a place where you can record not just what you learn but also the questions that arise during your writing and research activities.

For more on using journals, see Chapters 2 and 4.

Try to answer these questions while you do your invention work:

- What do I already know about the topic that I am writing about?

- What feelings or attitudes do I have about this topic? How can I keep them out of my text so that my writing is as free of bias as possible?

- What questions can I ask about the topic?

- Where might I learn more about this subject (in the library, on the Web)? What verifiable information on my topic is available?

- Who would know about my topic? What questions might I ask that person in an interview?

- What do I know about my audience? What don't I know that I should know? Why might they be interested in reading my text?

- What might my audience already know about my subject? Why might they care about it?

- To what extent will sensory details—color, shape, smell, taste, and so on—help my reader understand my topic? Why?

For more on descriptive writing, see Chapter 13.

- What visual aids might I use to better inform my readers?

Doing your invention work in electronic form, rather than on paper, lets you easily use this early writing as you construct a draft.

As with any kind of writing, invention activities improve with peer feedback and suggestions. Consider sharing the invention work you have done so far with several classmates or friends in order to understand your rhetorical situation more clearly and to generate more useful information.

Writing Activity

Brainstorming

Working with the questions on page 175, spend a few minutes brainstorming—jotting down everything you can think of about your topic.

Craig Broadbent's Brainstorming

Craig Broadbent, a first-year student, chose to respond to Scenario 1 on page 159. Broadbent decided that he would brainstorm to get onto paper what he already knew about the litter issue on his campus before he interviewed his friends about it:

—I see stuff every day—newspapers, those extra advertising things they put into the paper, cups, plates, and—especially—cigarette butts.

—It's always worst around where ashtrays are—that's really weird.

—The paper stuff is always worst around where the newspapers are.

—Oh—they do put a box or some container next to the paper stands for students to toss those inserts, if they don't want to read them. Not sure why so many end up on the ground.

—Bad in the men's rooms, too, at times—towels on the floor almost always.

—Classrooms: stuff tacked or taped to the walls, old soda cups and crumpled-up hamburger wrappers and old napkins and candy wrappers . . .

Broadbent also used freewriting and clustering to explore his topic. (See Chapter 6, page 135, for examples of these strategies.)

Exploring Your Ideas with Research

Although you can sometimes draw exclusively on your experience in a piece of informative writing, especially in personal writing contexts, in academic, professional, and civic writing situations, you will usually need to include information gained from outside research.

Assume, for example, that you would like to inform a group of your friends about a local homeless shelter. You would probably want to list the services the shelter provides, indicate the various ways people can become involved with the shelter, and cite financial data on what percentage of each cash donation goes to support the shelter's clients. To provide this information to your readers, you would need to conduct some form of research.

Research provides you with the statistical data, examples, and expert testimony that will enable you to give your audience enough information, and the right kind of information, on your topic. As with any other aspect of your writing, the kind and amount of research you will need to do will depend on your rhetorical situation: who your audience is and what you are trying to accomplish. If you are writing a paper for a sociology course on aspects of male group behavior, you will need to locate articles in scholarly journals, as well as statistical data, which you could present in a chart. If you are writing about a problem in your community, you will need to read articles and government documents, and you might also interview government officials.

ELECTRONIC ENVIRONMENTS | **Using a Search Engine to Narrow a Potential Topic**

The results of a general search for sources can let you know if your informative topic is unwieldy. If a search using a search engine such as Google or Yahoo! brings up thousands of Web sites with information about your topic, it is probably too broad. For example, when a search engine such as Google returns more than 2 million links for the topic "Avian influenza virus," you need to narrow it so that your ideas and research will be more focused. Adding search terms based on your specific interests and concerns can help narrow your exploratory Web search. (Tip: Separate your terms or phrases in the search window with quotation marks.) Adding the terms "Michigan" and "schools" to the search brings the number of results down to 1,300 sites, many of which are likely to provide information about possible exposure to the Avian influenza virus in Michigan schools, a more focused topic. This topic is still fairly broad, however. Adding the term "Detroit" brings the total down to 446 sites, and the top ten hits include Web sites on government policy that contain documents with information you could use in a paper about how local areas can prevent and prepare for an outbreak.

As you work on the scenario you have chosen (see pages 159–62), you could conduct several kinds of research. If you are researching a problem on campus or in your community, you might conduct interviews with students or residents affected by the problem. As an alternative, you might consider conducting a survey of a representative sample of students or community members. You will also need to observe the problem.

Gather, read, and take notes on your topic from outside sources. You might use an electronic journal to record images, URLs, and other information that you find as you do your research. Such an e-journal makes it easy for you to add that information once you start drafting your paper.

For help with locating sources of information, see Chapter 19; for help with documenting your sources, see Chapter 20.

Craig Broadbent's Research

For his informative paper on the litter problem on his campus, Craig Broadbent thought it would be useful to include data that show how long it takes certain waste products to decompose. By searching with the the phrase "How long does trash last?" in the search engine BING, he found this information at the Web site maintained by the National Park Service:

For more on using search engines, see Chapter 19.

Rate of Biodegradability	
Orange/banana Peels	Up to 2 years
Wool socks	1–5 years
Cigarette butts	1–5 years
Plastic-coated paper	5 years
Plastic bags	10–20 years
Plastic film containers	20–30 years
Nylon fabric	30–40 years
Leather	Up to 50 years
Tin cans	50 years

(continued)

STUDENT WRITING EXAMPLES

Brainstorming (pp. 176, 350)
Freewriting (pp. 48, 135, 261, 396)
Criteria (p. 307)
Listing (p. 95)
Table (p. 49)
Answers to Reporter's Questions (p. 261)
Organization (pp. 96, 181)
Clustering (pp. 135, 305)
Interviewing (p. 220)
Research (pp. 137, 177, 222, 263, 308, 398)
Reflection (p. 12)

Rate of Biodegradability	
Aluminum cans & tabs	80–100 years
Plastic six-pack holders	100 years
Glass bottles	1,000,000 years
Plastic bottles	Indefinitely
Styrofoam	Indefinitely

Broadbent realized that this information, though interesting, was probably more than he needed, so he decided that he would narrow it down a bit when he added it to his informative paper.

Reviewing Your Invention and Research

After you have conducted your research, review your invention work and notes, and think about the information you have collected from outside sources. At this time, you may be tempted to decide on a thesis statement—a statement that summarizes your main point. Even though you might already have a general idea of what you want your informative paper to focus on, until you get some of your ideas and research on paper, it is often hard to know what your thesis will be. Your thesis should come *from* the writing you do about your topic. Once you have done a lot of invention work (listing, brainstorming, clustering, and so on) and research, you may be ready to decide on your working thesis. Or you can wait until after you construct your first draft.

For more on deciding on a thesis, see Chapter 13.

Writing Activity

Using Your Invention and Research to Help Focus Your Ideas

To help develop your thesis, review your invention and research notes:

For more on synthesis, see Chapter 3.

- Look for connections between the pieces of information you have gathered. By doing so, you are synthesizing the information from your sources. Craig Broadbent noticed several instances where the recycling program on his campus seemed invisible. This discovery became the main idea of his paper.
- Decide on the most important piece of information you have collected. One approach is to start your paper with this information. To emphasize the invisibility of recycling on his campus, Craig Broadbent starts his paper with "We seem to have a case of invisible blue barrels on campus—when was the last time you saw one and what is unusual or unique about it?"

Craig Broadbent's Review of His Research

Craig Broadbent wanted his paper to include some of the information about recycling that he learned from his research. He investigated the issue on his campus, he interviewed two of his classmates about it, and he did a brief search of back issues of the campus's newspaper, the *Campus Reporter,* for information about campus recycling. His review of his research helped him decide on an effective way to start his paper. Here are some of his notes:

1. Jim Roberts (roommate) told me that no one had mentioned the school's recycling program to him, at orientation or anywhere else.
2. Tracy Worsam (friend and classmate) told me that she'd even asked about the program at her orientation, and no one there seemed to know much about it, other than "we have some blue barrels around campus."
3. The last ten or twelve issues of the *Campus Reporter* had only one small advertisement and no articles about the program. Why so little? All of those things make me wonder if I should start with a question, perhaps like, "Why doesn't anyone on campus know about our recycling program?" And, maybe a title something like, "A big campus secret: Our blue barrels."
4. I also looked on the Web and found this information on the Environmental Protection Agency's (WPA) Web site (http://www.epa.gov/epawaste/nonhaz/municipal/pubs/msw_2010_factsheet.pdf).

Every ton of mixed paper recycled can save the energy equivalent of 165 gallons of gasoline.

Recycling just 1 ton of aluminum cans conserves more than 207 million Btu, the equivalent of 36 barrels of oil, or 1,665 gallons of gasoline.

Maybe I can use these in my paper to help readers understand the information more easily.

Strategies FOR Success | Responsibility

Writers of successful informational papers are responsible writers: they present their information honestly, accurately, and without bias. That careful approach allows readers to make up their own minds about the information.

Readers often use the information from their reading to help them make a decision, to support an idea in their writing, or to teach someone else. It is important, therefore, that you as a writer present accurate information and that you are aware of any biases, or preconceived ideas, you may bring to your writing about a topic—biases that might cause you to present that information in a way that is other than neutral.

Responsible writers also take care to present reliable data. For example, you cannot say "the majority of students who attend this college think that the school does a good job of recycling on campus" unless you have asked a sufficiently large and representative group of your schoolmates and are reasonably certain that you are presenting a true majority opinion.

Organizing Your Information and Research

Once you have some sense of what you would like your informative paper to include, consider how you might organize this material. The questions to ask yourself when deciding on your organization are all rhetorical:

- Who is your audience?
- Why might they be interested in your subject, or how can you make them interested in it? (One way to indicate why your subject is important to your audience is to explain how your audience will be affected by it.)
- What is your purpose for writing—that is, what do you want to *inform* your readers about?
- What are the most important ideas, concepts, or statistics that you want your readers to learn about from your text?

The answers to these questions can help you decide what you need to emphasize, which in turn will help you choose an organization.

Here are three possible organizational approaches for writing an informative paper:

Options FOR Organization
Options for Organizing Informative Writing

Capture Your Readers' Attention	Question Your Readers	Create a Context
Start with an unusual or surprising piece of information about your subject.	Begin with a question to help readers see why they might want to read about your topic.	Set the stage. What is the situation that your readers may be interested in?
Present the information, starting from the least unusual or surprising idea and moving to the most.	Outline the information, starting with the least significant piece of information and working toward the most important.	Broaden your initial explanation with specific details, quotations, and examples so your reader can "see" what you are writing about.
Use specific examples, quotations, statistics, and so on to illustrate your topic.	Use specific examples, quotations, statistics, and so on to illustrate your topic.	Compare and contrast your subject with another one, to help readers understand the information.
End your paper by restating a unique or surprising aspect of your topic.	Conclude by answering the question that you started with.	Conclude your paper by reinforcing your reader's connection to your topic.

Craig Broadbent's Organization

Craig Broadbent reviewed his invention material and then put together a rough outline for his first draft. He decided to start with a question and to use the second approach described above.

> Set the stage, so to speak, by asking if readers know what the blue barrels are and how they work.
> State my purpose: informational.
> Explain recycling and how it works.
> Include tables, photos, charts to show my ideas.
> Explain the cost aspects of recycling.
> Let people know how to find out more information.

Constructing a Complete Draft

Once you have chosen the organizational approach that works best given your audience and purpose, you are ready to finish constructing your draft. Look back over the information you have generated through your invention activities and collected through your research, as well as any comments made by your classmates. You should also reexamine your focus or your thesis (if you have one) and decide whether you need to modify it. If you do not have a thesis yet, consider whether you are ready to develop a working thesis.

Remember that you will learn more about your subject as you write, and your ideas will probably change as you compose the first draft of your informative essay. Consider, too, what visual aids your readers might find useful.

Integrating Sources into Your Draft: Paraphrasing Information from Sources

One effective way to present information is to paraphrase it: to put information from a source into your own words. This is especially true for information from interviews. You will discover once you start interviewing people that interviewees often ramble. Paraphrasing can help you present only the information that is pertinent to your subject.

Look at the notes Craig Broadbent had from his interviews of students:

Tracy Worsam:
I've been active in recycling efforts both at my high school and in my church. I just assumed this university would have a full-scale program. So I asked a whole bunch of people at orientation about what this school did. One person, I'm not even sure who, just pointed and said "we have some blue barrels around campus." I was really disappointed.

Jim Roberts:
I'm kind of interested in recycling and all kinds of green activities. I was expecting to hear how I could help during orientation. Unless I missed it completely, no one mentioned recycling at all—neither during orientation nor since I've been here. You're the first person I've met who seems interested in it.

Group interview with James Wilson, Stacy Marble, and Sam Addams:
    Marble—Yeah, we and a few other guys all rent rooms in that house.
    Wilson—Those of us who live here try to keep the place neat—but, you know, it's really the landlord's job to clean up the front yard.
    Addams—No kidding. We wake up on Saturday morning and there are all those beer cans and other litter in the front yard. We hate it.
    Marble—We can't stay up all night to see who's trashing our yard.
    Addams—No, but you know, maybe a webcam would be cool.

Although the interviews provide relevant information, they also contain much extraneous detail. By paraphrasing, you can take only the relevant ideas you've gained from your interviews and state them in your own words. But remember: Even though the words are yours, you still need to cite where you found the ideas.

Notice how Craig Broadbent integrated parts of his interviews into his final draft. In addition to comments from Roberts and Worsam, Broadbent included a sentence in paragraph 9 that paraphrased interviews with three other students—Wilson, Marble, and Addams: "They all told me that *they* never littered even though their yard was a mess (Wilson, Marble, and Addams)." Notice that this paraphrase gets to the heart of the matter while eliminating unrelated comments.

Parts of a Complete Draft

Introduction: Successful informative writing grabs and holds readers' attention. The following strategies can help you hook your readers:

- **Define any important terms that the reader might not know.** Defining terms does not mean listing their dictionary definitions, but rather explaining those terms in the context of your explanation of your subject. For an especially effective opening, you might get readers' attention by defining a familiar term in an unexpected way.

- **Start your text with unusual or surprising information.** Dan Fletcher begins his article about *Wikipedia* by noting that with the addition of a recent entry about a Norwegian actress, the online encyclopedia had reached a milestone: 3 million entries.

- **Get down to business by bluntly stating your thesis.** A straightforward statement like "Denver's new sign code is causing businesses to lose money" often gets readers' attention. Journalists, who are trained to put the most important information up front, often use this approach.
- **Start with a provocative example or two.**

Body: Think of the body of your informative text as the place to provide all of the information that you want your readers to know and to understand. This is the section where you will present your data: quotations, graphs, tables, charts, and so on. The body of your paper is always the longest part, and although you are not trying to prove anything in an informative essay, you are providing information to your readers, and most of it will appear in this section. The body is also where you will synthesize the information you are providing.

For more on synthesis, see Chapter 3.

Conclusion: Your conclusion should tie your paper together for readers by explaining or suggesting the significance of the information you have given them: why it is useful or interesting to them. Here are some strategies for concluding an informative paper:

- **Summarize your main points.**
- **Explain the subject's most critical part.** Carol Ezzell uses a quotation from an expert to indicate what is most significant about her topic: "If you colonize time, you also colonize the future" (page 167).
- **Outline again the subject's most important aspects.**

Title: You might think that you need to craft a title before you start writing, but often it is more useful to get a first draft on paper or into a computer file and then consider possible titles. Your paper's title should indicate what your paper is about, but it should also capture your readers' interest and invite them to read further.

- **Use a title that readers will wonder about.** For example, "Clocking Cultures" makes readers wonder what this essay could be about.
- **Start with something current.** Dan Fletcher titles his article "A Brief History of *Wikipedia*." Anyone familiar with *Wikipedia* will want to read more.

Writing Activity

Constructing a Full Draft

Using the writing you did when selecting an organizational approach, write a complete draft of your informative paper.

VISUAL *Thinking* | Going Beyond Words to Achieve Your Goals

To help his readers understand the information in his paper, Craig Broadbent decided to look for *visual aids* on the topic of recycling. As noted above, he had already found good information about how long trash lasts (page 177) and located some useful graphics (page 179), both of which he decided to use. Broadbent also wondered whether a photograph of some litter or a blue barrel might help, perhaps right at the start of his paper. He tried several images to get a sense of whether or not they would fit within his paper:

Watch for the Blue Barrels
Craig Broadbent

None of these images seemed to be all that useful to Broadbent, so he kept searching on Google for images. Finally, he found a photograph that helped him show readers what he was discussing. He decided to put this image near the beginning of his paper.

Broadbent also deleted some of the information (such as "plastic film containers" and "plastic six-pack holders") from the data he found on how long trash lasts, so he would present only the most important information. He put that data into Table 1 in his final paper (page 191).

- Of the visuals Broadbent considered, which do you think best support his purpose?
- What kind of visual would you use to help readers understand the information about recycling?

Craig Broadbent's First Draft

After deciding on an organizational approach, Craig Broadbent was ready to begin his first, or working, draft. As he wrote, he did not worry about grammar, punctuation, mechanics, or proper documentation style; instead, he concentrated on getting his main ideas on paper. Here is the first draft of his recycling paper. (The numbers in circles refer to peer comments, which follow the draft below.)

Watch for the Blue Barrels
Craig Broadbent

Have you ever wondered what all of those blue barrels are, around campus . . . and if you know what they're for, do you wonder why students don't seem to use them? ①

Joan Meyers, who coordinates our campus recycling program, says that it has been around for more than ten years now, but receives little publicity (Meyers). My purpose here is to outline what we're doing here on campus, what the costs and income are from the program, and finally, based on several interviews, to suggest reasons why students don't use the blue barrels.

Our campus program not only keeps the campus cleaner, since items are collected in the blue barrels instead of perhaps being thrown on the ground, but also makes some $5,000 a year for the school (Meyers). Ms. Meyers also told me that our college could make as much as $30,000 a year from recycling, if we all recycled all the newspapers, cans, etc., that we now throw away. ② ③

Students, though, don't use the program, sometimes because they're not aware of it. Student Jim Roberts told me that at orientation or anywhere else no one had mentioned the school's recycling program to him (Roberts). And Tracy Worsam even asked about the program at her orientation, and no one there seemed to know much about it, other than "we have some blue barrels around campus" (Worsam). ④

A search of several issues of the *Campus Reporter* perhaps explains why not many students are really aware of the blue barrel program. During the last few months, there has been only one small advertisement about the campus recycling program, and no articles about the program were published.

In order to know about and understand the recycling program, Meyers suggests that information be provided at all orientation meetings, and that weekly advertisements are run in the *Campus Reporter* (Meyers). ⑤

Student Comments on Craig Broadbent's Draft

① "I thought your introduction 'worked' and made me want to read more."

❷ "It seems to me that the strongest parts of your paper are the examples, especially all the statistics."

❸ "Perhaps a table or chart would help me see what you mean."

❹ "The weakest part is the interview information, which made me want to read more of what other people had to say."

❺ "Your conclusion was weak—maybe you could add what students ought to be doing now? Put another way, what do you want your readers to do with this (interesting) information?"

Revising

Revising means reviewing and re-thinking your informative text. The most effective way to revise your work is to read it as if you are reading it for the first time. Reading your own work in this way is difficult to do, of course—which is why writers often put their work aside for a time. The more you can see your writing as if for the first time, the more you will respond to it as your real readers might, questioning and probing and exploring it. As you reread the first draft of your informative writing, here are some questions to ask yourself:

- What else might my audience want or need to know about my subject?
- How else might I encourage my audience to learn more about my subject?
- What information did I find that I did not include in my paper? (Effective research always results in more information than you can include, so consider what you left out that you might include in your next draft.)
- Have I clearly explained any terms my readers might not know?
- Have I clearly synthesized the information I collected from all of my different sources?
- Could some of my information be more effectively presented as a graph, a chart, or in a photograph?

Technology can help you revise and edit your writing more easily. Use your word processor's track-changes tool to try out revisions and editing changes. After you've had time to think about the possible changes, you can "accept" or "reject" them. Also, you can use your word processor's comment tool to write reminders to yourself when you get stuck with a revision or some editing task.

Because it is so difficult to see our own emerging writing with a fresh eye (even for experienced writers), it is almost always useful to ask classmates, friends, or family members to read and comment on drafts of your papers.

Responding to Readers' Comments

Once they have received feedback from peers, teachers, and others, writers have to decide what to do with that feedback. Because the text is *your* paper, you as the

WRITER'S *Workshop* | Responding to Full Drafts

As you read and respond to your classmates' papers (and as they comment on yours), focus on the informative nature of this assignment, but from a reader's perspective. Be sure to ask questions of their writing and to respond to their ideas by exploring your reactions and responses to their thoughts.

Working in pairs or groups of three, read each others' drafts, and then offer your classmates comments that will help them see both their papers' strengths and places where they need to develop their ideas further. Use the following questions to guide your responses to the writer's draft:

- What is your first impression of this draft? How effectively does the title draw you into the paper? Why?

- What do you like about the draft? Provide positive and encouraging feedback to the writer.

- What is the writer's focus? If the paper loses focus, where does it do so?

- What part(s) of the text are especially informative? What information was interesting and/or new to you?

- Comment specifically on the introduction: What is effective about it? What suggestions can you make on how to improve it?

- What do you think is the author's thesis or main point? How could it be expressed or supported more effectively?

- In the main part of the paper, are there parts that are confusing? Where would you like more details or examples to help you see what the author means? What parts could use more explanation or definitions?

- How clear is the author's informative writing? If there are places that seem wordy or unclear, how might the author revise to address those problems?

- How accurate does the information seem? How does the author indicate the sources of statistics and other information that are not common knowledge?

- Reread the conclusion: How well does it tie everything together? To what extent does it make you want to learn more about this topic?

- What do you see as the main weaknesses of this paper? How might the writer improve the text?

- If you are working with a nontraditional text (a Web page, for example, or a brochure), what special attributes are present, and how effective are they?

- If there are visual aspects of the document, how effectively do they illustrate the point being made? How much do the visuals add to a reader's overall understanding of the information?

writer are responsible for dealing with reader responses to your work. You may decide to reject some comments, of course, and that decision is yours. Some of your readers might not understand your main point, or they may misunderstand something you wrote—so it is up to you either to accept or to ignore their comments and suggestions. Other comments, though, deserve your attention, as they are the words of real readers speaking to you about how to improve your text. You may find that comments from more than one reader contradict each other. In that case, use your own judgment to decide which reader's comments are on the right track.

 # KNOWLEDGE OF CONVENTIONS

When effective writers edit their work, they attend to the conventions that will help readers—the table manners of writing. These include genre conventions, documentation, format, usage, grammar, punctuation, and mechanics. By attending to these conventions in your writing, you make reading your work a more pleasant experience.

Editing

The last task in any writing project is editing. When you edit and polish your writing, you make changes to your sentence structure and word choice to improve your style and to make your writing clearer and more concise. You also check your work to make sure it adheres to conventions of grammar, usage, punctuation, mechanics, and spelling. Use the spell-check function of your word-processing program, but be sure to double-check your spelling personally. If you have used sources in your paper, make sure you are following the documentation style your instructor requires.

See Chapter 20 for more on documenting sources.

As with overall revision of your work, this final editing and polishing is most effective if you can put your text aside for a few days and come back to it with fresh eyes. We strongly recommend that you ask classmates, friends, and tutors to read your work as well.

To assist you with editing, we offer here a round-robin editing activity focused on finding and correcting problems with modifiers.

 ## Genres, Documentation, and Format

For advice on writing in different genres, see Appendix C. For guidelines for formatting and documenting papers in MLA or APA style, see Chapter 20.

If you are writing an academic paper, follow the conventions for the discipline in which you are writing and the requirements of your instructor. If you are constructing a brochure for a local service organization (Scenario 3), refer to the guidelines presented in Appendix C. If you have used material from outside sources, including

WRITER'S *Workshop* | **Round-Robin Editing with a Focus on Modifiers**

Informative writing benefits from the careful use of **modifiers**—words or groups of words that describe or limit other words—such as adjectives, adverbs, infinitives, participles, prepositional phrases, and relative clauses. Working in small groups, read one another's papers, looking for two common problems: misplaced and dangling modifiers.

When a modifier is misplaced, it is too far away from the word or phrase it is modifying, so that it appears to be modifying something else. To correct the problem, the modifier needs to be moved.

MISPLACED Student Jim Roberts told me ~~at orientation or anywhere else~~ no one
                                                       at orientation or anywhere else
          had mentioned the school's recycling program to him ^ .

A modifier is dangling when the word or phrase it modifies does not appear in the sentence to all. You can correct the problem by adding the word or phrase.

                                              students need to be provided with
DANGLING In order to know about the recycling program, ^ ~~Meyers suggests that~~
                                                          ,according to Meyers
          information ~~be provided~~ at all orientation meetings ^ .

Compare notes to see if you have questions about modifiers, and consult a grammar handbook or ask your instructor for assistance.

visuals, give credit to those sources, using the documentation style required by the discipline you are working in and by your instructor.

A Writer Achieves His Goal: Craig Broadbent's Final Draft

The final draft of Craig Broadbent's essay "Watch for the Blue Barrels" follows. As you read Broadbent's essay, think about what makes it effective. Note, too, how he used the suggestions his classmates offered during peer review to make his informative paper more effective. Following the essay, you'll find some specific questions to consider.

CRAIG BROADBENT

INFORMATIVE ESSAY   Watch for the Blue Barrels

This is Broadbent's thesis sentence. Here he tells his readers that he will inform them about the campus recycling program and why they should take part.

Have you ever wondered what all of those blue barrels that are scattered around campus are for . . . and if you know what they're for, do you wonder why students don't seem to use them? Those blue barrels are the heart of our campus-wide recycling program, and it is critical not only that students know what they are, but also that they *use* the barrels (see Fig. 1).

Joan Meyers, who coordinates our campus recycling program, says that it has been in place for more than ten years now, but receives little publicity. My purpose here is to outline what we're doing about recycling on campus, to show what the costs and income are from the program, and finally, based on several interviews, to suggest the reasons that students don't use the blue barrels.

Fig. 1 A Blue Barrel for Recycling Waste. Source: Stockbyte/PunchStock RF

What is recycling and why should we care about it? Recycling is the reuse of some product. We all know that reusing plastic, aluminum cans, newspaper, glass, and other items by recycling them saves energy (and thus helps our air pollution problem) and can also save money. Recycling is environmentally sound—the more paper, plastic, and metal products that we can reuse, the less we have to make. That's the case even though things are usually not recycled into what they were to start with. That is, aluminum cans, Meyers told me, rarely are recycled to make more aluminum cans. But they *are* recycled and made into other products (frying pans, for instance). In addition to Meyers' examples, the United States Environmental Protection Agency mentions that there are more than 4500 products that are made from recycled material, including things such as car bumpers, egg cartons, and carpets. Therefore, recycling saves trees and other natural resources.

One peer suggestion Broadbent received was the following:

Perhaps a table or chart would help me see what you mean.

To address this reader's concern, Broadbent added this paragraph and also Table 1.

Not only that, but if certain items are *not* recycled, they can be around forever. That is, if we don't recycle some household items, they never seem to "waste away." For example, the National Park Service lists a number of items that can take close to forever to break down, or they *never* will go away, as shown in Table 1.

Even seemingly minor items like cigarette butts can last as long as five years, and empty soda cans—unless they are recycled—can last for up to 100 years. And styrofoam and plastic can last forever.

Joan Meyers notes that our recycling program not only keeps the campus cleaner, since items are collected in the blue barrels instead of perhaps being thrown on the ground, but it also generates some $5,000 a year in revenue for

Table 1. Amount of Time It Takes Common Items to Break Down

Cigarette butts	1–5 years
Plastic-coated candy wrappers	5 years
Plastic bags	10–20 years
Tin cans	50 years
Aluminum cans and tabs	80–100 years
Glass bottles	100,000 years
Plastic bottles	Indefinitely
Styrofoam	Indefinitely

Source: National Park Service, "How Long Does Litter Last?" 9 Sept. 2011; Web; 16 Jan. 2012; <http://www.nps.gov/tuma/forkids/upload/HowLongDoesLitterLast.pdf>.

the school. Ms. Meyers also told me that our college could make as much as $30,000 a year from recycling if we recycled all the newspapers, cans, and other waste that we now throw away. There is impressive savings involved in recycling: the University of Rochester was one of the EPA's Gold Achievement award winners for 2011, and they saved over $200,000 by recycling. The EPA provides details about UR's program:

> The university effectively utilized online social networking tools, posters, fact sheets, articles, student group initiatives, and university staff and faculty to encourage participation in events and campaigns, including RecycleMania, the Go Green Pledge, Earth Day, Water Week, and E-Cycle Day. Through these efforts, more than 5,000 UR undergraduates learned about the importance of waste reduction on their college campus. To keep the students involved in UR's sustainability initiatives, they are offered the opportunity to write and edit for the "UR Green News" newsletter.
>
> In all, UR's education and outreach efforts helped the university recycle nearly 3,400 tons of materials, resulting in a reduction of more than 8,000 metric tons of carbon dioxide equivalent. The university also saved more than $230,000 in 2010 through recycling revenues and avoiding disposal costs. ("2011 Wastewise Award Winners")

7

Recycling also saves in other ways, including energy (like gasoline and oil), as the EPA reports (see Fig. 2).

8

Students, though, don't use our recycling program, sometimes because they're not aware of it. Student Jim Roberts told me that no one had mentioned the school's recycling program to him, at orientation or anywhere else. Another student, Tracy Worsam, even asked about the program at her orientation, but no one there seemed to know much about it, other than to say "we have some blue barrels around campus." Finally, I interviewed several students who live in that old house on the edge of campus. It's not really a fraternity but more of a boardinghouse. They all told me that

9

Another comment Broadbent received from his peer review session pointed out a problem:

The weakest part is the interview information, which made me want to read more of what other people had to say.

Note how he has now included a good deal of information from the students he interviewed.

Recycling just 1 ton of aluminum cans conserves more than 207 million Btu, the equivalent of 36 barrels of oil, or 1,665 gallons of gasoline.

Fig. 2. Energy Savings from Recycling Aluminum. Illustration from "Municipal Solid Waste Generation, Recycling, and Disposal in the United States: Facts and Figures for 2010" (Environmental Protection Agency, Nov. 2011; Web; 17 Mar. 2012; http://www.epa.gov/epawaste/nonhaz/municipal/pubs/msw_2010_factsheet.pdf)

they never littered, even though their yard was a mess (Wilson, Marble, and Addams). Maybe my interview with them—and the information I gave them about the blue barrel program—will help. Maybe if they understood recycling and had blue barrels in a convenient location, they would recycle plastic, paper, glass, and so on.

A search through several back issues of the *Campus Reporter* may explain why not many students are really aware of the blue barrel program. During the last few months, only one small advertisement about the campus recycling program has appeared in the *Reporter*, and no articles about the program were published.   10

The EPA provides what might be a useful suggestion for our college: a program they sponsor called "RecycleMania." It is a "friendly competition among college and university recycling programs in North America and Canada. During 8 weeks each spring, schools compete to reduce waste, increase recycling and raise awareness of conservation issues across campus" ("Welcome"). Perhaps if we could get our own college involved we could make a huge difference in the environmental awareness of our own students.   11

In order to know about and understand the recycling program, students need to be provided with information at all orientation meetings, and weekly advertisements need to be run in the *Campus Reporter*, according to Joan Meyers. In the meantime, students who would like to learn more about the recycling program on campus, and how they can help, can contact Meyers at JoanMeyers@Ourcollege.edu.   12

Works Cited

"Buy Recycled." Environmental Protection Agency. 26 July 2011. Web. 16 Jan 2012. <http://www.epa.gov/osw/conserve/rrr/buyrecycled.htm>.

Environmental Protection Agency (EPA). "Municipal Solid Waste Generation, Recycling, and Disposal in the United States: Facts and Figures for 2010." Web. 16 Jan. 2012.

Broadbent's peer made this comment on his earlier draft:

Your conclusion was weak—maybe you could add what students ought to be doing now? Put another way, what do you want your readers to do with this (interesting) information?

Note how he now addresses what students can do to become more involved with their campus recycling program.

This paper follows MLA guidelines for in-text citations and works cited. Note that URLs are optional.

- - -. "2011 Wastewise Award Winners." 15 Nov. 2011. Web. 16 Jan. 2012. <http://www.epa.gov/epawaste/partnerships/wastewise/events/2011awardees.htm>.

- - -. "Welcome to the RecycleMania Website." Web. 16 Jan. 2012. <http://www.recyclemaniacs.org/Index.htm>.

"How Long Does Litter Last?" National Park Service. 9 Sept 2011. Web. 16 Jan 2012. <http://www.nps.gov/tuma/forkids/upload/HowLongDoesLitter-Last.pdf>.

Meyers, Joan. Personal interview. 17 Jan. 2012.

Roberts, Jim. Personal interview. 15 Jan. 2012.

Wilson, James, Stacy Marble, and Sam Addams. Personal interview. 17 Jan. 2012.

Worsam, Tracy. Personal interview. 15 Jan. 2012.

UNDERSTANDING A WRITER'S GOALS: QUESTIONS TO CONSIDER AND DISCUSS

Rhetorical Knowledge: The Writer's Situation and Rhetoric

1. **Audience:** How effective is Broadbent at appealing to the audience that this information is intended for—students at a college or university? What can you point to in the essay to demonstrate what you mean?

2. **Purpose:** In addition to its informative purpose, what other purposes does this paper have?

3. **Voice and tone:** What is Broadbent's attitude toward his subject? How does he indicate this attitude in his tone?

4. **Responsibility:** What can you point to in Broadbent's informational essay that gives the text its *ethos?* To what extent do you believe the information that Broadbent presents here? Why?

5. **Context, format, and genre:** How has Broadbent's context—his college campus—affected his paper? How might he have written about the same subject differently in another context? The first sentence of Broadbent's essay directly engages the reader in a personal way that wouldn't be found in a formal report. Do you think Broadbent's informality here is appropriate for his audience? Will it succeed in getting his audience more fully engaged?

Critical Thinking: The Writer's Ideas and Your Personal Response

6. What ideas in Broadbent's essay seem the most important to you? Why?

7. How effectively does Broadbent inform the reader? What examples can you point to in the text that provide useful information?

Composing Processes and Knowledge of Conventions: The Writer's Strategies

8. How effective are the visuals that Broadbent includes? What is your opinion of the sources he uses? What other sources might he have consulted?

9. What is your opinion of Broadbent's conclusion?

Inquiry and Research: Ideas for Further Exploration

10. Go to your college's main Web page and search for "recycling." In no more than one page, outline what you learn.

Self-Assessment: Reflecting on Your Goals

Now that you have constructed a piece of informative writing, go back and consider your learning goals, which you and your classmates may have considered at the beginning of this chapter (see pages 156–57). Write notes on what you have learned from this assignment.

 ### Rhetorical Knowledge

- *Audience:* What did you learn about your audience as you wrote your informative paper?
- *Purpose:* How successfully do you feel you fulfilled your informative purpose?
- *Rhetorical situation:* How did the writing context affect your informational text? How did your choice of topic affect the research you conducted and how you presented your information to your readers? What do you see as the strongest part of your paper? Why? The weakest? Why?
- *Voice and tone:* How would you describe your voice in this essay? Your tone? How do they contribute to the effectiveness of your informational essay?

 ### Critical Thinking, Reading, and Writing

- *Learning/inquiry:* How did you decide what to focus on in your informative paper? Describe the process you went through to focus on a main idea, or thesis.
- *Responsibility:* How did you fulfill your responsibility to your readers?
- *Reading and research:* What did you learn about informative writing from the reading selections you read for this chapter? What research did you conduct? Why? What additional research might you have done?

Writing Processes for Informative Writing

- *Invention:* What invention strategies were most useful to you? Why?
- *Organizing your ideas and details:* What organization did you use? How successful was it? Why?
- *Revising:* What one revision did you make that you are most satisfied with? Why? If you could make an additional revision, what would it be?
- *Working with peers:* How did your instructor or peer readers help you by making comments and suggestions about your writing? How could you have more effectively used the comments and suggestions you received?
- *Visuals:* Did you use photographs or other visuals to help you inform your readers? If so, what did you learn about incorporating these elements?
- *Writing habits:* What "writerly habits" have you developed, modified, or improved on as you constructed the writing assignment for this chapter?

 ## Knowledge of Conventions

- *Editing:* What sentence problem did you find most frequently in your writing? How will you avoid that problem in future assignments?
- *Genre:* What conventions of the genre you were using, if any, gave you problems?
- *Documentation:* Did you use sources for your paper? If so, what documentation style did you use? What problems, if any, did you have with it?

Refer to Chapter 1 (pages 12–13) for a sample reflection by a student.

Writing to Analyze

To more clearly understand a subject such as the irrational fear of spiders or snakes, scientists analyze it, or break it down. An **analysis** examines an issue or topic by identifying the parts that make up the whole. You can gain a clearer understanding of your subject when you look closely at the individual pieces that constitute the whole. An analysis of a *phobia,* defined as an uncontrollable (and sometimes irrational) fear of some situation, object, or activity, would require you to examine the various aspects of that phobia.

Analyzing phobias is an area of study at colleges and universities. Here is an excerpt from an essay about anxiety disorders, which includes phobias, by a researcher at the University of Texas at Austin:

Fear can be a good thing.
    Being afraid makes us heed severe weather warnings and keeps us from running across busy freeways. It is a survival mechanism for most, but for some people their fear has become consuming and out of control.

What are you afraid of?

when it interferes with daily functioning or when the response is above and beyond what is called for. Anxiety disorders are the largest—and one of the most treatable—classes of psychiatric disorders."

Rapid breathing, pounding heart and a desire to flee are typical—and reasonable—reactions to perceived danger, but for someone experiencing an anxiety disorder, these feelings become overwhelming. The fight or flight response kicks into overdrive when a person is experiencing the symptoms of an anxiety disorder. Research has shown that anxiety disorders in the U.S. cost more than $42 billion each year, about one third of the amount spent on mental health care in this country.

Although psychologists analyze subjects such as phobias to understand mental processes better, analysis can also be helpful in everyday life. You have probably analyzed the college you are currently attending: examining its catalogue to consider the variety of courses offered, perhaps reading through faculty lists to consider whom you might be able to study with, and considering other factors. Using analysis in your writing can help you come to a deeper understanding of your subject and share that understanding with your readers.

Since 1988 Dr. Michael Telch and the Laboratory for the Study of Anxiety Disorders (LSAD) in the Department of Psychology at The University of Texas at Austin have been researching treatments for anxiety-related disorders such as panic disorder, obsessive-compulsive disorder, social anxiety disorder, and specific phobias, including claustrophobia, arachnophobia and cynophobia (dog phobia).

"Anxiety is part of being a human being," Telch said. "The question is when does it become a disorder? Mother Nature gave us an alarm system of anxiety and panic to cope with threats. This signal system is critical to our survival. The bad news is that this mechanism is capable of sending a false alarm.

"It can become a disorder when the alarm is out of proportion to the threat," he added. "The hallmark is that the brain is receiving danger messages when the danger isn't there. While many people have these false alarms, it becomes a disorder

Setting Your Goals for *Analytical Writing*

Rhetorical Knowledge (pp. 200–4)

- **Audience:** Determine who will benefit from your analysis. What do the audience members probably already know? What will you need to tell them?
- **Purpose:** When you analyze a complex situation, process, or relationship, you can help others understand the subject more thoroughly.
- **Rhetorical situation:** In an analysis, you break down your subject into parts or categories to help your reader understand it more clearly. The situation that calls for the analysis helps you understand which details you need to look at most closely.
- **Voice and tone:** When you write an analysis, a detailed, thorough approach and a reasonable tone can increase your credibility to readers.
- **Context, medium, and genre:** Decide on the best medium and genre to use to present your analysis to the audience you want to reach.

Critical Thinking, Reading, and Writing (pp. 205–18)

- **Learning/inquiry:** By reading and writing analytically, you gain a deeper understanding of issues and the ability to make more informed decisions.
- **Responsibility:** Effective analysis leads to critical thinking. When you engage in analysis, you see the nuances of all the potential relationships involved in your subject.
- **Reading and research:** Analysis can involve close observation as well as interviews and online and library research.

Writing Processes (pp. 219–31)

- **Invention:** Use invention activities such as brainstorming, listing, and clustering to help you consider the parts of your subject and how they relate to one another.
- **Organizing your ideas and details:** If your subject is large, you might break it down into more understandable parts, or you might begin with individual parts and examine each one in detail.
- **Revising:** Read your work with a critical eye to make certain that it fulfills the assignment and displays the qualities of good analytical writing.
- **Working with peers:** Listen to your classmates to make sure that they understand your analysis.

 Knowledge of Conventions (pp. 231–32)

- **Editing:** The round-robin activity on page 232 will help you check your analysis for wordy sentences.
- **Genres for analytical writing:** Usually, analyses are written as formal documents, so most of the time your analysis will be a formal report or an academic essay.
- **Documentation:** If you have relied on sources outside of your own experience, cite them using the appropriate documentation style.

RHETORICAL KNOWLEDGE

An analysis is often an opportunity to help your readers understand a familiar topic in a new way. Whatever your topic, you will need to consider why you want them to gain this understanding. You will also need to decide what medium and genre will help you get your analysis across to your audience.

 ## Writing to Analyze in Your College Classes

Although academic disciplines vary widely, all of them require the use of analysis, because when you analyze something, you almost always come to understand it more completely. In your college career, you may be asked to construct written analyses in many of your classes:

- In a chemistry class, you might be asked to break down an unknown compound to find what elements are present and write a lab report on your findings.
- In a literature class, you might be asked to analyze how an author develops the hero of a novel to be a sympathetic character.
- In an American history class, you may analyze what political circumstances led to the ratification of an amendment to the U.S. Constitution.

Performing an analysis usually requires you to make close observations or conduct research so that you will have a command of your subject. Writing an analysis forces you to put your understanding of that subject into your own words.

The "Ways of Writing" feature presents different genres that can be used when writing to analyze in your college classes.

 ## Writing to Analyze for Life

In the professional, civic, and personal areas of your life, you also will construct analyses of various ideas, products, and situations.

The kind of analytical writing you do in your professional life will depend on your career, yet the odds are that at some point you will be asked to do an analysis and write a report on your findings. For example, an attorney analyzes legal rulings, the strengths and weaknesses of a client's case, and the arguments presented in court. A physician analyzes her patient's symptoms as she attempts to diagnose the illness and prescribe a cure.

Often the first impulse in civic life is emotional. You may get angry when the city council decides to demolish an old building, or you might enthusiastically support a local developer's plan to buy unused farmland. Your voice will be taken much more seriously by decision makers, however, if you engage in a balanced, in-depth analysis.

Interestingly, in our personal lives, we often tend to analyze events or conversations after they have happened. You may have had a conversation with a close

Ways of Writing to Analyze

Genres for Your College Classes	Sample Situation	Advantages of the Genre	Limitations of the Genre
Behavioral analysis	In your social psychology class, you are asked to construct a statistical analysis of the behavior in specific situations of male college students in groups, as compared to how they act individually in those same situations.	Your research and statistical analysis will provide your readers with useful information about behavior.	It is difficult to find enough reliable statistics for such an analysis; there sometimes are time constraints that limit your research.
Rhetorical analysis	Your writing professor asks you to analyze the rhetorical appeals on a Web site.	This analysis will help you to understand how a Web site appeals to its readers.	This is only one way to examine a Web site.
Nutrition analysis	In your health and nutrition class, your professor asks you to analyze several new diets.	You can provide useful information to readers.	Your analysis is not an evaluation of a diet, which often is what readers want.
Letter to your campus newspaper	Your ethics professor asks you to draft a letter to your college newspaper analyzing a campus problem.	Your college newspaper is a useful forum in which to publicize your analysis of the campus problem to the right audience.	A letter to the editor allows only limited space for your analysis. It might not be published.
Chemical analysis report	Your biology teacher asks you to construct a report on the toxicity of a specific group of chemicals when they are combined.	This report helps readers understand the interaction between chemicals. Such knowledge is critical whenever medicine is dispensed.	A chemical analysis report might not provide everything needed for your biology class.
Visual analysis	Your writing teacher asks you to analyze the visual features of advertisements for cellular phones.	A visual analysis will help you to understand that visuals can have as much impact on an audience as text.	A focus on visual elements can divert attention from verbal content.
Genres for Life	**Sample Situation**	**Advantages of the Genre**	**Limitations of the Genre**
Brochure	As part of a neighborhood group, you construct a brochure to analyze an issue for a school bond vote.	A brochure is a convenient format for distributing information.	A brochure offers limited space for your analysis of the school bond.
Web site	Your business offers a Web site that allows employees to input their salary, tax situation, and so on to help them determine the best way to invest their retirement funds.	This Web site is an interactive venue for employees to analyze their possible investment scenarios.	Sometimes Web sites can be difficult to use and take time to update with new information.
Wiki	You want to create a wiki that allows members of your community to share their analyses of a local issue.	A wiki is an uncomplicated way for interested parties to share their analyses.	Wikis can become long and convoluted; someone needs to monitor activity.
Brand analysis	Your company asks you to analyze several potential new lines of merchandise.	Your analysis will provide sufficient information to help the company make good business decisions.	It can be difficult to find adequate information for such an analysis.
Letter	In a letter that you will never send, you analyze a problem in a relationship with a friend to avoid similar problems in the future.	A "letter to yourself" helps you to honestly understand a problem.	Because you do not plan to send the letter, you might not put much effort into writing it.

friend that left both of you feeling unhappy. After the encounter, you replay the conversation in your mind, trying to take apart what was said by whom and figure out what went wrong. The "Ways of Writing" feature on page 201 presents different genres that can be used when writing to analyze in life.

Scenarios for Writing | Assignment Options

Your instructor may ask you to complete one or more of the following analytical writing assignments. Each assignment is a *scenario,* which provides some context for the analysis you will construct. The scenarios give you a sense of who your audience is and what you want to accomplish with your analytical writing, including your purpose; voice, tone, and point of view; context; and genre.

Starting on page 219, you will find guidelines for completing the assignment option that you choose or that is assigned to you.

Writing for College

SCENARIO 1   **Analysis of a Campus Issue**

Analysis helps people understand whether an idea is a good one or not, or whether a policy should be followed or not. For example, there was a discussion on our campus about giving the student government the responsibility to operate the student union. The university would allow the students to decide what restaurants and stores would operate in the building, how meeting rooms would be used, and other matters. Interested parties were considering whether this change would be beneficial. An analysis of the issues involved in a decision such as this one could help the decision makers understand what would be at stake, and they could then make an informed choice when they voted on the issue.

On your campus, there are many issues that you might analyze:

- Tuition increases: Tuition increases at one school declined over a period of five years—on a percentage basis—but the cumulative increase for the five years was about 44 percent.
- Extra fees: Why are they necessary? Where does that money go?
- Availability of professors during their office hours (and at other times).

Writing Assignment: Think about what is happening on your campus. Select a complex problem that affects you or others. Construct a report that analyzes the problem and offers insights about it.

SCENARIO 2   **A Visual Analysis**

Visuals are important and pervasive. Often, we see them in texts and use them in our own texts; sometimes, they stand alone. The visual elements of a text include not only photos, charts, and drawings but also the fonts used in that text. Here we will focus on an image.

To analyze an image, you would ask the same questions you would ask if you were to analyze a verbal text: What are the elements of the visual that make it work? How do those various aspects function together, complementing one another, to have the intended effect?

For practice, examine Figure 8.1, a billboard advertising a media player. Consider the elements that make up this ad and how they work together to tell a viewer about the product and to encourage that person to buy an iPod. See the "Genres Up Close" feature on page 215 for suggestions.

Writing Assignment: Assume you have been asked to complete an assignment for a class in which you have been discussing popular culture. For this assignment, select a visual image (a Web page, a photograph, an advertisement, or a drawing), and analyze how the aspects of that image work together. In your essay, start by outlining what you think the image is trying to do. Your analysis, then, should center on how effectively the aspects of the image function together to create that effect.

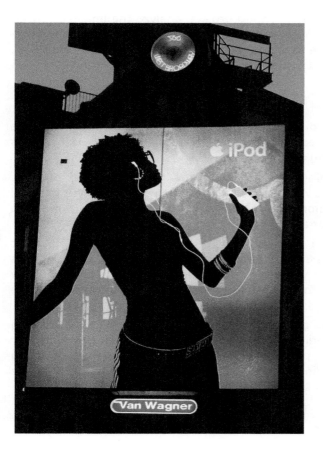

FIGURE 8.1
Billboard
Advertisement

Writing for Life

SCENARIO 3   Professional Writing: A Business Report Analyzing Part of Your Future Career

Think forward to the day when you are ready to apply for jobs in your chosen field. Select an image or advertisement related to your future career—the position you plan to seek after you graduate from college. You might select the following, for example:

- A movie advertisement, if you are planning to work as an actor, director, or screenwriter, or in another role in the film industry
- An advertisement for a product produced by or a service provided by the company you hope to work for
- An image from a company's annual report
- A company's logo
- A Web page from a nonprofit or government agency for which you hope to work

Writing Assignment: For this writing project, analyze the image or advertisement that you selected. Your task is not to evaluate the image or advertisement, but rather to analyze its various aspects (color, point of view, text, size, and shading) to understand how the image or advertisement works.

Rhetorical Considerations in Analytical Writing

Audience: Although your teacher and classmates are the initial audience for your analysis, also consider a wider audience. What kinds of analysis will be most interesting to this group of readers?

Purpose: By researching and analyzing the problem, issue, concept, options, or object, you will provide your readers with an analysis that will allow them to make more informed decisions. What kinds of information will you include in your analysis to support your purpose?

Voice, tone, and point of view: You have probably chosen your topic because you have a personal interest in the subject. What preconceptions do you have? How can you avoid letting them affect your analysis? How can you use voice and tone to establish credibility, so your readers believe your analysis?

For more on choosing a medium and genre, see Chapter 17.

Context, medium, and genre: Keeping the context of the assignment in mind, decide on a medium and a genre for your writing. How will your analysis be used? Who might be interested in reading your analysis? If you are writing for an audience beyond the classroom, consider what will be the most effective way to present your analysis to this audience.

CRITICAL THINKING, READING, AND WRITING

Before you begin to write your analysis, consider the qualities of successful analytic writing. It also helps to read one or more examples of analysis to see these qualities in action.

Learning the Qualities of Effective Analytical Writing

To help you and your readers better understand your subject, you need to make sure your analysis includes the following qualities:

- **A focus on a complex subject.** Any subject worth analyzing—a political position, a book, a war strategy—will consist of many parts or features, and these parts will interact with one another in complicated ways.

- **A thorough explanation of the parts and how they relate to one another.** Your first step will be to identify the component parts or aspects of your subject and then consider how those parts function separately and together. For a subject such as a new school tax bond, you might consider aspects like the following:
  - Benefits:
    - to the students
    - to the local tax base
    - to the teachers, administration, and support staff
  - Problems and costs:
    - costs in the form of debt that will need to be paid off
    - interest charges
  - What happens if the community does not fund the schools in this way?
    - Will school taxes need to be raised?
    - Will the quality of the school suffer?

  After you have identified the parts or aspects of your subject, you need to gain a thorough understanding of each one so that you can explain it to your readers.

- **Research-based rather than personal-based writing.** A formal analysis usually requires research. Your understanding of the subject is seldom enough to inform a thorough analysis. If you were analyzing the bond proposal, for example, you would need to read the entire proposal, interview the officials or citizen groups behind it, and examine recent school budgets.

For more on conducting research, see Chapters 19 and 20.

- **A focused, straightforward presentation.** An effective analysis focuses on the subject's component parts, always working to show how they combine to make up the whole. All aspects of your text must focus on some central theme or idea that links all parts or aspects of the analysis.

   An analysis is usually neutral in tone—the writer's primary purpose is not to persuade, but rather to explain how the subject functions.

- **Insights.** Taking something apart to analyze it provides insights into how each part functions, how each aspect relates to every other aspect and to the whole.

For more on thesis statements, see Chapter 13.

- **A conclusion that ties parts together.** In an analysis, your conclusion does much more than just state your major claim (as a *thesis statement* usually does). In your conclusion, you have the opportunity to outline *how* the parts function together and also to explain whether you believe they function effectively or not.

Reading, Inquiry, and Research: Learning from Texts That Analyze

The reading selections that follow are examples of analytical writing. As you read the texts, ask yourself the following questions:

- What makes this analysis effective?
- What qualities of an effective analysis (see pages 205–6) do the selections exhibit?
- What parts of the analysis leave me with questions?
- How can I use these analytical techniques in my writing?

JAMES M. LANG

Putting In the Hours

OPINION PIECE

Most casual observers of the North American pro- 1 fessor assume his natural habitat to be the class- room, where he engages in those behaviors commonly associated with his species: speaking to audiences of young people in a loud voice, marking with writing uten- sils on green or white boards, receiving and distributing pieces of paper.

But the casual observer may overlook that this spe- 2 cies usually spends an equal, if not greater, part of his week in his den, holding what his institution terms "office hours." At small, liberal-arts colleges in New England, like the one where our observations have been cen- tered, he and his colleagues are, in fact, required to hold 10 office hours each week—time set aside for advisees and students who want to consult with the professor outside of the normal classroom hours.

Working our way up and down the halls of one 3 faculty office building, checking out the office-hour schedules posted below the nameplates, and observing the work and leisure habits of these specimens through their half-opened doors, we have been able to classify, according to their office-hour behavior, some subspecies of the North American professor.

James M. Lang is a public speaker, work- shop leader, and assistant professor of English at Assumption College. Essays from his regular column for the *Chroni- cle of Higher Education* about life on the tenure track were compiled into the book *Life on the Tenure Track: Lessons from the First Year* (2005). Lang is also the author of *Learning Sickness: A Year with Crohn's Disease* (2004). This essay was originally published on May 16, 2003, as part of Lang's column in the *Chronicle*. We find that our students can often identify their own professors (and sometimes their friends) using Lang's catego- ries. Can you?

The Early Bird: Whether he actually likes morn- 4 ings or not, the Early Bird schedules all of his office hours before 10 a.m.—in other words, before most of his students have rolled out of bed. The Early Bird can be assured that he will have fewer office visits than his next-door neighbor, who has scheduled all of her hours after noon.

The Early Bird has done nothing technically wrong, of course; he probably 5 keeps his office hours more regularly than most faculty members. But the Early Bird also knows exactly what he is doing. He doesn't particularly want students visiting during office hours, and he has found the best legal means of ensuring that they don't.

The Door Closer: The Door Closer knows that students are far more likely 6 to knock on an open door than a closed one, so he wards off all but the most desperate and devoted of his students by keeping his door completely shut during office hours. For extra effect, he will lock it, forcing students to realize that they are interrupting him by compelling him to walk to the door and open it.

We have actually observed students walk up to a professor's office, see   7
the door closed, and walk away dispirited—only to watch the office's occupant
emerge moments later, heading to the departmental office for a coffee refill. Like
the Early Bird, the Door Closer has not violated the letter of his contract; he
relies instead upon simple and subtle discouragement.

The Counselor: The Door Closer's antithesis, the Counselor props his door   8
open as wide as it will allow, faces his desk towards the doorway, and peeks
out expectantly at every passing footfall. The Counselor wants students to visit
him in his office. The Counselor wants to know how they're doing. The students
actually divulge this information to the Counselor: They tell him about their
roommates, and their relationships, and their home lives. The Counselor loves it.

Other faculty members are baffled by the Counselor, and slightly suspicious   9
of him. They suspect—and they are probably right—that their own names come
up occasionally in the Counselor's office, and that the Counselor listens to student complaints about them with a sympathetic ear.

The Chatterer: Chatterers, whether they want students in their office or   10
not, like to spend their office hours socializing. They stop in to visit other colleagues who are having office hours, they linger in the departmental office to
check their mail or fill their coffee mug, and they welcome long lines at the copy
machine. As a rule, nonchattering faculty members tend to appreciate Chatterers most at paper-grading time, when frequent interruptions to their work are
happily tolerated. When they are trying to prepare for a class they have to
teach in 30 minutes, the average faculty member sees his Chattering neighbor
as a nuisance.

Most Chatterers are people who simply like to talk, and practice their chat-   11
ting habits in other realms of their lives as incessantly as they do at the office.

We have noticed a subspecies of Chatterers, though: people who live by   12
themselves, especially those newly arrived at the college, without much of a
social network outside the campus. For this species, the time they spend in the
office provides them with their primary socializing opportunity. Back in their
apartments, it's a book or the television. During office hours they get to communicate with other members of their species.

The Fugitive: The counterpart to the lonely Chatterer, the Fugitive has a   13
houseful of living creatures—spouses, children, dogs, cats, hermit crabs—and
sees the office as his refuge from the chaos that constantly threatens to overwhelm his home life. Fugitives can best be recognized by their relaxed attitude
during office hours. However much work they have to do at the office, it can't be
any more stressful than what they have to deal with at home. Fugitives usually
have at least one extremely comfortable chair in their office, and can occasionally
be spotted sitting in that chair and staring off into space, just enjoying the peace
and quiet.

In the interests of scientific objectivity, we should disclose that the author of   14
this paper is a Fugitive.

He has a recliner purchased from the Salvation Army, and the most relax-   15
ing part of his day are those moments when he can balance a cup of tea on the
armrest, kick off his shoes, and read the material he has assigned for class. He
has a little refrigerator in his office, and he has expressed his desire to install a
television/VCR as well.

"If you ever kick me out," he has been known to remark to his wife, with   16
just a hint of hopefulness, when he has all three kids in the tub and the phone
and the doorbell are ringing and the cats are scratching at the door, "I'll be able
to move right into my office."

"Don't get your hopes up," she has been known to respond.   17

But the truth of the matter is, he is not always or exclusively a Fugitive.   18
Sometimes he engages in behaviors associated with the Chatterer, and the Door
Closer, and sometimes the Early Bird too (he draws the line at the Counselor—
much as he loves his students, he does not want to hear about their latest relationship problems).

He holds one office hour on Friday morning from 8:30 to 9:30 a.m., before   19
his first class. In an entire semester, he has had one visitor during that office
hour, and she came under extreme duress, when all other options were
exhausted. He counts three Chatterers in his department among his closest
friends, so he often welcomes the opportunity to talk with them, even occasionally instigating such conversations. And he will close his door when he is having one of those weeks when the paper stack never seems to diminish, no
matter how many he grades. So we have begun to suspect that these observations are perhaps more appropriately classified as behaviors rather than subspecies types.

Most North American professors do have a dominant behavior that char-   20
acterizes their office-hour activity, but most also engage in multiple behaviors in
the course of a single week.

Given the early and exploratory nature of these observations, we would   21
welcome notes from fellow field researchers who have studied the office-hour
habits of the North American professor, and have observed other forms of both
common and unusual behaviors.

UNDERSTANDING A WRITER'S GOALS: QUESTIONS TO CONSIDER AND DISCUSS

Rhetorical Knowledge: The Writer's Situation and Rhetoric

1. **Audience:** The *Chronicle of Higher Education* is a weekly newspaper for college professors. How effectively does Lang understand and reach his audience? Who else—besides college teachers and students—might be interested in reading Lang's analysis?

2. **Purpose:** Why do you suppose Lang wrote this essay?

3. **Voice and tone:** What can you point to in Lang's tone that helps to establish his *ethos*?

4. **Responsibility:** What can you cite from the essay that shows how Lang was fulfilling his responsibilities as a writer when he wrote "Putting In the Hours"?

5. **Context, format, and genre:** Lang's essay appeared in a respected academic periodical, the *Chronicle of Higher Education*. Is his essay typical of the kind of writing you would expect in such a journal? Why? How does Lang twist the genre of the serious academic essay to make this a humorous piece?

Critical Thinking: The Writer's Ideas and Your Personal Response

6. What is your initial reaction to Lang's analysis? Do you find it humorous? Why?

7. How accurate are Lang's categories and subcategories? Why? Do you agree with his analysis? Why or why not?

Composing Processes and Knowledge of Conventions: The Writer's Strategies

8. Consider Lang's overall organization by making a sentence or scratch outline of it (outline the text by writing, in one sentence, what each paragraph has to say). How effective is his organization? Why? In what other way(s) might this essay be organized?

9. Lang starts his essay with this line: "Most casual observers of the North American professor assume his natural habitat to be the classroom . . ." (paragraph 1). What effect does Lang have by making his essay sound like an observation of animals in nature?

Inquiry and Research: Ideas for Further Exploration

10. Visit two of your professors in their offices. How do they compare to Lang's professors? Be specific in your description.

SUSAN CAIN

The Power of Introverts

Our lives are shaped as profoundly by personality as by gender or race. And the single most important aspect of personality—the "north and south of temperament," as one scientist put it—is where we fall on the introvert-extrovert spectrum. Our place on this continuum influences our choice of friends and mates, and how we make conversation, resolve differences, and show love. It affects the careers we choose and whether or not we succeed at them. It governs how likely we are to exercise, commit adultery, function well without sleep, learn from our mistakes, place big bets in the stock market, delay gratification, be a good leader, and ask "what if." It's reflected in our brain pathways, neurotransmitters, and remote corners of our nervous systems. Today introversion and extroversion are two of the most exhaustively researched subjects in personality psychology, arousing the curiosity of hundreds of scientists. 1

These researchers have made exciting discoveries aided by the latest technology, but they're part of a long and storied tradition. Poets and philosophers have been thinking about introverts and extroverts since the dawn of recorded time. Both personality types appear in the Bible and in the writings of Greek and Roman physicians, and some evolutionary psychologists say that the history of these types reaches back even farther than that: the animal kingdom also boasts "introverts" and "extroverts," from fruit flies to pumpkinseed fish to rhesus monkeys. As with other complementary pairings—masculinity and femininity, East and West, liberal and conservative—humanity would be unrecognizable, and vastly diminished, without both personality styles. 2

Take the partnership of Rosa Parks and Martin Luther King Jr.: a formidable orator refusing to give up his seat on a segregated bus wouldn't have had the same effect as a modest woman who'd clearly prefer to keep silent but for the exigencies of the situation. And Parks didn't have the stuff to thrill a crowd if she'd tried to stand up and announce that she had a dream. But with King's help, she didn't have to. 3

Yet today we make room for a remarkably narrow range of personality styles. We're told that to be great is to be bold, to be happy is to be sociable. We see ourselves as a nation of extroverts—which means that we've lost sight of 4

ANALYSIS

Susan Cain, a former corporate attorney and negotiations consultant, has turned her curiosity about human nature into a career as a writer and public speaker. Her book *Quiet: The Power of Introverts in a World That Can't Stop Talking* (2012), from which the following excerpt is taken, is the result of her own interest in how personality traits that may run counter to cultural norms can lead people to success. We find that many of our students realize that they share Cain's introverted traits. Her work helps them understand and make the most of their introversion while, at the same time, allows our extroverted students learn a new respect for introverts.

who we really are. Depending on which study you consult, one third to one half of Americans are introverts—in other words, *one out of every two or three people you know.* (Given that the United States is among the most extroverted of nations, the number must be at least as high in other parts of the world.) If you're not an introvert yourself, you are surely raising, managing, married to, or coupled with one.

If these statistics surprise you, that's probably because so many people   5 pretend to be extroverts. Closet introverts pass undetected on playgrounds, in high school locker rooms, and in the corridors of corporate America. Some fool even themselves, until some life event—a layoff, an empty nest, an inheritance that frees them to spend time as they like— jolts them into taking stock of their true natures. You have only to raise the subject with your friends and acquaintances to find that the most unlikely people consider themselves introverts.

It makes sense that so many introverts hide even from themselves. We live   6 with a value system that I call the Extrovert Ideal—the omnipresent belief that the ideal self is gregarious, alpha, and comfortable in the spotlight. The archetypal extrovert prefers action to contemplation, risk-taking to heed-taking, certainty to doubt. He favors quick decisions, even at the risk of being wrong. She works well in teams and socializes in groups. We like to think that we value individuality, but all too often we admire one *type* of individual—the kind who's comfortable "putting himself out there." Sure, we allow technologically gifted loners who launch companies in garages to have any personality they please, but they are the exceptions, not the rule, and our tolerance extends mainly to those who get fabulously wealthy or hold the promise of doing so.

Introversion—along with its cousins sensitivity, seriousness, and   7 shyness—is now a second-class personality trait, somewhere between a disappointment and a pathology. Introverts living under the Extrovert Ideal are like women in a man's world, discounted because of a trait that goes to the core of who they are. Extroversion is an enormously appealing personality style, but we've turned it into an oppressive standard to which most of us feel we must conform.

The Extrovert Ideal has been documented in many studies, though this   8 research has never been grouped under a single name. Talkative people, for example, are rated as smarter, better-looking, more interesting, and more desirable as friends. Velocity of speech counts as well as volume: we rank fast talkers as more competent and likable than slow ones. The same dynamics apply in groups, where research shows that the voluble are considered smarter than the reticent—even though there's zero correlation between the gift of gab and good ideas. Even the word *introvert* is stigmatized—one informal study, by psychologist Laurie Helgoe, found that introverts described their own physical appearance in vivid language ("green-blue eyes," "exotic," "high cheekbones"), but when asked to describe generic introverts they drew a bland and distasteful picture ("ungainly," "neutral colors," "skin problems").

But we make a grave mistake to embrace the Extrovert Ideal so unthinkingly. Some of our greatest ideas, art, and inventions—from the theory of evolution to van Gogh's sunflowers to the personal computer—came from quiet and cerebral people who knew how to tune in to their inner worlds and the treasures to be found there. Without introverts, the world would be devoid of: 9

the theory of gravity

the theory of relativity

W. B. Yeats's "The Second Coming"

Chopin's nocturnes

Proust's *In Search of Lost Time*

Peter Pan

Orwell's *Nineteen Eighty-Four* and *Animal Farm*

The Cat in the Hat

Charlie Brown

Schindler's List, E.T., and *Close Encounters of the Third Kind*

Google

Harry Potter*

As the science journalist Winifred Gallagher writes: "The glory of the   10 disposition that stops to consider stimuli rather than rushing to engage with them is its long association with intellectual and artistic achievement. Neither $E = mc^2$ nor *Paradise Lost* was dashed off by a party animal." Even in less obviously introverted occupations, like finance, politics, and activism, some of the greatest leaps forward were made by introverts. Figures like Eleanor Roosevelt, Al Gore, Warren Buffett. Gandhi—and Rosa Parks—achieved what they did not in spite of but *because of* their introversion.

---

*Sir Isaac Newton, Albert Einstein, W. B. Yeats, Frédéric Chopin, Marcel Proust, J. M. Barrie, George Orwell, Theodor Geisel (Dr. Seuss), Charles Schulz, Steven Spielberg, Larry Page, J. K. Rowling.

UNDERSTANDING A WRITER'S GOALS: QUESTIONS TO CONSIDER AND DISCUSS

Rhetorical Knowledge: The Writer's Situation and Rhetoric

1. **Audience:** From reading this short excerpt from *Quiet*, what inferences can you make about the intended audience of the book?

2. **Purpose:** Can you determine Cain's purpose in presenting the contributions of introverts?

3. **Voice and Tone:** How would you characterize Cain's tone in this piece? How does it affect her credibility?

4. **Responsibility:** Cain asserts that extroversion is culturally more valued than introversion. Do you think she is sensationalizing the situation? If so, what makes you think so?

5. **Context, format, and genre:** This piece is an excerpt from a book. What clues are there from the piece, if any, that indicate that this is an excerpt from a book, rather than a self-contained essay? What insights does Cain's analysis offer?

Critical Thinking: The Writer's Ideas and Your Personal Response

6. What point do you think Cain is trying to make here? What conclusions is Cain drawing from her analysis of the information she is presenting?

7. What is your own response to Cain's analysis? Do you consider yourself an introvert or an extrovert? How do you think whether you're an introvert or extrovert affects how others view you? How does it influence your chances of success?

Composing Processes and Knowledge of Conventions: The Writer's Strategies

8. Throughout this excerpt, Cain asserts that our culture encourages us to value extroverts more than introverts. Yet toward the end of the selection she presents a list of significant contributions made by introverts. What is the purpose of this list of contributions by introverts?

9. Cain asserts that extroversion is so valued that many introverts pretend to be extroverts. What evidence does she offer for this assertion? What evidence could she offer?

Inquiry and Research: Ideas for Further Exploration

10. Do some more reading on personality theory to see how other personality dimensions may have an impact on how individuals behave. Do these other dimensions align with the perspective Cain presents? The example she presents of Rosa Parks and Dr. Martin Luther King, Jr., is intriguing because it emphasizes the idea of complementarity in personality. Can you think of any other specific examples where complementary personality types might have led to a stronger group effort?

GENRES *Up Close* **Writing a Visual Analysis**

On any given day, you are likely to encounter hundreds or even thousands of texts with visuals such as photos, diagrams, charts, maps, and graphs. For example, advertisements with visual elements appear in magazines, in newspapers, on billboards, as part of Web sites, and in various other media. The visuals that you see each day are as rhetorical as the words that you read. Because these kinds of visual elements are pervasive and often persuasive, readers and viewers need skills for analyzing them. Writing visual analyses helps to develop these reading and viewing skills.

A visual analysis will usually include the following features:

- **A copy of the image.** Seeing the image helps the reader understand the analysis, and reading the analysis helps the reader gain new insights into the visual.

- **A written description of the image.** The description can help guide readers' attention to specific features.

- **An analysis of what the visual image is communicating—the rhetorical features of the visual.** As you craft your analysis, consider the material offered in Chapter 18, "Communicating with Design and Visuals." Also ask yourself the following kinds of questions:
  - What are the parts of the visual? How do the parts relate to the whole?
  - What story does the visual tell?
  - How do you react to the visual emotionally, intellectually, or in both ways?
  - What is the purpose of the visual?
  - How does the visual complement any verbal content in the text? (Most advertisements include both words and images.)
  - How is the visual placed in the text? Why do you think it is placed there?
  - How does this visual appeal to the intended audience? For example, a photo of Steve Lake (a catcher for the Chicago Cubs, Philadelphia Phillies, and St. Louis Cardinals in the 1980s and 1990s) playing in Game 7 of the 1987 World Series might appeal to a knowledgeable connoisseur of baseball, but it might not mean much to a casual fan of the game.
  - What would the text be like if the visual were missing?
  - What other visuals could work as well as, or even more effectively than, the current one? For example, in some situations a diagram might be more effective than a photo because it can reveal more details.
  - What design principles (see Chapter 18) has the writer used in the visual?

JESSE HASSENGER

VISUAL ANALYSIS   Irony As a Disguise

Jesse Hassenger writes about popular culture for *PopMatters*, AMC's filmcritic.com, and *The L Magazine*. Favorite topics include animation, sketch comedy, and *Veronica Mars;* his essay on the latter was published in the anthology *Neptune Noir*. This analysis has not been published previously.

When faced with a barrage of competing advertisements, often ad-makers will disguise their images in order to better stand out. Upon first glance, this anti-drug ad looks like another sort entirely: the kind of retro enticement once found on the backs of comic books and youth-oriented magazines. Rather than an advertisement for weight-gain pills or a miracle diet, however, it recruits readers to become a   1

Includes a copy of the advertisement.

professional "TV remote control operator," making hyperbolic claims about this dubious career path.

Even within this established framework, the central point may not be immediately clear to the reader—the piece could be construed as a public-service ad for any number of causes, such as encouraging exercise or discouraging the passive nature of TV watching. Those are both elements of the image, but it's only in the tagline at the bottom of the page that the ad's more specific goal becomes clear: "Hey, not trying to be your mom, but there aren't many jobs out there for potheads."

This is key to the ad's goal: to discourage drug use in a less hectoring tone than its audience may be accustomed to reading or hearing. The casual wording of that tagline—opening with "hey, not trying to be your mom"—seems designed to downplay the fact that the ad is, essentially, attempting to offer advice and guidance. This, combined with the humorous parody style of the ad, is arranged so that the reader might let his or her guard down and feel less resistant to the earnest and not necessarily "fashionable" message contained at its core.

Though the placement of its key, revealing tagline is subtle rather than attention-grabbing, the ad is actually quite text-heavy overall, using fonts, design, and fake-aging texture in place of too many images. Highlighting the flim-flam nature of its fake claim—that a fine living can be carved out from sitting on the couch and watching television—the ad's dominant images are a single greasy-looking fellow in a variety of ridiculous poses, with a few supporting images of a generic diploma and a hand holding a remote control. Though the text is enthusiastic, the spare and uninspiring (maybe even depressing) images signal the ad's irony.

The ad also uses its retro style to contribute to this sense of irony, since these types of ads are now recognized as silly and blatantly disingenuous. In fact, one potential problem with the ad would be if its target audience did not understand the reference to these kinds of old-timey huckster advertisements; the modern equivalent would likely be found in infomercial-style television spots, rather than a print source. However, the ad's sarcasm should be recognizable even without a familiarity with its inspiration, because of the prominent placement of the largest image, with the goofy-looking guy wielding two remotes. This image is the clearest immediate signal to readers that they are dealing with some kind of parody, and not a "real" advertisement—or rather, that the real advertisement will be revealed with closer attention. This sort of playful but decodable deception speaks to an image and advertising-saturated culture, where disguises can be the most efficient way to sneak a message across.

2   Provides a description of the advertisement.

3   Suggests how the advertisement might be perceived by its audience.

4   Explains how the parts of the advertisement contribute to its ironic message.

5

QUESTIONS FOR WRITING AND DISCUSSION: LEARNING OUTCOMES

Rhetorical Knowledge: The Writers' Situation and Rhetoric

1. **Audience:** What audience do you think Hassenger has in mind for this visual analysis? Why do you think that?

2. **Purpose:** What is Hassenger trying to accomplish in this visual analysis?

3. **Voice and Tone:** What is Hassenger's attitude toward his audience and the topic?

4. **Responsibility:** How seriously has Hassenger taken his responsibilities as a writer?

5. **Context and Format:** If Hassenger were to make this essay available in some other venue, such as a blog, how might he need to change the analysis?

6. **Genre:** A visual analysis usually includes the visual image, a description of the image, and some analysis of the image. To what extent does Hassenger's analysis do these three things?

Critical Thinking: The Writers' Ideas and Your Personal Response

7. To what extent do you agree with Hassenger's analysis? Why?

Composing Processes and Knowledge of Conventions

8. How has Hassenger organized his analysis? Why do you think that he organized it that way?

Inquiry and Research: Ideas for Further Exploration

9. Hassenger does not comment on the text in the middle of the ad elaborating on the advantages of being a TV remote control operator. What could be said about those words relative to the visual image?

10. Find other ads that include humor to stand out. How many of them use visuals, as Hassenger notes, to "signal to readers that they are dealing with some kind of parody, and not a 'real' advertisement – or rather, that the real advertisement will be revealed with closer attention"?

WRITING PROCESSES

As you work on the assignment you have chosen, remember the qualities of an effective analytical paper, which are listed on pages 205–6. Also remember that writing is rarely a neat series of well-defined steps. You might start with an invention activity or two and then conduct some research, which leads to more invention work and then a first draft; but then you might need to do more invention work to help flesh out your draft and conduct more research to fill in gaps in information; and then you will revise your draft and possibly find another gap or two. . . . So while the activities listed below imply that writers go through them step-by-step, the actual process of writing is usually messier.

Invention: Getting Started

Try to answer these questions while you do your invention work:

- What do I already know about the subject that I am considering for my analysis?
- What insights do I already have to offer?
- Where might I learn more about the topic I am considering? What verifiable information am I likely to find?
- What do I know about my audience?
- What might my audience already know about this topic? How can I make my insights convincing for them?
- What questions do I need to answer before I can begin (and complete) my analysis?

Writing Activity

Freewriting, Listing, and Interviewing

Using the questions above, jot down (freewrite) everything you can think of about your subject in ten minutes. Even if you cannot think of anything to say, keep writing.

Next, place your ideas in a sequence—whether from smallest to largest or least to most important. A list helps you categorize each aspect of your subject for an analysis. Once you have put your information in a list, you can move each item around as you see fit.

Finally, ask others what they know about your subject—what they see as its component parts, what they think are its important aspects, and how they think those parts or aspects work together. A useful way to conduct such interviews is to ask the *who, what, where, when, why,* and *how* questions that a newspaper reporter generally relies on.

Sarah Washington's Interviewing

Student writer Sarah Washington decided to respond to Scenario 1 (page 202) about a campus issue. When her instructor mentioned the issue of campus parking, Washington knew she had found her subject. In class, she used freewriting to get her initial ideas on paper and then decided to interview Michael Nguyen, who heads her college's Parking and Transit office. Here is a portion of that interview:

STUDENT WRITING EXAMPLES

Brainstorming (pp. 176, 350)

Freewriting (pp. 48, 135, 261, 396)

Criteria (p. 307)

Listing (p. 95)

Table (p. 49)

Answers to Reporter's Questions (p. 261)

Organization (pp. 96, 181)

Clustering (pp. 135, 305)

Interviewing (p. 220)

Research (pp. 137, 177, 222, 263, 308, 398)

Reflection (p. 12)

Question: Can you tell me a little about who you are and what your background is?

Answer: I have a degree—believe it or not—in Public Parking, and I'd worked with two businesses before I came here. When I started here, I had to start at the bottom and slowly worked my way up and I've had this position for nearly five years.

Q: What exactly does Parking & Transit do? What does it cost to park on campus?

A: P&T has 6,100 parking spaces available—most are in paved lots, but we also handle the Elm Street garage, which has six levels of covered parking, and the garage on Maple with five levels. We handle the cleaning, the paving and repair work, selling parking permits to students and faculty, and so on. We also patrol the campus, giving parking tickets to anyone illegally parked.

Lately, we've spent a lot of time talking to dorm residents, to see how we might provide better and more parking for their use. But it's a battle—we only have so much space on campus, and we're growing every semester in terms of students. That's a good problem to have.

Parking costs for the covered garage are $250 a semester; for the surface lots it's $200 a semester. However, it costs us about $150 a semester to maintain a surface parking space, and about $200 a semester to maintain a garage space in the garage—so we really lose money.

Q: When does most of your work take place?

A: Well, we're really busy right before classes start, selling permits. But we also get busy at mid-term as the lots and garages are pretty dirty by then—lots of litter—so there's an ongoing cleaning program. And we're busy all the time patrolling—we give out a lot of parking tickets.

Exploring Your Ideas with Research

Before you begin your research, consider what your focal point should be. For example, suppose you wanted to research how electronic telecommunications such as smartphones and the Internet are helping college students communicate electronically with their professors and classmates, enabling them to keep in touch and to share more information. You could choose to focus on how college students who take online courses communicate with classmates. Look over your invention work to remind yourself of all that you know about your subject, as well as the questions you came up with about it. Use the reporter's questions of *who, what, where, when, why,* and *how* to get started on your research. After you have decided what information you need, determine what kind of research you need to conduct in order to gather that information. Use an electronic journal to record images, URLs, interview notes, and other electronic pieces of information that you find as you conduct your research.

Writing Activity

Conducting Research

Consider your subject for analysis and, in no more than two pages, outline a research plan. In your plan, indicate the following:

- What you already know about your subject
- What questions you still have
- Who or what sources might be able to answer your questions
- Who (roommates, college staff, professors) might be able to provide other perspectives on your subject
- Where you might look for further information (library, Web, primary documents, other sources)
- When you plan to conduct your research

Sarah Washington's Research

Sarah Washington began her invention and research on college parking by writing down what she already knew and the questions she still had. During the early stages of her invention work, she realized that she was having an emotional response to the issue of parking—the lack of parking on campus made her frustrated and angry—and she really did not have good information about the reasons for the situation. She started her formal research by interviewing Michael Nguyen. She then interviewed others affected by college parking to find out what they thought about their situation, focusing on the reporter's *who, what, where, when, why,* and *how* questions; she also learned what other colleges do in terms of parking, examined how parking permits are issued, and determined whether the parking costs at her college are in line with what other, similar, colleges charge for parking.

After interviewing several people on campus, she made the following notes in her research journal.

> There needs to be sufficient parking for all the students who live in campus housing who have or are allowed to have cars. Of course, this number could vary from semester to semester.
>
> We have 6,100 parking places, in the garages and in surface lots (Nguyen interview).
>
> There also needs to be sufficient parking for the staff who drive to work during regular business hours. Faculty needs are more difficult to determine. Their time on campus is inconsistent. While it is easy to know when they teach and hold office hours, other times (class preparation, grading, writing, researching in labs or the

library, attending meetings, etc.) all vary from week to week. They need a parking spot, but they might not all be on campus at the same time. The trick is to figure out what percentage is likely to be on campus.

Mr. Nguyen told me that there were 13,845 total students enrolled this semester. Of that total, 6,735 live on campus. 2,700 of the resident students have cars. There are 512 full-time faculty and 193 part-time faculty. In addition, there are 398 staff people who work at the university.

Commuter students—there are about 6,500 of them, according to Mr. Nguyen—may be the group whose parking needs are most difficult to determine. They often lead complicated lives balancing school, work, and family obligations. They come to campus for class, but also likely come to campus at other times to use the library and other campus facilities, or to take part in other activities. It's difficult to determine when they will be on campus. I should ask some commuter students in my English class when they actually *are* at school—in class or at the library or whatever—to get some sense of how much that group of students is on campus.

Finally, all campuses need to provide parking spaces for visitors. Again, the needs of visitors vary. They can be prospective students, businesspeople, government employees, or industry leaders who need to meet with the faculty or administration. Sometimes they are members of the general public who want or need to use university facilities that may be open. Who can I talk to about how many visitors we have, on average?

Reviewing Your Invention and Research

For more on developing a thesis, see Chapter 13.

After you have conducted your research, review your invention work and notes, and think about the information you have collected from outside sources. You may be ready to decide on a working thesis statement—a statement that summarizes the main point of your analysis—at this point. Even though you might already have a general idea of the conclusion your analysis is leading you to, until you get

Strategies FOR Success   Persistence

Successful writers are persistent. They don't accept quick or easy answers. Instead, they take the time to delve deeply and thoughtfully into their subject. Since effective analytical writing is thorough, using persistence to examine and explain as many details as possible is necessary. If you are working in a field that has particular procedures in place, you have an obligation to use persistence in following the accepted procedures faithfully. For example, if you are working in a scientific field, you will need to document everything you do—from taking notes on your process, to constructing drawings that illustrate the process, to verifying measurements with specific instruments. You also must clearly and accurately present any statistical data, with all supporting evidence and detail, and you must explain relationships between variables in your experiment.

some of your ideas and research down on paper, it is often difficult to know what your thesis will be. It is helpful to decide on your thesis after you have done your invention work (listing, brainstorming, and clustering, for example) and research.

Organizing Your Information

When you have some sense of what your analysis will include, consider how you might organize this material. Here are some questions to ask yourself when deciding on your organization:

- Who is your audience?
- Why might they be interested in your analysis, or how can you make them interested in it?
- What is your purpose for writing—that is, why do your readers need this analysis?
- What is the most important aspect of your subject?

The answers to these questions can help you decide what you need to emphasize, which in turn will help you choose an organization.

Here are three organizational structures that you might consider.

For more on cause and effect, see Chapter 10; for more on classification, see Chapter 13.

Options FOR Organization
Options for Organizing an Analysis

Defining Parts	Classification	Relating Causes and Effects
Explain why the subject you are analyzing is important to your readers.	Start with a question about your subject that readers probably do not know the answer to.	Begin with information about your subject that may surprise your readers.
Provide examples of how readers might be affected by the subject.	Explain why knowing the answer to this question will benefit your readers.	Explain how an analysis of your subject will lead to more surprises and better understanding.
Provide background information so readers can see the whole subject of your analysis.	Use the writing strategy of *classification* to explain your subject, labeling and explaining each aspect or part.	Use the writing strategy of *cause and effect* to show how each aspect or part of your subject causes or is affected by the other aspects or parts.
Use a strategy of *description* to explain each aspect or part of your subject.	Provide specific examples to illustrate each category.	
Provide examples to show what you mean.	Conclude by showing how the aspects or parts function together to make up the whole of your subject.	Provide specific examples to show what you mean.
Conclude by showing how each aspect or part works with the others.		Conclude by outlining how parts of your subject function together.

Constructing a Complete Draft

Once you have chosen the most effective organizational approach, you are ready to construct your draft. Consider how you might use the invention materials you generated and how you might integrate the research information you gathered.

As you write your first draft, remember the main point that you are trying to make. In an analysis, you will want to make sure that your discussion of the aspects of your subject helps to support what it is that you are trying to say about the whole.

There are many ways to write a first draft. It may seem to make the most sense to you to start at the first sentence and then move to the end; however, many writers, once they decide on their organization, write individual pieces of their draft and then put them all together.

Synthesizing and Integrating Sources into Your Draft: Incorporating Numerical Data

When writers incorporate numerical data from sources, they do not need to enclose numbers in quotation marks because it is not possible to paraphrase numbers. However, if a writer uses the exact words of a source to comment on those data, then quotation marks are required. For example, in the essay "Campus Parking: Love It or Leave It" (pages 232–35), Sarah Washington includes numerical data, which she gathered from Michael Nguyen and from the Web sites of other universities. Notice that she reports the data without any commentary from Nguyen or anyone else. Therefore, readers can assume that the following section of her analytical essay includes the exact numbers that Nguyen provided, but that the words are Washington's:

> When I interviewed Mr. Michael Nguyen, head of Parking and Transit, he gave me the following background information:
> —A total of 13,845 students are registered this semester.
> —Of those, 6,735 live on campus.
> —A total of 2,700 resident students (that is, students who live on campus) have cars.
> —There are 512 full-time faculty members; 193 part-time faculty.
> —There are 398 staff employees.

Even though Washington does not quote Nguyen, she credits him as a source when she introduces the data. Of course, in her list of works cited at the end of the essay, Washington also includes information about the source:

> Nguyen, Michael. Personal interview. 12 March 2012.

When integrating numerical data into your writing projects, keep in mind the following guidelines:

1. Double-check the source to make certain that you have reported the data accurately.

2. Do not place numbers in quotation marks unless you include commentary from the source.

3. Indicate the source in the body of your text and in your list of works cited or references.

Parts of a Complete Draft

Introduction: Regardless of your organizational approach, begin with a strong introduction that captures your readers' attention and introduces the subject you are analyzing. To do so, you might use one of the following strategies:

- **Explain (briefly) why an analysis of your subject might be of interest.** In "Putting In the Hours" (pages 207–9), James Lang suggests that it might be interesting to consider the behavior of his subject, the North American college professor.
- **Provide a brief outline of what most people know about your subject.**
- **Explain (briefly) why your analysis is important.** In "The Power of Introverts" (pages 211–13), Susan Cain asserts that personality is as powerful a factor in life as gender and race. You may want to look at how the problem affects one person and then generalize to show how it affects many people.
- **Provide a fact about the subject you are analyzing that will surprise or concern your readers.**

Body: You can use various writing strategies to effectively analyze your subject:

- **Classify and label each aspect of your subject.** In "Putting In the Hours", James Lang organizes his descriptions of professors and their offices by labeling them: the "Early Bird," the "Door Closer," the "Chatterer," and so on. He then describes each type. In "The Power of Introverts," Susan Cain uses the classifications of "introversion" and "extroversion" and then lists some of the traits that define the two terms.
- **Define the various parts of your subject—explaining what each is and how it relates to the other parts.** If you were to analyze a smartphone, for example, you would probably focus on the input options (keypad or touch screen), texting and phone capability, audio, video, and web-browsing capability.
- **Compare and contrast each aspect of your subject, so readers can see the differences and similarities.** For instance, you might compare the functional features of two smartphones.
- **Focus on the cause-and-effect relationship of each aspect of your subject,** to show how one aspect causes, or is caused by, one or more other aspects. This approach would work well if you were analyzing a complex machine such as a car or an airplane.

For more on classification, definition, comparison and contrast, and causal analysis, see Chapter 13.

Conclusion: In your conclusion, review the major parts or aspects of your subject, explaining the following:

- How they relate to one another
- How they function together
- How all of the aspects of your subject lead to the conclusion you have reached

Title: As you compose your analysis, a title may emerge, but often it will not occur to you until late in the process. Because an analysis is by definition complex, you may not be able to summarize your main ideas in your title, but it should be something that catches your readers' attention.

VISUAL *Thinking* | Going Beyond Words to Achieve Your Goals

	Lots	Garages
MySchool	$200	$250
Texas	312	602
UAB	220	340
UTEP	140	295

You might discover that an effective way to show your analysis is by means of a chart or graph such as a flowchart, a pie chart, a bar graph, or a line graph. For example, Sarah Washington collected data when she was doing research for her analysis of campus parking. The data at the left is information Washington discovered about costs for parking at her school and three others. While collecting this data, she realized that comparing parking costs is difficult because some schools have a variety of parking options. This data reflects schools that offer both surface lots and parking garages.

If you wanted to show these data in a graph, you could present them in several ways. A line graph would look like this:

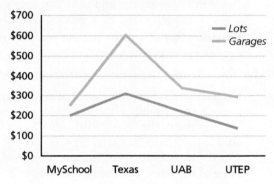

If you displayed the same data in a bar graph, the visual would look like this:

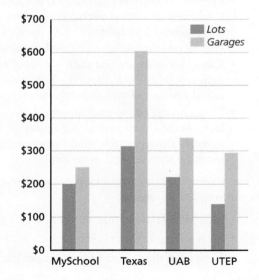

- What type of chart or graph most effectively shows and explains how the parking costs at Washington's school compare to costs at other schools? Why?
- How would it affect your audience's understanding if you used more than one kind of chart or graph in your analysis?

Using Excel to Convert Data into Visuals

If you are using numbers and quantities as support for your analysis, working with a spreadsheet program like Microsoft Office Excel can be most effective. The Excel program can quickly convert your data into tables, graphs, and charts. If you are taking a class that uses advanced spreadsheet software such as SPSS (originally Statistical Package for the Social Sciences), you may want to use it for creating charts and graphs that illustrate data you are including in your project.

Sarah Washington's First Draft

Sarah Washington decided to start her first draft with a portion of her original freewriting as an opening paragraph. Note also that she uses headings for her report, which is excerpted below.

Because this is a first draft, Washington did not worry about errors in usage, grammar, punctuation, or spelling. She concentrated on getting her ideas down. (The numbers in circles refer to peer comments, which follow the draft on page 229.)

Writing Activity

Constructing a Complete Draft

U sing the writing you did when selecting an organizational approach, write a complete draft of your analytical paper. Remember that your analysis will likely evolve as you write.

Campus Parking: Love It or Leave It
Sarah Washington

Like many others, I've been frustrated by the parking situation since I first started school here. . . . Every year it seems as though the parking fees go up, and every year it seems as though it's harder to find a good parking spot.❶

I finally decided to do something about it. I started by going to the Student Government Office to see if they had information on why the parking was so bad on this campus and what they were planning to do about it. I was told the best person to talk with was Michael Nguyen, the head of our parking department.

Campus Data

I interviewed Mr. Nguyen and received the following background information:

There were 13,845 total students enrolled this semester. Of that total, 6,735 live on campus. 2,700 of the resident students have cars. There are 512 full-time faculty and 193 part-time faculty. In addition, there are 398 staff people who work at the university.❷

Analysis

Looking at those numbers, I was able to make the following quick determinations. If everyone drove themselves to campus and needed to be there at the same time, the campus would need 10,913 parking spots (the total of all the faculty and staff and students who are either nonresidential or have cars). That means the university would have to be looking at close to 11,000 parking spots, which is especially important because Nguyen told me that the campus presently has 6,100 parking spots.

My initial response was no wonder I always felt I could never find a parking spot.③ However, I soon realized that even at 9:00 am on Monday not every one of those 11,000 people will be on campus and not everyone drives. I knew I had friends who lived in apartments close enough to campus that they walked to class. And, after talking to Nguyen, I realized that not only are all students not on campus at the same time, but all faculty aren't necessarily on campus at the same time either. In addition, some students, and to a lesser degree, faculty and staff, carpool. All of these variables act to reduce the number of parking spaces that is really needed.

We can get a better idea of how great the need really is by looking④ at the following scenario. By looking at staff surveys done by the Parking Office, we learn that 15% of the staff either carpool or use some other means of transportation. That gives us around 340 spots that are necessary to support employees not counting the faculty.

If we then assume, at the busiest time of day, 60% of the full time faculty and 50% of the part time faculty need to be on campus, and they all drive their own vehicles and don't carpool, that will cause us to have an additional need of around 410 spots.

It may be more difficult to determine the real number of spots that students need. However, if we assume that at the time of highest traffic, 70% of students are there, we can see there will then be a need for approximately 5,000 student spaces—not counting the necessary 2,700 spaces by the resident halls.

Adding all of these numbers, we discover that the campus may need around 8,450 parking spots, or a little more than 76% of the initial estimate of more 11,000 spots. It also becomes evident that the campus really can use a lot more parking at peak periods—not my initial thought of 4,900 spots. . . .

Conclusion

I also became acutely aware that determining how many parking spots are needed is not an exact science. There are many variables and they may change from semester to semester. In addition to the raw numbers, I discovered that part of the problem exists as a result of the desirability of the lots. Everyone wants to be close to where they're going, but that "where" keeps changing. During the morning, students all want to park in the lots closer to the academic buildings where their classes were being held. Later in the day, more vehicles could be found in the lot that serves the student union and the library. One thing that might help is simply having students plan their days on campus a little better. For example, if they have classes in the morning and plan on staying on campus for most of the day, they might have a much easier time looking for a parking spot over by the library rather than the classroom buildings. ⑤

Student Comments on Sarah Washington's First Draft

① "Interesting introduction, but I'm not sure what the purpose of your paper is. Are you going to try to inform readers of parking problems or persuade us to do something?"

② "These numbers are confusing like this—maybe put them into a list?"

③ "Also interesting, but you have a lot of your personal feelings in your paper. If I understood your paper's purpose, I'd know better whether it's appropriate for them to be in it."

④ "Who is 'we' here? I'm not sure why you're using 'we'—sounds strange."

⑤ "Now you're ending, and you're back to the number of parking spaces, without ever explaining what all that information about parking has to do with anything."

Revising

Many writers find that it is useful to let their work "sit" for a time—to put it aside for a day or two and then revise it. When you approach your work this way, you will find it easier to notice parts that are not explained in enough detail, or examples that are confusing, or places where an illustration or graph might show what you mean more clearly than the text does.

As you revise your early drafts, wait before doing any editing. When you revise, you will probably change the content and structure of your paper, so time spent working to fix problems with sentence style or grammar, punctuation, or mechanics at this stage is often wasted.

When you reread the first draft of your analysis, here are some questions to ask yourself:

- What else might my audience want or need to know about my subject?
- How else might I interest my audience in my analysis of this subject?
- What did I find out about my subject that I did not include in my paper?
- Have I clearly explained any terms my readers might not know?
- Could some aspects of my analysis be better presented as a graph or chart?

Use your word processor's track-changes tool to try out revisions and editing changes. After you have had time to think about the possible changes, you can "accept" or "reject" them. Also, you can use your word processor's comment tool to write reminders to yourself.

WRITER'S *Workshop* | Responding to Full Drafts

Working in pairs or groups of three, read one another's papers, and then offer your classmates comments that will help them see both their papers' strengths and places where they need to develop their ideas further. Use the following questions to guide your responses to the writer's draft:

- What is your first impression of this draft? How effectively does the title draw you into the paper? Why?

- What do you like about the draft?

- What is effective about the introduction? What suggestions can you make on how to improve it?

- How well do you understand what the author is trying to do in this paper? Does the paper wander a bit? Where? What questions are left unanswered?

- How has the writer demonstrated an awareness of readers' knowledge, needs, and/or expectations for the analysis?

- How effective is this paper as an analysis? How has the writer covered—or failed to cover—all of the parts or aspects of the subject adequately? What *other* aspects of the subject should be included?

- What is your opinion of the author's insight into the subject? How meaningful is it?

- What do you think is the author's thesis or main claim for the analysis? How could it be expressed or supported more effectively?

- In the main part of the paper, are there parts that are confusing or concepts that are unclear? Where would you like more details or examples to help you see what the author means?

- Is the writer's tone straightforward and neutral?

- How accurate and appropriate is the supporting evidence? Are there any questionable statistics, inaccurate facts, or questionable authorities? How clearly does the author indicate the sources for statistics and other supporting information?

- How well does the conclusion tie everything together?

- If there are visual aspects of the document, how effectively do they illustrate the point being made?

- What do you see as the main weaknesses of this paper? How might the writer improve the text?

Because it is so difficult to see emerging writing with a fresh eye (even for experienced writers), it is almost always useful to ask classmates, friends, or family members to read drafts of your papers and comment on them.

Responding to Readers' Comments

Once they have received feedback from peers, teachers, and others, writers have to decide how to deal with those comments and suggestions. It is important to consider carefully what your readers are saying to you. You may decide to reject some comments, of course, because they are not consistent with your goals for your paper. For example, some readers may disagree with your point of view or conclusion. You may find that comments from more than one reader contradict each other. In that case, use your own judgment to decide which reader's comments are on the right track.

In the final draft of Sarah Washington's paper, on pages 232–35, you can see how Washington responded to readers' comments, as well as to her own review of her first draft.

 KNOWLEDGE OF CONVENTIONS

When effective writers edit their work, they attend to the conventions that will help readers. These include genre conventions, documentation, format, usage, grammar, punctuation, and mechanics. By attending to these conventions in your writing, you make reading a more pleasant experience for your audience.

 Editing

The last task in any writing project is editing—the final polishing of your document. When you edit and polish your writing, you change your sentence structures and word choices to improve your style and to make your writing clearer and more concise. You also check your work to make sure it adheres to conventions of grammar, usage, punctuation, mechanics, and spelling. Use the spell-check function of your word-processing program, but be sure to double-check your spelling personally. If you have used sources in your paper, make sure you are following the documentation style your instructor requires.

See Chapter 20 for more on documenting sources.

As with overall revision of your work, this final editing and polishing is most effective if you can put your text aside for a time and come back to it with fresh eyes. It also helps to ask classmates, friends, and tutors to read your work as well.

To assist you with editing, we offer here a round-robin editing activity focused on finding and correcting problems with wordy sentences, a constant challenge for many writers (See page 232.)

Genres, Documentation, and Format

If you are writing an academic paper, follow the conventions for the discipline in which you are writing and the requirements of your instructor. If you are constructing a formal business report for Scenario 3, follow the model for a business analysis report.

If you have used material from outside sources, including visuals, credit those sources, using the documentation style required by the discipline you are working in and by your instructor.

For advice on writing in different genres, see the Appendix C. For guidelines for formatting and documenting papers in MLA or APA style, see Chapter 20.

WRITER'S *Workshop* | Round-Robin Editing with a Focus on Wordiness

Wordiness—using more words than necessary—is a common concern for writers and their readers. Wordy sentences take longer to read, and having a large number of them in your paper will increase your reader's workload and decrease your paper's effectiveness.

Work with two peers to edit one another's papers for wordiness. Ask yourself questions like "Is the writer repeating herself?" and "Has the writer included phrases that don't add meaning to the sentence?" Circle sentences that can be made more concise, and make suggestions on how to tighten them. Compare notes to see if you have any questions about wordiness, and ask your instructor for assistance.

A Writer Achieves Her Goal: Sarah Washington's Final Draft

After meeting with peer reviewers, Sarah Washington continued to revise her paper and eventually constructed a finished draft. The final draft of "Campus Parking: Love It or Leave it" follows. As you read the essay, think about what makes it effective.

SARAHWASHINGTON

ANALYTICAL ESSAY

Campus Parking: Love It or Leave It

One classmate wrote this comment on Washington's paper:

Interesting introduction, but I'm not sure what the purpose of your paper is. Are you going to try to inform readers of parking problems or persuade us to do something?

In her revision, Washington clearly indicates what she is trying to accomplish: to analyze the parking situation.

L ike many others, I've been frustrated by the parking   1
situation since I first started school here. While talking to other students, I've discovered that we're all not very happy about the parking. It's too expensive, and there are never enough spots. I've talked to other students who are juniors and seniors, and they say it's been like this since they started. Every year it seems as though the parking fees go up, and every year it seems as though it's harder to find a good parking spot. An analysis of the parking situation on campus will help anyone concerned with parking (and that includes most students) understand how parking "works" at our college. I am focusing my analysis on two aspects of campus parking: the number of spaces, including how many spaces are actually needed, and also the costs for parking on campus, especially compared to what other colleges charge.

Campus Data

When I interviewed Mr. Michael Nguyen, head of Parking and Transit, he gave   2
me the following background information:

A total of 13,845 students are registered this semester.

Of those, 6,735 live on campus.

A total of 2,700 resident students (that is, students who live on campus) have cars.

There are 512 full-time faculty members, 193 part-time faculty.

There are 398 staff employees.

Analysis

Looking at the numbers Mr. Nguyen provided, I was able to make the following quick determinations. If everyone drove to campus and needed to be there at the same time, the campus would need 10,913 parking spots (the total of all the faculty, staff, and students who are either nonresidential or have cars). That means the university would have to provide close to 11,000 parking spots, or around 4,900 additional spots. This is especially important because, according to Nguyen, the campus presently has 6,100 parking spots.

However, even at 9:00 a.m. on Monday not every one of those 11,000 people will be on campus, and not everyone who is on campus drives. I have friends who live in apartments close enough to campus to allow them to walk to class. And, after talking to Nguyen, I realized that not only are all students not on campus at the same time, but all faculty aren't necessarily on campus at the same time either. In addition, some students, and to a lesser degree, faculty and staff, carpool. All of these variables act to reduce the number of parking spaces really needed on campus. Clearly we need further analysis to understand the severity of the parking problem.

Staff surveys done by the Parking office indicate that 15% of the staff either carpool or use some other means of transportation. Therefore, around 340 spots are necessary to support employees, not counting the faculty. If we then assume that, at the busiest time of day, 60% of the full-time faculty and 50% of the part-time faculty need to be on campus, and they all drive their own vehicles and don't carpool, then the campus will need around 410 additional spots.

It may be more difficult to determine the real number of spots that students need. However, assuming that at the time of highest traffic there are 70% of the nonresident students present on campus, we can estimate that those students need parking. At these times, then, the campus will need approximately 5,000 student spaces—not counting the necessary 2,700 spaces by the resident halls.

Adding all of these numbers, we determine that the campus may need in the neighborhood of 8,450 parking spots, or a little more than 76% of the initial estimate of more 11,000 spots. It is evident that the campus really can use some more parking at peak periods, perhaps as many as 2,300 spots—not my initial estimate of 4,900 spots.

Parking Costs

This analysis reveals that the college is close to the number of parking spots it needs, but cost is another part of the whole campus parking picture. Parking on our campus—which for students runs $400 per year—seems to be in the midrange. Some universities such as Iowa State University only charge students

Washington responded to one of her peer reviewers by placing this information in a list to make it more readable.

In her earlier draft, Washington got this comment from one of her peer reviewers to this sentence from her first draft: "My initial response was no wonder I always felt I could never find a parking spot."

Also interesting but you have a lot of your personal feelings in your paper. If I understood your paper's purpose I'd know better whether it's appropriate for them to be in it.

Note that in her final version she has removed her personal comment as she continues to outline the details of her analysis.

A classmate asked this question and made this comment on Washington's draft:

Who is "we" here? I'm not sure why you're using "we" so much—sounds strange.

She revised her draft to cut back on her use of the word *we*, which also helped to make her sentences more concise.

$111 per year to park (Iowa State University). However, the University of Oregon charges students $750 for yearly parking (University of Oregon).

Other schools charge varying amounts: 9

The University of Nebraska: "perimeter parking " is $312 per year while "reserved parking" is $936 per year. There are two other levels, $504 and $612 per year, in between (University of Nebraska).

The University of Texas at Austin: students can park in surface lots for $120 or $180 a year, but if they want garage parking, it runs from $602 per year for commuters and $677 to $743 per year for residential students (University of Texas).

Parking costs at our school, it appears, are not out of line with other colleges.

We can look at the graph in Fig. 1 to see how our school's costs compare to some others when looking at the difference in costs for parking in surface lots and parking garages.

Conclusion

Determining how many parking spots are needed on a campus is not an exact   10
science. There are many variables involved and those variables may change from semester to semester. In addition to the raw numbers, I discovered that part of the problem with parking exists as a result of the desirability of the lots.

Fig. 1 The other schools, in addition to MySchool, are the University of Texas at Austin (Texas), the University of Alabama at Birmingham (UAB), and the University of Texas at El Paso (UTEP).

Everyone wants to be close to where they're going, but that "where" keeps changing. During the morning, students all seem to want to park in the lots closer to the academic buildings where their classes are being held. Later in the day, more vehicles can be found in the lot that serves the student union and the library. Students can help the situation by simply planning their days on campus a little better. For example, if they have classes in the morning and plan on staying on campus for most of the day, they might have a much easier time finding a parking spot over by the library rather than in crowded lots near the classroom buildings. Where parking is concerned, a little strategy can go a long way.

In her first draft, Washington received this comment from a classmate:

Now you're ending, and you're back to the number of parking spaces, without ever explaining what all that information about parking has to do with anything.

Note how she now offers a more effective conclusion to her text.

Washington has provided a synthesis of the information she has analyzed.

Works Cited

Iowa State University Parking Division. "2011–2012 Parking Permit Price List." Web. 28 March 2012. <http://www.parking.iastate.edu/permit/fees>.

Nguyen, Michael. Personal interview. 12 March 2012.

University of Alabama at Birmingham. "Parking." Web. 28 March 2012. <http://www.uab.edu/parking/parking/students/fees-location>.

University of Nebraska—Lincoln Parking and Transit Services. "Permit Costs." Web. 28 March 2012. <http://parking.unl.edu/permits/cost.shtml>.

University of Oregon Department of Public Safety Office of Parking and Transportation. "Permits." Web. 28 March 2012. <https://parking.uoregon.edu/content/permits>.

University of Texas at Austin. "Parking and Transportation Services." Web. 28 March 2012. <http://www.utexas.edu/parking/parking/student/>.

University of Texas at El Paso. "Parking and Transportation Services." Web. 28 March 2012. <http://admin.utep.edu/Default.aspx?tabid=50699>.

This paper follows MLA guidelines for in-text citations and works cited. Note that URLs are optional

UNDERSTANDING A WRITER'S GOALS: QUESTIONS TO CONSIDER AND DISCUSS

Rhetorical Knowledge: The Writer's Situation and Rhetoric

1. **Audience:** What audience does Washington have in mind for this essay? How can you tell?

2. **Purpose:** What can you point to in Washington's paper that indicates her purpose?

3. **Voice and tone:** How would you describe the tone Washington uses in her paper? Would a different tone (more strident, perhaps, or more subdued) have made her analysis more, or less, effective? Why?

4. **Responsibility:** How accurately does Washington represent statistical information? How credible is Washington's analysis? Why?

5. **Context, format, and genre:** Washington is writing as a college student concerned about parking on her campus. How does this context affect her use of language, and evidence in her analysis? Washington chose to write her analysis as an informal report. What impact does this genre have on you as a reader? Can you explain how by using this genre Washington's paper is more or less understandable than if she had chosen to just write an essay?

Critical Thinking: The Writer's Ideas and Your Personal Response

6. What is your initial response to Washington's analysis? What in her text causes your response?

7. To what extent does Washington's report give you insight into how parking might work at other public places serving large groups of drivers?

Composing Processes and Knowledge of Conventions: The Writer's Strategies

8. Construct a brief outline of Washington's analysis. How effective is her organization? Why?

9. How effectively does Washington use statistics or data to support her claims?

Inquiry and Research: Ideas for Further Exploration

10. At your library, find a journal or magazine that covers the area you think you want to major in, and locate an example of an analysis. In no more than two pages, explain why that text is or is not an effective analysis.

Self-Assessment: Reflecting on Your Goals

Now that you have constructed a piece of analytical writing, go back and consider your learning goals. Write notes on what you have learned from this assignment.

 ### Rhetorical Knowledge

- *Audience:* What have you learned about addressing an audience in analytical writing?
- *Purpose:* What have you learned about the purposes for constructing an analysis?
- *Rhetorical situation:* How did the writing context affect your analytical text? How did your choice of topic affect the research you conducted and the way you presented your analysis to your readers? What do you see as the strongest part of your analysis? Why? The weakest? Why?
- *Voice and tone:* How would you describe your voice in this essay? Your tone? How do they contribute to the effectiveness of your analysis?

 ### Critical Thinking, Reading, and Writing

- *Learning/inquiry:* What process did you go through to focus on a main idea, or thesis? How did you judge what was most and least important?
- *Responsibility:* How did you fulfill your responsibility to your readers?
- *Reading and research:* What did you learn about analytical writing from the reading selections you read for this chapter? What research did you conduct? How sufficient was the research you did?
- *Skills:* As a result of writing this analysis, how have you become a more critical thinker, reader, and writer?

Writing Processes

- *Invention:* What invention strategies were most useful to you?
- *Organizing your ideas and details:* What organization did you use? How successful was it?
- *Revising:* What one revision did you make that you are most satisfied with? Why? If you could make an additional revision, what would it be?
- *Working with peers:* How did your instructor or peer readers help you by making comments and suggestions about your writing? How could you have made better use of the comments and suggestions you received?
- *Visuals:* Did you use photographs or other visuals to help explain your analysis to readers? If so, what did you learn about incorporating them?
- *Writing habits:* What "writerly habits" have you developed, modified, or improved on as you completed the writing assignment for this chapter?

 ## Knowledge of Conventions

- *Editing:* What sentence problem did you find most frequently in your writing? How will you avoid that problem in future assignments?
- *Genre:* What conventions of the genre you were using, if any, gave you problems?
- *Documentation:* Did you use sources for your paper? If so, what documentation style did you use? What problems, if any, did you have with it?

Refer to Chapter 1 (pages 12–13) for a sample reflection by a student.

Writing to Convince

CHOLULA, PUEBLA

Think of the last time you wrote something. Whether it was a formal academic paper, a letter, or an informal note such as a text message to a friend, your writing was most likely designed to convince someone about something—to persuade your reader that he or she should accept your particular point of view. In fact, most purposes for writing—to inform, to explain, to analyze—to some degree almost always involve persuasion.

You encounter **persuasive writing**—writing designed to convince readers to agree with the writer's position—many times a day. Notice, for example, the persuasive appeals in the advertisement here. The top line noting that Cholula, Puebla, has the "biggest pyramid in the world" and has "a church on top" is an ethical appeal because it shows that the ad writers are knowledgeable about the area's history and geography. At the same time, these historical details can be considered logical appeals because they are pieces of information. "The place you thought you knew" is, of course, an emotional appeal, as is the color photograph that

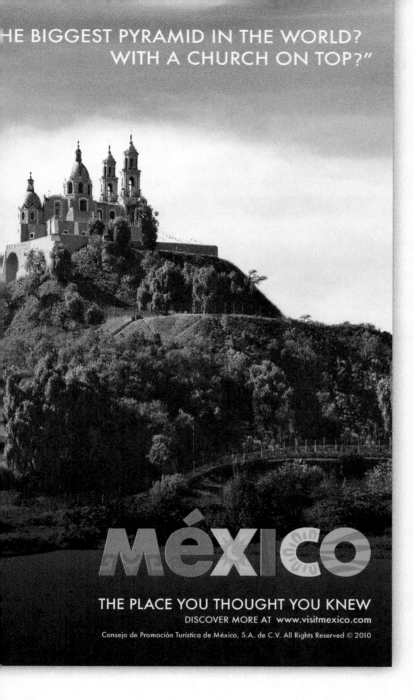

HE BIGGEST PYRAMID IN THE WORLD?
WITH A CHURCH ON TOP?"

MÉXICO

THE PLACE YOU THOUGHT YOU KNEW
DISCOVER MORE AT www.visitmexico.com

showcases the breathtaking beauty of Cholula. How effectively does this advertisement convince you to visit this place?

Advertisements, of course, are clearly intended to convince the reader to buy something—a product or service or trip to Mexico. For most of the persuasive writing you will do, you will have a more limited audience than the audience for an advertisement or a newspaper editorial, but the strategies that you will use to assert your point of view and persuade readers are the same.

Setting Your Goals for *Persuasive Writing*

Rhetorical Knowledge (pp. 242–46)

- **Audience:** When you write to convince your readers, your success depends on how accurately you have analyzed your audience: their knowledge of and attitudes toward your topic.
- **Purpose:** A convincing text is meant to persuade readers to accept your point of view, but it can also include an element of action—what you want readers to do once you've convinced them.
- **Rhetorical situation:** Think about all of the factors that affect where you stand in relation to your subject—you (the writer), your readers (the audience), the topic (the issue you are writing about), your purpose (what you wish to accomplish), and the exigency (what is compelling you to write your persuasive essay).
- **Voice and tone:** When you write to persuade, you are trying to convince readers to think or act in a certain way. The tone you use will influence how they react to your writing, so you should consider carefully how you want to sound to your readers. If your tone is subdued and natural, will that convince your readers? What if you come across as loud and shrill?
- **Context, medium, and genre:** Decide on the most effective medium and genre to present your persuasive essay to the audience you want to reach. Often, you can use photographs, tables, charts, and graphs as well as words to provide evidence that supports your position.

Critical Thinking, Reading, and Writing (pp. 246–59)

- **Learning/inquiry:** Writing to persuade helps you learn the important arguments on all sides of an issue, so such writing deepens your understanding.
- **Responsibility:** As you prepare to write persuasively, you will naturally begin to think critically about your position on the subject you are writing about, forcing you to examine your initial ideas, based on what you learn through your research. Persuasive writing, then, is a way of learning and growing, not just of presenting information.
- **Reading and research:** You will usually need to conduct interviews and online and library research to gather evidence to support the claims you are making in your persuasive writing.

Writing Processes (pp. 260–72)

- **Invention:** Use various invention activities, such as questioning or freewriting, to help you consider the arguments that you might use to support your persuasive essay or the opposing arguments you need to accommodate or refute.
- **Organizing your ideas and details:** Most often, you will state the main point—your thesis—clearly at the start of your persuasive essay and then present the evidence supporting that point. Other methods of organization are useful, however, depending on your audience and context.
- **Revising:** Read your work with a critical eye to make certain that it fulfills the assignment and displays the qualities of effective persuasive writing.
- **Working with peers:** Listen to your classmates as they tell you how much you have persuaded them, and why. They will give you useful advice on how to make your essay more persuasive and, therefore, more effective.

Knowledge of Conventions (pp. 272–73)

- **Editing:** Citing sources correctly adds authority to your persuasive writing. The round-robin activity on page 273 will help you edit your work to correct problems with your in-text citations and your works-cited or references list.
- **Genres for persuasive writing:** Possible genres include academic essays, editorials, position papers, letters to the editor, newspaper and magazine essays—even e-mails or letters you might send to friends or family members to persuade them about a problem or issue.
- **Documentation:** You will probably need to rely on sources outside of your experience, and if you are writing an academic essay, you will be required to cite them using the appropriate documentation style.

RHETORICAL KNOWLEDGE

When you write to persuade, you need to have a specific purpose in mind, a strong sense of your audience, and an idea of what might be an effective way to persuade that audience. You need to make a point and provide evidence to support that point, with the goal of persuading your readers to agree with your position.

Writing to Convince in Your College Classes

Many—if not most—of the papers you will be asked to write for your college classes will be persuasive. Although your college assignments will often specifically require that you inform or analyze, they will frequently include an element of persuasion. Here are some examples:

- In a literature course, your instructor might ask you to argue that the concept of the Oedipal complex is appropriate for analyzing Hamlet's behavior.
- Your sociology professor might ask you to develop and support a thesis about deviant behavior in prisons.
- Your mechanical engineering professor might ask you to argue for or against using a particular material in a specific situation.

Writing to Convince for Life

Although persuasive writing is common in college and university courses, it plays an even larger role in professional, civic, and personal settings. Consider these examples of professional writing:

- A product development team needs to convince company executives to manufacture a product it has designed and tested.
- An attorney needs to ask fellow members of the local bar association to work *pro bono* (for free) for a specific group.
- A division manager needs to convince the human resources manager to hire a particular applicant.

Civic leaders and other participants in the political process—mayors, city council members, school board members, town supervisors, volunteers, and ordinary citizens—are also constantly involved in persuasion. In fact, it is difficult to imagine a political process without persuasion as its major component. For instance, concerned citizens might write to their city council to argue that a stoplight needs to be installed at an intersection where many accidents have occurred.

In personal settings, you constantly negotiate with those around you as you make life decisions, often working to convince others that your views ought to be accepted or that your ideas are more effective than theirs. For example, you might write to persuade a family member to send you money for tuition. Or you might write to a friend or family member to encourage him or her to have a medical test if that person is having trouble making a decision.

The "Ways of Writing" feature presents different genres that can be used when writing to convince in college and in other areas of life.

Ways of Writing to Convince

Genres for Your College Classes	Sample Situation	Advantages of this Genre	Limitations of the Genre
History essay	Your world history professor asks you to construct a paper in which you argue that specific events caused the Iraq war of 2003.	Your research will provide documented details of what led up to the war. It will help your readers understand the causal relationships.	Your essay may not offer a broad enough overview to give readers an idea of the total picture.
Letter to your campus newspaper	Your political science professor asks you to send a letter to your college newspaper encouraging your classmates to change the form of student government.	Anything published in a college newspaper will have a wide audience of people who have an interest in campus affairs.	You will have to make your argument in a limited amount of space. It might not be published.
Editorial for your local newspaper	For your writing class, you are asked to construct an editorial responding to public criticism about your campus: students driving fast through neighborhoods, loud parties at student-occupied apartment buildings, and so on.	Editorials are read by a local audience and are therefore useful for convincing local readers about an issue that is important to them.	You will have to make your argument in a limited amount of space and without visuals. It might not be published.
Oral presentation	Your environmental science professor asks you to prepare a ten-minute speech that convinces your classmates to attend a rally for a community clean-up.	Talking to your audience gives you the opportunity to engage them and gauge their level of interest.	Some listeners will "tune out," so you have to work to keep their attention.
Genres for Life	Sample Situation	Advantages of the Genre	Limitations of the Genre
Brochure	With several of your neighbors, you decide to construct a brochure that presents the benefits of raising taxes for your local schools.	A brochure can provide a quick overview of the arguments in favor of a tax increase.	Your argument must be presented in a limited amount of space.
Business letter	Your business is moving to a neighboring state, and you want as many employees as possible to make the move with your company.	A letter is a personalized way to explain the benefits of the new location.	Asking employees to make such a move is a difficult task; a letter might be too brief to be convincing.
Poster	To encourage people to attend an upcoming school event, you construct a poster that you will copy and place in various locations on campus.	A poster is a visual way to get readers interested. Posters can be placed in many places, ensuring broad exposure to your message.	A limited number of people will actually see and read the posters.
Web site	You want to create a Web site that will convince your community to vote for a mayoral candidate.	Your Web site can provide useful information for a particular demographic that is otherwise difficult to reach.	Some readers will only skim a Web site, and some do not have access.
Job application cover letter	You need to construct a cover letter in response to a job ad.	A cover letter lets you discuss and explain your background and experiences in a positive way, specific to the particular job.	Your background might not be a good match for the job, forcing you to "stretch" in your letter.

Scenarios for Writing | Assignment Options

Your instructor may ask you to complete one or more of the following assignments that call for persuasive writing. Each of these assignments is a *scenario,* which gives you a sense of who your audience is and what you need to accomplish with your persuasive writing.

Starting on page 260, you will find guidelines for completing whatever scenario you decide—or are asked—to complete.

Writing for College

SCENARIO 1 **Academic Argument about a Controversial Issue**

What controversial issues have you learned about in other college classes? Here are some possibilities:

- Political science: In what ways did the controversy over the Affordable Care Act, passed by Congress early in 2010, affect the results of the 2010 election?
- Business ethics: How effective is the threat of criminal punishment in preventing insider trading of stocks?
- Psychology: How should the courts use the concept of insanity to determine culpability in criminal cases?

Writing Assignment: Select a controversial issue or problem from one of your classes, and compose a paper convincing readers in that class that your position on the issue is valid.

SCENARIO 2 **An Oral Presentation on an Issue That Matters to You**

This scenario asks you to select an issue or a problem that matters to you and to construct and present a brief but convincing oral presentation to your class. Choose an issue that you are interested in, feel strongly about, and would like to explore in more detail. You can find some issues to choose from by filling in the blanks in these statements:

- I really wish someone would do something about _____.
- I'm always puzzled when I see _____.
- I hate it when someone tells me to _____.
- Downtown, _____ is a real problem.
- In the campus union, I wish they would _____.

As you construct your oral presentation, consider your audience. What might they already know about your subject? What are you trying to convince them of? Do you want them to take some action or simply to hear your argument? What kind of information (texts, statements, pictures, handouts) might be effective for this audience, your purpose, and your topic? What might be an effective way to present such information?

Writing Assignment: Construct a convincing oral presentation about an issue that is important to you. Your instructors will let you know if you can use PowerPoint and will provide a time limit for your presentation.

Writing for Life

SCENARIO 3   Civic Writing: An Editorial about a Campus—Community Problem

Every college campus has problems, ranging from scarce parking, to over-crowded computer labs, to under-age drinking, to too little community involvement. Some campus problems, such as too much traffic, extend into the surrounding neighborhoods.

Writing Assignment: Using the list of features of an editorial on page 254, write an editorial for your school newspaper in which you identify a campus problem that also affects the surrounding community and then persuade your readers that the problem exists and that it needs to be taken seriously. Although you need to do more than simply provide information about the problem (that is an informative paper, covered in Chapter 7), you do not need to suggest detailed solutions to the problem (that is a proposal, covered in Chapter 12). Your goal is to convince your readers that your campus has a problem and that this problem has a negative impact on the surrounding neighborhoods.

Underage drinking is an issue on many college campuses.

Rhetorical Considerations in Persuasive Writing

Audience: Although your instructor and classmates are your initial audience for this assignment, you might also consider other audiences for your persuasive writing. What would you like them to believe or do? How might they respond to your argument? How might you best convince them?

Purpose: Your main purpose is to make your audience aware of the issue and to convince them that it is significant and that your position is the most reasonable one. How can you achieve this goal? You might also want to convince them to *do something* about it. What are different ways to accomplish this goal?

Voice, tone, and point of view: Why are you interested in the issue? What are your attitudes toward the issue and the audience? How will you convey those attitudes to your audience?

Context, medium, and genre: Although you are writing this persuasive paper to fulfill a college assignment, most issues worth writing about are important beyond the classroom. How might your views make a difference to your community? Keeping the context of the assignment in mind, decide on

For more on choosing a medium and genre, see Chapter 17.

the most appropriate medium and genre for your writing. If you are writing for an audience beyond the classroom, consider what will be the most effective way to present your argument to this audience. You might write an e-mail message to a friend, prepare a memo for colleagues at work, or write a brochure or op-ed piece for members of your community.

 # CRITICAL THINKING, READING, AND WRITING

As we have seen, effective persuasive writing focuses on an issue and provides sufficient and compelling evidence to convince readers that the writer's position on that issue is correct, or at least worthy of respect. Before you begin to write your own persuasive paper, read one or more persuasive essays to get a feel for this kind of writing.

Learning the Qualities of Effective Persuasive Writing

Much of the writing that you do is intended to convince someone to agree with you about something, typically about an issue. An **issue** is a subject or problem area that people care about and about which they hold differing views. Issues of current concern in the United States include tax cuts, campaign finance reform, and school vouchers. Subjects about which people tend to agree—for example, the importance of education in general—are not usually worth writing arguments about.

Persuasive writing that achieves the goal of convincing readers has the following qualities:

- Presentation of the issue. Present your issue in a way that will grab your readers' attention and help them understand that the issue exists and that they should be concerned about it. For example, if you are attempting to convince buyers to purchase smartphones with antivirus protection, you first need to demonstrate the prevalence of smartphone viruses. Another way to present the issue is to share an anecdote about it or to offer some statistics that clearly demonstrate the existence and danger of viruses.

- A clearly stated, arguable claim. A **claim** is the assertion you are making about the issue. Your claim should be clear, of course; a confusing claim will not convince readers. Any claim worth writing about also needs to be arguable: a statement about which reasonable people may disagree. For example, "All smartphone users should purchase antivirus software" is an arguable claim; a reader could disagree by saying, "Smartphone viruses are not a major threat." However, no one would disagree with the statement "Computer viruses can be annoying and disruptive." Therefore, it is not arguable and so is not an effective claim for a piece of persuasive writing.

- An awareness of audience. **Because your task as a writer is to convince other people, it is crucial to be aware of the needs, situations, and perspectives of your audience. In any audience, you can expect some members to be more open to your claim than others:**

  - If someone already agrees with you, persuasion is unnecessary.
  - If someone mildly disagrees with you or is undecided, persuasion has a good chance of working.
  - If someone strongly disagrees with you, there is little chance that persuasion will work.

  Savvy writers devote their time and energy to addressing the second group of readers. It's usually not an effective use of time to address the first or third groups.

- Convincing reasons. **Writers of convincing arguments offer support for what they are asking their reader to believe or to do. Think of the reasons you use to support your point as the other part of a *because* statement, with the claim being the first part. Here's an example: "Animal fur should not be used in clothing *because* synthetic fur is available and looks like real fur."**

- Sufficient evidence for each reason. **After considering the degree to which the audience agrees or disagrees with your claim, provide enough evidence, and the right kind(s) of evidence to convince your readers and, if applicable, persuade them to act accordingly. Evidence includes statistics, expert opinion, examples, and anecdotes (stories).**

- Appeals based on the writer's logic, emotion, and character. **Effective persuasive writers carefully decide when to use three kinds of appeals— *logos* (appeals based on logic), *pathos* (appeals to the audience's emotions), and *ethos* (appeals based on the writer's character or credibility). Appeals based on logic are generally the most effective. Emotional appeals can be effective with audience members who are predisposed to accept your claims. Appealing to an audience's emotions is risky, however, because critical thinkers will reject this type of appeal unless it is accompanied by logical and ethical appeals. Appeals based on the writer's authority and credibility—ethical appeals—can be powerful, especially when coupled with logical appeals.**

ELECTRONIC ENVIRONMENTS) **Political-Discussion Posts**

One way to see argumentation and persuasion in action is to look at political-discussion posts on news Web sites. Choose a topic thread or news article, and as you skim or read the posts, ask yourself three questions about each post: (1) How much credibility does the writer seem to have on the topic he or she is discussing (ethos)? (2) How does the writer use factual information and logic to make his or her points (logos)? (3) What is your emotional reaction to the writer's remarks (pathos)? You can determine the weight a writer's comments probably carry with others by assessing that writer's credibility, reasoning, and emotional integrity. Be sure to assess the language writers use in response to each other as well.

For more on strategies for argument, including dealing with opposing views, see Chapter 14.

- **An honest discussion of other views.** For any arguable claim or thesis, there will be at least one other point of view besides yours. To be effective, the writer of a persuasive text needs to acknowledge and deal with possible objections from the other side. You already make this kind of **counterargument** naturally. For example, when you are told that you "cannot register for this course because you have not completed the prerequisite," you probably already have an answer to that objection such as, "You're right, but I received approval from the dean because of my prior professional experience."

  If you think that another perspective has merit, you should certainly *acknowledge* it and even *concede* that it is valid. Another possibility is a Rogerian approach (see Chapter 14), in which both sides negotiate a compromise position. Perhaps you can offer a compromise by incorporating aspects of the other perspective into your thesis. Of course, if other perspectives on your issue are without merit, you will need to *refute* them by indicating how they are inappropriate, inadequate, or ineffective.

- **A desired result.** The goal of persuasive writing is to convince readers to change their minds about an issue or at least to give your view serious consideration. Often the goal is to get your reader to act in some way—vote for a candidate, write a letter to the school board, or buy some product.

Reading, Inquiry, and Research: Learning from Texts That Persuade

The readings that follow are examples of persuasive writing. As you read the persuasive selections your instructor assigns, consider the following questions:

- What makes this selection convincing?
- To what extent am I convinced by the writer's reasons and evidence? Why?
- What parts of the selection could be improved? In what ways?
- How can I use the techniques of persuasive writing exemplified here in my writing?

MARIAN WRIGHT EDELMAN

Still Hungry in America

OPINION PIECE

"There were some times where, you know, we wouldn't have that much food, and I would tell my mom, 'I'm not hungry, don't worry about it,' and I lost a lot of weight. I remember I used to be a size five, and I went from a size five to a size zero," a New York high school senior said in December.

In 1967, a s a young civil rights lawyer in Mississippi, I was asked to testify before the Senate Subcommittee on Employment, Manpower, and Poverty in Washington about how the anti-poverty program in Mississippi was working. The Head Start program was under attack by the powerful Mississippi segregationist delegation because it was operated by church, civil rights, and Black community groups after the state turned it down. After defending the Head Start program, I told the committee I had become increasingly concerned about the growing hunger in the Mississippi Delta. The convergence of efforts to register Black citizens to vote, Black parents' challenges to segregated schools, the development of chemical weed killers and farm mechanization, and recent passage of a minimum wage law covering agriculture workers on large farms had resulted in many Black sharecroppers being pushed off their near feudal plantations, which no longer needed their cheap labor. Many displaced sharecroppers were illiterate and had no skills. Free federal food commodities like cheese, powdered milk, flour, and peanut butter were all that stood between them and starvation. I invited the Senators to come to Mississippi and hear directly from local people about the positive impact the anti-poverty program was making. They did.

Marian Wright Edelman, founding president of the Children's Defense Fund, has degrees from Spellman College and Yale Law School. She was the first African-American woman admitted to the Mississippi Bar. An activist for children's issues, she has convinced Congress to improve foster care, adoption policies, and child care. She has also advocated to protect children with disabilities, as well as children who are neglected, abused, and homeless.

In the following opinion piece, which appeared in the *Huffington Post* in February 2012, she writes to convince readers to take action to support federal programs that provide food to hungry children in America. As you read her opinion piece, consider whether she convinces you to support her cause.

I testified again with local community leaders in their subsequent hearing in Jackson—again sharing the desperate plight of hungry people—and urged the Senators to visit the Mississippi Delta with me to experience for themselves the hungry poor in our very rich nation, to visit the shacks and look into the deadened eyes of hungry children with bloated bellies, a level of hunger many people did not believe could exist in America. "They are starving and someone has to help them," I said.

Senator Robert Kennedy responded as did Senator Joseph Clark and   4
Republican Senator George Murphy. So in April 1967 they visited homes in
Cleveland, Mississippi, asking respectfully of each dweller what he or she had
had for breakfast, lunch, or dinner the night before. Robert Kennedy opened
their empty ice boxes and cupboards after asking permission. I watched him
hover, visibly moved, on a dirt floor in a dirty dark shack out of television-cam-
era range over a listless baby with a bloated belly from whom he tried in vain
to get a response. He lightly touched the cheeks, shoulders, and hands of the
children clad in ragged clothes outside who responded to his question "What did
you have for breakfast?" saying "We haven't had breakfast yet," although it was
nearly noon. And he tried to offer words of encouragement to their hopeless
mothers.

He kept his word to try to help Mississippi's hungry children and went   5
immediately to see Secretary of Agriculture Orville Freeman the next day and
urged him to get some food down there and to eliminate any charges for food
stamps for people who had no income. Robert Kennedy's pushing, passion, and
visibility helped set in motion a chain of events including a *60 Minutes* documentary on "Hunger in America" that led to reforms. But change was slow and
incremental. Secretary Freeman did not believe there were people in Mississippi with no income who could not afford to pay $2 for food stamps and sent his
own staff back with Peter Edelman, Robert Kennedy's legislative assistant, to
retrace the Senators' trip. A series of reports in ensuing months funded by the
Field Foundation and visits by doctors, including Robert Coles,[1] to examine poor
children in Mississippi and other southern states documented that hunger was
widespread not just in Mississippi but throughout the south and elsewhere in
America.

But as more months passed without enough federal response, I complained   6
in frustration during a visit with Senator Kennedy in Washington. When I told
him I was stopping in Atlanta to see Dr. King, he urged me to tell Dr. King to
bring the poor people to Washington to make hunger and poverty visible since
the country's attention had turned to the Vietnam War and put poverty and
hunger on the back burner. Dr. King responded positively and immediately, and
began planning for the campaign. After Dr. King's assassination, the Poor People's Campaign was carried on by his staff, and I moved to Washington to help
as Counsel and federal policy liaison. It was a watershed coming together of
White, Black, Native American, and Latino poor seeking jobs and adequate
income and an end to hunger.

Many have pronounced it a failure, but I differ and believe it made hunger a   7
national issue and set into motion a number of positive steps that led to major
expansions of the federal food safety net programs so many depend on today.

---

[1]Child psychiatrist and author who chronicled the struggle to integrate schools in the South during the 1960s.

After Robert Kennedy's assassination, the bipartisan McGovern committee continued hearings around the country, a range of hunger activists kept pushing the Nixon administration and Congress to improve the nutrition safety net, and President Nixon appointed a task force headed by Pat Moynihan, his Domestic Policy Advisor, which affirmed hunger was a major problem. President Nixon gave a speech saying hunger had no place in our rich land. A prod towards these steps was a second quiet Poor People's Campaign delegation, which came to Washington in 1969 and met with President Nixon and his Cabinet in the White House. In that meeting, Rev. Ralph Abernathy and other leaders urged action to end hunger, and President Nixon kept responding by saying he was seeking peace in Vietnam. A contentious press conference followed and a series of Congressional visits criticizing the President's weak response helped catalyze a series of steps, including a White House conference on nutrition and incremental expansions of child and family nutrition programs that made a huge difference for millions until they came under attack from Reagan administration budget assaults and attempts to eliminate a range of federal safety net programs.

8   Today, crucial programs like food stamps, the Women, Infants and Children (WIC) nutrition program, and school lunch, breakfast and summer feeding programs continue working to combat child and family hunger. Their implementation could be significantly improved, but in the current recession, they have proved to be indispensable lifelines for the millions of jobless families with no cash income in our rich nation—about six million or 1 in 50 Americans, the *New York Times* reported in 2010—for whom food stamps are the only defense against the wolves of hunger. Last year more Americans relied on food stamps to eat than at any time since the program began in 1939—*46 million*. Yet once again some voices are starting to wonder whether we *really* need robust anti-hunger programs in America, and whether there are *really* so many children out there who might otherwise go hungry. A recent skeptical *Wall Street Journal* article was titled "The Myth of Starving Americans."

9   The safety net has indeed made it harder to find starving children with bloated bellies like those Senator Kennedy met in Mississippi in 1967—thank God. But the quiet pangs of hunger and the documented signs of chronic malnutrition are still here, from rural Mississippi to inner cities to middle class suburbs where families have fallen on hard times. Hungry boys and girls are not imaginary figures like the fictional Dick and Jane but very real children like *Jane Soliternik*, a New York City high school senior and the recent recipient of a Children's Defense Fund's Beat the Odds® scholarship award. Jane has overcome many odds in her young life, including cardiac surgery, her father's death, and poverty—especially after her widowed mother was laid off from her job as a medical assistant during the Great Recession and couldn't find another job for more than two years. When unemployment benefits were exhausted, Jane and her mother lived on the Social Security payments Jane received following the

death of her father. Jane was already facing multiple challenges, and then hunger was added to the list: "There were some times where, you know, we wouldn't have that much food, and I would tell my mom, 'I'm not hungry, don't worry about it,' and I lost a lot of weight. I remember I used to be a size five, and I went from a size five to a size zero. So, you know, I try to not eat too much. I try to eat in school. They give me free lunch in school."

This makes Jane just 1 of 14 million children who participate in free or   10
reduced price school lunch programs during the year and are often "at nutritional risk" and go hungry when those meals aren't provided. Without this vital safety net, we might return to the scenes Senator Kennedy witnessed. Hunger in America is real and widespread and pretending hungry children do not exist or that families should be ashamed of their needs is shameful. Unemployed parents unable to find a job when jobs are scarce should not be blamed for their inability to put food on the table. Robert Kennedy always understood that in addressing the hunger emergency the real culprit was poverty and lack of jobs, wages, training, and education to provide hope for restless youths trapped into failure and jail rather than given opportunities. The same is true now. Until we solve that crisis, we will still have jobless parents, poor families, and hungry children in America. For now, when more than 16 million American children, one of every four children, are not sure where the next meal will come from, we have urgent work to do.

The Food Research and Action Council (FRAC) did release one small   11
piece of good news in January: a new poll showing American voters overwhelmingly oppose cutting food stamp assistance as a way to reduce government spending. "What this poll tells us is that, despite rhetoric and false claims about the program, Americans across the country see food stamps as a program that works and that is making a real difference for people," said FRAC President Jim Weill. "American voters won't tolerate hunger in our midst, and across party lines they support this valuable program." You and I need to make sure our leaders hear this message loudly and clearly.

UNDERSTANDING A WRITER'S GOALS: QUESTIONS TO CONSIDER AND DISCUSS

Rhetorical Knowledge: The Writer's Situation and Rhetoric

1. **Audience:** Who is the audience for this opinion piece? Whom is Edelman trying to convince?

2. **Purpose:** What is Edelman's primary purpose for writing this opinion piece? What does she want her audience to do?

3. **Voice and Tone:** How does Edelman's voice come through in this reading? What evidence supports your view of her voice?

4. **Responsibility:** How has Edelman responsibly presented the issue of hunger to readers?

5. **Context, format, and genre:** Edelman wrote this column for the *Huffington Post,* a widely read online newsmagazine that publishes many opinion pieces. Why do you think the *Huffington Post* published this particular one?

Critical Thinking: The Writer's Ideas and Your Personal Response

6. What do you find most interesting in Edelman's column? Why?

7. How do you respond to the details about Edelman's own experience? How do those details support or undermine her case?

Composing Process and Knowledge of Conventions: The Writer's Strategies

8. How does Edelman use quotations in her column?

9. What persuasive appeals does Edelman use—*logos, ethos, pathos*? How effectively does she use appeals? Why do you think so?

Inquiry and Research: Ideas for Further Research

10. Read other columns by Marian Wright Edelman. What do they have in common with this opinion piece?

GENRES *Up Close* **Writing an Editorial**

Writers use a range of genres to convince in professional, civic, and personal situations including editorials/opinion pieces, position papers, job reference letters, and business letters. Editorials are appropriate when you want to convince readers that you have a valid position on a controversial or debatable topic. An op-ed piece appears on the page opposite the editorial page in a newspaper or magazine; thus "op-ed" is short for "opposite editorial." However, it can also mean "opinions and editorials."

Features of effective op-eds or editorials include the following:

- They often respond to a previously published article in a newspaper.
- They are usually short (250–800 words).
- They include an opinion or stance.
- They make a point in the first few sentences.
- They indicate why the issue is important.
- They show respect for other points of view.
- They suggest or imply an action that readers can take.

As you read the following example of an editorial, consider in what ways Dowd's text matches the description above of an editorial or op-ed piece.

MAUREEN DOWD

Our Own Warrior Princess

EDITORIAL

Jennifer showed me her scar Friday. It's the most beautiful scar I've ever seen. A huge stapled gash on her stomach, shaped like the Mercedes logo. A red badge of courage. Jennifer is my niece, a 33-year-old lawyer. On Wednesday, she had half her liver taken out at Georgetown University Hospital to save the life of her uncle (my brother Michael), who had gotten hepatitis years ago from a tainted blood transfusion.

The complicated and risky operation for the two, side by side, went from 7:30 am. until after 10 pm. Then, when a Medivac helicopter arrived with a matching liver for another patient, the same team of doctors had to start on another emergency six-hour liver transplant.

The night nurse told Jennifer she was an oddity. "We don't see many live donors," she said. "Not many people are that generous."

Or brave. Jennifer's morphine drip wasn't attached properly the first night after the operation, and no one knew it. She felt pain, but didn't want to be a wimp by complaining too loudly. Instead, she was Reaganesque, cracking jokes and wondering where the cute doctors were.

She survived the first night after this excruciating operation au naturel, like Xena the Warrior Princess. If all goes well, her liver will grow whole again in several weeks, as will Michael's half.

Unlike her father, who charged people a nickel to see his appendix scar when he was 10, she let me look for free. As we sat in her room, watching Mariah Carey singing with a bare midriff on the "Today" show, I worried a little how she would take the disfigurement.

She's a fitness fanatic, who works as a personal trainer in her spare time. She's single, out in the cruel dating world. And we live in an airbrush culture, where women erase lines with Botox, wrinkles with lasers, and fat with liposuction. I told Jen scars are sexy; consider that

Maureen Dowd won the Pulitzer Prize for Commentary in 1999. In 1992, she received the Breakthrough Award from Women, Men and Media at Columbia University. She won the Matrix Award from New York Women in Communications in 1994. In 1996, she was named one of *Glamour's* Women of the Year. In 1992, she was also a Pulitzer Prize finalist for national reporting.

In the following column, which first appeared in the *New York Times* on June 1, 2003, Dowd writes in a personal way about organ donation—telling the story of what her niece, Jennifer, did to help her brother, Michael. Although persuasive writing most often uses facts, statistics, and hard evidence to make its case, as you read Dowd's column, consider how effective she is in using emotional appeals to persuade you. Is Dowd's column persuasive enough for you to sign up to be an organ donor? Why or why not?

Paragraphs 1 and 2: Description of Dowd's niece's transplant indicates the importance of the issue.

great love scene in "Lethal Weapon 3" when Mel Gibson and Rene Russo, as police officers, compare scars.

Jennifer has every quality of heart, spirit, mind and body a woman could want. She's smart, funny, generous, loyal, principled, great looking and, obviously, adventurous.   8

"Write a column about me," she smiled, tubes coming out of every part of her body, as I left her room.   9

Includes an opinion or stance.

I knew what she meant. She didn't want me to write about her guts, but to encourage others to have the guts to donate organs. When she came to, she asked for the green ribbon pin that encourages organ donation. Her exquisite doll-like transplant surgeon, Dr. Amy Lu, in white coat and black high-heeled mules, still on the job after 21 hours in the operating room, removed her pin and gave it to Jennifer.   10

Quotations from expert sources reinforce the importance of the issue.

As Neal Conan said on NPR Thursday: "More than 80,000 Americans are on waiting lists for organ donations, and most will never get them. Thousands on those lists die every year. One big reason for the shortage is that families are reluctant to give up their relatives' organs. Even when people filled out a donor card or checked the organ donor box on their driver's license, family members often refuse. The need is so acute and so frustrating that more and more doctors are wondering whether financial incentives might persuade some families to change their minds and save lives." (Iran has wiped out its kidney transplant wait by offering rewards.)   11

As the New York Organ Donor Network Web site notes: "One donor can save up to eight lives through organ donation and improve dozens of lives through corneal, bone, skin and other tissue transplants. Across the U.S., 17 men, women and children of all races and ethnic backgrounds die every day for lack of a donated organ."   12

I'm one of the scaredy-cats who never checked the organ donation box or filled out the organ and tissue donor card.   13

Usually short—this piece is under 600 words long.

Some people don't do it because they have irrational fears that doctors will be so eager to harvest their organs, they'll receive subpar care after an accident.   14

Suggested action is implied: fill out a donor card.

I had nutty fears, too, straight out of a Robin Cook medical thriller, that they might come and pluck out my eyes or grab my kidney before I was through with them.   15

On Friday, Michael's birthday, I got the card online, filled it out and stuck it in my wallet. If Jennifer is brave enough to do it alive, how can I be scared of doing it dead?   16

UNDERSTANDING A WRITER'S GOALS: QUESTIONS TO CONSIDER AND DISCUSS

Rhetorical Knowledge: The Writer's Situation and Rhetoric

1. **Audience:** How effective is Dowd in reaching the audience for whom this information is intended—someone reading the *New York Times* and perhaps interested in organ donation? What can you point to in Dowd's column to demonstrate what you mean?

2. **Purpose:** In what area of life (academic, professional, civic, personal) does "Our Own Warrior Princess" best fit? What is Dowd trying to convince the reader to believe or do? What can you point to in the column to support your opinion?

3. **Voice and tone:** What is Dowd's attitude toward people who don't offer to donate organs? How does she attempt to reach them?

4. **Responsibility:** Dowd's primary evidence consists of the story of her niece's sacrifice, which is an emotional appeal to her readers. How justified is Dowd's use of *pathos*—an appeal to readers' emotions? How effective is it? Why?

5. **Context, format, and genre:** Newspaper columns such as Dowd's have specific length limits (as compared to, say, an essay that might appear in a journal). How might such a form constrain Dowd? How might it benefit her?

Critical Thinking: The Writer's Ideas and Your Personal Response

6. How has Dowd's column affected your views about becoming an organ donor?

7. Consider other persuasive writing that you have read. In what way(s) are they similar to or different from Dowd's column?

Composing Processes and Knowledge of Conventions: The Writer's Strategies

8. How does Dowd establish her *ethos* in this article?

9. Dowd uses a personal story to make her point. How effective is this writing strategy? Why?

Inquiry and Research: Ideas for Further Exploration

10. What questions do you still have about organ donation? Where can you go to get answers to those questions?

Organ Donation

Although Allsup, Inc. is a corporation that assists people seeking Social Security benefits, it sometimes runs public-service campaigns, such as the one below for organ donation. Most readers would assume the mother in this photograph was donating an organ for her child. But what if it was the other way around? Would you support a child donating an organ to a parent? Why?

You're donating more than an organ. You're giving someone a second chance at life.

April is National Donate Life Month.

An estimated 77 people get organ transplants every day, yet more than 98,000 people are still waiting for organ, tissue, marrow and blood donors. During National Donate Life Month, we thank all those who have given the gift of life...and encourage everyone to register to become organ donors. This simple act today can give someone in need a lifetime of tomorrows.

Allsup
Life Reclaimed
www.allsup.com

UNDERSTANDING A WRITER'S GOALS: QUESTIONS TO CONSIDER AND DISCUSS

Rhetorical Knowledge: The Writer's Situation and Rhetoric

1. **Audience:** Who is the audience for this advertisement? What makes you think that?
2. **Purpose:** What language in the poster most clearly indicates the purpose of the advertisement?
3. **Voice and tone:** What attitude does Allsup have toward the audience?
4. **Responsibility:** To whom does Allsup seem to feel responsible?
5. **Context, format, and genre:** Advertisements that appear on posters or in other venues frequently include visual elements such as photos. What does the photo add to this advertisement?

Critical Thinking: The Writer's Ideas and Your Personal Response

6. How persuasive do you find this advertisement? Why?
7. How do the persuasive features of this advertisement compare to those in Maureen Dowd's editorial on pages 255–56?

Composing Processes and Knowledge of Conventions: The Writer's Strategies

8. Why does the advertisement include the numerical information that appears in the copy at the bottom?
9. Why does the advertisement use the relatively informal contraction "You're" instead of the more formal "You are"?

Inquiry and Research: Ideas for Further Exploration

10. Conduct a Web search to find other advertisements for organ donation. How do their appeals (*ethos, logos, pathos*) compare to the appeals in this advertisement?

WRITING PROCESSES

As you work on the assignment that you have chosen, remember the qualities of an effective and convincing persuasive paper, listed on pages 246–48. Also remember that while the activities listed below imply that writers proceed step-by-step, the actual process of writing is usually messier: You will keep coming back to your earlier work, adding to it, modifying the information to be more accurate as you conduct additional research and become more familiar with your issue.

If you are considering several issues for your persuasive text, put your notes into a separate computer document for each one. Once you determine the focus of your paper, it will be easy to access and use the notes on that issue.

Invention: Getting Started

The invention activities below are strategies that you can use to help you get some sense of what you already know about the issue you have chosen. Whatever invention method(s) you use (or that your instructor asks you to use), try to answer questions such as these:

- What do I already know about this issue?
- What is my point of view on this issue?
- Where might I learn more about this issue? What verifiable information is available?
- What might my audience already know? What might their point of view be?
- What do I know about my audience? What don't I know that I should know?
- What questions do I have about the issue?
- What are some other views on this issue?

For more on strategies for discovery and learning, see Chapter 4.

Doing your invention work in electronic form, rather than on paper, lets you easily use your invention work as you construct a draft.

 Writing Activity

Questioning and Freewriting

Spend a few minutes jotting down answers to the reporter's questions about your issue: *who, what, where, when, why,* and *how.* You may find that your answers to these questions lead to more questions, which will help you focus on additional aspects of your subject to research.

Then, using the answers you noted above, freewrite about *one side* of your issue for ten minutes. Then freewrite about the *opposing side* of your issue, again for ten minutes. This activity will help you better understand and appreciate the arguments on both sides.

Student writer Santi DeRosa read an article in his college paper about how female students help recruit male athletes for his school. DeRosa had concerns about the ethics of this practice, so he decided to respond by writing an essay on the issue for his writing class.

Santi DeRosa's Answers to the Reporter's Questions

Santi DeRosa might ask—and answer—the reporter's questions as follows:

- Who is involved? Whom do they affect, and how are they affected? Who has control over recruiting practices? Who might change the situation?

  Female students volunteer, and I wonder how people perceive this. How do the women feel about doing this? Who decides who gets to "volunteer"? What does the president of the university think about this?

- What do they do?

  They act as guides and escorts. Nothing sexual—or is there? I wonder how their boyfriends feel about their participation.

- Where does the recruiting occur?

  Taking someone to a local fast-food restaurant seems pretty harmless, while visiting other places may not.

- When does the recruiting happen? What sequence of events is involved?

  I think that recruiting is in the fall, but I'm not certain. How do the people get matched up? Do they work (escort) in groups, and if not, is there a chaperone?

- Why does this happen? Why are these particular students involved?

  How well does this form of "recruiting" really work? Some young men might be influenced if attractive young women showed them around the campus and the city. Why do the young women volunteer? They must get some satisfaction—a sense of civic responsibility and pride in the school, which is a good thing.

- How do the female students act when they are with the athletes? React?

  I need to find out more about the logistics of these recruiting visits. Do NCAA rules and regulations apply? How are the female students trained for this work?

Santi DeRosa's Freewriting

DeRosa also used freewriting to explore his ideas. A portion of his freewriting appears here:

Interesting that women are used to recruit male athletes here, and that they volunteer. Is this a good idea? Are the women being used and objectified? What if they want to do it? What if the whole process is pretty innocent? The newspaper sensationalized it, which bothers me. I can't think of what to write, I can't think—hey, do they use males to recruit female athletes? I need to find out about that. . . .

STUDENT WRITING EXAMPLES

Brainstorming (pp. 176, 350)
Freewriting (pp. 48, 135, 261, 396)
Criteria (p. 307)
Listing (p. 95)
Table (p. 49)
Answers to Reporter's Questions (p. 261)
Organization (pp. 96, 181)
Clustering (pp. 135, 305)
Interviewing (p. 220)
Research (pp. 137, 177, 222, 263, 308, 398)
Reflection (p. 12)

STUDENT WRITING EXAMPLES

Brainstorming (pp. 176, 350)
Freewriting (pp. 48, 135, 261, 396)
Criteria (p. 307)
Listing (p. 95)
Table (p. 49)
Answers to Reporter's Questions (p. 261)
Organization (pp. 96, 181)
Clustering (pp. 135, 305)
Interviewing (p. 220)
Research (pp. 137, 177, 222, 263, 308, 398)
Reflection (p. 12)

Exploring Your Ideas with Research

Research is critical to any persuasive text, for if you cannot provide evidence to support your position, you probably will not convince your reading audience.

Although you may be able to use information from your own experience as evidence, you will usually need to offer verifiable information from sources, such as facts, statistics, expert testimony, and examples.

To find evidence outside of your own experience that you need to support your claim, look for answers to the following questions:

For help with locating sources of information, see Chapter 19; for help with documenting your sources, see Chapter 20.

- What facts or other verifiable information can I find that will provide solid evidence to convince my readers to agree with my position?
- What expert testimony can I provide to support my claim? What authorities on my issue might I interview?
- What statistical data support my position?
- What are other people doing in response to this issue or problem?

The subject you focus on and the kind of essay you are constructing help to determine the research you conduct. For example, for the scenarios earlier in this chapter, you could conduct several kinds of research:

- For Scenario 1 (page 244), which asks you to focus on a controversial issue, assume that you have decided to write about whether the threat of criminal punishment helps to prevent insider trading of stocks. What kinds of research might you conduct? At your library, a search of business publications such as the *Wall Street Journal, BusinessWeek,* and *Forbes* would be a good place to start. But you could also interview some local business executives to get their perspectives for your paper. And you could interview local law enforcement officials and attorneys to get their take on whether the threat of punishment helps stop insider trading.
- For Scenario 3 (page 245), where you focus on a problem in your campus community, that same kind of local research—interviewing your classmates, for example—will provide useful information for your paper. Consider the comments you could get, for instance, if you were writing about an issue involving your classrooms, such as the condition of the building or the time classes are scheduled, or a campus issue, such as campus safety, student fees, or athletics. Speaking with campus officials and administrators will also give you useful information. In addition, a search of the campus newspaper archives in your college's library may provide good background information on your issue.
- One way to learn about other perspectives on your subject is to read online blogs or join e-mail lists that focus on your topic. These ongoing electronic conversations often can provide multiple perspectives and ideas on the issue you are writing about—which then can help you with your own thinking and research.

Writing Activity

Conducting Research

Using the list of qualities of effective persuasive writing, go through your invention activity notes to find the questions you still have and want to ask. Now is the time to determine the best way(s) to answer those questions. Would it be useful to:

- Conduct more library research in books?
- Interview people about your subject?
- Conduct more library research in journals?

Make a research plan. Where will you conduct your research, and when will you do so?

STUDENT WRITING EXAMPLES

Brainstorming (pp. 176, 350)

Freewriting (pp. 48, 135, 261, 396)

Criteria (p. 307)

Listing (p. 95)

Table (p. 49)

Answers to Reporter's Questions (p. 261)

Organization (pp. 96, 181)

Clustering (pp. 135, 305)

Interviewing (p. 220)

Research (pp. 137, 177, 222, 263, 308, 398)

Reflection (p. 12)

Student Example: An Excerpt from Santi DeRosa's Research

For my paper, I can use some of the details from the school newspaper's articles. Those articles offer a clear narrative account of recruiting activities. They also help to demonstrate that there is an issue.

I also found some information about the same kind of thing at Colorado State University (Lambert article).

I will need to research how to define the concept of "objectification," a term I've read about. I need to be clearer on this concept. I did check the *American Heritage Dictionary* through Dictionary.com and they had this great quotation under the word's definition that I could include in my paper:

> To present or regard as an object: "Because we have objectified animals, we are able to treat them impersonally" (Barry Lopez).

I like how that really connects to the point I'm trying to make in my paper.

Reviewing Your Invention and Research

After you have conducted your research, review your invention work and notes and the information you collected from outside sources. Once you have a general idea of the conclusion your research is leading you to, you can develop a "working" thesis statement: If you had to make a point now, based on what you have learned, what would it be? It is called a working thesis because your main point or thesis will inevitably change as you continue to conduct research and learn more. And, as you know, through the process of writing itself, you will

Writing Activity

Considering Your Research and Focusing Your Ideas

Using your research notes as a starting point, again use the reporter's questions of *who*, *what*, *where*, *when*, *why*, and *how* to get onto paper or into a computer file what you know about your issue. For example, if you were focusing on a campus-community problem, some of your research notes might look like these:

Who: Students and neighbors alike who are affected when lots of student cars are going through the neighborhood, often too fast, both when they come to campus and when they leave.

What: The biggest issues seem to be too many cars on neighborhood streets, too many of them speeding, and too many of them parking where they should not.

For more on deciding on a thesis, see Chapter 13.

learn about your topic, so give yourself permission to modify and develop this initial thesis statement as you draft and revise your text. Once you have written several drafts, received feedback on them, and revised them, you will be better able to determine what your final thesis statement should be.

Strategies FOR Success: Openness

Successful writers are open to new ideas and a wide range of perspectives. In writing to convince, openness is especially important because readers are more likely to accept your ideas if they think that you are open-minded. As you consider other perspectives, think about how they compare and contrast with your own ways of looking at the world. How does viewing an issue from another perspective enable you to see the world in new ways? If you find a new idea easy to accept, why is that the case? If you find a new idea difficult to accept, why is that so? If a perspective differs from yours, what distinguishes the two? What are the points of agreement? How can the two perspectives be combined to form yet another way of looking at the world?

Openness also applies to a writers' strategies for finding, gathering, using, and presenting information. For example, if you usually begin looking for information by doing a Google search, try a different approach, such as using some of the strategies described in Chapter 19, "Finding and Evaluating Information."

Open-minded writers listen to the ideas of others, and they consider the validity of those ideas without automatically ruling them out. An open-minded writer acknowledges opposing views and is willing to accept those that withstand critical scrutiny. Of course, it's important to know when to refute ideas that do not withstand critical analysis.

If you ignore or distort opposing views, readers will think you are either unaware or dishonest, which will quickly weaken or destroy your *ethos*—your credibility. Ignoring the other side of an issue, the objections that others might have to your point of view, actually weakens your position, as your readers may be aware of the objections and wonder why you did not deal with these other perspectives.

Organizing Your Information

Because the purpose of writing a persuasive text is to convince your readers to accept your point of view, you will need to organize your reasons and evidence strategically. The questions that you need to ask yourself when deciding on your organization are all rhetorical:

- Who is your audience? What is your readers' position on your issue likely to be? If they are undecided, you might try a classical or an inductive approach, both of which are discussed below. If they are likely to hold an opposing view, then a refutation approach, also discussed below, may be the better choice.

- Why might they be interested in your persuasive writing, or how can you make them interested in it?

- What is your purpose for writing—that is, why do you want to convince readers of this position?

When you construct a persuasive paper, determine the most effective organizational approach for your purpose and audience. One method of organizing an argument, called the *classical scheme*, was first outlined by Aristotle nearly 2,400 years ago. If you are using the classical scheme, this is the sequence you will follow:

See more on Aristotelian organization in Chapter 14.

> introduction → main claim → evidence supporting claim → discussion of other perspectives (acknowledging, conceding, and/or refuting them) → conclusion

Aristotle's approach is also called the **deductive method** because you state your claim and then help the reader understand, or deduce, how the evidence supports your claim. The advantage of this method is that you state your position and make your case early, before your reader starts thinking about other perspectives.

Another organizational approach is commonly known as the **inductive method.** When using this approach, you first present and explain all of your reasons and evidence, then draw your conclusion—your main claim. The advantage is that your reader may come to the same conclusion before you explicitly state your position and will therefore be more inclined to agree with your point of view.

Because persuasive writing must usually acknowledge and incorporate or refute opposing viewpoints, a third organizational method starts by presenting the views of the other side. In this method, you first deal with objections to your claim and then state your position and provide reasons and evidence to support it. This is an especially effective strategy if the opposing view or views are widely held.

Here are three organizational structures that you might consider for your persuasive paper.

Options FOR Organization
Organizing a Persuasive Paper

The Classical (Deductive) Approach	The Inductive Approach	The Refutation Approach
Introduce the issue and state your thesis.	Introduce the issue.	Introduce the issue.
Explain the importance of the issue.	Offer reasons and evidence for your claim.	List opposing views.
Present your reasons and evidence—why readers should agree with you.	Draw your conclusion—your main claim.	Deal with each objection in turn.
Answer objections—either incorporating or refuting other points of view.	Deal with other viewpoints either before or after presenting your claim.	Introduce your position and explain why it makes sense, offering reasons and evidence.
Conclude—often with a call to action.	Conclude—often with a call to action.	Conclude—often with a call to action.

Constructing a Complete Draft

Once you have chosen the best organizational approach for your audience and purpose, you are ready to construct your draft. After you have reviewed your invention writing and research notes, developed a working thesis, and carefully considered all of the reasons and evidence you generated, construct a complete first draft.

As you work, keep the following in mind:

- You may discover that you need to do more invention work and/or more research as you write.

- As you try out tentative claims and reasons, ask your classmates and other readers about the kinds of supporting evidence they consider convincing.

For more on choosing visuals, see Chapter 18.

- Consider whether photographs or other visuals might help support your thesis.

- If you become tired and the quality of your thinking or your productivity is affected, take a break.

Synthesizing and Integrating Sources: Incorporating Partial Quotes in Your Sentences

Often, your research will provide you with lots of quotations, which means you have to determine how to incorporate the quotations you want to use into your text. One way to use quotations, whether they come from a source you interviewed or from source you read, is to incorporate them into your sentences, a using a phrase such as "she said" or "Johnson comments":

> I interviewed Joy Watson and she said, "The recycling program is working."

Another method of incorporating a quotation is to integrate it into the structure of your sentence. For instance, in the following example, Santi DeRosa quotes Joe Watson from an article in the campus newspaper by integrating the quotation within his own sentence, and then he repeats part of the quotation that he wants to emphasize in his next sentence:

> The people interviewed for the article who support the "hostess" program defend it by saying that "the recruiters perform respectable duties during high school recruits' campus visits" (Watson). Does the responsibility of "performing respectable duties" end when they leave the campus for a party? (paragraph 5)

Using only part of the quotation the second time allows DeRosa to focus on a phrase that he thinks is important and that he wants the reader to pay special attention to.

When you incorporate quotations into your own writing, remember the following:

1. Always introduce the quotation (never just put it into your text without some words of introduction).

2. Accurately report and document where the quotation came from.

Parts of a Complete Draft

Introduction: Regardless of your organizational approach, you need to have a strong introduction to capture your readers' attention and introduce the issue. To accomplish these two goals in an introduction, you might do one or more of the following:

- **Share an anecdote that clearly exemplifies the issue.** Maureen Dowd begins her column on organ donation (page 255) with the story of her niece's bravery in choosing to donate part of her liver to her uncle.

- **Provide a brief history of the issue.** Marian Wright Edelman begins her argument (p. 249) with a history of efforts to protect and expand antipoverty programs.

- **Provide a fact or statistic about the issue that will surprise—and possibly concern—readers.**

- **Explain (briefly) why your persuasive text is important.**

- **Ask an intriguing question about your subject.** Santi DeRosa opens his paper (page 274) by asking a key question:

  Are women at the university being treated as objects by the very university that has a responsibility to treat them with equality and dignity and not as second-class citizens?

Body: You can use various writing strategies, including defining all terms your reader might not understand within the body of your text, to effectively persuade your reader. This is the area of your paper where you will need to provide supporting examples or other types of evidence for each reason you offer, use visual aids (photographs, charts, tables) to support your position, and use rhetorical appeals—*ethos, logos, pathos* (page 29)—to help convince your readers.

For more on rhetorical appeals and argument strategies, see Chapter 14.

Conclusion: In your conclusion, you need to restate or allude to your thesis and let your readers know what you would like them to do with the information they learned from your essay. Conclusions in persuasive writing often do the following:

- **Explain your main thesis or point—what you want to persuade your reader about.**

- **Summarize how each supporting point adds evidence to support your main point.** In a long, involved argument, a summary can help readers recall the main points that you are making.

- **Reach out to the audience.** Marian Wright Edelman ends with an appeal to readers to make sure that "our leaders" hear the message about hunger.

- **Include a "call to action."** Maureen Dowd ends "Our Own Warrior Princess" with a description of herself filling out an organ donor card and the strong implication that readers should do so as well.

Title: As you compose your persuasive writing, a title should emerge at some point—perhaps late in the process. The title should reflect the point you are trying to make, and it should catch your readers' attention and make them want to read your essay. It may be risky to state your major claim in the title: If you state a controversial claim in your title, you run the risk that some readers will choose not to read your argument. However, there are times when stating a bold claim in the title is appropriate—especially if readers may not have even considered the topic.

| VISUAL *Thinking* | Going Beyond Words to Achieve Your Goals |

In his essay about the objectification of women, Santi DeRosa notes how the advertising industry has portrayed women in gratuitous ways (paragraph 8), especially in commercials for alcoholic beverages and automobiles. To illustrate his point, DeRosa could include some examples of advertisements where the visual portrayal of attractive women is gratuitous, but he may not need to include such visuals because most people reading his essay are familiar with this type of ad.

The essay discusses how young women in sororities sometimes participate in recruiting male student athletes. Here he might include a photo of a female student talking with a male student athlete, as in Figure 9.1.

- What other visuals might DeRosa use in his essay?
- In what ways, if any, would the addition of visuals support DeRosa's claim (see his final draft on pages 274–76)?

FIGURE 9.1
A male athlete talking
to a female student

| Writing Activity |

Constructing a Complete Draft

Using your invention work, your research, and the writing you did when selecting an organizational approach for your persuasive paper, write a complete first draft. Remember that your argument will evolve as you write, so your ideas will most likely change as you draft.

Santi DeRosa's First Draft

In this brief draft, note how Santi DeRosa incorporates information and examples from his life, as well as from outside sources. As he wrote, DeRosa did not worry about grammar, punctuation, and mechanics; instead, he concentrated on getting his main ideas on paper.

The Objectification of Woman. Who's Fault Is it?
Santi DeRosa

Are women being objectified by a university that has a responsibility to treat women with equality and not as second class citizens?

I say yes. All you need to do is look at the athletics department to see the way women are treated. What I don't understand is why women allow themselves to be used in such a way

In the past week I have read a couple of news articles from the campus newspaper that got me a little perplexed. Maybe it's the fact that I have a son the age of the female students in the articles. Or, maybe it's the fact that I have a wife, a sister, a mother, and nieces that I respect as people and as women. The articles upset my sense of right and wrong.

Joe Watson wrote the first article, "Risky behavior not policed in university recruiting" and explains how high school football players that visit the university for the purpose of being recruited are met by coeds, of which, thirty-five of the thirty-seven are females. Is this just a coincidence? No, I don't think so. It is no coincidence when schools from all over the country use the same practices to recruit high school players. The reporter took an informal survey of 117 Division 1-A football programs nationwide and found many with the same recruiter make-up. Louisiana State has 55 females; Alabama leads the way with 100 females. The university advertises every spring for new recruiters. Most come from sororities. The football coaches say they prefer using females because that's the way the other schools do it and the players coming to campus to be recruited would be uncomfortable if they were greeted by males because they are used to female recruiters. I think that this is just an excuse to turn a blind eye to a potential problem. Most of the players who come to be recruited are 17 and 18 years old. There have been many reports of under-age drinking at local clubs and parties and sometimes sex according to some senior recruiters. The people interviewed for the article who are in support of the "hostess" program defend it by saying that "the recruiters perform respectable duties during high school recruits' campus visits." Does the responsibility of "performing respectable duties" end when they leave the campus for a party? I believe that Becky Stoltz, a fourth year recruiter said it best when interviewed, "It's a disaster waiting to happen."

The second news article I read was by Megan Rudebeck. The story titled "'Hot' recruiters draw prospects" seems to be defending the program. Ms. Rudebeck not only talked to the coaches that run the program; she spoke with recruiters and players as well. She almost had me convinced that I might have been over reacting. I started to think that here is a woman writing a story that seems to be in defense of the way the recruiting program works. Maybe I am reacting wrongly. That is until the last line of the story when she quotes Zach Krula, a freshman offensive lineman. Zach says, "We've got a lot of hot girls, we might as well utilize them." After a few minutes I started to think to myself, why isn't Ms. Rudebeck insulted by that comment? Is she, as well as the women that are part of the program, so brain-washed with the need to get quality players into the football program that they are willing to overlook the fact that they are being "utilized."

As ideas for further development, Santi made these notes at the end of his initial draft:

Short history of women's struggle for equality.
Use family stories to tell history of strong women?
Define the objectification of women.
Conclusion.

Revising

Once you have a full draft of your persuasive text, you still have much to do. First, however, you should set the draft aside so that you can gain some critical distance. You can then read it with fresh eyes. When you approach your work this way, you will find it easier to notice reasons that are irrelevant, evidence that is not fully developed, or places where a compelling visual might add to the impact of your argument.

As you work to revise your early drafts, do not be concerned about doing a great deal of heavy editing. When you revise, you will probably change the content and structure of your paper, so time spent fixing problems with sentence style or grammar, punctuation, or mechanics at this stage is often wasted.

When you reread the first draft of your persuasive writing, here are some questions to ask yourself:

- How clearly and persuasively am I making my point? Am I sure my readers can understand it? How easily will they be able to restate the thesis?

- How effectively does all of my evidence support that main point? (Have I included evidence that seems persuasive but that does not support the point I am arguing for.)

- Are there photographs, charts, or graphs that might help me make my point?

- Are there parts of my paper that might confuse a reader? If so, how might I clarify them?

- Do I restate or allude to my main point at the end of my paper and also explain to the reader what I would like him or her to *do* (to vote, to write a letter to the editor, to *do* what I have been arguing for)?

Technology can help you revise and edit your writing more easily. Use your word processor's track-changes tool to try out revisions and editing changes. After you have had time to think about the possible changes, you can "accept" or "reject" them. Also, you can use your word processor's comment tool to write reminders to yourself when you get stuck with a revision or some editing task.

Because it is so difficult even for experienced writers to see their emerging writing with a fresh eye, it is almost always useful to ask classmates, friends, or family members to read and comment on drafts of your persuasive writing.

WRITER'S *Workshop* | **Responding to Full Drafts**

Working with one or two classmates, read each paper, and offer comments and questions that will help each of you see your papers' strengths and weaknesses. Consider the following questions as you do:

- What is your first impression of this draft? How effective is the title at drawing you in? Why? What are your overall suggestions for improvement? What part(s) of the text are especially persuasive? What reasons could use more support? Indicate what you like about the draft, and provide positive and encouraging feedback to the writer.

- How tight is the writer's focus? Does the paper wander a bit? If so, where?

- How effective is the introduction? What suggestions can you make to improve it?

- What is the author's thesis or main claim? How could it be expressed or supported more effectively?

- Are there parts that are confusing? Where would you like more details or examples to help clarify the writer's meaning?

- How accurate and appropriate is the supporting evidence? How clearly does the author indicate the sources of statistics and other supporting evidence?

- Might visuals such as charts, tables, photographs, or cartoons make the text more convincing?

- How clearly and effectively does the writer present any opposing points of view? How effectively does the writer answer opposing viewpoints? How might the writer acknowledge, concede, and/or refute them more effectively?

- How well has the writer demonstrated an awareness of readers' knowledge, needs, and/or expectations? How might the writer demonstrate greater awareness?

- How carefully has the writer avoided logical fallacies?

- What could be added to or changed in the conclusion to make it more effective? How well does it tie everything together? If action is called for, to what extent does it make you want to take action?

Notes on Santi DeRosa's First Draft, from a Conference with His Instructor

After writing his first draft, DeRosa met with his instructor, who thought his topic was promising but indicated that he needed more support on recruiting practices at his school and at other campuses. Together they brainstormed more ideas to develop his paper in more depth. The practice of using female students to help recruit male athletes led to these objections, which are more completely developed in DeRosa's final draft (see pages 274–77):

1. Using women for their bodies
2. Manipulation
3. A program that reinforces age-old notions of exploitation
4. Limits and defines women's roles
5. Under the guise of school spirit
6. Better add some more extensive research info

Responding to Readers' Comments

Once they have received feedback on their writing from peers, instructors, friends, and others, all writers have to figure out what to do with that feedback.

The first thing to do with any feedback is to consider carefully what your readers have said about your text. In his case, DeRosa arranged a conference with his writing teacher, who helped him brainstorm some specific objections to the recruiting program at his school to give his argument more depth.

As with all feedback, it is important to listen to it carefully and consider what your reader has to say. Then it is up to you, as the author, to decide how to come to terms with these suggestions. It is especially important to deal with comments from readers indicating that they are unconvinced by your argument. You sometimes may find that comments from more than one reader contradict each other. In that case, you need to use your own judgment to decide which reader's comments are on the right track.

In the final version of his paper, you can see how Santi DeRosa responded to his instructor's comments, as well as to his own review of his first draft.

KNOWLEDGE OF CONVENTIONS

When effective writers edit, they attend to the conventions that will help readers process their work. These include genre conventions, documentation, format, usage, grammar, and mechanics. By attending to these conventions in your writing, you make reading a more pleasant experience for readers.

Editing

The final tasks in any writing project are editing and proofreading—the final polishing of your document. When you edit and polish your writing, you make changes to your sentence structures and word choices to improve your style and to make your writing clearer and more concise. You also check your work to make sure it adheres to conventions of grammar, usage, punctuation, mechanics, and spelling. Use the spell-check function of your word-processing program, but be sure to double-check your spelling personally. If you have used sources in your paper, make sure you are following the documentation style your instructor requires.

As with overall revision of your work, this final editing and polishing is most effective if you can put your text aside for a few days and come back to it with fresh eyes. Because checking conventions is easier said than done, though, we strongly recommend that you ask classmates, friends, and tutors to read your work as well.

To assist you with editing, we offer here a round-robin editing activity focused on citing sources correctly.

See Chapter 20 for more on documenting sources using MLA or APA style.

WRITER'S *Workshop*	**Round-Robin Editing with a Focus on Citing Sources**

Working in small groups, look over both the in-text citations and the works-cited or references lists in your papers. For example, you might notice a problem with an in-text citation that is supposed to be in MLA style, such as this one:

> In the last line of the story, however, Rudebeck quotes Zach Krula, a freshman offensive lineman. Zach says,

"We've got a lot of hot girls, we might as well utilize them" (Rudebeck).

In MLA style, it is not necessary to include the source's name in parentheses if the name has been given within the text.

As you work with your peers, consult Chapter 20 of this text, which provides guidelines for using MLA or APA style when citing sources.

ROUND-ROBIN EDITING WITH A FOCUS ON

Fragments (p. 146)
Modifiers (p. 189)
Wordiness (p. 232)
Citing Sources (p. 273)
Careful Word Choice (p. 319)
Subordinate Clauses (p. 363)
Inclusive Language (p. 411)

Genres, Documentation, and Format

If you are writing an academic paper in response to Scenario 1, you will need to follow the conventions for the discipline in which you are writing and the requirements of your instructor. If you are writing an editorial for your college newspaper (Scenario 3), you should check the newspaper's editorial page or its Web site to see what the requirements are for length and format and what information you need to include when you submit the editorial.

A Writer Achieves His Goal: Santi DeRosa's Final Draft

Santi DeRosa continued to revise and edit his paper, and constructed a finished draft, which follows. As you read the essay, think about what makes it effective. Following the essay, you'll find some specific questions to consider.

SANTI DEROSA

PERSUASIVE ESSAY   # The Objectification of Women: Whose Fault Is It?

Are women being treated as objects by the very university that has a responsibility to treat them with equality and dignity and not as second-class citizens? All anyone needs to do is look at the athletics department to see the way women are treated here. What I don't understand is why women allow themselves to be used in such a way.

In the past week I have read two news articles in the campus newspaper about recruiting practices that made me a little perplexed. Maybe it's because I have a son the age of the female students in the articles, or maybe it's because I have a wife, a sister, a mother, and nieces whom I respect as people and as women, but these articles upset my sense of right and wrong. Objectification of women, sexual or otherwise, should never be allowed or condoned.

In the first article I read, "Risky Behavior Not Policed in Recruiting," reporter Joe Watson explains how high school football players who visit campus for the purpose of being recruited are met by coeds. Thirty-five of thirty-seven student recruiters are females. Is this just a coincidence? I don't think so. Schools from all over the country use the same practices to recruit high school players. Watson conducted an informal survey of 117 Division 1-A football programs nationwide and found many with similar proportions of female to male recruiters. Louisiana State has 55 females; Alabama leads the way with 100 females.

As Watson reports, the university advertises every spring for new recruiters. Most come from sororities. The football coaches say they prefer using women because that's the way the other schools do it. They maintain that the players coming to campus to be recruited would be uncomfortable if they were greeted by men because they are used to female recruiters.

This justification is just an excuse to ignore a potential problem. Most of the players who come to campus to be recruited are 17 and 18 years old. There have been many reports of under-age drinking at local clubs and parties and sometimes sex, according to some senior recruiters. The people interviewed for the article who support the "hostess" program defend it by saying that "the recruiters perform respectable duties during high school recruits' campus visits" (Watson). Does the responsibility of "performing respectable duties" end when they leave the campus for a party? I believe that Becky Stoltz, a fourth-year recruiter who was interviewed for the article said it best: "It's a disaster waiting to happen." Big problems have in fact already happened at the University of Colorado, where a recruiting aide was indicted for improper conduct after a three-month grand-jury investigation of illegal recruiting practices, including allegations of sexual assault (Lambert).

1

2

3

4

5

DeRosa and his instructor brainstormed a number of objections to the recruiting practices for him to develop in his revised draft, including this one:

I need to develop the idea that these practices use women for their bodies.

Note how DeRosa develops this objection.

Here DeRosa paraphrases a newspaper article.

DeRosa and his instructor also came up with the following objection for him to develop:

The program reinforces age-old notions of exploitation.

Note how he adds details and specific examples to support this part of his persuasive text.

Over the last hundred years, women have traveled a rocky road to greater 6
equality. At the turn of the twentieth century women didn't have many of the rights
we take for granted today, such as the right to own property and the right to vote.
By staying strong, working together, and maintaining their dignity, women eventually gained these rights for themselves and their daughters and granddaughters.

In my own family, my grandmother and great-grandmother took care of their 7
family in Italy while my grandfather came to America to set up a decent life for
them. My grandmother held things together for six years until her husband was
able to go back and get her. Although she did not have the same rights as a man of
that time, she never gave up hope and never lost her pride. In this country she
worked as a seamstress, as so many Italian women did, in order to help the family
make it through bad times and to provide a better life for her children. My mother
also worked a full-time job as a seamstress in a factory while taking care of her
home and family, as women did in the 1950s and 1960s. However, women of that
time were being taken for granted, and their roles had to change. Women wanted
more, and through their strength of conviction, they got it—more equitable pay for
their work. However, over the last forty years, the great strides women have made
have been somewhat squandered. Women have made impressive gains in their
professional lives, but they have also come to be seen, more and more, as objects.

The objectification of women in popular culture and sports is not new. Dur- 8
ing the 1950s and 1960s, the advertising industry started to portray women in
roles outside the kitchen, but it also created a perspective on women that objectified them. To consider women in terms of the way they look is objectification.
Examples of this are common: (1) Female newscasters chosen for their appearance, (2) the Dallas Cowboy cheerleaders—and cheerleading squads for other
teams, and (3) beautiful women appearing in advertisements for beer and
automobiles.

Amanda Bonzo, in an opinion piece in the online journal *The Digital Colle-* 9
gian, writes the following about this process of objectification:

> In our society, a woman's body is objectified daily on television, music vid-
> eos, advertisements. What do we do with objects? We buy, sell, trade
> them. . . . We tame them through rape and domestic abuse. Finally, we
> destroy them.

And Casey Jacketta, writing for the University of New Mexico's *Daily* 10
Lobo, notes the following:

> I was pleased that my favorite show, "Law and Order," was on. Then, as I
> kept watching, I realized that the assistant district attorney, played by
> Angie Harmon—a woman—didn't say a word in court. This troubled me,
> so I changed the channel to MTV. This upset me even more! All I saw was
> a bunch of barely clothed women shaking their bodies for the male singer's
> pleasure.

DeRosa effectively
uses quotations to
help make his point.

We see what these writers are talking about daily in advertising and in other media such as television, movies, and music. It is unfortunate that the sexual objectification of women sells products, and unless women understand that advertisers, filmmakers, college athletic departments, and others are taking advantage of them, this exploitation will never change. Barbara Fredrickson and her colleagues explain that this process causes women to start to view themselves the way others view them; as a consequence, "[a] woman views her own body as an object (or each piece as a separate object)" (274). 11

Objectification is often disguised as free speech and free expression, which are both noble principles, although they are often misused. What I don't understand is how any woman would allow herself to be used in this way. In the case of recruiters, objectification is disguised as school spirit. 12

DeRosa also needed to develop this objection to the recruiting program:

It operates under the guise of school spirit.

He added information from another article (by Megan Rudebeck) that puts a positive spin on the practice DeRosa is criticizing and provides a defense of the program; he then refutes Rudebeck's argument.

In the second news article I read, "'Hot' Recruiters Draw Prospects," Megan Rudebeck seems to be defending the program. Ms. Rudebeck not only talked to the coaches that run the program; she spoke with recruiters and players as well. She almost had me convinced that I might be over-reacting. After all, here is a woman who is defending the way the recruiting program works. In the last line of the story, however, Rudebeck quotes Zach Krula, a freshman offensive lineman. Zach says, "We've got a lot of hot girls, we might as well utilize them." That quotation made me wonder why Ms. Rudebeck wasn't insulted by that comment. Is she, as well as the women who are part of the program, so brainwashed by the need to get quality players onto the football team that they are willing to overlook the fact that they are being "utilize[d]"? 13

The use of women as sexual objects in mass media advertising, television, and music has made the practice so commonplace that we fail to see that it degrades our society. It amazes me that the women of the recruiting staff have not made the connection. It amazes me that Ms. Rudebeck and the coaching staff say they don't see what's going on, and that students, faculty, the alumni, and the administration buy into this degrading and potentially dangerous practice. I hope that a copy of Joe Watson's article makes it into the hands of each of the recruiter's parents and the Board of Regents. This practice is an insult to the women of the university, as well as to every woman in the last century who has sacrificed in order to achieve social equality. 14

This paper follows MLA guidelines for in-text citations and works cited.

Works Cited

Bonzo, Amanda. Letter. *The Digital Collegian*. The Daily Collegian, 20 Nov. 2000. Web. 4 Feb. 2012.

Fredrickson, Barbara L., Tomi-Ann Roberts, Stephanie M. Noll, Diane M. Quinn, and Jean M. Twenge. "That Swimsuit Becomes You: Sex Differences in Self-Objectification, Restrained Eating, and Math Performance." *Journal of Personality and Social Psychology* 75 (1998): 269–84. Print.

Jacketta, Casey. "Women's Lib Has Not Ended Objectification." *Daily Lobo.* New Mexico Daily Lobo, 25 Nov. 2002. Web. 3 Feb. 2012.

Lambert, Liz. "Maxcey Indicted in CU Grand Jury Probe." 9 *News.com.* KUSA-TV, 6 Sept. 2004. Web. 3 Feb. 2012.

Rudebeck, Megan. "'Hot' Recruiters Draw Prospects." *The State Press.* The State Press, 18 Oct. 2002. Web. 3 Feb. 2012.

Watson, Joe. "Risky Behavior Not Policed in Football Recruiting." The State Press. *The State Press.* 9 Dec. 2002. Web. 3 Feb. 2012.

UNDERSTANDING A WRITER'S GOALS: QUESTIONS TO CONSIDER AND DISCUSS

Rhetorical Knowledge: The Writer's Situation and Rhetoric

1. **Audience:** What audience does DeRosa have in mind for this essay? How can you tell?

2. **Purpose:** What purpose(s) does DeRosa have for writing this essay? How well does he achieve his purpose(s)?

3. **Voice and tone:** How does DeRosa's voice and tone help to establish his *ethos*? Is his tone appropriate? Why or why not?

4. **Responsibility:** How effectively does DeRosa represent opposing views on the issue of using female students as recruiters? In what ways, if any, could he represent their views more fairly?

5. **Context, format, and genre:** DeRosa is writing as a student but also as a husband and father. How does this context affect his use of language, appeals, and evidence? DeRosa has written an academic essay that argues for a specific change. Does DeRosa convince you that a problem exists? Do you think his essay will spur those he names in his last paragraph to action?

Critical Thinking: The Writer's Ideas and Your Personal Response

6. To what extent does DeRosa's text appeal to your emotions? In what way(s)?

7. What is DeRosa's main point, or claim? To what extent do you agree with it? Why?

Composing Processes and Knowledge of Conventions: The Writer's Strategies

8. How convincing is the evidence DeRosa supplies? What other evidence might he have used?

9. What organizational method does DeRosa use? How effective is it? What other method(s) might he have used?

Inquiry and Research: Ideas for Further Exploration

10. Conduct a search (at your school library or on the Web), focusing on the events that DeRosa describes in his family history (paragraph 7). What similarities can you find to the family story that DeRosa relates in his text?

Self-Assessment: Reflecting on Your Goals

Now that you have constructed a piece of writing designed to convince your readers, review your learning goals, which you and your classmates may have considered at the beginning of this chapter (pages 240–41). Then reflect on all the thinking and writing that you have done in constructing your persuasive paper. To help reflect on the learning goals that you have achieved, respond in writing to the following questions:

Rhetorical Knowledge

- *Audience:* What have you learned about addressing an audience in persuasive writing?
- *Purpose:* What have you learned about the purposes for constructing an effective persuasive text?
- *Rhetorical situation:* How did the writing context affect your persuasive text?
- *Voice and tone:* How would you describe your voice in this essay? Your tone? How do they contribute to the effectiveness of your persuasive essay?
- *Context, medium, and genre:* How did your context determine the medium and genre you chose, and how did those decisions affect your writing?

Critical Thinking, Reading, and Writing

- *Learning/inquiry:* How did you decide what to focus on for your persuasive text? Describe the process you went through to focus on a main idea, or thesis.
- *Responsibility:* How did you fulfill your responsibilities to your readers?
- *Reading and research:* What did you learn about persuasive writing from the reading selections in this chapter? What research did you conduct? How sufficient was the research you did?
- *Skills:* As a result of writing this paper, how have you become a more critical thinker, reader, and writer? What skills do you hope to develop further?

Writing Processes

- *Invention:* What invention strategies were most useful to you?
- *Organizing your ideas and details:* What organizational approach did you use? How successful was it?
- *Revising:* What one revision did you make that you are most satisfied with? If you could go back and make an additional revision, what would it be?
- *Working with peers:* How did your instructor and peer readers help you by making comments and suggestions about your writing? List some examples of how you revised your text based on comments from your instructor and your peer readers. How could you have made better use of the comments and suggestions you received? How could your peer readers help you more on your next assignment? How might you help them more, in the future, with the comments and suggestions you make on their texts?
- *Visuals:* Did you use photographs, charts, graphs, or other visuals to help you convince your readers? If so, what did you learn about incorporating these elements?
- *Writing habits:* What "writerly habits" have you developed, modified, or improved on as you constructed the writing assignment for this chapter? How will you change your future writing activities based on what you have learned about yourself?

 ## Knowledge of Conventions

- *Editing:* What sentence problem did you find most frequently in your writing? How will you avoid that problem in future assignments?
- *Genre:* What conventions of the genre you were using, if any, gave you problems?
- *Documentation:* Did you use sources for your paper? If so, what documentation style did you use? What problems, if any, did you have with it?

If you are constructing a course portfolio, file your written reflections so that you can return to them when you next work on your portfolio. Refer to Chapter 1 (pages 12–13) for a sample reflection by a student.

Writing to Evaluate

In 1997, the American Film Institute (AFI) announced a list of the hundred greatest American films. The list was chosen by a panel of "leaders from across the film community." In 2007, the AFI updated this list, which now includes one film released since 2000: *Lord of the Rings: The Fellowship of the Ring. Citizen Kane,* however, retained its spot at the top of the list. Following are the top twenty-five:

American Film Institute's Greatest Movies, 1–25

1. *Citizen Kane* (1941)
2. *The Godfather (1972)*
3. *Casablanca (1942)*
4. *Raging Bull (1980)*
5. *Singin' in the Rain* (1952)
6. *Gone with the Wind* (1939)
7. *Lawrence of Arabia* (1962)
8. *Schindler's List* (1993)
9. *Vertigo* (1958)
10. *The Wizard of Oz* (1939)
11. *City Lights* (1931)
12. *The Searchers* (1956)
13. *Star Wars* (1977)
14. *Psycho* (1960)
15. *2001: A Space Odyssey* (1968)
16. *Sunset Boulevard* (1950)
17. *The Graduate* (1967)
18. *The General* (1927)
19. *On the Waterfront* (1954)

Source: *AFI's 100 YEARS . . . 100 MOVIES* (1998).

20. *It's a Wonderful Life* (1946)
21. *Chinatown* (1974)
22. *Some Like It Hot* (1959)
23. *The Grapes of Wrath* (1940)
24. *E.T.—The Extra-Terrestrial* (1982)
25. *To Kill a Mockingbird* (1962)

Whether you agree with these rankings or not, for the AFI to compile the list, people had to evaluate movies based on specific criteria.

Evaluations are part of everyday life. When you decide which classes to take, what to eat for breakfast, or which candidate to support in an election, you decide which choice is best for you and act accordingly. As you think about the choices you confront in your life, consider why you make the ones that you do.

You make such decisions by evaluating your available choices based on certain **criteria,** or standards. For example, if you are evaluating a product, you may consider factors such as price, brand name, location, and size. Usually, you will base your evaluation on a combination of criteria—and you will inevitably weigh some criteria more heavily than others.

Whether you realize it or not, you have years of practice in judging the trustworthiness of others' evaluations and the relevance of the criteria they use. When a newspaper endorses a political candidate, your familiarity with the newspaper and its editorial policy influences your view of that endorsement. If you are a movie fan, you have probably already come to some conclusions about the excerpt from the AFI's evaluation of the "Greatest Movies" based on your agreement or disagreement with its list of films. Your experience with everyday evaluations will help you determine the criteria for the evaluations you write.

Rhetorical Knowledge (pp. 284–88)

- **Audience:** Determine who will benefit from your evaluation. Who needs to make decisions about the subject of your evaluation? What do the audience members probably already know about your subject? What will you need to tell them?
- **Purpose:** When you evaluate, you make a judgment based on specific criteria. Your purpose is not simply to say, "I think the Toyota truck is better than the Chevy," but to convince your reader to agree.
- **Rhetorical situation:** Consider the many factors that affect where you stand in relation to your subject. If you have some personal interest in your evaluation, you will have a different stance from that of a more neutral party.
- **Voice and tone:** When you construct an evaluation, you are trying to explain your reasoned judgment. You always want to support that judgment with specific examples and details so your readers can understand why your evaluation says what it does. Your tone should present your evaluation thoughtfully and reasonably—if you seem to "shout" at your readers, they will not agree with your evaluation.
- **Context, medium, and genre:** Decide on the best medium and genre to use to present your evaluation to the audience you want to reach.

Critical Thinking, Reading, and Writing (pp. 288–303)

- **Learning/inquiry:** By observing, listening to, and/or reading about the subject of your evaluation, and then by writing about it, you gain a deeper understanding of its qualities and the ability to make more informed judgments about it.
- **Responsibility:** Effective evaluative writing leads naturally to critical thinking. When you evaluate something, you have to consider all aspects of your subject, not only to determine the criteria on which you will base your evaluation but also to construct a reasoned argument for your judgment.
- **Reading and research:** To evaluate a subject, you need not only to examine it in detail but also to examine similar items.

Writing Processes (pp. 304–18)

- **Invention:** Various invention activities can help you consider all aspects of the subject you are evaluating.
- **Organizing your ideas and details:** The act of evaluating necessarily means that you think about the various aspects of your subject. That process can help you organize your thinking, and later your writing, into categories, based on your criteria.
- **Revising:** Read your work with a critical eye to make certain that it fulfills the assignment and displays the qualities of effective evaluative writing.
- **Working with peers:** Listen to your classmates' thoughts and suggestions carefully to make sure that they understand your evaluation.

 ## Knowledge of Conventions (pp. 318–19)

- **Editing:** Effective evaluations usually require careful word choice. The round-robin activity on page 319 will help you check your evaluation for word choice.
- **Genres for evaluative writing:** In many situations, your evaluation will be a formal report or an academic paper. Evaluations written about movies, restaurants, or other products or services are not quite as formal as college assignments, however.
- **Documentation:** If you relied on sources outside of your experience, cite them using the appropriate documentation style.

RHETORICAL KNOWLEDGE

When you write an evaluation, you need to consider the criteria on which you will base your evaluation as well as how you will develop those criteria. What aspects of the work, product, service, or idea should you examine for your evaluation? How can you best make an evaluative judgment about it? You will also need to decide what medium and genre will help you get your evaluation across to your audience most effectively.

Writing to Evaluate in Your College Classes

As a college student, you will be expected to read and write evaluations in many of your classes:

- Your psychology instructor might ask you to read brief summaries of experiments and evaluate how well each experiment's design served to answer the research question.
- Your political science instructor might ask you to rate the effectiveness of a political campaign.
- Your business and marketing instructor might ask you to evaluate several potential store locations.

In much of your academic writing, you will also have to evaluate the sources and evidence you select to support your thesis statements.

The "Ways of Writing" feature on page 286 presents different genres that can be used when writing to evaluate in your college classes.

Writing to Evaluate for Life

In addition to the evaluations you will consider and write while in college, you will no doubt make evaluations every day in the professional, civic, and personal areas of your life.

In your professional life, your writing will often have an evaluative purpose. For example, if you are a manager with employees reporting to you, you will probably be asked to evaluate their performance. You may consider criteria that include both verifiable information (does your employee arrive at work on time?) and opinions (is he or she an effective leader?). You will need to provide evidence to support your judgments while sufficiently explaining your opinions.

In your civic life, you will often evaluate the political positions of local and national candidates for public office, along with ballot initiatives and referendums, and then make decisions or recommendations.

Without realizing it, we often make evaluations when writing in our personal life. An e-mail to a relative may include comments about favorite restaurants, teachers, or newfound friends. On the one hand, we might feel more comfortable making evaluations for our friends and family. On the other, we may feel especially obligated to provide a useful evaluation because we care about the relationship.

The "Ways of Writing" feature on page 286 presents different genres that can be used when writing to evaluate in life.

Scenarios for Writing | Assignment Options

Your instructor may ask you to complete one or more of the following writing assignments that call for evaluation. Each of these assignments is in the form of a *scenario*, which gives you a sense of who your audience is and what you need to accomplish with your evaluative writing.

Starting on page 304, you will find guidelines for completing whatever scenario you decide—or are asked—to complete. Additional scenarios for college and life are online.

Writing for College

SCENARIO 1   Academic Evaluation: What Are the Rules?

You may currently live (or may previously have lived) in a communal setting such as a dormitory, a military barracks, a summer camp, or a house or apartment with roommates. In that setting, you are probably aware of rules and regulations, yet you may not have thought about whether they are fair or not, or even if there are punishments for not obeying the rules. Or you may be living with one or both of your parents, who probably insist on certain rules.

Consider questions such as these:

- What are the rules for living in the particular setting (communal or parental)? Are they fair and reasonable?
- Who is paying for the living quarters? Do they (should they) have total control of what happens in them?
- Should parents be allowed to place restrictions on college-age students who live at home? What rules would be reasonable?
- If an organization such as a college or the government controls the living quarters, can or should it monitor e-mail? Internet access?

Writing Assignment: Write an evaluation of the rules of the communal setting in which you currently live or once lived, or of your parent's or parents' rules. You will need to do some research on what the rules are and consider what you might use as criteria for evaluating them. Your audience will be your instructor and your classmates.

Ways of Writing to Evaluate

Genres for Your College Classes	Sample Situation	Advantages of the Genre	Limitations of the Genre
Career assessment	In your career and life planning class, you are asked to construct an evaluation focusing on possible careers you might pursue after you graduate: the kind of work, the pay, the possibilities for advancement, and so on.	The assignment requires you to think through your criteria and conclusions carefully and thoroughly.	You might not have time to gather really meaningful data if you lack the time to interview people pursuing the careers you are investigating.
History essay	In your world history class, you are asked to evaluate the perceived benefits of manned space flight	This evaluation will require you to develop and apply valid criteria to reach a historical conclusion.	Historical events rarely occur in isolation, and no set of criteria will be all inclusive.
Letter to your campus newspaper	Your mathematics professor asks you to write a letter using statistics drawn from interviews to evaluate a specific aspect of campus life (dining, grounds, and so on).	Anything published in a college newspaper will have a wide audience of people who have an interest in campus affairs.	A letter to the editor gives you limited space for your evaluation, and you may not have enough room to adequately make your case. It might not be published.
Business report	Your business instructor asks you to evaluate several marketing plans for a new product for college students.	An evaluative report allows you to identify criteria and then research what students might and might not purchase.	It does not allow for extraneous factors that may not be included in your research.

Genres for Life	Sample Situation	Advantages of this Genre	Limitations of the Genre
Brochure	As part of a community group, you want to publicize your evaluation of a sales tax increase that your community will be voting on.	Your evaluation, often with illustrations and in a compact form, will provide readers with evaluative criteria that will enable them to make a more informed decision.	A brochure provides limited space for your evaluation.
Letter	You are planning a family reunion, at which you expect nearly a hundred family members from around the country, and you want to evaluate possible locations.	A letter is an effective way to share information and to explain the criteria on which you are basing your evaluation.	Letters and responses to letters are slow; sending the letter by e-mail or posting it to a Web site is another option, but that may exclude some family members.
Blog	You start a blog that evaluates software programs used for education.	A blog is an easy and uncomplicated way for you to share your evaluations with a wide and interested audience.	Blogs often need monitoring for improper comments; sometimes a lot of information is generated that takes time to read through.
E-mail	You send an e-mail to coworkers that evaluates several digital storage options for your company.	An e-mail allows you to input links to the prospective companies' Web sites and ask for feedback.	Some people might feel they need more information than the e-mail includes.
Performance review	You are required to submit a performance review for several employees whom you supervise.	Often there is a form that provides specific criteria you can use to construct your evaluation.	Sometimes the criteria for an evaluation no longer fits the work the employee does; forms provide limited room for originality or extra comments and suggestions.

Writing for Life

SCENARIO 2 An Evaluation of a Subject You Are Curious About

For this scenario, select a work of art, a film, a television program, a product, a service, an event, or a place to evaluate—something you are interested in and would like to know more about. Your audience will be your instructor and your fellow classmates.

Writing Assignment: Choose a subject whose value you would like to consider. You may value it highly and want others to know about it, or you may think that it is highly overrated and want others to see why. Construct an evaluation in which you make your judgment known. Be sure to explain clearly the criteria on which you will make your evaluation, and then show how your subject meets—or does not meet—those criteria.

SCENARIO 3 Personal Writing: Evaluating a Cultural Event or Performance

In your personal life, you attend any number of cultural events: museum exhibits, art shows (whether those of professional artists, photographers, or sculptors, or those of your friends), musical performances, plays, dance performances, and so on. Your college or university is a wonderful source of cultural events. How do you evaluate such cultural performances or events? On what criteria *should* they be evaluated? How much weight should you give one criterion in relation to others? How might your own criteria match up with those of other students who also attend the event or performance?

Writing Assignment: For this assignment, assume that your local newspaper or a local magazine has asked you to evaluate a recent cultural event or performance. In no more than 1,200 words, explain the criteria that you see as important, and then give your evaluation of that event or performance. Consider how you might use visuals to help illustrate your evaluation.

RHETORICAL CONSIDERATIONS IN EVALUATIVE WRITING

Audience: Although your instructor and classmates are your initial audience for this assignment, who are other possible audiences? Consider whether the members of your audience will agree with you about the criteria for evaluating your subject, or whether you will need to convince them to accept your criteria.

Purpose: Your main purpose is to evaluate your subject in terms of the criteria you decide on. How will you persuade your audience to accept your judgment of it?

Voice, tone, and point of view: You have probably chosen your subject because you have a personal interest in it. What preconceptions about it do you have? How can you avoid letting them color your evaluation? How can you use voice and tone to establish credibility?

For more on choosing a medium and genre, see Chapter 17 and Appendix C.

Context, medium, and genre: Keeping the context of the assignment in mind, decide on a medium and genre for your evaluation. How will your evaluation be used? If you are writing for an audience beyond the classroom, consider what will be the most effective way to present your evaluation to this audience.

 # CRITICAL THINKING, READING, AND WRITING

Before you begin to write your evaluation, read one or more evaluations to get a feel for this kind of writing.

To write an effective, responsible evaluation, you need to understand your subject and the reasons for your evaluation of it. You will need to choose valid criteria, organize your writing logically, and present your evaluation in a way that fulfills your responsibility to your readers. To do this, you need to think critically about your own views, as well as those of any outside sources. Thinking critically does not necessarily mean that you will criticize, but rather that you will carefully consider which criteria are most and least important and how different aspects of your subject relate to each other.

 ## Learning the Qualities of Effective Evaluative Writing

As we have seen, most writing is purposeful. Focusing on the outcome should be the starting point for everything you write, and for an evaluation, you want to make a reasoned, thoughtful, and justifiable judgment. You need to outline the criteria on which you will base your evaluation and then explain how the subject of your evaluation fits the criteria.

Evaluative writing that achieves its goal has the following qualities:

- **Clearly defined and explained criteria.** Readers expect an evaluation to be based on specific criteria that are germane to the item being evaluated. You would evaluate an array of backpacks in a sporting-goods store using different criteria from those you would use to evaluate, say, a set of luggage. Readers deserve to have the criteria you use defined in detail so they can understand your reasoning.

  If you are evaluating a work of art, you should use—and explain—criteria appropriate for evaluating art—for example, aesthetic appeal, the impact the work has on the viewer, and how well it represents a specific genre.

- **Comparisons based on the criteria.** Especially when you are evaluating products or services, you will need to show how your subject can be measured against similar subjects and then explain this basis of comparison. You will compare like with like, showing how each aspect of the item you are evaluating rates in comparison with the same (or a similar) aspect of a similar item.

  You can make comparisons based on numerical information ("Tire brand C has a 50 percent longer tread life rating than Brand B, and twice as long as Brand A"). A table can help your readers see the basis of your claim.

Tire Brand	Tread Life Rating
Brand A	30,000 miles
Brand B	40,000 miles
Brand C	60,000 miles

Because numerical information is verifiable and is not a matter of opinion, it can be persuasive evidence for your overall evaluation.

Finally, you can make comparisons based on more subjective criteria, such as your definition of "quality": You might note that a backpack "should have this kind of fabric, this type of zipper, a lifetime warranty, and straps made out of this material." Then you could go on to outline how each backpack you are evaluating matches (or perhaps does not match) each of your criteria.

When you compare, it is important not to slant your evaluation by leaving out negative information or highlighting only those details that make the product, service, or work you favor seem to be the best. Instead, explain and compare honestly so your readers can reach their own conclusions about the effectiveness of your evaluation. You may find that the item you judge to be best is weak when measured on the basis of one or more of your criteria. It is vital to your overall credibility to account for such shortcomings. Just because something is comparatively weak in one or more areas does not mean that it cannot still come out on top in your evaluation.

- Evidence that supports your claims. To accept your evaluation, readers need to understand that you are not just making assertions about your subject, but that you have evidence to support your claims. Evidence can include the following:

  - *Testimony:* "I've owned Ford automobiles for twenty years, and they've never let me down."

  - *Statistical information:* "A recent study by the National Highway Traffic Safety Administration found that nearly 50 percent of the 11,500 cars, pickup trucks, vans, and sport-utility vehicles the agency checked had at least one tire with half-worn tread. Another 10 percent had at least one bald tire" (*Consumer Reports*).

  - *Detailed description:* The more details you can provide, the easier it will be for a reader to understand what you mean. For example, if you were evaluating netbook computers, you might explain your evaluation by discussing in detail the amount of memory in each netbook, the processor speed, screen size and quality, and price.

- An analysis and explanation of how any visual elements affect your evaluation. When they evaluate textbooks, teachers often consider how the visual elements in the books might help students learn more effectively. If you were a science teacher, for example, you might focus on the photographs or drawings in the various books under consideration and cite examples from the texts in your evaluative comments.

- A clearly stated judgment. Readers can either agree or disagree with your conclusions, but if you have written a successful evaluation, they will understand how you arrived at your judgment.

Reading, Inquiry, and Research: Learning from Texts That Evaluate

The following reading selections are examples of evaluative writing. As you read through the selections, consider the following questions:

- How clearly are the evaluative criteria explained?
- To what extent do I agree with the evaluation? Why?
- How well do I understand why the writer evaluated this subject as he did? That is, how clearly has the writer explained his judgment?
- How familiar am I with the subject that is being evaluated?
- What else would I like to know about the subject being evaluated?
- How can I use the techniques of evaluative writing, as demonstrated here, in my own writing?

JONATHAN H. LIU

The 5 Best Toys of All Time

OPINION PIECE

Here at GeekDad we review a lot of products—books, toys, gadgets, software—and I know it's impossible for most parents to actually afford all of the cool stuff that gets written up. Heck, most of us can't afford it either, and we're envious of the person who scored a review copy of a cool board game or awesome gizmo. (Disclosure: that person is probably me.) So while we love telling you about all the cool stuff that's out there, I understand that as parents we all have limited budgets and we sometimes need help narrowing down our wishlists. 1

A senior editor at *Wired* magazine, Jonathan Liu writes the column "GeekDad" for *Wired*. He is also an artist who works with Etch-a-Sketch drawings and other media. He lives in Portland, Oregon, and is a stay-at-home dad. The following article appeared in *Wired* in January 2011.

So to help you out, I've worked really hard to narrow down this list to five items that no kid should be without. All five should fit easily within any budget and are appropriate for a wide age range, so you get the most play out of each one. These are time-tested and kid-approved! And as a bonus, these five can be combined for extra-super-happy-fun-time. 2

1. Stick

What's brown and sticky? A Stick. 3

This versatile toy is a real classic—chances are your great-great-grandparents played with one, and your kids have probably discovered it for themselves as well. It's a required ingredient for Stickball, of course, but it's so much more. Stick works really well as a poker, digger and reach-extender. It can also be combined with many other toys (both from this list and otherwise) to perform even more functions. 4

Stick comes in an almost bewildering variety of sizes and shapes, but you can amass a whole collection without too much of an investment. You may want to avoid the smallest sizes—I've found that they break easily and are impossible to repair. Talk about planned obsolescence. But at least the classic wooden version is biodegradable so you don't have to feel so bad about pitching them into your yard waste or just using them for kindling. Larger, multi-tipped Sticks are particularly useful as snowman arms. (Note: requires Snow, which is not included and may not be available in Florida.) 5

As with most things these days, there are higher-end models of Sticks if 6 you're a big spender, from the smoothly-sanded wooden models (which are more uniformly straight than the classic model) to more durable materials such as plastic or even metal. But for most kids the classic model should do fine. My own kids have several Sticks (but are always eager to pick up a couple more when we find them).

One warning: the Stick can also be used as a sword or club, so parents 7 who avoid toy weapons might want to steer clear of the larger models. (On the other hand, many experts agree that creative children will just find something else to substitute for Stick, so this may be somewhat unavoidable.)

Although she is not generally known as a toy expert, Antoinette Portis has writ- 8 ten this helpful user manual for those needing some assistance in using their Stick.[1]

Wired: Finally, something that *does* grow on trees.   9
Tired: You could put someone's eye out.   10

Disclosure: I have received several samples of Sticks from one manufac- 11 *turer for review.*

2. Box

Another toy that is quite versatile, Box also comes in a variety of shapes and 12 sizes. Need proof? Depending on the number and size you have, Boxes can be turned into furniture or a kitchen playset. You can turn your kids into cardboard robots or create elaborate *Star Wars* costumes. A large Box can be used as a fort or house and the smaller Box can be used to hide away a special treasure. Got a Stick? Use it as an oar and Box becomes a boat. One particularly famous kid has used the Box as a key component of a time machine, a duplicator and a transmogrifier, among other things.

Still stuck for ideas? Check out this Box user manual by Antoinette Portis 13 for a few more ideas.[2]

The Box may be the most expensive item on my list, available from many retail- 14 ers and shipping companies, but they can often be had cheaper if you know where to look. Amazon is one of my main sources of the small- to medium-sized Box; I include one with virtually every order I place there. If you don't mind second-hand toys, the grocery store, bookstores and recycling centers are also great sources for Boxes. Oh, and the best place for the extra-large version is an appliance store (though sometimes they'll try to sell you an appliance along with it, which could get pricey.)

Note: If you're in a pinch, Laundry Basket is a similar item and can often be 15 substituted for Box in some instances, though it's generally not as great for costumes (other than a turtle). And if you're thinking of using Box for your next building project, Mr. McGroovy's Box Rivets make a great optional accessory.

---

[1]A reference to Antoinette Portis's children's book *Not a Stick*.
[2]A reference to Portis's book *Not a Box*.

Wired: Best celebrity endorsement: Calvin & Hobbes. 16

Tired: Paradox: what do you put Box in when you're done playing with it? 17

3. String

My kids absolutely love String—and when they can't find it, sometimes they substitute other things for it such as scarves or blankets, but what they're really after is String. Now, I should start off by saying that String is *not* intended for toddlers and babies: it is a strangulation hazard and your kids must be old enough to know not to put it around their necks. However, when used properly your kids can really have a ball with String. 18

The most obvious use of String is tying things together, which my kids love to do. You can use it to hang things from doorknobs or tie little siblings to chairs or make leashes for your stuffed animals. Use String with two Cans for a telephone (and teach your kids about sound waves), or with Stick to make a fishing pole. You'll need String for certain games like Cat's Cradle—there's even an International String Figure Association for lots more information. String is a huge part of what makes some toys so fun—try using a yo-yo or a kite without String and you'll see what I mean. Try the heavy-duty version of String (commonly branded Rope) for skipping, climbing, swinging from trees or just for dragging things around. 19

Although you can buy String at a store, it's generally sold in much larger quantities than your children will probably need—usually my kids are happy with roughly two or three feet of it. I actually have no idea where it comes from, because I don't remember buying them any, so it must be pretty easy to come by. 20

Wired: It really ties everything together. 21

Tired: There's a reason "no strings attached" is a benefit. 22

4. Cardboard Tube

Ah, the Cardboard Tube. These are kind of like the toy at the bottom of a box of Cracker Jacks—they come free with a roll of paper towels and other products but you have to wait until you get to the end of the roll before you can finally claim the toy. (Perhaps this explains why my kids—who love the small size—go through toilet paper so quickly.) The small- and medium-sized are most common, but the large versions that come with wrapping paper can be more difficult to obtain—I had a roll of Christmas wrapping paper that lasted about three years before my kids finally got the Tube. There's also an extra-large size that is sometimes sold with posters, and a super-sized industrial version which you'll generally only find from carpet suppliers. (Of course, carpet stores aren't toy stores, and while their product also goes by the name Cardboard Tube it's hardly the same thing and probably shouldn't be considered a toy.) 23

My kids have nicknamed the Cardboard Tube the "Spyer" for its most common use in our house, as a telescope. (Or tape two of them together for use as 24 binoculars.) But if you happen to be lucky enough to get a large size, the best use is probably whacking things. Granted, Stick is also great for whacking, but the nice thing about Cardboard Tube is that it generally won't do any permanent damage. It's sort of a Nerf Stick, if you will. If that sounds up your alley, look up the Cardboard Tube Fighting League—currently there are only official events in Seattle, San Francisco and Sydney, but you could probably get something started up in your own neighborhood if you wanted. Or if you're more of a loner, perhaps the way of the Cardboard Tube Samurai is a better path.

Obviously if your own kids are younger you'll want to exercise discretion   25
about these more organized activities, but it probably wouldn't hurt to provide them with a Cardboard Tube or two just so they'll get used to the feel of it. You never know if your kid will be the Wayne Gretzky or Tiger Woods of Cardboard Tube Fighting, right? Best to give them the opportunity so that if they show some particular aptitudes they'll have that early advantage. And if not, well, there are still plenty of people who enjoy playing with Cardboard Tubes casually without all that pressure.

Wired: Comes free with purchase of toilet paper, paper towels, and wrapping paper.   26
Tired: Doesn't hold up to enthusiastic play.   27

5. Dirt

When I was a kid one of my favorite things to play with was Dirt. At some point I   28
picked up an interest in cleanliness, and I have to admit that I'm personally not such a fan of Dirt anymore—many parents (particularly indoor people like me) aren't so fond of it either. But you can't argue with success. Dirt has been around longer than any of the other toys on this list, and shows no signs of going away. There's just no getting rid of it, so you might as well learn to live with it.

First off, playing with Dirt is actually good for you. It's even sort of edible (in   29
the way that Play-doh and crayons are edible). But some studies have shown that kids who play with Dirt have stronger immune systems than those who don't. So even if it means doing some more laundry (Dirt is notorious for the stains it causes) it might be worth getting your kids some Dirt.

So what can you do with Dirt? Well, it's great for digging and piling and   30
making piles. We've got a number of outdoor toys in our backyard, but my kids spend most of their time outside just playing with Dirt. Use it with Stick as a large-format ephemeral art form. (Didn't I tell you how versatile Stick was?) Dirt makes a great play surface for toy trucks and cars. Need something a little gloopier? Just add water and—presto!—you've got Mud!

Dirt is definitely an outdoor toy, despite your kids' frequent attempts to bring   31
it indoors. If they insist, you'll probably want to get the optional accessories Broom and Dustpan. But as long as it's kept in its proper place, Dirt can be loads of fun.

Wired: Cheap as dirt.   32
Tired: Dirty.   33

UNDERSTANDING A WRITER'S GOALS: QUESTIONS TO CONSIDER AND DISCUSS

Rhetorical Knowledge: The Writer's Situation and Rhetoric

1. **Audience:** This article originally appeared in *Wired*, a magazine whose readers are interested in the latest technology. Can you see why this article might appeal to them? Why or why not?

2. **Purpose:** Why do you think Liu is writing to his high-tech audience about everyday items such as toys?

3. **Voice and Tone:** Do you think Liu is serious in his evaluation of what he calls toys? What can you point to in his use of language that makes you feel that way?

4. **Responsibility:** Is Liu fulfilling his responsibility as a writer when he advocates using these everyday items as toys? Why or why not?

5. **Context, format, and genre:** At first glance, this article is written for parents who are interested in toys for their children. Yet, it appeared in *Wired*. Do you think this article might have been very different if it had appeared in *Parents® Magazine*? If so, in what ways?

Critical Thinking: The Writer's Ideas and Your Personal Response

6. Do you think sticks, boxes, string, cardboard tubes, and dirt are really good toys? If so, would you expect your kids to play with them? If not, then why do you think Liu is making his argument in favor of them?

7. Look at the evaluation that Liu has done for just one of the five toys. Do you think it's accurate? Do you think it's fair? Do you agree with him that the item is a good toy? If you don't agree, why don't you agree?

Composing Processes and Knowledge of Conventions: The Writer's Strategies

8. In paragraph 2, Liu clearly states the criteria on which he will make his evaluations about "good toys." They are toys that
   - fit easily within any budget
   - are appropriate for a wide age range
   - are time-tested
   - are "kid-approved"
   - can be combined with other toys

   Is Liu's strategy of putting his criteria at the start of his evaluation a useful one? Why?

9. Liu begins his piece by admitting that many cool toys are expensive, so he's going to look at more reasonably priced toys. He then presents five distinct but similarly organized sections. Do you find this organization to be effective? If so, why? If not, why not?

10. At the end of each of the five sections, there is a brief comment called Wired and Tired. Do you think this strategy helps Liu to make his point? Why or why not?

Inquiry and Research: Ideas for Further Exploration

11. We often feel inundated and overwhelmed by what seems to be the never-ending need to have the newest, the brightest, the most high tech, the most current version of everything. Can you think of a list of five of the best type of product or service that are neither the newest, brightest, most high tech, or most current versions of that product or service? Like Liu, you could list five toys (if you come up with five different toys), or you might think about fashion, food or food preparation, study materials, automobile accessories, or a type of product or service from any other area of daily life.

GENRES *Up Close*   Writing a Review

Critical reviews play an important role in daily life. Before people go to restaurants, movie theaters, concert halls, bookstores, or music stores, they often read reviews to help them make thoughtful decisions about how to spend their money. Before employers decide to hire job applicants, renew employees' contracts, or offer employees salary increases, they read reviews of those applicants and employees, in the form of letters of recommendation and annual performance evaluations. And before people spend large amounts of money on major repairs or renovations to their homes or apartments, they go online to read reviews of the contractors they are considering.

Although many critical reviews appear in print (newspapers, magazines, letters, reports), many also appear in audio form on radio shows such as *All Things Considered* and *Weekend Edition* on National Public Radio. They also appear in video form on television shows such as *Anderson Cooper 360* (CNN), *The O'Reilly Factor* (Fox), and *E News* (E! TV). On the Internet, they can appear in written, audio, or video formats.

The critical review has some standard features:

- **A brief summary of what's being reviewed.** A summary helps readers make sense of the evaluation. For example, before passing judgment on a restaurant's décor, a reviewer needs to describe it so that readers can understand the points the writer is making about it—that the lighting is too dim or the bold color scheme is unattractive. Such a summary also helps readers decide if they are likely to agree with the reviewer's taste in restaurant décor. However, keep in mind that for some types of reviews, the reviewer needs to be careful not to provide too many details, or "spoilers." For example, giving away the ending of a mystery could ruin the film for some people who had planned to see it.

- **An evaluation or critique.** The evaluation focuses on the criteria that matter most to readers. Of course, the focus will vary depending on what is being reviewed. A movie review focuses on such criteria as acting, set design, sound track, special effects, character development, plot, directing, and editing. A restaurant review, however, focuses on décor, atmosphere, service, cost, menu, and flavor.

In the reviews that follow, notice how the reviewers attend to these genre criteria. In the two film reviews, for example, notice what standard film elements they summarize and critique. Consider how the writers' choices of what they evaluate affect your impressions.

ROGER EBERT

Harry Potter and the Deathly Hallows: Part 2

REVIEW

A fter seven earlier films reaching back a decade, the Harry Potter saga comes to a solid and satisfying conclusion in *Harry Potter and the Deathly Hallows: Part 2*. The finale conjures up enough awe and solemnity to serve as an appropriate finale and a dramatic contrast to the lighthearted (relative) innocence of *Harry Potter and the Sorcerer's Stone* all those magical years ago.

Harry, Hermione and Ron are grown up now, and Harry has even grown the facial stubble required of all epic heroes. The time has come for him to face Lord Voldemort in their final showdown, and their conflict is staged in a series of special effects sequences containing power and conviction. I am still not sure what the bolts discharged by magic wands actually consist of, but never mind. They look wicked and lethal.

I dare not reveal a single crucial detail about the story itself, lest I offend the Spoiler Police, who have been on my case lately. Besides, you never know. Maybe they've completely rewritten J. K. Rowling's final book in the series. Maybe Harry dies, Voldemort is triumphant, and evil reigns.

What I can observe is that this final film is a reunion of sorts for a great many characters we've come to know over the years. So many distinguished British actors have played roles in the Potter films that those who haven't may be fitfully resentful. Here we see once again characters whose names were once new and now resonate with associations: Bellatrix Lestrange, Rubeus Hagrid, Professor Dumbledore, Ollivander, Lucius Malfoy, Sirius Black, Severus Snape, Remus Lupin and even Prof. Minerva McGonagall, who is called upon to summon her powers and shield Hogwarts School from the powers of Voldemort.

You don't want to know what happens to Hogwarts here. Many of its shining spires and noble gothic arches are reduced to ruin and ashes, providing an apocalyptic battleground. The school also seems to have mysteriously relocated adjacent to

Roger Ebert is America's most famous and widely-read film critic. He has been the film critic for the *Chicago Sun-Times* since 1967 and first gained national fame for his partnership with the late Gene Siskel in the television show "Siskel and Ebert at the Movies," which popularized the simple thumbs-up, thumbs-down critique of films. Ebert has written fifteen books and is a lecturer at the University of Chicago Fine Arts Program. Despite lengthy and debilitating cancer treatment and radiation in 2004, Ebert continues to write and publish film reviews, including this one from 2011. Ebert's review covers the last of the Harry Potter films, and you will notice how he connects the whole series of films through a discussion of how the characters change over time.

Paragraph 1: Provides an evaluation of the movie at the beginning of the review.

Paragraphs 2 and 3: Summarizes the movie briefly without giving away too many details, or "spoilers."

towering heights that permit vertiginous falls to the earth far below. There is no place in Britain that fits this geography, but then is Hogwarts quite in the real Britain?

What it does occupy is a Britain of the imagination. The series has remained faithful to J. K. Rowling's original conception, and resisted temptations to cheapen its action or simplify its complexity. She created a fictional world with its own logic and consistency, and here at the finale, there is some satisfaction in seeing loose ends tied up, lingering mysteries explained and suspicions confirmed. 6

In a dreamy sequence, we are allowed to see the characters as they were in the beginning. They were so young. By spanning something like real time, the story has grown older along with them. Daniel Radcliffe, born 1989, was 11 when he first played Harry Potter, is 21 now, and he and Ron Weasley (Rupert Grint) and Hermione Granger (Emma Watson) have luckily remained recognizable and soldiered on through what involved a great deal of hard labor. Not many young actors have worked so relentlessly for a decade. 7

That said, it's apparent again in this film that the three leads are upstaged by the supporting characters. 8

Their role is to be plucky, clean-cut and stalwart. They sneak around and observe things. They eavesdrop. They speculate. They are lectured to. They endure a little low-key puberty. Harry struggles to master his magic. Meanwhile, such British legends as Maggie Smith, Helena Bonham Carter, Michael Gambon, Alan Rickman and Ralph Fiennes steal scenes just by standing there. What chance does Harry or anybody have against Voldemort's smashed face with its nostril slits? Late in the film, leaving nothing to chance, Voldemort even appears as his own fetus, looking like it's been simmered in red sauce. 9

It is Fiennes' Voldemort who dominates this last installment, illustrating the old actors' axiom that it is better to play the villain than the hero. It takes a considerable villain to hold his own in the crumbled ruins of Hogwarts, and force the remaining students to choose between the friends of Harry or joining him on the dark side. Considering what has happened to Hogwarts, it's a little surprising that the students haven't been sent home, but then Dumbledore has had other things on his mind. 10

This movie is impressively staged, the dialogue is given proper weight and not hurried through, there are surprises which, in hindsight, seem fair enough, and *Harry Potter* now possesses an end that befits the most profitable series in movie history. These films will be around for a long time. And without spoiling a single thing, let me just observe that the final scene clearly leaves an opening for a sequel. I know, Rowling says there won't be one. Just sayin'. 11

Note: This entire movie is dark, gloomy and filled with shadows. So it should be. That makes it particularly inappropriate for the additional dimness of 3-D. There are a few shots that benefit from 3-D (I like the unfolding of the little magical globe) but none that require it. Avoid the surcharge and see the film in proper 2-D with brighter color. 12

Focuses on the acting, a key criterion in film reviews.

ANDREW O'HEHIR

Harry Potter and the Deathly Hallows: Part 2: An Action-Packed Curtain Call

REVIEW

Andrew O'Hehir has written about films and media for more than twenty years. Currently O'Hehir focuses on films (including film reviews) for *Salon.com* and also has written for *Art & Antiques, Spin,* the *New York Times,* the *Hollywood Reporter,* and other journals. O'Hehir graduated from the Johns Hopkins University. This review was published in *Salon* in 2011. O'Hehir's review is an interesting contrast to Roger Ebert's evaluation of the film. As you read it, look for the aspects of this review that disagree with what Ebert has to say about this final Harry Potter film.

Conclusions to fantasy epics and quest narratives pose a diabolical problem for their creators, one that calls to mind a remark I once read in a journal by Edmund Wilson, one of the 20th century's greatest cultural critics. Late in his life Wilson had decided to give up reading history, he wrote, because "I know the kinds of things that happen." Epic fantasy is, if possible, even more familiar than history, in that we know *exactly* what will happen: Good will triumph over evil at great price, but only after the hero endures a crisis of self-doubt and agrees to sacrifice himself for the greater good. So the execution of such a conclusion becomes largely a technical matter, a matter of How more than What, and still less Why. In the case of *Harry Potter and the Deathly Hallows: Part 2*, a movie with no beginning and no middle but two-plus hours of thundering, momentous ending, all of this is carried to a comical extreme.

I'm not trying to wage some kind of King Canute battle against the tide of approbation for this remarkable series and its final chapter, honest. I am suggesting that we're all congratulating the filmmakers for not having screwed the whole thing up too badly. (Which is something to be celebrated: Consider the ever-dwindling *Chronicles of Narnia* series, or the disastrous efforts to turn Philip Pullman's *His Dark Materials* and Lemony Snicket's *Series of Unfortunate Events* into movie franchises.) Director David Yates, screenwriter Steve Kloves and their formerly young cast—Daniel Radcliffe, Rupert Grint and Emma Watson began this enterprise as schoolchildren and now seem ready for divorces and rehab clinics—bring the Potter cycle to rest with a great cinematic clash of cymbals (and symbols). *Harry Potter and the Deathly Hallows: Part 2* is a grave and violent picture built around the large-scale destruction of Hogwarts, Harry's beloved alma mater, and the final confrontation between Harry (Radcliffe) and the reptile-headed Dark Lord Voldemort (Ralph Fiennes), who are linked to each other in ways they don't quite understand.

As he began to do in *Deathly Hallows: Part 1*, Yates deliberately recalls the inspirational movies about the blitz of London and the lonely courage with which the British faced Hitler in the dark early years of World War II. I don't know

Summarizes the movie.

3

whether J. K. Rowling has ever discussed the Battle of Britain as an influence on her fantasy universe, but she's precisely the right age to have been raised on such national mythological tales of Churchill-era nobility and sacrifice. While most of *Deathly Hallows: Part 2* is set in and around the climactic siege of Hogwarts—in which, yes, some beloved Potterworld personages will die—we also see Harry, red-headed Ron (Grint) and shockingly grown-up Hermione (Watson, of course, but in this sequence also played by Helena Bonham Carter, and don't make me explain) stage a daring raid on the Gringotts Wizarding Bank, which ends with an abused captive dragon totally destroying the place. Any consonance with current events, which renders it especially satisfying to witness a bank reduced to rubble, is presumably coincidental. (As we now know, many financial institutions in the Muggle universe are also run by greedy and untrustworthy goblins.)

Focuses on special effects, a key criterion in fantasy films.

If the Gringotts raid is one of the Potter series' most effective uses of large-scale CGI effects, I found much of the final battle at Hogwarts, including the O.K. Corral showdown between Harry and Voldemort, disappointingly generic. Oh, I don't mean that it's boring to sit through, exactly. There's a whole lot of spellcasting and Death-Eating and exploding Gothic architecture and Fiennes' lizard-man Voldemort howling in pain and pointlessly murdering underlings as Harry and friends gradually discover and destroy the Horcruxes that contain fragments of his soul. (I can't stop myself: The next-to-last Horcrux is inside . . . mmrp! Stifled by the Spoiler Cops, just in time.) Yates and cinematographer Eduardo Serra do a nice job of keeping the viewer oriented in space and time, no mean feat when space is an imaginary digital artifact and time is completely elastic. There's a lovely and crucial flashback sequence into the memories of über-Goth potions expert turned Hogwarts headmaster Severus Snape (Alan Rickman)—for my money the most compelling character in the whole series—whose long-running and ambiguous role in the Potter mythos is finally revealed.

Along with Rickman, numerous other beloved players make final cameos, making this peculiar film—which is simultaneously too short and too long—feel an awful lot like an extended curtain call. Maggie Smith as Prof. McGonagall and Jim Broadbent as Prof. Slughorn, Robbie Coltrane as Hagrid, Tom Felton as the chastened Draco Malfoy, Bonham Carter as the adorably evil Bellatrix Lestrange, David Thewlis as lycanthrope Remus Lupin and Evanna Lynch as New Agey Celtic seer Luna Lovegood all get a few seconds of screen time. So do various departed characters, including Harry's long-dead parents, Gary Oldman as Sirius Black and of course Michael Gambon as Albus Dumbledore, who appears in a misty-moisty afterlife scene where Yates simultaneously manages to screw up a crucial plot point and render the spiritual underpinnings of the entire Potter franchise as total bollocks. (We also meet Dumbledore's grouchy brother, nicely played by Ciarán Hinds, a personal favorite.) And I *guess* Harry's so-called paramour Ginny Weasley (Bonnie Wright) makes an appearance, but not so you'd notice it. (Potter fans hate me for this one, but the submerged sexual tension between Harry, Hermione and Ron is a central element of this universe, and one Rowling herself seems barely aware of. Ginny is a transparent and inadequate attempt to defuse it.)

What bugs me about *Deathly Hallows: Part 2* may be an inevitable consequence of the fact that Yates and Kloves, previous directors Chris Columbus, Mike Newell and Alfonso Cuarón, and everybody else who's worked on this amazing 14-year, eight-film odyssey has had to serve so many masters. Loyalty to both the letter and spirit of Rowling's books was more important than it almost ever is in a Hollywood production, because the universe of Potter fandom is so large, so well-organized and so vocal. But the filmmakers also had to appeal to moviegoers who hadn't read the books and were absorbing the whole story on-screen, as well as casual viewers who might dip in and out, depending on reviews or what their friends said, in search of an exciting yarn but without much caring about the history of the Diadem of Ravenclaw or the backstage intrigue among the Hogwarts faculty.

6

Viewed in that light, *Harry Potter and the Deathly Hallows: Part 2* is an adequate and often artful exercise in checking off boxes. If you haven't imbibed a minimum of four or five other Potter books and/or movies, including *Deathly Hallows: Part 1*, then the exposition surrounding the action sequences will be total gibberish and you shouldn't even bother. (By the way, I saw it in Imax 3-D, and unless you can't stop yourself don't spend the extra money.) This is almost entirely a movie for the Potter fan base, which may have been the only possible outcome in adapting Rowling's torrents of verbiage, dense plotting and encyclopedic arcana. But this final installment, driven far less by acting and characterization than any of the preceding seven, fails the Peter Jackson test of becoming an affecting and absorbing work on its own terms.

7

Provides an evaluation of the movie, comparing it with another movie in the series.

The "O Children" sequence in *Deathly Hallows: Part 1*, and indeed the entire haunted, lonely middle section of that vastly superior movie, have stayed with me powerfully. Hours after seeing this one, I don't look back on it with any emotion, or even much in the way of sense-memory. Radcliffe as Harry, and even more so Fiennes as the wounded Voldemort, who feels victory escaping his grasp as evil wizards always will, are both splendid. But the final confrontation between these intertwined geniuses, at least as we see it here, has no moral or intellectual heft; it's a lightning-bolt battle out of a 1980s *Doctor Strange* comic. (I'm not saying that's the worst thing in the world.) Seconds later, I was out on the sidewalk in front of the theater, feeling a little baffled and irritated: Wait, Dumbledore said what to Snape and what to Harry? Voldemort is incapable of killing Harry because . . . why, exactly? Which Horcrux is the giant snake and which one is the Magic Cup of H.R. Pufnstuf? What the Sam Hill are the Deathly Hallows again, and what do they have to do with anything? (Answer: They don't.)

8

So ends this enormously important, and enormously extended, chapter of   9
pop culture, with a combination of bang and whimper. Nothing quite like this
series has ever been tried before in cinema history, and as I wrote last year,
following the central trio of Radcliffe, Grint and Watson through the aging process has itself forced the movies to confront Rowling's central themes, which I
take to be "the painful transition from childhood to adulthood, the loss of parents
and loved ones, the first intimations of personal mortality." For better or worse,
Rowling's books and the hit-and-miss movies based on them have reshaped not
just the marketplace for fiction and film but the contemporary cultural imagination, re-establishing fantasy as the central narrative mode (arguably for the first
time since the Middle Ages). I suspect that Rowling will remain popular for a
long time while the films fade a lot more rapidly into the background. But we
have only begun to live in the world they made.

UNDERSTANDING A WRITER'S GOALS: QUESTIONS TO CONSIDER AND DISCUSS

Rhetorical Knowledge: The Writers' Situation and Rhetoric

1. **Audience:** In their reviews, both Ebert and O'Hehir discuss the success of the series of Harry Potter films. Does this technique help audiences better understand their reviews?

2. **Purpose:** How similar are Ebert's and O'Hehir's purposes for writing their reviews?

3. **Voice and tone:** How do Ebert and O'Hehir reveal their attitudes toward the film and toward their readers? Does O'Hehir's generally negative review make you want to see the film? Discourage you from wanting to see the film? Why?

4. **Responsibility:** To what extent do Ebert and O'Hehir seem responsible to their readers? How responsible should movie reviewers be to their readers? Why?

5. **Context and genre:** Consider how this film has been highly anticipated by a huge audience. How does that anticipation seem to affect both reviews? A movie review typically includes some plot summary to help readers who have not seen the film. How effectively has each reviewer summarized the plot of *Harry Potter and the Deathly Hallows: Part 2*?

Critical Thinking: The Writers' Ideas and Your Personal Response

6. What are the relative strengths and weaknesses of each review?

7. If you have seen *Harry Potter and the Deathly Hallows: Part 2,* on what points do you agree and disagree most strongly with Ebert and with O'Hehir? If you have not seen the film, which review is most effective in convincing you to see or not see the film?

Composing Processes and Knowledge of Conventions: The Writers' Strategies

8. Compare the attention that Ebert and O'Hehir pay to plot and characters. How do they differ?

9. How clearly do Ebert and O'Hehir state their criteria for evaluating *Harry Potter and the Deathly Hallows: Part 2*? Where in each review do you find their criteria indicated?

Inquiry and Research: Ideas for Further Exploration

10. Conduct a Web search to find other reviews of *Harry Potter and the Deathly Hallows: Part 2.* How are those reviews similar to or different from the ones that Ebert and O'Hehir wrote?

11. Look up O'Hehir's review of *Harry Potter and the Deathly Hallows: Part 1* and compare it to this review of *Part 2.* Which is a more effective review, and why?

12. If you saw *Harry Potter and the Deathly Hallows: Part 2* in 3-D, watch the film again in 2-D. Explain why you agree or disagree with Ebert's "Note," at the end of his review, where he writes, "There are a few shots that benefit from 3-D (I like the unfolding of the little magical globe) but none that require it. Avoid the surcharge and see the film in proper 2-D with brighter color," or with O'Hehir, who writes, "By the way, I saw it in Imax 3-D, and unless you can't stop yourself don't spend the extra money."

WRITING PROCESSES

As you work on the assignment that you have chosen, remember the qualities of an effective and convincing evaluative paper, which are listed on pages 288–90. Also remember that while the activities listed below imply that writers proceed step-by-step, as you write, you will keep coming back to your earlier work, modifying your criteria and strengthening the support for your claim.

Strategies FOR Success | Engagement

Successful writers find ways to engage with their subject matter: they are interested in and involved with what they are writing about. To be engaged in your subject, it helps to select a topic to evaluate that interests you (if you have a choice of topic). If you have an interest in cars, for example, evaluating a particular car or some aspect of the automotive industry could be an engaging topic for you. If you are interested in a specific major or a particular career goal (to become an attorney, for example), then that subject will probably engage your interest. If you enjoy a particular genre of film, or a specific type of video game, that interest can inform your choice of topics.

Selecting a topic that engages you will help you ask pertinent questions about that subject, to explore all of its most important features, and to effectively compare or contrast it with other similar subjects. And selecting, focusing on, and working with an engaging subject will be more interesting and fun for you as you examine that subject in detail and then evaluate it. A successful evaluation also engages readers, so work with your classmates to determine what they think about your evaluation—and pay close attention to their comments and suggestions on how to improve your text.

Invention: Getting Started

For more on discovery and learning, see Chapter 4.

Invention activities can help you clarify what you might want to evaluate before you begin your evaluation. Writers often find it useful to work through several invention activities for any particular writing task. Regardless of the invention activities you do, try to answer these questions while you work:

- What do I already know about the subject that I am thinking about evaluating?
- What makes each potential subject suitable for evaluation?
- What criteria can I establish for my evaluation? On what basis should I make my judgment? How can I compare it with similar items?
- What kinds of explanation can I provide about each of my criteria?
- Where might I learn more about this subject?
- What verifiable information about my subject is available?

- Are any of my criteria potentially just a matter of opinion, and if so, how might I explain them?
- What might my audience already know about my subject? What do I know about my audience? What don't I know that I should know?

Writing Activity

Clustering

Clustering is an invention technique that can help you focus on a subject to evaluate and come up with criteria for your evaluation. Working with the questions here, spend a few minutes jotting down everything you can think of about the subject or subjects you want to evaluate or discussing them with classmates. Don't worry about putting this information into sentences or paragraphs; simply record it using any words that come to mind. Or try freewriting, which is writing continuously.

Once you have some ideas, you can then use clustering to see relationships between or among them. Put the subject you are focusing on into a circle in the center of a piece of paper, and spend a few minutes creating a cluster of your ideas about the subject.

Annlee Lawrence's Clustering

Annlee Lawrence decided to write an evaluation of meals at some local fast-food restaurants. To get started, Lawrence brainstormed her initial thoughts, which turned out to be a series of questions. She continued her invention work by doing some freewriting and then clustering her ideas. Below is an example of a cluster Lawrence might have done for her evaluation of fast-food restaurants.

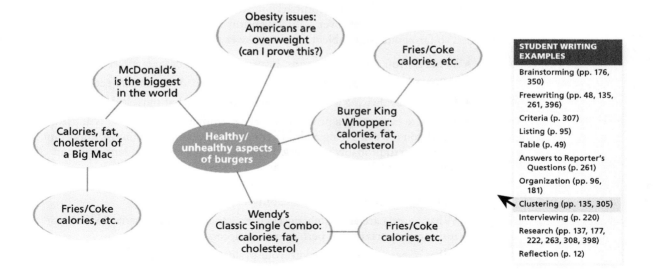

STUDENT WRITING EXAMPLES

Brainstorming (pp. 176, 350)
Freewriting (pp. 48, 135, 261, 396)
Criteria (p. 307)
Listing (p. 95)
Table (p. 49)
Answers to Reporter's Questions (p. 261)
Organization (pp. 96, 181)
Clustering (pp. 135, 305)
Interviewing (p. 220)
Research (pp. 137, 177, 222, 263, 308, 398)
Reflection (p. 12)

Constructing and Supporting Evaluative Criteria

To evaluate any subject, you need to begin by considering the basis on which you will make your evaluation, as well as how you might support your criteria. Consider the various aspects of the subject on which you might base your evaluation. Here are just a few possibilities:

- Physical aspects such as size, weight, shape, taste, smell, and sound (these criteria are often used in evaluating food products and restaurant meals, for example)
- Quality (often measured by the warranty period, both in length of time and which parts of the product are covered under the manufacturer's warranty)
- Aesthetic aspects (for example, how the item feels to use, drive, listen to, sit in, wear), color, and proportion (you use these kinds of criteria when you purchase clothing)
- Entertainment-value aspects (If you are evaluating a TV action drama, for example, you might use criteria such as quality of the acting, number of action scenes in each episode, and level of interest in and appeal of the main characters.)
- Comparative aspects, such as the following:
  - Which career would give me the greatest satisfaction? Why?
  - What is the best place to study? Why?
  - Which political candidate should get my vote? Why?

For more on making comparisons, see Chapter 13.

In most evaluations, you will need to show how your subject can be measured against similar subjects and explain the basis of your comparison. If you are comparing two automobiles, for example, you could compare them in terms of price, gas mileage, and maintenance, among other criteria.

Once you have a basis for comparison, the first step in deciding the criteria for your evaluation is to look over your invention work and consider what you have learned so far about your subject. Try to answer these questions:

- What do you consider the most important aspect of your subject?
- What other qualities, either positive or negative, does this subject have?
- If you are evaluating a subject for its usefulness, what must it do?
- If you are evaluating a product or service, think about what you will use it for. If you are evaluating a child's car seat, for example, the most important criterion will probably be safety. What do you mean by the term *safe*, and how can you tell if a particular car seat is safe?
- If a product or service needs to be reliable, what do you mean by that term, and how can you determine reliability?
- What criteria are absolutely necessary for the subject to possess? What criteria are important, but perhaps not as necessary?
- What research might help with your evaluation? Will a search of the Web help? What would you gain from talking with others or conducting a survey?

Writing Activity

Constructing and Supporting Criteria

Construct a list of possible criteria for your evaluation. For each of your criteria, explain, in no more than one sentence, why it is important in evaluating your subject. Also, in no more than one sentence, outline what kind of evidence you might use to support each criterion.

Annlee Lawrence's Criteria

After Annlee Lawrence completed some brainstorming and freewriting about her subject, she made a list of the criteria for evaluating fast-food restaurants and did some additional freewriting to discover what they meant and what she thought about each one. Here is an excerpt:

- Why should anyone care about eating a burger?
- What does "obesity" mean? Who says it's important?
- Why is "fat" bad and are there different kinds of fat?
- How does cholesterol hurt people? And I read somewhere that there is both good and bad cholesterol—I wonder if any of each is in a burger?
- And everyone knows that we want to consume fewer calories, right?
- Does any of this affect taste?
- What about the other stuff we usually eat with a burger? Fries? A Coke?

I guess I know it's important to not be overweight and all, but I wonder if eating a burger now and then really matters. Aren't there some people who eat them all the time, though? I mean, with fries and all? How bad could that be? I need to learn more about fat and calories and things, so I can point to what is bad (and if anything is good) about America's burgers.

Once I learn some stuff—now, where can I learn the fat content, etc. of burgers? Does McDonald's and Wendy's and Burger King post them some where? Online? It'd be kind of funny if I had to go and buy a burger at each place, just to find out how unhealthy it might be!

And once I have some information, how can I present it so readers can understand and make a wise choice, based on my evaluation?

STUDENT WRITING EXAMPLES

Brainstorming (pp. 176, 350)
Freewriting (pp. 48, 135, 261, 396)
Criteria (p. 307)
Listing (p. 95)
Table (p. 49)
Answers to Reporter's Questions (p. 261)
Organization (pp. 96, 181)
Clustering (pp. 135, 305)
Interviewing (p. 220)
Research (pp. 137, 177, 222, 263, 308, 398)
Reflection (p. 12)

Exploring Your Ideas with Research

Although personal opinions are sometimes sufficient evidence for an evaluation, in more formal settings, you will need to support your claims with outside research. One advantage of conducting research is that the information you find will help you form your judgment about your subject. It's important not to make that judgment too soon; often you won't know what you really think until you have done a lot of invention work, conducted much of your research, and have even written a draft or two.

Research, of course, can give you solid evidence—verifiable information, such as figures, statistics, data, or expert testimony—to help support your final evaluation.

For help with locating sources of information and with field research, see Chapter 19; for help with taking notes and documenting your sources, see Chapter 20.

The kind and amount of research you will need to do will vary according to the rhetorical situation: who your audience is and what you are trying to accomplish. Use the reporter's questions of *who, what, when, where, why,* and *how* to get started on your research. After you have determined the information you need, decide what kind of research you should conduct to gather that information, in the library and on the Internet. You may also need to do field research.

As you review your notes, look for information that will help you show to what degree your subject does, or does not, meet a given criterion. Look as well for any conclusions that others have drawn about the subject of your evaluation—and consider if and how your evaluation differs from theirs. While you can use others' opinions in support of your conclusion, hearing and reading what others have said will often provide new ideas and suggest additional avenues for research.

As you conduct your research, you may find that other writers have reached judgments that differ from yours. You will want to address—and counter—their opinions in your comments, in order to strengthen your evaluation.

Writing Activity

Conducting Research

Using the list of qualities of effective evaluative writing on pages 288–90, review your invention writing and your list of criteria, and note what you already know about your subject. Next, determine whether you need to do research to come up with additional criteria or evidence, learn more about similar subjects, or muster stronger counterarguments.

In no more than two pages, outline a research plan. In your plan, indicate the following:

- What you already know about your subject
- What questions you still have
- Who or what sources might answer your questions
- Who might provide other perspectives on your subject
- Where you might look for further information
- When you plan to conduct your research

Gather, read, and take notes on your subject from these outside sources. Use an electronic journal to record images, URLs, and other information that you find as you conduct your research.

Annlee Lawrence's Research Strategy

Annlee Lawrence needed to research the nutritional content of typical meals available from the three restaurants she was evaluating. She developed the following research plan:

- I'll check both online and at the stores themselves, to see if the information is provided.
- I need to try to compare apples-to-apples as much as I can—that is, I want to compare similar-size hamburgers, and similar-size fries and drinks (otherwise it

would be an unfair evaluation and my readers would not benefit and probably wouldn't believe me).

- I should check in the library for information on why these things (calories, fat, cholesterol) are bad for people.
- I may also find in the library some useful information about the companies I'm focusing on (McDonald's, Wendy's, Burger King). I know there are others (Sonic, A&W), but I want to concentrate on the big three, as they're everywhere.

Reviewing Your Invention and Research

After you have conducted your research, review your invention work and notes and think about the information you collected from outside sources and how that information matches the criteria you have for your evaluation. You may be ready to decide on a working thesis statement—a statement that summarizes the main point of your evaluation—at this point. Even though you might already have a general idea of the conclusion your evaluation is leading you to, your thesis should come *from* your complete evaluation. It is best to decide on your thesis when you have done a lot of invention work (listing, brainstorming, clustering, and other strategies) and research. You might even wait until after you construct your first draft.

Writing Activity

Considering Your Research and Focusing Your Ideas

Examine the notes you have taken from your research. Then, using your criteria as a starting point, see how your information matches the criteria you have established.

Organizing Your Evaluation

Once you have some sense of the criteria you will use and how your subject matches those criteria, consider how you might organize your evaluation. Here are some questions to ask yourself when deciding on your organization:

- Who is the audience for your evaluation?
- Why might readers be interested in your evaluation, or how you can make them interested in it?
- What is your purpose for writing—that is, what will your readers learn about your subject by reading your evaluation? How will that knowledge help them as they write their own evaluations?

ELECTRONIC ENVIRONMENTS ⎬ **Using Computer Software to Create Hierarchies**

If there's one thing computers are good at, it's establishing hierarchies (systems of ranking, prioritizing, and organizing things). When you're writing an essay that evaluates something, the computer screen can serve as a workshop space, where you can move around ideas and concepts.

You can use a variety of software programs—and sometimes different windows within the same software application—to design charts, outlines, tables, Venn diagrams, timelines, and other visual space-holders for your information. Use color, line, shape, and space to code information, defining categories and interesting interrelations among your ideas and segments of information.

For more on design and visuals, including examples of different kinds of graphics, see Chapter 18.

The answers to these questions can help you decide what you need to emphasize, which in turn will help you choose an organizational approach.

For more on the inductive and deductive methods, see Chapter 9.

Here is a brief outline of three possible organizational approaches for writing an evaluation:

Options FOR Organization
Options for Organizing Evaluations

First Inductive Approach	Second Inductive Approach	Deductive Approach
Outline why you are making the evaluation.	Begin with a discussion of the subject or subjects that you are evaluating.	Begin with the conclusion that you have reached about the subject or subjects (your thesis statement).
Discuss/explain the criteria.	Explain its or their strengths and weaknesses.	Explain why and how you reached that conclusion using a compare-and-contrast format; compare and contrast each aspect of what you are evaluating in relation to the criteria.
Explain how well your subject or subjects match (or fail to match) the various criteria.	Outline how the positive and negative points match each of your criteria.	
Discuss which subjects are "best," according to the evaluative criteria you have established. Explain your thesis statement in your conclusion.	Explain how the subject or subjects you are evaluating fulfill those criteria (this, then, is your thesis statement).	

Constructing a Complete Draft

Once you have generated some initial thoughts and ideas, selected the criteria for judging your subject, and reviewed your notes from your reading and research, your next step is to write a first draft, which is often called a working draft. Your first draft is your opportunity to expand, explain, and develop your ideas.

Before beginning your draft, review the writing you have done so far. What are the relative advantages of evaluating several items or of concentrating on just one? Why? Review the criteria that you have developed and decide which you want to emphasize. If your instructor and/or peers have given you suggestions, consider how you will incorporate their advice into your evaluation. As you prepare to write, ask yourself the following questions:

- What is the most effective way to explain my criteria?
- In what ways does the subject of my evaluation match up with (or fail to match up with) the criteria I have selected?
- What is my final evaluation?
- How can I express my main point effectively as a thesis statement?

As you draft your evaluation, stop occasionally to read your work, imagining that you are reading it for the first time. Because your draft is an exploratory text, ask yourself the following questions:

- How have I compared my subject with similar items?
- How effectively have I added details demonstrating how well the subject matches my criteria?
- What visual information might I use to explain my evaluation?
- How clear is my final judgment?

For more on comparison, definition, and description, see Chapter 13.

Synthesizing and Integrating Sources into Your Draft: Creating Visuals to Show Your Data

INTEGRATING SOURCES

Including Others' Perspectives in Narratives (p. 97)

Quoting Sources (p. 139)

Paraphrasing Sources (p. 181)

Incorporating Numerical Data (p. 224)

Incorporating Partial Quotes (p. 266)

Creating Visuals to Show Your Data (p. 311)

Summarizing Information from Sources (p. 356)

Including Research Information (p. 401)

In many ways, simply doing an evaluation is a kind of synthesis—the act of taking pieces of information and putting them together to form a new way of looking at your subject. The specific details of the subject that you are evaluating, taken together, will enable you to make the determining judgments needed for your evaluation. These details from your research will then help your readers follow your line of thought and understand the reasoning behind your judgments.

When researching and writing an evaluation, you may find that some of your evaluation will be based on numerical data. One useful way to show those data is in the form of a graph or a table. We can see how Annlee Lawrence incorporates numerical data into her evaluative narrative both to explain to and to show her readers the total caloric intake of some popular fast-food meals:

> When I researched the nutritional content of these three meals, I found that all three have high calorie content (see fig. 1). The Whopper Combo from Burger King has been a favorite of Americans for generations. But is it as good for your body as it is to your taste buds? When I researched the nutritional information, I discovered that this meal has a grand total of 1230 calories. In contrast, Wendy's Classic Single Combo has 1060 calories, and McDonald's Quarter Pounder Combo has 1000.

Lawrence lists the meals in descending order based on number of calories. Some readers simply get overwhelmed with reading numbers, however. One way to make a clearer argument is to do what Lawrence did: incorporate numbers into your narrative, but also use graphs or tables to visually depict the data. Lawrence could total the caloric intake of each of the fast-food meals and show the results in a table, for example:

Table 1 Calories in a Fast Food Meal

Fast-Food Meal	Total calories
Burger King's Whopper Combo	1230
Wendy's Classic	1060
McDonald's Quarter Pounder Combo	1000

Consider how such a table makes it easy for readers to see what Lawrence found out about the calorie content of various fast-food combination meals.

Parts of a Complete Draft

Introduction: One of the qualities of a successful evaluation is that it grabs and holds readers' attention. Strategies that will help you hook your readers include the following:

- **Begin by explaining why you are making the evaluation—your rhetorical purpose—followed by a discussion of your criteria.** It is also often helpful to include an explanation of why you selected these criteria. This is usually the approach taken by articles in consumer magazines such as *Consumer Reports.* Jonathan Liu uses this approach in "The 5 Best Toys of All Time," indicating that his criteria are that the five toys he is discussing "should fit easily within any budget, and are appropriate for a wide age range so you get the most play out of each one. These are time-tested and kid-approved!"
- **Indicate your conclusion at the beginning.** You will then explain in the body of your text why and how you reached that conclusion. Roger Ebert uses this type of introduction in his review: "After seven earlier films reaching back a decade, the Harry Potter saga comes to a solid and satisfying conclusion in *Harry Potter and the Deathly Hallows: Part 2.*"
- **Set the scene for your evaluation.** Depending on your topic, you might open your evaluation with a description of your subject.

Body: If you are using the inductive approach, indicate what you want to evaluate and on what basis at the beginning, and then work through the process (and through the body of your evaluation) as you go. If you are using the deductive method, begin by stating your judgment, and then use the body of your paper to support it, often by comparing and contrasting your subject with other subjects of the same type.

Conclusion: Regardless of the organizational method you employ, make sure that your judgment of your subject—your evaluation—is clearly stated. Remember that in an evaluation, your ultimate conclusion is usually your thesis statement, or main point, but your conclusion can serve other purposes as well. A conclusion in evaluative writing often does the following:

- **Summarizes how each supporting piece of evidence helps support your main point.** In a lengthy, detailed evaluation, a summary of your findings can help readers recall the main points that you are making.
- **Reaches out to your audience.** An appeal to the audience is an especially effective way to end an evaluation, as often you want them not only to agree with your evaluation but also to do something with what they have learned.

Title: As you compose your evaluative writing, a title should emerge at some point—perhaps late in the process. The title should reflect your judgment of your subject, and it should catch your readers' attention and make them want to read your essay.

ELECTRONIC ENVIRONMENTS) **Storing Image Files**

It is always a good idea to store the photographs you find in your research in a separate computer file, so you will have easy access to them when you start constructing your evaluation. Name your images and folders so that you can easily find the pictures you wish to use. For example: "Rodeo_rider. jpg," or "calfroper1. gif" will help you more easily find images you've saved than "pic1" or "image_3".

Be aware that image files come in different formats: .jpg, .gif, .bmp, and .tif are some common image file extensions. If a picture will not open on your computer, it may be because you don't have a program on your computer that is capable of handling that image's format.

VISUAL *Thinking* | Going Beyond Words to Achieve Your Goals

For more on using visuals, see Chapter 18.

As a result of her research, Annlee Lawrence found a number of statistics that she wanted to use in her paper to help readers understand her evaluation.

While writers can often present statistical information in sentences within their text, presenting that information in a table organizes the data for readers and makes it easier for them to understand. For example, the information on calories, cholesterol, and fat in the second paragraph of Lawrence's first draft (see page 315) could be presented like this:

Food item	calories	milligrams of salt	fat (grams)
Whopper	670	980	40
Fries (salted)	410	530	18
Coke	290		

She could also put her information in the form of a column or bar graph, or if Lawrence wanted to show how the total calories of these three food items make up a meal, she could use a pie chart.

- While Lawrence selected a pie chart to display this data, would a line or bar chart be as effective?

- What other kind of visual—such as a drawing or photograph—might help readers understand this information?

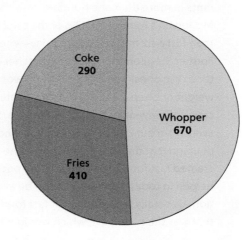

Calories from Parts of a Meal

Writing Activity

Constructing a Full Draft

After reviewing your notes, invention activities, and research, and carefully considering all of the information that you generated and the comments you received, construct a complete first draft of your evaluation, using the organizational approach that you have decided on. Remember that your evaluation will evolve as you write, so your ideas will most likely change as you compose this first draft. Remember also that you will be learning as you write. While you may have some sense of whether your subject fits your criteria, expect to modify your position as you develop your evaluation essay.

Annlee Lawrence's First Draft

After deciding on an organizational approach and a tentative thesis, Annlee Lawrence was ready to begin her first, or working, draft. She did not worry about errors and instead concentrated on getting her main ideas on paper. Note that she started her paper by outlining what she was going to do, without revealing her conclusions. This inductive approach is one of the possible organizational methods described on page 310. As she wrote, Lawrence did not worry about grammar, punctuation, and mechanics; instead, she concentrated on getting her main ideas into her draft. (The numbers in circles refer to peer comments, which follow the draft on page 316.)

Who Has the Better Burger?
Annlee Lawrence

Did you know that McDonald's operates more than thirty thousand restaurants in more than one hundred countries on six continents? In the United States, McDonald's represents 43% of the total fast-food market. McDonald's feeds more than forty-six million people a day—more than the entire population of Spain! Former Surgeon General David Satcher comments, "Fast food is a major contributor to the obesity epidemic." It's no wonder that sixty percent of America is overweight or obese. Obesity, if left unabated, will surpass smoking as the leading cause of preventable death in America. So why is it that we can't seem to stay away from our beloved Big Macs or Whoppers? Probably because our lives demand it at times. We don't have time to prepare a full-blown meal, so we have created fast food to fit with our fast-paced lives. So unfortunately, obesity can't be helped in today's society, but can be avoided through moderation of consumption. Generally speaking, most fast food is unhealthy. But if you had to pick one that was the healthiest, which would it be? I felt that for this evaluation, the most important criteria for determining a "healthy" burger should be calories, total fat, and cholesterol. I chose some of the favorite meals to evaluate: the Whopper Combo from Burger King, Wendy's Classic Single Combo, and McDonald's Quarter Pounder Combo.①

The Whopper Combo from Burger King has been a favorite of Americans for generations. But is it as good to your body as it is to your taste buds? When I researched the nutritional information, I discovered that the sandwich itself has 670 calories, 75 milligrams of cholesterol, 40 grams of total fat, and 980 milligrams of sodium. A medium order of salted fries has 410 calories, 18 grams of fat, and 530 milligrams of sodium. Not to mention the medium Coke that contains 290 calories. All this adds up to be a grand total of 1370 calories, 58 grams of fat, and 75 milligrams of cholesterol (Burger King Nutritional Information).②

Because I used the Burger King Whopper, I picked a similar sandwich from Wendy's, Dave's Hot 'N Juicy 1/4 lb. Single. The burger has 580 calories, 33 grams of total fat, 105 milligrams of cholesterol, and 2480 grams of sodium. A medium fry has 420 calories, 21 grams of fat, and a medium coke has 240 calories. This all adds up to 1240 calories, 51 grams of total fat, and 105 milligrams of cholesterol (Wendy's Nutrition Facts).

Last but not least, there is the McDonald's Quarter Pounder with cheese. Despite popular opinion, this burger is the best for you. It has 510 calories, 26 grams of fat, and 1190 milligrams of sodium, which is 50% of what people are supposed to have, each day, salt-wise. A medium fry has 380 calories, 19 grams of fat, and 270 milligrams of sodium. And a 16 ounce Coke has 150 calories. The total calories would be 1040, total fat 35, and total sodium of 1460, which is about 60% of the recommended daily sodium intake ("Get the Nutrition").

So if you do get caught up in a hurry and feel like grabbing a burger and you are counting calories, then get the McDonald's Quarter Pounder. The McDonald's Quarter Pounder has 70 fewer calories than the Wendy's "Dave's Hot 'N Juicy 1/4 lb. Single" and 160 fewer calories than the Burger King Whopper. Even their fries have 30 fewer calories than Wendy's and 40 fewer than Burger King. This doesn't mean that you should go and buy out McDonald's. Obviously, as the movie *Super-Size Me* proved, even the "healthy" fast food isn't good for you. But if eaten in moderation, fast food is one of the best things to happen to America.③

Works Cited ④

Burger King Nutritional Information. Web. 21 January 2012. <http://www.bk.com/en/us/ menu-nutrition/index.html>.

McDonald's Corporation. "McDonald's USA Nutrition Facts for Popular Menu Items." Web. 2 Aug. 2012. <http://nutrition.mcdonalds.com/getnutrition/nutritionfacts.pdf>

*"Getting to Know Us." Web. 29 January 2012. <http://www.aboutmcdonalds.com/mcd/
our_company.html>.*

*McDonalds (NYSE:MCD) report: Market share, margins on the rise." 16 November 2010.
Web. 29 January 2012. <http://www.stockmarketsreview.com/recommendations/
mcdonalds_report_20101115_59520/>.*

*"McDonald's 24/7." 5 February 2007. Web. 29 January 2012. <http://www.businessweek.com/
magazine/content/07_06/b4020001.htm>.*

*Wendy's Nutrition Facts & Topics. Web. 21 January 2012. <http://www.wendys
.com/food/Nutrition.jsp.mcdon>.*

Student Comments on Annlee Lawrence's First Draft

1. "These seem like good criteria, but why did you choose them? Do you need a stronger reason for your criteria here?"

2. "These are a lot of statistics to digest at once (sorry!). I got lost. Can you give all this in a table or chart?"

3. "Seems like the ending contradicts the rest of your essay. Why is fast food good for America? The ending seems wrong here."

4. "You should check your formatting here. I think the dates might be wrong. Also, don't you have a quote in the first paragraph from the Surgeon General? There's no citation for it here."

Revising

Once you have a full draft of your evaluation, you still have much to do. First, however, you should set the draft aside so that you can gain some critical distance. You can then read it with fresh eyes.

As you revise your early drafts, hold off on doing a great deal of heavy editing. When you revise, you will probably change the content and structure of your paper, so time spent working to fix problems with grammar, punctuation, or mechanics at this stage is often wasted.

When you reread the first draft of your evaluation, here are some questions to ask yourself:

- How effectively have I explained or indicated my criteria?
- What else might my audience want or need to know about my subject?
- How else might I interest my audience in my evaluation of this subject?
- What did I find out about my subject that I did not include in my evaluation?

WRITER'S *Workshop* | Responding to Full Drafts

Working with one or two other classmates, read each evaluation and offer comments and questions that will help each of you see your papers' strengths and weaknesses. Consider the following questions as you do:

- What is your first impression of this draft? How effective is the title at drawing you in? Why? What are your overall suggestions for improvement? What part(s) of the text are especially strong?
- How clear and understandable is the point of the evaluation?
- How has the writer explained the subject of the evaluation? How might he or she develop the explanation further to make it more effective?
- How clearly and thoroughly has the writer explained and justified the criteria? What details need to be added or clarified?
- How effectively has the writer applied his or her criteria?

- How adequately are all assertions supported with evidence?
- If the writer makes comparisons, how clear are they? Where might additional comparisons be called for?
- How could the writer more clearly match the criteria to the subject? Are there any criteria that the writer discusses but never applies to the subject?
- What terms need to be defined?
- How effective is the organization of this evaluation? Why?
- How might visuals help the writer support his or her criteria more effectively?
- How clearly does the writer present and discuss any opposing points of view on this subject?
- How adequately is the writer's overall evaluation supported by the evidence he or she has presented?

- How clearly have I defined any terms my readers might not know?
- Could some aspects of my evaluation be more effectively presented as a graph or chart?

Technology can help you revise and edit your writing more easily. Use your word processor's track-changes tool to try out revisions and editing changes. After you have had time to think about the possible changes, you can "accept" or "reject" them. Also, you can use your word processor's comment tool to write reminders to yourself when you get stuck with a revision or some editing task.

Because it is so difficult even for experienced writers to see their emerging writing with a fresh eye, it is almost always useful to ask classmates, friends, or family members to read drafts of your evaluative writing.

Responding to Readers' Comments

Once they have received feedback on their writing from peers, instructors, friends, and others, all writers have to decide what to do with that feedback. Since your writing is your responsibility, you must determine how to deal with reader responses to your work.

The first thing to do with any feedback is to consider carefully what your readers have to say about your text. For example, Annlee Lawrence's readers had the following reactions:

- One reader wondered why she chose the criteria she did. Lawrence needs to think about whether she needs to justify her criteria for her readers.
- Another reader felt overwhelmed by all of the statistical information in the paper and suggested a chart. Lawrence needs to think about what one or more charts might add to her paper, and what type of chart or graph she might use.
- A reader felt dissatisfied with her ending. How might Lawrence improve her conclusion?
- A reader pointed out problems with Lawrence's documentation, which affected the credibility of her evaluation.

You may decide to reject some comments, of course; other comments, though, may deserve your attention. You may find that comments from more than one reader contradict each other. In that case, use your judgment to decide which reader's comments are on the right track.

In the final version of her paper on pages 320–23, you can see how Annlee Lawrence responded to her reader's comments.

 # KNOWLEDGE OF CONVENTIONS

When effective writers edit their work, they attend to genre conventions, documentation, format, usage, grammar, and mechanics. By attending to these conventions in your writing, you make reading a more pleasant experience for readers.

 ## Editing

After you revise, you have one more important step—editing and polishing. When you edit and polish, you make changes to your sentence structure and word choice to improve your style and to make your writing clearer and more concise. You also check your work to make sure it adheres to conventions of grammar, usage, punctuation, mechanics, and spelling. If you have used sources in your paper, you should make sure you are following the documentation style your instructor requires.

Because it is sometimes difficult to identify small problems in a familiar text, it often helps to distance yourself so that you can approach your draft with fresh eyes. Some people read from the last sentence to the first so that the content, and their familiarity with it, doesn't cause them to overlook an error. We strongly recommend that you ask classmates, friends, and tutors to read your work to help you find editing problems that you may not see.

To assist you with editing, we offer here a round-robin editing activity focused on careful word choice, which is a common concern in writing to evaluate.

See Chapter 20 for more on documenting sources using MLA or APA style.

WRITER'S *Workshop* | **Round-Robin Editing with a Focus on Careful Word Choice**

Evaluative writing often requires careful word choice (diction). It is critical to select words that clearly represent what you intend to say. For example, notice how the revision to this sentence improves its clarity:

> *rely on*
> We don't have time to prepare a full-blown meal, so we have created fast food to fit with our fast-paced lives.

People in general have not "created" fast food, but they have come to rely on the convenience that it provides.

Working with several peers, consult a good college dictionary and the portion of a handbook that covers word choice. If you are uncertain about a specific word choice, ask your instructor for help.

ROUND-ROBIN EDITING WITH A FOCUS ON

Fragments (p. 146)
Modifiers (p. 189)
Wordiness (p. 232)
Citing Sources (p. 273)
Careful Word Choice (p. 319)
Subordinate Clauses (p. 363)
Inclusive Language (p. 411)

Genres, Documentation, and Format

If you are writing an academic paper in response to Scenarios 1 or 2, you will need to follow the conventions for the discipline in which you are writing and the requirements of your instructor. If you are working on Scenario 3, a review, you can be somewhat more informal than you would be in an academic paper.

If you have used material from outside sources, including visuals, you will need to give credit to those sources, using the documentation style required by the discipline you are working in and by your instructor.

For advice on writing in different genres, see the Appendix C. For guidelines for formatting and documenting papers in MLA or APA style, see Chapter 20.

A Writer Achieves Her Goal: Annlee Lawrence's Final Draft

Here is Annlee Lawrence's final draft. Note that she has addressed the questions and concerns that her classmates had.

ANNLEE LAWRENCE

EVALUATIVE ESSAY   **Who Has the Healthier Burger?**

Notice how Lawrence offers support for her criteria: information from the Surgeon General's guidelines.

In the following section, Lawrence has incorporated information from external sources to support her thesis.

One of Lawrence's classmates commented on her criteria:

These seem like good criteria, but why did you choose them? Do you need a stronger reason for your criteria here?

Lawrence has added information about why she chose calories as a criterion in response to this comment.

D id you know that McDonald's operates more than thirty-three thousand restaurants in more than one hundred countries on six continents ("Getting to Know Us")? Around the world, McDonald's represents nearly 13% of the total fast-food market ("McDonald's Report"). McDonald's feeds more than 27 million people a day—more than the entire population of Spain ("McDonald's 24/7")! Former Surgeon General David Satcher comments, "Fast food is a major contributor to the obesity epidemic" (*Super Size Me*). 1

It's no wonder that 60% of Americans are overweight or obese. Obesity, if left unchecked, will soon surpass smoking as the leading cause of preventable death in America. So why can't we seem to stay away from our beloved Big Macs or Whoppers? Probably because our lives demand it at times. Busy Americans often don't have time to prepare a home-cooked meal, so they rely on fast food to fit in with their fast-paced lives. Unfortunately, then, fast food is a part of today's society, but obesity can be avoided through moderation of consumption. Generally speaking, according to the Office of the Surgeon General, most fast food contains high—and therefore unhealthy—levels of calories, fat, and cholesterol, three dangerous aspects of an unhealthy lifestyle. But some fast-food meals are not as bad for you as others. For this evaluation, I chose three popular meals: the Whopper Combo from Burger King, Wendy's "Dave's Hot and Juicy" meal, and McDonald's Quarter Pounder Combo. 2

When I researched the nutritional content of these three meals, I found that all three have high calorie content (see fig. 1)—and since most everyone is concerned with calories, they are the starting point for my evaluation. The Whopper from Burger King has been a favorite of Americans for generations. But is it as good for your body as it is to your taste buds? When I researched the nutritional information, I discovered that this burger has a grand total of 1370 calories. In contrast, Wendy's "Dave's Hot and Juicy" meal has 1240 calories, and the McDonald's Quarter Pounder with cheese combo has 1040. 3

TOTAL CALORIES

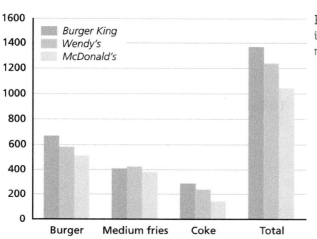

Fig. 1. Total calories in three fast-food meals

One peer reviewer had this comment:

These are a lot of statistics . . . Can you maybe give all this in a table or chart?

Note how Lawrence put that data into three charts.

The Burger King Whopper meal not only has the highest calorie count, it also has the highest fat content at 57 grams of total fat (see fig. 2). The next lowest is Wendy's Combo meal at 40 grams of total fat. The lowest of the three is McDonald's Quarter Pounder Combo at 35 grams of fat. 4

TOTAL FAT

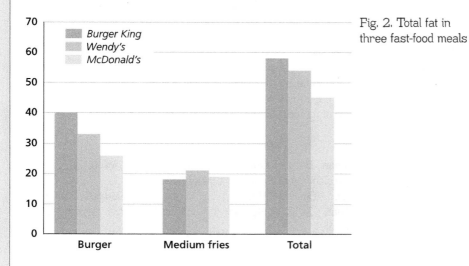

Fig. 2. Total fat in three fast-food meals

Last but not least is the sodium content (see fig. 3). Americans generally 5 take in way too much sodium: the government's Centers for Disease Control recommends that the average person's daily sodium intake should be no more than 2300 milligrams per day.

Wendy's hamburger clearly has more sodium than either of the other two burgers, probably because it includes bacon. Note that Wendy's burger alone 6 has more sodium than the average person should have for an entire day.

TOTAL SODIUM (SALT)

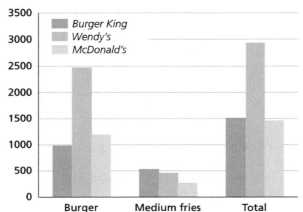

Fig. 3. Total sodium in three fast-food meals

So if you are in a hurry and feel like grabbing a burger, you are probably 7 better off getting the McDonald's Quarter Pounder meal, which has fewer calories and lower fat content than the other two meals. This doesn't mean, however, that you should make a habit of eating at McDonald's or any other fast-food restaurant chain, especially if you have a genetic predisposition to high cholesterol levels. Obviously, as the movie *Super Size Me* proved, even "healthy" fast food isn't good for you when consumed on a regular basis. Even if eaten in moderation, fast food is not one of the best things to happen to busy Americans.

Works Cited

Burger King Corporation. *Burger King Nutritional Information*. Web. 21 Jan. 2012. <http://www.bk.com/en/us/menu-nutrition/index.html>.

McDonald's Corporation. *Get the Nutrition Facts for a McDonald's Menu Item*. Web. 21 Jan. 2012. <http://nutrition.mcdonalds.com/bagamcmeal/chooseCustomize.do>.

---. "Getting to Know Us." Web. 21 Jan. 2012. <http://www.aboutmcdonalds.com/mcd/our_company.html>.

Lawrence's classmate felt the ending of her first draft had problems:

Seems like the ending contradicts the rest of your essay. Why is fast food good for America? The ending seems wrong here.

She has made a slight change here to address this comment.

This paper follows MLA guidelines for in-text citations and works cited.

One of Lawrence's classmates pointed out that she had problems with her documentation:

Don't you have a quote in the first paragraph from the Surgeon General? There's no citation for it here.

Her revised list includes a citation for the Surgeon General's *Dietary Guidelines*.

"McDonalds (NYSE:MCD) Report: Market Share, Margins on the Rise." *StockMarketsReview.com* 16 Nov. 2010. Web. 29 Jan. 2012.

"McDonald's 24/7." *Businessweek.com*. Business Week. 5 Feb. 2007. Web. 29 Jan. 2012.

Super Size Me. Dir. Morgan Spurlock. Hart Sharp Video. 2004. Film.

United States. Centers for Disease Control and Prevention. *Americans Consume Too Much Sodium (Salt)*. 24 Feb. 2011. Web. 29 Jan. 2012.

---. Office of the Surgeon General. *Dietary Guidelines for Americans, 2010*. 31 Jan. 2011. Web. 21 Jan. 2012.

Wendy's Company. *Wendy's Nutrition Facts & Topics*. Web. 21 Jan. 2012. <http://www.wendys.com/food/Nutrition.jsp.mcdon>.

UNDERSTANDING A WRITER'S GOALS: QUESTIONS TO CONSIDER AND DISCUSS

Rhetorical Knowledge: The Writer's Situation and Rhetoric

1. **Audience:** Who do you see as Lawrence's audience?

2. **Purpose:** Lawrence seems to have another purpose for her evaluation, in addition to writing this paper for a class assignment: to help her classmates. How well does she fulfill that larger purpose?

3. **Voice and tone:** How does Lawrence use voice and tone to establish her *ethos?*

4. **Responsibility:** How effectively does Lawrence represent the facts about calories and other nutritional data in her evaluation?

5. **Context, format, and genre:** Lawrence is writing as a college student who eats fast food. How does that affect her credibility in this evaluation? Can you tell what genre Lawrence's evaluation might be? Is it a report? While Lawrence makes effective use of graphs—usually a sign of a report—she does not use heads or subheads.

Critical Thinking: The Writer's Ideas and Your Personal Response

6. What is your initial response to Lawrence's essay?

7. Lawrence focuses on only three criteria for her evaluation. How sufficient are they , do you think, for her to construct an effective evaluation? Why?

Composing Processes and Knowledge of Conventions: The Writer's Strategies

8. How effective is the evidence that Lawrence provides? What other evidence might she have used?

9. How effectively does Lawrence use the quotation and information from the former Surgeon General?

Inquiry and Research: Ideas for Further Exploration

10. Interview several of your classmates, explaining Lawrence's conclusions. What is their reaction to her evaluation? Might it influence their dining decisions in the future?

Self-Assessment: Reflecting on Your Goals

Now that you have constructed a piece of evaluative writing, go back and reconsider your goals. To help reflect on the goals that you have achieved, respond in writing to the following questions:

 ## Rhetorical Knowledge

- *Audience:* What have you learned about addressing an audience in evaluative writing?
- *Purpose:* What have you learned about the purposes for constructing an evaluation?
- *Rhetorical situation:* How did the writing context affect your evaluative text? How did your choice of subject affect the research you conducted and the way you presented your evaluation?
- *Voice and tone:* How would you describe your voice in this essay? Your tone? How do they contribute to the effectiveness of your evaluation?
- *Context, medium, and genre:* How did your context determine the medium and genre you chose, and how did those decisions affect your writing?

 ## Critical Thinking, Reading, and Writing

- *Learning/inquiry:* What process did you go through to focus on a main idea, or thesis? How did you judge what was the most and least important criterion in your evaluation?
- *Responsibility:* How did you fulfill your responsibility to your readers?
- *Reading and research:* What did you learn about evaluative writing from the reading selections in this chapter? What research did you conduct? How sufficient was the research you did?
- *Skills:* As a result of writing this evaluation, how have you become a more critical thinker, reader, and writer? What skills do you hope to develop further in your next writing project?

Writing Processes

- *Invention:* What invention strategies were most useful to you?
- *Organizing your ideas and details:* What organization did you use? How successful was it?
- *Revising:* What are the strongest and the weakest parts of your essay? Why? If you could go back and make an additional revision, what would it be?
- *Working with peers:* How did your instructor or peer readers help you by making comments and suggestions about your writing? List some examples of useful comments that you received. How could you have made better use of the comments and suggestions you received?
- *Visuals:* Did you use photographs or other visuals to help explain your evaluation to readers? If so, what did you learn about incorporating these elements?
- *Writing habits:* What "writerly habits" have you developed, modified, or improved on as you constructed the writing assignment for this chapter? How will you change your future writing activities, based on what you have learned about yourself?

Knowledge of Conventions

- *Editing:* What sentence problem did you find most frequently in your writing? How will you avoid that problem in future assignments?
- *Genre:* What conventions of the genre you were using, if any, gave you problems?
- *Documentation:* Did you use sources for your paper? If so, what documentation style did you use? What problems, if any, did you have with it?

If you are preparing a course portfolio, file your written reflections so that you can return to them when you next work on your portfolio. Refer to Chapter 1 (pages 12–13) for a sample reflection by a student.

CHAPTER

11

Writing to Explain Causes and Effects

We are often curious about how and why things happen. We wonder what causes natural phenomena such as the northern lights (aurora borealis) that sometimes blaze across the night sky, we want to know what caused the extinction of certain species, and we have a vested interest in knowing the causes of diseases such as cancer, Alzheimer's, or schizophrenia.

Consider the events that take place in your life: You are surrounded by

changes that occur, *trends* you can observe (and wonder why they happen), *behavior* that is unusual or surprising. All have *causes,* reasons why they happened or are happening. In fact, *why* is probably the best question you can ask as you explore any cause-and-effect relationship.

In some cases, discovering the cause is an end in itself. For instance, we may one day know precisely why the dinosaurs became extinct about

60 million years ago, but we may not be able to use that information to change life as it is currently lived on Earth. In other cases, though, we can use information gained from causal analysis to eliminate or avoid the causes of certain effects. For instance, in recent years, scientists have come to understand—and share with the public—the strong cause-and-effect relationship between tobacco use and certain kinds of cancer. Although identifying and understanding relationships between causes and effects can be challenging, the act of writing will help you to become more aware of them. Because life includes many causes and effects, writing about them can help you to make sense of sequences of related events.

Setting Your Goals for *Causal Analysis*

Rhetorical Knowledge (pp. 330–35)

- **Audience:** Your success will partially depend on how well you have analyzed your audience. How can you make your audience interested in this cause-and-effect relationship?
- **Purpose:** Your main purpose is to convince readers that a cause-and-effect relationship exists. Your purpose may be to identify a cause and determine its effect(s). Or your purpose may be to determine a series of causes and effects—often called a *causal chain.*
- **Rhetorical situation:** Think about the factors that affect where you stand in relation to your subject.
- **Voice and tone:** Present yourself as a logical writer who provides reliable information.
- **Context, medium, and genre:** Decide on the most effective medium and genre to use to present your causal analysis. Visuals such as flowcharts are often an effective way of helping audiences understand causal relationships.

Critical Thinking, Reading, and Writing (pp. 335–49)

- **Learning/inquiry:** Think critically about whether an actual cause-and-effect relationship exists. It may be coincidental that one event happens right after another or that two phenomena often occur together.
- **Responsibility:** Recognize that causes and effects may be more complex than you first realize. Any given phenomenon or event is likely to have many causes and to produce many effects.
- **Reading and research:** As you conduct research about a causal relationship, make sure you understand the nature of the relationship well enough to be able to document the causality.

Writing Processes (pp. 350–62)

- **Invention:** Begin by recording possible answers to the question you are considering, using an invention strategy such as brainstorming or listing.
- **Organizing your ideas and details:** Once you have recorded some ideas, think about how to organize your main points and what supporting evidence you need to provide.
- **Revising:** Read your work with a critical eye, to make certain that it displays the qualities of a good causal analysis.
- **Working with peers:** Peer review is a crucial part of the process of writing a causal analysis because it enables you to get a sense of how an audience will respond to your claim that a cause-and-effect relationship exists.

Knowledge of Conventions (pp. 362–63)

- **Editing:** When you edit a causal analysis, make sure that the subordinate clauses are attached to independent clauses and are therefore part of complete sentences.
- **Genres for cause-and-effect writing:** In your college classes, you will be required to follow the conventions for an academic essay. Other, nonacademic writing situations may call for a variety of genres.
- **Documentation:** You will probably need to rely on sources outside of your experience, and if you are writing an academic essay, you will be required to cite them using the appropriate documentation style.

RHETORICAL KNOWLEDGE

When you write about causes and effects, you need to have a specific purpose in mind, some sense of your audience, and an idea of an effective way to substantiate the cause-and-effect relationships you are considering. How can you prove your claim that a cause-and-effect relationship exists?

 ## Writing about Causes and Effects in Your College Classes

Many of the assignments for your college classes will ask you to determine the causes of an event, a trend, or a phenomenon. Here are some examples:

- Your theater history instructor may ask you to explain why and how a type of stage has evolved over time.
- Your biology instructor may ask you to explain what causes leaves to turn color and drop from trees in certain parts of the world in the fall.
- In a sociology course, you might investigate the possible effects of anti-poverty programs on the crime rate in low-income neighborhoods.

The "Ways of Writing" feature on page 332 presents different genres that can be used when writing about causes and effects in your college classes.

 ## Writing about Causes and Effects for Life

Much of the writing constructed in professional settings is designed to solve problems. The first step in solving any problem is determining why the problem exists. Many professionals in the work world spend a good deal of their time determining causes and effects:

- A team of medical researchers writes a paper reporting on a study that reveals a cause-and-effect relationship between vitamin C deficiency and osteoporosis.
- A teacher wonders why some students have difficulty reading and studies them to find out the causes of their problems.

When writers focus on community issues, they often need to find and explain answers to *why* questions:

- A citizens' group submits a written report to the county health board arguing that more restaurant inspections lead to fewer incidences of *E. coli* food poisoning.
- A homeowner writes a letter to the editor of a county newspaper arguing that a nearby golf course is the source of the chemical residue recently discovered in local well water.

You will also encounter many occasions for thinking and writing about causes and effects in personal settings. It is critical to understand why things happen, and journals are an excellent place to explore such cause–and–effect relationships. For example, a young couple might keep a daily journal on the activities of their infant daughter. After a few weeks, when they reread their entries, they might notice a pattern suggesting that when they feed their daughter one kind of formula, she sleeps fewer hours at night.

The "Ways of Writing" feature on page 332 presents different genres that can be used when writing about causes and effects in life.

Scenarios for Writing | Assignment Options

Your instructor may ask you to complete one or both of the following assignments, in the form of *scenarios*, that call for writing about causes and effects. Each scenario gives you a sense of who your audience is and what you need to accomplish with your causal analysis.

Starting on page 350, you will find guidelines for responding to whatever scenarios you decide—or are asked—to complete. Additional scenarios for college and life may be found online.

Writing for College

SCENARIO 1 Academic Paper: Causes and Effects in One of Your Other College Courses

Consider the topics that you are studying this semester that involve causes and effects. Choose a topic that interests you, and then come up with a question about that topic that will lead you to investigate causes and/or effects. Here are some possibilities:

- **Geology:** What causes an earthquake?
- **Music:** How did hip-hop change popular music?
- **Art:** How did the invention of the camera affect the kinds of painting that artists did in the nineteenth century?
- **Physics:** What causes the lift that makes it possible for airplanes to fly?

Alternatively, you might consider some general cause-and-effect relationships that you have noticed. Here are a few examples:

- **College:** Why does the cost of attending college always seem to increase?
- **Community:** Why do some neighbors around the college resent having students rent homes nearby?
- **Classroom:** Why do some students take so long to finish college?

Ways of Writing to Explain Cause and Effect

Genres for Your College Classes	Sample Situation	Advantages of the Genre	Limitations of the Genre
Academic essay	Your health and wellness professor asks you to explain the possible causes of eating disorders in college-age female students.	In an academic essay you can examine an important issue in detail to determine cause.	Effective academic essays require substantial supporting evidence.
PowerPoint presentation	Your writing professor asks you to prepare a presentation on how professional athletes influence the actions of teenage males.	A *PowerPoint* presentation allows you to provide visuals that accompany your talk.	You'll need to be careful not to offer too many or too few details.
Brochure	To promote an expanded campus recycling program, your brochure needs to explain the cause(s) for the expanded program and its benefits.	A brochure is an effective medium for concisely presenting material in words and visuals.	A brochure allows only limited space for presenting an argument.
Formal laboratory report	Your botany professor asks you to construct a formal lab report showing the relationship of a warmer climate to the recent increase in the number of elm trees infested with bark beetles in your community.	A formal lab report is a common venue for showing such a cause-and-effect relationship.	Lab reports typically do not appeal to a wide audience.
Genres for Life	Sample Situation	Advantages of the Genre	Limitations of the Genre
Brochure	You decide to construct a brochure that explains why a certain stretch of highway is dangerous and causes more accidents.	A brochure gives readers a quick overview of your topic.	A brochure provides limited space to explain causes and effects.
Formal business plan	To get a loan for a new product line, you construct a business plan showing how these new products will increase profits.	Lending institutions often require a formal business plan before they decide whether to offer a loan.	Some intangibles—such as the work ethic of employees—cannot easily be documented in a business plan.
Poster	To help children understand that they need to wash their hands before eating, you construct a poster showing how germs can cause them to become sick.	A poster is a useful visual teaching tool for young readers.	Posters offer limited space for presenting material.
Web site	You want to create a Web site that explains how high school dropouts hurt the community because they often cannot find jobs that pay well.	A Web site can have a large school-age readership.	Constructing effective Web sites is time-consuming, and a Web site might not reach the entire target group.
Editorial	By writing an editorial, you hope to convince residents of your town that a slight increase in the sales tax will benefit the community.	An editorial lets you outline details about the cause-and-effect relationship between the small tax increase and the benefits for your community.	Because editorials tend to be short, it can be difficult to present enough evidence to support your position.

Writing Assignment: For this assignment, you can choose among several options. One possibility is to select an effect and then write about its causes. Another possibility is to select a cause and then write about its effects. Your goal is to convince an audience of instructors and students in the discipline that your causal analysis is credible.

SCENARIO 2 Laboratory Report

You are likely to be asked to construct laboratory reports during your college career, especially in your science classes. While your instructor will give you specific guidelines for the report he or she asks you to construct, lab reports generally are just what the name implies: Written observations.

Lab reports typically include these main headings:

- **Introduction:** a general guide to your experiment and the report that follows
- **Method:** a step-by-step outline of the process followed so that your experient could be replicated
- **Results:** your findings, often including presentations of data in tables and graphs
- **Analysis:** an explanation and outline of the mathematics involved
- **Discussion:** the relevance of your findings in relation to those of others, as well as any problems with your lab work
- **Conclusion:** a discussion of the extent to which the experiment met your initial goals

Lab reports can also include an abstract (a brief summary) and a review of the current literature (results of related studies and experiments). All sources (textbooks, papers, and so on) must be cited.

Writing Assignment: For one of your science classes, construct a formal laboratory report based on an experiment that you conducted. Your instructor will provide specific guidelines for you to follow.

Writing for Life

SCENARIO 3 Personal Writing: A Poster to Describe a Campus Club

A poster is an effective medium for conveying a brief message. Posters often include photographs or other visual elements, and they sometimes are printed in full color and on glossy paper. Figure 11.1 shows a poster for a chess club.

Small businesses use posters as sales tools to explain a product or service. Health agencies use posters to inform clients about health-related issues. Graduate schools provide posters to help potential students understand program and graduation requirements. Nonprofit agencies use posters to explain the work they do and sometimes to solicit contributions. College clubs (the rugby team, the botany club, the debating team, and so on) often design posters to serve as recruiting tools for potential members.

FIGURE 11.1
Poster for a
Chess Club

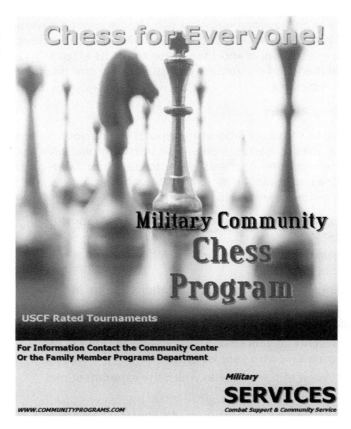

Writing Assignment: For a college or university club of which you are a member, design a poster that outlines what the club does, explain the benefits of joining, and include a brief form that students who would like to join can fill in and send to your club.

Rhetorical Considerations in Cause-and-Effect Writing

Audience: While your instructor and classmates are your initial audience, you should also consider other audiences for your causal analysis. What evidence will convince your readers that you are making a valid claim about a cause-and-effect relationship?

Purpose: Your general purpose is to convince readers that a cause-and-effect relationship exists. How can you establish the causes of something (an effect), establish the effects of something (a cause), or show how a series of causes and effects are related?

Voice, tone, and point of view: Why are you interested in the cause-and-effect relationship that you have chosen to write about? What preconceptions about it do you have? What are your attitudes toward the topic and the audience? How will you convey those attitudes?

Context, medium, and genre: Keeping the context of the assignment in mind, decide on a medium and a genre for your writing. How will your writing be used? If you are writing for an audience beyond the classroom, consider what will be the most effective way to present your information to this audience.

For more on choosing a medium and genre, see Chapter 17 and Appendix C.

 # CRITICAL THINKING, READING, AND WRITING

Before you begin to write your causal analysis, read examples of writing about causes and effects to get a feel for this kind of writing. The qualities of writing about causes and/or effects include a focused presentation of the effect(s) or cause(s), a clearly stated claim that a cause-and-effect relationship exists, and sufficient evidence to support the claim. The writer also has the responsibility to research carefully, to avoid logical fallacies, and to consider other points of view.

 ## Learning the Qualities of Effective Writing about Causes and Effects

When you consider what causes what, or what the effects of something are, you need to convince others that the relationship you see in fact exists. Here are the qualities of writing that analyzes causes and/or effects successfully:

- Presentation of focused cause(s) or effect(s). At the beginning of your essay, introduce the event, activity, or phenomenon for which you wish to establish cause(s), or effect(s), or both. To focus the causes or effects, you should limit the time period that you are considering. This does not mean you cannot write about long periods of time (for a geology paper, you often have to do so). Rather, always keep the time period in mind as you determine exactly what to focus on so you can reasonably cover your topic given the limits of your assignment.

- A clearly stated claim that a cause-and-effect relationship exists. After you have done enough research to be certain that a cause-and-effect relationship exists, you will be prepared to state the nature of that relationship. State the claim so that readers understand it, especially since they may know little or nothing about your topic. For example, "The terrorist attack on September 11, 2001, led to tighter security screening at airports in the United States" asserts a clear cause-and-effect relationship.

- Sufficient evidence to support your claim. To support your claim, present evidence that readers will consider persuasive. Such evidence may consist of the following:

  - The results of empirical studies or historical research found in scholarly and popular books, in journals, and on Web sites
  - Your own observations, experience, or reading
  - Testimony from interested or affected parties ("Interviews with other students indicate that . . .") or experts ("Professor X, a noted authority, asserts that . . .")
  - The use of examples that demonstrate that your suggested cause or causes actually do cause the effect

- Clear, logical thinking. People often jump to conclusions when they see two events happening at the same time and assume there is a cause-and-effect relationship (see the discussion of *post hoc, ergo propter hoc* in the box on page 354). So consider these issues as you search for cause-and-effect relationships:

  - **Does the effect have a single cause, or multiple causes?** Things are rarely as simple as they first appear to be. More often than not, an effect will have multiple causes. Carefully analyze and research all the causes that may contribute to a particular effect.
  - **What are the contributing causes, and do they lead to a precipitating cause?** Often, a number of causes together contribute to what might be called a *precipitating cause,* the final cause that sets the effect in motion. Several contributing causes might set up a single precipitating cause. Although the football fan might blame the kicker who missed a last-second field goal for the team's loss of the important game, there surely were many other reasons that contributed to the loss (for example, dropped passes, poor execution of running plays, missed tackles).
  - **Is a particular cause remote or immediate?** It is sometimes useful to examine a chain of causes so that you understand what came first, what happened next, and so on. Writing down the sequence of causes and effects will help you see the events in the **causal chain** as they happened over time.
  - **Is a particular cause necessary or sufficient?** A **necessary cause** is one that must be present for the effect to occur. A **sufficient cause** is one that, if present, always triggers a particular effect. For example, for a teenager to be able to borrow the family car, his or her family must have a car—that cause is *necessary* to the effect of the teenager being able to borrow it. The teenager's forgetting to put gas into the family car before bringing it back, however, is a *sufficient* cause for the parents to refuse to lend it again; other causes would be sufficient as well (bringing the car home dirty or running into a utility pole and denting the fender are also possible causes for the parents' decision), so forgetfulness is not a necessary cause.

- Anticipation of possible objections or alternative explanations. While your causal analysis may be highly plausible, there are almost always other possible causes for the same effect or other possible effects of the cause that you are considering. Be prepared to acknowledge those other potential causes or effects and to show why your causes or effects are more likely.

For more on writing effective arguments, including claims, evidence, types of appeals, and counterarguments, see Chapter 14.

Reading, Inquiry, and Research: Learning from Texts That Explain Cause-and-Effect Relationships

The readings that follow are examples of writing about causes and effects. As you read them, consider the following questions:

- To what extent has the writer focused on causes, on effects, or on both causes and effects?
- What parts of the selection seem the strongest? Why do you think so?
- How can you use the techniques of cause-and-effect writing exemplified here in your writing?

JUAN WILLIAMS

The Ruling That Changed America

Juan Williams is the author of *Thurgood Marshall: American Revolutionary,* the nonfiction bestseller *Eyes on the Prize: America's Civil Rights Years, 1954–1965,* and *This Far by Faith: Stories from the African American Religious Experience.* He was born in Colon, Panama, but moved to Brooklyn, New York, in 1958. In an interview for the Web site *Tolerance.org,* Williams said, "Since I was born in 1954 my whole education is tied to the *Brown* case. I attended public schools in Brooklyn, New York, during the 1960s [and] those schools were very integrated. . . . I went to schools with Jewish children, Irish children, Italian children, and a stunning range of immigrant children from around the world."

Williams attended Haverford College and graduated with a degree in philosophy in 1976. For more than twenty years, Williams was an editorial writer, op-ed contributor, and White House reporter for the *Washington Post.* His work has appeared in *Newsweek, Fortune, Atlantic Monthly, Ebony, Gentlemen's Quarterly,* and the *New Republic.* Williams is currently a political analyst for Fox News and a panelist on *Fox News Sunday.*

This essay originally appeared in the April 2004 issue of the *American School Board Journal.*

Fifty years later, the *Brown* decision looks different. At a distance from the volcanic heat of May 17, 1954, the real impact of the legal, political, and cultural eruption that changed America is not exactly what it first appeared to be. 1

On that Monday in May, the high court's ruling outlawing school segregation in the United States generated urgent news flashes on the radio and frenzied black headlines in special editions of afternoon newspapers. One swift and unanimous decision by the top judges in the land was going to end segregation in public schools. Southern politicians reacted with such fury and fear that they immediately called the day "Black Monday." 2

South Carolina Gov. James Byrnes, who rose to political power with passionate advocacy of segregation, said the decision was "the end of civilization in the South as we have known it." Georgia Gov. Herman Talmadge struck an angry tone. He said Georgia had no intention of allowing "mixed race" schools as long as he was governor. And he touched on Confederate pride from the days when the South went to war with the federal government over slavery by telling supporters that the Supreme Court's ruling was not law in his state; he said it was "the first step toward national suicide." The *Brown* decision should be regarded, he said, as nothing but a "mere scrap of paper." 3

Meanwhile, newspapers for black readers reacted with exultation. "The Supreme Court decision is the greatest victory for the Negro people since the Emancipation Proclamation," said Harlem's *Amsterdam News.* A writer in the *Chicago Defender* explained, "neither the atomic bomb nor the hydrogen bomb will ever be as meaningful to our democracy." And Thurgood Marshall, the NAACP lawyer who directed the legal fight that led to *Brown,* predicted the end of segregation in all American public schools by the fall of 1955. 4

Slow Progress, Backward Steps

Ten years later, however, very little school integration had taken place. True to the defiant words of segregationist governors, the Southern states had hunkered down in a massive resistance campaign against school integration. Some Southern counties closed their schools instead of allowing blacks and whites into the same classrooms. In other towns, segregationist academies opened, and most if not all of the white children left the public schools for the racially exclusive alternatives. And in most places, the governors, mayors, and school boards found it easy enough to just ask for more time before integrating schools. 5

That slow-as-molasses approach worked. In 1957, President Eisenhower had to send troops from the 101st Airborne into Little Rock just to get nine black children safely into Central High School. Only in the late '60s, under the threat of losing federal funding, did large-scale school integration begin in Southern public schools. And in many places, in both the North and the South, black and white students did not go to school together until a federal court ordered schoolchildren to ride buses across town to bring the races together. 6

Today, 50 years later, a study by the Civil Rights Project at Harvard University finds that the percentage of white students attending public schools with Hispanic or black students has steadily declined since 1988. In fact, the report concludes that school integration in the United States is "lower in 2000 than in 1970, before busing for racial balance began." In the South, home to the majority of America's black population, there is now less school integration than there was in 1970. The Harvard report concluded, "At the beginning of the 21st century, American schools are now 12 years into the process of continuous resegregation." 7

Today, America's schools are so heavily segregated that more than two-thirds of black and Hispanic students are in schools where a majority of the students are not white. And today, most of the nation's white children attend a school that is almost 80 percent white. Hispanics are now the most segregated group of students in the nation because they live in highly concentrated clusters. 8

At the start of the new century, 50 years after *Brown* shook the nation, segregated housing patterns and an increase in the number of black and brown immigrants have concentrated minorities in impoverished big cities and created a new reality of public schools segregated by race and class. 9

The Real Impact of *Brown*

So, if *Brown* didn't break apart school segregation, was it really the earthquake that it first appeared to be? 10

Yes. Today, it is hard to even remember America before *Brown* because the ruling completely changed the nation. It still stands as the laser beam that first signaled that the federal government no longer gave its support to racial segregation among Americans. 11

Before *Brown*, the federal government lent its power to enforcing the laws of segregation under an 1896 Supreme Court ruling that permitted "separate 12 but equal" treatment of blacks and whites. Blacks and whites who tried to integrate factories, unions, public buses and trains, parks, the military, restaurants, department stores, and more found that the power of the federal government was with the segregationists.

Before *Brown*, the federal government had struggled even to pass a law banning lynching. 13

But after the Supreme Court ruled that segregation in public schools was a violation of the Constitution, the federal attitude toward enforcing second-class citizenship for blacks shifted on the scale of a change in the ocean's tide or a movement in the plates of the continents. Once the highest court in the land said equal treatment for all did not allow for segregation, then the lower courts, the Justice Department, and federal prosecutors, as well as the FBI, all switched sides. They didn't always act to promote integration, but they no longer used their power to stop it. 14

An irreversible shift had begun, and it was the direct result of the *Brown* decision. 15

The change in the attitude of federal officials created a wave of anticipation among black people, who became alert to the possibility of achieving the long-desired goal of racial equality. There is no way to offer a hard measure of a change in attitude. But the year after *Brown*, Rosa Parks refused to give up her seat to a white man on a racially segregated bus in Montgomery, Ala. That led to a yearlong bus boycott and the emergence of massive, nonviolent protests for equal rights. That same year, Martin Luther King Jr. emerged as the nation's prophet of civil rights for all Americans. 16

Even when a black 14-year-old, Emmit Till, was killed in Mississippi for supposedly whistling at a white woman, there was a new reaction to old racial brutality. One of Till's elderly relatives broke with small-town Southern tradition and dared to take the witness stand and testify against the white men he saw abduct the boy. Until *Brown*, the simple act of a black man standing up to speak against a white man in Mississippi was viewed as futile and likely to result in more white-on-black violence. 17

The sense among black people—and many whites as well—that a new era had opened created a new boldness. Most black parents in Little Rock did not want to risk harm to their children by allowing them to join in efforts to integrate Central High. But working with local NAACP officials, the parents of nine children decided it was a new day and time to make history. That same spirit of new horizons was at work in 1962 when James Meredith became the first black student to enroll at the University of Mississippi. And in another lurch away from the traditional support of segregation, the federal government sent troops as well as Justice Department officials to the university to protect Meredith's rights. 18

The next year, when Alabama Gov. George Wallace felt the political necessity of making a public stand against integration at the University of Alabama, 19 he stood only briefly in the door to block black students and then stepped aside in the face of federal authority. That was another shift toward a world of high hopes for racial equality; again, from the perspective of the 21st century, it looks like another aftershock of the *Brown* decision.

The same psychology of hope infected young people, black and white, nation-   20 wide in the early '60s. The Freedom Rides, lunch-counter sit-ins, and protest marches for voting rights all find their roots in *Brown*. So, too, did the racially integrated 1963 March on Washington at which Martin Luther King Jr. famously said he had a vision of a promised land where the sons of slaves and the sons of slave owners could finally join together in peace. The desire for change became a demand for change in the impatient voice of Malcolm X, the militant Black Muslim who called for immediate change by violent means if necessary.

In 1964, a decade after *Brown*, the Civil Rights Act was passed by a Con-   21 gress beginning to respond to the changing politics brought about by the land-mark decision. The next year, 1965, the wave of change had swelled to the point that Congress passed the Voting Rights Act.

Closer to the Mountaintop

This sea change in black and white attitudes toward race also had an impact on   22 culture. Churches began to grapple with the Christian and Jewish principles of loving thy neighbor, even if thy neighbor had a different color skin. Major league baseball teams no longer feared a fan revolt if they allowed more than one black player on a team. Black writers, actors, athletes, and musicians—ranging from James Baldwin to the Supremes and Muhammad Ali—began to cross over into the mainstream of American culture.

The other side of the change in racial attitudes was white support for equal   23 rights. College-educated young white people in the '60s often defined themselves by their willingness to embrace racial equality. Bob Dylan sang about the changing times as answers "blowing in the wind." Movies like "Guess Who's Coming to Dinner" found major audiences among all races. And previously all-white private colleges and universities began opening their doors to black students. The resulting arguments over affirmative action in college admissions led to the Supreme Court's 1978 decision in the *Bakke* case, which outlawed the use of quotas, and its recent ruling that the University of Michigan can take race into account as one factor in admitting students to its law school. The court has also had to deal with affirmative action in the business world, in both hiring and contracts—again as a result of questions of equality under the Constitution raised by *Brown*.

But the most important legacy of the *Brown* decision, by far, is the growth   24 of an educated black middle class. The number of black people graduating from high school and college has soared since *Brown*, and the incomes of blacks have climbed steadily as a result. Home ownership and investment in the stock market among black Americans have rocketed since the 1980s. The political and economic clout of that black middle class continues to bring America closer to the mountaintop vision of racial equality that Dr. King might have dreamed of 50 years ago.

The Supreme Court's May 17, 1954, ruling in *Brown* remains a landmark   25
legal decision. But it is much more than that. It is the "Big Bang" of all American history in the 20th century.

UNDERSTANDING A WRITER'S GOALS: QUESTIONS TO CONSIDER AND DISCUSS

Rhetorical Knowledge: The Writer's Situation and Rhetoric

1. **Audience:** Williams is writing for an audience that, more likely than not, takes the decision in *Brown vs. Board of Education* for granted. How does he show his audience the real importance of the decision?

2. **Purpose:** Williams wants readers to understand that even if U.S. public schools are still largely segregated, *Brown vs. Board of Education* was perhaps the most important Supreme Court decision of the twentieth century. How successful is he in convincing you?

3. **Voice and tone:** Williams begins his article with measured language, much as you'd expect from a newspaper reporter. He then intersperses his reporting with several short, one-sentence paragraphs of commentary (for example, see paragraphs 13 and 15). How does this tone affect your response to what you read?

4. **Responsibility:** Williams needs to make sure his readers understand the social situation in the United States in 1954. How effectively does he do that?

5. **Context, format, and genre:** This essay is written as a retrospective, looking back over U.S. history in the fifty years since the Supreme Court decision. How sufficiently does Williams provide the historical background for you as readers today? How well does he establish the appropriate context? How does he use the conventions of an academic essay?

Critical Thinking: The Writer's Ideas and Your Personal Response

6. Before reading Williams's article, how aware were you of the impact of *Brown vs. Board of Education*? Can you think of another Supreme Court ruling that has had as significant an impact?

7. At the end, Williams asserts that *Brown vs. Board of Education* was instrumental in helping to establish the emerging black middle class. How do your experiences relate to Williams's observation?

Composing Processes and Knowledge of Conventions: The Writer's Strategies

8. Because for many people, fifty years after the fact, *Brown vs. Board of Education* is simply an entry in history books, how does Williams make the decision real for his current readers?

9. Williams structures his argument to show that *Brown vs. Board of Education* did not accomplish what it intended, but that it eventually did more. How effective is his argument? Why?

Inquiry and Research: Ideas for Further Exploration

10. Investigate other Supreme Court decisions. Which seem to have had a greater impact than expected at the time they were made?

NEAL GABLER

How Urban Myths Reveal Society's Fears

CAUSE-AND-EFFECT ESSAY

A well-known film critic and television personality, Neal Gabler has written articles for a number of publications, including the *New York Times, Esquire, New York Magazine, Vogue, Salon, Us,* and *Playboy.* His books include *An Empire of Their Own: How the Jews Invented Hollywood* (1988), *Winchell: Gossip, Power and the Culture of Celebrity* (1994), *Life the Movie: How Entertainment Conquered Reality* (1998), and *Walt Disney: The Triumph of American Imagination* (2006). The following essay was originally published in the *Los Angeles Times* in 1995. It offers insights into the origins of some popular urban myths.

1   The story goes like this: During dinner at an opulent wedding reception, the groom rises from the head table and shushes the crowd. Everyone naturally assumes he is about to toast his bride and thank his guests. Instead, he solemnly announces that there has been a change of plan. He and his bride will be taking separate honeymoons and, when they return, the marriage will be annulled. The reason for this sudden turn of events, he says, is taped to the bottom of everyone's plate. The stunned guests quickly flip their dinnerware to discover a photo—of the bride *in flagrante*[1] with the best man.

2   At least that is the story that has been recently making the rounds up and down the Eastern seaboard and as far west as Chicago. Did this really happen? A *Washington Post* reporter who tracked the story was told by one source that it happened at a New Hampshire hotel. But then another source swears it happened in Medford, Mass. Then again another suggests a banquet hall outside Schenectady, N.Y. Meanwhile, a sophisticated couple in Manhattan has heard it happened at the Pierre.

3   In short, the whole thing appears to be another urban myth, one of those weird tales that periodically catch the public imagination. Alligators swarming the sewers after people have flushed the baby reptiles down the toilet. The babysitter who gets threatening phone calls that turn out to be coming from inside the house. The woman who turns out to have a nest of black-widow spiders in her beehive hairdo. The man who fails asleep and awakens to find his kidney has been removed. The rat that gets deep fried and served by a fast-food outlet. Or, in a variation, the mouse that has somehow drowned in a closed Coca-Cola bottle.

4   These tales are preposterous, but in a mass society like ours, where stories are usually manufactured by Hollywood, they just may be the most genuine form of folklore we have. Like traditional folklore, they are narratives crafted by the collective consciousness. Like traditional folklore, they give expression to the national mind. And like traditional folklore, they blend the fantastic with the routine,

---

[1]Caught in the act of being unfaithful with the best man.

if only to demonstrate, in the words of University of Utah folklorist Jan Harold Brunvand, the nation's leading expert on urban legends, "that the prosaic contemporary scene is capable of producing shocking or amazing occurrences."

Shocking and amazing, yes. But in these stories, anything can happen not because the world is a magical place rich with wonder—as in folk tales of yore—but because our world is so utterly terrifying. Here, nothing is reliable and no laws of morality govern. The alligators in the sewers present an image of an urban hell inhabited by beasts—an image that might have come directly from Hades and the River Styx in Greek mythology. The babysitter and the man upstairs exploits fears that we are not even safe in our own homes these days. The spider in the hairdo says that even on our own persons, dangers lurk. The man who loses his kidney plays to our fears of the night and the real bogymen who prowl them. The mouse in the soda warns us of the perils of an impersonal mass-production society. 5

As for the wedding-reception tale, which one hacker on the Internet has dubbed "Wedding Revenge," it may address the greatest terror of all: that love and commitment are chimerical and even friendship is meaningless. These are timeless issues, but the sudden promulgation of the tale suggests its special relevance in the age of AIDS, when commitment means even more than it used to, and in the age of feminism, when some men are feeling increasingly threatened by women's freedom. Thus, the groom not only suffers betrayal and humiliation; his plight carries the hint of danger and emasculation, too. Surely, a legend for our time. 6

Of course, folklore and fairy tales have long subsisted on terror, and even the treacly cartoons of Walt Disney are actually, when you parse them, dark and complex expressions of fear—from Snow White racing through the treacherous forest to Pinocchio gobbled by the whale to Dumbo being separated from his mother. But these crystallize the fears of childhood, the fears one must overcome to make the difficult transition to adulthood. Thus, the haunted forest of the fairy tales is a trope for haunted adolescence; the witch or crone, a trope for the spent generation one must vanquish to claim one's place in the world; and the prince who comes to the rescue, a trope for the adult responsibilities that the heroine must now assume. 7

Though urban legends frequently originate with college students about to enter the real world, they are different from traditional fairy tales because their terrors are not really obstacles on the road to understanding, and they are different from folklore because they cannot even be interpreted as cautionary. In urban legends, obstacles aren't overcome, perhaps can't be overcome, and there is nothing we can do differently to avoid the consequences. The woman, not knowing any better, eats the fried rat. The babysitter is terrorized by the stranger hiding in the house. The black widow bites the woman 8 with the beehive hairdo. The alligators prowl the sewers. The marriage in Wedding Revenge breaks up.

It is not just our fears, then, that these stories exploit. Like so much else in modern life—tabloids, exploitalk programs, real-life crime best-sellers—urban legends testify to an overwhelming condition of fear and to a sense of our own impotence within it. That is why there is no accommodation in these stories, no lesson or wisdom imparted. What there is, is the stark impression that our world is anomic. We live in a haunted forest of skyscrapers or of suburban lawns and ranch houses, but there is no one to exorcise the evil and no prince to break the spell. 9

Given the pressures of modern life, it isn't surprising that we have created myths to express our malaise. But what is surprising is how many people seem committed to these myths. The *Post* reporter found people insisting they personally knew someone who had attended the doomed wedding reception. Others went further. They maintained they had actually attended the reception—though no such reception ever took place. Yet even those who didn't claim to have been personally involved seemed to feel duty bound to assert the tale's plausibility. 10

Why this insistence? Perhaps the short answer is that people want to believe in a cosmology of dysfunction because it is the best way of explaining the inexplicable in our lives. A world in which alligators roam sewers and wedding receptions end in shock is at once terrifying and soothing—terrifying because these things happen, soothing because we are absolved of any responsibility for them. It is just the way it is. 11

But there may be an additional reason why some people seem so willing to suspend their disbelief in the face of logic. This one has less to do with the content of these tales than with their creation. However they start, urban legends rapidly enter a national conversation in which they are embellished, heightened, reconfigured. Everyone can participate—from the people who spread the tale on talk radio to the people who discuss it on the Internet to the people who tell it to their neighbors. In effect, these legends are the product of a giant campfire around which we trade tales of terror. 12

If this makes each of us a co-creator of the tales, it also provides us with a certain pride of authorship. Like all authors, we don't want to see the spell of our creation broken—especially when we have formed a little community around it. It doesn't matter whether these tales are true or not. What matters is that they plausibly reflect our world, that they have been generated from the grass roots and that we can pass them along. 13

In a way, then, these tales of powerlessness ultimately assert a kind of authority. Urban legends permit us to become our own Stephen Kings, terrorizing ourselves to confirm one of the few powers we still possess: the power to tell stories about our world. 14

UNDERSTANDING A WRITER'S GOALS: QUESTIONS TO CONSIDER AND DISCUSS

Rhetorical Knowledge: The Writer's Situation and Rhetoric

1. **Audience:** When we selected Gabler's essay for this textbook, we thought it was about a topic that college students would be interested in. To what extent do you agree or disagree? Why?

2. **Purpose:** What do you see as Gabler's purpose in writing this essay?

3. **Voice and tone:** How would you describe Gabler's tone in this essay?

4. **Responsibility:** How does Gabler's use of Disney characters (paragraph 7) help or hurt his credibility?

5. **Context, format, and genre:** Because Gabler's essay was originally published in a newspaper, it is fairly brief, as most newspaper articles are. How does that conciseness affect how Gabler presents his information? What additional information would you like to have? Why? How does Gabler use the conventions of an essay?

Critical Thinking: The Writer's Ideas and Your Personal Response

6. Do you agree with Gabler that urban myths are the current version of "the most genuine form of folklore [traditional beliefs, myths, legends, and tales that are shared orally] we have" (paragraph 4)? Why or why not?

7. Gabler argues that urban myths require us to "suspend . . . disbelief in the face of logic" (paragraph 12). What instances can you think of in your life where you have suspended your disbelief? How willingly do you suspend disbelief? Why?

Composing Processes and Knowledge of Conventions: The Writer's Strategies

8. What kind of evidence in Gabler's essay do you find the most convincing? The least?

9. Gabler says that urban myths allow us each to become "a co-creator of the tales" (paragraph 13) and that they "permit us to become our own Stephen Kings, terrorizing ourselves . . ." (paragraph 14). How effective is this cause-and-effect argument?

Inquiry and Research: Ideas for Further Exploration

10. Interview several of your friends about myths they are familiar with. Outline them and make a brief report to your class.

GENRES *Up Close* **Writing an Educational Poster**

Because people are busy juggling the demands of the professional, civic, and personal areas of their lives, they sometimes do not have time to read lengthy texts such as full academic essays. At other times, writers need to grab readers' attention when they are on the go—walking on sidewalks or down hallways, riding on buses or trains, or standing in a checkout line at a store or diner. To reach busy readers on the go, writers sometimes use educational posters, which provide information in a condensed form, with a mix of visual and verbal elements. Effective educational posters have the following features:

- **A focus on a single narrow topic.** A typical poster only has room for one very specific message.
- **A balance of elements.** Words, images, and white space (space with out words or images) all appear in harmony, without clutter.
- **Relatively few words.** They include just enough to make a point.
- **Large type.** They can be read from a distance—at least ten feet away—when displayed on a wall.

The type size should be at least 24-point.

As you read the following poster, consider how these features are implemented.

APRILYUS

CAUSE-AND-EFFECT POSTER   **Anti-Smoking Poster**

Octavian, also known as Aprilyus, is an art student in Romania. His favorite art style is impressionism, and his favorite artists are Grigorescu, Edgar Degas, and Igor Vieru. He enjoys digital arts and photography and believes that "a good artist is like an encyclopedia." We chose this poster by Aprilyus because it demonstrates the power of using both words and visual elements in texts.

The poster focuses on a single, narrow topic—why you should not smoke.

The words, images, and white space in the poster are balanced.

The type size is large enough to be read at a distance.

UNDERSTANDING A WRITER'S GOALS: QUESTIONS TO CONSIDER AND DISCUSS

Rhetorical Knowledge: The Writer's Situation and Rhetoric

1. **Audience:** What effect will this poster have on smokers? What effect will it have on non-smokers of various ages?
2. **Purpose:** What is the primary purpose for this poster? Is it to encourage smokers to quit? Is it to prevent people from starting smoking? How does it establish a cause-effect relationship?
3. **Voice and Tone:** What is Aprilyus's attitude toward the topic?
4. **Responsibility:** What does Aprilyus consider his responsibilities to be? Why do you think that?
5. **Context, format, and genre:** If you were asked to convert this poster to a magazine ad, what changes would you make? Why?

Critical Thinking: The Writer's Ideas and Your Personal Response

6. How to you respond to this poster? Why?
7. What is the most striking feature of the poster? What makes you think that?

Composing Process and Knowledge of Conventions: The Writer's Strategies

8. How do the image and the words on the poster reflect Aprilyus's interest in Impressionism?
9. Why does Aprilyus use so few words on the poster?

Inquiry and Research: Ideas for Further Research

10. Find other works by Aprilyus. What common elements run through his work?
11. Conduct a Web search to learn more about the causes of lung cancer.

WRITING PROCESSES

As you work on your assignment, revisit the qualities of an effective cause-and-effect paper (see pages 335–37), and remember that the writing process is recursive—that is, writers move back and forth among all of the activities. After you engage in invention strategies and conduct some research, you may start writing, or you may decide to do some more research.

Invention: Getting Started

As you work, try to answer these questions:

- What do I already know about this event, phenomenon, or trend?
- What do I know about its cause(s) or effect(s)?
- Where can I learn more about the causal relationships involved? What relevant personal experiences or observations can I contribute?
- What might my audience already know about the cause-and-effect relationship I am exploring?
- What might my audience's point of view be?
- What questions do I have? What do I want and need to find out?

As with any kind of writing, invention activities improve with peer feedback and suggestions. Consider sharing the invention work you have done so far with

STUDENT WRITING EXAMPLE

Brainstorming (pp. 176, 350)

Freewriting (pp. 48, 135, 261, 396)

Criteria (p. 307)

Listing (p. 95)

Table (p. 49)

Answers to Reporter's Questions (p. 261)

Organization (pp. 96, 181)

Clustering (pp. 135, 305)

Interviewing (p. 220)

Research (pp. 137, 177, 222, 263, 308, 398)

Reflection (p. 12)

Writing Activity

Brainstorming

Brainstorming is an invention technique that can help you focus your causal analysis and come up with possible causes and/or effects. Working with the questions above, spend a few minutes writing everything you can think of about the causal relationship you plan to discuss. Don't worry about putting this information into sentences or paragraphs; simply record it using any words that come to mind.

several classmates or friends in order to understand your rhetorical situation more clearly and to generate more useful information.

Hanna Lake's Research and Brainstorming

Earlier in her writing course, Hanna Lake wrote a paper about Irish and Norwegian customs in her family's history. Her interest in family history led her to wonder how people develop their definitions of family. She became particularly interested in how life experiences shaped the concepts of family for Black Hawk, the famous Sauk leader, and Harriet Jacobs, a nineteenth-century slave born in North Carolina, two figures she had learned about in her American history course.

Lake began by brainstorming the following lists. Notice that she is working to understand Black Hawk's and Harriet Jacobs' definitions of "family."

"Family"

<u>Black Hawk:</u>
Definition: ???
Evidence:

- British are their father (45); "furnished them with goods"
- French are their father (45); those who supply/provide for them
- Americans are their brother
- not all Indian tribes are automatically their brethren (47)
- their tribe is a united front (48)
- Spanish father has always been a good friend (51)
- "myself or nation" (54) uses "we" a lot

Role:

Not so much the nuclear family
The entire tribe, who holds a common interest
Anyone who offers help*

<u>Jacobs:</u>
Definition: ???
Evidence: ???
Role:
Nuclear family is her support system
Masters can be "like" family
Anyone who offers help*
Chapter 14 pg 525
The family is a haven in a heartless world. ~ Attributed to Christopher Lasch

<u>My response:</u>
Strange that both Jacobs and Black Hawk would see those who have power over them as "family."

Hanna Lake's Freewriting: A Letter to Her Grandfather

To organize her thinking for her project, Hanna Lake wrote a short letter to her grandfather because she knew that he was interested in family and family history. Note how she describes her project in this brief note.

Hi, Grandpa. For my class, I am writing about what caused a Native American leader named Black Hawk and a slave named Harriet Jacobs to develop their concepts of family. I'm looking at what family means to them and what roles family plays in their lives.

As for Black Hawk, I think that family was a broad concept. Family ties were different from what I have experienced in my life. He was not as close to his wife and children, but he did consider his whole tribe and some Europeans as loosely-affiliated family members. He has Spanish "fathers," and the U.S. President is known as the "Great Father." I know this sounds kind of weird, but I think using the "family metaphor" was the best way he could relate to other people. He also felt that the son of one of his old friends was like an adopted son. He called his tribe (the Fox tribe) "our" tribe and they live in "our" village. This shows that his tribe was a big support network. However, not all Indian tribes were like family. They sometimes warred against other tribes. The terms "father" and "brother" are used frequently in his autobiography and tend to designate people who provided support and supplies for Black Hawk and his tribe. Basically, for Black Hawk family was a broad concept, encompassing blood relations, his tribe, and his allies.

Harriet Jacobs had a dissimilar concept of family. She spent most of her time with her grandma and other close kin. She mostly views family as her blood relations although there are some masters whom she seems to consider like family. Again, this is kind of weird, but it may be that Jacobs could relate to family relationships.

Exploring Your Ideas with Research

Usually, when you are writing about cause-and-effect relationships, you will need to provide evidence to support your claims. Although you may be able to draw on your own experience to provide evidence, you will also need to offer verifiable information such as facts, statistics, expert testimony, experimental results, and examples. For instance, if you were writing about cause-and-effect relationships in the areas of health or safety, two good sources of information are the Centers for Disease Control and the U.S. Department of Transportation, both of which have Web sites filled with reliable information.

To find evidence from outside of your own experience, you will need to do research to answer questions such as the following:

- What facts or other verifiable information will provide solid evidence that a cause-and-effect relationship actually exists? Where can I find this information? What sources will be most reliable?

- What expert testimony can I provide to support my thesis about causes or effects, or both? What authorities might I interview?

- What statistical data support my contention that a cause-and-effect relationship exists?

- How can I best explain the data to my readers so that (1) they can easily understand them and (2) my evidence supports my conclusions?

The subject you focus on, and the kind of essay you are constructing, helps to determine the kind of research you conduct. For example, you could conduct several kinds of research:

- For Scenario 1, in which you focus on a topic in one of your courses, interviewing classmates, professors, and/or administrators is a useful way to learn about different perspectives.

- For Scenario 3, in which you create a poster, look at posters on and off campus. Which are particularly effective?

As we have seen, Hanna Lake already had an interest in Black Hawk and Harriet Jacobs and their ideas about family when she began her cause-and-effect assignment. She wanted to explore this topic in more depth and detail. At her college library, she searched the library's online catalog for sources using the keywords "Black Hawk" and "Harriet Jacobs" and found some books that might be helpful. Sources she located included the following slave narrative:

> Brent, Linda. *Incidents in the Life of a Slave Girl*. Ed. L. Maria Child. *The Classic Slave Narratives*. Ed. Henry Louis Gates, Jr. New York: New American Library, 2002. 437–668. Print.

Writing Activity

Conducting Research

What sources could help you answer the questions you have about your topic and formulate a working thesis? The following questions will help you focus your research:

- What do you already know about the subject from your invention work?
- What cause-and-effect connections can you make?
- For what cause-and-effect connections do you need to provide some evidence?
- Whom might you quote as an expert?
- Where can you find statistics that will support your claim?
- Where might you look for more information and evidence?

Reviewing Your Invention and Research

After you have conducted your research, review your invention work and the information you collected from outside sources. Once you have a general idea of the cause(s) and/or effect(s) your research is leading you to, try to develop what is called a *working thesis statement:* If you had to explain the cause-and-effect relationship now, based on what you have learned, what would it be? Through the process of writing itself, you will learn more about your topic and possible cause-and-effect relationships, so you will modify and develop the working thesis statement as you draft and revise your text.

Writing Activity

Considering Your Research and Focusing Your Ideas

Examine the notes you have made based on your research. Then, using the *who, what, where, when, why,* and *how* questions as a starting point, see what information you have. For example, if you were preparing a brochure for a campus group that is working to make your campus smoke-free, here are the kinds of questions you might ask to get started on your brochure:

- **Who:** Who is affected by smoking on campus?
- **What:** What are the effects of smoking on campus?

(continued)

Writing Activity

Considering Your Research and Focusing Your Ideas *(continued)*

- **Where:** Where do people smoke on campus?
- **When:** When is smoking on campus most detrimental to the health of others?
- **Why:** Why is it important to make ours a smoke-free campus?
- **How:** How can making our campus smoke-free lead to a healthier place to study and to work?

Strategies FOR Success   Self-Reflection

Self-reflection, also called *metacognition,* is thinking about thinking. Effective writers, readers, thinkers, and learners reflect on what they do because they know that reflection leads to better performance. Writers, in particular, benefit from reflecting on what they do when they compose, as well as the texts that they produce. Reflection is especially important when you are writing about cause-and-effect relationships because it is important to think beyond the obvious: causes can have many effects and effects can have multiple causes. To help you reflect more critically on causes and effects, consider the following kinds of questions: What are all of the possible causes of this phenomenon? What are the most likely causes? What are the most obvious causes? What are some possible causes that may have been overlooked?

Events that happen at the same time may or may not be related causally—be sure you are not asserting a relationship that does not in fact exist, or mistaking a cause for an effect, or vice versa. A thoughtful writer works diligently to avoid the logical fallacy of *post hoc, ergo propter hoc,* a Latin phrase meaning "after this, therefore because of this." If you argue that X caused Y simply because X preceded Y, you are guilty of this logical fallacy. What are some examples of *post hoc, ergo propter hoc* thinking that you have recently witnessed?

Often, in cases where two events happen at the same time and are probably causally related, it still may not be obvious which is the cause and which is the effect. For instance, educational experts have observed that students with low self-esteem often underperform in school. But do people who have low self-esteem perform poorly in school because they have low self-esteem, as has been assumed in the past? Or do they have low self-esteem because they perform poorly in school, as some psychologists now believe? A reflective writer needs to consider both of these possibilities.

Organizing Your Cause-and-Effect Paper

Once you have a working thesis and supporting evidence for your cause-and-effect paper, you need to consider how you might organize your text. The questions to ask yourself are all rhetorical:

- Who is the audience for your paper?
- Why might they be interested in your reasoning about causes and/or effects, or how can you make them interested in it?

- What is your purpose for writing—that is, why do your readers need to understand this cause-and-effect relationship? What will your readers learn about your subject by reading your paper?

Once you have determined your purpose, you can choose the organizational approach that is best suited to it. Here are three possible organizational approaches that you might choose for your paper.

Options FOR Organization
Organizing a Cause-and-Effect Essay

Identify an Effect and Then Determine Its Cause(s)	Identify a Cause and Then Determine Its Effect(s)	Determine a Series of Causes and Effects
Introduce the effect.	Introduce the cause.	Introduce one of the causes or one of the effects.
Explain the importance of the effect.	Explain the importance of the cause.	Explain the importance of the cause or the effect that you have identified.
List possible causes.	List possible effects.	List possible causes and effects.
Assert probable cause-and-effect relationship(s).	Assert probable cause-and-effect relationship(s).	Assert probable chain of causes and effects.
Note that there may be several causes.	Note that there may be several effects.	Provide evidence to support your claim about series of causes and effects.
Provide evidence to support your claim about cause-and-effect relationship(s).	Provide evidence to support your claim about cause-and-effect relationship(s).	Address skeptics' doubts.
Address skeptics' doubts—others say these causes do not cause the effect, so address those objections.	If others might see different effects from your cause, address their objections.	Conclude by summarizing the cause-and-effect relationships you discussed in your paper.
Conclude by summarizing the cause-and-effect relationships you discussed in your paper.	Conclude by summarizing the cause-and-effect relationships you discussed in your paper.	

Constructing a Complete Draft

Once you have chosen the most effective organizational approach for your audience and purpose, you are ready to construct the rest of draft. As you work, keep the following in mind:

- Draw on your invention work and your research. If necessary, do more invention work and/or more research.
- As you try out tentative ideas about possible causes and/or possible effects, ask peers about what they consider necessary to support your ideas.
- Ask yourself and peers whether visuals might help make your case.

For more on constructing visuals, see Chapter 18.

Synthesizing and Integrating Sources into Your Draft: Summarizing Information from Sources

When considering cause-and-effect relationships, effective writers integrate a variety of sources into their texts to support their claims. Although writers can quote or paraphrase source material, they often find it best to summarize source information about cause-and-effect relationships because such explanations can be too long to integrate effectively as quotations or paraphrases. As noted on pages 553–54 in Chapter 20, summaries need to encapsulate others' ideas accurately and concisely.

On pages 363–68 in this chapter, Hanna Lake quotes, paraphrases, and summarizes source material in her essay on the causes of Black Hawk's and Harriet Jacobs's ideas about family. When she summarizes source material, she clearly strives to be accurate and concise, as illustrated in the following passage (paragraph 7) from her essay:

> As with many American Indian nations of the time, European powers played a large role in the everyday lives of Black Hawk and the Sauk. The Spanish, French, English, and Americans all engage in diplomacy with Black Hawk throughout his autobiography. The Europeans supplied the Sauk with goods, weaponry, and even luxury items in exchange for trade and alliances (Black Hawk, 43, 45). Though today we would see the Europeans' treatment of the Native Americans as controlling and oppressive, Black Hawk viewed this system of support as akin to the care taken by parents looking after their children; their support earns the European ambassadors the moniker of "father," and the President of the United States is known as their "Great Father," who oversaw his "red and white children" (Black Hawk, 150). The general population of American whites were the Sauk's brothers—a familial relationship characterized by alternating periods of amity and conflict—and those in power who provided aid, presents, and allegiance were considered the Sauk's fathers. Some of Black Hawk's struggles were due to conflicts with his white brothers, but his "fathers" aid Black Hawk with allegiance and supplies during these times of struggle. For Black Hawk, these relationships were just as important as veritable blood bonds.

Notice how the summary includes source citations, enclosed in parentheses to set them off from Lake's words. The citations indicate to readers that this paragraph is a summary of someone else's words and ideas, rather than Lake's original ideas. (The paragraph also includes quotations, which are integrated into Lake's sentence and set off with quotation marks.)

In short, when you summarize and integrate others' ideas into your texts, you should aim to do the following:

- Concisely condense the source material.
- Accurately encapsulate the information in the source material.
- Cite the source of the information.
- Indicate how the summary supports your claim(s).

Parts of a Complete Draft

Introduction: To write an introduction that captures readers' attention, you might want to try one of the following strategies:

- **Give your audience a reason for being interested by vividly portraying how this topic makes a difference in their lives.**
- **Make a statement that suggests the unexpected.** Juan Williams uses this strategy in "The Ruling That Changed America" (page 338):

  Fifty years later, the *Brown* decision looks different. At a distance from the volcanic heat of May 17, 1954, the real impact of the legal, political, and cultural eruption that changed America is not exactly what it first appeared to be.

- **Examine a surprising causal relationship (that you can substantiate) to hold an audience's interest.**

Body: There are many strategies you can use to show cause and effect. In the body of your causal analysis, you may list and discuss possible causes and effects. You will likely also refute skeptics' claims. For example, in a causal analysis on the dangers of smoking, you might note that while many smokers may feel their habit endangers only themselves, research data indicates the harmful effects of second-hand smoke. You could then present the data as evidence.

ELECTRONIC ENVIRONMENTS	**Using Graphics and Video to Explain Cause-and-Effect Relationships**

Graphics, and even video, can help you explain complex cause-and-effect relationships. If your instructor allows, see if you can find a short video clip (one to three minutes long) that shows the causal relationship you are explaining. Many Web search engines include video searches. Or you might explore a large video site such as YouTube (http://youtube.com). If you have access to a digital video camera or own a video-capable cell phone or smartphone, you can create a short video clip. For example, if you are writing about the effects of proper grip, motion, and follow-through on curveball execution in baseball, you could ask a campus baseball player to demonstrate while you record a video of various techniques. Consider recording a voice-over that explains the movements involved.

Conclusion: In your conclusion, you need to reinforce the connections between the causes and effects that you have established. Do not assume your reader will make the same connections you have. Ask yourself the following questions:

- How effectively have you shown that the effect was a result of the cause?
- How well have you tied together all of the different ideas you have been working with?
- How clearly have you articulated your perspective so your audience has no doubt about what you have been trying to prove?
- Have you given your reader a sense of closure?

Title: As you construct your cause-and-effect paper, a title should emerge at some point—often late in the process. The title should reflect the cause-and-effect claim that you are considering.

For more on oral presentations, including the use of PowerPoint, see Chapter 16.

VISUAL *Thinking*	Going Beyond Words to Achieve Your Goals

For this assignment Hanna Lake wrote a causal analysis in which she examined how life experiences influenced Black Hawk's and Harriet Jacobs's concepts of family. Fortunately, painted portraits of Black Hawk and photographs of Harriet Jacobs exist, and Lake easily found them on the Web. She did need to make choices, however, because multiple images of these two historical figures are available. For Black Hawk, she chose an illustration that appears in *History of the Indian Tribes of North America,* a three-volume set published between 1836 and 1844. For Harriet Jacobs, Lake chose a photo that appears on the cover of an edition of Jacobs' autobiography. Lake considered these publications to be reliable sources of historically accurate images. By adding these visuals to her causal analysis, Lake made Black Hawk and Jacobs seem more real for readers.

- What other criteria could Lake use to select visuals for her analysis?
- What visuals would you recommend that Lake use in her analysis?

Writing Activity

Constructing a Full Draft

After reviewing your notes and research and invention activities, and carefully considering all of the information that you have generated, you are ready to construct a first complete draft, using the organizational approach that you have decided on. Remember that your thinking about the nature of the cause-and-effect relationship may evolve as you draft your paper, so your ideas will most likely change as you compose the first draft of your essay.

As you draft, keep in mind that you are proving that something occurred as a direct result of something else. Make sure you have support for your claims about cause-and-effect relationships.

There is no one right way to start composing. However, if you have an organizational plan that you are comfortable with, you might begin by filling in parts of the sections that you feel best about or those where you feel you have the best information. You can always put everything together later.

An Excerpt from Hanna Lake's Early Draft

In this excerpt from an early draft, note how Hanna Lake incorporates evidence from her sources to prove her claim. As she wrote, Lake did not worry about grammar, punctuation, and mechanics; instead, she concentrated on getting her main ideas onto paper. (The numbers in circles refer to peer comments, which follow the draft on page 360.)

Brothers, Brethren, and Kin: The Role of Family in the Lives of Harriet Jacobs and Black Hawk❶
Hanna Lake

Family serves a valuable function in a person's life; it fosters personal identity, provides support, and functions as a group of loyal confidants. Family has no strict definition and varies from individual to individual. The mechanisms that act on one's interpretation of family are life forces and life-shaping events. Harriet Jacobs, who wrote under the pseudonym Linda Brent, is a female slave in a slaveholding Southern state in the mid-nineteenth century.❷ During her enslavement she must endure undue advances from her master, grueling labor, and seven years confined in an attic while she is trying to escape. For Jacobs, the institution of slavery is the main force that produces her unique view on family. Black Hawk is a member of the Sauk tribe in the Western territory of the United States near present-day Illinois (Black Hawk 41). He is a war chief in his tribe; this position brings him frequently to battle and into talks with various political and military leaders. Black Hawk's views on family are formed mostly in his relations with others—tribes, countries, and cultures. He considers family to be a broad term that encompasses his nuclear family (though less so than the traditional sense), any group with common interests, or who looks to help Black Hawk and his tribe. Indeed, Black Hawk's broad sense of family, and his use of familial terms to define nonfamilial relationships, may make modern readers of his autobiography uncomfortable. Harriet Jacobs views family in a slightly more traditional sense: her close blood relations, with some benevolent individuals passing into the realm of *family*. Jacobs and Black Hawk grew up in diametrically different environments and, thus, even their translations of family—one of the most basic concepts—are deviating.

Jacobs' Nuclear Family❸

For Jacobs, her reality is bleak and wrought with turmoil. Slavery places her existence in the hands of white slaveholders who consider her property to be bought, sold, and mistreated—sexually and otherwise. It is because of this unfortunate circumstance that her view of family is more conventional. She needs a strong support system to keep her resolve firm and, luckily, she is blessed with the relatively uncommon opportunity to have her actual family on the same plantation. Her grandmother, Martha, is an industrious free Black woman who keeps her own home near the house of the Flint family plantation whom Harriet considers to be a "great treasure" (Jacobs 445); she serves as Harriet's rock and confidante throughout the narrative. MORE ABOUT PRESENT FAMILY. Even her mother and father, who both die when Jacobs is still an adolescent, remain on Jacobs' mind all throughout her everyday life.

Black Hawk's lack of close family

While Jacob's clings to the blood-related family she does have, Black Hawk does not seem to have the similar deeply rooted ties to his nuclear family and thus, his definition of *family* is less nuclear family-centric. Children, his wife, and other close relations are rarely mentioned, save for mainly the opening narration of previous generations of men in his family (Black Hawk 41–46). And even then there is little emotion or affection shown towards his great grandfather and his progeny. On another occasion, Black Hawk offers to trade his son for the son of a friend in his tribe (Black Hawk 61). When his own son is mentioned, no name is given and no sadness is expressed over losing his son (his own flesh and blood!) for a time. And when this adopted son is later killed, Black Hawk is determined to avenge his death with the help of braves in his tribe (Black Hawk 70). However, when Black Hawk loses his father in a battle with the Cherokees, he "blacken[s] his face, fast[s], and pray[s] to the Great Spirit for five years." As stated in the footnotes, tradition in the Sauk nation calls for a mourning period for close kin of up to a year; Black Hawk quintuples this period to grieve for his father (Black Hawk 49). Later, Black Hawk loses both his son and daughter in a short span of time. He describes this as "a hard stroke, because [he] loved [his] children" and resolves to live in seclusion with his family—this is one of the few instances when he refers to his wife, children, or nuclear family at all (Black Hawk 96). These prolonged times of mourning demonstrate that Black Hawk is deeply affected by the deaths of his father and children. Also, these episodes show that he considers his nuclear family to hold a dearer place in his life than he indicates; maybe it is just more difficult for him to translate those strong emotions of love into words than it is for Jacobs.❹

Student Comments on Hanna Lake's Early Draft

❶ "I'd like to see what Jacobs and Black Hawk look like."

❷ "When you talk about events in Jacobs's and Black Hawk's lives, use past-tense verbs. However, when you refer to the autobiographies, you can use present-tense verbs because the texts still exist."

❸ "You might consider eliminating the headings in the paper so that it flows more smoothly."

❹ "Your essay needs a conclusion to tie some of your points together."

▮ Revising

Once you have a draft, put it aside for a day or so. This break will give you the chance to come back to your text as a new reader might. Read through and revise your work, looking especially for ideas that are not explained completely, terms that are not defined, and other problem areas. As you revise your early drafts, hold off on doing a great deal of heavy editing.

When you reread the first draft of your paper, here are some questions to ask yourself:

- How effectively have I explained my thesis so the reader knows what I intend to prove?
- What else might my audience want or need to know about my subject?
- How else might I interest my audience in my causal analysis?
- What did I find out about my subject that I did not include in my causal analysis?
- Have I clearly explained and defined any terms my readers might not know?
- Would any aspects of my causal analysis be more effective if presented visually?

WRITER'S *Workshop* | **Responding to Full Drafts**

Working with one or two classmates, read each paper and offer comments and questions that will help each of you see your paper's strengths and weaknesses. Consider the following questions as you do:

- What is your first impression of this draft? How effectively does the title draw you into the paper? Why? What part(s) of the text are especially effective for showing a cause-and-effect relationship?

- How well does the writer stay on track? If he or she loses focus, where does it happen?

- How logical is the paper? What strengths and weaknesses do you see in the writer's logic?

- How effective is the introduction? What suggestions can you make to improve the introduction?

- What do you think is the author's thesis or main point? How could it be expressed or supported more effectively?

- In the main part of the paper, are there parts that need more explanation? Where would you like more details or examples?

- How credible is the writer's case that a relationship exists? How credible are his or her sources?

- Might visuals such as charts, tables, graphs, or photographs help the writer to explain or support his or her claims about causes and/or effects more simply and clearly?

- How clearly and effectively does the writer present any opposing points of view on this subject? How effectively does he or she answer opposing viewpoints?

- What could be added or changed to make the conclusion more effective? To what extent does it make you want to learn more about this topic?

- What are the main weaknesses of this paper?—How might the writer improve the text?

Use your word processor's track-changes tool to try out revisions and editing changes. After you've had time to think about the possible changes, you can "accept" or "reject" them. Also, you can use your word processor's comment tool to write reminders to yourself when you get stuck with a revision or some editing task.

Responding to Readers' Comments

Once they have received feedback on their writing from peers, teachers, friends, and others, writers have to figure out what to do with that feedback. Because your writing is your responsibility, you must determine how to deal with reader responses to your work. The first thing to do with any feedback is to consider seriously what your reader has to say. Then it is up to you, as the author, to decide *how* to come to terms with these suggestions as you revise your causal analysis. You may decide to reject some comments, of course; other comments, though, may deserve your attention. You may find that comments from several readers contradict each other. In that case, use your own judgment to decide which reader's comments are on the right track. It is especially important to determine how well you have helped readers understand a cause-effect relationship.

In the final version of Lake's paper on pages 363–68, you can see how she responded to her reader's comments, as well as to her own review of her early draft.

 # KNOWLEDGE OF CONVENTIONS

In your college classes, writing about a cause-and-effect relationship is usually academic writing, so you will be required to follow the conventions for an academic essay. Other situations may call for a variety of genres, including memos, essays, blog postings, letters to the editor, and even formal position papers. Such documents often include tables, charts, graphs, or photos. Be aware of the conventions for any genre you use.

 ## Editing

After you revise, you have one more important task—editing and polishing. At the editing stage, make changes to your sentence structures and word choices to improve your style and to make your writing clearer and more concise. Also check your work to make sure it adheres to conventions of grammar, usage, punctuation, mechanics, and spelling. Use the spell-check function of your word-processing program, but be sure to double-check your spelling personally (your computer cannot tell the difference between, say, *compliment* and *complement*). If you have used sources in your paper, make sure you are following the documentation style your instructor requires.

See Chapter 20 for more on documenting sources using MLA or APA style.

As with overall revision of your work, this final editing and polishing is most effective if you can put your text aside for a few days and come back to it with fresh eyes. We strongly recommend that you ask classmates, friends, and tutors to read your work to find editing problems that you may not see. To assist you with editing, we offer here a round-robin editing activity focused on making sure that subordinate clauses are attached to independent clauses.

WRITER'S *Workshop*	Round-Robin Editing with a Focus on Subordinate Clauses

ROUND-ROBIN EDITING WITH A FOCUS ON

Fragments (p. 146)
Modifiers (p. 189)
Wordiness (p. 232)
Citing Sources (p. 273)
Careful Word Choice (p. 319)
Subordinate Clauses (p. 363)
Inclusive Language (p. 411)

Writing about causes and effects benefits from the careful use of **subordinate clauses**. A subordinate clause has a subject and a verb, but it cannot stand on its own because it begins with a subordinating conjunction such as *although*, *because, while, if,* or *since*). When it appears on its own, it is a sentence fragment:

FRAGMENT *Because my car did not start this morning.*

Because subordinate clauses cannot stand on their own, they need to be attached to an independent clause:

SENTENCE *Because my car did not start this morning,* I was late for class.

or

SENTENCE I was late for class *because my car did not start this morning.*

Working with several classmates, look for the subordinate clauses in your papers, and make sure they are attached to independent clauses. If you are uncertain about a specific convention for using subordinate clauses, consult a handbook or ask your instructor.

Genres, Documentation, and Format

If you are writing an academic paper in response to Scenario 1, follow the conventions appropriate for the discipline in which you are writing and the requirements of your instructor. However, if you are responding to Scenario 3, follow the guidelines for educational posters so that it meets the needs and requirements of your intended audience.

If you have used material from outside sources, including visuals, give credit to those sources, using the documentation style required by the discipline you are working in and by your instructor.

For advice on writing in different genres, see Appendix C. For guidelines for formatting and documenting papers in MLA or APA style, see Chapter 20.

A Writer Achieves Her Goal: Hanna Lake's Final Draft

Here is Hanna Lake's finished cause-and-effect paper, in which she argues that life experiences shaped Harriet Jacobs' and Black Hawk's definitions of family.

HANNA LAKE

Brothers, Brethren, and Kin: The Role of Family in the Lives of Harriet Jacobs and Black Hawk

Harriet Jacobs, who wrote a famous narrative under the pseudonym Linda Brent, was a slave in a slaveholding Southern state in the mid-nineteenth century (fig. 1). During her enslavement she endured undue advances from her master, grueling labor, and confinement in an attic for seven years while trying to escape. For Jacobs, the institution of slavery was the major force that shaped her concept of family. Black Hawk (fig. 2) was a member of the Sauk tribe in the Western territory of the United States (Black Hawk 41). He was a war chief in his tribe, a position that brought him frequently into battle and into talks with political and military leaders. For Black Hawk, "family" represented a proud tradition that could help keep his tribe harmonious and strong, and he used the context of family strategically to move the Sauk forward on the national and world stage. "Family" for Jacobs, which included blood relations and a small number of benevolent whites, served as a source of great emotional strength, protection, and strategic help to break out of slavery. Harriet Jacobs and Black Hawk grew up in diametrically different environments and entered adulthood at extreme ends of the power spectrum—Jacobs as a powerless slave and Black Hawk as the leader of an independent nation. For these two nineteenth-century Americans, the challenges they faced in their adult lives shaped their perceptions of "family" and the role it played in their struggles.

Harriet Jacobs' reality was bleak and wrought with turmoil. Slavery placed her destiny in the hands of white slaveholders who considered her to be property that can be bought, sold, and mistreated—sexually and otherwise. Because of this unfortunate circumstance, her view of family was fairly conventional. She needed a strong support system to keep her resolve firm, and luckily she was blessed with the relatively uncommon opportunity to have her blood relatives on the same plantation. Her grandmother, Martha, was an industrious free Black woman who kept her own home near the house of the Flint family plantation, and Harriet considered her

1

2

Lake has changed some verb tenses in her essay. When referring to the events in the lives of Jacobs and Black Hawk, she uses past-tense verbs. However, when she refers to the autobiographies, she uses present-tense verbs because the autobiographies still exist.

Because a classmate asked what Jacobs and Black Hawk looked like, Lake added a photo of Jacobs and a portrait of Black Hawk.

Fig. 1   Harriet Jacobs

Fig. 2   Black Hawk

to be a "great treasure" (Jacobs 445); she serves as Harriet's rock and confidante throughout the narrative. Her grandmother also alleviated part of the greatest struggle Harriet had to deal with: the unwanted advances from Dr. Flint. Because of her grandmother's demeanor and constant presence, Dr. Flint, out of fear, did not pursue Harriet (Jacobs 472).

However, Jacobs' family was so close-knit that Dr. Flint used their closeness to his advantage. When Harriet ran away, he jailed her two young children and her uncle Phillip, hoping to distress her so much that she would come out of hiding to rescue the family that she held so dear (Jacobs 553, 563). Even her mother and father, who both died when Jacobs was still an adolescent, remained on Jacobs' mind throughout her everyday life. She thought about her parents with fond memories and lamented that her own children "cannot remember [her] with such entire satisfaction as [she] remembered [her] mother" (Jacobs 541). "Family" in *Incidents in the Life of a Slave Girl* means family in the most literal and traditional sense of the word: parents, grandparents, children, and all other blood relations who love each other, look out for one another's well-being, and minimize the effects of constant struggles. For Harriet Jacobs, family was her source of strength and happiness in a life made hopeless by slavery.

While Jacobs clung to the blood-related family she did have, Black Hawk did not seem to have similarly deeply rooted ties to his nuclear family and, thus, his definition of "family" was less centered on them. Indeed, Black Hawk's broad sense of family, and his use of familial terms to define nonfamilial relationships, may make modern readers of his autobiography uncomfortable. He rarely mentions his wife, children, and other close relations in his autobiography. In the opening narration he does describe previous generations of men in his family (Black Hawk 41–46), but even then Black Hawk shows little emotion or affection toward his great-grandfather and his progeny. On another occasion in the narrative, Black Hawk offers to trade his son for the son of a friend in his tribe (Black Hawk 61). When he mentions his own son, he doesn't even give his name and expresses no sadness over losing him. But when his adopted son is later killed, Black Hawk is determined to avenge his death with the help of

3

4

Lake removed the headings in her essay to make it flow more smoothly.

braves in his tribe (Black Hawk 70), signifying a strong attachment. When Black Hawk loses his father in a battle with the Cherokees, he "blacken[s] his face, fast[s], and pray[s] to the Great Spirit for five years." As stated in the footnotes, Sauk tradition called for a mourning period for close kin of up to a year; Black Hawk quintupled this period to grieve for his father (Black Hawk 49). Later, Black Hawk lost both his son and daughter in a short span of time. He describes this as "a hard stroke, because [he] loved [his] children" and resolves to live in seclusion with his family—this is one of the few instances when he refers to his wife, children, or nuclear family (Black Hawk 96). These prolonged times of mourning demonstrate that Black Hawk was deeply affected by the deaths of his father and children and that his nuclear family might have held a dearer place in his life than he indicates elsewhere in his writings; maybe it was more difficult for him to translate strong emotions of love into words than it was for Jacobs. But, unlike Jacobs, Black Hawk's greatest challenges extended far beyond the realm of his personal well-being, so the solace and support that were vital to his struggles also went beyond what members of a nuclear family can offer.

While Black Hawk included his close blood relations in his idea of 5 "family," he also included members of the Sauk tribe. This group is most important to Black Hawk's fight for his goals. He consistently uses the word *our*, which signifies a unity between Black Hawk and the other Sauks: "our village" and "our people" (Black Hawk 77, 69). They were a people of common ancestry; people who had the same father in Muk-a-tà-quet; people who owed their success to Na-nà-ma-kee, another late war chief (Black Hawk 129). This reference to their shared forefathers is interesting because Na-nà-ma-kee was also Black Hawk's great-grandfather (Black Hawk 41). The fact that Black Hawk does not mention this link while addressing the men of his tribe shows that their common roots were more important than his notable heritage. Even though there were disagreements among the Sauk, they generally stood as a united front against enemies, much like a family unit. Black Hawk found a constant source of support from his tribe in the ongoing struggles against land-grabbing whites and rival tribes; while his tribe was a close-knit family system, there were conflicts with nearby tribes such as the Osage and the Sioux (Black Hawk 47, 140). The tribe had common enemies, and they worked together to avenge deaths of murdered members of the tribe (Black Hawk 123).

Like Black Hawk, Harriet Jacobs did find some support beyond her 6 nuclear family, and she expresses appreciation and fondness for the additional support she finds in benevolent whites. Early in life, Jacobs was graced with a kind mistress who had also been her mother's mistress before her death. This generous woman provided Harriet with a life similar to "that of any free-born white child" and even taught her how to read and write

Lake added the names *Osage* and *Sioux* after a peer reviewer suggested that this would be useful information.

(Jacobs 448). Again, even during her harrowing time under the eye of Dr. Flint, Jacobs found some solace in the "large, loyal heart" of Miss Fanny, the woman who set her grandmother free and who visits Harriet to ensure she is being treated well (Jacobs 539). And during her escape Jacobs receives help from compassionate white friends—at a time when she most needs it. A dear friend of her grandmother promises to keep Harriet hidden, despite the illegality of harboring fugitive slaves. When Jacobs first meets her, the benefactress assures her that "[she] will be safe here" (Jacobs 552). These words of encouragement, along with a promise of security, establish a backup family for Harriet—a family with more privilege who can help her escape the perils of slavery. These white women, while mentioned only a few times in the narrative, were extremely powerful in Jacobs' life. They provided assistance and useful tools not often available to a slave. To Jacobs these women were extensions of her family, like a kindly aunt or another strong grandmother. While they were not as consistently valuable to Jacobs emotionally as her immediate family, they did assist her with her greatest struggles at opportune times.

As with many American Indian nations of the time, European powers   7 played a large role in the everyday lives of Black Hawk and the Sauk. The Spanish, French, English, and Americans all engage in diplomacy with Black Hawk throughout his autobiography. The Europeans supplied the Sauk with goods, weaponry, and even luxury items in exchange for trade and alliances (Black Hawk 43, 45). Though today we would say the Europeans' treatment of the Native Americans was controlling and oppressive, Black Hawk viewed this system of support as akin to the care taken by parents looking after their children; their support earns the European ambassadors the moniker of "father," and the president of the United States is known as their "Great Father," who oversaw his "red and white children" (Black Hawk 150). The general population of American whites were the Sauk's brothers—a familial relationship characterized by alternating periods of amity and conflict—and those in power who provided aid, presents, and allegiance were considered the Sauk's fathers. Again, this definition, which implies a subservience of one group to another, makes us uncomfortable. However, it becomes understandable in the context of Black Hawk's use of the "family metaphor" to define broad relationships. Also, as Native American scholar Mark Wallace notes, Black Hawk's voice was "mediated" and "restrained by whites before it was even conceived" (481). Further, as literary scholar J. Gerald Kennedy observes, "The restrained voice we hear in the narrative is that of an old man filled with pride, remorse, and anger" (xxi). Some of Black Hawk's struggles were due to conflicts with his white brothers, but his "fathers" aid Black Hawk with allegiance and supplies during these times of struggle. For Black Hawk, these relationships were just as important as veritable blood bonds.

Lake consulted some other scholarly sources to provide context for some of Black Hawk's observations.

The diverging opinions of the two authors about the definition and role of   8
family in their lives can be attributed to their social foundations and basic life
experiences. For Jacobs, family was a constant source of support, but at the
same time, its presence was always a matter of uncertainty. She could never be
confident that her family members would be in her life from one day to the next.
Since slavery was such a terrible institution, it hardened the slaves emotionally
and limited the circle of those people they could trust and depend on. But the
family system she did have aided her in her struggles with a life of hard labor,
sexual harassment, and eventual escape. Although Black Hawk was impris-
oned later in his life and witnessed horrible atrocities committed by whites
(Trask), during his formative years he was not subjected to captivity as a slave
on a Southern plantation. As a result, he viewed family as a broader support
system. For Black Hawk, family also encompassed members of his tribe and
nations who offered assistance. His family structure assisted in his struggles
with enemies, which included the United States government during portions of
his life, and advanced the well-being of the greater Sauk community. However,
we need to keep in mind historian Kerry A. Trask's observation that in his
autobiography "Black Hawk thereby unwittingly enabled white people to feel
good about themselves" (303), replacing their guilt with admiration for the Sauk
leader.

When a classmate noted that the essay stopped, rather than concluded, Lake added this paragraph.

Black Hawk and Jacobs had contrasting concepts of family, which reflected   9
some of the differences in their life experiences. However, focusing on the
differences may cause readers to overlook some similarities in their lives.
For example, both of them came from oppressed groups who were treated
unjustly. Perhaps most importantly, though, both of them wrote autobiographies that include many keen insights about the roles that families can play.
Both of them offer observations that encourage contemporary readers to
think about what it means to be part of a family, no matter how the term *family*
is defined.

Works Cited

Black Hawk. *Black Hawk: An Autobiography.* Ed. Donald Jackson. Urbana-
    Champaign: University of Illinois, 1955. Print.

Brent, Linda. *Incidents in the Life of a Slave Girl.* Ed. L. Maria Child. *The Classic
    Slave Narratives.* Ed. Henry Louis Gates, Jr. New York: New American
    Library, 2002. 437–668. Print.

Kennedy, J. Gerald. Introduction. *Life of Black Hawk, or Mà-ka-tai-me-she-kià-
    kiàk: Dictated by Himself.* By Black Hawk. Ed. J. Gerald Kennedy. New
    York: Penguin, 2008. vii–xxviii. Print.

Trask, Kerry A. *Black Hawk: The Battle for the Heart of America.* New York:
    Holt, 2006. Print.

Wallace, Mark. "Black Hawk's *An Autobiography*: The Production and Use of
    an 'Indian' Voice." *American Indian Quarterly* 18 (1994): 481–94. Print.

UNDERSTANDING A WRITER'S GOALS: QUESTIONS TO CONSIDER AND DISCUSS

Rhetorical Knowledge: The Writer's Situation and Rhetoric

1. **Audience:** How does Lake acknowledge what her audience does and does not already know?

2. **Purpose:** Although Lake has considered the concept of family by studying her own family's history, in this paper she studies the concepts of family for two people whose experiences differ dramatically from hers. What do you think she has accomplished by studying these diverse perspectives?

3. **Voice and tone:** What is Lake's attitude toward her subject?

4. **Responsibility:** How does Lake responsibly represent the content of the two autobiographies?

5. **Context, format, and genre:** Lake is aware that both Jacobs and Black Hawk come from different cultures and different contexts from those of twenty-first century Americans. Because Lake relies on autobiographical material, it is only natural that Jacobs's and Black Hawk's perspectives will be revealed and might be at odds with our own view. How adequately does Lake explain her sources' contexts? How might she do so even more effectively?

Critical Thinking: The Writer's Ideas and Your Personal Response

6. How does your concept of family compare or contrast with the two concepts that Roen describes?

7. Which of the two concepts of family is easier for you to understand? Why?

Composing Processes and Knowledge of Conventions: The Writer's Strategies

8. To write her causal analysis, Lake drew on two autobiographies—primary sources—as well as secondary sources. What does she gain by incorporating secondary sources?

9. How does Lake draw connections between Black Hawk's and Jacobs' life experiences and their view of family?

Inquiry and Research: Ideas for Further Exploration

10. Interview several friends to find out how their life experiences have shaped their ideas about family. Write about the similarities and differences that the interviews reveal.

Self-Assessment: Reflecting on Your Goals

Now that you have constructed a piece of writing that explains causes and effects, review your learning goals, which you and your classmates may have considered at the beginning of this chapter (see pages 328–29). To help reflect on the learning goals that you have achieved, respond in writing to the following questions:

 ### Rhetorical Knowledge

- *Audience:* What have you learned about addressing an audience in this kind of writing?
- *Purpose:* What have you learned about the purposes for writing about causes and effects?
- *Rhetorical situation:* How did the writing context affect your writing about cause(s) and/or effect(s)? How did your choice of subject affect the research you conducted?
- *Voice and tone:* How would you describe your voice in this essay? Your tone? How do they contribute to the effectiveness of your writing?
- *Context, medium, and genre:* How did your context determine the medium and genre you chose, and how did those decisions affect your writing?

 ### Critical Thinking, Reading, and Writing

- *Learning/inquiry:* While working on your paper, what did you learn about the causal relationship you focused on that you could generalize about?
- *Responsibility:* How did you show that the effect or effects you wrote about were really the result of the cause or causes you identified?
- *Reading and research:* What did you learn from the reading selections in this chapter? What research did you conduct? What additional research might you have done?
- *Skills:* What skills have you learned while you were engaged in this project? How do you hope to develop them further in your next writing project?

Writing Processes

- *Invention:* What invention skills have you learned in writing about causes and effects? Which skills were most useful to you?

- *Organizing your ideas and details:* Describe the process you used to identify the causes and then the effects you wrote about. How did you decide to organize your paper, and how successful was your organization?

- *Revising:* What one revision did you make that you are most satisfied with? If you could go back and make an additional revision, what would it be?

- *Working with peers:* How have you developed your skills in working with peers? How did you make use of feedback you received from both your instructor and your peers? How could your peer readers help you more with your next assignment? How might you help them more, in the future, with the comments and suggestions you make on their texts?

- *Visuals:* Did you use visuals to explain your cause(s) or effect(s) to readers? If so, what did you learn about incorporating these elements?

- *Writing habits:* What "writerly habits" have you developed, modified, or improved on as you constructed the writing assignment for this chapter? How will you change your future writing activities, based on what you have learned about yourself?

Knowledge of Conventions

- *Editing:* What sentence problem did you find most frequently in your writing? How will you avoid that problem in future assignments?

- *Genre:* What conventions of the genre you were using, if any, gave you problems?

- *Documentation:* Did you use sources for your paper? If so, what documentation style did you use? What problems, if any, did you have with it?

If you are constructing a course portfolio, file your written reflections so that you can return to them when you next work on your portfolio. Refer to Chapter 1 (pages 12–13) for a sample reflection by a student.

CHAPTER 12

Writing to Solve Problems

You see, hear, and read about problems and possible solutions to those problems all the time. In developing countries, governments and nongovernmental organizations struggle with problems such as widespread poverty or disease. Closer to home, your community might experience a high dropout rate in your local high school or a shortage of affordable housing. When you write to propose solutions, you first identify an existing problem and then suggest one or more possible ways to solve it. For example, the Web site for ACCION International has identified world poverty as a problem and has proposed a possible solution. ACCION started its lending program more than forty years ago, providing loans to what it calls "Microentrepreneurs," so those business owners can grow their own small companies. In turn, the interest they pay provides funding for even more small-business loans.

When you are faced with a smaller-scale problem than world poverty,

Industry Initiatives   Our Impact   Make a Donation   Get Involved   Media Center

go

Mission and Vision

on
a private, nonprofit organization with the mission of
ple the financial tools they need to improve their

n
sion is to build a financially inclusive world with
economic opportunity for all.

e in a financially inclusive world—one in which
idual can seize the opportunity to access a full
igh-quality, affordable financial services. Through
ach person we serve can capitalize on his or her
oility and drive to achieve real economic gains—
brighter futures for themselves and their families.

e about what we do and how we work »

Voices
FROM THE FIELD

This Is What We Do
Accion brings access to financial
services to some of the poorest
people in the most challenging
environments in the world, from China
to Brazil to India. *3:21*

Website Feedback | Sitemap | Privacy Policy

perhaps one in your own life or your friends' lives, you will often propose your own solution to it. When you suggest counseling to an unhappy friend, you are proposing a solution—a known treatment—to an emotional problem: depression. When you recommend a heating and air conditioning repair company to a friend with a broken furnace, you are proposing a solution—the repair company—to a more practical problem: the faulty furnace.

When you propose any solution, however, others may already have suggested different solutions to the same problem. Therefore, you must support your own proposal with convincing evidence—not just opinions—and demonstrate that the proposal has a reasonable chance of success.

373

Setting Your Goals for a *Proposal*

 Rhetorical Knowledge (pp. 376–80)

- **Audience:** To convince your audience to accept your solution, pay careful attention to your readers' views on and attitudes toward the problem. Who will be interested in your solution? What are their needs, values, and resources? What arguments are most likely to convince this audience?
- **Purpose:** One purpose of any proposal is to convince readers of the existence of a problem and the need for a solution. Another purpose is to convince readers that the solution(s) you propose is (are) the best one(s) possible.
- **Rhetorical situation:** Think about the factors that affect where you stand in relation to your subject. What is compelling you to write your proposal essay?
- **Voice and tone:** When you write to solve problems, you will need to be persuasive. As a result, make sure your tone engages your readers and does not in any way threaten or offend them.
- **Context, medium, and genre:** Decide on the most effective medium and genre to use to present your proposal to the audience you want to reach. Visuals such as charts, graphs, and photographs may help you make your case.

 Critical Thinking, Reading, and Writing (pp. 381–95)

- **Learning/inquiry:** When you propose a solution, you first need to think critically to determine whether the problem exists and needs to be solved and whether your proposed solution is viable. Also think critically about the kind of evidence that will convince your readers. Further, evaluate a range of possible solutions to find one or more that are not only viable but effective.
- **Responsibility:** As you read solutions proposed by others, you have the responsibility to consider their solutions fairly as well as critically. You cannot ignore other good ideas simply because you do not agree with them.
- **Reading and research:** Readers will find your solution more acceptable if you have carefully and critically examined the problem and the issues surrounding your solution, supporting it with strong evidence, not unproven assumptions and assertions.

Writing Processes (pp. 396–410)

- **Invention:** Start by recording the ideas that you have about your problem, using an invention strategy such as brainstorming or listing. After recording your initial ideas and findings, you will also need to conduct research.
- **Organizing your ideas and details:** Once you have some ideas down, think about how you might organize your main points, what evidence you might need to provide to support them, and how you might deal with competing solutions to the problem.
- **Revising:** As you write, you may change your opinion about your problem and solution. Once you have a draft, read your work with a critical eye to make certain that it displays the qualities of an effective proposal.
- **Working with peers:** "Test" your solution on your classmates.

Knowledge of Conventions (p. 411)

- **Editing:** One of the hallmarks of effective proposals to solve problems is the use of inclusive language—language that makes diverse readers feel like part of the team that is solving the problem.
- **Genres for writing to solve problems:** In your college classes, proposing a solution usually involves academic writing, so you will probably be required to follow the conventions for an academic essay. Nonacademic writing situations may call for a variety of genres such as a formal proposal to provide funding for a specific solution or an informal memo to suggest an internal policy change.
- **Documentation:** When writing to solve problems, you will probably need to rely on sources outside of your own experience. Make sure you document them using the appropriate style.

RHETORICAL KNOWLEDGE

Readers of any proposal may ask themselves, "Why should I believe *you*?" All successful proposals have one important aspect in common: the establishment of a credible *ethos*. The nature of your subject and your audience will help you decide how best to maintain a balance between logical arguments and appeals to your readers' emotions.

Writing to Solve Problems in Your College Classes

In many of your college classes, your instructor will present you with a problem and ask you to propose a solution. For your classes, you will be expected to examine any problem in depth, with academic rigor and an appropriate level of detail so that readers understand the problem. After all, if readers cannot understand the problem and see how it affects them, then why should they pay any attention to your proposed solution(s)? Here are some examples of problems you could write about in your college classes:

- In your political science class, you may be asked to propose a solution to the problems associated with the electoral college.
- In a course in environmental studies, you might be asked to propose ways to reduce U.S. dependence on fossil fuels.
- In your geology course, you might be asked to write a research proposal to study the problem of erosion in a nearby canyon.
- In your botany course, you might be assigned a problem/solution paper to examine the effects of climate change on the oak trees that surround your county courthouse and plaza.

The "Ways of Writing" feature presents different genres that can be used when writing to solve problems in your college classes.

Writing to Solve Problems for Life

Writing to solve problems is prevalent in all areas of your life. Many people feel that all they ever do in their professional lives is propose solutions to problems. Consider the following examples:

- An employee writes to her company's personnel director to propose a solution to the high turnover rate in her division.
- A new member of a company's product development division writes to his supervisor to suggest ways to reduce the time and costs required to develop and test new products.

People who are active in their communities often propose solutions as part of their civic life. Because problems continually emerge, every community constantly needs ideas to help solve its problems. You might, for example, write a letter to a local newspaper in which you propose a plan for raising funds for a nonprofit organization.

In your personal life, you will also encounter problems that need to be solved. Some will no doubt be large and potentially life altering. Suppose your mother, who lives alone, is suffering from Alzheimer's disease. You might send an e-mail to your siblings, proposing several possible solutions that you will discuss in a conference call. Or suppose your child is having a problem at school. You might send a letter to your child's teacher.

The "Ways of Writing" feature presents different genres that can be used when writing to solve problems in life.

Scenarios for Writing | Assignment Options

Your instructor may ask you to complete one or both of the following assignments that call for a solution to a problem. Each of these assignments is in the form of a *scenario*. The list of rhetorical considerations on page 380 encourages you to think about your audience; purpose; voice, tone, and point of view; and context, medium, and genre.

Starting on page 396, you will find guidelines for completing whatever scenario you decide—or are asked—to complete. Additional scenarios for college and life may be found online.

Writing for College

SCENARIO 1 **Solving a Social Problem from One of Your Courses**

Think about a problem that you have learned about in another class you are taking this term. To complete this assignment, assume that the instructor has asked you to choose a problem and propose a solution for it, which you will present to your classmates. You must first decide which problem you wish to address and then look at various options for solving the problem. Here are some possible social problems to consider:

- **Education:** In some states, the dropout rate is relatively high.
- **Criminal justice:** In some cities, motorists run red lights more frequently than they do in other communities.
- **Business administration:** In many sectors of the U.S. economy, relatively few women have attained high-level management positions.
- **Health:** The incidence of diabetes is relatively high among some segments of the population in the United States.

Writing Assignment: Propose a solution to the problem that you have selected. Be sure to focus on solving one aspect of the problem, thus narrowing it down to a manageable size.

Ways of Writing to Solve Problems

Genres for Your College Classes	Sample Situation	Advantages of the Genre	Limitations of the Genre
Academic essay	In your sociology class, your professor asks you to examine some social problem (the effect of television violence or advertising on young people; eating disorders; and so on) and suggest possible solutions.	Your research on both the problem and potential solutions will be useful to young people who may engage in potentially unhealthy behaviors.	Some societal problems are too large to cover in one paper.
Proposal	The professor in your college success class asks you to write a paper detailing why some students leave school and to propose some ways to keep them enrolled.	A proposal is a good way to define a problem and then present research on potential solutions.	To get information from your fellow students, you will need to interview them—perhaps many of them—which is time-consuming.
Oral presentation	Create an oral presentation for your international relations class outlining a problem in another country and suggesting some solutions to that problem.	This oral presentation will force you to define the problem succinctly and then present possible solutions to it.	Illustrations will be crucial, and some problems are difficult to define orally and to show visually.
Letter to your campus newspaper	Your writing professor asks you to draft a letter to the editor of your campus newspaper about a problem on campus (litter, speeding cars, and so on).	Your school newspaper is a useful arena to publicize the problem and to ask fellow students to help with the solution.	A letter allows only limited space, and some problems and solutions are hard to describe briefly. It might not be published.
Recommendation report	Your business instructor asks you to outline an unusual business problem and to suggest a solution.	Finding a unique problem in the business world may help you and your readers understand how to solve unusual issues.	To make a good recommendation you will need to choose from multiple solutions, which may be difficult if the problem is unique.
Genres for Life	Sample Situation	Advantages of the Genre	Limitations of the Genre
Brochure	With several neighbors, you decide to construct a brochure in which you outline a local problem and suggest possible solutions.	A brochure provides a quick and easy way to share information about the problem, as well as your proposed solution.	A brochure provides limited space to present both the problem and the solution.
Memo	You have been asked to write a memo to the president of your firm, telling her about a serious problem and suggesting possible solutions.	A memo forces you to write concisely and specifically.	A memo is restrictive in terms of space (no one wants to read a ten-page memo).
Wiki	You want to construct a wiki that allows people in your area to share information on problems that affect them (graffiti, dangerous intersections, and so on) and to suggest and comment on possible solutions.	A wiki is an easy and uncomplicated way for people to share what they know about problems and potential solutions.	Someone will need to monitor the wiki for improper comments; readers need a reason to return to read and post on the wiki.
Web page	Every five years your extended family has a large-scale reunion, but there are always problems (travel time and cost, location for the reunion, and so on). Construct a Web page outlining these problems and and suggesting possible solutions.	A Web page gives everyone the same information at the same time; you can constantly update it, and you can provide links so you do not need to type all details into the page.	A static Web page does not allow for interaction (as a wiki does).
Performance improvement plan	A person you supervise at work has low sales for the quarter. You need to explain the problem and suggest solutions to it.	You can use your plan to outline both the problem and suggested solutions in sufficient detail so your employee has a real opportunity to improve his performance.	If your "plan for improvement" is incomplete, your employee might not do what he needs to do to solve the problem.

SCENARIO 2   Academic Writing: A Problem That Matters to You

For this scenario, decide on a problem for which you would like to propose a solution. You may choose a problem from any area of your life. Here are some suggestions:

- Your campus lacks adequate services for students with various kinds of disabilities.
- Your college needs daycare facilities for students with children.
- Your city's public library has too few computers, which means that patrons often must wait a long time for one to become available.
- The hourly pay rate for student workers on campus is relatively low.
- The number of arrests for driving under the influence rises dramatically in your city during holiday weekends.

Writing Assignment: Do you have a problem on your mind? What do you think should be done about it? Answering these two questions may lead you to a topic that you will want to write about. Your audience will be the community affected by the problem as well as the person or organization that has the power and resources to implement your solution.

Writing for Life

SCENARIO 3   Civic Writing: Proposal to Solve a Community Problem

Think about some problem in your community, such as litter that does not get picked up, a shortage of shelters or food banks for the homeless, gang violence, job losses, high housing prices, a lack of parks, or big-box stores moving in or closing down. As you consider a local problem, keep in mind that you will need to define that problem and prove that it exists to your readers. Unless they can understand the problem, your solution will not make any sense. Figure 12.1 gives an example of one possible local problem.

Writing Assignment: Write a formal proposal, which you plan to present to the city council, outlining and explaining the problem, as well as your suggested solution. For more on the format of a formal proposal, see pages 381–82. In your proposal, be sure to do the following:

- State the problem in enough detail that readers will understand it and its importance to your community.
- If your research turns up any background information (what the causes of the problem are, how long it has been a problem, what others have done to try to solve the problem, and so on), also outline that background information.
- List possible solutions with their strengths and weaknesses (and costs, if applicable).

FIGURE 12.1
An increase in the number of mortgage foreclosures during an economic downturn can be problematic in communities with high unemployment.

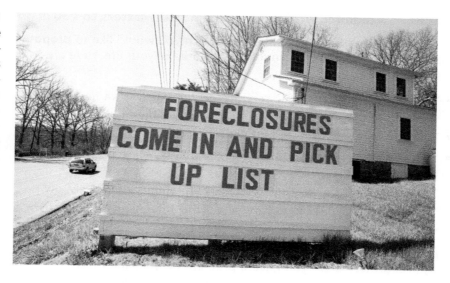

- Explain why your suggested solution is the most effective one to solve the problem.
- Ask for action of some kind (for example, further study or funding for the solution).

Rhetorical Considerations

Audience: While your instructor and classmates will be the primary audience, you should also consider other audiences for your proposal, depending on the scenario you have chosen. What will your audience know about this problem? Why should they be concerned about it? How can you make your solution(s) seem reasonable to them? What kinds of responses would you expect them to have to your proposal?

Purpose: Your purpose is to identify a particular problem and propose a viable solution. How will you convince your audience the problem needs attention?

Voice, tone, and point of view: You may choose to write about a problem that you have strong feelings about. How much has your view of the problem—or even your view that it *is* a problem—been determined by your value system? How will you deal with your preconceptions about the problem, and how might these preconceptions affect your tone? What attitudes, if any, do you have toward members of your audience, and how might that affect how you present your information?

For more on choosing a medium and genre, see Chapter 17 and Appendix C.

Context, medium, and genre: Keeping the context of the assignment in mind, decide on a medium and a genre for your writing. How will your writing be used? If you are writing for an audience beyond the classroom, consider what will be the most effective way to present your proposal to this audience.

CRITICAL THINKING, READING, AND WRITING

Before you begin to write your proposal, consider the qualities of a successful proposal. It also helps to read one or more proposals to get a feel for this kind of writing.

Effective writing that solves problems contains a clearly defined problem and a well-articulated solution that is targeted for a specific audience. In addition, this kind of writing will include convincing evidence for the proposed solution's effectiveness, as well as a well-documented review of alternative solutions. Finally, an effective proposal will include a call to action.

Learning the Qualities of Effective Proposals

A proposed solution to a problem should include the following qualities:

- A clearly defined problem. An effective proposal first establishes the existence of a problem that is both understandable and manageable within the scope of the assignment.

- An awareness of the audience. Your readers need to believe that the problem you are writing about actually exists and that your proposed solution will work. Therefore, use what your audience already knows and believes to shape your proposal. For instance, if your audience readily accepts the existence and importance of the problem, you can focus almost exclusively on the proposed solution. If, however, your readers may be unaware of the problem, or may not believe it *is* a problem, you will need to spend time making them aware of it and convincing them to be concerned about it.

- A well-explained solution. Your readers need both to understand your solution and to find it reasonable. One way to help any audience understand your proposal is to use language that the audience understands and to provide definitions of unfamiliar terms.

- Convincing evidence for the effectiveness of the solution. You will need to prove that your solution is viable and that it is the best answer to the problem by supporting your assertions with evidence such as expert testimony, case studies, experimental studies, and examples of similar solutions to similar problems. A solution needs to be feasible, affordable, and effective.

  You will also need to anticipate readers' objections to your proposed solutions so that you can address them. The cost of any solution almost always comes up as an objection, so you need to be prepared to deal with that concern ("While this solution is expensive in the near future, I will demonstrate how paying the extra money now will actually save us money in the long run").

For more information on cause and effect, see Chapter 11.

- A well-documented review of alternative solutions. While your proposed solution should stand on its own merits, for your proposal to convince the most skeptical readers, you must also acknowledge alternative ways to solve the problem and then carefully show why the alternatives will not work, or work as well, thus demonstrating that your solution is the best option.
- A call to action. There is little point to proposing a solution to a problem unless someone actually implements that solution. At the end of your proposal, you should urge those who can take action to solve the problem to do so.

Reading, Inquiry, and Research: Learning from Texts That Propose Solutions

As you read the selections, consider the following questions:

- How effective is the writer at convincing you that there is a problem that needs to be addressed?
- To what extent has the writer offered a workable solution?
- How convincing is the evidence? Why?
- How effectively does the writer anticipate opposing views and look at alternative solutions?
- How can you use the techniques of proposal writing exemplified here in your own writing?

ANYA KAMENETZ

The Case for Girls

PROPOSAL ESSAY

Anya Kamenetz is at *Fast Company* magazine. She is the author of *Generation Debt* (2006) and *DIY U: Edupunks, Entrepreneurs, and the Coming Transformation of Higher Education* (2010). She also maintains a blog, DIY U, where she writes about how technology is changing the landscape of higher education. We chose this essay because it gives a possible solution to a global problem.

On December 11, according to my doctors' best guesstimate, I am due to give birth to a baby girl. My husband and I couldn't be happier. Most parents, however? They'd rather have a boy.

It may not be surprising that there's a lingering preference for baby boys over baby girls worldwide. What's alarming, however, is that this global inclination is manifesting more strongly than ever. Historically, when nature is allowed to determine sex all on its own, about 105 boys are born for every 100 girls (and because women live longer, the ratio of people on the planet evens out over time, even tilting slightly toward females). But the balance of nature has shifted in Asia, thanks to wider availability of affordable ultrasound equipment, which detects gender as early as 15 weeks, and widespread abortion. In China, after 30-plus years of the country's One Child Policy, the ratio of boys to girls is a highly unnatural 120:100 (it's even reached 150:100 in one province). In India, 109 boys are born for every 100 girls. Demographers calculate that roughly 160 million Asian females have gone what they euphemistically categorize as "missing." There's growing evidence that this pattern of sex selection is being followed in Eastern Europe and the former Soviet Union, and similar trends seem likely in Africa and the Middle East.

Lest we think this is some sort of second and third-world predicament, it turns out boys are still No. 1 in the United States too. A 2011 Gallup poll revealed that if American men between the ages of 18 and 49 could have only one child, 54% would want a boy; "no preference," at 26%, beat out girls, who rated a measly 19%. According to the same poll, women don't have a preference; but since it takes two to tango, as the song goes, that makes for heavy pressure in favor of "a masculine child," as Luca Brasi so eloquently put it in *The Godfather*. These figures have remained essentially unchanged for 70 years—the stats were the same in 1941. While it may be culturally taboo here to openly reject or abort a child based on gender, fears of second-class status and doubts of a daughter's potential value are remarkably persistent.

In India and China, the preference for sons is seen as pragmatic and economically sound, a choice often exercised by educated, upwardly mobile parents, making this a form of "consumer eugenics" (a term coined by Mara Hvistendahl, the author of the 2011 book *Unnatural Selection*). Cultures with such a pronounced boy bias tend to also have a tradition of "patrilocality," where daughters go to live with their husbands' families, while sons stay at home and inherit property. In China, where one-child families have been official policy since 1979, the aging population has resulted in the so-called 4-2-1 problem: four grandparents, two parents, and just one child. According to the old customs, that one child, the economic mainstay, had better be a boy. The situation in India is similar. As one newspaper ad for sonograms put it: "Spend 500 rupees now or 500,000 rupees later"—on a dowry.

That consumer preference turns into disaster when repeated across a   5
society. Unnatural Selection does a frightening, thorough job of documenting the consequences for countries full of men: sex trafficking in Albania, mail-order brides in Vietnam, crime in "bachelor towns" in rural China. The future portends aging populations short of nurses and teachers.

By the Numbers

44%: the increase in a U.S. woman's paycheck from 1970 to 2007

6%: the salary increase for an American man over the same period

2024: the year when the average American woman may outearn the average American man

45%: Swedish government officials who are women

51.4%: American managers who are women (way up from a meager 26.1% in 1980)

33: countries that have had a female president. (But not, of course, the U.S.!)

51%: U.S. personal wealth held by women

83%: U.S. consumer purchases made by women

$0.63: what a Wyoming woman gets for every dollar a man earns

$0.84: what a woman gets in Vermont

5: average number of children for an American mother in the 1960s; it's down to 2.5 now

21: average age of a first-time mom in 1970; it's up to 25 now

87: life expectancy (in years) of the average Japanese woman

8.5%: unemployment rate for U.S. women

9.5%: unemployment rate for U.S. men

74%: women on teams that created ads for this article

3%: female creative directors in the ad industry

Fact is, the desire and the data don't match up. In the 21st century, there's 6 a compelling case for girls as the equal—and in some cases, optimal—gender for roles in leadership, innovation, and economic growth. Women excel in education, the most crucial factor in tomorrow's workforce; we are 56% of undergraduates in the U.S. and approaching parity in China and India. Our socialization is geared toward the right stuff for the changing requirements of success in the 21st century: Women are likely to have a more balanced, empathetic leadership style, better communication skills, a knack for fostering innovation through collaboration. Consider the results of a recent study by psychologists at MIT and Carnegie Mellon, who divided people into teams and asked them to complete intelligence tasks together. The IQ scores of the groups' members barely affected collective performance. The number of women on a team, however, affected it a lot—the more women, the better.

The evidence is mounting that baby girls are a strong investment. "An 7 important future indicator for a developing economy is its treatment of women," says Sheryl WuDunn, coauthor with husband Nicholas Kristof of Half the Sky, a best seller turned PBS series turned online game that dubs girl power "the best way to fight poverty and extremism." A country that gives girls equal opportunity has twice as much talent and brainpower to draw on and is likely to be more open and flexible in ways that promote international trade. World Bank numbers also show that development dollars invested in projects that target girls and women show a 90% return; the figure for projects focused on men and boys hovers between 30% and 40%. The Grameen Bank, the best-known microfinancier, makes 97% of its loans to women, whose repayment rates are much higher.

Thankfully this kind of reasoning is gaining influence, resulting in many 8 creative efforts to brighten the image of daughters. China has attacked the 4-2-1 problem head-on. The government has started a pension program benefitting rural people over age 60 with daughters, and not sons. The amounts match or beat what the typical son would send home to his folks from the city. In the Chinese version of Medicare, insurance premiums are now discounted or in some cases eliminated for the lucky parents of girls. India offers the "Indira Gandhi Scholarship Scheme for Single Girl Child"—only daughters may apply. So far these well-meaning efforts have enjoyed limited success. After five years, China's national Care for Girls program has barely nudged the sex imbalance.

Government incentives and private-sector funding are important parts of an 9 effort to rectify this problem. But there's also a place for branding; in countries like China, India, and South Korea, pro-girl advertising has been added to the mix—mostly simplistic propaganda. If better executed, these ads could shape social attitudes in ways subtle and overt. "If handled correctly, the most sensitive issue can be dealt with," says Priscilla Natkins of the Ad Council, which brought the world Rosie the Riveter and Smokey the Bear. She points to recent success-ful U.S. campaigns about drunk driving ("Friends Don't Let Friends . . ."), autism, and seat-belt use. "When we took on our seat-belt campaign, usage was in the low–20 percents—now it's way up in the mid-80s. Advertising didn't do that alone, but we planted the seed with consumers that led to legislation."

That's why, as a thought experiment, *Fast Company* asked some top adver-tising, marketing, branding, and digital agencies to make the case for baby girls in the language of the global consumer—a challenge they took very seriously.   10

"As we tried to understand the issue better," says Rei Inamoto from AKQA,   11
"we realized that this is not an issue of daughters versus sons. It's an issue of the self-perpetuating and devastating belief that women have little value."

My daughter will be brought up to understand her true value. That's a   12
promise. As for all the little girls to be born around the world, the creation of these ads is an effort to show how imagination can change the conversation around their lives.

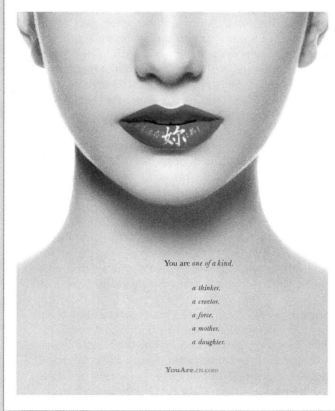

An ad created by AKQA, a digital agency located in San Francisco. The ad targets Chinese women; the charac-ter on the woman's mouth means "you."

You are *one of a kind.*

a thinker.

a creator.

a force.

a mother.

a daughter.

YouAre.cn.com

UNDERSTANDING A WRITER'S GOALS: QUESTIONS TO CONSIDER AND DISCUSS

Rhetorical Knowledge: The Writer's Situation and Rhetoric

1. **Audience:** Who do you think is Kamenetz's audience? This essay originally appeared in *Fast Company,* an American business magazine. Is this article what you imagine readers of a business magazine expect? Why or why not?

2. **Purpose:** Kamenetz reveals her purpose late in her essay when she mentions that *Fast Company* is calling for a global advertising campaign to promote the value of women. Do you think there are any other agendas present in this essay? If so, what might they be?

3. **Voice and Tone:** Throughout her essay, Kamanetz presents readers with facts and statistics. Yet she chooses to begin by informing readers that she is about to give birth to a baby girl. How does this fact affect her *ethos?* Do you consider it as important as the other facts she presents? If so, why? If not, why not?

4. **Responsibility:** In many ways, Kamenetz's entire essay is about social responsibility on a global level. She suggests that since public service announcements and ads have worked in the United States, they can also work globally. Can you think of any previous global public service ad campaign? If so, what was it? Do you think any global public service ad campaign can be successful? If so, why? If not, why not?

5. **Context, format, and genre:** This essay is really a call to action to the international advertising community. Do you think it's effective? Why or why not? What might Kamenetz have done to make it more effective?

Critical Thinking: The Writer's Ideas and Your Personal Response

6. Kamenetz's main premise is that the devaluation of women in many parts of the world can be alleviated by a global advertising campaign. To be successful it would mean changing age-old cultural patterns. Do you think this type of change is possible through advertising?

7. Can you think of other ways to address the global issue that Kamenetz writes about? What other methods might be as effective or more effective than advertising?

Composing Processes and Knowledge of Conventions: The Writer's Strategies

8. Kamenetz uses many different statistics throughout her essay. Do you find all the numerical data to be helpful? Compelling? Trivial? What data does she present that you find more compelling than any other?

9. Kamenetz begins by citing statistics that demonstrate a problem. She then mentions some potential solutions that are being tried. Finally, she proposes her solution: a global public service ad campaign. Do you find this organizational method effective? Why or why not?

Inquiry and Research: Ideas for Further Exploration

10. Kamenetz uses different kinds of statistics to demonstrate that women are not valued as much as men both in the United States and globally. Can you find more statistics to corroborate what Kamenetz presents? What statistics would you present to make the most compelling case? In what context would you present those statistics?

VIRGINIA HEFFERNAN

OPINION PIECE

Education Needs a Digital-Age Upgrade

Virginia Heffernan is a national correspondent for *Yahoo! News*. Previously, she was a regular contributor for the *New York Times*. Her most common topics are the Internet and pop culture. This essay originally appeared in the "Opinionator" section of *NYTimes.com* in August 2011. As many columnists occasionally do, Heffernan discusses a book she has recently read, presenting what might be considered a book review.

1   If you have a child entering grade school this fall, file away just one number with all those back-to-school forms: 65 percent.

2   Chances are just that good that, in spite of anything you do, little Oliver or Abigail won't end up a doctor or lawyer—or, indeed, anything else you've ever heard of. According to Cathy N. Davidson, co-director of the annual MacArthur Foundation Digital Media and Learning Competitions, fully 65 percent of today's grade-school kids may end up doing work that hasn't been invented yet.

3   So Abigail won't be doing genetic counseling. Oliver won't be developing Android apps for currency traders or co-chairing Google's philanthropic division.

4   Even those digital-age careers will be old hat. Maybe the grown-up Oliver and Abigail will program Web-enabled barrettes or quilt with scraps of Berber tents. Or maybe they'll be plying a trade none of us old-timers will even recognize as work.

5   For those two-thirds of grade-school kids, if for no one else, it's high time we redesigned American education.

6   As Ms. Davidson puts it: "Pundits may be asking if the Internet is bad for our children's mental development, but the better question is whether the form of learning and knowledge-making we are instilling in our children is useful to their future."

7   In her galvanic new book, *Now You See It*, Ms. Davidson asks, and ingeniously answers, that question. One of the nation's great digital minds, she has written an immensely enjoyable omni-manifesto that's officially about the brain science of attention. But the book also challenges nearly every assumption about American education.

8   Don't worry: She doesn't conclude that students should study Photoshop instead of geometry, or Linux instead of Pax Romana. What she recommends,

in fact, looks much more like a classical education than it does the industrial-era holdover system that still informs our unrenovated classrooms.

Simply put, we can't keep preparing students for a world that doesn't exist. We can't keep ignoring the formidable cognitive skills they're developing on their own. And above all, we must stop disparaging digital prowess just because some of us over 40 don't happen to possess it. An institutional grudge match with the young can sabotage an entire culture.   9

When we criticize students for making digital videos instead of reading *Gravity's Rainbow,* or squabbling on *Politico.com* instead of watching *The Candidate,* we are blinding ourselves to the world as it is. And then we're punishing students for our blindness. Those hallowed artifacts—the Thomas Pynchon novel and the Michael Ritchie film—had a place in earlier social environments. While they may one day resurface as relevant, they are now chiefly of interest to cultural historians. But digital video and Web politics are intellectually robust and stimulating, profitable and even pleasurable.   10

The contemporary American classroom, with its grades and deference to the clock, is an inheritance from the late 19th century. During that period of titanic change, machines suddenly needed to run on time. Individual workers needed to willingly perform discrete operations as opposed to whole jobs. The industrial-era classroom, as a training ground for future factory workers, was retooled to teach tasks, obedience, hierarchy and schedules.   11

That curriculum represented a dramatic departure from earlier approaches to education. In *Now You See It,* Ms. Davidson cites the elite Socratic system of questions and answers, the agrarian method of problem-solving and the apprenticeship program of imitating a master. It's possible that *any* of these educational approaches would be more appropriate to the digital era than the one we have now.   12

To take an example of just one classroom convention that might be inhibiting today's students: Teachers and professors regularly ask students to write papers. Semester after semester, year after year, "papers" are styled as the highest form of writing. And semester after semester, teachers and professors are freshly appalled when they turn up terrible.   13

Ms. Davidson herself was appalled not long ago when her students at Duke, who produced witty and incisive blogs for their peers, turned in disgraceful, unpublishable term papers. But instead of simply carping about students with colleagues in the great faculty-lounge tradition, Ms. Davidson questioned the whole form of the research paper. "What if bad writing is a product of the form of writing required in school—the term paper—and not necessarily intrinsic to a student's natural writing style or thought process?" She adds: "What if 'research paper' is a category that invites, even requires, linguistic and syntactic gobbledygook?"   14

What if, indeed. After studying the matter, Ms. Davidson concluded, "Online   15
blogs directed at peers exhibit fewer typographical and factual errors, less plagiarism, and generally better, more elegant and persuasive prose than classroom assignments by the same writers."

In response to this and other research and classroom discoveries,   16
Ms. Davidson has proposed various ways to overhaul schoolwork, grading
and testing. Her recommendations center on one of the most astounding revelations of the digital age: Even academically reticent students publish work prolifi-
cally, subject it to critique and improve it on the Internet. This goes for everything
from political commentary to still photography to satirical videos—all the stuff
that parents and teachers habitually read as "distraction."

A classroom suited to today's students should deemphasize solitary piece-   17
work. It should facilitate the kind of collaboration that helps individuals compensate for their blindnesses, instead of cultivating them. That classroom needs
new ways of measuring progress, tailored to digital times—rather than to the
industrial age or to some artsy utopia where everyone gets an Awesome for
effort.

The new classroom should teach the huge array of complex skills that   18
come under the heading of digital literacy. And it should make students account-
able on the Web, where they should regularly be aiming, from grade-school on,
to contribute to a wide range of wiki projects.

As scholarly as *Now You See It* is—as rooted in field experience, as well   19
as rigorous history, philosophy and science—this book about education happens
to double as an optimistic, even thrilling, summer read. It supplies reasons for
hope about the future. Take it to the beach. That much hope, plus that much
scholarship, amounts to a distinctly unguilty pleasure.

UNDERSTANDING A WRITER'S GOALS: QUESTIONS TO CONSIDER AND DISCUSS

Rhetorical Knowledge: The Writer's Situation and Rhetoric

1. **Audience:** Do you think Heffernan is writing for a general population (the readership of the online *New York Times*) or does she have a more specific audience in mind? What makes you think so?

2. **Purpose:** Heffernan sees a problem with our nineteenth-century educational system, which was designed to train workers for an industrial economy. To address the problem, she reviews a book, *Now You See It,* that presents a solution. Do you think Heffernan accomplishes her purpose, suggesting a new educational system? Why or why not?

3. **Voice and tone:** Heffernan is writing about a serious problem: the apparent disconnect between the current educational system and what twenty-first–century students need to learn. Do you feel her tone is appropriate for her topic? Why or why not?

4. **Responsibility:** Heffernan begins by citing the prediction that 65% of future careers will be in fields that don't exist today. As a result, in her view, the current educational system is not designed to meet future needs. She then presents a review of a book that presents some solutions. Should Heffernan have offered her readers more options? Are the suggestions provided by the author of one book enough?

5. **Context, format, and genre:** This essay originally appeared as an opinion piece on a newspaper's Web site; it could easily be seen as a book review, however. Can you identify what also makes this a piece of writing that looks for a solution to solve a problem? What makes you come to your conclusion?

Critical Thinking: The Writer's Ideas and Your Personal Response

6. As a student who is looking to enter the workforce in the future or who is currently balancing school and work, how do you feel about the notion that 65% of future careers haven't even been invented yet? How do you think you can prepare for careers that don't yet exist?

7. Do you agree with Heffernan that digital literacy is the answer? How would you define digital literacy? What skills does someone need to possess to be considered digitally literate? Why do you think studying Photoshop and Linux might not be the answer?

Composing Processes and Knowledge of Conventions: The Writer's Strategies

8. Since Heffernan is presenting some of the solutions that Cathy N. Davidson mentions in her book *Now You See It,* readers need to get a sense of both Heffernan's and Davidson's *ethos* on this topic. How does Heffernan establish both her own *ethos* and Davidson's as well?

9. Explain what strategy Heffernan uses to establish that a problem exists with education. Then describe how she encourages her audience to agree that the problem exists.

Inquiry and Research: Ideas for Further Exploration

10. Check out the *Occupational Outlook Handbook* published by the U.S. Bureau of Labor Statistics (www.bls.gov/ooh/). How does the government's projection of where jobs will open up in the next ten years match up with what Heffernan is saying? Is Davidson's solution likely to produce good candidates for the jobs that the Bureau of Labor Statistics is projecting? Why or why not?

GENRES *Up Close*   Writing a Proposal

Proposals often offer solutions to problems, but they also can suggest actions to take in situations where there is no real problem. For example, you can propose that you and your friends watch a particular sporting event or attend an upcoming concert. If you and your friends have similar tastes in sports or music, you may not have to support your proposal with reasons—for example, "This is being billed as the most competitive game of the season" or "I've heard it's the group's best concert yet."

Other kinds of proposals can outline future research projects, suggest ways to improve a company's already strong productivity, put forward ideas for enhancing an organization's marketing procedures, or seek funding for a research project. Such proposals are not designed to solve problems; instead, they suggest ways to seize opportunities.

Whether you are writing a proposal to solve a problem or to seize an opportunity, the genre features are similar. In particular, proposals do the following:

- Define a problem to be solved or an opportunity to be seized.
- Delineate a plan of action for solving the problem or seizing the opportunity.
- Make the case that the proposed solution is the most practical, feasible, and effective.
- Anticipate questions, objections, and alternative solutions/methods of seizing opportunities.
- Conclude with what the writer would like to happen next.

How does the following proposal memo fit these conventions?

AMY BASKIN AND HEATHER FAWCETT

Request for a Work Schedule Change

Background

1 **K**aren works weekdays 9:00 to 5:30 as a technical writer for an aerospace plant. Karen's husband, Murray, doesn't start work until 9:30, but often must work late into the evening. They have two school-age children. Their youngest, Helen, has cerebral palsy.

2 Karen would like to work flextime, so that she can be home with her daughters after school. That would allow her to schedule more therapy appointments for Helen, as well as help the girls with their homework. It would also save the family significant babysitting costs.

3 She will request a 6:00 a.m. to 2:30 p.m. workday.

Proposal Memo

To: John Doe
From: Karen MacDonald
Re: Request for Flextime
Date: May 17, 2006

4 As a team member of HI-Tech's Technical Writing Division for six years, I'd like to propose changing my work hours to 6:00 a.m. to 2:30 p.m., instead of 9:00 to 5:30.

5 I believe that, with this earlier schedule, I would be able to improve my written output by at least a third. As I'm sure you know, writing and editing requires a great deal of solitary concentration. Although I enjoy the camaraderie of our open-concept office, I am frequently disrupted by nearby phone calls and discussions. With the earlier schedule, I would have several hours to work without distraction before most of my coworkers arrive each day.

6 An earlier schedule would also allow me to schedule my daughter's medical appointments after work, meaning I'd be able to take significantly less time off, yet still see to her needs.

MEMO

Amy Baskin is a freelance writer who has published in magazines such as *Canadian Parent, Canadian Living, Today's Parent, Canadian Family,* and *Education Today.* She has also taught children and adults for more than two decades.

Heather Fawcett is a writer and an advocate for children with special needs. Early in her career, she was a technical writer in the computer industry. Her textbook *Techniques for Technical Communicators* has been used on college and university campuses in Canada and the United States.

This proposal memo is excerpted from Baskin and Fawcett's book *More Than a Mom—Living a Full and Balanced Life When Your Child Has Special Needs. www.morethanamom.net.*

Do you or someone you know have flexible work hours? What benefits and problems can you see with such an arrangement?

Overview of the memo—defines the problem/opportunity.

Delineates a plan of action to solve the problem/seize the opportunity.

Anticipates questions and objections.

Concludes with what the writer would like to happen next.

I feel that my work record as a reliable, self-directed, and self- disciplined employee makes me an ideal candidate for flextime work.   7

Since I rarely interact directly with customers, customer service should not be compromised. Should an urgent matter arise after I'd left work for the day, I would still be accessible by cell phone.   8

My meetings with engineers can be easily rescheduled to take place before 2:30. I could still arrange to work a later schedule on days when my presence would be critical in the late afternoon—for example, if a client requested a 3:00 meeting.   9

To ensure success, I propose we meet weekly in the first month to review the arrangement. I would continue to report on my progress in weekly department meetings.   10

We can use the timelines currently in our product schedule to track my projects and measure productivity.   11

I would like to discuss this proposal with you further to address any potential concerns you might have. I understand that you are responsible for the success of this department and must determine whether this plan works for our team as a whole. I suggest a trial period of one month, after which the arrangement could be assessed and revised, if necessary. I understand that if the plan is not working, I might be required to return to my original schedule.   12

UNDERSTANDING A WRITER'S GOALS: QUESTIONS TO CONSIDER AND DISCUSS

Rhetorical Knowledge: The Writer's Situation and Rhetoric

1. **Audience:** The audience for Karen Mac-Donald's proposal memo is her supervisor. How has MacDonald shaped the memo to address the supervisor's needs?

2. **Purpose:** MacDonald's goal is stated in the "Re" line—she is requesting flextime. Besides announcing her goal with the phrase "Request for Flextime," what other phrases might be effective in the "Re" line?

3. **Voice and tone:** How does MacDonald's tone affect the persuasiveness of her proposal memo?

4. **Responsibility:** How does MacDonald demonstrate that she is a responsible parent and employee?

5. **Context, format, and genre:** If MacDonald had decided to make this request in a face-to-face meeting rather than in a memo, what would be different? If there is a follow-up meeting with her supervisor to discuss the proposal, what more might MacDonald say to strengthen her case? If MacDonald had written a letter rather than a memo to make her proposal, how would the letter differ from the memo?

Critical Thinking: The Writer's Ideas and Your Personal Response

6. If you were MacDonald's supervisor, how would you respond to her proposal? Why?

7. What is the most compelling section of MacDonald's proposal?

Composing Processes and Knowledge of Conventions: The Writer's Strategies

8. How does MacDonald address potential objections to her proposal? How effectively does she do that?

9. How does MacDonald establish her *ethos* in the proposal? How effectively does she do that?

Inquiry and Research: Ideas for Further Exploration

10. Conduct a Web search to see how some companies use flextime. Who seems to benefit from flextime?

WRITING PROCESSES

As you work on your assignment, remember the qualities of an effective proposal (see page 381). Also recall the recursive nature of the writing process—that is, after you engage in invention and conduct some research, you may start writing, or you may decide to do some more research. In fact, the more writing experience you get, the more you will realize that no piece of writing is ever finished until your final draft.

Invention: Getting Started

As with any writing that you do, the more invention activities that you can draw on, the more effective your paper will be. Try to answer these questions while you do your invention work:

- What do I already know about the problem?
- What possible solutions do I already have in mind to propose?
- Where might I learn more about this problem? What personal experience might I have that is relevant?
- What might my audience already know about this problem?
- What might their point of view be?
- What questions do I have about the problem or about possible solutions?

 ### **Writing** Activity

Freewriting

For more on freewriting and other strategies for discovery and learning, see Chapter 4.

Keeping the questions above in mind, freewrite to jot down everything you know about the problem. Be sure to list any questions you still have as well. Your freewriting and listing should give you a good sense of what research you still need to conduct. Once you jot down what you know about the problem, you not only can focus on what else you need to understand about it (for more research), but you also can start thinking about possible solutions. Do not worry about putting what you know, what questions you have, and so on into complete sentences; the idea is to get down on paper or in a computer file everything you know about the problem and potential solutions. That invention work will give you a useful starting point.

Susan DeMedeiros's Freewriting

Student writer Susan DeMedeiros decided to look at the problem of identity theft caused by illegal skimming devices—as well as solutions to this problem. She began with the following short piece of freewriting:

> Who would have ever thought I'd have my identity stolen on vacation? And that
> I wouldn't even realize it until my husband and I got home? I never expected to be a

victim of a crime—especially a crime that was also taking place in our safe and comfortable suburb of Santa Clara, California. Yet that's exactly what happened. My husband and I both had our cards skimmed at a hotel restaurant. We were just like the unfortunate supermarket customers at a Lucky grocery store who used a self-service checkout machine that had an illegal skimming device embedded in it. I think consumers need to know how to protect themselves from this kind of identity theft.

STUDENT WRITING EXAMPLES

Brainstorming (pp. 176, 350)

Freewriting (pp. 48, 135, 261, 396)

Criteria (p. 307)

Listing (p. 95)

Table (p. 49)

Answers to Reporter's Questions (p. 261)

Organization (pp. 96, 181)

Clustering (pp. 135, 305)

Interviewing (p. 220)

Research (pp. 137, 177, 222, 263, 308, 398)

Reflection (p. 12)

Exploring Your Ideas with Research

Once you have used invention techniques to decide on a problem and explore what you know about it, you need to conduct research to investigate the problem further and develop possible solutions to it.

Although your own experience may provide some evidence for the effectiveness of your proposed solution, personal experience usually needs to be supplemented by other forms of evidence: quotations from experts, examples, statistics, and estimates of the time and financial resources needed to implement the solution drawn from reliable sources. One way to organize your research is to use the qualities of effective proposals to guide your research activities. Here are some possibilities:

- **A clearly defined problem:** As you do research on your problem, look at how others have defined it and narrowed it to make it more manageable.

- **An awareness of the audience:** Your research should give you a sense of how other writers have defined and addressed their audiences. Also, you should note how other writers have treated people's perceptions of the problem that you are trying to solve. What do they assume that people know about the problem? What do they assume that people do not know about the problem? How much do they assume that people care about the problem?

- **A well-articulated solution:** For most kinds of problems in the world, you will not be the first person to propose solutions. Look at how other writers have articulated their solutions.

- **Convincing evidence for the solution's effectiveness:** You will need to find evidence that your proposed solution is viable. Look for expert testimony, the results of experimental research, and case studies.

- **A well-documented review of alternative solutions:** You cannot be certain that your proposed solution is the most effective one unless you have carefully reviewed a range of possible solutions. As you consider them, keep an open mind—you might find a solution that is more effective than the one that you first offered.

- **A call to action:** As you do your research, look at the language that other writers have used to inspire their readers to action.

For advice on conducting primary research, see Chapter 19.

> **ELECTRONIC ENVIRONMENTS**   **Conducting Primary Research Online**
>
> Your writing about problems and solutions can be improved if you investigate the kinds of solutions that would satisfy the larger community. To do so, you can use online resources to conduct primary research. To collect data or feedback from members of the community that will be affected by your solution, you can create a survey to collect their opinions, observations, and ideas, either by developing a simple e-mail distribution list and sending a small number of questions to targeted respondents or taking advantage of free spaces for collecting peoples' opinions and reactions on popular sites such as *Facebook*, *Twitter*, or *SurveyMonkey*.

Writing Activity

Conducting Research

Using the list of qualities for effective writing to solve problems, begin by listing what you already know about the problem and potential solutions. Then note what research you still need to conduct and possible sources to consult.

Susan DeMedeiros's Notes on Her Research

Reminder to self: Don't forget to include all the citations for the sources that I'm planning to use. Do this for everything or I'll be sorry later.

A clearly defined problem: I learned about the problem first-hand by being a victim. I can see from information in the news and by talking to people at my bank that it's a big problem. However, to get more hard data the U.S. Bureau of Justice Statistics looks like a good place to check.

An awareness of the audience: I think that I have a pretty good handle on the audience for this; it's pretty much everyone who uses credit cards and debit cards. However, I should look at how others have addressed audiences. I think I can get an idea of this by looking at the articles in local and national newspapers.

A well-articulated solution: I need to read a little more here and talk to more people. I also want to think about this a little more. I have sort of a sense of what might be a possible solution, but I need to think about how to write about it. I definitely want to see what the professional law enforcement agencies and bank security experts have to say.

Convincing evidence for the solution's effectiveness: Here I need to read what people with multiple perspectives are writing. If I do that, I'll have more options at a potential solution. That article that talks about a former skimmer should help here. I also need to figure out if sites like Mint.com provide greater security or put you more at risk.

A well-documented review of alternative solutions: If I don't look at a range of solutions, I might miss a really good solution. I need to keep an open mind. Also, I'm aware the best solution for me might not be the best solution for everyone.

A call to action: I'll rely a lot on others here. I'll see how others have called for action—and how folks have responded to those calls. I think that conversations with the bank and police department will include calls to action.

Reviewing Your Invention and Research

After finding sources and reading them critically, reconsider your thinking about your problem and your proposed solution in light of the qualities of an effective solution. Also begin thinking about a tentative thesis—your statement of your proposed solution. Keep an open mind, though. As you draft and revise your proposal, you may continue to refine your thesis. In some cases, you might even change it drastically. People who develop the best solutions usually leave open the possibility that a better solution could occur to them at any time.

For more on developing a thesis, see Chapter 13.

Susan DeMedeiros Considers Her Research and Focuses Her Ideas

After reading through various sources and taking notes, DeMedeiros wrote the following in her research journal:

> My reading has given me a better handle on the problem and its possible solutions. I think I'm ready to state that the best solution is text alerts, though I understand that there are other options. Even though I'm recommending text alerts, I'll mention the other options.

Strategies FOR Success | Flexibility

Successful writers are flexible, especially when they are proposing a solution to a problem. Often when looking at a problem and then proposing a solution, writers may be tempted to fall back on their preconceived ideas. However, successful writers are flexible enough to put aside their own preconceived perspectives and to be honest about the scope and magnitude of the problem. Once they are willing to do so, they may become aware of solutions that never would have occurred to them otherwise.

Likewise, it's important to be flexible about a range of viable solutions and to evaluate carefully the effectiveness, affordability, and limitations of each. By being flexible in this way, you establish your credibility with your readers by demonstrating that you have thoroughly investigated a range of solutions and have made a carefully considered recommendation. By presenting each option fairly and by showing how *your* solution is the best, you also make your own position more credible and believable.

Organizing Your Information

Once you know the problem you will be writing about and the solution you will be proposing, you need to consider how you might organize this material. Here are some questions to ask yourself:

- Who is your audience?
- Why might they be concerned about the problem you are discussing, and why might they be willing to accept your solution? Is it in your audience's best interest to find a solution for your problem?

- What is your purpose for writing—that is, why do your readers need this solution?
- What is the most important aspect of the problem you are proposing to solve?

One method for organizing a solution to a problem is the **whole-problem pattern.** If you are following this pattern, you first grab the readers' attention and introduce the problem and then use the paragraphs that follow to explain and illustrate it. If you think that readers are already familiar with the problem, this part of the paper could be fairly short, consisting of only a paragraph or two. If you think that readers are not familiar with the problem, however, then you might need to devote several pages to explaining and illustrating it. Then offer your proposed solution or set of solutions, respond to objections that you think readers might have, and conclude with a call to action.

A second organizational approach is to **segment the problem.** This approach is useful if the problem is relatively complex and has several components. First, you explain and illustrate the problem, but in a general way. Next, you focus on each part of the problem that needs special attention, offering a solution and responding to objections that you anticipate that are specific to each part. Finally, you offer suggestions for implementation and conclude with a call to action.

A third organizational approach, which involves a **sequence of steps,** is appropriate if the solution has multiple steps. After introducing the problem, you offer an overview of a series of steps that will solve the problem. You then explain each step in detail, provide evidence that it will work, and address any objections to it.

Here is a summary of these three organizational structures.

Options FOR Organization
Organizing a Proposal Essay

Whole-Problem Pattern	Segmenting the Problem	Sequence of Steps
Introduce the problem and its background.	Introduce the problem and its background.	Introduce the problem and its background.
Explain the problem.	Explain the problem.	Explain the problem.
Offer a solution or set of solutions.	Explain one part of the problem, offer a solution, and respond to objections.	Offer a multistep solution with an overview of the steps.
Respond to anticipated objections to the solution.	Explain another part, offer a solution, and respond to objections.	Offer a detailed explanation of the first step.
Offer suggestions for implementing the solution.	Deal similarly with remaining parts.	Offer a detailed explanation of the second step.
Conclude with a call to action.	Offer suggestions for implementing the solution.	Deal with any additional steps that might be necessary.
	Conclude with a call to action.	Conclude with a call to action.

Constructing a Complete Draft

Once you have chosen the organizational approach that works best given your audience and purpose, you are ready to construct your draft. Remember that your thinking about the problem and its solution(s) will evolve as you write, so as you work on the draft, keep the following in mind:

- Draw on your invention work and your research. As you draft, you may discover that you need to do more invention work and/or more research.

- As you try out tentative solutions to the problem, ask peers about the kinds of evidence you need to demonstrate that the solution is viable.

- Ask yourself and peers whether visuals might help make your case.

Synthesizing and Integrating Sources into Your Draft: Including Research Information

If you are working on a large research assignment, you will end up with a wealth of information, so using that information in your text can be a challenge: How can you condense it to help the reader understand it? This problem is especially acute when some of your research comes from texts that provide you with a large amount of information. One way to condense such research is to summarize what you learn and then to use those summaries in your text (for more on summarizing, see pages 553–54).

When faced with a mountain of information, student writers often try to use it all—and so the information overwhelms the text. The student has turned over control of the text to the ideas from the sources she or he found, and the text is no longer the writer's. You can avoid giving up control of your text by using summaries of information from sources to support your claims.

After gathering extensive information provided by the U.S. Bureau of Justice Statistics, Susan DeMedeiros might have been tempted to take on the entire problem of identity theft, a huge subject. However, since she was herself a victim of a skimming machine, similar to what had happened in her local supermarket, she was able to concentrate on this one particular method of identity theft and avoid the temptation of trying to attack the entire problem. Doing so helped DeMedeiros select the most important ideas and present that information to her readers in an understandable manner.

In order to get a better handle on the information she had learned and what part of that information she wanted to present to her readers, DeMedeiros summarized what she felt would be important for her readers to know. She was able to use her summaries as she began to draft her paper. Here is an example of what DeMedeiros summarized:

> I didn't realize the extent of identity theft until I found myself to be a victim. What was even worse was my bank tried to notify me by leaving voicemail on my home phone, but that happened when I was on vacation. I've since learned that I was a

INTEGRATING SOURCES

Including Others' Perspectives in Narratives (p. 97)

Quoting Sources (p. 139)

Paraphrasing Sources (p. 181)

Incorporating Numerical Data (p. 224)

Incorporating Partial Quotes (p. 266)

Creating Visuals to Show Your Data (p. 311)

Summarizing Information from Sources (p. 356)

Including Research Information (p. 401)

victim of a skimming machine that had been placed in a card reader at a hotel restaurant. I've since learned that there are at least five different steps to take to protect yourself from identity theft:

- Pay close attention to card readers (Service, 2012).
- Monitor all accounts using a consolidated service such as Mint.com (Schultz).
- Educate yourself about identity theft and ways to prevent it (Federal, 2012).
- Shred bills, receipts, and bank statements (Shapiro, 2012).
- Set up message alerts that inform you of unauthorized account transactions (Ayala, 2012).

Note that DeMedeiros has defined the problem and her personal connection with it and then lists the potential solutions in a format—a summary—that makes them clear and understandable to the reader. DeMedeiros will end up recommending the final solution she lists.

To use summaries in your writing, do the following:

- Introduce the summarized information (never just put it into your text without some of your words as an introduction).
- Connect the summary back to your main point, so your readers can easily see how the summarized information supports your argument.
- Accurately report and document where the information came from.

Parts of a Complete Draft

Introduction: Regardless of your organizational approach, begin with a strong introduction to capture your readers' attention and introduce the problem that you are proposing to solve. To accomplish these two goals, you might do one or more of the following:

- **Provide a brief history of the problem.**
- **Quote an authority who knows the problem well.** In the second paragraph of "The Case for Girls," Anya Kamenetz cites the book *Unnatural Selection* by Mara Hvistendahl for reasons parents prefer sons (page 383).
- **Cite salient statistics that demonstrate the nature of the problem.** Kamenetz begins her article by citing statistics that show how males are preferred over females in many modern societies, including the United States.
- **Provide information about the problem that will surprise—and possibly concern—readers.** Virginia Heffernan begins her article (page 388) with the announcement that "fully 65 percent of today's grade-school kids may end up doing work that hasn't been invented yet."

Body: When you propose a solution to a problem, you should determine the most effective organizational approach for the purpose you are trying to achieve and the audience you are addressing. The reading selections in this chapter, for example, use the organizational approaches outlined on page 400 to good effect. Whether you present a whole problem, segment the problem, or give a step-by-step solution, be sure to show why other solutions will not work or have already failed. Sometimes a problem has not been solved because previous solutions addressed only its symptoms, not its root cause. If this is the case, you need to show that your solution will take care of the root problem.

- **Present a whole problem and then give solutions.** Heffernan presents the problem by describing the work of Cathy N. Davidson, who maintains that the current educational model is based on preparing workers for late nineteenth-century industries. Heffernan then suggests that several other educational models might be more relevant today.

- **Give a segmented view of the problem and solutions.** Kamenetz presents how the preference for boys exists in different cultures. She then discusses solutions that have been tried. Finally, she gives a call to action for her solution of implementing a global public service campaign.

Conclusion: In your conclusion, review your proposed solution, reach out to your audience, and, usually, call for readers to take action to implement the proposal. Your conclusion could include the following:

- An outline of the problem you are working to solve
- A summary of your main points, with an explanation of why your solution would work
- A call to action—what you would like your reader to *do* now that he or she knows about the problem and your suggested solution

Title: As you compose your proposal, a title should emerge at some point—often very late in the process. The title should, of course, reflect the problem that you are addressing and might or might not hint at the solution. If you hint at a controversial solution in the title, however, you risk alienating readers whom you might otherwise win over with the strength of your argument.

Writing Activity

Constructing a Complete Draft

After reviewing your notes, invention activities, and research, and carefully considering the possible solutions you have generated, write a complete first draft of your paper. Be sure to explain your problem in detail and to outline your solution and explain why it is the best way to solve the problem your paper focuses on.

Susan DeMedeiros's First Draft

In her first draft, note how Susan DeMedeiros presents the problem to her audience. As she wrote, DeMedeiros did not worry about grammar, usage, punctuation, and mechanics; instead, she concentrated on getting her main ideas into her draft. (The numbers in circles refer to peer comments, which follow the student draft on page 409.)

VISUAL *Thinking* | Going Beyond Words to Achieve Your Goals

While researching her proposal on preventing identity theft, Susan DeMedeiros found the report "Identity Theft Reported by Households, 2005–2010" on the Web site of the Bureau of Justice Statistics, a part of the U.S. Department of Justice. Along with other statistical data, she found the following figures and table shown below and on page 405.

You can see that these three visuals, for the most part, present the same information in three different formats: a table, a stacked bar chart, and a line graph.

Type of identity theft experienced by victimized households, and total financial loss attributed to each type of identity theft, 2010

Types of identity theft	Percent of identify theft victimizations*	Financial Loss	
		Total loss (in thousands)	Percent of total loss
All types	100.0%	$13,257,487	100.0%
Existing credit card	54.0	$4,214,848	31.8
Other existing account	25.6	$2,306,165	17.4
Personal information	9.0	$3,901,016	29.4
Multiple types	11.4	$2,835,459	21.4

*Percent of identity theft victimizations by type of theft does not match the percentages by type shown in figure 2 due to the inclusion of the multiple types category.

Percent of households that experienced identity theft, by type of theft, 2005, 2007, 2009, and 2010

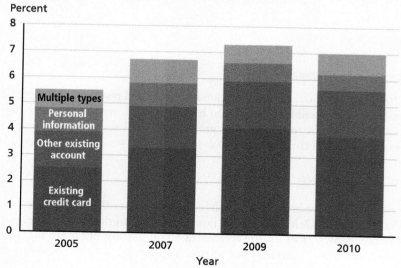

VISUAL *Thinking* | Going Beyond Words to Achieve Your Goals

Household identity theft victimizations, 2005, 2007, 2009, and 2010

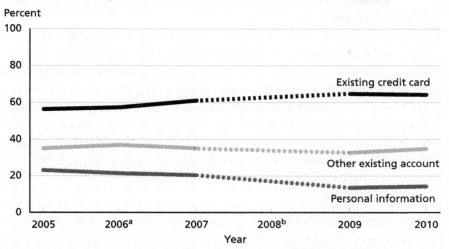

ªDue to methodological changes in the 2006 NCVS, use caution when comparing 2006 criminal victimizaton estimates to other years. See Criminal Victimization, 2006, http://www.bjs.gov, for more information.

ᵇAnnual estimates are not available for 2008 because 6 months of identity theft data were collected.

From "Identity Theft Reported by Households, 2005–2010," by L Langton, November 2011, Crime Data Brief, Bureau of Justice Statistics, U.S. Department of Justice. Retrieved from http://bjs.ojp.usdoj.gov/content/pub/pdf/itrh0510.pdf

- Which of these three visual representations do you think most effectively presents the data to a general audience? Why?

- What do you think are the strengths and weaknesses of the

  - bar chart
  - line graph
  - table

- Which do you think DeMedeiros should use in her proposal? (To see which one she did use, turn to page 413.)

Staying Ahead of Skimming Scams
Susan DeMedeiros

Identity Theft History ❶

According to the U.S. Bureau of Justice Statistics, various forms of identity theft have become more widespread over the past five years. In 2010, 8.6 million American households had at least one person who was a victim of identity theft. Five years earlier, in 2005, persons in 6.4 million households were victimized (Langton, 2011). This increase is primarily due to the growing un-authorized use of credit and debit cards. Identity theft is defined by the Bureau of Justice as having three components: unauthorized use of credit and debit cards, fraudulently impersonating another for the purpose of opening new accounts, and a combination of the two components. It is a global problem.

What Is Skimming?

Criminals use a tactic called "skimming" to steal personal information from consumers who swipe their cards at locations such as ATMs, grocery stores, and gas pumps. Skimming is when thieves attach data reading devices on digital card readers either internally or externally, or use handheld magnetic readers to collect the personal data stored in the magnetic stripe on the back of credit or debit cards. They then sell this data for $10 to $50 each to higher end criminals who use encoders to transfer your data to counterfeit cards (Poulsen, 2009). This creates a nightmare for the consumer. Not only does this create fraudulent charges on their credit cards, it swiftly wipes out cash from their bank accounts. ❷

My Story

Visiting New York was a trip my husband and I had looked forward to for many months. I was excited about experiencing the energy of the Big Apple and shopping on 5th Avenue. My husband could not wait to listen to jazz music at the Village Vanguard. We stayed in a nice hotel on Long Island, and took the railroad into the city each day. When we returned home to California, there was a voice mail message from our bank to contact them regarding possible fraud on our account. I went online to view our bank account and discovered, to my horror, there were hundreds of dollars missing. I informed my bank that they were indeed fraudulent transactions. My husband's debit card was skimmed as well. Both cards were skimmed at the hotel restaurant where we had stayed, as we later discovered. The excitement from our vacation was replaced by anger and shock. Thieves ruined our vacation.

What Consumers can do

There are several possible solutions to this problem for consumers to consider:

- Pay close attention to card readers (Service, 2012).
- Monitor all accounts using a consolidated service such as Mint.com (Schultz).
- Educate yourself about identity theft and ways to prevent it (Federal, 2012).
- Shred bills, receipts and bank statements (Shapiro, 2012).
- Set up message alerts that inform you of unauthorized account transactions (Ayala, 2012).

  Let's examine each one of these options . . .

The U.S. Secret Service suggests paying close attention to card readers.

Although it is important to know what a tampered device may look like, there have been card readers found with no external modifications such as the ones removed from Lucky grocery stores in California. Those units had internal cameras and electronics added to the circuitry that were discovered by the grocery employees during scheduled machine maintenance only after the units were opened. In such cases, the consumer would not see any difference in the external view of the card reader and would not know if it had been tampered with (Service, 2012).

Former skimmer suggests monitoring your accounts using Mint.com.

Convicted skimmer Dan DeFelippe now helps the government fight identity theft. Although he makes an important point of being vigilant about monitoring bank account activity, consolidating accounts at Mint.com has its drawbacks. At Mint.com, the user is required to provide all of their user names and passwords, so this solution may not be safe enough for the consumer even though the company claims they encrypt the data stored on their servers (Schultz). Providing private account log in data and passwords to an outside company makes sensitive data vulnerable to a breach. Furthermore, referring consumers to outside account consolidation services does not respond directly to consumer actions against card skimming at point of sale purchases.

The Federal Trade Commission promotes consumer education.

The Federal Trade Commission does indeed have an informative website www.ftc.gov, which offers the consumers a plethora of helpful information. However, if credit or debit cards have been compromised due to skimming of digital card readers, the FTC offers solutions only after the consumer has been notified of the breach by their respective financial institutions (Federal, 2012).

The Santa Clara Police Department suggests shredding sensitive documents.

The SCPD focuses on careful handling of paper items such as shredding bills, receipts, bank statements, and watching your mail (Shapiro, 2012).

The Best Solution ?

MessageAlerts

Wells Fargo Bank suggests message alerts delivered to your email or mobile device. Wells Fargo Bank offers customers the best solution to protect their accounts. The Rapid Alerts program offers consumers free message alerts delivered by email or text. Alerts notify customers instantly of transactions to their accounts. This empowers consumers to take action should they see unauthorized activity (Ayala, 2012).

- Consumers can instantly detect fraudulent transactions and take immediate action.
- Rapid Alerts identify the merchant, date, amount, and location.
- Transactions originating from international locations are instantly identified
- Consumers are instantly alerted of online purchases, ATM withdrawals, and telephone transactions.

Are message alerts effective?

According to Peter Ho, product manager for Wells Fargo Card Services and Consumer Lending, "We piloted Rapid Alerts in 2009 and received an overwhelming positive response from participants who said text alerts were an invaluable tool for monitoring their accounts . . ." (Ho)

Why would receiving a text message be the solution to focus on?

What is the point if the thieves already have my card data?

What do message alerts NOT do?

Message alerts do not prevent someone from opening new accounts in your name. Message alerts do not lock or close your account. It's up to you to take action. ④

Solution	Benefit	Cost
Look for fake card readers	You choose not to swipe your card if the reader looks suspicious. The benefit is that your card is not tampered with if you don't swipe it.	Many card skimming devices are internal and cannot be seen externally, so the cost is not using your card at paypoint locations.
Consolidate accounts on Mint.com	One stop shopping. Monitor all of your accounts on one site.	Loss of privacy and security of your user names and passwords carries risk of breaching all your accounts.
Sign up for credit reports	Can view activity to see if someone is opening up accounts in your name, or using your cards fraudulently.	From $12.00 to $40.00 per month. Reports are sent monthly or quarterly, not instantly.
Shred mail	Thieves cannot go through trash and retrieve your personal data to open accounts of their own if your mail is shredded.	Shredders and shredding services run from $25 to thousands of dollars depending on the level of quality. Shredding has no impact on card skimming.
Monitor accounts and bank statements	Keeps you up to date with the status of your accounts.	Fraud can occur at anytime day or night. The consumer won't know when it happens and can miss it unless they go into their bank sites constantly, which is impractical.
Text and Email alerts	Instant notification of unusual activity monitored by the bank. Activity can be quickly ceased and reimbursed.	No cost courtesy service offered by most banks and financial institutions. Set up takes minutes and can be done online.

The point is this . . . ⑤

1) Text message alerts are the first line of defense. You will be alerted the moment unusual activity occurs.

2) Bank software programs keep track of your purchasing habits and can detect when activity does not fit your patterns.

3) Without message alerts, if your card is compromised, the potential for thieves to charge up your account or deplete your cash increases as time ticks on.

 , ⑦

Student Comments on Susan DeMedeiros's First Draft

① "You probably need an introduction that grabs our attention more than this does."

② "I think some kind of graphic might help explain all these numbers."

③ "Why isn't the 'Best Solution' in with the other solutions?"

④ "I really like the way you present information in this table but is it in the best place?"

⑤ "These are important points. Is this the best way to introduce them?"

⑥ "You need some sort of conclusion to tie things up more."

⑦ "Of course, in your revised version, you'll need to include all of your citations."

Revising

Once you have a draft, put it aside for a day or so. This break will give you the chance to come back to your text as a new reader might. Reread and revise your work, looking especially for ideas that are not explained completely, terms that are not defined, and other problem areas. As you work to revise your early drafts, postpone doing a great deal of heavy editing. When you revise, you will probably change the content and structure of your paper, so time spent working to fix problems with sentence style or grammar, punctuation, or mechanics at this stage is often wasted.

As you revise, here are some questions to ask yourself:

- How effectively have I explained and outlined the problem(s), so my readers can understand those issues?
- What else might my audience want or need to know about my subject?
- How might I explain my solution(s) in sufficient detail and with enough examples so my readers can see how my ideas are logical solutions to the problem?
- How clearly have I explained and defined any terms my readers might not know?
- What other visual aids might help explain the problem and/or my solution(s)?

Responding to Readers' Comments

Once you have received feedback from your classmates, your instructor, and others about how to improve your text, you have to determine what to *do* with their suggestions and ideas. The first thing to do with any feedback is to really listen to it

WRITER'S *Workshop* | **Responding to Full Drafts**

Working with one or two other class-mates, read each paper and offer comments and questions that will help each of you see your papers' strengths and weaknesses. Consider the following questions as you do:

- What is your first impression of this draft? How effectively does the title draw you into the paper? What part(s) of the text are especially effective at explaining the problem or the writer's proposed solution?

- How successfully does the introduction grab readers' attention? What other attention grabbers might the writer try?

- How well has the writer explained the problem to someone who is unfamiliar with it? How might the writer explain it more effectively?

- How effective is the organizational approach?

- How carefully did the writer document sources in this draft?

- How well has the writer explained the proposed solution(s)?

- How well has the writer addressed objections that skeptics might raise?

- How has the writer suggested ways to implement the proposed solution(s)?

- Might visuals help the writer to present the problem or its solution(s) more effectively?

- How effectively does the conclusion call people to action?

- What do you see as the main weaknesses of this paper? How might the writer improve the text?

and consider carefully what your readers have to say. For example, how might Susan DeMedeiros have responded to these reader suggestions?

- One reader was not drawn in by DeMedeiros's introduction. When a peer reviewer indicates that an introduction does not excite him or her, that comment means that *some* readers might just stop reading at that point.

- Another reader asked about the possibility of using a graphic to help explain data.

- A reader requested a conclusion that ties all of DeMedeiros's information together.

All of these questions or concerns were issues that DeMedeiros needed to address.

As with any feedback, it is important to listen to it carefully and consider what your reader has to say. Then it is up to you, as the author, to decide *how* to deal with these suggestions. You may decide to reject some of them and respond to others. You may find that comments from more than one reader contradict each other. In that case, you need to use your own judgment to decide which reader's comments are on the right track.

In the final version of her paper on pages 412–18, you can see how Susan DeMedeiros responded to her readers' comments, as well as to her own review of her first draft.

KNOWLEDGE OF CONVENTIONS

By paying attention to conventions when they edit their work, effective writers help to meet their readers' expectations. Experienced readers expect proposals to follow accepted conventions.

Editing

When you edit and polish your writing, you make changes to improve your style and to make your writing clearer and more concise. You also check your work to make sure it adheres to conventions of grammar, usage, punctuation, mechanics, and spelling. If you have used sources in your paper, make sure you are following the documentation style your instructor requires.

See Chapter 20 for more on documenting sources using MLA or APA style.

Because it can be difficult to identify small problems in a familiar text, it often helps to distance yourself from it so that you can approach the draft with fresh eyes. Some people like to put the text aside for a day or so; others try reading aloud; and some even read from the last sentence to the first so that the content, and their familiarity with it, doesn't cause them to overlook an error. We strongly recommend that you ask classmates, friends, and tutors to read your work to help find editing problems.

To assist you with editing, we offer here a round-robin editing activity on inclusive language.

WRITER'S *Workshop* | **Round-Robin Editing with a Focus on Inclusive Language**

When you propose solutions to problems, be especially careful to use inclusive language—language that does not exclude people based on gender, ethnicity, marital status, or disability. Using inclusive language makes readers feel that they are included in the group that is solving the problem.

Look for instances in your work where you may have inadvertently used language that excludes a group based on gender, ethnicity, marital status, or disability. If you are uncertain about whether a particular word or phrase is a problem, consult a grammar handbook or ask your instructor.

ROUND-ROBIN EDITING WITH A FOCUS ON

Fragments (p. 146)
Modifiers (p. 189)
Wordiness (p. 232)
Citing Sources (p. 273)
Careful Word Choice (p. 319)
Subordinate Clauses (p. 363)
Inclusive Language (p. 411)

Genres, Documentation, and Format

If you are writing an academic paper in response to Scenarios 1 or 2, you will need to follow the conventions appropriate for the discipline in which you are writing. For Scenario 3, you may need to follow the conventions of a formal proposal.

For advice on writing in different genres, see Appendix C.
For guidelines for formatting and documenting papers in MLA or APA style, see Chapter 20.

A Writer Achieves Her Goal: Susan DeMedeiros's Final Draft

Below is the final draft of Susan DeMedeiros's proposal. As you read her essay, consider whether you think her solutions will work.

SUSAN DEMEDEIROS

PROPOSAL ESSAY   **Staying Ahead of Skimming Scams**

Abstract

On November 11, 2011, California-based Lucky grocery stores discovered skimming devices embedded in their self-service check-out machines during routine maintenance. Readers in 24 stores in California were breached. Two of them were in my community, and one is where I shop regularly. This incident is the inspiration for my topic for this project. I interviewed the Santa Clara store manager where the tampering occurred, the police, and the local Wells Fargo Bank for their perspective and advice. In addition to offering members of the public what I think is the best solution to protect their assets, I include statistical data on the prevalence of identity theft, information on card skimming, and a list of other possible solutions.

Staying Ahead of Skimming Scams

Santa Clara, California, is one of the safest places to live, but it is not immune to card skimming thieves. In November 2011, store employees discovered tampered card readers in check-out stands at the Lucky grocery store on Saratoga Avenue (S. Fein, personal communication, February 4, 2012). These card readers contained internal skimming devices that recorded credit and debit card data the moment they were swiped. Local shoppers were swindled out of thousands of dollars, but this turned out to be more than a local problem. Skimming devices were discovered in 24 Lucky stores throughout California (Delevett, 2011; Tumposky, 2011). Communities need to learn how to protect themselves from this growing problem. These days, people use credit and debit cards regularly at pay point locations such as grocery stores, gas pumps, ATMs, and movie theaters. In order to protect themselves, consumers should be vigilant and know what to do to avoid becoming victims of fraud. Several solutions are available, all

One of DeMedeiros's classmates made the following comment on her initial draft:

You probably need an introduction that grabs our attention more than this does.

DeMedeiros responded with a new opening paragraph that attempts to catch the reader's attention by presenting the situation that led to her interest in the topic.

of them outlined below, but the one that is most effective is setting up text and e-mail alerts that instantly notify consumers the moment an unauthorized transaction is attempted on their accounts. This solution is not only fast, easy, and inexpensive, it is critical.

Identity Theft History

According to a report by Lynn Langton (2011), a statistician for the U.S. Bureau of Justice Statistics, various forms of identity theft have become more widespread over the past five years. In 2010, 8.6 million American households had at least one person who was a victim of identity theft. Five years earlier, in 2005, persons in 6.4 million households were victimized. This increase is primarily due to the growing unauthorized use of credit and debit cards. Identity theft is defined by the Bureau of Justice Statistics as having three components: unauthorized use of credit and debit cards, fraudulently impersonating another for the purpose of opening new accounts, and a combination of these two components. It is a global problem. We can see the growth of identity theft in the chart from the U.S. Bureau of Justice Statistics shown in Figure 1 (Langton, 2011)

3

DeMedeiros received this comment from a classmate:

I think some kind of graphic might help explain all these numbers.

Her response was to add this graphic.

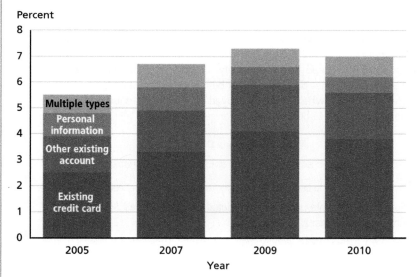

Figure 1 Percent of households that experienced identity theft, by type of identity theft, 2004, 2007, 2009, and 2010. From "Identity Theft Reported by Households, 2005-2010," by L. Langton, November 2011, *Crime Data Brief*, Bureau of Justice Statistics, U.S. Department of Justice. Retrieved from http://bjs.ojp.usdoj.gov/content/pub/pdf/itrh0510.pdf.

What Is Skimming?

Criminals use a tactic called "skimming" to steal personal information from consumers who swipe their cards at locations such as ATMs, grocery stores, and gas pumps. Skimming happens when thieves attach data-reading devices to digital card readers either internally or externally or use handheld magnetic readers to collect the personal data stored in the magnetic stripe on the back of credit or debit cards. They then sell this data for $10 to $50 each to higher-end criminals who use encoders to transfer consumers' data to counterfeit cards (Poulsen, 2009). This creates a nightmare for the consumer. Not only does skimming create fraudulent charges on their credit cards, it swiftly wipes out cash from their bank accounts.

My Story

I've had my own experience with this type of identity theft. Visiting New York was a trip my husband and I had looked forward to for many months. I was excited about experiencing the energy of the Big Apple and shopping on 5th Avenue. My husband could not wait to listen to jazz music at the Village Vanguard. We stayed in a nice hotel on Long Island, and took the railroad into the city each day. When we returned home to California, however, there was a voice-mail message from our bank asking us to contact them regarding possible fraud on our account. I went online to view our bank account and discovered, to my horror, that hundreds of dollars were missing. I informed my bank that the transactions were indeed fraudulent. My husband's debit card had been skimmed as well. We later discovered that both of our cards had been skimmed at the hotel restaurant where we had stayed. Thieves had caused the excitement from our vacation to be replaced by anger and shock.

What Consumers Can Do

Consumers can consider several possible solutions to this problem:

- Pay close attention to card readers as you use them (U.S. Secret Service, 2012).
- Monitor all accounts using a consolidated service such as *Mint.com* (Krantz, 2011; Schultz, 2010).
- Educate yourself about identity theft and ways to prevent it (Federal Trade Commission, 2012).
- Shred all bills, receipts, and bank statements (C. Shapiro, personal communication, February 4, 2012).
- Set up message alerts that inform you of unauthorized account transactions (M. Ayala, personal communication, February 4, 2012).

Each of these options has advantages and disadvantages, as indicated by the following review and table.

The U.S. Secret Service suggests paying close attention to card readers.

Although it is important to know what a tampered device may look like, some card readers have no external modifications, such as the ones removed from Lucky grocery stores in California. Those units, which had internal cameras and electronics added to their circuitry, were discovered by the grocery employees during scheduled machine maintenance only after the units were opened. In such cases, the consumer would not see any difference by looking at the card reader and would not know if it had been tampered with (U.S. Secret Service, 2012). 8

Former skimmer suggests monitoring your accounts using *Mint.com*.

Convicted skimmer Dan DeFelippe (Crouch, 2011) now helps the government fight identity theft. Although he makes an important point about being vigilant and monitoring all bank account activity, consolidating accounts at *Mint.com* (a website that manages money and monitors all of its users' financial accounts) has its drawbacks. At *Mint.com*, the user is required to provide the user names and passwords to all of their accounts, so this solution may not be safe enough for the consumer even though the company claims they encrypt the data stored on their servers (Krantz, 2011; Schultz, 2010). Providing private account log-in data and passwords to an outside company makes sensitive data vulnerable to a breach. Furthermore, outside account consolidation services do not protect consumers directly from card skimming at point-of-sale purchases. 9

The Federal Trade Commission promotes consumer education.

The Federal Trade Commission has an informative website (www.ftc.gov) that offers consumers a wide range of helpful information. However, if credit or debit cards have been compromised due to skimming of digital card readers, the FTC offers assistance only after the consumer has been notified of the breach by the respective financial institutions (Federal Trade Commission, 2012). 10

The Santa Clara Police Department suggests shredding sensitive documents.

The SCPD advises consumers to shred all paper items such as bills, receipts, and bank statements, and to watch your mail carefully (C. Shapiro, personal communication, February 4, 2012). These precautions will help consumers avoid some forms of identity theft, but they won't prevent skimming scams. 11

Wells Fargo Bank suggests message alerts delivered to your e-mail or mobile device.

Wells Fargo Bank offers customers the best solution to protect their accounts. The Rapid Alerts program offers consumers free message alerts delivered by e-mail or text. Alerts notify customers instantly of unusual transactions to their accounts. This service empowers consumers to take 12

Here one of DeMedeiros's classmates asked the following question:

Why isn't the "Best Solution" in with the other solutions?

DeMedeiros responded by placing her "best solution" in with the others.

Here one of DeMedeiros's classmates wondered if the table were placed in the best spot:

I really like the way you present information in this table but is it in the best place?

DeMedeiros moved the table up to where its placement made more sense.

action should they see unauthorized activity (M. Ayala, personal communication, February 4, 2012).

- Consumers can instantly detect fraudulent transactions and take immediate action.
- Rapid Alerts identify the merchant, date, amount, and location.
- Transactions originating from international locations are instantly identified.
- Consumers are instantly alerted of online purchases, ATM withdrawals, and telephone transactions.

I think receiving message alerts is the best solution. However, the following table presents the benefits and costs of each solution.   13

Solution	Benefit	Cost
Look for fake card readers	You choose not to swipe your card if the reader looks suspicious. The benefit is that your card is not tampered with if you don't swipe it.	Many card-skimming devices are internal and cannot be seen externally, so the cost is not using your card at a pay-point location that might be suspicious.
Consolidate accounts on *Mint.com*	This solution offers one-stop shopping. You can monitor all of your accounts on one site.	This solution requires loss of privacy and the security of your user names and passwords; it carries the risk of breaching all your accounts.
Sign up for credit reports	You can view activity to see if someone is opening up accounts in your name or using your cards fraudulently.	Credit reports cost from $12.00 to $40.00 per month. Reports are sent monthly or quarterly, not instantly.
Shred mail	Thieves cannot go through trash and retrieve your personal data to open accounts of their own if your mail is shredded.	Shredders and shredding services run from $25 to thousands of dollars, depending on quality. Shredding has no impact on card skimming.

(continued)

Monitor accounts and bank statements	This solution keeps you up to date on the status of your accounts.	Fraud can occur at any time day or night. Consumers won't know when it happens and can miss it unless they go into their bank sites constantly, which is impractical.
Text and e-mail alerts	Instant notification of unusual activity, monitored by the bank. Activity can be quickly stopped and losses reimbursed.	This no-cost courtesy service is offered by most banks and financial institutions. Set up takes minutes and can be done online.

Are message alerts effective?

According to Peter Ho (2010), product manager for Wells Fargo Card Services   14
and Consumer Lending, "We piloted Rapid Alerts in 2009 and received an
overwhelming positive response from participants who said text alerts were an
invaluable tool for monitoring their accounts." However, it's important to remember these limitations:

- Message alerts do not prevent someone from opening new accounts in your name.
- Message alerts do not lock or close your account. It's up to you to take action.

Even with their limitations, message alerts can protect you in the following
ways:

(1) Text message alerts are the first line of defense. You will be alerted the moment unusual activity occurs.

(2) Bank software programs keep track of your purchasing habits and can detect when activity does not fit your patterns.

(3) You will be alerted if your card is compromised, so the potential for thieves to charge items to your account or deplete your cash as time passes is greatly reduced.

Take Action

The sooner people take action, the better. Consumers should call or visit their   15
financial institution today and sign up for message alerts to be sent to their cell
phones or e-mail addresses. The public must be vigilant and protect their assets
and credit by taking advantage of the tools that are available to help them stay
ahead of the countless thieves who commit these crimes.

One of DeMedeiros's classmates asked:

These are important points. Is this the best way to introduce them?

DeMedeiros changed her introduction to these points to make it more formal.

One classmate pointed out that DeMedeiros didn't really have a conclusion in her initial draft. She responded with a concluding paragraph.

The paper follows APA guidelines for in-text citations and references.

Since the draft originally submitted to classmates didn't contain any formal documentation, one classmate reminded DeMederios to add it:

Of course, in your revised version, you'll need to include all of your citations.

DeMedeiros included a formal list of references in her final draft.

References

Crouch, M. (2011, January 6). Secrets of a former credit card thief. CreditCards.com. Retrieved from CreditCards.com website: http://www.creditcards.com/credit-card-news/secrets-former-credit-card-thief-dan-defelippi-1282.php.

Delevett, P. (2011, December 7). Lucky urges some customers to close bank accounts in wake of hacking. *San Jose Mercury News*. Retrieved from http://www.mercurynews.com/business/ci_19480050.

Federal Trade Commission. (2012). Fighting back against identity theft. Retrieved from http://www.ftc.gov/bcp/edu/microsites/idtheft/consumers/about-identity-theft.html.

Ho, P. (2010, March 23). Wells Fargo and Visa rollout rapid alerts for credit card-holders. Retrieved from Visa website: http://corporate.visa.com/media-center/press-releases/press1009.jsp.

Krantz, M. (2011, February 25). How safe are online financial sites like Mint.com? *USA Today*. Retrieved from http://www.usatoday.com/money/perfi/columnist/krantz/2011-02-22-financial-software-safety_N.htm.

Langton, L. (2011, November). Identity theft reported by households, 2005–2010. Retrieved from U.S. Bureau of Justice Statistics http://bjs.ojp.usdoj.gov/content/pub/pdf/itrh0510.pdf.

Poulsen, K. (2009, October 2). Credit card skimming survey: What's your magstripe worth? *Wired*. Retrieved from http://www.wired.com/threatlevel/2009/10/florida_skimming/?utm_source5Contextly&utm_medium=RelatedLinks&utm_campaign=Previous.

Schultz, J. (2010, July 6). Should you trust Mint.com? *The New York Times*. Retrieved from http://bucks.blogs.nytimes.com/2010/07/06/should-you-trust-mint-com/.

Tumposky, E. (2011, December 9). Lucky's customers hit by card-skimming thieves. Retrieved from ABC News website: http://abcnews.go.com/US/luckys-supermarket-chain-hit-card-skimmer-thieves/story?id=15123679#.Ty3bb1wV3gU.

U.S. Secret Service. (2012). Beware of skimming fraud. Retrieved from http://www.secretservice.gov/Skimming%20Fraud.pdf.

UNDERSTANDING A WRITER'S GOALS: QUESTIONS TO CONSIDER AND DISCUSS

Rhetorical Knowledge: The Writer's Situation and Rhetoric

1. **Audience:** Who is the intended audience for DeMedeiros's proposal? What makes you think that?

2. **Purpose:** What does DeMedeiros hope will happen when people read her proposal?

3. **Voice and tone:** How has DeMedeiros used language to help establish her *ethos* as someone who is knowledgeable about the problem of this particular form of identity theft?

4. **Responsibility:** Comment on DeMedeiros's use of sources to support her proposal. How responsibly has she used her sources? Why?

5. **Context, format, and genre:** DeMedeiros wrote this paper for a first-year writing course. If she were to convert this piece of writing to an article for her local newspaper, what revisions would she need to make? Effective problem/solution papers feature a well-defined problem and then present a viable solution. Does DeMedeiros do both in her paper? If so, how? If not, what could she do?

Critical Thinking: The Writer's Ideas and Your Personal Response

6. What is your initial response to DeMedeiros's proposal?

7. How is DeMedeiros's paper similar to other proposed solutions that you have read?

Composing Processes and Knowledge of Conventions: The Writer's Strategies

8. How effectively does DeMedeiros organize her proposal? What other organization would have worked?

9. Do you find the table that DeMedeiros uses to explain the different security options to be helpful? Can you think of any other visuals DeMedeiros might have used to help her argument? What might they be?

Inquiry and Research: Ideas for Further Exploration

10. Interview family members and neighbors about their feelings on how identity theft is affecting them and what measures they are taking to avoid it.

Self-Assessment: Reflecting on Your Goals

Having finished your proposal assignment, take some time to reflect on the thinking and writing you have done. It is often useful to go back and reconsider your learning goals (see pages 374–75). In order to better reflect on these learning goals, respond in writing to the following questions:

 ## Rhetorical Knowledge

- *Purpose:* What have you learned about the purposes for writing a proposal?
- *Audience:* What have you learned about addressing an audience for a proposal?
- *Rhetorical situation:* How did the writing context affect your writing about the problem you chose and the solution you proposed? How did your choice of problem and solution affect the research you conducted and how you made your case to your readers?
- *Voice and tone:* What have you learned about the writer's voice in writing a proposal?

 ## Critical Thinking, Reading, and Writing

- *Learning/inquiry:* As a result of writing a proposal, how have you become a more critical thinker, reader, and writer?
- *Responsibility:* What have you learned about a writer's responsibility to propose a good and workable solution?
- *Reading and research:* What research did you conduct for your proposal? Why? What additional research might you have done?
- *Skills:* What critical thinking, reading, and writing skills do you hope to develop further in your next writing project? How will you work on them?

Writing Processes

- *Invention:* What process did you go through to identify the problem and the solution you wrote about? How helpful was this process? What research skills have you developed while writing your proposal?

- *Organizing your ideas and details:* How successful was your organization? What drafting skills have you improved? How will you continue to improve them?

- *Revising:* What revising skills have you improved? If you could go back and make an additional revision, what would it be?

- *Working with peers:* How did you make use of the feedback you received? How have you developed your skills in working with peers? How could your peer readers help you more on your next assignment? How might you help them more?

- *Visuals:* Did you use visuals to help explain your problem and solution? If so, what did you learn about incorporating these elements?

- *Writing habits:* What "writerly habits" have you developed, modified, or improved on as you constructed the writing assignment for this chapter? How will you change your future writing activities, based on what you have learned about yourself?

 ## Knowledge of Conventions

- *Editing:* What sentence problem did you find most frequently in your writing? How will you avoid that problem in future assignments?

- *Genre:* What conventions of the genre you were using, if any, gave you problems?

- *Documentation:* Did you use sources for your paper? If so, what documentation style did you use? What problems, if any, did you have with it?

If you are constructing a course portfolio, file your written reflections so that you can return to them when you next work on your portfolio. Refer to Chapter 1 (pages 12–13) for a sample reflection by a student.

13

Using Strategies That Guide Readers

Whatever your purpose, you can use a range of rhetorical strategies to help readers understand your writing. Whether you use them within a sentence, a paragraph, or a complete piece of writing, these strategies help readers make connections. This chapter starts by focusing on the basic building blocks of any piece of writing—the thesis statement and the paragraph. Next, we look at how to link sentences and paragraphs together using cohesive devices. Then we explore strategies to narrate, describe, define, classify, compare, and contrast. Finally, we look at different ways you can outline and map your writing to ensure that the writing strategies you use are effective. All of these strategies can be used for the writing projects in Chapters 5–12.

Announcing a Thesis or Controlling Idea

A **thesis** announces the main point, major claim, or controlling idea in an essay. A clear thesis helps readers because it prepares them for what they will be reading.

Although a thesis statement can focus your attention as you write, it is usually helpful to write your thesis statement after you have done invention work and research. Invention activities can help you clarify your thinking about a topic. Research can help you learn more about it. Once you have done invention and research, a thesis statement can help you construct a well-focused draft. Of course, the exact wording of your thesis statement might change as you draft your paper.

The best thesis statements are limited and focused and offer some sense of the support that is forthcoming. If your thesis statement merely states a fact, it just informs the reader about that fact; it is not arguable. If you offer a personal feeling as a thesis ("I don't like coffee"), people could certainly argue with it, but your evidence would be purely subjective ("I don't care for the flavor") and therefore not persuasive. If your thesis statement is general and vague ("Movies are more expensive now than they were last year"), you probably won't be able to write much in support for it. Providing two figures—the average price of movies last year and the average price this year—proves your assertion.

Here are two examples of weak thesis statements that have been revised to make them stronger:

WEAK	I can't stand war movies.
REVISED	*Letters from Iwo Jima* is an effective war movie because it forces Americans to view, and even sympathize with, combatants traditionally seen as enemies.
REASON	There is no way to support your personal feeling—that you do not like war movies—with evidence. But you could provide evidence for the ways *Letters from Iwo Jima* helps viewers see enemy combatants in a new light.
WEAK	The National Football League is in trouble.
REVISED	The National Football League is in trouble because of highly publicized head injuries.
REASON	The weak version is too general and vague. The revised version gives a specific reason for the trouble.

It is important to *qualify* your thesis statement by using terms such as *probably* or *likely* to make it more acceptable to an audience.

EXAMPLE	Abraham Lincoln probably experienced more stress than any other U.S. president.

Writing Activity

Revising Weak Thesis Statements

Revise each of the following thesis statements, and explain how your revision has strengthened each statement.

New York City has a larger population than Chicago.
Pizza is better than pasta.
There are many weight-loss drugs available to consumers.
I don't like windy days.
Women's sports are growing in popularity.

Writing Paragraphs

A **paragraph** is a collection of connected sentences that focus on a single idea. With few exceptions, your writing projects will consist of paragraphs, each developing an idea related to your topic. In your writing, you need to think about both the effectiveness of individual paragraphs and the way they are organized and connected to support your purpose. Consider the following example, which might appear in a paper about Abraham Lincoln's career:

> During his years as president, 1861–1865, Abraham Lincoln experienced great stress from a combination of causes. **First,** the Civil War, which broke out weeks after his March 1861 inauguration, wore on him daily until its end in April 1865. **Second,** typhoid took the life of Willie, his beloved eleven-year-old son, in February 1862. **Third,** his wife, Mary Todd Lincoln, suffered from depression and other forms of mental illness, problems that became more acute during the years in the White House.

Although the specifics may vary, effective paragraphs generally have the following features:

- A Focus on a single main idea. The more tightly you focus a paragraph on a main idea, the more you will help readers navigate the paragraph. Note that in the example paragraph every sentence is focused on the causes of Lincoln's stress. If you want to alert your readers to other information that will come later in your paper, use a *forecasting sentence*. In the example about Lincoln, the sentence that mentions Mary Lincoln's depression could forecast that the paper will have more to say about that topic.

- A topic sentence. A topic sentence guides readers by expressing a paragraph's main idea, the idea that the other sentences in the paragraph support or develop. In the example about Lincoln, the first sentence, which is underlined, serves as the topic sentence.

- **Different levels of specificity.** All paragraphs have at least two levels of specificity. In the paragraph about Lincoln, the topic sentence clearly introduces the idea of stress and its various causes, and the second, third, and fourth sentences are more specific.
- **Connective words and phrases.** Used within a paragraph, connective words and phrases, discussed in more detail on pages 428–30, can show precisely how the sentences in the paragraph support the topic sentence and relate to one another. In the example paragraph, the words *First, Second,* and *Third* (in bold type) tell readers that each of the sentences they begin offers a separate cause of Lincoln's stress.
- **A logical connection to the next paragraph.** When readers finish a paragraph, they expect that the next paragraph will be connected to it in some readily apparent way. After reading the paragraph that focuses on the sources of stress that Lincoln experienced, readers expect that the next paragraph will also be related to Lincoln's stress.

Placement of Topic Sentences

In the paragraph about Lincoln, the topic sentence is the first sentence, a placement that lets readers know right away what the paragraph will be about. Sometimes, however, a topic sentence is more effective at the end of a paragraph, where it can serve to develop suspense or summarize information. This strategy can be especially useful in persuasive writing because it allows the writer to present evidence before making an assertion. Here is an example:

> Less than a quarter of our agricultural land is used to feed people directly. The rest is devoted to grazing and growing food for animals. Ecosystems of forest, wetland and grassland have been decimated to fuel the demand for land. Using so much land heightens topsoil loss, the use of harsh fertilizers and pesticides, and the need for irrigation water from dammed rivers. <u>If people can shift away from meat, much of this land could be converted back to wilderness.</u>
>
> Joseph Pace, "Let's Go Veggie!"

Sometimes when the point is fairly clear to readers, a writer may decide to leave it unstated. In the following paragraph, the implied (unstated) topic sentence could be something like, "Lynn had endured an abusive marriage":

> When I first met Lynn, she seemed withdrawn and disoriented. She had just taken the biggest step of her 25 years; she had left an abusive husband and she was scared: Scared about whether she could survive on her own and scared of her estranged husband. He owned a small restaurant; she was a high school dropout who had been a waitress when she met him. During their three years of marriage

he had beaten her repeatedly. Only after he threw her down a flight of stairs had she realized that her life was in danger and moved out. I don't think I fully grasped the terror she had lived until one summer day when he chased Lynn to the door of my house with a drawn gun.

Barbara Ehrenreich, "A Step Back to the Workhouse"

Moving to a New Paragraph

Paragraph breaks signal that a writer is moving from one idea to another. Consider again the example paragraph on Lincoln in which every sentence is related to causes of stress. We could develop that paragraph further by adding sentences that maintain that focus. Look at what happens, though, when we add a sentence that does not fit the focus on causes of stress:

> . . . Third, his wife, Mary Todd Lincoln, suffered from depression and other forms of mental illness, problems that became more acute during the years in the White House. <u>To alleviate the stress, Lincoln often read the plays of Shakespeare.</u>

The last sentence in this paragraph does fit the general topic of Lincoln's experience with stress, but it does not fit the tight focus on causes in this paragraph. Instead, it introduces a related but new idea. The solution is to make the last sentence the topic sentence of the next paragraph:

> . . . Third, his wife, Mary Todd Lincoln, suffered from depression and other forms of mental illness, problems that became more acute during the years in the White House.
>   <u>To alleviate the stress, Lincoln often read the plays of Shakespeare.</u> Among those that he read most frequently were *King Lear, Richard III, Henry VIII, Hamlet,* and *Macbeth.* About his favorite play, *Macbeth,* he wrote the following in a letter to the actor James H. Hackett on August 17, 1863: "I think nothing equals *Macbeth.* It is wonderful."

Notice that this new paragraph provides details about Lincoln and stress that are even more specific than the ones in the preceding paragraph.

Opening Paragraphs

The opening paragraphs of an essay announce the topic and the writer's approach to it. In an opening paragraph the writer needs to establish a relationship with readers and help them connect the topic to what they already know and care about. Some common strategies for opening paragraphs include the following:

- Tell an interesting anecdote.
- Raise a thought-provoking question.
- Provide salient background information.

Writing Activity

Introductions

For each of the following excerpts from opening paragraphs, describe the strategy that the writer is using. Does it make you want to read more? Why or why not?

The official poverty rate in 2003 was 12.5 percent, up from 12.1 percent in 2002. In 2003, 35.9 million people were in poverty, up 1.3 million from 2002. For children under 18 years old, both the poverty rate and the number in poverty rose between 2002 and 2003, from 16.7 percent to 17.6 percent, and from 12.1 million to 12.9 million, respectively.

U.S. Census Bureau, "Poverty: 2003 Highlights"

The most vulnerable victims of poverty are the world's children. Nearly 28,000 children die *every day*—more than 10 million per year—most from preventable diseases and malnutrition. Yet, the handful of preventable diseases that kill the majority of these children can be treated and prevented at very little cost. Measles can be prevented with a vaccine costing just 26 cents. Diarrheal disease, which results from poor sanitation and unsafe drinking water, can be treated with pennies' worth of oral rehydration salts. Malaria kills nearly one million children each year, despite the fact that treatment for acute malaria costs just pennies.

results.org

Tina Taylor was a model of what welfare reform was supposed to do. Taylor, 44, a single mother, had spent six years on public assistance. After 1996, when changes were made in welfare law to push people into work, she got a job that paid $400 a week and allowed her family to live independently. For the first time in a long time, she could afford to clothe and feed her two children, and even rent a duplex on the beach in Norfolk.

Griff Witte, "Poverty Up as Welfare Enrollment Declines; Nation's Social Safety Net in Tatters as More People Lose Their Jobs"

- Offer a view that the writer and readers hold in common.
- Forecast the rest of the essay.

Concluding Paragraphs

Readers remember best what they read last. Although it is not that memorable to simply restate what your essay is about in your conclusion, you can use it to do the following:

- Restate your thesis and remind readers of your key points.
- Emphasize the significance of your perspective on your topic.
- Bring your writing to closure by recalling the opening.

Writing Activity

Conclusions

For each of the following concluding paragraphs, explain what the writer has done and decide how effective you think each conclusion is.

> Each day of my life there are times when I reflect back to working on the farm. And every day people notice that I am different from the rest of my peers. At school, teachers and organization leaders are impressed by my time management skills and the amount of responsibility I take on. At work, my boss continues to ask me where he can find some more hard working people. I simply tell him, "Try hiring some farm girls. I hear they turn out pretty good."
>
> Jessica Hemauer, "Farm Girl"

> The Supreme Court's May 17, 1954, ruling in *Brown* remains a landmark legal decision. But it is much more than that. It is the "Big Bang" of all American history in the 20th century.
>
> Juan Williams, "The Ruling That Changed America"

Using Cohesive Devices

Within paragraphs, effective writers use a variety of cohesive devices to show readers how sentences are connected to one another. The major devices include connective words and phrases, word repetition, and pronoun reference. To help readers understand how paragraphs are related to one another, writers use transitional sentences as well as headings.

Using Connective Words and Phrases

You can guide readers with logically connected sentences and paragraphs, making these connections explicit through the use of **connective words and phrases.** These connections fall into three main categories: temporal, spatial, and logical.

TEMPORAL CONNECTIONS

Time: now, then, during, meanwhile, at this moment

> I worked all weekend. <u>Meanwhile,</u> my colleagues watched football all day Saturday and Sunday.

Frequency: often, occasionally, frequently, sometimes

> Sally likes unplanned trips. <u>Sometimes,</u> she'll even show up at the airport and then decide where to fly for the weekend.

Temporal order: first, second . . . ; next; before (that); after (that); last; finally

> Let's eat dinner. <u>After that</u>, let's see a movie.

SPATIAL CONNECTIONS

Location: nearby, outside, inside

> I stood by the window. <u>Outside</u>, a moose ran down the street.

Spatial order: first, second . . . ; last, next

> Jane sat in the corner. <u>Next to her</u> sat Jill.

LOGICAL CONNECTIONS

Addition: further, furthermore, moreover, additionally, in addition, and, also

> Martha Flynn is a powerful council member in our city. <u>In addition</u>, she may be headed for other powerful positions in the future.

Opposition/contrast: on the other hand, however, in contrast, on the contrary, but, conversely, nevertheless, yet, instead, rather

> I don't eat meat for ethical reasons. <u>On the other hand</u>, I do wear leather shoes.

Comparison: likewise, similarly, analogously

> George H. W. Bush led the United States to war in the 1990s. <u>Likewise</u>, George W. Bush led the United States to war in 2001.

Causation: because, as a result, as a consequence, therefore, thus, accordingly, consequently, so, then, on account of

> He didn't pay his phone bill. <u>As a result</u>, the phone company discontinued his service.

Clarification: in other words, that is,

> He rarely does his homework. <u>In other words</u>, he's not a very good student.

Qualification: under the (these) circumstances, under other circumstances, under these conditions, in this context

> John McCain spent years as a prisoner of war in North Vietnam. <u>Under these circumstances</u>, it's remarkable that he is so well adjusted.

Conclusion: finally, in summary, to sum up, in conclusion, therefore

> The new Toyota Camry has been rated one of the safest cars on the road. <u>Therefore,</u> we should consider buying one.

Illustration: for example, for instance, in particular, specifically

> Luz wears colorful clothes. <u>For example,</u> yesterday she wore a bright red sweater to her math class.

Using Word Repetition

Repeating a word or phrase from one sentence to the next helps readers make a connection between those two sentences:

> In a new study on the occurrence of dating **violence** among teenagers, University of Arkansas researchers found that 50 percent of high schoolers have experienced some form of physically **violent** behavior in their relationships. More surprising, the research revealed that male and female students perpetrate **violence** at an equal rate and that, of the two, females may be inflicting more serious forms of abuse on their partners.
>
> Megan Mooney and Patricia Petretic-Jackson, "Half of High School Students Experience Dating Violence, UA Study Shows"

Using Pronoun Reference

Pronouns substitute for nouns. When writers use pronouns to replace nouns, those pronouns point backward or forward to the nouns that they replace:

> During **his** years as president, 1861–1865, Abraham Lincoln experienced great stress from a combination of causes. First, the Civil War, which broke out weeks after **his** March 1861 inauguration, wore on **him** daily until its end in April 1865. Second, typhoid took the life of Willie, **his** beloved eleven-year-old son, in February 1862. Third, **his** wife, Mary Todd Lincoln, suffered from depression and other forms of mental illness, problems that became more acute during the years in the White House.

Writing Activity

Focusing on Cohesive Words

Working alone or with one or two classmates, identify the cohesive devices (and lack of cohesive devices) in the following paragraph. Also, edit the paragraph by adding cohesive devices that you think might strengthen connections between sentences.

(continued)

Writing Activity

Focusing on Cohesive Words *(continued)*

> The want to consume is nothing new. It has been around for millennia. People need to consume resources to survive. However, consumption has evolved as people have ingeniously found ways to help make their lives simpler and/or to use their resources more efficiently. Of course, with this has come the want to control such means. Hence, the consumption patterns have evolved over time based on the influence of those who can control it. As a result, there is tremendous waste within this system, to maintain such control and such disparities.
>
> Anup Shaw, "Creating the Consumer"

Using Transitional Sentences and Paragraphs

Writers use **transitions** to help readers move from one section of an essay to another. These sentences or paragraphs often summarize what has come before and forecast what will come next. Here are two examples:

> Those are the advantages of an interest-only home loan. However, there are several disadvantages as well.

> Although after that presentation I admired her intellect even more, her next decision caused me seriously to question her judgment.

Using Headings

In short pieces of writing, you may not need to use headings. For longer pieces of writing and in certain genres, though, headings and even subheadings can help readers more quickly understand the focus of the paragraphs that follow them. They tell readers that the paragraphs they precede are a related group and are all on the same topic.

Keep the following guidelines in mind when you write headings:

- Generally, use only one level of heading for a five-page paper.
- Be sure all content under a heading relates to that heading.
- Make your headings specific.

VAGUE	Properties of Glass
SPECIFIC	Chemical Properties of Glass

- At each level, make headings parallel in grammatical structure, font, and level of specificity.

NOT PARALLEL	The Chemistry of Glass, Physical Properties
PARALLEL	Chemical Properties of Glass, Physical Properties of Glass

- Design headings so that they stand out from the text.

DOESN'T STAND OUT	Common Uses of Glass
DOES STAND OUT	**Common Uses of Glass**

For more on headings in MLA and APA style, see Chapter 20.

If you are writing an academic paper, you should follow the requirements of the documentation style you are using for the style of your headings.

Writing Activity

Focusing on Headings and Subheadings

Working on your own or with several classmates, consider the headings in "Staying ahead of Skimming Scams" (pages 412–18 in Chapter 12). How do the headings help guide readers?

Writing Narratives

Both in everyday speech and in many kinds of writing, **narration** is a common strategy. When you narrate, you relate an event or a series of events or, in the case of a process, you give a series of steps. Most narratives are organized by time, or **chronologically,** from the beginning to the end of an event, a series of events, or a process. Obviously, narration is relevant to much of our discourse in all areas of our lives because our lives are filled with events and processes:

- At dinner, you tell your family or friends about an event at school or work that day.
- In a science course, you record what happened when you conducted a laboratory experiment.
- As a witness to a traffic accident, you tell the investigating police officers what happened.

In this section we consider two kinds of narratives: narratives that relate an event or a series of events and narratives that relate a process.

Narrating Single Events or a Series of Events

Often in everyday conversation, you narrate single events. Narrating a single event is also a common way of organizing part or all of a piece of writing. You might write an essay about an event that affected your life, an article on the opening of a store in your neighborhood, or a research report on the Montgomery bus boycott in 1955. You can also narrate a series of events such as an account of your life, of the growth of the McDonald's restaurant chain, or of the American civil rights movement in the 1950s and 1960s.

For more on narrating an event or a series of events, see Chapter 5.

When you narrate an event or a series of events, you will most often order your details chronologically—what happened first, what happened next, and so on. As an alternative, however, you might discuss the importance of the event or events first, and then proceed to the details so that your readers will understand why they, too, ought to be interested in what happened.

Chronological Structure: Because life's events occur chronologically, it is usually easiest to narrate them that way. It is also usually easier for readers to process narratives mentally when they unfold chronologically. Even a short narrative paragraph such as the following one can suggest a chronological ordering of events:

> Once my aunt found a freckle on her chin, at a spot that the almanac said predestined her for unhappiness. She dug it out with a hot needle and washed the wound with peroxide.
>
> Maxine Hong Kingston, "No Name Woman"

Point of View: The narrator of a story can have any of several points of view, so when you construct a narrative, select a point of view to write from.

In the *first-person* point of view, the narrator tells the story from the perspective of a participant or character in the story:

> When I went to kindergarten and had to speak English for the first time, I became silent.
>
> Maxine Hong Kingston, "Tongue Tied"

In a narrative told from a *third-person* point of view, the narrator is not a participant or character in the story. The narrator consistently uses third person pronouns or proper nouns to talk about the actions of characters:

> On December 1, 1963, shortly after President Kennedy's assassination, Malcolm X addressed a public rally in New York City. He was speaking as a replacement for Elijah Muhammad as he had done many times before. After the speech, during a question and answer period, Malcolm X made the remark that led to his suspension as a Muslim minister. In answer to a question, "What do you think about President Kennedy's assassination?" Malcolm X answered that he saw the case as "The chickens coming home to roost." Soon after the remark, Malcolm X was suspended by Elijah Muhammad and directed to stop speaking for ninety days.
>
> John Henrik Clarke, from the Introduction to
> *Malcolm X: The Man and His Times*

Developing Tension: Narrative tension is the feeling readers have when they are concerned about what will happen to a character. The more readers care about a character, the more they want to know how the character will get through a conflict. Narratives with tension are more interesting to readers. To establish tension in narratives, writers show conflicts between characters who hold differing values or perspectives. For example, the following sentences develop tension:

> My mother's parents didn't want her to marry my father, so the young couple eloped on a blustery day in November.

> Tom and I were best friends, but then one day I saw him stuff a DVD into his shirt in a department store.

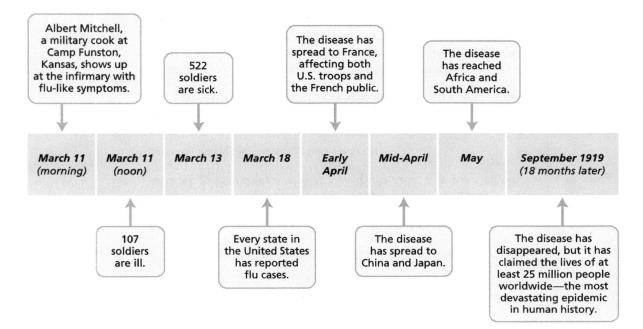

FIGURE 13.1
Timeline for the
1918 Flu Epidemic

Resolving the Tension or Conflict: Just as readers are intrigued by narrative tension, they are interested in seeing how tensions are resolved. Most readers look forward to a sense of closure by the end of the story.

Incorporating Visuals in Narratives: When you narrate a series of events, you have the opportunity to cover a significant period of time, as well as the complications involved in a more extended narration. If the chronology becomes complex, you might find it useful to guide readers with a summarizing visual such as a timeline. Figure 13.1, for instance, is a brief timeline for the flu epidemic of 1918.

Writing Activity

Analyzing Narrative Strategies

After reading the following narrative, which was posted in the business section of *DenverPost.com*, on March 13, 2007, respond in writing to the following questions:

1. What does the image of SpongeBob SquarePants add to the article? Why?
2. Why does the writer end with a report on stock prices?
3. How does the writer indicate various chronologies of events in the narrative?
4. How do verb tenses function in the narrative?

For more on a type of writing that uses narration extensively, see Chapter 5, "Writing to Share Experiences."

Viacom Sues YouTube for $1 Billion
Seth Sutel AP Business Writer

NEW YORK—MTV owner Viacom Inc. sued the popular video-sharing site YouTube and its corporate parent, Google Inc., on Tuesday, seeking more than $1 billion in damages on claims of widespread copyright infringement.

Viacom claims that YouTube has displayed more than 160,000 unauthorized video clips from its cable networks, which also include Comedy Central, VH1 and Nickelodeon.

The lawsuit, filed in U.S. District Court in New York, marks a sharp escalation of long-simmering tensions between Viacom and YouTube and represents the biggest confrontation to date between a major media company and the hugely popular videosharing site, which Google bought in November for $1.76 billion.

YouTube's soaring popularity has been a cause of fascination but also fear among the owners of traditional media outlets, who worry that YouTube's displaying of clips from their programs—without compensation— will lure away viewers and ad dollars from cable and broadcast TV.

Viacom is especially at risk because much of its programming is aimed at younger audiences who also are heavy Internet users. Last month Viacom demanded that YouTube remove more than 100,000

Fans of SpongeBob SquarePants and his friends, shown here in a scene from *The SpongeBob SquarePants Movie,* are not able to view scenes from the popular Nickelodeon cartoon show on the YouTube Web site. Viacom Inc., which owns Nickelodeon, has insisted that all of its content be removed from YouTube and is suing the popular video sharing site for more than $1 billion, claiming copyright infringement.

unauthorized clips after several months of talks between the companies broke down.

YouTube said at the time that it would comply with the request and said it cooperates with all copyright holders to remove programming as soon as they're notified.

In a statement, Viacom lashed out at YouTube's business practices, saying it has "built a lucrative business out of exploiting the devotion of fans to others' creative works in order to enrich itself and its corporate parent Google."

Viacom said YouTube's business model, "which is based on building traffic and selling advertising off of unlicensed content, is clearly illegal and is in obvious conflict with copyright laws."

Viacom said YouTube has avoided taking the initiative to curtail copyright infringement on its site, instead shifting the burden and costs of monitoring the video-sharing site for unauthorized clips onto the "victims of its infringement."

A representative for Google didn't immediately respond to a request for comment.

Other media companies have also clashed with YouTube over copyrights, but some, including CBS Corp. and General Electric Co.'s NBC Universal, have reached deals with the videosharing site to license their material. CBS Corp. used to be part of Viacom but has since split off into a separate company.

Universal Music Group, a unit of France's Vivendi SA, had threatened to sue YouTube, saying it was a hub for pirated music videos, but later reached a licensing deal with the company.

In addition to damages, Viacom is also seeking an injunction prohibiting Google and YouTube from using its clips.

Google shares dropped $4.82, or 1.1 percent, to $449.93 in Tuesday morning trading on the Nasdaq Stock Market, while Viacom's Class B shares rose 43 cents, or 1.1 percent, to $40 on the New York Stock Exchange.

Narrating Processes

When you narrate a process, you tell how something is done (informative/explanatory process narrative), or you tell others how to do something (instructional/directive process narrative).

Informative/Explanatory Process Narratives: Informative or explanatory process narratives tell readers how something is done so that they can understand a process, not so that they can replicate it. For example, you might write an informative process analysis to explain how a legislative bill becomes a law or how a seed germinates.

Instructional/Directive Process Narratives: In contrast to informative or explanatory process narratives, the purpose of instructional or directive process narratives is to help readers learn how to do something. For instance, you might explain how to make a great pizza or how to used the online library catalog at your school so that readers can replicate these processes.

Writing Descriptions

When you describe, you sketch people, places, and things verbally. Usually, you will aim to establish an overall feeling about what you are describing, such as the feeling evoked in the following passage:

> A dark mist lay over the Black Hills, and the land was like iron. At the top of the ridge I caught sight of Devil's Tower upthrust against the gray sky as if in the birth time the core of the earth had broken through its crust and the motion of the world was begun. There are many things in nature that engender an awful quiet in the heart of man; Devil's Tower is one of them.

N. Scott Momaday, *The Way to Rainy Mountain*

Because it is so common, **description** will be part of many of your writing projects. However, the approach you take to description will depend on what you are describing. Here we focus on three approaches that can be effective—naming people, things, or features; providing sensory details; and giving spatial dimensions.

Naming in Description

When you describe someone or something, you need to name that person or thing, as well as its features. For example, if you were to describe the room where you sleep, you might name objects such as the bed, dresser, chair, artwork, walls, ceiling, and floor. Consider the effect of naming in the following excerpt from Robert Sullivan's book *Rats:*

> A rat is a rodent, the most common mammal in the world. *Rattus norvegicus* is one of the approximately four hundred different kinds of rodents, and it is known by many names, each of which describes a trait or a perceived trait or sometimes a habitat: the earth rat, the roving rat, the barn rat, the field rat, the migratory rat, the house rat, the sewer rat, the water rat, the wharf rat, the alley rat, the gray rat, the brown rat, and the common rat. The average brown rat is large and stocky; it grows to be approximately sixteen inches long from its nose to its tail—the size of a large adult human male's foot—and weighs about a pound, though brown rats have been measured by scientists and exterminators at twenty inches and up to two pounds. The brown rat is sometimes confused with the black rat, or *Rattus rattus,* which is smaller and once inhabited New York City and all of the cities of America but, since *Rattus norvegicus* pushed it out, is now relegated to a minor role.

A Sensory Approach to Description

A thorough sensory description includes details from all five senses—sight, sound, taste, smell, and touch. In a vivid sensory description, the reader experiences vicariously what the writer has described. To generate such a description, you might use the questions in the following table. With minor modifications, you can use these questions to develop descriptions of a wide range of items.

Sense	Questions to Consider	Responses
Sight	What does it look like?	
	What do I see when I look at it?	
Hearing	What sounds does it make?	
	What sounds are associated with it?	
Taste	How does it taste?	
	What tastes are similar to it?	
	What tastes are associated with it?	
Smell	What does it smell like?	
	What smells are similar to it?	
	What smells are associated with it?	
Touch	What does it feel like to the touch?	
	What tactile associations do I have with it?	

Of course, for some subjects, you will rely on details from only one or two senses. The sense you will use most often when writing description is sight. Remember that other senses can also have an impact on readers, however. The sense of smell, for example, tends to evoke memory in humans more powerfully than any other sense.

In the following description, notice how the writer appeals to several senses:

> Good bread. Its pleasure is deeply soul satisfying. It's not a superficial pleasure. It's down deeper than that. It may come from a perfect crust, with texture, definition, a caramelized crusty crunch with just the right give and not too thick. And it may come from a light, airy crumb, and you know it's been crafted by gentle, knowing hands that have shaped thousands of loaves just like this. And it may come from that lingering, wheaty fullness that makes you think of a soft sun-tinted breeze flowing its tide through a field of just-ripe, golden, amber-at-sunset wheat, ready for harvest.
>
> Ken's Artisan Bakery and Café (Portland, Oregon), "What Is Good Bread?"

A Spatial Approach to Description

When you describe something *spatially*, you describe it in terms of both its own physical dimensions and its relationship to the objects around it. An approach that is primarily spatial can include sensory details or a visual, which may even be the predominant part of the description. For example, Figure 13.2 is an x-ray of a child's hand. Below is a brief spatial description of the x-ray.

FIGURE 13.2
An X-ray of a
Child's Hand

The hand is composed of many small *bones* called carpals, metacarpals and phalanges. The two bones of the lower arm—the radius and the ulna—meet at the hand to form the wrist.

The *carpal bones* are a set of eight short bones forming the wrist; they are disposed on two rows of four bones each. These bones, the size of a marble, provide the wrist's litheness and mobility.

The palm of the hand is composed of five *metacarpal bones* laid out from the wrist, as a fan. The articulation of the first metacarpal bone with the carpal bones, permits the movement of touching, with the thumb, the tips of all fingers.

It is from this movement that the human hand can acquire the efficiency necessary to grab and manipulate objects.

Every hand is composed of 14 long bones named the *phalanges.* These bones compose the fingers and the thumb. Each finger has three phalanges and the thumb only two.

McGill University, School of Architecture

Writing Activity

Writing an Effective Description

Working on your own or with several classmates, choose a topic to describe. First, generate a list of questions that an interested reader might have about the topic. Second, answer each of the questions to generate descriptive details. Third, use those details to write a short descriptive paragraph, using the approaches described above.

For more on two types of writing that use description extensively, see Chapter 5, "Writing to Share Experiences," and Chapter 8, "Writing to Analyze."

Writing Definitions

Definitions help your readers understand the terms that you are using. Clear definitions are especially important if you are writing about a topic that you know more about than your readers do, about an issue over which there are differences of opinion—including over the meanings of terms—or about a topic for which precision is crucial. You will find occasions to use definitions in all four areas of life:

- In a letter to one of your U.S. senators, you define "the working poor" as you argue for legislation to assist low-income families.
- When you take a friend to a baseball game, you define "earned run average" when "ERA" appears after a pitcher's name on the big screen in left field.
- In an economics course, you define "gross domestic product" in a paper about economic growth in India and China.

Kinds of Definitions

You can use any of several kinds of definitions depending on how much information your readers need. Sometimes you can define a term simply by giving your readers a **synonym,** a more familiar word or phrase that could be used in place of the term you are defining. However, defining a word with a synonym has limitations. Consider some synonyms for the word *war: warfare, combat, conflict, fighting, confrontation, hostilities,* and *battle.* Depending on the context, these words cannot necessarily be used interchangeably.

More useful than a synonym in many cases is an essential definition. **Essential definitions** are sentence definitions that include three parts: (1) the name of what is being defined, (2) the general category for the item being defined, and (3) the form or function that distinguishes the item being defined from similar items in the same general category. Here are some examples:

Name	Category	Form or Function
A toaster	is a small kitchen appliance	that browns bread.
A mixer	is a small kitchen appliance	that combines ingredients.

If a synonym or an essential definition is sufficient, you can incorporate it in an extended definition. An **extended definition,** which can take up one or more paragraphs, may include both of these briefer types of definition, as well as additional information and examples. It is especially helpful when you need to define a concept that is abstract or complex. For instance, here is an extended definition of a *mugwump:*

> This archetypal American word derives from the Algonquian dialect of a group of Native Americans in Massachusetts. In their language, it meant "war leader." The Puritan missionary John Eliot used it in his translation of the Bible into their language in 1661–63 to convey the English words *"officer"* and *"captain."*

Mugwump was brought into English in the early nineteenth century as a humorous term for a boss, bigwig, grand panjandrum, or other person in authority, often one of a minor and inconsequential sort. This example comes from a story in an 1867 issue of *Atlantic Monthly:* "I've got one of your gang in irons—the Great Mugwump himself, I reckon—strongly guarded by men armed to the teeth; so you just ride up here and surrender."

It hit the big time in 1884, during the presidential election that set Grover Cleveland against the Republican James G. Blaine. Some Republicans refused to support Blaine, changed sides, and the *New York Sun* labelled them *little mugwumps*. Almost overnight, the sense of the word changed to *turncoat*. Later, it came to mean a politician who either could not or would not make up his mind on some important issue, or who refused to take a stand when expected to do so. Hence the old joke that a mugwump is a person sitting on the fence, with his mug on one side and his wump on the other.

Michael Quinion, *World Wide Words*

Notice that the definition indicates what a mugwump is, explains the origin of the word and its history, and provides concrete examples.

Writing Activity

Identifying Features of a Definition

Consider the following definition of a Luddite:

A Luddite is a person who fears or loathes technology, especially new forms of technology that threaten existing jobs. During the Industrial Revolution, textile workers in England who claimed to be following the example of a man named Ned Ludd destroyed factory equipment to protest changes in the workplace brought about by labor-saving technology. The term *Luddite* is derived from Ludd's surname. Today, the term Luddite is reserved for a person who regards technology as causing more harm than good in society, and who behaves accordingly.

Tech Target Network

For more on a type of writing that uses definitions extensively, see Chapter 9, "Writing to Convince."

1. What are the features of this definition?
2. How might you clarify the definition?

Writing Classifications

When you classify, you group—or divide—items into categories based on one or more of three principles—completeness, exclusiveness, or consistency:

- **Completeness** means that all items need to be included in a classification. If you were classifying automobiles, you would need to make certain that SUVs were included in your scheme.

FIGURE 13.3
The Five Food
Groups That Make
Up a Healthy Diet

Source: http://www.choosemyplate.gov/index.html

- **Exclusiveness** means that none of your categories should overlap with any other category. If you were classifying movies, for example, the categories *movies about monsters* and *scary movies* don't work because some movies about monsters are scary (*The Thing*) and would fit in both categories.
- **Consistency** means that the same criteria need to be used to determine the contents of each category. If you are classifying animals and two of your categories are *mammals* and *birds,* your third category should not be *extinct animals* because that introduces different criteria into your system.

For more on a type of writing that uses classification extensively, see Chapter 8, "Writing to Analyze."

Many topics can be classified, which means that you will find classification a useful organizing strategy for many kinds of writing:

- Before purchasing a laptop computer for business travel, you might classify some possible laptops you are considering by weight—ultra-light (under three pounds), light (three to five pounds), moderate (six to eight pounds), and heavy (more than eight pounds).
- In deciding which candidates to support in an election, you might classify them according to their stated positions on issues that are important to you.
- As you write a menu for your next week's meals, you could use the categories in the diagram shown in Figure 13.3.

Writing about Comparisons and Contrasts

The related strategies of **comparison**—looking at how subjects are similar—and **contrast**—looking at how they are different—are common not just in writing but in thinking. People find that they are crucial tools in thinking about and differentiating many aspects of the world around them.

In all areas of life, you will use comparison and contrast:

- In an art history class, you might compare and contrast the features of two schools of art such as impressionism and surrealism.
- In an e-mail to a friend, you might compare and contrast two romantic comedies that you recently saw at movie theaters.
- You might compare and contrast the features of two network servers that your company is considering for purchase.

Approaches to Comparison and Contrast

The two major approaches to comparing and contrasting two items are point-by-point and block. In the **point-by-point approach,** you discuss the two items together for each point of comparison/contrast. In the **block approach,** you discuss all of your points of comparison/contrast about one item first and then all points about the other item second. Here are two abbreviated outlines for a paper comparing the sports of baseball and fast-pitch softball, each using one of the two organizational approaches.

Point-by-Point Approach

I. Pitching
   A. Method
      1. Overhand or sidearm in baseball
      2. Underhand in fast-pitch softball
   B. Speed
      1. Up to 100 miles per hour in baseball
      2. Up to 70 miles per hour in fast-pitch softball
II. Field dimensions
   A. Mound
      1. Elevated to about 12 inches in baseball
      2. Level with the field in fast-pitch softball
   B. Infield
      1. Ninety feet between bases in baseball
      2. Sixty feet between bases in fast-pitch softball
   C. Outfield
      1. Over 400 feet to the centerfield fence in baseball
      2. Usually no more than 300 feet to the centerfield fence in fast-pitch softball

(continued)

III. Equipment
   A. Balls
      1. A baseball is approximately 2.75 inches in diameter
      2. A fast-pitch softball is approximately 3.5 inches in diameter
   B. Bats
      1. Baseball bats are usually over 2.5 inches in diameter
      2. Fast-pitch softball bats are usually under 2.3 inches in diameter

Block Approach
   I. Baseball
      A. Pitching
         1. Overhand or sidearm
         2. Up to 100 miles per hour
      B. Field dimensions
         1. Pitcher's mound approximately 12 inches high
         2. Ninety feet between bases
         3. Over 400 feet to centerfield fence
      C. Equipment
         1. Baseball approximately 2.75 inches in diameter
         2. Bats usually over 2.5 inches in diameter
   II. Fast-Pitch Softball
      A. Pitching
         1. Underhand
         2. Up to 70 miles per hour
      B. Field dimensions
         1. Pitcher's circle level with the field
         2. Sixty feet between bases
         3. Usually no more than 300 feet to centerfield fence
      C. Equipment
         1. Softball approximately 3.5 inches in diameter
         2. Bats usually under 2.3 inches in diameter

If you compare two items with many features, you should usually use the point-by-point approach. Regardless of the approach that you use, however, you can help guide your readers by doing the following:

- Focusing on the major similarities and differences
- Including the same points of comparison/contrast for both items
- Covering the points in the same order for both subjects
- Using transition words to move from point to point

Comparing/Contrasting

Read the excerpt from *Quiet: The Power of Introverts in a World That Can't Stop Talking* on pages 211–13 in Chapter 8, "Writing to Analyze." Construct an outline of the major points of comparison/contrast that Susan Cain offers when she compares introverts and extroverts. Does she use a point-by-point approach or a block approach?

Using Outlines and Maps to Organize Your Writing

Regardless of the organizing strategies that you use, outlines and visual maps can be helpful tools. Commonly used outlines and maps include scratch outlines, formal outlines, and tree diagrams.

SCRATCH OUTLINES

Scratch outlines work well early in the process of composing. As rough sketches of your thoughts, they can help you get ideas on paper without much concern for the final organization of the project. A scratch outline might be little more than a list of ideas in the order in which they might appear in the final project. Here is an example:

Solving the Problem of Childhood Obesity

- Open with a story about obesity to grab readers' attention.
- Provide some background/history.
- Describe the problem with statistics.
- Explain the causes of the problem: poor nutrition (five food groups), large serving sizes, lack of exercise.
- Describe the consequences of childhood obesity: diabetes, adult cardio vascular problems.
- For each cause, offer a possible solution: teaching parents how to read nutritional labels; educating children and parents about serving sizes; persuading schools to require physical education; and persuading parents to engage their children in more exercise.
- Conclude.

FORMAL OUTLINES

Formal outlines can be useful once you have done some invention work and research. In a formal outline, you arrange your ideas in a series of levels. The first level is marked with roman numerals (I, II, III), the second level with capital letters (A, B, C), the third level with numbers (1, 2, 3), and the fourth level with lowercase letters (a, b, c). Each level must have at least two entries. The entries in a formal outline can be in sentences (a sentence outline) or in words or phrases (a topic outline) as in the following example:

Solving the Problem of Childhood Obesity

I.   Opening story about obesity
II. Background/history of obesity
III. Description and explanation of the problem
   A. Statistical overview of the problem
   B. Causes of the problem
     1. Poor nutrition (five food groups)
     2. Large serving sizes
     3. Lack of exercise
   C. Consequences of problem
     1. Diabetes
     2. Cardiovascular problems in adulthood
IV. Possible solutions
   A. Instruction for parents on how to read nutritional labels
   B. Education for children and parents about serving sizes
   C. Recommendation that schools require physical education and that parents engage their children in more exercise
V.   Conclusion

If you wanted a more detailed plan, with sentences that you could actually use in your paper, you could prepare a sentence outline like the following:

Solving the Problem of Childhood Obesity

I.   Many children, such as Heather H., begin the cycle of dieting and gaining weight as early as age 10.
II. Obesity has been increasing in the United States, especially among children and adolescents.
III. Here are some recent, and quite startling, statistics about childhood obesity.
IV. There are several reasons for this problem, including poor nutrition, ever increasing portion sizes, and children's reluctance to exercise.
   A. The first reason is that today's children, who live in one of the wealthiest countries in the world, suffer from poor nutrition.
   B. Another reason is that we all seem to expect large serving sizes in every restaurant these days.
   C. Finally, many children don't exercise, preferring to stay indoors for video games and online chats with their friends.
V.   The consequences of childhood obesity can be dire.
   A. Diabetes can be one major and severe consequence.
   B. Childhood obesity also leads to cardiovascular problems when children grow up.

VI. Fortunately, some doctors and other experts are turning their time and attention to this problem, and have come up with some unique ideas.
   A. Parents need to learn how to read food labels, so here are some instructions for doing so.
   B. Both children and parents need to understand what a reasonable "serving size" looks like.
   C. Several exercise programs are available that schools can provide to young students—exercise that will be fun and helpful to them.

VII. Childhood is too important a time to spend obsessing about weight, but children should be encouraged to eat a healthful diet and exercise regularly to avoid the dieting treadmill that Heather H. and others like her are on.

TREE DIAGRAMS

Like outlines, tree diagrams show hierarchical relationships among ideas; Figure 13.4 gives an example.

FIGURE 13.4
Tree Diagram for a Paper on Childhood Obesity

CHAPTER

14 Using Strategies for Argument

Often in our culture, the word *argument* has a negative connotation, as if to *argue* really means to *fight* about something. But the term *argument* in many academic, professional, and civic settings and in most writing situations means to debate with someone about an issue or to attempt to convince someone to accept your point of view. That does not mean your debating partners, listeners, or readers will end up agreeing with you (or you with them), but rather that, at the end of your argument, your audience will say, "I understand what you mean and can appreciate your position. I don't necessarily agree with everything you've said, but I can see where you're coming from." This kind of argument must have as its thesis an assertion that is debatable, not a certainty, and must generate responses somewhere on the following continuum:

**Strongly   Strongly
Disagree   Agree**

Assertions that are capable of evoking such responses are appro

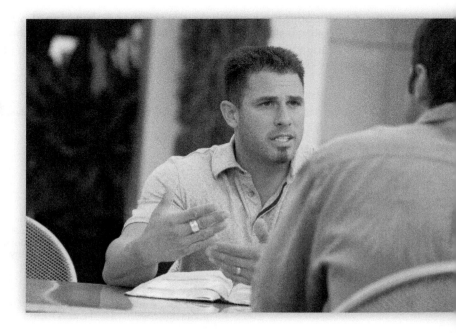

priate **thesis statements** or **claims** for arguments. The fundamental aim of an argument is to move the audience along this continuum of responses toward agreement.

Effective arguers get to know their audiences well enough to understand where on this continuum their responses are likely to lie, and they choose argument strategies based on that knowledge.

Of course, some members of the audience will be willing to move farther along the continuum than others.

If "winning" an argument means that the other side sees, understands, and appreciates your position, then your goal is to present your thesis and supporting evidence in a logical manner, so that your reader can at least understand—and perhaps agree with—your position.

Argument and Persuasion

When you present an argument, you want readers at a minimum to understand what you mean and to see your perspective. The concept of **argument,** then, is somewhat different from and broader than that of **persuasion.** When you have persuaded someone, you have convinced that person to believe something (this legislative bill is better than that one) or to do something (provide the funding needed for longer library hours).

In a sense, an argument is the means of persuasion: You cannot persuade someone about anything without an effective argument. So while you certainly hope that you will be able to persuade the president of your school to increase the hours that the library is open, your overall goal is to construct and present a sound, effective argument. Put another way, after members of your audience read your argument, they may or may not agree with you in part or in full, but if your argument is effective, they will at least think, "I understand this writer's position, and he or she has made a strong case."

Each of the chapters in Part 3 of this book asks you to construct a certain kind of argument, with the goal of attempting to persuade your readers in a variety of ways. For example, Chapter 9 ("Writing to Convince") asks you to argue for a position on a controversial issue, while Chapter 10 ("Writing to Evaluate") asks for your judgment on the quality of a product, event, place, or other subject. In both cases, you may not necessarily cause your readers to change their minds—by switching sides on the issue or rushing out to see the film you recommended. Rather, they will understand your position and the reasons and evidence that support that position. Likewise, for Chapter 11 ("Writing to Explain Causes and Effects"), and Chapter 12 ("Writing to Solve Problems"), you are asked to argue a debatable claim, whether it be a cause-and-effect relationship or a solution to a problem. Readers may not completely agree with your claim, but if it is soundly argued, they should at least be willing to consider it.

Rhetorical Appeals

The philosopher Aristotle was one of the first to notice that effective speakers use three kinds of appeals to help make their arguments convincing. An **appeal** in this sense is a means of convincing your audience to agree with your argument, and perhaps of convincing them to do something. We introduced the three kinds of appeals—*logos, ethos,* and *pathos*—in Chapter 2 (pages 27–30) in the context of rhetorical analysis. Here we focus on using them to construct an effective written argument. You already use these various appeals when you want to convince your friends to do something with you, for example, or to talk your parents or children into going somewhere.

Logical Appeals

Logical appeals, or, using the Greek word, *logos,* are appeals made through your use of solid reasoning and appropriate evidence, including statistical and other types of data, expert testimony, and illustrative examples.

No matter what kind of evidence you use to support your argument, that evidence must come from reliable sources. For more information on evaluating sources, see Chapter 19.

Consider what kind(s) of evidence will best convince your audience. For example, if you are writing to evaluate something (perhaps a film, a restaurant, or an art museum), quoting known and accepted authorities on the subject is often persuasive. If you are writing to solve a problem, historical information also can be useful by demonstrating, for instance, how other communities have dealt with similar issues or problems.

Ethical Appeals

Ethical appeals, or appeals to *ethos,* focus on your character. When you establish your *ethos,* you communicate to readers that you are credible, intelligent, knowledgeable, fair, and perhaps even altruistic, concerned about the welfare of others. You can establish your ethos by doing the following:

- Present yourself as knowledgeable about your subject matter.
- Acknowledge points of view that differ from yours, and deal fairly with them. For example, you might write, "Other people might say that _____ is less costly than what I'm proposing, and they would be right—my plan does cost more. But the benefits far outweigh the cost, and here is why. . . ."
- Provide appropriate information, including facts and statistics. Some audiences will be receptive to statistical information; others will be more receptive to quotations from experts in the field. Still others might look for both types of evidence.

Emotional Appeals

Appeals to readers' emotions, or *pathos,* can help readers connect with and accept your argument. However, effective arguers use emotional appeals judiciously, avoiding appeals that astute readers might consider exploitive.

There are many ways to appeal to readers' emotions. Here are some possibilities:

- Identify who is or will be affected positively or negatively by a situation or course of action that you are arguing for and ask the audience to identify with them.
- Show how the situation or course of action has emotionally affected people elsewhere.
- Arouse indignation over a current situation by showing how it is inconsistent with a community's value or concerns.

You use all three appeals frequently in everyday life. To convince a friend to go to see a film with you, for example, you might mention that the film, although new and relatively unknown, received an award from the Sundance Film Festival, an appeal in which you draw on the *ethos* of the famous film festival; you might point out that the early showings cost only half as much as the nighttime shows (*logos*); or you might plead that you have no one else to go with and hate going to movies alone (*pathos*).

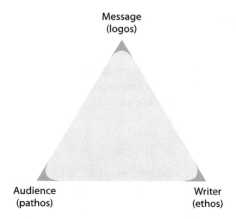

Message
(logos)

Audience
(pathos)

Writer
(ethos)

FIGURE 14.1
The Rhetorical
Triangle

The Rhetorical Triangle: Considering the Appeals Together

Most effective arguments combine rhetorical appeals because audiences respond to a variety of appeals. The three kinds of appeal complement one another, as is suggested by the rhetorical triangle shown in Figure 14.1. Each aspect of an act of communication—the writer, the reader, the message—is connected to the other two aspects.

Writing Activity

Considering Your Audience

Construct two brief letters, each no longer than a page. For each letter, assume that you want twenty-four-hour, seven-day-a-week access to your college's library.

- For your first letter, your audience is your classmates. How would you argue for your position in a letter to them? What needs would you list, to show those you have in common?

- For your second letter, your audience is the president of your college or university. How would you argue for your position to him or her?

  With several classmates, discuss the differences between your letters.

Three Approaches to Argument

In this chapter, we cover three ways to conceptualize argument: classical, Toulmin, and Rogerian. All three approaches are widely used as ways to think about and to design effective arguments. Understanding how they function will help you not only to understand the arguments you read or hear but also to construct your own written arguments.*

- The *classical* approach is a way of organizing an argument to make sure you, as a writer, have covered all important aspects of your argument.

---

*Thanks to our good friend and colleague Doug Downs for reminding us of the differences among these three concepts.

- The *Toulmin* way of considering an argument examines how the argument functions: how one aspect provides reasons and evidence for another and what assumptions underlie the writer's claims.

- The *Rogerian* approach to argument helps those involved in any argument understand and perhaps appreciate other points of view and how those might relate to their own positions.

Classical Strategies for Arguing

Aristotle

About 2,400 years ago, the Greek philosopher Aristotle formalized what we now call the **classical scheme** of argument by listening to effective public speakers and then figuring out what made their arguments successful. Amazingly, Aristotle's ideas remain relevant today. If you are using the classical scheme, this is the sequence you follow:

- Introduction
- Main claim
- Evidence supporting claim
- Discussion of other perspectives
- Conclusion

This approach is called the **deductive** way to reason because you state your claim and then help the reader understand (or deduce) how the evidence supports your claim. Here is a simplified example of how the deductive approach might work in asking for a raise:

• Introduction and main claim	I'd like to talk with you about raising my salary. I've been with the company for two years now, and for several reasons I feel that I deserve a raise at this point in my career here.
• Evidence supporting claim	First, I am very effective now at doing work in the office as well as working with customers outside the office.
	Second, I've taken classes to learn several new software programs, and I'm now fully proficient at using them.
	Third, I've shown that I can take on lots of responsibility because I've handled several important projects in the past two years.
	Fourth, my end-of-year rankings have consistently improved.

• Discussion of other perspectives (acknowledging, conceding, and/or refuting them)	Now, I know there was that one dissatisfied customer, but if you'll recall, I managed to satisfy her (at last!) by providing extra service.
• Conclusion	Therefore, I deserve a raise.

The advantage of the deductive method is that you state your position and make your case before your reader starts thinking about other perspectives. Because readers understand what your point is *early* in your text, they find it easier to follow your argument.

If you are using another method, commonly known as the **inductive** approach, you first present and explain all of your reasons and evidence, then draw your conclusion—your main claim. In other words, you provide the evidence first and then the conclusion at the end. The advantage is that your reader may come to the same conclusion before you explicitly state your position and will therefore be more inclined to agree with your view.

For more on deductive and inductive reasoning, see Chapter 9.

An inductive approach to asking for a raise could use the same evidence to support the claim, discussion of other perspectives, and conclusion, but begin without a main claim:

- • Introduction   I'd like to speak with you about my job performance here at our company now that I've been here for two years.

Parts of a Classical Argument

Thinking about the parts of an argument makes the task of arguing more manageable. When you put the parts together, the results can lead to an effective whole.

The classical argument as presented here has five parts occurring in a certain order. However, as you write your own arguments, you may find that not every part is essential in every case and you may also find it useful to rearrange or combine the parts. The five parts are as follows:

1. **Introduction** (*exordium*): In the introduction, you gain the attention of the audience and begin to establish your credibility. To accomplish this task, you need to have analyzed your audience carefully. Your overall goal in the introduction is to prepare your audience to be receptive to your case.

    Here are some strategies that can work well in introductions for arguments:

    - • Show how the issue affects the audience.
    - • Show how the issue affects the community in general.
    - • Outline what a reader might do about the issue.
    - • Ask a question to grab the reader's attention.
    - • Explain what will happen if the reader does not get involved and take action.
    - • Begin with a compelling quotation.

> **ELECTRONIC ENVIRONMENTS**   **Using Music in Arguments**
>
> If you have ever listened closely to the words of popular songs, whether they are examples of rock, blues, jazz, musical theater, hip-hop, or rhythm and blues, you've probably noticed that many song lyrics follow the patterns of argument. Mining popular culture for examples that can help you build an argument can be quite effective.
>
> If you are asked to write an essay that persuades, consider searching your music collection for interesting and powerful metaphors, statements, and stories you can use as quotations. Whether you collect CDs, download tunes, call up videos on YouTube, listen to podcasts, or even write and produce your own
>
> music, it is possible to consider your collection of music as a collection of arguments. Be careful, though, to provide context and reasons for choosing the particular quotations that seem to support your view.
>
> Often, you can insert a sound file into a PowerPoint presentation, which can add an interesting dimension to a persuasive oral presentation. Additionally, you can produce an audio argument by using Audacity, a free audio editing program available online. Be cautious about posting any music online, however. All music—no matter how brief the excerpt—is protected by copyright and is not considered fair use unless it is in the public domain.

2. **Narration** (*narratio*): Here you briefly explain the issue and provide some background or context for the argument you will make, as well as explain why it is important. If your readers understand why the issue is important to *them*, they are more likely to be interested and involved in your argument. You can use a narrative to do the following:

   • State the crucial facts that are generally agreed on.

   • List the main issues or aspects that you will consider in your argument.

   • Introduce the main reasons that support your argument.

3. **Confirmation** (*confirmatio*): This is the main body of your argument. Here you offer evidence to support your thesis or claim. Evidence can consist of facts, statistics, expert opinion, and other information. For example, if you are arguing that students should get involved in the upcoming campus elections, statistics on an issue that affects them personally can help them understand the importance of the campaign.

4. **Refutation** (*refutatio*): If you can argue about a statement, that means ideas or values are in dispute—that is, an issue is undecided and there is another side to your argument. Dealing with that other side, or **counterargument,** is a crucial step: If you fail to deal with the opposition's counterarguments, your readers may think that you are unaware of them or that you are trying to conceal their existence.

   To refute counterarguments, you first need to discover what they are through research or audience analysis. For example, as you share ideas and drafts with your classmates, ask them what arguments the other side might make to address this issue or problem.

   As you consider opposing viewpoints, you need to decide how to handle them. Refutation is only one of several options. Some counterarguments may not be significant enough to merit further consideration; it may be enough simply to acknowledge them. If you are trying to convince students to vote in a campus election, you might simply acknowledge the objection that one vote does not make a difference: "I understand what you mean, because I used to think that way. And it's true that one vote rarely makes 'the difference' in any election." Or you might decide to refute the objection, noting that "what one person can do is to talk to other people, and convince them that they need to vote, and talk to them about the issues, and then all of a sudden that one person has gotten a lot of other people involved."

Other ways to deal with objections to your argument include the following:

- Agree that *part* of the opposing view is valid, and then demonstrate how the rest of the argument is unsound.

- Accept that the opposing view is valid, but note that what the opposition suggests costs too much / is impractical / will not work because _____ has been tried and been unsuccessful in other places or has some other problem.

- Discredit any authorities they cite in their favor ("Since Jones wrote that, three studies have been published showing that his conclusions were incorrect . . .").

5. **Conclusion** (*peroration*): Here you conclude your argument and, possibly, call for action. In the conclusion, you can do one or more of the following:

- Summarize your case.
- Stir readers' emotions.
- Suggest an action or actions that the audience might take.
- Refer back to the start of your essay, tying everything together.
- List your main points, touching on your evidence for each.

Example: The Classical Scheme in Action

DAVID WOLMAN

Time to Cash Out: Why Paper Money Hurts the Economy

David Wolman is a contributing editor at *Wired,* where this essay first appeared. He is the author of *Righting the Mother Tongue* and *A Left-Hand Turn Around the World,* and he has written for magazines such as *Newsweek, Discover, Outside,* and *Forbes.* Wolman's work has also been anthologized in the *Best American Science Writing* series.

Introduction: Here Wolman sets the stage, so to speak, as he introduces his argument.

Narration: Wolman states his point about the outmoded nature of physical currency. Wolman tries to get readers thinking: Does physical currency cost more than it's worth? Is it bad for the environment? What examples from your own experience suggest that physical currency no longer makes sense?

Two years ago, Hasbro came out with an electronic version of Monopoly. Want to buy a house? Just put your debit card into the mag-stripe reader. Bing! No more pastel-colored cash tucked under the board. Turns out it wasn't Lehman Brothers but Parker Brothers that could smell the future. At least, that's what participants at this year's Digital Money Forum believe. In March, after a long day of talks with titles like "Currency 2.0" and "Going Live With Voice Payments," forum attendees at London's plush Charing Cross Hotel gathered for drinks—and, yes, a few rounds of Monopoly Electronic Banking Edition.

Unfortunately, the world's governments remain stuck in the past. To maintain our stock of hard currency, the US Treasury creates hundreds of billions of dollars worth of new bills and coins each year. And that ain't money for nothing: The cost to taxpayers in 2008 alone was $848 million, more than two-thirds of which was spent minting coins that many people regard as a nuisance. (The process also used up more than 14,823 tons of zinc, 23,879 tons of copper, and 2,514 tons of nickel.) In an era when books, movies, music, and newsprint are transmuting from atoms to bits, money remains irritatingly analog. Physical currency is a bulky, germ-smeared, carbon-intensive, expensive medium of exchange. Let's dump it.

Markets are already moving that way. Between 2003 and 2006, noncash payments in the US increased 4.6 percent annually, while the percentage of payments made using checks dropped 13.2 percent. Two years ago, card-based payments exceeded paper-based ones—cash, checks, food stamps—for the first time. Nearly 15 percent of all US online commerce goes through PayPal. Smart-card technologies like EagleCash and FreedomPay allow military personnel and college students to ignore paper money, and the institutions that run dining halls and PXs save a bundle by not having to manage bills and coins or pay transaction fees for credit cards. Small communities from British Columbia to the

British Isles are experimenting with alternative currencies that allow residents to swap work hours, food, or other assets of value.

But walled-garden economies are a long way from a fully cashless society. As *Wired* first noted 15 years ago, to rely exclusively on an emoney system, we need a ubiquitous and secure network of places where people can transact electronically, and that system has to be as convenient as— and more efficient than—cash. The infrastructure didn't exist back then. But today that network is in place. In fact, it's already in your pocket. "The cell phone is the best point-of-sale terminal ever," says Mark Pickens, a microfinance analyst with the Consultative Group to Assist the Poor. Mobile phone penetration is 50 percent worldwide, and mobile money programs already enable millions of people to receive money from or "flash" it to other people, banks, and merchants. An added convenience is that cell phones can easily calculate exchange rates among the myriad currencies at play in our world. Imagine someday paying for a beer with frequent flier miles.

Opponents used to argue that killing cash would hurt low-income workers— for instance, by eliminating cash tips. But a modest increase in the minimum wage would offset that loss; government savings from not printing money could go toward lower taxes for employers. And let's not forget the transaction costs of paper currency, especially for the poor. If you're less well off, check-cashing fees and 10-mile bus rides to make payments or purchases are not trivial. Yes, panhandlers will be out of luck, but to use that as a reason for preserving a costly, outdated technology would be a sad admission, as if tossing spare change is the best we can do for the homeless.

Killing currency wouldn't be a trauma; it'd be euthanasia. We have the technology to move to a more efficient, convenient, freely flowing medium of exchange. Emoney is no longer just a matter of geeks playing games.

4

5

Confirmation: Wolman provides multiple examples of how governments, businesses, and individuals are moving to electronic currency.

Objection and Refutation: Wolman himself offers an objection to his argument and then refutes the objection by giving a specific example of a new technology that is now available.

Objection and Refutation: Wolman gives a second objection. He then answers with a potential solution. What other solutions would you suggest?

Conclusion: Asks the readers to think about how we can use existing technologies to make life better. Notice the "value charged" language he uses.

Writing Activity

Identifying a Classical Argument

With several of your classmates, find an essay in a newsmagazine (such as *Time* or *Newsweek*) that is written in the form of a classical argument. Identify each part of the argument:

- Introduction
- Narration
- Confirmation
- Refutation
- Conclusion

Toulmin Approach to Argument

Stephen Toulmin

Another important approach to argument was developed by philosopher Stephen Toulmin in his 1958 book *The Uses of Argument.* As with Aristotle's classical scheme, you already use the main aspects of Toulmin's approach: Every day you make assertions ("All students need to be involved in the upcoming election") and then use "*because* statements" to provide support for those assertions ("because if they are not, they won't have their needs and positions represented to those in power"). Toulmin called your assertion a **claim** and the *because* statement **data.** For example, if you are trying to convince your classmates to become involved in campus politics, you might claim that their involvement is vital to their own interests. But unless your classmates believe that getting involved will affect them (in amount of tuition they pay, for example), they will not be able to understand why they ought to take the time and make the effort to become involved. So you, as the person making the argument, must consider whether your audience will know why it is important for them to participate, and if you determine that they may not, it is up to you to provide those specific reasons.

What Toulmin adds to this fairly intuitive way of constructing any text is the notion of a **warrant:** *why* the data support the claim. Sometimes you need to say why explicitly; other times you can assume that your reader understands this connection.

In **Toulmin's model of argumentation,** then, three components are considered essential to any argument:

- **Claim:** the conclusion or point that you will argue and hope to convince readers to agree with. For example, your claim might be "A major objective of this country's space program should be to land a crew of astronauts on Mars."
- **Data:** the reasons you give to support your claim. Your data may take the form of *because* statements. You might support your claim about Mars by saying "because knowing about Mars will help us understand our own planet and the life it supports because Mars may have had water—and life—at one time."

- **Warrant:** the connection between the claim and the data, explaining why the data support the claim. Often this connection is obvious and can go unstated. For example, the data and claim above are connected by the idea that it is important that we understand our planet.

Three other components of an argument are considered optional: the backing, the rebuttal, and the qualifier:

- **Backing:** If you are not sure that your readers will see the connection between data and claim, you need to state the warrant and support it as well. The support for the warrant is the backing. If you felt you could not assume the warrant about understanding our planet, you might need to state it explicitly: "Understanding our own planet and the life it supports is crucial to our survival as a species, and knowing about Mars will help us gain that understanding."

- **Rebuttal:** When you rebut the opposition's position, you prove that your position is more effective—for example, that it is acceptable to more people. You might acknowledge the potential objection that space missions with astronauts are costly but argue that the potential benefits outweigh the costs: "While space flight with astronauts is expensive, in terms of our total economy those costs are small and the possible knowledge that we would gain by putting a human being instead of a machine in charge of data collection is priceless."

- **Qualifier:** In response to opposing positions and points, you may need to in some way limit or modify, or qualify, your claim. You can do this by indicating precisely the conditions under which your claim does and does not apply. Qualifiers often include words such as *sometimes, possibly, may,* and *perhaps.*

Example: The Toulmin Model in Action

JORDAN WEISSMAN

The Myth of Energy Independence: Why We Can't Drill Our Way to Oil Autonomy

Jordan Weissmann received his degree in journalism from Northwest University and currently is an associate editor at *The Atlantic.* Weissmann served as a reporting intern for several newspapers, including the *Milwaukee Journal Sentinel.* He has written for a number of publications, including *The Washington Post* and *The National Law Journal.*

American energy independence makes for great political rhetoric. And not much else.   1

We can thank President Nixon for the term. During the dark days of the   2 1973 Arab oil embargo, he publicly vowed to wean the United States off foreign energy sources by the end of the decade, an initiative he dubbed "Project Independence." While things didn't quite pan out the way he imagined, the dream he conjured has lived on with presidents from both parties ever since.

These days, though, it's not just politicians who are dreaming. Over the last   3 year, it's become respectable—even chic, in a geeky, Washington think-tank sort of way—to suggest that the United States might indeed be close to kicking its foreign energy habit. Take this Bloomberg headline from Monday: "America Gaining Energy Independence." Or this *Financial Times* article from October: "Pendulum Swings On American Oil Independence." Daniel Yergin, the renowned oil analyst and Pulitzer Prize winner, now argues that the center of world oil production may be moving from the Middle East to the Western hemisphere.

Claim Weissman will rebut: The U.S. might just be able to "kick" its foreign energy habit.

There are plenty of good reasons for the optimism. With the development   4 of its massive shale deposits, the United States has become the world's single largest producer of natural gas. We're so awash in it that domestic prices have plummeted to historic lows. Advances in drilling technology have also made it possible to access hard-to-tap "tight" oil reserves in states such as North Dakota. Analysts believe those fresh crude sources could yield 2.9 million barrels of oil a day by 2020, up from 900,000 today. Meanwhile, cars are getting more efficient, and fuel use has dropped after soaring during the last decade, which frees up more energy production for export. According to Bloomberg, the U.S. is already getting 81% of its energy from domestic sources, the largest share since 1992, and up 10 percentage points since 2005. Then, there's Canada, which now claims the world's third largest oil reserves thanks to Alberta's petroleum rich tar sands. That's important because Canada and the U.S. are family when it comes to global trade. They're currently our single largest oil supplier. We sell them 75% of their imports and buy 75% of their exports. The National Petroleum Council, which advises the White House on energy issues, believes that by 2035, the two countries combined could more than double their oil production to 22.5 million barrels a day, enough to satisfy their current total consumption.

If you're not too concerned about how much carbon gets pumped into the atmosphere over the next few decades, these are all great developments. (If you do care about global warming, these are all reasons to have a stiff drink, and perhaps consider moving far from the coasts.) But even if we're approaching energy independence, the chances of ever actually getting there are rather slim, especially if our economy is still running on oil in 20 years.

5

MANAGE YOUR EXPECTATIONS

It may theoretically be possible for the U.S. and Canada to more than double our oil output, as the NPC suggests. To put that in perspective, we'd be adding the rough equivalent of another Saudi Arabia to the world oil market. To do it, the countries would have to pretty much tap every resource they have, both onshore and off. Obviously, the old "drill baby drill" crowd would love that approach. But it's still controversial in coastal swing states like Florida. Beyond that, accessing some of the resources would require technology we don't have yet.

6

In the most likely scenarios, North American oil production will get a big boost in the coming years. It just won't be enough for us to start waving good-bye to OPEC. The U.S. Energy Information Administration forecasts that the American oil production will reach 6.7 million barrels a day by 2020, up from 5.5 million in 2010, then drop back to 6.1 million by 2035. Canada's National Energy Board foresees future production doubling to 6.0 million barrels per day by that year. So we'd end up with about 12.1 million barrels a day, around two-thirds* of what the United States currently chugs through on its own.

7

But let's not be realistic for a moment. Let's assume the U.S. and Canada did manage to drill enough oil that we could tell Saudi Arabia to take its light sweet crude and shove it. What then? Well, we'd still be exposed to all the ugliness of the global oil market. American and Canadian crude would be priced just like everywhere else—based on what the world's highest bidders are willing to pay for it. Americans would continue to feel pain at the pump every time a war broke out in the Middle East or African militants blew up a pipeline.

8

*An earlier version of this story said 12.1 million barrels would account for "a bit more than half" of what the U.S. currently uses each day. The fraction is closer to two-thirds.

Warrant: Less reliance on foreign energy sources would be beneficial.

Claim: Our chances of actually achieving energy independence are slim.

Data: Evidence in the form of forecasts from the U.S. Energy Information Administration shows that energy production will increase, then drop off.

Data: Even with additional oil resources, the U.S. would still be subject to the international market. Price would still be an issue and a problem.

Qualifier: Greater energy independence would be beneficial, easing unemployment and helping our trade balance.

WHAT WE CAN EXPECT

This isn't to say there wouldn't be benefits to greater energy independence. 9
Because natural gas is so difficult to ship, it's not sold on a truly global market, so a big supply at home means cheaper prices. Our abundance of gas has already started luring manufacturers back to the United States in industries, such as chemicals, that rely on it for production. Domestic oil supplies would also help our trade balance. Crude imports account for 44% of the U.S. current account deficit, and buying oil from North Dakota instead of, say, Nigeria would obviously shrink that figure.

But it would still be wise to moderate our hopes, both about North 10
America's ability to drill its way to energy independence, and about what that would even accomplish. Perhaps we can cut down on what we buy from the Middle East. Perhaps we can cut it down significantly. But believing that will save us from the world's problems? That's still just a dream.

Writing Activity

Using a Toulmin Argument

Consider an issue you think is important to your classmates. Construct a brief Toulmin argument in which you identify your claim and the warrants your classmates need to believe in order to accept your argument. This issue could be something of local interest, such as online courses, or a matter of national significance, such as health care.

Rogerian Strategies for Arguing

Rogerian argument, which is based on the work of psychologist and mediator Carl Rogers, allows for the fact that at times we will take perspectives on issues that conflict with the views of people with whom we have important relationships. Suppose you and a close friend disagree about how to solve the problem of alcohol-related traffic fatalities. Although you could use classical argumentative strategies to win this argument, in the long term, your relationship might be better served by a conversation in which you try to see the other point of view.

Carl Rogers

Differences of opinion occur in all four areas of life—the academic, the professional, the civic, and the personal. And in all four areas, we have relationships that we want to maintain. We might therefore do better to resolve our differences without trying to "win." Although the strategies of classical argument may work well in settings where the participants are clearly opponents trying to convince a third party (two lawyers making their case to a jury, for instance), they do not work so well when the participants need to maintain a collegial, friendly, or even loving relationship. And although such strategies may work well when your topic is relatively uncontroversial or your audience is disposed to agree with your claim, they may be more likely to alienate than to persuade your audience when your topic is controversial and your audience is hostile to your claim. You might think of Rogerian argument as a "kinder, gentler" way to argue—and one that might often serve you well.

The ultimate goal of Rogerian argument is to negotiate differences and cooperate to reach a resolution that benefits or is in some way acceptable to both parties. Thus, in Rogerian argument, it is useful to begin by thinking about commonalities—that is, by thinking about and understanding opposing views and asking yourself, "Even though we may have some differences, what do we have in common?" or "Even though we may not think alike, how can we work together effectively to solve this problem?" Rogerian argument asks you to "feed back" opposing arguments. This approach requires you to understand the other person's position and to think enough about that position to articulate it. Stating the other person's position does not mean that you agree with it, of course, but that you understand it and that you recognize the other side of the argument.

Rogerian arguments have several components:

- **Introduction:** The introduction includes a description of the issue you hope to come to a consensus on. As you state a goal, keep your tone positive and invite others to participate in solving the problem or reaching agreement.

- **Summary of opposing views:** Be as accurate and as neutral as you can in stating the views of those who may disagree with you. Show that you have the skills, character, and fairness to see and appreciate the merits of opposing views.

- **Statement of understanding:** After you have stated the opposing views, demonstrate that you understand why others might hold such views. If possible, indicate the conditions under which you too could share those views.

- **Statement of writer's position:** The previous three parts have prepared your readers to listen to your views, and here is the place to state them. Invite your audience to consider your views in the same way that you have considered theirs.

- **Statement of contexts:** Building on the statement of your position, be specific about the kinds of conditions under which you hope others will find merit in your position.

- **Statement of benefit:** Explain how your position or solution will benefit those who might oppose you. End on a positive and hopeful note.

Example: Rogerian Strategies in Action

RICK REILLY

Nothing but Nets

Rick Reilly has been voted National Sportswriter of the Year eight times. He wrote the weekly "Life of Reilly" column for *Sports Illustrated* for many years, and he frequently contributes to *Time* magazine. Reilly's nonfiction books include *Who's Your Caddy?* and *The Life of Reilly: The Best of* Sports *Illustrated's Rick Reilly.* Reilly also has published the novel *Missing Links* and is the winner of many awards, including the New York Newspaper Guild's Page One Award for Best Magazine Story. The following article was first published in *Sports Illustrated* in 2006. Our students find this essay humorous and enlightening.

I've never asked for anything before, right? Well, sorry, I'm asking now. 1

We need nets. Not hoop nets, soccer nets or lacrosse nets. Not New 2 Jersey Nets or dot-nets or clarinets. *Mosquito* nets.

See, nearly 3,000 kids die every day in Africa from malaria. And accord- 3 ing to the World Health Organization, transmission of the disease would be reduced by 60% with the use of mosquito nets and prompt treatment for the infected.

Three thousand kids! That's a 9/11 every day! 4

Put it this way: Let's say your little Justin's Kickin' Kangaroos have a big 5 youth soccer tournament on Saturday. There are 15 kids on the team, 10 teams in the tourney. And there are 20 of these tournaments going on all over town. Suddenly, every one of these kids gets chills and fever, then starts throwing up and then gets short of breath. And in seven to 10 days, they're all dead of malaria.

We *gotta* get these nets. They're coated with an insecticide and cost 6 between $4 and $6. You need about $10, all told, to get them shipped and installed. Some nets can cover a family of four. And they last four years. If we can cut the spread of disease, 10 bucks means a kid might get to live. Make it $20 and more kids are saved.

So, here's the ask: If you have ever gotten a thrill by throwing, kicking, 7 knocking, dunking, slamming, putting up, cutting down or jumping over a net, please go to a special site we've set up through the United Nations Foundation. The address is: *UNFoundation.org/malaria.* Then just look for the big *SI's Nothing But Net* logo (or call 202–887–9040) and donate $20. *Bang.* You might have just saved a kid's life.

Problem: Reilly is a sportswriter who is not writing about game nets, but the need for mosquito nets.

Introduction: Reilly outlines the severity of the problem.

Reilly works hard to put the problem into a language that everyone can understand.

Reilly points out how inexpensive the nets are.

Benefit: For $10 you can save a child's life.

Note how Reilly writes about a shared, common ground with any reader who ever played a sport (which would include almost everyone).

Or would you rather have the new Beastie Boys CD? 8

You're a coach, parent, player, gym teacher or even just a fan who likes 9 watching balls fly into nets, send $20. You saved a life. Take the rest of the day off.

You have *ever* had a net in the driveway, front lawn or on your head at 10 McDonald's, send $20. You ever imagined Angelina Jolie in fishnets, $20. So you stay home and eat on the dinette. You'll live.

Hey, Dick's Sporting Goods. You have 255 stores. How about you kick in 11 a dime every time you sell a net? Hey, NBA players, hockey stars and tennis pros, how about you donate $20 every time one of your shots hits the net? Maria Sharapova, you don't think this applies to you just because you're Russian? Nyet!

I tried to think how many times I have said or written the word "net" in 12 28 years of sports writing, and I came up with, conservatively, 20,000. So I've already started us off with a $20,000 donation. That's a whole lot of lives. Together, we could come up with $1 million, net. How many lives would that save? More than 50 times the population of Nett Lake, Minn.

I know what you're thinking: *Yeah, but bottom line, how much of our $1 million* 13 *goes to nets?* All of it. Thanks to Ted Turner, who donated $1 billion to create the U.N. Foundation, which covers *all* the overhead. "Every cent will go to nets," says Andrea Gay, the U.N. Foundation's Director of Children's Health.

Nets work! Bill and Melinda Gates have just about finished singlehandedly 14 covering every bed in Zambia. Maybe we can't cover an entire Zambia, but I bet we could put a serious dent in Malawi.

It's not like we're betting on some scientist somewhere coming up with a 15 cure. And it's not like warlords are going to hijack a truckload of nets. "Theoretically, if every person in Africa slept at night under a net," says Gay, "nobody need ever die of malaria again." You talk about a net profit.

My God, think of all the nets that are taken for granted in sports! PingPong 16 nets. Batting cage nets. Terrell Owens's bassinet. If you sit behind the plate at a baseball game, you watch the action *through* a net. You download the highlights on Netscape and forward it on the net to your friend Ben-net while eating Raisinets. Sports is nothing *but* net. So next time you think of a net, go to that website and click yourself happy. Way more fun than your fantasy bowling league, dude.

One last vignette: A few years back, we took the family to Tanzania, which 17 is ravaged by malaria now. We visited a school and played soccer with the kids. Must've been 50 on each team, running and laughing. A taped-up wad of newspapers was the ball and two rocks were the goal. Most fun I ever had getting whupped. When we got home, we sent some balls and nets.

I kick myself now for that. How many of those kids are dead because we 18 sent the wrong nets?

Writer's position: Reilly works to defuse the money objection to his proposal, and he does so in a humorous way. Sure, he says, he wants to raise a million dollars . . . but then he shows how that large amount can come from many small donations.

Benefit: no overhead costs— all donations pay for nets.

Benefit: Look at how many lives could be saved.

Writing Activity

Writing Activity

Constructing a Rogerian Argument

With several of your classmates, construct a Rogerian argument, focusing on some campus or national issue or problem.

Some Common Flaws in Arguments

Any argument, no matter how effective, can be marred by **logical fallacies,** or flaws in reasoning. Although sometimes introduced deliberately into an argument with the aim of misleading readers, such flaws are often inadvertent, and avoiding them requires the kinds of critical thinking discussed in Chapter 2. The following list includes the most common and easily avoided fallacies.

- **Appealing to irrational fears:** All humans have fears, and it is often easy to exploit those fears. Someone making the argument that cattle ranchers should test each cow every month, even though there have been only a few isolated cases of mad cow disease in the United States, would be exploiting an irrational fear.

- **Appealing to pity:** Although appeals to pity and other emotions can be justified at times, this kind of appeal can mask an otherwise weak case. If a student who is failing a course because she has missed many classes and performed poorly on exams appeals to her instructor by pleading, "If I fail this course, I won't graduate on time," she is obviously masking a weak case.

- **Appealing to prejudice:** Also known as *ad populum*, this fallacy occurs when the writer appeals to a preexisting prejudice. A common example is the practice of putting an image of the American flag on a bumper sticker that advocates a particular product or stance, with an appeal to patriotism thus substituting for an argument for the product or stance. For example, Figure 14.2 is an advertisement for the American Civil Liberties Union (ACLU) that uses the American flag to indicate that their cause is patriotic. How does this image influence your initial reaction to the ad?

- **Appealing to tradition:** The most common form of this appeal is the statement "We've always done it this way in the past."

FIGURE 14.2 An advertisement for the ACLU, using the familiar stars and stripes as part of its appeal

- **Arguing from a lack of knowledge or evidence:** We can illustrate both forms of this flaw with the following example: You have looked for a needle in a haystack, and your search has been unsuccessful. From this lack of evidence, one person might argue that there must be a needle in that haystack if you would only search more carefully. From the same lack of evidence, a second person might argue that there is no needle in the haystack. In reality, of course, neither conclusion can be supported.

- **Attacking the opponent's character:** Often called an *ad hominem* attack, this fallacy is sometimes used in an attempt to direct attention away from the logic of a case—usually a strong case—by evoking a negative emotional response to the person making the case. In an effort to make an opponent seem like a hypocrite, a person might say, "My opponent argues that vegetarianism is a moral choice, but I notice that he wears leather shoes—so it is acceptable to *wear* part of an animal, but not to eat part of one? That is hypocritical!" The opposite fallacy (*pro hominem*), which is also common, involves directing attention away from a case—usually a weak case—by evoking a positive emotional response to the person making it. A legislator might appeal to the public to support an unworthy bill by praising the record of the colleague who introduced it: "Because Representative Smithers has advocated good ideas in the past, we should vote for her plan to drill for oil in Central Park."

- **Attributing false causes:** Usually called *post hoc, ergo propter hoc* ("after this, therefore because of this"), this fallacy occurs when someone assumes that event A caused event B because event A occurred before event B. A common example is superstitious thinking: "I've been having so much bad luck recently because I broke a mirror/walked under a ladder/crossed the path of a black cat." This fallacy is common in civic life. In political campaigns, for example, an incumbent will often claim that his or her policies have caused the economy to improve, whereas a challenger will charge that the incumbent's policies have caused crime rates to increase. All sorts of events occur before other events in the world, but that does not mean that they cause those other events.

- **Bandwagon appeal:** Here the arguer is essentially saying, "Many people are doing it, especially people whom you admire, so it must be a good thing to do. You should do it too." Television beer commercials frequently use this appeal when they show a group of young, attractive people having a great time at a party: If those people are having such a good time drinking that brand of beer, anyone who drinks it will also have a good time.

- **Begging the question (circular reasoning):** This fallacy treats a questionable assertion as if it has already been answered or fully explained, as in the following example: "My friend would never cheat because he's an honest person." To assert that someone is honest is not to provide evidence that he did not or would not cheat; this assertion merely restates the idea that the person would not cheat but has nothing to do with whether he actually did cheat.

- **Complex question:** In this ploy, an arguer asks a question that actually has two parts and demands a one-part response. For instance, the question "When did you stop beating your dog?" has embedded in it the assumption that you used to beat your dog. The person to whom it is addressed would be right to reply, "Hold on. Let's first establish whether I have ever beaten my dog in the first place."

- **Either-or reasoning:** Also known as "false dichotomy," this fallacy occurs when writers give readers two opposing choices (either A or B) when other possibilities also exist. For instance, a person might state, "You can major in business administration, or you can plan on getting a crummy job."

- **Faulty analogy:** In this fallacy, the writer makes a comparison that is in some way misleading or incomplete—or that does not even relate to the topic being discussed. A columnist who writes, "Leading a country is like running a business. In both cases, the bottom line is the most important consideration" is using a faulty analogy because governments and businesses are different in significant ways.

- **Guilt by association:** This fallacy occurs when a writer seeks to discredit an opponent by associating the opponent with some unpopular person, group, or idea, as when politicians attempt to brand their opponents with labels such as "free-spending liberal" or "hard-right conservative." Such labels imply that *all* liberals are "free spending" or that all conservatives are "hard-right"—and both labels have negative connotations.

- **Overgeneralization:** This fallacy occurs when someone reaches a conclusion based on insufficient evidence, especially atypical examples. For instance, your friend engages in overgeneralization when, after an automobile accident in which she was not wearing a seat belt but sustained only minor injuries, she says, "See. Seat belts aren't necessary."

- **Oversimplification:** People sometimes search for simple answers to complex problems. For instance, some might say that the solution to gang violence in high schools would be simply to require students to wear uniforms in school. Of course, the problem of gang violence is complex, and its solution will not be that easy.

- **Red herring (or non sequitur):** This fallacy occurs when the writer introduces an irrelevant point to divert attention from the issue being considered. The fallacy gets its name from the practice of dragging a red herring—a fish—along the ground to distract hunting dogs from the scent that they are following. A student who says to his teacher, "I know that I was late for class today, but I've been on time every other day" is using a red herring to throw the teacher off the scent of the real issue: The student is late.

- **Slippery slope:** This fallacy claims that once something starts, it must continue, just like a person sliding down a slippery slope. An example is the student who says, "We've got to fight that proposed fee for using the computer center. If that fee is enacted, pretty soon they'll be charging fees for using the restrooms on campus."

- **Stacking the deck:** Here the writer presents evidence for only one side of the case. A student who says, "I should get an A because I handed in all my homework," while neglecting to mention that she got a C on the midterm and final exams, is stacking the deck.

- **Straw person:** This fallacy occurs when an arguer distorts the opponent's argument and then attacks that distorted argument. For instance, a few decades ago, when equal rights for women was a hotly contested issue, some people made statements such as "Equal rights for women means that women will have the right to use men's restrooms. What is this country coming to?" Unisex restrooms were not part of what women's rights advocates were arguing for.

- **Universal statements:** Such statements often include words such as *always, never, all, everyone, everybody, none,* or *no one.* Of course, some statements that include those words are true—for instance, "All humans are mammals." However, when writers use those words to describe human behavior or beliefs, those statements are usually problematic. For example, the statement "Men never share their feelings, but women always do" could be easily contradicted with just one or two cases.

Writing Activity

Searching for Logical Fallacies

To help you learn to identify logical fallacies, find several instances of them in your local or campus newspaper. (Hint: Often, letters to the editor provide rich material!). Bring copies to class, share them, and explain the logical fallacies to your classmates.

15

Using Strategies for Collaboration

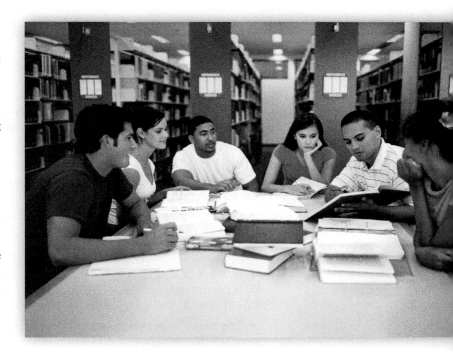

Although writing can be a solitary activity, it is often a collaborative endeavor. For instance, researchers in the sciences, education, and engineering often co-author research proposals and reports. In business, teams often write project proposals and reports. In local, state, or national legislatures, many people collaborate to write bills to present to their colleagues. When groups of neighbors or parents are concerned about some local problem, they will often collaborate on a letter to the editor of their local newspaper or to the school board. In your writing classroom, you will probably have the opportunity to get feedback from your classmates, and in other courses, you are likely to encounter assignments that require you to work as part of a team.

Working with Peers on Your Single-Authored Projects

As you craft your own writing projects, working with peers can yield many benefits. Early in the process of crafting a project, peers can help you generate ideas by challenging you to consider other perspectives. Later in the process, peers can point out ways to revise your writing so that readers will find it more understandable, informative, or persuasive. Peers can also help edit your prose.

In the chapters in Parts 2 and 3 of this book, "Writer's Workshop" activities help you solicit feedback from peers. It is your responsibility to encourage peers to offer candid assessments of your work. Peers should not be nasty, of course, but they *should* give you a clear sense of how well your writing is fulfilling its purpose.

Strategies for Working with Peers on Your Projects

Feedback from peers can help you at any point in a project. Although it is important to seek and use the perspectives that peers can offer, it is equally important to remember that *you* are ultimately responsible for the project. Given this principle, the following guidelines can be useful:

- Peers can indicate what is working well—and not so well. When peers ask for more information, you should consider adding that information to your next draft.
- Peers' questions are usually more helpful than their suggestions.

Using Digital Tools for Peer Review

If it is difficult to find time to meet face-to-face with peers outside of class, digital tools for peer review can help. Even if it is easy to meet face-to-face, though, writers still can use digital tools. Here are some common tools that you can use:

- The track-changes feature of your word-processing software makes it easy to see the changes that different reviewers are suggesting in a document. You can then accept or reject any or all suggested changes.
- The "comment" feature of most word-processing software makes it easy to offer a suggestion or pose a question to the writer.
- Many instructors use a course-management system to offer courses either completely or partially online.
- Wikis offer writers the opportunity for peer review. Changes to documents in wikis are automatically tracked. Changes can easily be made by anyone with access to the document.

Working with Peers on Multiple-Authored Projects

Working with your classmates on multiple-authored projects can have many benefits. One long-term benefit is that it will prepare you for co-authoring documents with your colleagues in the workplace. Another benefit is that working with a group can infuse a project with a rich array of perspectives.

Group work also presents challenges, however. Some members of the writing team may be inclined to contribute too much to the project while others sometimes seem to contribute too little. Some co-authors may insist on doing things their way without listening to potentially effective ideas from others.

Strategies for Working with Peers Effectively

Working with peers can be challenging because they may question your thinking in new and sometimes uncomfortable ways. In college, this kind of interaction is especially likely because your classmates may have personalities and/or cultural backgrounds that differ substantially from yours. Although encountering a variety of backgrounds and perspectives can move you out of your comfort zone, it can also be a catalyst for learning.

Collaboration can take place in several ways. You might find yourself working on an entire project with the same team. Or you might find yourself using one classmate or a small group of your classmates as peer reviewers for drafts of one another's works. The "Writer's Workshop" sections in Parts 2 and 3 suggest strategies for peer review of single-authored works.

To make the most of your work with peers, try the following strategies:

- **Listen empathically to your group members' comments and questions.** Empathetic listeners strive to understand why someone is making a particular comment or raising a particular question.

- **Assign roles to members of the group.** One member of the group can be the *recorder*, whose duty is to keep track of who says what. Another member of the group can be the *question-asker*, posing questions to encourage everyone to think more critically or deeply. Yet another group member can be the *facilitator*, whose role is to keep the discussion focused and moving forward. It is important that every group member have some *specific responsibility* to perform.

- **Provide positive and constructive feedback.** Every piece of feedback can be stated more or less negatively or more or less positively. Further, every negative or less positive statement can be recast into a more positive form:

ELECTRONIC ENVIRONMENTS) **Using a Wiki to Collaborate**

Working in groups can be a challenge, especially when you are in an online class or your group members are trying to schedule out-of-class work time together. You might want to consider using a free online groupware site, or even a wiki. A wiki is an interactive Web site that allows members to create, add, delete, and change content. Each group member can edit existing content and develop separate materials on linked pages. Wikis and groupware document sites eliminate the confusion of keeping track of multiple e-mails in your inbox. Some popular sites to try out free of charge include *Google Groups* (http://groups.google.com), *Google Docs* (http://docs.google.com), *Wikidot* (http://www.wikidot.com/), and *Wikispaces* (http:// www.wikispaces.com).

Less Positive	More Positive
There's an error in his sentence.	You could edit the sentence this way:
This paragraph is underdeveloped.	You could develop this paragraph by adding this:
You don't have a conclusion.	What are you planning to say in the conclusion?

- **Pay attention to interpersonal dynamics.** Before the group begins discussing the assigned topic, ask each member of the group to respond to the following kinds of questions:
  - What can the group do to function most effectively?
  - What seems to impede our group from functioning effectively?
  - What encourages you to contribute effectively to the group?
- **Do round-robin sharing.** To ensure that every member of the group contributes equally, go around the table clockwise, with each person contributing one after the other. Do this as many times as necessary to solicit everyone's contributions.
- **If possible, keep the group relatively small—three or four members.** Larger groups become hard to manage, and it becomes difficult to coordinate calendars or to reach consensus.
- **Consider your class and your peer group to be intertwined communities.** Make a commitment to improve the work of each community and each member of the community. If every member makes such a commitment, everyone will benefit.
- **Celebrate your accomplishment.** When the project is completed, treat yourselves, perhaps by enjoying coffee or lunch together.

One way to ensure the success of any group endeavor is to plan. The tasks that follow will help you to plan various aspects of your work with your group.

DEFINE SUCCESS FOR THE GROUP

What will count as success, and how can the group achieve it? You might use the following chart, for example, to define success and to identify the means for achieving it.

Defining Group Success

Sign of Success	Method(s) for Achieving
Everyone shows up for our meetings at the agreed-on time.	Add meetings to daily planners and/or smartphones.
Everyone participates equally.	Use a round-robin approach for sharing ideas during discussions.

DEVELOP A PLAN FOR DEALING WITH GROUP PROBLEMS

Potential problems include a group member who dominates a discussion, doesn't carry a fair share of the load, or misses a deadline. If a problem does surface, deal with it immediately. Dealing with small problems immediately can keep them from becoming bigger problems. If a problem arises, do *not* focus on who is to blame; instead, focus on finding a solution.

SET SHORT-TERM AND LONG-TERM GOALS

Before the group begins a particular work session, decide what you want to accomplish in the session—your short-term goal. As you work, stay focused on that goal until you achieve it. If the group will work together over multiple sessions, decide on a long-term goal to achieve by the last session. Then establish short-term goals for each session along the way.

Project Goals	
Long-Term Goals	**Short-Term Goals**
Complete the project by November 16.	Complete library research by October 3.
	Complete interviews by October 10.

DEVELOP A PLAN FOR COMPLETING THE PROJECT

Identify the subtasks that need to be completed along the way, as well as a timeline for completing each subtask. Write down who is responsible for each task, and make certain that each member of the group has a list of everyone's responsibilities. As each deadline for a subtask approaches, ask the responsible member or members to report on progress.

MAKE A CALENDAR OF GROUP MEETINGS

Group meetings can be held face-to-face, by telephone, or in online chat rooms. For each meeting, establish an agenda and identify what each person needs to do before the meeting. Also, decide who will serve as the discussion leader for each meeting, and assign a different discussion leader for each meeting.

Calendar for Meetings			
Meeting Date	**Agenda Item(s)**	**Individuals' Preparation**	**Discussion Leader**
October 11	Examine interviews	Hanna: Bring three copies of transcripts of interviews with rental-property owners.	Hanna
		Molly: Bring three copies of transcripts of interviews with renters.	Molly
		Meghan: Bring three copies of transcript of interview with city attorney.	Meghan

Using Digital Tools to Facilitate Multiple-Authored Projects

Whether or not collaborative meetings are held in person, digital tools can support the process. Here are some tried-and-true suggestions for using digital tools:

- Agree on a sequence for working on each digital file to avoid duplication of effort.
- For revising, use the track-changes and comment features of your word-processing software. That way other members of the group can see the changes that you are making.
- When you send a file to another member of the group for revising or editing, copy the other members of the group so that they can be certain who is working on the document and can see the progress on the project.
- When you name files, include the current date in the file name, such as "rental_paper_10–18–12." Don't delete older versions of files because you may need them to recover a deleted paragraph or to recover a file that has become corrupted.

Making Effective Oral Presentations

Along with invention, arrangement, memory, and style, *delivery*—the way you present a message—is one of the five canons of rhetoric. In most of this book, we have dealt with written or visual forms of delivery. In this chapter, however, we will consider oral presentations, a form of delivery that is becoming increasingly important in all areas of life.

- In your academic life, you will be asked to make presentations in some of your classes.
- In your professional life, you will often be asked to present your ideas to your colleagues and to clients.
- In your civic life, you may speak before the local school board, or to the city council, or in front of any number of civic or political organizations.
- In your personal life, you may be called on to give a speech at an occasion such as a wedding, a funeral, or a school reunion, or you may speak at a less formal gathering of your family or friends.

As with written communication, oral presentations are *rhetorical acts*. To prepare an effective oral presentation, you need to ask yourself the same questions that you would ask for any writing situation:

- What do I want to accomplish? In other words, what is the purpose of this presentation?
- Who is my audience? What do they already know about my topic?
- What is the context surrounding this presentation?

- How much do I already know about my topic, and what else do I need to learn about it?

Once you have decided what you want to accomplish with a particular audience on a specific occasion, you will have a better understanding of how you need to prepare: what kind of research you need to conduct, what types of information you need to collect, and what kinds of visuals you should prepare.

477

Developing Your Presentation

You can use several approaches to develop an oral presentation. For more formal presentations on complex topics, you might decide to write the full text of your presentation. In some situations, you might choose to read your full text, especially if you have to use specific words at specific moments during your presentation. In other situations, you might write the full text and then prepare an outline of it. You might then speak from that outline, which is written on a sheet of paper, appears on a set of PowerPoint slides, or both.

Establishing a Clear Structure

As with any piece of discourse that you construct, an oral presentation needs to have a clear organization that helps you to achieve your purpose. For most oral presentations, you will need to do the following:

- Construct an effective, thought-provoking, and attention-grabbing *introduction.* Remember that during your presentation, your listeners may be tempted to let their attention wander. Therefore, part of your job is to draw them in, to tell them something that will interest them, and to indicate quickly how your topic affects them.

- Let your audience know the *main point(s)* that you plan to make. Often called **forecasting,** this technique is especially important in oral presentations. If you have five main points that you want to cover, name them. Each time you move to the next point, make note of that, too ("The third point I want to make is . . . "). It often helps to provide the audience with a written outline of your points.

For more on supporting claims with evidence, see Chapters 9 and 14.

For more on using transitions, see Chapter 13.

- Include sufficient evidence to *support* each one of your claims. You will be much more credible as a speaker if you support your claims with facts, examples, statistics, and testimony from experts.

- Be sure to *point back* to your main point so that it will be easy for your listeners to understand exactly how each point that you make or piece of information that you provide relates to your thesis.

- Use *visual aids* to outline the structure of your talk, if the situation calls for them. Your PowerPoint slides should outline the points you want to make, which you will then elaborate on. The message of each visual needs to be readily apparent.

- Use your *conclusion* to summarize and emphasize your main point, and to outline briefly how everything in your presentation supports it.

VISUAL *Thinking* | *PowerPoint* Presentations

Consider the most *ineffective* ways to use or a PowerPoint presentation:

- The speaker uses very small type, so any text would be hard for the audience to read.
- The speaker spends part of the designated speaking time setting up or becoming familiar with the projection equipment.
- The speaker simply reads the visuals to the audience.
- The speaker uses every PowerPoint special effect on every slide.
- The speaker faces *away from* the audience while reading the text on the screen.
- The speaker walks to the screen and uses a finger to point to words on the screen.

Now contrast that presentation with an effective one:

- Each visual aid uses appropriate type sizes, colors, and graphics to illustrate the speaker's main points.
- Before the presentation, the speaker learns how to use the equipment and sets it up.
- The speaker talks directly to the audience, using the text on each visual only as a starting point, which he or she then elaborates and explains.
- The speaker uses PowerPoint special effects sparingly.
- The speaker talks directly to the audience, making eye contact and looking for signs that the audience is "getting" what the presentation is about.
- If necessary, the speaker uses an inexpensive laser pointer to point to specific words on the screen.

Suppose you were assigned to write an academic paper focusing on whether students litter on your campus, and you needed to prepare an oral presentation as part of that assignment. The slide in Figure 16.1 on page 479 is one possible way for you to start a PowerPoint presentation on that topic.

The photograph can help you get your audience's attention and focus them on your topic. Each subsequent PowerPoint slide can contain the same heading, but provide the points you want to discuss in your presentation. Your second slide (Figure 16.2) might offer examples that suggest that students really are *not* slobs.

You will elaborate on these **talking points** as you make your presentation, discussing each one in detail and providing more information to support each point as you make it. For example, for the first point you could add the following information:

For more on visuals for presentations, see Chapter 18.

- Student organizations collect all recycled products in classrooms and office buildings.
- Student groups make money through this recycling effort.

(continued)

(continued)

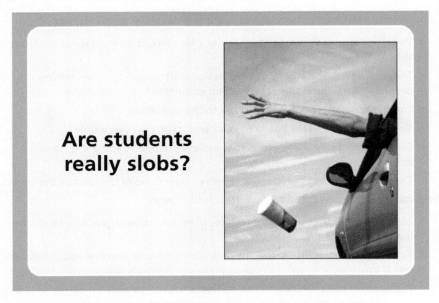

FIGURE 16.1   An Opening Slide for a Presentation

Are students really slobs?

Not necessarily. At our college, students

- help with the campus recycling program.
- are responsible for cleaning their dorm rooms.
- are subject to weekly inspections.
- are fined if their bathrooms are not clean.
- serve on a task force to keep our campus beautiful.

FIGURE 16.2   A Second Slide

- Students work together in the dorms to collect recycled products.
- Several student leaders serve on the Campus Recycling Board (CRB).

As you speak, then, you will flesh out each point with specific examples that are not on the slide but that provide information and details for your audience.

Considering Your Audience

Your *audience* is your primary concern as you plan, develop, and deliver your presentation. Every decision you make depends on your awareness of that audience, from considering what they already know about your subject, to what they need to know to believe what you tell them, to how you should present yourself to that audience. So consider: How do you want to come across to your audience? As informed and logical? As thoughtful? Probably. Or as someone shouting at them? Or droning at them? Probably not.

ELECTRONIC ENVIRONMENTS | **Enhancing Oral Presentations with Visuals and Audio**

Using graphic, audio, and video files to enhance your oral presentations is not just a good idea—in this day and age, it's often expected. Audiences are not usually critical of video that is less than perfect as long as it illustrates an important point. Before incorporating media into your oral presentation, however, use the following checklist to make sure your presentation goes smoothly:

- Examine the room, lecture hall, or space where you will be presenting. Note the size and shape of the room, the seating arrangements, and the available equipment.

- If you are using video or sound media, make sure you have allowed enough time for the video or audio clip to play.

- Keep it brief. Do not give the audience time to get uncomfortable or restless while the video or sound is playing.

- *Always* plan a fallback handout, visual chart, or anecdote in the event that the technologies available in the room suddenly fail.

- Choose music, video clips, and images that are relevant to your presentation and that strengthen your claims and positions.

- Practice your presentation, including the time it takes to start and stop each video or sound element.

- Once you feel that you have developed and practiced your presentation sufficiently, ask a friend, co-worker, or classmate to be your test audience. Be open to this person's feedback. Video and sound elements should illustrate, add meaning to, and clarify main points, not distract or confuse your audience. If your test audience tells you that it's not clear why you have incorporated media, ask for comments and suggestions.

- Give the audience time to react. If they *do* enjoy the media you've incorporated, give them a moment to laugh or applaud before you continue with your presentation.

One way to move your audience in the direction you would like them to go is through what magician and author Steve Cohen calls "command [of] the room." He recommends that you do the following:

- Look listeners in the eye. This might seem hard to do, especially if you are speaking before a large crowd, but you can always find someone to look at and speak to directly. Find these folks in several parts of your audience, and soon it will look like you are speaking personally to *everyone* in that audience.
- Hold that eye contact longer than you might expect to.
- Speak in a conversational tone and manner.
- Remember the 45-degree rule: If you are concerned that you might wobble as you speak, make sure to put one foot in front of the other, at about a 45-degree angle. It's impossible to wobble when you stand that way.

Finally, always make certain that your listeners can hear you, projecting your voice to the farthest member of your audience. To make certain that the audience can hear you, begin your presentation by asking, "Can folks in the back of the room hear me if I speak at this volume?" It's also a good idea to ask people to raise their hands and cup their ears if they can't hear you.

Writing Activity

Analyzing and Evaluating a Speech

Author Dale Dauten suggests listening to the "top 100 speeches" and other speeches available at http://www.americanrhetoric.com/. Visit that Web site and listen to a famous speech. In no more than two pages, write a brief analysis by responding to the following questions:

- What do you think made this speech famous?
- How effective do you think it was? Why?
- How effective do you think its original audience found it? Why?
- How was it organized?
- What were the main points of the speech?

Eliminating the Fear of Speaking in Public

The fear of speaking in public is always at or close to the top of lists of common fears. However, a bit of nervousness before a presentation can be a positive thing. If you are not nervous, you can be overconfident and not do a very effective job. Here are some techniques that can help you overcome stage fright:

- Be overprepared. Know what you want to say. Know your subject. If you plan to use visual aids, be prepared for the unexpected—for example, a broken projector.

- Practice *out loud* several times before your presentation. The more you practice, the better your presentation will be, period. *Thinking* what you want to say and actually *saying it aloud* are really two different things. When you just think about a presentation, your mind tends to fill in the words you leave out. But when you force yourself to practice out loud, you will end up with a much more polished presentation.

- Time your presentation so you know that it fits whatever time parameters you have been given. You want to avoid having your host hold up a sign that says "TWO MINUTES LEFT" when you still have eight minutes of material to deliver in your presentation.

- Another way to eliminate the fear of speaking, or at least to avoid showing that fear, is to use a clipboard to hold your notes. A piece of paper held in your hand might shake, but a clipboard will not.

- *Visualize* making a successful presentation before you make it. *See yourself* in front of your audience. *Listen* to them applaud. *See* audience members nod in agreement. *See yourself speaking with them* afterward. Picture what you want to happen, and it will.

- As you speak, do not let minor distractions bother you. If you hear noise from an adjoining room or from the street outside, ignore it. Do not assume that the person in the back row who appears to be laughing is laughing at you. Any number of things will distract you. You need to ignore them and concentrate on what you want to say.

Other Tips for Making Effective Oral Presentations

- Show enthusiasm.
- Use hand gestures purposefully.
- Become aware of any tics (such as, saying "um," playing with your hair, or rubbing your nose) and eliminate them. One strategy is to video record your speech and then watch it with a friend or classmate. Another strategy is to watch for these distracting behaviors while practicing in front of a mirror.
- Before a presentation and immediately following it, invite members of the audience to ask questions at the end of the presentation.
- Do not rely solely on visuals, especially a PowerPoint presentation. Because digital technology can fail, be prepared to give a presentation even if the computer or the projector fails to function properly.
- After practicing your presentation with a script or notes, also practice giving it with a bulleted list of your main points. Put that list on a 3" × 5" card.
- Always say "thank you" at the end of your presentation. You will find it to be surprisingly effective (and thoughtful).

Online Presentations

It's not uncommon now for people to make online presentations. Whether you're taking an online class or being asked to make a presentation to a group of people who can't gather in the same place at the same time, you can now use digital technologies to record and deliver a presentation. (You might use the recording function in PowerPoint or choose a screen recording program such as Quicktime Player or Camtasia.) When you create an online presentation, follow the same general guidelines you would use when making a face-to-face presentation. However, make sure to pay close attention to the following points.

- Make sure your audio track matches the text on your slides.
- Make sure any visuals you use on your slides enhance the point you are trying to make.
- Make sure to script your presentation before you record it. Then practice reading it several times before recording it. You are much more likely to give a professional-sounding presentation if it's scripted and you have practiced it.
- Make sure to keep your digital presentation under eight minutes. People tend to stop paying attention to online presentations that last longer than eight minutes.

Writing Activity

Making an Oral Presentation

Using one of the papers that you wrote for Part 2 or 3 of this textbook, prepare and deliver an oral presentation. Revise and adapt your paper to suit your new medium and purpose by establishing a clear structure, using effective visual aids, and considering your audience according to the strategies described in this chapter.

If you have a video camera and can record your presentation so you can play it back and critique yourself, so much the better. But in any case, when you practice, think of your work as *rehearsal:* Go through your presentation from start to finish, without stopping. If you get tongue-tied or drop your notes or the projector does not work, just continue as if you were actually giving your speech.

CHAPTER 17

Choosing a Medium, Genre, and Technology for Your Communication

As long as humans have recorded their experiences, they have used technologies that act as tools to record their ideas.

The image that opens this chapter is a portion of a prehistoric cave painting from caves in Lascaux, France. The paintings are approximately 17,000 years old. Although we know little about the person or people who made this image, we can surmise that painting was a useful technology for communicating with the intended audience. We do know that this medium (painting on a cave wall) allowed ancient humans to record images that might be decorative, might be symbolic, might tell a story, or might have performed a combination of these functions. Although cave painting is a type of communication—or **genre**—that has been lost, its medium is certainly durable, having survived for thousands of years.

Communication technologies are as varied as paint on a cave wall or a canvas, a piece of chalk, a ballpoint pen, or a word-processing program. Whatever a writer's purpose, the availability of a particular tool often helps to determine what **medium**—method of delivery—that writer uses to communicate.

When writers use a specific communication technology, they need to understand the impact that the technology will have on that communication. You do not always have a choice of which technology or medium you can use. But when you do, you need to understand the potential and limitations of each, and you need to make your choice in a rhetorically sound way. This chapter will provide an overview of communication technologies, suggestions on evaluating publishing options, and guidelines for choosing the most effective genre and medium for your work. This chapter will also discuss design considerations and computer-mediated technologies.

Communication Technologies

Communication technology is not necessarily an electronic device. Because writing is itself a technology, every tool that we use to compose is a kind of communication technology. Some communication technologies, such as word-processing software, encourage revision while others, such as pen and paper, make revision more difficult. On the other hand, a handwritten letter, while difficult to revise, may make a more personal connection with your reader than a word-processed document. And pens and note paper are easier to carry than laptop computers and do not require an electrical outlet, a battery, or an Internet connection to function.

For an overview of technologies for computer-mediated communication, see pages 489–96.

Writing is inextricably linked to the technology that produces it. Understanding your own process and what communication technologies will work most effectively and efficiently for you in a given writing situation is important to your success as a writer.

Publishing Your Work

When you write letters or even when you write for an academic purpose, you are usually writing to one person or to a small number of people. As a result, your communication is generally private. When you *publish* your written work, however, you make it public. You can publish your writing in a variety of ways, from printing a newsletter and distributing copies to a limited group of people to constructing a page on the Web that is accessible to anyone. Although publishing your work can be exciting, it also involves both responsibilities and risks.

As recently as the 1970s, the only way to publish a piece of writing was in some kind of print medium. Publishing meant typesetting a manuscript and reproducing it on a printing press, a process that was both time-consuming and expensive. With the advent of the Internet, specifically the hypertext environment of the Web, today's students have technology and publishing options and opportunities that were unheard of in the past. Now anyone who constructs a Web page on a server connected to the Internet publishes a document that is available to the entire world. If you are like our students, for example, you probably spend some time on Facebook and Twitter. While these are not academic "publishing" by any means, they are a way for you—a student—to publish and share information with students everywhere.

If you publish to a broad audience, and especially if you publish online, you need to remember that those who view your work will be forming an opinion of you and your ideas that is based solely on what they see and read. Comments made in haste, without thought and reflection, can sometimes come back to haunt their authors. Members of your audience will also respond in some way to the design of your document or Web page—to the colors, the typeface, the size of type, the arrangement of items on the page or screen, and so on. If you make assertions, they will expect you to provide proof. As with any other form of written communication, they will also expect you to follow the conventions of spelling, grammar, punctuation, and mechanics. If you do not, you will weaken your credibility. Whether you publish in print or in an electronic medium, you will enhance your credibility if you choose an appropriate genre.

Selecting a Genre and a Medium

At the beginning of any writing task that has an audience beyond their immediate circle, writers need to decide which established form, or genre, to write in and the best medium in which to publish their work.

The chapters in Parts 2 and 3 include further details about genres.

In choosing a genre and medium, you need to consider carefully the audience, the context, and the purpose for your writing. For example, if you are writing a set of instructions for the operation of a propane camp stove, you can expect that the people who will read those instructions will usually be outdoors and often in isolated locations. The instructions will be more useful and effective if they are published in print and in a size that is easy to pack and carry. On the other hand, if you are providing information about the academic support resources available on your campus and most of the students on the campus have high-speed Internet access, the best way to reach this audience may be to publish the information on a Web site.

Deciding on a Genre for Your Work

The genre you use for your writing is usually determined by your rhetorical purpose: Who is your audience, and what are you trying to accomplish with that audience? Sometimes, of course, whoever asks you to write will dictate the genre:

- Your employer asks you to construct a formal proposal.
- Your art teacher asks you to construct and present an oral report that uses visuals in the form of handouts or a PowerPoint presentation (for more on presentation software, see page 495).
- Your Aunt Hanna asks you to send her a letter about your recent move to a new city, and she especially requests that you print photographs in the letter.
- Your college president requests e-mail responses to a proposed new student fee.

Much of the time, though, you will select the appropriate genre based on your audience and rhetorical purpose:

- If you want to suggest to the president of your college that your campus cafeteria needs a healthier selection of food, a formal letter or proposal is probably the best approach (Chapter 9 focuses on persuasive writing).
- If you want to provide information to your community about an upcoming campus art exhibit, a brochure or poster might be the best genre (Chapter 7 focuses on informative writing).
- If you want to analyze an upcoming proposal to raise school taxes, a wiki or blog might be useful genres with which to present your analysis—and either one would allow others to chime in as well (Chapter 8 focuses on analytical writing; for more on blogs and wikis see page 491).

For more on some common genres, see Appendix C.

Once you have decided on the genre, you will have to decide which medium will be the most effective in presenting the information (or your argument, evaluation, request, and so on). And your writing might take several forms. For example, if you are writing to share an experience (see Chapter 5), you might outline your shared experience in one of these forms:

- In print form, as an essay for your writing class or a newsletter to your extended family
- On the Web, including several pictures, to share with family and friends
- As a PDF file on the Web that readers can download and print
- In an audio or video clip that you can e-mail to readers and/or make available as a Web link

Deciding Whether to Use Print, Electronic, or Oral Media

Few academic papers are handwritten these days. Usually, you need to turn in an assignment printed in type on paper or in some kind of electronic medium. Often you have no choice; your instructor will specify a medium and format. However, in other situations your instructor might not specify the medium and format and instead will expect you to make the proper rhetorical choice.

Because the same information can usually be provided in both print and electronic forms, the medium you choose often depends on how that information is going to be used. Consider how each one also helps you accomplish different tasks better than the other.

Features of Paper and Electronic Documents

Criteria	Medium: Print on paper	Medium: Electronic
Portability	Easily portable	Can be sent almost instantly over the Internet; needs devices for portability such as a laptop, e-reader, or smartphone
Control of design	Relatively easy to control	Less easy to control—issues can be screen size and resolution
Ability to search	More difficult to search—needs a good index	Easy to search—can use linked keywords
Revision	Once printed, difficult to revise—have to go back to the electronic version	Easy to revise

Paper documents work best when you are providing information in a narrative or sequential organization. Much academic writing, which is often argumentative, works well in print form because argument, which involves stating and supporting a thesis, is best presented as a linear sequence of points. On the other hand, if you are providing information that does not need to be read sequentially or chronologically, then hypertextual electronic formats, in which readers can use links to move easily from one section to another, offer an advantage over paper documents.

Writing Activity

Selecting a Medium

With several of your classmates, consider the following writing tasks. For each one, decide what genre and medium might be appropriate to get your message across to the audience indicated.

- A group consisting of you and your neighbors wants to collect comments and information on a problem with an illegal dump near a school and present them to the town council.

- To increase public awareness of the different organizations on campus, your group has been asked to send information to various civic clubs such as the Rotary, Kiwanis, and Elks. With the material will be a request for donations to your school organizations.

Considering Design

In addition to choosing a genre and medium for your work, you will need to decide on a design for it. We know that many people absorb information more readily when it is presented in a diagram or a chart. And we know that how a document looks will affect our response to it. Chapter 18 covers the principles of effective design and provides guidelines for incorporating visual material in your writing. No matter what design functions you use, your goal in using them should be to make your message more effective.

Technologies for Computer-Mediated Communication

Your choice of a medium for your work may depend not only on the writing situation and the genre you have chosen but also on the availability of computers and the Internet to you and your audience, and on your—and their—comfort level with using them.

When you think about the way you use computers during your writing process, you probably think about using word-processing software to compose, revise, and edit your various drafts. Although these uses are important, they are not the only way that computers can help you during your writing process. You might use a computer to find information on the Internet or to access library databases. In addition, you can use word-processing software at other times besides composing, such as when you are taking notes or brainstorming, listing, and doing other invention work. You can even use other technologies, such as e-mail, blogs, wikis, or instant messages, for exploring topics and sharing ideas and drafts with peers.

The following technologies give you additional tools and options for writing and publishing your work.

E-mail

Many of us use e-mail frequently. Familiar though it may be, e-mail is a powerful technology. To make the best use of it, you need to be aware of some basic rhetorical issues.

- **Tone:** E-mail messages range from very informal to formal, depending on your audience. If you are writing to a close friend, a family member, or even a classmate, you may feel comfortable using nonstandard words such as "gonna" or "dunno" or acronyms such as BTW (by the way) or ASAP (as soon as possible). However, using nonstandard language in your e-mail correspondence with supervisors, instructors, or people you don't know may harm your credibility with your audience.

- **Audience:** While you may send an e-mail to a specific person, *that* person might forward your e-mail or include it in another e-mail to someone you don't even know, so be aware of and cautious about what you say. If you have a sensitive message to convey or want to address serious issues, pick up the telephone.

- **Ethos:** Your e-mail address will be seen by everyone to whom you send e-mail. If you send e-mail from work or school, your address is often assigned to you—and usually consists of a form of your name. However, when you set up a personal e-mail account, you can choose your own address, which will therefore say something about you. Like a vanity license plate on a car, addresses that are overly cute are inappropriate in a professional environment. Consider using different personal addresses for different purposes. When you are looking for a job, be sure to use a personal e-mail address instead of your work e-mail since your current employer may have access to your e-mail account.

For more on e-mail as a genre, see Appendix C.

Threaded Discussions

A **threaded discussion** is simply e-mail that, instead of being sent to individual addresses, is posted on the virtual equivalent of a bulletin board. Participants add their comments in the appropriate place—either as an extension of a previous message or as a new topic or "thread." The advantage is that everyone can see what the other participants are saying.

Threaded discussions can help instructors and students perform a variety of writing tasks. If the class is being offered entirely online, threaded discussions are a substitute for in-class discussions. If the class meets face-to-face, threaded discussions are one way to work collaboratively on a class assignment or participate in a discussion outside of class.

Synchronous Chat

At its most basic level, **synchronous chat** is simply a way to communicate with someone else in real time using text. Synchronous chat brings individuals together in a space to communicate. Programs like Second Life allow you to "teleport" to a virtual world and interact through the use of avatars. These days most people who use synchronous chat are likely to be using some kind of instant messaging (IM).

Although instant messaging and other forms of synchronous chat are a great way to communicate with distant friends or relatives, you can also use the same technology for a variety of group or team activities including classroom and work-place tasks. Synchronous chat provides an incredibly powerful environment for brainstorming. Because most chat software has a logging function, you can keep a written record of your conversation or brainstorming session and use it later in your writing. The convenience of having a record of what has been said can also be used by employers to terminate employees who misuse company equipment. When using IM in the workplace, always be professional and appropriate with your keystrokes.

For a definition of brainstorming, see Chapter 4, page 65.

Blogs

Blogs are a type of online journal. Like pen-and-paper journals, blogs often feature personal, reflective writing, but blogs are posted on the Web and are therefore public documents. Because blogs are consciously written as public documents, they are often about subjects that might interest large numbers of people, such as politics or sports or the entertainment industry. However, they tend to retain their personal flavor because there is seldom, if ever, any accountability for what gets written in a blog. Some blogs are the work of a single author, others are interactive. They allow, and even encourage, multiple writers to take part in the conversation. An Internet site like Globe of Blogs (www.globeofblogs.com) lists thousands of blogs on a wide variety of topics.

Wikis

A **wiki** is "a page or collection of Web pages designed to enable anyone who accesses it to contribute or modify content" (http://en.wikipedia.org/wiki/Wiki). A wiki allows readers not only to read what is posted (as in a blog) but also to add or modify the content. In a real sense, then, a wiki is a living document that changes according to the thoughts about and written responses to information and ideas already posted. Although the most famous wiki is probably the online encyclopedia *Wikipedia*, there are many other uses for a wiki:

- Businesses use wikis to share information and to let employees add and correct information.
- Families, especially extended families, can use a wiki to post information on family members, family reunions, and important occasions.
- College students can use a wiki to share information, to work on collaborative writing assignments, and for other purposes related to their course work.
- Teachers use wikis to share curricular material, lesson plans, and assignment prompts and to encourage students to have online discussions about key topics in the discipline.

Word-Processing Software

Word processors such as Microsoft *Word, OpenOffice,* and *WordPerfect* have always performed four basic functions: inserting text, deleting text, copying and moving text, and formatting text. One important advantage that word processors offer is that they are a very forgiving technology. Changes are easy to make. This ability to revise texts easily opens up all kinds of possibilities for writers. Major revisions become easier because moving chunks of text from one place to another takes only a few simple clicks. Editing your text becomes easier because you can make minor changes with just a few keystrokes, instead of having to retype or handwrite the entire paper. In addition, other functions allow a writer or writers to edit a text and peer reviewers to make comments on it.

For more on effective document design and the use of visuals, see Chapter 18.

While all documents need to be well written, readers now expect word-processed documents to look professional as well. Formatting options include, but are not limited to, type fonts and sizes, tables, boxes, and visual effects such as numbered and bulleted lists. If a writer needs to include graphics, they can be inserted directly into the word-processed document. Options for designing a document continue to increase as technology improves.

ELECTRONIC ENVIRONMENTS   **Learning New Software Programs**

Use the "barter system" to discover how you and your classmates can help one another become more proficient with various software applications. Make a list of all the computer programs (software applications) you have used, and compare the list with those made by your friends. Are there programs you would like to learn to use? Are there programs you can show someone else how to use more effectively? Take advantage of any free time you have in the computer classroom or computer lab to help someone else—or ask for someone's help—in using unfamiliar programs that will aid your peers in their classes or on the job.

Writing Activity

Using Editing Features

Using whatever word-processing software you have available, investigate some of its editing features. Is there a "track-changes" feature? If so, try it. Is there a "comment" feature?

Working in teams of two, each student should write a paragraph or two on what you think is the most interesting or challenging feature of your word-processing program. Save your writing as an electronic file, and then share it with your teammate. Edit your teammate's file, using the track-changes and comment features.

Peer-Review Applications

As increasing numbers of writers use computer software to collaborate, the software keeps improving. The programs that writers use for this purpose fall into two distinct categories: collaborative tools built into standard word-processing programs, as discussed on page 492, and Web-based editing programs.

One type of Web-based editing program is a wiki—software that allows open editing of Web documents. A wiki is useful when writing teams work over distance and do not necessarily share the same computer operating systems or Web-browsing software. This flexibility makes wikis useful for student projects. You may also find *Google Docs* helpful; the "see revision history" feature allows collaborators to return to previous drafts and see what changes have been made to the file.

One Web-based program that allows peers to comment on your work is available to you as part of *Connect Composition,* which is available with this text. This software permits you and the other members of your assigned peer group to make comments about one another's writing and to view and respond to those comments.

Graphics Software

Today, it is possible to enhance your documents using a variety of visual information: tables, charts, graphs, photos, drawings, and other visual images. Although you can design some tables using a word-processing program and graphs and charts using a spreadsheet, other images need to be digitized (that is, put into a form that can be read by a computer). The easiest way to render many visuals in a digital format is to use a graphics program such as *PaintShop-Pro, Illustrator,* or *FreeHand.* If you are taking photographs yourself, you can use a digital camera. If you have a printed image, however, you can easily digitize it by using a scanner.

Once the image is digitized, you can manipulate it by using graphic editing software such as *PhotoShop.* Image-editing software allows you to change the size or resolution of the digital image, crop out unneeded elements, or change the contrast. However, image-editing software also makes it possible to change images inappropriately. Just because it is easy to change a photo does not mean that you *should* change it. The ease with which we can alter images raises serious ethical questions.

ELECTRONIC ENVIRONMENTS **Protecting Your Computer**

Letting someone use your computer can result in downloads and icons you don't want or need popping up on your screen or freezing your computer when you least expect it. Especially when your school computer is used for "recreational" purposes, files and programs can clog up your machine, causing resource issues that can mean an expensive trip to the tech support service. It's better to limit the number of people who use your computer and to resist the urge to use someone else's computer. Most colleges provide computer labs on campus, and the staff at the computer lab can usually help you with any problems that arise. In order to avoid corruption and loss of your data, be sure to back up all of your documents often. Besides saving documents to an external device, you can e-mail copies of documents to yourself.

FIGURE 17.1
The photograph in this
Newsweek cover has been
altered to show the late Princess
Diana walking next to the
former Kate Middleton, now
her daughter-in-law.

We have all seen examples of famous photographs that have been altered to include a person who was not in the original image or to change a person's appearance in some way. Some doctored photos might be considered funny, or may make some point, as in the *Newsweek* cover shown in Figure 17.1. The magazine cover shows Kate Middleton, recently married to Prince William of Great Britain, walking next to William's mother, Princess Diana, who died in a tragic traffic accident in 1997. The provocative image helps readers to imagine what might have been if Diana were still alive, the topic of an article within the magazine. Other images, however, are fabricated with the intention of misleading readers.

Desktop Publishing Software

Desktop publishing software such as *Quark* and *InDesign* allows writers to produce documents on their personal computers that are ready to be professionally printed. Although people who are comfortable with computers and have some training in layout and design can readily do some simple desktop publishing tasks, most people need training or practice in its use. Most desktop publishing programs are designed to construct short documents, and people often use them to prepare flyers, brochures, and newsletters. Such software gives you control over your document, including more precision in placing and manipulating images and more control over *leading* (the spacing between the lines) and *kerning* (the spacing between letters).

VISUAL *Thinking* | Using Image-Editing Software Ethically

If you are thinking of altering a photo, the first question you need to ask yourself has both ethical and legal implications: Do I have the right to change someone else's image without that person's permission? Unless you already own the image or have the owner's permission to use it and alter it, making changes may very well violate the creator's copyright. Because you will need the owner's permission to use the image, make sure you also get permission to change the image if you would like to do so. You may think that cropping out what you consider to be unnecessary parts of a photo might not be an issue, but the copyright owner might see the issue differently. Second, you need to be sure that by making changes you are not misrepresenting your subject or misleading your readers.

Presentation Software

At some point in their careers, almost all professionals make oral presentations. Sometimes professionals need to make a presentation to an audience of peers or higher-level employees. At other times they may need to do a sales presentation or present a report on a project in a more informal setting. Most professional presenters include some kind of visual component to help keep their audience's attention focused on the presentation. In the past, presenters often used large charts or posters, slides, or overhead transparencies. Now, most professionals use presentation software such as *PowerPoint* or *Prezi.* Presentation software allows you to format slides for a presentation easily and professionally. If you do not have access to *PowerPoint,* you can use *Impress,* a compatible, open-source (free) program that is part of the *OpenOffice* desktop software suite. *Google Docs,* another free Web-based presentation program, allows you to import *PowerPoint* files and easily share and collaborate on presentations online.

When using presentation software, you need to remember that your slides should complement your presentation, not be its focus. When you give a presentation, you want your listeners to focus primarily on what you say. If you use a graphic, the graphic should add to, not detract from, the content of the slide. Think of your bullet points as "talking points" or even as hyperlinks. What you actually say is the equivalent of clicking on a link in a Web page for more information. Take care not to use your slides as speaking notes for your presentation, and use only a limited amount of text on each slide.

For more on oral presentations and presentation software, see Chapter 16.

Technologies for Constructing Web Pages

Web pages are computer files that can be viewed using software called a **browser.** Examples of browsers are *Internet Explorer, Safari,* and *Firefox.* Web pages are coded using hypertext markup language (html). The html coding places information in the document that allows the browser to display the page properly. There are many ways to construct a Web page:

- Use the "save as a Web page" option in your word-processing software. This option has the advantage of being easy and is appropriate for very simple, straightforward Web pages.

- "Hand code" the hypertext markup language (html) (this means writing the actual mark-up tags in a text editor like *Notepad* or *TextEdit*). This option gives you more control over the design of your site, but it is time-consuming.

- Use an html editor like *Dreamweaver.* Because html has become increasingly complex, most professionals now use html editors.

- Use a Web-based page construction tool like *Google Sites*. Web-based tools usually have both visual (word processor–like) and html editor modes. They have the added advantage of instantly providing you with an opportunity to view your page exactly as it will appear online before you publish it.

For more on writing Web pages, see Appendix C.

Although you need to be sensitive to the look and feel of your Web pages, ultimately what will matter most is their content. The most important question will be, "How effectively am I getting my message across to the audience that I am targeting?"

Communicating with Design and Visuals

The two documents on this page combine written and visual elements. The poster at the top of the page was created with specialized graphics software, commonly available in university or college computing labs. The flyer below uses one of several widely available word-processing software programs.

Whether you are designing an elaborate poster or a simpler one, you can use the same standard design principles that are the focus of this chapter.

When you apply the principles of design, you need to consider your writing situation and make rhetorical choices. Here are some questions to consider:

- What are you trying to accomplish with your text, and how might design and images help you achieve your goals?
- What kind(s) of design elements and images might appeal to your audience?
- How will the available technology affect the design and image choices you make?

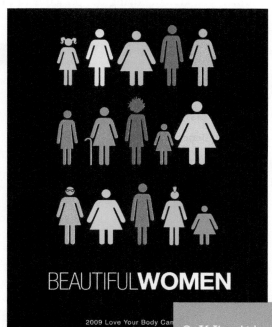

BEAUTIFUL**WOMEN**

2009 Love Your Body Can
www.nowfoundation.org

For a discussion of reading visuals critically, see Chapter 2.

Principles of Document Design

Whatever their rhetorical choices might be, writers can use the design principles of proximity, contrast, alignment, and repetition to craft more effective texts.

Proximity

Whenever you vary the amount of space between and around text elements so that related items are close to one another and unrelated items are separated from one another, you are employing the principle of **proximity**. For instance, consider the following three versions of a shopping list:

Version A	Version B	Version C
wireless network router	wireless network router	wireless network router
watercolors	wireless mouse	wireless mouse
English dictionary	blank CDs	blank CDs
blank CDs	English dictionary	English dictionary
pastels	thesaurus	thesaurus
thesaurus	book of quotations	book of quotations
wireless mouse	oil paints	oil paints
oil paints	watercolors	watercolors
book of quotations	pastels	pastels

Which list would make it easier for you to find these nine items in the shortest amount of time? Most people would probably find the third list easiest to use because the information is organized into three categories. We might label those categories "Computer Equipment," "Reference Books," and "Art Supplies." The spaces between the three categories help separate one group from another.

For some documents, such as brochures and newsletters, writers can also use borders and color to group common items and separate them from dissimilar items. (Color type may not be appropriate for many academic papers.)

As illustrated by the flyer advertising tutoring services at the beginning of this chapter, borders can also make sections of your written text stand out.

Contrast

Contrast is the design feature that sets some aspects of a page apart from others. You can use contrast by employing design features such as bold or italic type,

FIGURE 18.1
The Color Wheel

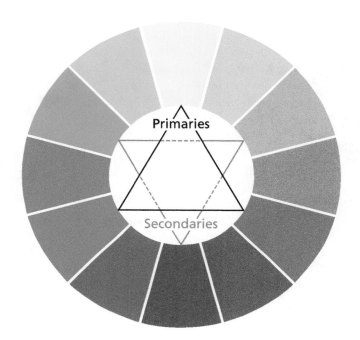

underlining, indentation, and color to indicate the hierarchy of importance among text elements and to create certain effects. For instance, you can use contrast to make headings at different levels of importance visually distinct.

Color can also add visual interest and contrast to your texts. If you use more than one color in a document, however, consult the color wheel shown in Figure 18.1 to determine which colors work best together.

As the color wheel indicates, the **primary colors** are red, yellow, and blue. The **secondary colors,** located at points halfway between the three primary colors on the wheel, are formed by combining primary colors: Red and yellow combine to make orange; blue and yellow combine to make green; and red and blue combine to make violet. Other colors are formed by combining primary colors with secondary colors.

Complementary colors are directly across from each other on the wheel— for instance, yellow and violet, red and green, and blue and orange. Placing complementary colors next to each other has the effect of *jarring* the reader. Placing adjacent colors together, on the other hand, has a *pleasing* effect. Pairing colors separated by two or three positions on the color wheel can have a *vivid* or *bold* effect.

Colors are sometimes considered to be warm and cool. *Warm* colors—red, orange, and yellow—are energetic and bold. *Cool* colors—green, blue, and violet—sometimes have a soothing, calming effect. Consider the poster shown in

FIGURE 18.3 A Poster Using Cool Colors

FIGURE 18.2 A Poster Using Warm Colors

Figure 18.2 above. Two warm colors, yellow and red, appear together in this poster. Because red and yellow are also both primary colors, the red text on the yellow background is especially eye-catching.

Now consider the poster shown in Figure 18.3. The background for this poster is in shades of blue and the turtle is mostly green, both cool colors that have a calming effect.

Alignment

Alignment is the design feature that provides consistency in the placement of text and graphical elements on a page. Writers also use alignment to indicate relationships among text elements. As readers of English, we are accustomed to text that is aligned on the left side of the page. Other alignments are possible, however, and you can vary alignments to achieve different effects.

Unless your text is very brief, your best choice for most academic writing is usually to align your text at the left margin to make it easier for your readers to process. For other contexts—for example, a professional report—you might align your text at both margins, or *justify* it, for a professional look; most books and periodicals make extensive use of this type of alignment. If your text is short and you want to achieve an eye-catching effect on a poster or a brochure, you might consider using right or center alignment.

Repetition (or Consistency)

When you use **repetition** or **consistency,** you apply the same design features to text elements with similar rhetorical functions, doing so consistently throughout the text. Note how the consistent use of bullets in front of the items in our shopping list sets them off even more for readers.

Shopping List

Computer Store	Bookstore	Art Supply Store
• Wireless network router	• English dictionary	• Oil paints
• Wireless mouse	• Thesaurus	• Watercolors
• Blank CDs	• Book of quotations	• Pastels

There are many ways to adhere to the principle of repetition or consistency in a document: following a documentation style accurately; designing to make text easier to read; using typefaces and fonts consistently; using a carefully developed heading structure; and using bullets, numbers, letters, graphics, and white space consistently.

USING A SINGLE DOCUMENTATION FORMAT

Chapter 20 provides guidelines for citing sources and formatting academic papers. Following a single, consistent format throughout your paper makes it easier for readers to determine the type of source you are citing, find it in your works-cited or references list, and consult it themselves if they choose to do so.

DESIGNING TO MAKE DOCUMENTS EASIER TO READ

The principles of proximity, contrast, alignment, and repetition aren't the only means that document designers use to help make texts more readable. The appropriate typeface (serif for print, sans serif for electronic), and the use of headings, bullets, and white space (any space that does not have text or graphics) all act to shape a document that is easier to read. While good design principles help readers read more quickly, they also enable readers to find information in long documents more easily.

USING TYPEFACES AND TYPE SIZES CONSISTENTLY

A **typeface** is a design for the letters of the alphabet, numbers, and other symbols. A **type font** consists of all the available styles and sizes of a typeface. For most academic documents, you should use no more than two typefaces. Typefaces belong to one of two general categories: serif and sans serif. A **serif** typeface has small strokes or extenders at the top and the bottom of the letter, and letters may vary in thickness. **Sans serif** (without serif) type has no small strokes or extenders, and the letters may have a uniform thickness. Usually, serif type is considered easier to read, especially in longer texts. For that reason, most newspapers, magazines, and books, including this one, use serif type for body text and sans serif type in headings and other kinds of displayed type, for contrast. Here are some examples of serif and sans serif type:

Serif Typefaces	Sample Sentence
Times New Roman	Carefully select the typeface that you use in your texts because the type can affect how easily readers can process your text.
Cambria	Carefully select the typeface that you use in your texts because the type can affect how easily readers can process your text.

Sans Serif Type	Sample Sentence
Arial	Carefully select the typeface that you use in your texts because the type can affect how easily readers can process your text.
Calibri	Carefully select the typeface that you use in your texts because the type can affect how easily readers can process your text.

All of the samples above are in 12-point type, which is a standard size for academic papers (1 point is equivalent to 1/72 of an inch). Notice that different typefaces take up different amounts of space. In some writing situations, space costs money; if so, you should consider a smaller face such as Times New Roman or Calibri over a larger one such as Cambria or Arial. In other situations, such as a slide presentation, you may need a larger face.

Most computer programs offer a wide range of typefaces to choose from, including unusual and ornate varieties. You should use these typefaces sparingly, however, because they can be difficult to read, especially for longer texts.

USING HEADINGS CONSISTENTLY

Headings signal the content of your paper and help readers understand its organization. When headings are worded and styled consistently, readers know which sections are at a higher or lower level of generality than others. You can use different sizes of type; different typefaces; and underlining, bold, and italic type to signal different levels of generality. Treat headings at the same level the same way—the same font size and style, the same location on the page, and the same capitalization.

You should also use parallel structure for all headings at a given level, as in the following example:

Parts of the City
    Shopping in the Business District
    Discovering the Residential Areas
    Enjoying the Waterfront
    Relaxing in the Parks

ELECTRONIC ENVIRONMENTS | **Integrating Visual and Graphical Elements**

Projects written for digital media should integrate visual and graphical elements in ways that make logical and rhetorical sense. Here are some suggestions:

- Choose appropriate color schemes. See the discussion of contrast on pages 498–500.

- Use *labels* and *captions* that clarify visual information.

- Use elements that *explain* and *create context* for images, video, and sound that you use. Use media that *support* your main ideas and arguments, rather than simply accompanying them.

- Be prepared to prove ownership and/or rights to the media you have incorporated.

USING BULLETS, NUMBERS, ROMAN NUMERALS, AND LETTERS CONSISTENTLY

You can use bullets, numbers, Roman numerals, or letters—or some combination of these elements—for a variety of purposes. Most frequently, they are used to indicate items in a list or an outline. Any of these markers can be effective for a short list of items, as shown on page 504.

If you are presenting steps in a process or items in a certain order, numbers are usually a more effective choice, and a combination of Roman numerals, letters, and numbers is standard in outlines. Bullets can be used to set off the items in a list effectively, although they can be problematic in longer lists because readers may have to count down the list of items if they need to discuss a particular point in the list. Of course, you should use bullets, numbers, Roman numerals, and/or letters consistently throughout a text.

For more on how to construct an outline, see Chapter 13.

USING WHITE SPACE CONSISTENTLY

White space is any part of a document that is not covered by type or graphics. The margins at the edges of a document are white space, as are the spaces between lines and above and below titles, headings, and other elements. Use white space consistently and intentionally throughout a document to help readers process information. You should always leave the same amount of space above headings at the same level. (If you are using MLA or APA style, you will need to follow the guidelines provided by the style you are following for margins and spacing—see Chapter 20.)

Bullets	Numbers (with Bullets)	Roman Numerals (with Letters)	Letters (with Numbers)
Car Models	Car Models	Car Models	Car Models
• Ford	1. Ford	I. Ford	A. Ford
• Taurus	• Taurus	A. Taurus	1. Taurus
• Focus	• Focus	B. Focus	2. Focus
• Mustang	• Mustang	C. Mustang	3. Mustang
• Chevrolet	2. Chevrolet	II. Chevrolet	B. Chevrolet
• Impala	• Impala	A. Impala	1. Impala
• Malibu	• Malibu	B. Malibu	2. Malibu
• Corvette	• Corvette	C. Corvette	3. Corvette

USING GRAPHICS EFFECTIVELY

Graphics can appear in academic papers as well as a number of other types of documents. The different kinds of graphics are discussed on pages 506–17. Generally, you should use the same kind of graphic to illustrate similar points or concepts. To achieve consistency, you need to consider the following:

- What you want to accomplish with each graphic
- What the overall look of each image is
- How the graphics are marked with labels and captions
- How you should introduce the graphics within your text

Select the kind of graphic that best accomplishes your purpose. To most effectively indicate the composition of a pizza, for example, you might choose a pie chart like the one in Figure 18.4, which shows the ingredients used to make a sausage and

FIGURE 18.4
A Pie Chart Showing the Composition of Pizza
Source: Math League[1]

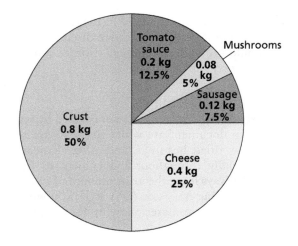

---

[1] Complete source information for the figures in this section can be found in the Credits on pages 633–36.

FIGURE 18.5
A Bar Graph
Presenting the
Same Data as the
Pie Chart

mushroom pizza weighing 1.6 kg. The sum of the numbers in the segments equals 1.6 kg, the weight of the pizza. The size of each slice shows us the fraction of the pizza made up from that ingredient. Figure 18.5 shows the same data but displayed as a bar graph—as you can tell, the bar graph does not explain or present the information as effectively as the pie chart does.

To present graphics effectively, follow these guidelines:

- **Give the graphics in your document a consistent look.** For example, use one-color or multicolor drawings rather than mixing one-color and multi-color drawings. If you use multiple colors, use the same ones in each graphic (for more on the use of color, see pages 498–500).

- **Introduce and explain each graphic.** Think about the meaning you intend to convey to readers with the graphic. If you do not do so, then it is possible that your readers will not understand why you have included the image. For the bar graph in Figure 18.5, for example, you should introduce it before it appears in your text ("This next graph shows how mushrooms make up the least amount, in weight, of the ingredients in a typical pizza") and follow the image with an explanation of how the bar graph connects to your topic.

- **Place graphics in a document strategically.** Place each visual as close as possible to the text discussion that refers to it. If you are following APA style, however, you have the option of placing visuals at the end of your paper.

Designing New Media

Most of the principles of good design for print texts still hold for new media with minor exceptions. For example, serif fonts appear to be more readable in print while sans serif fonts are more readable online. Whether you are crafting Web pages, *PowerPoint* presentations (meant to be presented as static presentations or as videos), or any other forms of new digital media, you should keep basic principles of effective design in mind.

There is a school of thought, championed by Web usability expert Jakob Neilsen, recommending that Web pages should err on the side of simplicity and avoid "bells and whistles." There are valid arguments for this point of view. However, remember that design is a rhetorical decision. How you design anything, whether it is a static Web page or a video, should be driven by your understanding of how to get your message across to your intended audience most effectively. Strike a balance between being engaging and eye-catching while not being overpowering.

The best way to achieve this visual balance is to think rhetorically. Is your target audience likely to respond most positively to a background of bright or muted colors? Will they most likely prefer to read long passages of text, or might they respond better to salient points in a bulleted list accompanied by a carefully scripted audio track?

Common Kinds of Visual Texts

When you consider adding a visual image or images to a document, you should do so to help accomplish your overall purpose. Do not add a visual just to have a picture or chart or table in your text; rather, use it as a way to support your thesis and achieve your goal for that piece of writing. Visuals such as tables, bar and line graphs, drawings, diagrams, maps, and cartoons can be effective tools.

Tables

Tables organize information in columns and rows for readers, helping them make comparisons between or among pieces of information or sets of numerical data. Consider, for instance, Table 18.1, which compares health care in seven countries based on quality, efficiency, access, length and health of people's lives, and expenditures per capita. The same data given in a paragraph would be difficult to compare. By reviewing the table, however, readers can easily make comparisons up and down rows, across columns, and across rows and columns. The table makes it easy to see that although the United States spends significantly more per person for health care, it clearly gets much less for its money.

USING TABLES EFFECTIVELY IN YOUR TEXTS

Word-processing programs will usually allow you to format information into tables automatically—consult the Help screen for the program you are using. Spreadsheet programs also allow you to construct tables.

To decide if a table will be appropriate for your purpose and audience, answer the following questions:

- Do I have data or information that could appear in tabular form?
- How would a table help me organize this data or information for readers?
- How can I organize the data or information in the table so that readers can find the information they need and make the comparisons I want them to see?

Bar and Line Graphs

Bar and line graphs provide another way to present numerical information to your readers. Both types of graphs plot data along a horizontal line (the x-axis) and a vertical line (the y-axis). Like a table, a **bar graph** allows readers to make comparisons.

Table 18.1 The United States Ranks Last Among Seven Countries on Health Sysytem Performance Based on Measures of Quality, Efficiency, Access, Equity, and Healthy Lives.

	AUS	CAN	GER	NETH	NZ	UK	US
OVERALL RANKING (2010)	3	6	4	1	5	2	7
Quality Care	4	7	5	2	1	3	6
Effective Care	2	7	6	3	5	1	4
Safe Care	6	5	3	1	4	2	7
Coordinated Care	4	5	7	2	1	3	6
Patient-Centered Care	2	5	3	6	1	7	4
Access	6.5	5	3	1	4	2	6.5
Cost-Related problem	6	3.5	3.5	2	5	1	7
Timeliness of Care	6	7	2	1	3	4	5
Efficiency	2	6	5	3	4	1	7
Equity	4	5	3	1	6	2	7
Long, Healthy, Productive Lives	1	2	3	4	5	6	7
Health Expenditures/ Capita, 2007	$3,357	$3,895	$3,588	$3,837*	$2,454	$2,992	$7,290

Note: * Estimate, Expenditure shown in $US PPP (Purchasing power parity.)
Source: Calculated by The Commonwealth Fund based on 2007 International Health Policy Survey; 2008 International Health Policy Survey of Sicker Adults, 2009 International Health Policy Survey of Primary Care Physicians; Commonwealth Fund Commission on a High Performance Health System National Scorecard; and Organization for Economic Cooperation and Development, OECD Health Data, 2009 (Paris: OECD, Nov. 2009). http://www.commonwealthfund.org/News/News-Releases/2010/Jun/US-Ranks-Last-Among-Seven-Countries.aspx

For example, the graph in Figure 18.6 on page 508 allows readers to compare actual or projected energy use in three different parts of the world over a period of fifty years.

Writing Activity

Analyzing Bar and Line Graphs

Analyze the bar and line graphs on page 508 by responding to the following questions:

- What are the components of the graphs?
- How has the writer used color in the bar graph?
- How has the writer organized the data in the graphs?
- What would happen if the writer reversed the *x*-axis and the *y*-axis in either of the graphs?
- What stories do these graphs tell?

FIGURE 18.6
Bar Graph
Showing Energy
Consumption in
the World from
1970 to 2020

Source: U.S. Government Energy Information Administration

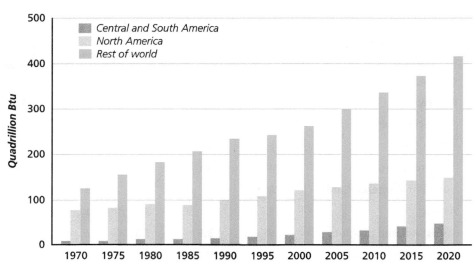

FIGURE 18.7
A Line Graph
Illustrating the
Relationship
between Mileage
and Value

Source: Math League

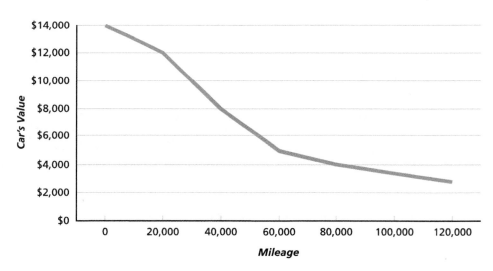

A **line graph** shows readers a change or changes over a period of time. Figure 18.7 is a line graph illustrating the relationship between a car's mileage and its value.

USING GRAPHS EFFECTIVELY IN YOUR TEXTS

You can use bar or line graphs that have been constructed by others in your project as long as you give proper credit to the source. You can also use a spreadsheet program, like *Excel,* or *PowerPoint* to construct graphs from data you have discovered or generated on your own. Consider using an online graphing site, such as "Create a Graph" (http://nces.ed.gov/nceskids/Graphing/), hosted by the National Center for Educational Statistics. If you do not have access to a computer, however, you can construct the graph yourself, using graph paper. If you use data from a source to construct your graph, you need to give credit to that source.

To use bar and line graphs effectively in your texts, consider the following questions:

See Chapter 20 for help with citing sources for your data.

- Do I have sets of numerical data that I would like readers to compare?
- Do I have data that indicate a change over a period of time?
- What could a bar or line graph add to my text?
- If I am using a bar graph, how should I organize it?
- How should I explain the graph in my text?
- Do I have access to the technology (a color printer, for example) that will enable me to construct the graph and present it effectively?

Charts

A **chart** is a visual text that allows you to show the relationships among different items or among the parts of a whole. Consider Figure 18.8, which shows what various stain colors look like on oak. Notice how the chart holds one variable constant—the kind of wood—so that readers can make consistent comparisons among stain colors.

Two kinds of charts that are very common in academic writing, as well as in writing for other areas, are pie charts and flowcharts. A **pie chart** shows readers the components that make up the whole of something. Pie charts, like the one shown in Figure 18.4 (page 504), are ideal for showing the percentages of each part of an item.

A **flowchart** shows how a process works. Many readers find it easier to understand processes when they see flowcharts. Figure 18.9 on page 510 illustrates the complex process of launching a water rocket. Notice that the chart is also a kind of *decision tree,* with yes or no responses that direct readers' progress through the chart.

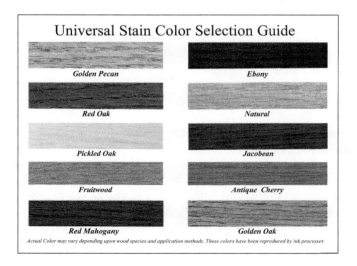

FIGURE 18.8
Chart Showing Wood Stains

FIGURE 18.9
Flowchart That Is
Also a Decision
Tree
Source: Gary
Ensmenger

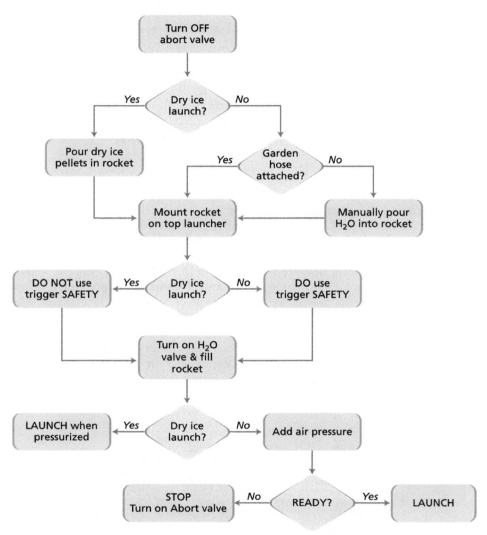

**H₂O Rocket Launcher Flowchart
(when alternative propellants are available)**

USING CHARTS EFFECTIVELY IN YOUR TEXTS

As with graphs, you can use charts that have been produced by others in your paper as long as you give proper credit to the source. You can construct your own charts the old-fashioned way—drawing them by hand—or you can use a drawing program. Spreadsheet programs and *PowerPoint* also enable you to produce charts and import them into your paper.

To use charts effectively in your texts, consider the following questions:

- Is there a process, a key relationship, or the components of something within my text that I could illustrate with a chart?

- How will the chart help my audience better understand a particular point in my paper?
- How can I organize the chart so that readers can see patterns in the information?
- Do I have access to the technology (a color printer, for example) that will enable me to construct the chart and present it effectively?

Photographs

Photographs are common in our lives. We see them daily in magazines and newspapers, as well as on Web sites, billboards, and posters. Because photographs are filled with details, a single photograph can replace hundreds or even thousands of words. Imagine how difficult it would be to describe your best friend's physical appearance to a stranger using words alone. On the other hand, a photograph could not give your reader a detailed view of your friend's personality.

Consider two well-known photographs of Abraham Lincoln. The first Figure 18.10) portrays Lincoln with his son Tad. The second (Figure 18.11) portrays Lincoln with Allan Pinkerton, who headed the Union spying operations, and Major General John A. McClernand. A writer could use either photograph to illustrate what Lincoln's life was like during the Civil War years, which corresponded with his years in the White House. The photograph that shows Lincoln with his son gives readers a sense of his personal life. It does not tell the whole story, however, including his love for Tad and his other two children—Willie and Robert—and his heartbreak when his favorite child, Willie, died from typhoid fever in 1862, at age eleven. These are details that a writer would include in the text. Similarly, the photograph of Lincoln with Pinkerton and McClernand does not give a complete picture of his working relationship with them; for that, words are needed.

FIGURE 18.10 Abraham Lincoln with His Son Tad

FIGURE 18.11 Lincoln with Allan Pinkerton (left) and Major General John A. McClernand

Writing Activity

Considering Photos

With your classmates, prepare a list of six well-known places, people, or objects. Bring one photograph of each place, person, or object to class. Compare and contrast your photos with those that other students have brought by responding to the following questions:

- What does each photograph reveal about its subject? What does each photograph leave out?
- What does each photograph reveal about the person who took it?
- How could you use each photograph in a piece of writing?
- What purposes could each photograph have in a given type of writing?

USING PHOTOGRAPHS EFFECTIVELY IN YOUR WRITING PROJECTS

With the advent of inexpensive digital photography, it is easy to store, retrieve, manipulate, and send photographs. Although it is easy to integrate digital photographs into your documents, note that low-resolution photos are grainy when printed on paper. *Resolution* refers to the number of pixels (or dots) in the image. High-resolution photos have more pixels per inch than low-resolution photos. The following table gives the recommended resolutions (300 dots per inch) for several photograph sizes:

Size of Photo	Recommended Resolution for Printed Photograph
2" × 2"	600 × 600 pixels
2" × 3"	600 × 900 pixels
4" × 6"	1200 × 1800 pixels
5" × 7"	1500 × 2100 pixels

In your written texts, you may use photographs that have been produced by others if you give proper credit to the source of the photograph. If you are publishing the photograph on a Web site or in some other print or electronic medium, you will need to obtain permission to use it from the copyright holder unless it is in the public domain. If a photograph is in the **public domain,** no one owns the copyright for the image, and you may use it without obtaining permission. You may find photos available for public use in Creative Commons (http://creative commons.org/).

To decide when and how to use photographs in your writing, consider the following questions:

- What kind of photograph will most effectively support my purpose?
- What impact will a photograph have on my text?

- How will my audience respond to each of the photographs that I am considering?
- Where might I place the photograph in my text? Why?
- Do I need permission to use a particular photograph?
- How might I ethically manipulate the photograph to use in my text? For example, can I crop, or cut out, part of the photograph that includes extraneous material?
- If the photograph is an electronic document, is the resolution high enough for use in a print document?
- Will the technology that is available to me accurately reproduce the photograph?

Drawings

Like photographs, **drawings** enable readers to visualize a subject. Drawings are common in technical and scientific writing because writers in those fields frequently need to give readers detailed descriptions of objects, many of which are so small or so far away that it is difficult to see and photograph them. Consider the drawing of a cell nucleus in Figure 18.12. Notice how this drawing includes **labels**—words that name its parts. What is missing from this drawing, however, is an explanation of the functions of the nucleus and its many parts. Only words can provide that information. In other words, the visual and verbal elements in a text should serve to complement and supplement each other.

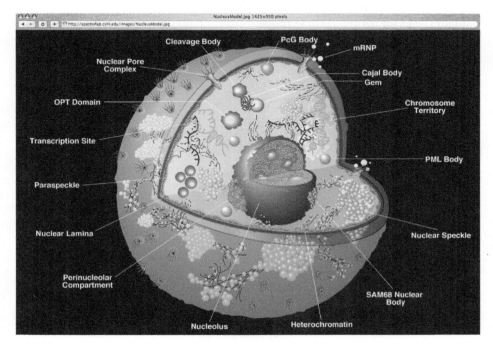

FIGURE 18.12
Drawing of a Cell Nucleus
Source: Spector Lab

Writing Activity

Considering Drawings

Find an example of a drawing in one of your textbooks, in a newspaper or magazine, or on a Web site. Discuss how successfully the text and drawing you have found work together to achieve the writer's purpose.

USING DRAWINGS EFFECTIVELY IN YOUR TEXTS

You can produce a drawing by hand. If you have access to a scanner, you can then scan your finished drawing, generating a computer file. Or you can use a drawing program that allows you to generate a digital file directly on your computer. If you pick up a drawing from a source for use in your paper, you will need to give proper credit to that source. If you are publishing the drawing, you will need to obtain permission to use it.

To use drawings effectively in your texts, consider the following questions:

- What in my text could I illustrate with a drawing?
- How could a drawing meet the needs of my audience?
- Can I use an existing drawing, or do I need to construct one?
- Do I need permission to use an existing drawing?
- Do I have access to software that I can use to construct the drawing?

Diagrams

Diagrams are drawings that illustrate and explain the arrangement of and relationships among parts of a system. Venn diagrams, for example, consist of circles representing relationships among sets. Consider the Venn diagram in Figure 18.13, which illustrates how sustainable development depends on relationships among the environment, the economy, and equity. Of course, this diagram by itself does not explain the exact nature of these relationships. To do that, a writer needs to define

FIGURE 18.13
Venn Diagram
Illustrating
Sustainable
Development
Source: Manchester
Development Education
Project

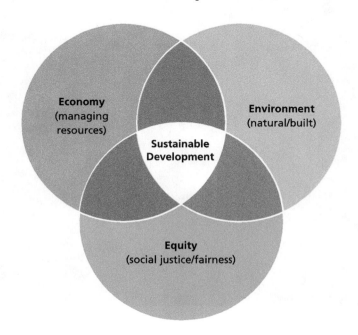

each of the terms in the diagram—*environment, economy, equity*—and then explain how they interact to form sustainable development.

USING DIAGRAMS EFFECTIVELY IN YOUR WRITING

As with drawings, you can either construct a diagram by hand and scan it or use a drawing program. If you use a diagram from a source, you will need to give proper credit to that source. If you are publishing the diagram, you will need to obtain permission to use it.

To use diagrams effectively in your writing, consider the following questions:

- What in my text could I illustrate with a diagram?
- What effect will the diagram have on my readers?
- Can I use an existing diagram, or do I need to construct one?
- Do I need permission to use an existing diagram?
- Do I have access to software that I can use to construct the diagram?

Maps

Cartographers use **maps** to record and show where countries, cities, streets, buildings, colleges, lakes, rivers, and mountains are located in the world or in a particular part of it. Of course, consumers of maps use them to find these places. We use printed or downloaded maps to drive from one location to another. On the evening news, we see maps showing where events take place and what kind of weather is occurring in neighboring states and countries. We even use maps to help us visualize fictional places such as the territories described in the *Lord of the Rings* trilogy (Figure 18.14).

FIGURE 18.14
Map from the *Lord of the Rings* Trilogy

FIGURE 18.15
Neanderthal
Range Map
Source: Richard G. Klein

Maps are used in many different academic disciplines, including sociology, political science, history, and geology. Anthropologists use maps to illustrate where species have lived, as in Figure 18.15, which shows the range of the Neanderthals—an extinct species of humans—in Europe.

Writing Activity

Analyzing Maps

Choose one of the two maps in Figures 18.14 and 18.15 or a map in one of your textbooks and respond to the following questions:

- What is the purpose of this map?
- What additional information would make the map more useful?
- What would a writer need to explain to readers so that readers could use the map effectively?
- How does the map adhere to the principles of proximity and contrast (see pages 498–500)?
- How might the captions for the maps be revised to be more informative?

USING MAPS EFFECTIVELY IN YOUR TEXTS

In most cases, you will need to use maps from other sources, giving credit and obtaining permission to use them if necessary. To use maps effectively in your texts, consider the following questions:

- What information could a map offer to my audience?
- If there is an existing map that will serve my purpose, do I need permission to use it?

- If I have to draw my own map, what tools do I need?
- What data do I need to construct the map?
- What information do I need to include in the caption for the map?
- What technology do I need to present the map effectively?

Cartoons

To find evidence of how much people enjoy cartoons, you need only walk the halls of any office building on your campus. You will notice that people display cartoons on their office doors, cubicle walls, and bulletin boards. **Cartoons** make humorous—and sometimes poignant—observations about people and events. Consider the cartoon in Figure 18.16. One feature of most cartoons is that their visual and verbal elements complement each other. The visual part of the cartoon gives the topic a human or humanlike face, and the verbal part offers a specific comment.

USING CARTOONS EFFECTIVELY IN YOUR TEXTS

In most cases, when you use cartoons in your text, they probably will have been produced by other people. Make sure that you are able to give the source information for any cartoon that you include. If you are publishing your project online or in another medium, you will need to obtain permission to use the cartoon from the copyright holder. If you draw your own cartoon, you will need to do so by hand and then scan it to produce a computer file that you can incorporate into your text.

To use cartoons effectively in your texts, consider the following questions:

- How will a cartoon support my purpose?
- Given that readers usually associate cartoons with humor or satire, how might humor or satire affect my readers?
- Do I need permission to use a published cartoon, or is it in the public domain?

FIGURE 18.16
Cartoon
Reprinted by permission of Randy Glasbergen

"My presentation lacks power and it has no point.
I assumed the software would take care of that!"

Using Visuals Rhetorically

See Chapter 1 for a discussion of audience, purpose, and the rhetorical situation.

As you consider using visuals, think about using them rhetorically to achieve a specific purpose with a specific audience.

Considering Your Audience

Readers are more likely to expect visuals in some genres than in others. Lab reports, for example, commonly include tables and graphs. This principle applies to any visuals that you plan to use in your writing. As you consider using a particular visual, ask yourself the following questions:

- Does my audience need this visual, or is it showing something that my readers already know very well? What information might a visual add?
- How will this audience respond to this visual?
- What other visual might they respond to more favorably?
- Will this audience understand the subtleties of this visual?
- How do I need to explain this visual for this particular audience?

Considering Your Purpose

As we saw in Parts 2 and 3 of this book, you will have a general purpose for any writing project—to record and share experiences, to explore, to inform, to analyze, to convince or persuade, to evaluate, to explain causes and effects, to solve problems, or to analyze creative works. To the extent possible, every part of your paper should contribute to that purpose. Any phrase, clause, sentence, paragraph, or section of your paper that does not support your purpose needs to be revised or deleted. The same principle applies to any visual that you are considering. Diagrams, for example, most often have an informative purpose. A cartoon, in contrast, is almost

FIGURE 18.17
A Photograph from the Web Page for Feed the Children, a Charitable Organization

always humorous but often makes a statement. Photographs are often used to make the rhetorical appeal of *pathos,* as they can evoke an emotional response in the reader. Figure 18.17, for example, is a photograph from the Web page for Feed the Children, a charitable organization.

Before using any visual, ask yourself these questions:

- How will this visual support my purpose?
- How might this visual detract from my purpose?
- Why is this visual necessary?
- What other visual or visuals might support my purpose more effectively?

Using Visuals Responsibly

Just as you need to consider the purpose for using any visual, you also need to consider how using visuals responsibly will enhance your credibility as a writer.

Permissions

Whenever you plan to use a visual, you need to make certain that you have permission to use it. If you have constructed a table, graph, or chart from data that you have gathered, then permission is not needed. If you use a visual prepared by someone else, or use data from a source to produce a visual, you should always give credit to your source, even if the visual or data are from a government source or are in the public domain (that is, outside of copyright and available to anyone who wants to use it). For most academic papers, it is usually not necessary to request permission to use a visual. However, if your writing will be made available to an audience beyond your classroom, including online, you will need to ask for permission to use any visual from a source that you include. Some visuals that you find on the Web are in the public domain, but if you are in doubt about a particular visual, contact the Web manager of the site where you found it to ask what permissions are required.

The subjects of photographs have certain rights as well. If you take a photograph of a friend, you need to ask your friend for permission to use it if your project will have an audience beyond the two of you. If your friend does not want the photo used in a course paper or on a Web site, you are ethically and legally obligated to honor those wishes. To be certain that there is no misunderstanding, ask your friend to sign an agreement granting you permission to use the photo for clearly specified purposes. If you later want to use the photo for other purposes, ask your friend to sign another agreement. But you should never put undue pressure on someone to sign such an agreement.

Distortions

Just as you should not distort quoted or paraphrased material (see Chapter 20), you should also be careful not to distort the content and the physical properties of any visuals you include in your paper. Sometimes the data in charts and graphs is misrepresented—consider, for example, Figure 18.18, which shows the pass rates for students in English 101. Clearly, the pass rate improved by year 3 and remained fairly stable afterward. *If* this chart maker wants to show a dramatic improvement in the pass rate, then it makes sense to use a scale that runs from 75% to 95%. On the other hand, a full scale (from 0 to 100%) makes the improvement in pass rates much less obvious and dramatic, as shown in Figure 18.19.

There may be times, however, when some forms of distortion can be helpful and ethical. For instance, consider the two maps shown in Figure 18.20. The first one shows the forty-eight contiguous states as they typically appear on a map. Such maps show the relative sizes—measured in square miles—of the states. The second map is designed to show the distribution of wire-service news stories about certain cities and states. Notice that New York and Washington, DC, get lots of attention in wire-service news stories. This deliberately distorted image helps to make a serious point about the news.

Writing Activity

D o a Web search to find a distorted map that presents information in a way that you think is interesting and useful. Write a brief explanation of why the distorted map is useful to share with friends who might also find the map interesting.

FIGURE 18.18
Chart That Distorts
Information

FIGURE 18.19
Chart That
Presents the Same
Information
Honestly

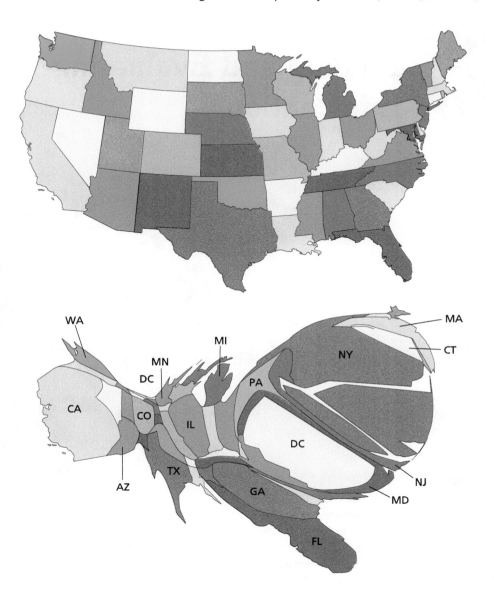

FIGURE 18.20
Regular Map of the United States and Distorted Map That Illustrates a Point about the News
Source: Maps by M. E. J. Newman and M. T. Gastner

19

Finding and Evaluating Information

In the past, **research** meant searching through actual library stacks. Because of the almost instant access to a wealth of sources that technology makes possible, finding information today may appear to be much easier than it was in the past, but the reality is that it is simply different. Although you can still find books and print journals on library shelves, and they are still useful resources, today researchers often start a project with a search of the library's online catalog or database or a search of the World Wide Web.

Before the advent of electronic sources, researchers usually assumed that they could generally rely on the accuracy of the printed texts found in college or university libraries. Although those sources still exist, anyone can now publish anything on the Web or more easily self-publish content as a book. So much information is available on the Internet that it is vital to focus your search as carefully as possible so that you turn up only the most relevant sources. It is also more critical than ever for

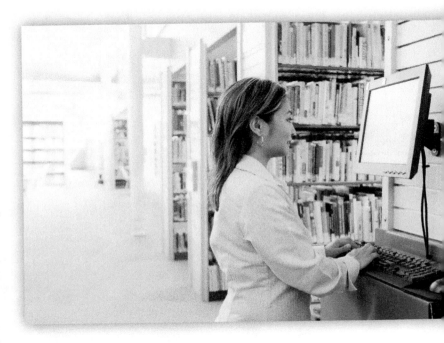

you to evaluate the quality of what you do find.

Also, many researchers go out into the field to conduct other kinds of research. Depending on the project and the discipline, you might gather information through observation or experimentation. If you are working with human subjects, you might use interviews and surveys.

Conducting Effective Library and Web-Based Research: An Example

You already have plenty of experience in conducting research. Have you ever used a classmate's opinion of an author or a band to influence a friend to read that author's book or to see that band? If so, you were using the results of a type of field research called **interviewing** as evidence.

For more on field research, see pages 541–46.

The research that you do for any writing task is a rhetorical act. That is, you conduct research for a specific purpose, with a particular audience in mind, in a specific writing situation. Consider how you might approach the following assignment for a psychology class:

> Respond to this question: Why do adolescent males (and sometimes females) change their behavior when they join a gang? Based on your research, write a 3-to 4-page paper that provides compelling reasons for this behavior, providing specific evidence to support your position.

This assignment is fairly straightforward: Your purpose is to fulfill this assignment, and your audience is your psychology professor. The assignment even provides you with a **research question.** Your answer to this question will form the thesis of your research paper. But where will you find the evidence that will help you decide on your answer to this question—your thesis—and support that thesis? How will you locate it? How will you be able to tell if the evidence is credible and reliable?

Often it will be your responsibility to formulate a research question. When you find yourself in that situation, keep these principles in mind:

- Keep the question focused. For example, "What caused the Civil War?" is a huge question. However, "Why did Confederate forces fire on Fort Sumter on April 12, 1861?" is much more manageable.

- Make sure you will be able to get good information on your question. You may be interested in the role Venezuelan oil plays in the U.S. economy, especially from the Venezuelan perspective. However, if you discover that most of the information for this topic is in Spanish and you can't read that language, you will probably not be able to go forward with this question.

- Consider whether you can find an adequate number of resources to answer your question. For example, are the people you hope to interview available and willing to speak with you? Can you really arrange to do field research at some far-off location?

Library Research

Usually the first place to look when conducting research to answer a question is the reference section of your college library. There you will find sources such as general and specialized encyclopedias and dictionaries. For example, you might start your research for the psychology paper about gangs and adolescents by defining "adolescent," perhaps by looking it up in a medical dictionary:

> A young person who has undergone puberty but who has not reached full maturity; a teenager.
>
> —American Heritage Medical Dictionary®

Based on this definition, you determine that your research will focus on males and females between the ages of thirteen and nineteen. You decide to conduct a search in your online college library catalog. (Librarians are also available online in many libraries.) Almost every library has a reference librarian, and he or she is a truly useful resource. It is always helpful to discuss your research question with the reference librarian. He or she will probably be able to point you to some reference sources that might be useful.

All college libraries have a book **catalog** of some kind. In addition to the book catalog, your library probably subscribes to various electronic **databases** such as *Academic Search Complete*. Databases are indexes of articles that are available in periodicals; many also provide complete texts of the articles themselves. To look for articles in popular or trade magazines, for instance, you would search one database, while you would use another database to find articles in academic journals, and still another database for articles in newspapers.

ELECTRONIC ENVIRONMENTS   **Using Academic Databases**

The following are popular academic databases that can help you with research in different disciplines. Keep in mind that the names of academic databases do change; your reference librarian can help you find a database that will be useful for your particular project.

- *Academic* Search *Complete*
- *ERIC*

- *General Science Index*
- *Google Scholar*
- *Humanities Index*
- *JSTOR*
- *LexisNexis Academic*
- *Social Science Index*

SEARCHING A LIBRARY CATALOG

For any electronic search, you need to come up with an appropriate word or phrase, or **keyword,** that will be found in the kind of source you are seeking. To find useful keywords for a search of your library's catalog, it is often a good idea to start by consulting the *Library of Congress Subject Headings (LCSH),* a book that lists subject headings in use in most library systems. It will tell you how subject areas are categorized in the library and will therefore help you come up with search terms that will turn up books on your subject.

Note that the search term "gang behavior" is just one of a range of possibilities. It is often useful to use a number of search terms. You can also pull up more information on each entry and examine other relevant references that might be useful to your research.

Here is a research hint: Whenever you find a book on your research subject in your college library, spend a few minutes examining the *other* texts that surround the one you just located. Books about the same topic are shelved together, so once you find one book on the topic you are researching, many others will be nearby.

SEARCHING AN ONLINE DATABASE

Now that you have several books that you might want to examine for information on gang behavior, you should also search one or more of the databases your college's library subscribes to. A search of a typical database—in this case, *Academic Search Complete*—using the keywords "male" and "gang" might turn up abstracts (summaries) of articles like this one:

> "GANG WORLD". By: Papachristos, Andrew V.. Foreign Policy, Mar/Apr2005 Issue 147, p48–55, 8p, 3c, 1bw; Abstract: The article discusses the rise of street **gangs** around the world. The image of a young, minority, "innercity," **male gang** member is transmitted, exploited, and glamorized across the world. The increasing mobility of information via cyberspace, films, and music makes it easy for **gangs, gang** members, and others to get information, adapt personalities, and distort **gang** behaviors. Two images of street **gangs** dominate the popular consciousness—**gangs** as posses of drug-dealing thugs and, more recently, **gangs** as terrorist organizations. Although the media like to link **gangs** and drugs, only a small portion of all **gangs** actually deal in them. Similarly, the name Jose Padilla is inevitably followed by two epithets—al Qaeda terror suspect and street **gang** member. The link between the two is extremely misleading. One of the most urgent challenges for policymakers is distinguishing between the average street **gang** and groups that operate as criminal networks. Globalization and street **gangs** exist in a paradox: **Gangs** are a global phenomenon not because the groups themselves have become transnational organizations, but because of the recent hypermobility of **gang** members and their culture. Individual **gangs** flaunt their Internet savvy by posting complex Web sites, including some with password protection. As the global economy creates a growing number of disenfranchised groups, some will inevitably meet their needs in a **gang.** INSETS: Want to Know More?; When **Gangs** Go Bad.; (*AN 16195307*)
> 📄 **HTML Full Text** 📄 **PDF Full Text** (1.7 MB)

Note that the abstract indicates that this article deals with "gang culture," so this one seems especially promising (and because the full text of the article is available online, you can print the essay with a click of your mouse). Note also that *Academic Search Complete,* the search database we used for this search, may not be available in all libraries. We use it here to illustrate a possible search database; your college or university will provide a similar search database.

Another online database that many colleges offer their students is *JStor*, which indexes a wide range of academic journals (about 175). Figure 19.1 shows the first part of a search using the keyword "adolescent gangs."

Several of the articles listed by *JStor* appear to be potentially useful. Since they are available as full-text articles, you can click on the title and immediately check them for relevance. Generally, you should also look for recent articles because their information will be more up to date.

FIGURE 19.1
Search of the *JStor*
Database Using
the Search Term
"Adolescent
Gangs"

Research on the Web

You continue your search on the Web, which is the largest part of the global network of computers known as the Internet. The Web is hyperlinked, which means that one useful site will often provide links to many more.

If you have conducted Web searches, you probably quickly learned that different **search engines,** software programs that find sites on the Web, locate different information—that the results provided by Google (www.google.com), Yahoo!

(www.yahoo.com), and Bing (www.bing.com) often vary. You may also have used a "meta-search" engine such as Dogpile (www.dogpile.com), which searches *other* search engines, so the results you retrieve are from a range of searches. Usually, it is a good idea to use several different search engines.

A search of the Web using Google and the keywords "gang behavior," for example, turns up over 18 *million* hits. This result provides an unmanageable number of choices. The best way to limit the number of hits that a search engine returns is to narrow what the search engine is looking for. You can narrow your search easily on Google by enclosing multiple keywords within quotation marks so that the search engine looks for them when they appear together as a phrase. Simply by enclosing the search term "gang behavior" in quotation marks, you can limit the result to 39,400 hits, for example. This helps, but 39,400 options are still far too many. As a next step, you might qualify the search even more. If you are looking for information about female gangs, for example, you might try searching with the keywords "gang behavior" and "female." Doing so gives you a list of 17,900 hits. Although that number is better, it's still not really good enough. You can then modify the search even further by trying this combination of keywords: "gang behavior" and "adolescent female." This time the response, shown in Figure 19.2, is only 234 hits, a more man-

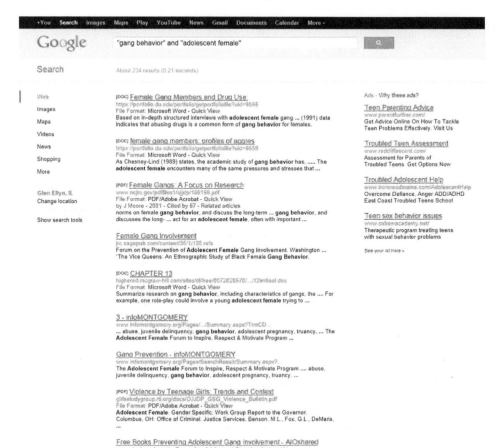

FIGURE 19.2
Result of a Search Using the Google Search Engine and the Keywords "Gang Behavior" and "Adolescent Female"

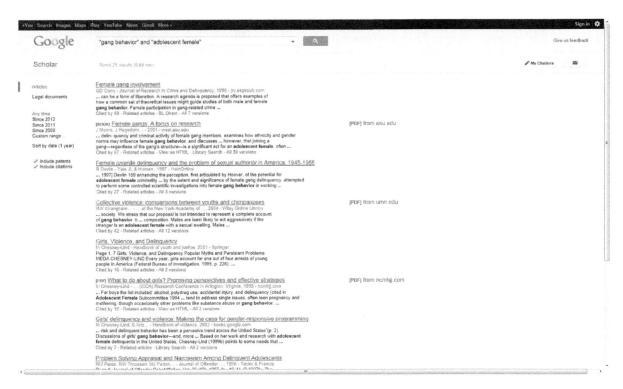

FIGURE 19.3 Result of a Search Using the Google Scholar Search Engine and the Keywords "Gang Behavior" and "Adolescent Female"

ageable number. By closely defining your search terms and using them in combination, you can narrow your search and come up with the best possible online sources.

One other option you might consider if you are working on an academic paper is Google Scholar, which searches only scholarly Web sites. Searching Google Scholar using the keywords "gang behavior" and "adolescent female" gives you the result shown in Figure 19.3. You can also search for images on the Web. Using an image search on Google, for example, you may find a photo of gang activity that you can use to illustrate your paper.

Writing Activity

Developing a List of Questions and a Research Plan

For one of your current writing projects, develop a list of intriguing research questions. These are questions that require complex answers, not just facts. After each question, indicate where you would go to find answers (your library's online catalog? a search engine?) and what you would do there.

Selecting Sources

Whenever you do research, you will encounter a wide range of sources. You have to determine what sources will be useful to you for your particular writing situation. We will outline a number of sources here and then discuss how you might *evaluate* the various kinds of information you locate.

The kind(s) of sources that you select depend on what you are trying to learn. You would not, for example, expect to find in books information on events that took place less than a year ago. For that kind of information, you would need to look for publications that publish more current information.

Each type of source has advantages and disadvantages, so it is usually best to use a variety of sources.

Books

Book from Oxford University Press

Books such as the one shown here have historically been a researcher's first choice for much academic research because they are almost always well researched and contain statistical information that has been validated. However, even books have to be subjected to more intensive questioning these days because it is now relatively easy for just about anyone to publish a book. Books in an academic library, however, have been carefully evaluated by librarians and are usually reputable. One disadvantage of the research you will find in a printed book is that it often takes several years to write, review, and publish a book—so the information often is not as current as that contained in other sources.

Academic Journals

The New York Times newspaper

Academic essays appear in **journals** such as the *American Journal of Psychiatry*. Journals are most often sponsored by universities. Essays in most academic journals are written by scholars in the field and are "peer reviewed," which means that other scholars have read the article, commented on it, and made a judgment about its validity and usefulness. Journal articles are usually well-researched. Also, academic essays usually come with a "works cited" or "references" page, which lists all of the sources the writer used. Often, these lists point to useful sources about the topic you are working on.

For example, your library search focusing on adolescent males and females and gangs might turn up this essay, published in the *American Journal of Psychiatry:* "What Happens to 'Bad' Girls? A Review of the Adult Outcomes of Antisocial Adolescent Girls" by Kathleen A. Pajer, M.D., M.P.H. In addition to the essay, you find a "works cited" section with eighty-three entries, references to other journal articles and books that Dr. Pajer used in her text. These will lead you to more information about teenage gangs.

Newspapers

Newspapers, especially those with a national focus such as the *New York Times,* are considered reliable sources. Often, local papers will get their information from national sources.

LexisNexis is a database that indexes newspapers, other periodicals, and a wide range of other kinds of documents. A *LexisNexis* search for newspaper articles on a topic will provide you with recent information. You need to remember, however, that while newspapers are very current sources, because they are following stories in progress, sometimes the information they provide may change as more complete information on a story becomes available.

Popular Magazines

Magazines, especially newsmagazines such as *Time* and *Newsweek,* have a broad perspective on national issues and often provide useful background and historical information, as well as their own editorial commentary. Many make the contents of the print magazine available online. Often the magazine will offer additional content online, as well as forums for readers to respond to articles and to one another.

A search at Time.com, for example, turns up possible sources for your paper on gangs, as shown in Figure 19.4.

Newsweek
Magazine

FIGURE 19.4
Search of the
Time.com Web Site
Using the Keyword
"Gangs"
From the Time.com
website, September 4,
2007. Copyright © 2007
Time Inc. Used under
license.

Trade or Commercial Magazines

Trade or commercial/professional magazines, such as *Business Traveler*, have a specific audience, which consists of the members of a group with a common interest or profession. If the magazine is published for a professional organization, a portion of the members' dues usually pays for the magazine. Other magazines are for-profit publications that serve the industry as a whole. These publications often are written specifically for their target audience. They also can provide lots of information from an insider's perspective, so you may need to be very familiar with the field.

Business Traveler
Magazine

Public Affairs Magazines

Magazines that focus on public affairs, such as *Foreign Affairs,* generally publish articles on national issues, so they are useful sources for papers about these issues. Their essays are usually thoughtfully researched and documented.

Specialty Magazines

Magazines about travel, different regions of the country, cooking, and other specialized topics are often useful if you are searching for the kinds of information they provide. Examples include *Arizona Highways*. Others, such as *BusinessWeek*, cater to a specific field and often have useful statistics and other types of information related to that field.

Foreign Affairs
Magazine

The Internet

The Internet, especially the Web, offers a huge range of information, all available very quickly. As you will see on pages 534–41, it sometimes takes a bit of work to figure out exactly who controls a Web site and the information it presents, so information you obtain from the Web must be used with caution.

It is extremely difficult to generalize about the Internet because it remains a dynamic, ever-evolving source of information and, often, misinformation. Any attempt to categorize Internet sources is, at best, a rough estimate, but we can point to at least five different kinds of online resources.

Arizona Highways
Magazine

- **Web sites that serve as what used to be called the "home page" of an organization.** Most of these are now much more complex and sophisticated than they were in the early years of the Web, but they may very well be the first place you choose to look for information about any organization or group. Although the quality of the information you find on these Web sites may be good, you need to remember that because they are maintained by the organization itself, they tend to give a very positive view of the organization.

- **Web sites that provide information to the general public.** Many of these Web sites are maintained by government agencies. Their subject matter and complexity vary depending on whether they are constructed and maintained by local municipalities, state agencies, or the federal government. In most instances,

FIGURE 19.5
Home Page for the
Internal Revenue
Service

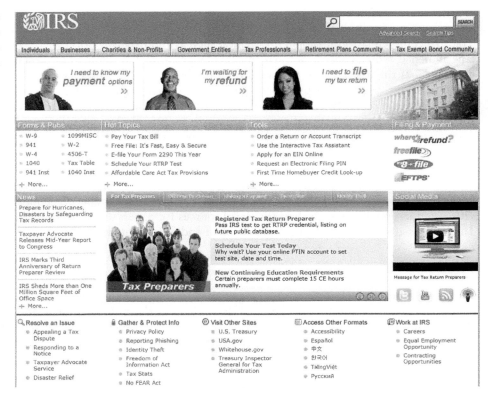

the information found on these sites is very reliable. Figure 19.5, for example, is the home page for the site maintained by the Internal Revenue Service.

- **Online periodicals and newspapers.** As noted earlier, almost every print publication now has an online version. Some local newspapers have a free news section that is available to all and a section that is available only for paid subscribers. Subscribers to the *New York Times* print edition receive the digital edition of the *Times* free. The *Times* also offers digital-only subscription plans (www.nytimes.com). Many magazines allow online viewers to read most of their articles, while others publish snippets online and allow full access only to subscribers.

   Some academic journals, such as *Kairos* (http://english.ttu.edu/Kairos/), are published only online. Like most academic journals, they are peer-reviewed, and the information in them is as reliable as that found in print academic journals.

- **Blogs.** A blog is usually maintained by one person who shares his or her thoughts on a given topic or set of topics and may post links to other sites on the Web as well as comments from other writers. While some blogs are maintained by experts in a particular field, others are written by people who want to communicate their own point of view on anything from politics to what kind of software is better. Be cautious about using them as sources. Figure 19.6 is an example of a blog on dieting.

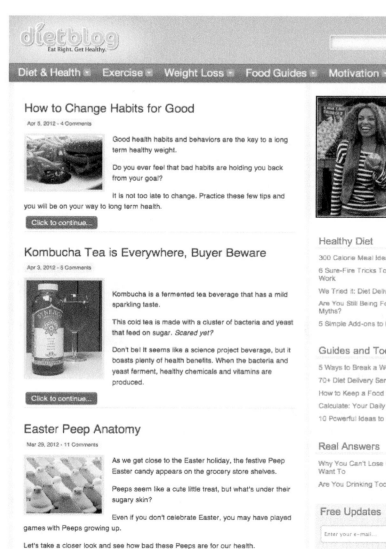

FIGURE 19.6
Page from *Diet Blog*
Reprinted by permission of Jim Foster, Editor, www.diet-blog.com/page/5

- **Wikipedia.** *Wikipedia* is a collaborative online encyclopedia. The articles on *Wikipedia* are written by volunteers, and it is possible for anyone to edit already existing articles. Although there are some safeguards to protect certain pages, some information found on *Wikipedia* may be suspect. You may think of it as a good starting place, in much the same way that a traditional encyclopedia is a place to start for background, but you should not rely on it for all of your information on a topic. It is always wise to look for

For more information on evaluating sources see pages 534–41.

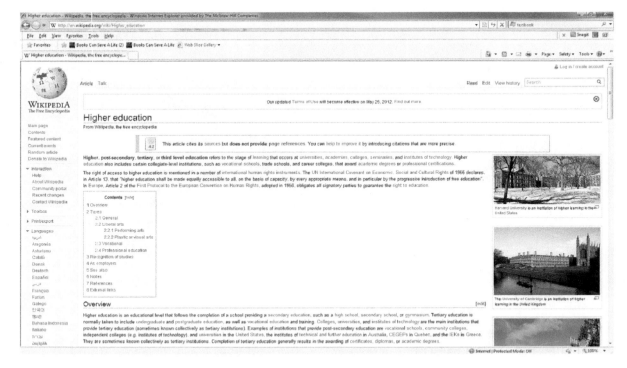

FIGURE 19.7 *Wikipedia* Entry for "Higher Education"

For more about Wikipedia, see "A Brief History of Wikipedia" by Dan Fletcher, pages 169–70 in Chapter 7.

additional sources of information beyond *Wikipedia*. You should also be cautious about citing it as a source in your academic papers. Figure 19.7 shows the *Wikipedia* entry for "higher education."

Writing Activity

Planning Your Research

For a college class in which you have been asked to conduct research on a particular topic, select a potential topic, and then list the sources you might look at and what you might expect to find in them. Also plan when and where you will conduct your research.

Evaluating Your Sources: Asking the Reporter's Questions

Finding sources is only the beginning of your task in conducting research; you also need to evaluate the information you locate. How do you determine that a source is credible and accurate? Usually, asking the questions reporters ask when they are working on a story will help you.

Who Is the Author?

Who is the author of the research? What can you learn about that author? If the work is an essay or an entire book, you may be able to find biographical information about the author or authors. For example, let's say you are conducting research on gangs and find this book in your college library: *Teen Gangs: A Global View*, edited by Maureen P. Duffy and Scott Edward Gillig, and published by Greenwood Press, now ABC-CLIO/Greenwood. Here is what you are able to find out about the two editors from examining the book:

> **MAUREEN P. DUFFY** is Associate Professor and Chair of the Counseling Department at Barry University, Miami Shores, Florida.
> **SCOTT EDWARD GILLIG** is Professor and Coordinator of the mental health counseling specialization at Barry University.

Scholarly Book on the Subject of Gangs

Both editors are university professors, which means the book most likely contains thoroughly researched and well-documented articles by respected authors. If you examine ABC-CLIO/Greenwood's catalog or Web site, you will see that it specializes in nonfiction books primarily for schools and that it also publishes library reference titles. Your investigation indicates that the editors are both professors and the book is not self-published. Although you cannot tell much about the reputation of ABC-CLIO/Greenwood from its Web site alone, all of the information you have found suggests that the articles in this text were probably written by people who are credible authorities in their field.

What Is the Text About? What Is the Quality of the Information?

To determine the answer to this question, you will need to ask the following additional questions:

- What is the focus of the printed or online text you are considering?
- How thoughtful and research-based is it?
- Does the text take a balanced, thoughtful approach?

You'll also want to make sure the text is relevant to your topic.

For instance, in your research on why adolescent males or females change their behavior when they join gangs, suppose you visit the Web site at www.streetgangs .com. The mission statement shown in Figure 19.8 on page 536 indicates that the site appears to be controlled by an individual and has been since 1995. This does not mean that the information on the site is not credible, only that you will need to consider the source if you decide to use anything from this Web site.

The final paragraph of the section about the history of the Web site adds this information:

> We receive dozens of email every day so forgive us if we cannot personally respond to your message, but we will do our best to answer ALL serious questions. We receive over 6 million page visits monthly so please do not email us to help you

FIGURE 19.8
Mission Statement
for the Web Site
Streetgangs.com
Reprinted by permission
of Alex Alonso, Editor,
www. streetgangs.com
/contacts/mission-
statement

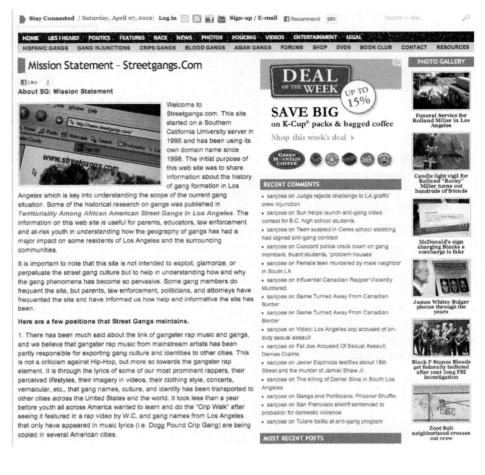

with your high school paper or to ask silly questions. Please see the *bibliography* for tips on good books to read and for articles to download, or visit the *topics* to read recent news articles. If you have a serious question about gangs visit the *billboard* where your question may have already been asked. If you would like to write an article for *Street Gangs Magazine* please follow the *submission guidelines* and forward your essay. Media requests should be made from the *contact page*.

With so much interest in street gangs, it is certainly possible that this Web site gets "over 6 million page visits monthly." How does the tone of these comments affect your view of this site?

Even at sites or blogs maintained by individuals, you can sometimes learn valuable information and find useful links. For example, *Streetgangs.com* offers (through the StreetGang.com Book Club) a publication titled *Territoriality Among African-American Street Gangs in Los Angeles.* The 184-page book "provides a thorough discussion of the history of Black gangs in Los Angeles from the late 1940s to the early 1970s, when the contemporary Black gangs emerged." Of course you would need to assess the reliability of all such sources.

When Was the Text Published or the Web Site Last Updated?

Generally, the more current the information a source provides, the more useful it is to you. In academic research, new data are generally a response to *older* data. In fact, one of the benefits of reading books and articles by university scholars is that they almost always refer to earlier research as they outline how their new research relates to it.

At www.streetgangs.com/contacts/copyrights, there is no notice of when the Web page was last updated, but in the copyright section you will find this notice:

Copyright © 1995–2012, Street Gangs,
P.O. Box 18238,
Los Angeles CA, 90018, USA
http://www.streetgangs.com/contacts/copyrights

This notice tells you that someone has worked on this Web site sometime in 2011. The page also includes a link to the biography and contact information for A. Alonso, who is evidently responsible for the site, another bit of evidence that the site is controlled by an individual.

Why Was This Information Published?

What can you determine about why the information was published? What is the text's purpose? Who appears to be the target audience? If you can determine to whom the text appeals, you might gain a sense of its purpose.

You cannot know for sure why an essay was published, or a book printed, or a Web site constructed, but you can make some good guesses:

- **Essays in academic journals** are often published to share new knowledge. This is especially true of articles in scientific journals, which publish the results of scientific research, but even in journals that focus on the humanities or on professional fields, professors publish what they have learned from their reading and thinking.

    Because articles in academic journals are peer-reviewed, other scholars in the field will get the chance to comment on, make suggestions about, and offer criticisms of any essay before it is published. So generally you can expect the information in journal articles to be credible. Journals are also major venues that scholars and practitioners use to communicate and share information within professional and scientific fields.

- **Academic books** provide professors with a way to distribute large amounts of information and insight to their peers, and while some make money for their author and publisher, many do not, so the profit motive is not a strong factor in publishing an academic text. Academic texts are also peer-reviewed, so other scholars in the field will have examined the information, data, and conclusions in a text prior to publication. During the publishing process, those peer reviewers will have the opportunity to contribute their ideas, criticisms, and suggestions. Academic texts are generally published by university presses.

- **Articles in newsmagazines and newspapers** present items in the local, national, or worldwide news. Most often, editors work diligently to present the news in an unbiased manner, but most newspapers and even some magazines have editorial pages or sections.

As with anyone else, newspaper and magazine editors and writers have their own particular viewpoints and ways of looking at what they report on—in other words, there is always *some* bias in anything that is said or written. At any particular time and place, you might be able to label newspapers and magazines according to their general tendencies. But these ways of seeing and writing about the news vary over time, as editors and writers come and go.

How can you, as a reader, get some sense of the biases of the news-magazines and newspapers you read for your research? One way is to compare how the same information is presented in different magazines or newspapers. Read two or more editorials on the same topic. Look for facts related to a story that appear in one publication but not in the other: What might the omission or inclusion of an important fact tell you about each newpaper's or magazine's biases? Consider how the same story is presented in two different publications. How big is the headline? How much space is devoted to the article? Is it on the front page or on an interior page?

- **Web sites** provide all kinds of information. However, not all Web sites give completely accurate and reliable information. You have to evaluate a Web site just as you would any other source. For information on evaluating Web sites, see "Electronic Environments" (page 541).

Writing Activity

Analyzing Newspapers

Most newspapers have a particular political slant, which is often clear in their editorials but is also evident in the way various news stories are presented. If you examine the newspapers from several large cities, such differences will be readily apparent. Select a major story that is currently in the news, and compare how three newspapers cover it. What kind of photographs accompany the story? What do their editorials say about it? How much "newsprint" or online space is devoted to the story? Where do the stories appear?

Compare what you have learned with the information that several of your class-mates have gathered about coverage of the same story or a similar story.

Writing Activity

Examining a Web Site to Determine Its Audience

Select one of the following Web sites and, in no more than two pages, outline who you think is the intended audience for the site, what you think its purpose is, and why you make that assertion. Indicate who maintains the site (if you can tell) and when it was last updated.

http://www.gangwar.com/dynamics.htm
http://www.csun.edu/~hcchs006/gang.html
http://www.gangstyle.com/

Where Was the Item Published?

It is becoming increasingly difficult to differentiate between library research and online research because so many traditional library resources are now located online. In addition, many libraries provide portals to online databases and other online sites. As a result, whether information resides in a physical building or is stored on a server, you will need your critical thinking skills more than ever to determine its value.

As with any research activity, your decision about where to search for information depends on what you are trying to learn. If the answer to your research question requires demographic data, you might find that all the reliable and most current census information is on different Web sites maintained by various agencies of the U.S. government. Web-based research is rarely sufficient for a project of any depth, however. For example, you probably can learn more about local census trends and data from your local newspaper (which may also be available on the Web).

Articles and other source materials published on the Web can appear professional and unbiased, but it is often difficult to find information that allows you to fully evaluate the credibility of a Web page. To do so, you need to determine what person, company, or organization constructed the site and stands behind it. If you learn that you are examining a personal Web site instead of one sponsored by a government agency or a university, you need to take that fact into account. Although organizations will often have their own agenda, they usually can devote more resources to the construction and maintenance of a Web site than an individual can. Web suffixes generally indicate the source of a Web site:

- **.edu** indicates an educational institution. Information you find at such a location has generally been approved by the school. However, many colleges and universities also provide Web space for students and faculty members, and those individuals may post information that has *not* necessarily been approved by the school.
- **.com** indicates a for-profit company. The suffix *.com* is a shortened form of *commercial* and usually designates a business-oriented site.
- **.org** indicates an organization. The *.org* Web suffix is generally used for nonprofit organizations.
- **.gov** indicates some level of government (state, national, or local).
- **.net** indicates Web sites generally used by Internet service providers (ISPs) and companies that provide Web hosting, like www.concentric.net. Some commercial businesses also use the *.net* extension, but usually not as their main Web site. Some Internet service providers allow their customers to use their "net" extension for sharing things like photographs, such as www.photo.net.
- **.biz** is most often used for small-business Web sites.
- **.info** is, like *.com*, an unrestricted domain: Anyone can use it. According to Network Associates, the company that assigns and allocates Web addresses, *.info* is the most popular extension beyond *.com*, *.net*, and *.org*.

For more information on Web suffixes and addresses, see http://www .networksolutions.com/. Network Solutions offers a "WhoIs" search function for nearly all sites on the Web except personal ones. Conducting a "WhoIs" search will give you information about the sponsor of any particular Web page. This search not only tells you who "owns" the domain name, but also provides e-mail contact information. If the Web page you're looking for is not listed, then it is probably a personal page.[1]

How Accurate Is the Information in This Source?

Anyone who stands in a supermarket check-out line and sees tabloid headlines about aliens and Elvis sightings understands that not all news stories that appear in print are necessarily accurate. How do you know what information to believe and what information to view with skepticism?

- One of the best ways of determining the accuracy of the information in any publication is to find out who published it. As we have noted, books published by university presses and articles published in academic journals are peer-reviewed. You can usually expect that large newspapers, such as the *New York Times*, will print the most accurate information available at the time each issue is published. Over time, some information published in reliable periodicals or newspapers may change or need to be corrected. The publication is then likely to publish the updated information.

- Another way of determining accuracy is to investigate the author's track record. Of course, it's important to make sure that the author's area of expertise is in the subject you are researching. A famous actor who writes a diet book may or may not be a credible source of information on proper nutrition.

To determine the accuracy of information on a Web site, you might consider the Web sites it provides links to. Often, following some of the links will give you information about the site's credibility. For example, the Web site *Streetgangs.com* showed these links in April 2012:

- ➤ The killing of Daniel Silva in South Los Angeles, April 3, 2012
- ➤ Pro Zimmerman advocates complain about media bias, March 30, 2012
- ➤ Photos of a Chinese gangster are anonymously posted from lost cell phone, March 26, 2012
- ➤ Armenian Power member convicted of identity theft charges, March 25, 2012

Links that connect to reputable newspapers or television stations would indicate that whoever is maintaining the Web site is providing readers with connections to legitimate news articles, thus adding to the credibility of the Web site. However, the links listed above lead to stories that have bylines but give little

---

[1]Thanks to William Sherman, University of Northern Colorado, for this information.

indication of what organization the writer works for. Some simply say "Times Staff." What impact do links such as these have on the way you view the information available on this site?

ELECTRONIC ENVIRONMENTS   **Evaluating Web Sites**

Ask yourself the following questions when evaluating the credibility of a Web site.

- Who is the author or sponsor of the site? What can you find out about the author or sponsor? Why might this person or organization sponsor the site? What benefit might the sponsor receive from the Web site?

- What does the site's address tell you about it? What does the suffix that appears at the end of the address tell you about it: *.edu* for educational, for example, or *.com* for commercial? Is there a tilde (~) in the address, which indicates a personal site?

- What is the purpose of the site? Is the purpose to provide information? To sell a product or service? To persuade readers to accept a particular point of view?

- How professional is the tone, and how well designed is the site? How carefully has it been edited and proofread? How many grammatical and spelling errors are there?

- Consider the quality of the author's arguments. Does the content contain logical fallacies? How fairly does the author deal with opposing views?

- Can you find a date when the site was published or most recently updated?

- What kinds of links does the site provide? How legitimate or credible are the sites the links lead to?

Field Research

As we have seen, much of the time you will gather information for your research projects from books, periodicals, the Web, and other preexisting sources. At other times, you may need to gather first-hand information. Sometimes you can get the information you need by simply observing people, wildlife, or natural phenomena. At other times, the best method of gathering information from human subjects may be to ask questions of individual people or groups of people, either directly or in writing. However you do it, the act of gathering information on your own is called **field research** because you need to go out "into the field." The most common kinds of field research you might find yourself doing are observation, personal interviews, and surveys.

Working with Human Participants

Much field research has to do with human behavior. Any time you are doing research that involves human participants, you are expected to behave ethically and to do or say nothing that might in any way harm your participants. To ensure that researchers follow ethical practices, all academic institutions (and many private organizations) have Institutional Review Boards (IRBs). All research projects that use human participants must be approved by your organization's IRB or its designated representative. All IRBs have their own rules. Check with your instructor about your school's human participants policy.

Informed Consent

Whether you are required to submit a formal proposal to your school's IRB or simply need to work closely with your instructor, if you are going to be working with human participants, you need to get their permission by having all of the participants in your field research sign an Informed Consent Form. Most institutions have templates for these forms readily available.

Observations

Watching and recording what you see might be the most effective way to help you answer your research question. If viewing people, animals, or other phenomena over a short time will provide you with useful information, you may choose observation as your research method.

OBSERVING HUMANS

If you are writing an informative or analytical paper, you may need to observe human behavior as part of your research. To make your observations, you might station yourself at a particular place in a shopping mall, at an athletic event, or at a busy intersection and record, in detail, certain behaviors. For example, you might record how many vehicles passing through an intersection near your college actually come to a complete stop at the stop sign. You would need to keep track of the total number of vehicles passing by as well as the specific number of vehicles that demonstrate the particular behavior you are watching for. It is, of course, possible to make even more detailed observations, such as what car models drivers who run stop signs are driving. To make detailed observations such as these, it helps to prepare by setting up categories. Once you are in the field observing and recording, you probably won't have time to develop new ones.

OBSERVING OTHER PHENOMENA

For writing projects that lend themselves to observation, see Chapters 6, 7, and 8.

You can also observe other natural and human-influenced phenomena. Some researchers observe animal behavior; others watch tornadoes and other weather patterns. The specific nature of what you are observing will determine the tools you will need and the methods you will use.

Writing Activity

Conduct an Observation

People often comment on how students are tied to technology. How valid is this assertion? One way to test this assumption might be to sit for an hour in your student union or some other place where students from your campus gather. Watch the behavior of the students. Are they talking with one another in person, or are they using technology to communicate, listen to music, or watch videos? Take notes of what you see. You might want to establish some categories. Are students talking on cell phones? Are they texting? Are they using laptops? Are they listening to iPods? Write a short report on your findings.

Interviews

Because most of us are comfortable talking with other people, we often think that interviewing someone will be easy. However, interviews are rarely an easy way to do meaningful research. Effective interviews that yield useful information happen only when the interviewer prepares ahead of time. As you prepare, it's important to remember that some of the interviews you may see on television or hear on the radio are not necessarily good examples of interviewing.

You can employ several strategies to prepare and conduct a successful interview:

- Call ahead to make an appointment instead of just showing up in your subject's office. You might obtain more information than you might otherwise have been able to get.

- Do your homework ahead of time so that you have good questions ready to ask, have anticipated the nature of the responses, and have good follow-up questions at hand. Being able to anticipate the nature of the interview will enable you to steer it in the direction in which you need it to go.

- Be prepared to take notes. Before you interview someone for an assignment, practice (using your interview questions) with a classmate or a friend.

- Consider bringing along some kind of recording device. If you plan to record the interview, make sure you have your subject's permission before the interview begins. Some people are willing to talk but do not wish to be recorded.

- Be polite and friendly during the interview. It is usually a good idea to follow up an interview with a thank-you note.

Although your specific interview questions will depend on your topic and the person you are interviewing, you will usually want to prepare two kinds of questions: open-ended and directed. **Open-ended questions** let the person being interviewed develop his or her answers at length. **Directed questions** seek more specific kinds of information. As part of her research for a paper on violence in the movies, for example, Magda was interested in learning about how people react when they are watching violent movies. To find out, she decided to interview the local manager of a theater chain that sometimes shows violent, R-rated movies. To prepare for the interview, Magda developed the following list of questions:

1. What would you consider a violent movie?

2. What specific content in a movie makes it violent?

3. Are all movies that contain scenes with (the content from the previous questions) necessarily violent? If not, why not? What's the determining factor?

4. Do you show many movies like that? If so, how many per month?

5. Why do you think people watch violent movies?

6. What age groups seem to watch violent movies?

7. Do audiences at violent movies behave differently from audiences at other types of movies, such as comedies?

8. Are audiences at violent movies more or less likely to buy more at the concession stand?

9. Do audiences at violent movies leave behind more or less trash in the theater?

10. Are audiences at violent movies more or less likely to leave through an unauthorized exit?

11. Are audiences at violent movies generally noisier or quieter?

Some of the questions in Magda's list, such as 1–3, were open-ended. Others, such as questions 7–11, were more directed, perhaps indicating the direction of her thinking as she developed her thesis.

Avoid what can be called "forced-choice questions," questions that presuppose only a few specific choices and force your subject to answer one of them. Asking "Do you think the football team is bad or just plain awful this year?" assumes the team really is bad and that your subject will agree. A better question would be "What's your opinion of the football team this year?"

Also stay away from leading questions that have built-in *assumptions* the person you are interviewing might not agree with. A question like "Don't you think that conducting surveys provides a richness that other research methods can't match?" assumes (1) that the interviewee will interpret "richness" in the same way you do, and (2) that both of your definitions of "can't match" will also agree. It would be more effective to ask the question in a more neutral way: "Are there any advantages, in your view, to surveys over other kinds of field research? If so, what might they be?"

Writing Activity

Conducting an Interview

Assume that you are a reporter for your school's newspaper. Your editor has assigned you to interview the president of your campus on a topic of your choice. Develop a list of ten questions, some open-ended, some directed, that you want to ask the president.

Surveys

Although interviews are useful sources of information and have the advantage of enabling a direct exchange between the subject and the interviewer, the number of people that one person can interview is limited. Some research projects require you to collect information from a larger number of people than you could possibly interview. To get information from a large number of people quickly and efficiently, you can use a **survey**. Although on the surface a survey may look like just a set of questions, an effective survey is carefully designed, and its questions are very specifically framed. A good survey will either target a particular group of people or solicit information about the participants to provide you with a context for their answers.

CONSTRUCTING A SURVEY

Several strategies will enable you to put together an effective survey:

- Keep the survey a reasonable length. Ask only those questions that are necessary. Many people think that all surveys need to start with questions that ask for certain basic demographic information, but you need gather only information that is important for your research.

- Make sure the questions you ask call for an appropriate response. If a reasonable answer to the question is "yes," or "no," make sure there are only two possible responses. If a wider range of responses is appropriate, a scale such as "strongly agree, agree, no opinion, disagree, strongly disagree" may be more useful.

- Consider whether you want to ask only *closed-ended* or *directed* questions that call for specific answers, such as "List your age," or if you also want to ask *open-ended* questions, such as "Describe your experience at the Math Testing Center." Closed-ended questions are easier to tabulate, but open-ended questions will provide you with more examples and narrative detail.

- If you ask open-ended questions that call for written responses, give your respondents enough room on the form to answer fully.

- The question itself should not influence the response. Asking a question like "Do you think there are not enough parking spaces on campus?" leads the respondent to say "yes." A more effective way to get the same information would be to ask, "What is your opinion of the campus parking situation?"

- Have a strategy for tabulating the open-ended responses. Are you going to try to categorize them? Are you planning to use them as anecdotal examples?

- Consider using an electronic survey, such as those provided by SurveyMonkey.com. These companies often allow you to conduct free surveys but limit the number of responses you can receive to 100 or so. An electronic survey lets you reach a wider audience: You can simply e-mail the survey link. Also, you may find that those you want to complete your survey are more likely to fill out an electronic form than a paper one—and the electronic survey will help you collect and collate your data.

ADMINISTERING YOUR SURVEY

Test your survey before you administer it. That way, if a question or two proves to be faulty, you can make changes. Have several people respond to your survey, asking them to indicate any confusing questions. Also consider whom you would like to respond to your survey, targeting your audience as specifically as possible. A general rule of thumb is that the more people you can ask to take your survey—the larger the data set—the more useful the results will be. It is also important to make sure that you are surveying the right population. If you are looking for information on what kind of coffee drinks are most popular on your campus, for example, you should survey only coffee drinkers.

Writing Activity

Develop a Survey

Often people who are thinking of opening a small business conduct a survey of their potential clientele to test their business plan's chances for success. Think of a possible product or service that seems to be lacking in your community. Then identify the customers your business will serve. Develop a set of survey questions that will give you a good sense of whether others share your perceived need for this business.

20

Synthesizing and Documenting Sources

Effective academic writing does not just emerge out of a writer's mind. Academic writers are expected to know what others have said about their topic, using the work of other writers to help establish a foundation for an argument, substantiate an argument, or set up a point that they will then challenge or support. This process of building your own arguments using support and arguments from other writers is called **synthesis**. As they synthesize ideas, academic writers need to use sources, acknowledging the thinking that already exists on an issue and giving credit to those who developed it. When developing an argument in an academic essay, for instance, you will be expected to review the relevant work of previous researchers and summarize their results.

You will then be able to build your own arguments, working from

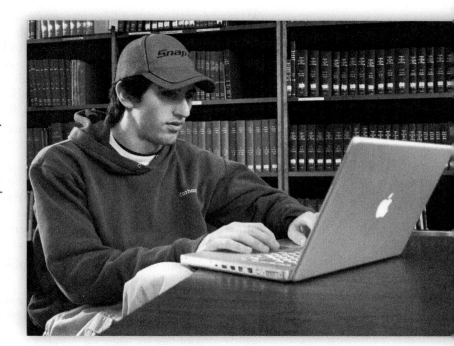

theirs. And you will need to give these researchers credit. To help you synthesize other people's writing and document your sources, this chapter covers plagiarism, quotations, paraphrasing, and

summaries, as well as the MLA and APA documentation styles.

For more on synthesis, see Chapters 2 and 3.

An Overview of Documentation

When you document sources appropriately, you accomplish several important purposes:

- Documentation indicates what you as the writer did not produce—in effect, it indicates where you have used summary and paraphrase: "This isn't my idea and here is where it came from." Or it indicates a quotation: "These aren't my words, and here is the name of the person who wrote or said them."

- Documentation that follows a system such as the one recommended by the Modern Language Association (MLA) or the American Psychological Association (APA) provides readers with a list of sources—called the list of Works Cited in MLA style or References in APA style—so they can consult the works listed. Proper documentation, within the text and in the list of sources, makes it easy for the reader to locate and read a particular source the writer has cited or even a specific quotation in that source.

- Proper documentation of appropriate sources lends *ethos* (credibility) to you as a writer and enhances your argument.

Different academic disciplines have different style guides that offer a range of conventions for writers to follow, including conventions for documentation. Here we will present the conventions for documentation given in the style guides of the MLA and the APA. MLA style is used for papers in humanities disciplines, including English; APA style is used for papers in social science disciplines. The current editions of both manuals are as follows:

Gibaldi, Joseph. *MLA Handbook for Writers of Research Papers.* 7th ed. New York: MLA, 2009.

American Psychological Association. (2010). *Publication manual of the American Psychological Association* (6th ed.). Washington, DC: Author.

Other disciplines recommend a variety of styles. Here are some of those other options:

- *Scientific Style and Format: The CSE Manual for Authors, Editors and Publishers* (7th ed.). If your academic work is in the sciences, you may be required to use the style suggested by the Council of Scientific Editors (CSE), formerly the Council of Biology Editors (CBE).

- *Information for Authors.* This volume, published by the Institute of Electrical and Electronics Engineers (IEEE), is used by engineers.

- *The Chicago Manual of Style* (16th ed.). *CMS* is another widely used style. In fact, if you are expected to do on-the-job writing that requires documentation, more likely than not you will use *CMS*.

When you use information from sources to support your thesis, you must be careful to give appropriate credit to the author of each source. Failing to do so is plagiarism. You can choose from among several options for presenting information that you have taken from other writers' work: quotations, paraphrases, or summaries.

Plagiarism

We've all heard lots of discussion about plagiarism. It's important, however, to have a firm grasp of exactly what constitutes plagiarism, which can mean different things to different people. The best definition of **plagiarism** is from the Council of Writing Program Administrators in their "Defining and Avoiding Plagiarism: The WPA Statement on Best Practices": "In an instructional setting, plagiarism occurs when a writer deliberately uses someone else's language, ideas, or other original (not common-knowledge) material without acknowledging its source" (http://www.wpacouncil.org/positions/WPAplagiarism.pdf). As the statement implies, the key concept in plagiarism is the *intent to deceive*: the act of knowingly submitting someone else's work as your own is the basic ingredient of what constitutes plagiarism. There are two somewhat related problems that students, especially those who are new to using research in their writing, often have problems with: inadequate or incorrect citations, and "patchwriting."

Inadequate or Incorrect Citations

One of the most common problems students have when they are integrating material from sources into their writing is inadequate or incorrect citations. Citation systems such as MLA can be confusing to new researchers, and instructors often see students make mistakes when they are citing sources. If you are integrating material from sources, whether you are using a direct quotation, a paraphrase, or a summary, you must cite it appropriately. You'll also need to have the appropriate citation in your list of works cited or references at the end of your paper. Refer to the guidelines on pages 556-79 for MLA or pages 580-99 for APA, and ask your instructor or a tutor in the writing center if you are unsure about how to cite a specific source.

Patchwriting

Rhetoric and composition scholar Rebecca Moore Howard uses the term "patchwriting" to describe what happens when students unintentionally put passages from sources into their own writing without proper attribution. This problem commonly occurs when students use paraphrases or summaries inappropriately or simply aren't quite sure how to incorporate the ideas of others into their work. To avoid patchwriting, make sure your paraphrases and summaries are really in your words and are properly cited when you incorporate the ideas of others into your work.

Anti-plagiarism Software

Search technologies that enable all of us to find information more quickly and thoroughly on the Internet than ever before can also be used by instructors to check whether the writing students are turning in is original or taken from another writer's work. Anyone who finds a suspicious passage in a piece of writing can easily enter the passage into a search engine such as Google, making sure the whole passage is enclosed in quotation marks, to see if it appears elsewhere on the Internet. Using similar search technologies, some companies have marketed what has come to be called *anti-plagiarism software* such as *Turnitin* or *SafeAssign*, which is part of *Blackboard*. Instructors who use this kind of software commonly let their students know that they are going to submit the students' papers. In fact, many instructors encourage their students to submit drafts of assignments so that the software can point out potentially problematic passages and inadequate citation. Using anti-plagiarism software in this way gives students the opportunity to have their drafts checked for both patchwriting and inadequate citation, so they can revise their papers before submitting the final draft.

Quotations

When the most effective way to make a point is to use another author's exact words, you are using a **quotation.** Use a direct quotation in the following situations:

- When the exact wording is particularly striking
- When the author is considered to be especially authoritative
- When you take issue with the author's statement

If you are using MLA style and your quotation is shorter than five lines, you should enclose it in quotation marks and incorporate it into your text. Because the quotation is incorporated into the sentence, a comma is used after the introductory phrase. At first it might feel a bit awkward or clumsy when you integrate quoted material into your writing; however, you will get better with practice. Using verbs such as *notes, comments, observes,* and *explains,* will help you introduce quotations smoothly and meaningfully.

For information on how to cite quotations, paraphrases, and summaries within text, see pages 556–58 for MLA style and pages 580–82 for APA style.

Commenting on the early days of Barack Obama's presidency, David Corn notes, "Politics is not a meritocracy, and Obama realized no president was guaranteed credit or lucky bounces" (15).

When the quotation is longer than four lines and you are using MLA style, start the quotation on a new line and indent all lines of the quotation one inch. The quotation should be double spaced and does not need to be enclosed in quotation marks. If the quotation is introduced with an independent clause, that clause is followed by a colon.

A political observer explains an analogy from the early days of Barack Obama's presidency:

> Politics is not a meritocracy, and Obama realized no president was guaranteed credit or lucky bounces. But at times he couldn't help feeling, as

> he told one associate, a kinship with the protagonist in Ernest Heming-
> way's *The Old Man and the Sea*. He had, against tremendous odds, caught
> a big fish, but on the long voyage back to shore, his prized catch had
> been picked to pieces by sharks. (Corn 15)

If you are using APA style, quotations of fewer than forty words should be enclosed in quotation marks and incorporated into the text, as follows:

> Commenting on the early days of Barack Obama's presidency, David Corn (2012)
> notes, "Politics is not a meritocracy, and Obama realized no president was guaran-
> teed credit or lucky bounces" (p. 15).

Block quotations are used in APA style when the quotation is at least forty words long. They are indented only five spaces and double spaced, and are not enclosed in quotation marks.

> A political observer explains an analogy from the early days of Barack Obama's
> presidency:
>
> > Politics is not a meritocracy, and Obama realized no president was guaranteed
> > credit or lucky bounces. But at times he couldn't help feeling, as he told one
> > associate, a kinship with the protagonist in Ernest Hemingway's *The Old Man
> > and the Sea*. He had, against tremendous odds, caught a big fish, but on the
> > long voyage back to shore, his prized catch had been picked to pieces by
> > sharks. (Corn, 2012, p. 15)

Paraphrases

Use a **paraphrase** to put someone else's ideas into your own words. Because you are using someone else's ideas, you need to include an appropriate citation. However, in a paraphrase you need to use your own words and sentence structure. If you choose to borrow unique phrases from the original, those phrases should be placed in quotation marks. Here, for example, is a block quotation in MLA style:

> In his book *The World Is Flat, New York Times* columnist Thomas L. Friedman notes
> that when Netscape went public in 1995, it had significant ramifications for the
> emerging global economy:
>
> > Looking back, what enabled Netscape to take off was the existence,
> > from the earlier phase, of millions of PC's, many already equipped

> with modems. Those are the shoulders Netscape stood on. What
> Netscape did was bring a new killer app—the browser—to this
> installed base of PC's making the computer and its connectivity inher-
> ently more useful for millions of people. (57)

If you don't want to use a direct quotation, you can paraphrase Friedman's information by changing it into your own words. However, in paraphrasing, you need to
be careful that you do not commit **plagiarism** by using language, sentence structures, or both that are too close to the original. The following paraphrase uses
language that too closely mimics the original.

Faulty Paraphrase

> In *The World Is Flat,* Thomas L. Friedman looks back to 1995 and notes that what
> enabled Netscape to take off when it went public was that it could stand on the
> shoulders of the millions of already existing PC's, many already equipped with
> modems. Its new killer app—the browser—helped millions of people make
> connecting more useful (57).

In contrast, the following paraphrase is entirely in the writer's own words and sentence structures:

Acceptable Paraphrase

> In *The World Is Flat,* Thomas L. Friedman looks back to 1995 and notes that Netscape
> could make a significant impact on the emerging global economy when it went
> public because of its browser. When Netscape brought this new software
> application—the browser—to the users of modem enhanced PC's, it made those
> connected computers much more useful (57).

Suppose you were writing about the film *Harry Potter and the Deathly Hallows:
Part 2* and wanted to cite ideas from Roger Ebert's review of it. Here is the first
paragraph from Ebert's review (page 297):

> After seven earlier films reaching back a decade, the Harry Potter saga comes
> to a solid and satisfying conclusion in *Harry Potter and the Deathly Hallows: Part 2.*
> The finale conjures up enough awe and solemnity to serve as an appropriate finale
> and a dramatic contrast to the lighthearted (relative) innocence of *Harry Potter and
> the Sorcerer's Stone* all those magical years ago.

Faulty Paraphrase

A faulty paraphrase of Ebert's second sentence would mimic his sentence structure in the original text and would look similar:

> According to Ebert, the final film conjures up both awe and solemnity to work as an appropriate finale as well as a dramatic contrast to the innocence of *Harry Potter and the Sorcerer's Stone* and the other earlier films.

The following acceptable version conveys Ebert's idea but with a different sentence structure.

Acceptable Paraphrase

> According to Ebert, the film both connects to the previous films and serves as a contrast to their original sense of innocence.

ELECTRONIC ENVIRONMENTS   **Managing Research Notes**

You can use a Word document while you are conducting research to help record notes and to document your research sources. Use an outline of your project to help organize information. While you may be tempted to copy and paste information from your sources, it is best to paraphrase or summarize from them and note why the information is relevant to your project's topic as well as the exact source the information came from. You can record source documentation for your list of works cited (MLA) or references (APA) in a Word file as you proceed.

Summaries

When you include a **summary** of your source's ideas, you condense the material presented by another author into a briefer form. While similar to paraphrasing, summaries reduce information into a substantially smaller number of words. You might summarize a paragraph or even a page of material in only a sentence or two. To summarize a chapter, you might need several paragraphs. A summary of a larger work might be several pages in length. Once again, however, the summary must be entirely in your own words and sentence structures to avoid plagiarizing the original. Here are unacceptable and acceptable summaries of the Ebert passage.

Unacceptable Summary

> After seven earlier films that go back ten years, the Harry Potter stories end with a solid and satisfying conclusion in *Harry Potter and the Deathly Hallows: Part 2.* The finale provides seriousness and surprise and so works to appropriately end the series that began with the lighthearted (relative) innocence of *Harry Potter and the Sorcerer's Stone* many years ago.

Acceptable Summary

> In Roger Ebert's opinion, the film is a fitting ending for the series of Harry Potter stories, and it provides a useful contrast to their earlier sense of innocence.

For more on writing a summary, see Chapter 2, pages 23 and 25

Note that if you use phrases from the original in your summary, you should enclose them in quotation marks.

Syntheses

As noted on pages 25–26 in Chapter 2, **synthesis** is the act of blending information from multiple sources and melding it with the writer's own ideas. A synthesis could involve quoting, paraphrasing, and/or summarizing source material. To avoid plagiarism when synthesizing source material, you need to clarify which ideas are taken from which sources and which ideas are your own. For example, in the opening paragraph of his essay on gangs and adolescent behaviors (page 596), writer Aaron Zook reviews some of the literature on the topic:

For more on synthesis, see Chapter 3.

> Since the early 1920s, researchers have closely studied the relationship between street gangs and violent crime from a variety of perspectives: criminological, sociological, and psychological (Thabit, 2005). Whatever the underlying causes for gang membership, the results seem clear; members of street gangs admit to a far greater rate of serious crime, and to far more severe acts of violence (Penly Hall, Thornberry, & Lizotte, 2006) than non-gang members of the same age, race, and socioeconomic background. According to the Web site Safeyouth.org (n.d.), gang violence is certainly cause for concern:
>
> > Gang members are responsible for much of the serious violence in the United States. . . . Teens that are gang members are much more likely than other teens to commit serious and violent crimes. For example, a survey in Denver found that while only 14% of teens were gang members, they were responsible for committing 89% of the serious violent crimes.
>
> Many researchers have therefore come to the conclusion that gangs necessarily cause violence and deviant behavior.

Notice how Zook uses parenthetical citations to identify the sources for information that he has taken from multiple sources. Notice too in the last sentence that Zook uses his own words to draw a conclusion from the material that he summarized and quoted earlier in the paragraph. However, if his sentence had read, "Many researchers have therefore come to the conclusion that gang members are responsible for much of the serious violence in the United States," he would have been plagiarizing because the sentence includes exact words and phrases from the original block quotation.

UNACCEPTABLE SYNTHESIS

Many researchers have therefore come to the conclusion that gang members are responsible for much of the serious violence in the United States.

ACCEPTABLE SYNTHESIS

Many researchers have therefore come to the conclusion that gangs necessarily cause violence and deviant behavior.

or

Many researchers have therefore come to the conclusion that "gang members are responsible for much of the serious violence in the United States."

Ellipses

If you decide that a quotation is too long and want to condense it, you can do so by placing an ellipsis (three periods with a space between each) in place of the omitted words. If the ellipsis occurs at the end of the sentence, you will need to place the sentence's period before the first ellipsis with a space between the period and the first ellipsis point. Make sure when you use an ellipsis that you do not change the meaning of the original quotation. For example, compare the original quotation from Marshall McLuhan and the condensed version to see how an ellipsis should be used properly.

ORIGINAL QUOTATION

As the alphabet neutralized the divergencies of primitive cultures by translation of their complexities into simple visual terms, so representative money reduced the moral values in the nineteenth century.

CONDENSED VERSION

In *Understanding Media,* Marshall McLuhan compares the visual technology inherent in the alphabet with money, saying, "As the alphabet neutralized the divergencies of primitive cultures . . . so representative money reduced moral values in the nineteenth century" (141).

Brackets

If you find that a quotation is not clear and you need to add information so that your readers will understand it better, you can do so by using square brackets [ ]:

> In their book *Freakonomics,* Steven D. Leavitt and Stephen J. Dubner confirm that often commonly held stereotypes seem to apply to reality:
>
>> For instance, men [on online dating sites] who say they want a longterm relationship do much better than men looking for an occasional lover. But women [on the same sites] looking for an occasional lover do great. (82)

MLA Documentation Style

There are two components to MLA style: parenthetical in-text citations and a works-cited list that appears at the end of the paper. Every source cited within the body of the paper appears in the works-cited list.

MLA Style: In-Text Citation

In MLA style, parenthetical in-text citations are used in conjunction with the list of works cited to give readers the information they would need to locate the sources that you have quoted, paraphrased, or summarized. The intent in MLA style is to give only as much information in the text as the reader needs to find the detailed bibliographical information in the list of works cited—generally, the author and the page number of the material cited. The following are examples of how to cite different types of sources within your text using MLA style, starting with the most basic citation: a work with one author.

A WORK WITH ONE AUTHOR

Suppose that you quote from page 173 of *Midnight Rising* by Tony Horwitz, published in 2011. In MLA style, your in-text citation would be "(Horwitz 173)." MLA in-text citations do not include punctuation, and the page number is given simply as a number.

The parenthetical citation is placed directly after the cited material. Here is an example using a block quotation in MLA style:

> The scene at Harpers Ferry, Virginia, in 1859 is described as one of confusion:
>
>> When the word of trouble in Harpers Ferry first spread on the morning of October 17, the response of white Virginians nearby was swift and instinctive. Their neighbors were under attack, blacks were rumored to be rising up, and that was all any able-bodied man needed to know before grabbing a gun and rushing to the scene. (Horwitz 173)

In this example, the author's name is not mentioned in the text that precedes the quotation. When the author's name is mentioned in the sentence preceding a quote, however, the parenthetical citation includes only the page number, as in the following example:

> Tony Horwitz describes the first reaction to rumors by those living near Harpers Ferry, Virginia, as both "swift and instinctive" (173).

If a parenthetical citation follows a quotation that ends a sentence, place the period after the parenthetical citation. However, if the quotation appears as a block (see above), place the period before the citation.

A WORK WITH MORE THAN ONE AUTHOR
Use all the authors' last names. If there are more than three authors, you can use the first author's last name with *et al.* following it.

> Glassick, Huber, and Maeroff state that "teaching, too, must in the end be judged not merely by process but by results, however eloquent a teacher's performance" (29).

> Ultimately, it is the results of teaching, not the method or the quality of the teacher's performance, that we must evaluate (Glassick, Huber, and Maeroff 29).

TWO OR MORE WORKS BY THE SAME AUTHOR
If you are citing ideas from two or more works by the same author, use the title of the work to distinguish which source you are citing.

> It is important to establish good relations with the people you work with by engaging in non-work related conversation. Both men and women do so, but the subjects of their conversations differ (Tannen, *Talking from 9 to 5* 64).

AN UNKNOWN AUTHOR
Use a shortened version of the title.

> Employees of Google believe their corporate culture to be antithetical to that of Microsoft ("Google" 15).

A GOVERNMENT AGENCY OR A CORPORATE AUTHOR
Use the name of the organization.

> Policy makers and citizens are warned that "Arizona is not positioned well to attract and keep the knowledge workers it needs" (Morrison Institute 6).

AN ANTHOLOGIZED WORK

Cite the author of the anthologized piece, not the editor of the collection. However, give the page numbers used in the collection.

> John Perry Barlow asks the important question: "The enigma is this: If our property
> can be infinitely reproduced and instantaneously distributed all over the planet
> without cost, without our knowledge, without its even leaving our possession, how
> can we protect it?" (319).

A SECONDARY SOURCE

Whenever possible, cite the original source. However, if you do need to use a quotation from a secondary source, use *qtd. in.*

> Jonathan Shaw muses, "I don't think mankind is ready, spiritually or mentally, for
> the transformations it's undergoing in the technological era: tattooing is a mute
> plea for a return to human values" (qtd. in Dery 284).

AN ONLINE SOURCE

Unless your source has some kind of numbering system or is a pdf file, you will not usually be able to provide page numbers for your quotation or paraphrase. Give the author or, if the author's name is not available, the title of the online work you are citing.

> According to Christopher Beam, there are a number of methods that Internet ser-
> vice providers can use to block Web sites if a government orders them to do so.

MLA Style: Constructing a List of Works Cited

Because the list of works cited at the end of your paper is intended to work together with your in-text citations, it includes only the sources you cite within your text, not the works that you read but did not cite. The list should be double-spaced, and its entries are listed alphabetically by the last name of the first author. The first line of each entry is even with the left margin; any subsequent lines are indented by one-half inch.

All entries in the list are formatted according to the same rules. In the following pages, you will find, for each common type of entry, a sample entry for a work in MLA style and, on pages 582-94, for many of the same works in APA style. First, though, to see some important differences between the two styles, consider these pairs of entries:

MLA   Horwitz, Tony. *Midnight Rising.* New York: Holt, 2012. Print.

APA   Horwitz, T. (2012). *Midnight rising.* New York: Henry Holt and Company.

MLA   Stine, Linda J. "Teaching Basic Writing in a Web-Enhanced Environment."
       Journal of Basic Writing 29.1 (2010): 33–55. Print.

APA   Stine, L. J. (2010). Teaching basic writing in a web-enhanced environment.
       Journal of Basic Writing 29(1), 33–55.

Notice in particular the following:

- In both styles, entries consist of three essential pieces of information, separated by periods: author, source, and publication information for the source (place of publication and publisher for the book; journal title and volume and issue number for the article). Note the difference in the placement of information: In APA style, the year of publication follows the author's name rather than coming later in the entry as it does in MLA style.

- In MLA style, authors' first and middle names are given in full if that is how they are given in the source; in APA style, only initials are given.

- In MLA style, all major words in titles are capitalized; in APA style, only the first word, words following a colon, and proper nouns are capitalized in the titles of books and articles. All major words are capitalized in the titles of periodicals, however.

- In both styles, titles of books and periodicals are given in italics. In MLA style, titles of articles are enclosed in quotation marks; in APA style, they are not.

- In MLA style, the medium of the source is identified—for example, Print, DVD, or Web.

The section that follows includes model entries for different types of print and nonprint sources in MLA style. Figure 20.1 provides you with a flowchart that will help you find the model entry that is closest to the source that you need to cite.

PRINT DOCUMENTS

Books

The basic items in an entry for a book are the author's name or authors' names, the title, and the publication information, consisting of the place of publication, publisher, date of publication, and medium. See Figure 20.2 on pages 562–63 for guidelines on where to find the elements of a works-cited entry for a book in MLA style.

1. Book with one author: The most basic form includes the author's name, the title of the book, in italics, and the publication information.

publication information

author   title city publisher date

Maddow, Rachel. *Drift*. New York: Crown, 2012. Print.

2. Two books by the same author: In MLA style, the author's name appears only in the first entry. For all subsequent entries, three hyphens are used instead of the name. The entries are listed in alphabetical order according to title.

Kissinger, Henry. *On China*. New York: Penguin, 2011. Print.

- - -. *White House Years*. New York: Simon, 1979. Print.

Is My Source a Complete Print Book or Part of a Print Book?

No	Yes, go to the next question below.	Go to this entry.
	Is it a book with only one author?	1
	Are you citing more than one book by this author?	2
	Is it a book with multiple authors?	3
	Is the book by an organization of some kind?	4
	Is the author unknown or unnamed?	5
	Does the book also have a translator?	11
	Is it a later publication or edition of the book?	6, 7
	Is it a multivolume work or part of a multivolume work?	13
	Is it part of a series?	14
	Does the book have an editor or a translator?	8, 11
	Is the book an edited collection or anthology?	8
	Is it a work in a collection or an anthology?	9
	Is it an introduction, a preface, a foreword, or an afterword?	12
	Is it an entry in a dictionary or reference work?	22
	Is it a published interview?	10

Is My Source from a Print Periodical Such as a Journal, a Magazine, or a Newspaper?

No	Yes, go to the next question below.	Go to this entry.
	Is it from a scholarly journal?	
	Is it a journal with volume and issue numbers?	15
	Is it a journal with only issue numbers?	16
	Is it from a magazine?	17
	Is it a review?	20
	Is it from a newspaper?	18
	Is it an editorial?	19
	Is it a letter to the editor?	21

3. Book with multiple authors: In MLA style, only the first author's name is inverted; the other authors' names are given first name first. MLA style uses *and* before the last author's name. In MLA style, if a book has more than three authors, you may give all the names or give the name of the first author followed by *et al.* (For an example of the use of *et al.*, see no. 8.)

> Grafton, Anthony, Glenn W. Most, and Salvatore Settis. *The Classical Tradition.*
> Cambridge: Harvard UP, 2010. Print.

4. Book by a corporate entity or organization:

> Adobe Systems Inc. *Adobe Acrobat 5.0: Getting Started.* San Jose: Adobe, 2001. Print.

Is My Source a Print Source but Not from a Journal, a Magazine, or a Newspaper?

No	Yes, go to the next question below.	Go to this entry.
	Is it an entry in a dictionary or reference work?	22
	Is it a government document?	23
	Is it a pamphlet?	24
	Is it the proceedings from a conference?	25
	Is it an unpublished doctoral dissertation?	26
	Is it a published or an unpublished letter?	27
	Is it a map or chart?	28
	Is it a cartoon?	29
	Is it an advertisement?	30

Is My Source a Nonprint Source from an Online Subscription Database or the World Wide Web?

No	Yes, go to the next question below.	Go to this entry.
	Is it a professional or personal Web site?	31
	Is it an article?	
	Is it a scholarly article retrieved from a database?	32
	Is it an article from an online journal?	34
	Is it an article from an online magazine?	35
	Is it an article from an online newspaper?	36
	Is it an online book?	33
	Is it a blog entry?	37
	Is it an entry on a wiki?	38
	Is it a posting to an electronic forum?	39
	Is it an e-mail message?	40

Is My Source a Nonprint Source That Is Not Published Online?

No	Yes, go to the next question below.	Go to this entry.
	Is it a television or radio program?	41
	Is it an audio recording?	42
	Is it a film, DVD, or Blu-ray?	43
	Is it a nonperiodical publication on CD-ROM?	44
	Is it a personal, e-mail, or telephone interview?	45
	Is it an oral presentation?	46
	Is it a performance?	47
	Is it a work of art?	48

Consult with Your Instructor about How to Cite Your Source.

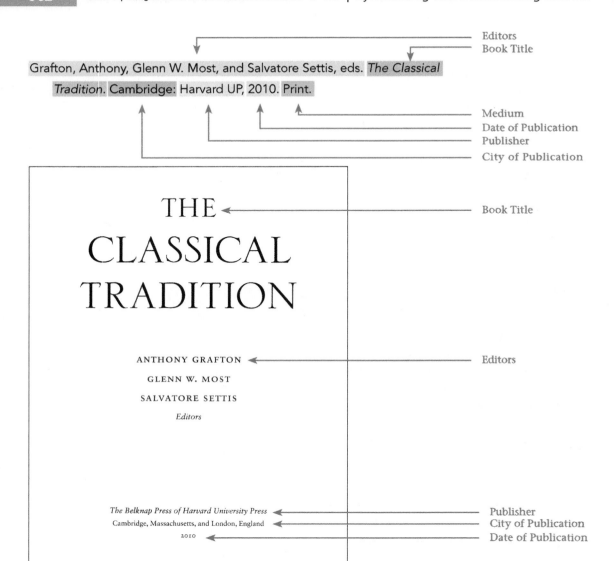

FIGURE 20.2   The Parts of a Works-Cited Entry for a Book in MLA Style

5. Book by an unknown author:

The Chicago Manual of Style: The Essential Guide for Writers, Editors, and Publishers.
16th ed. Chicago: Chicago UP, 2010. Print.

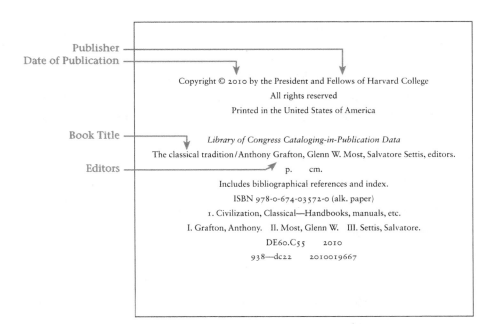

FIGURE 20.2 The Parts of a Works-Cited Entry for a Book in MLA Style *(Continued)*

6. Republished book: Including the original date of publication is optional in MLA style. If you do include this date, place it immediately following the title.

Darwin, Charles. *On the Origin of Species.* 1859. New York: Sterling, 2008. Print.

7. Book in a later edition:

Roen, Duane H., Gregory R. Glau, and Barry M. Maid. *The McGraw-Hill Guide to Writing: Writing for College, Writing for Life.* 3rd ed. New York: McGraw, 2013. Print.

8. Edited collection:

Inman, James A., and Donna N. Sewell, eds. *Taking Flight with Owls: Examining Electronic Writing Center Work.* Mahwah: Erlbaum, 2000. Print.

Harrington, Susanmarie, et al., eds. *The Outcomes Book: Debate and Consensus after the WPA Outcomes Statement.* Logan: Utah State UP, 2005. Print.

9. Work in a collection or an anthology: Include the full range of pages for the work you are citing, not just the pages you used or quoted from.

> Anson, Chris M., and Richard Jewell. "Shadows of the Mountain." *Moving a Mountain: Transforming the Role of Contingent Faculty in Composition Studies and Higher Education.* Ed. Eileen E. Schell and Patricia Lambert Stock. Urbana: NCTE, 2001. 47-75. Print.

10. Published interview:

> Banderas, Antonio. "America's Hottest Husband." Interview by Meg Grant. *AARP The Magazine* Nov. 2011: 64. Print.

11. Translation:

> Larsson, Stieg. *The Girl Who Kicked the Hornet's Nest.* Trans. Reg Keeland. New York: Knopf, 2010. Print.

12. Introduction, preface, foreword, or afterword:

> Campbell, T. Colin. Foreword. *Prevent and Reverse Heart Disease.* By Caldwell B. Esselstyn, Jr. New York: Avery, 2008. viii-ix. Print.

13. Multivolume work: If you have used more than one volume of a multivolume work, note the total number of volumes in the work after the title or editor information. (Refer to the actual volume and page numbers used in your in-text citation.)

> Caro, Robert A. *The Years of Lyndon Johnson.* 4 vols. New York: Vintage, 2003. Print.

If you have used only one volume of a multivolume work, cite only the volume you have used.

> Elias, Norbert. *The History of Manners.* Vol. 1. New York: Pantheon, 1982. Print.

14. Book in a series: If you are using a book that is part of a series, include the title of the series with no italics or quotation marks after the publication information and medium. Include the number of the series if it is present.

> Shortand, Michael, ed. *Science and Nature: Essays in the History of the Environmental Sciences.* Oxford: British Society for the History of Science, 1993. Print. BSHS Monograph Ser. 8.

Periodical Articles

The basic items in an entry for a periodical article are the author's name or authors' names, the title of the article, and information about the publication in which the article appeared, including its title, volume number (if applicable), date, page range, and publication medium. See Figure 20.3 on page 566 for guidelines on where to find the elements of a works-cited entry for a periodical article in MLA style.

15. Article in a scholarly journal with volume numbers: The issue number follows the volume number and a period.

author   title of article

Peters, Bradley. "Lessons about Writing to Learn from a University-High School

title of periodical

Partnership." *Journal of the Council of Writing Program Administrators*

34.2 (2011): 59-88. Print.

volume and issue no. and date   page range   medium

16. Article in a scholarly journal that has only issue numbers: Include only the issue number following the title of the journal.

Lousley, Cheryl. "Knowledge, Power, and Place." *Canadian Literature* 195 (2007):

11-30. Print.

17. Magazine article: Magazines may or may not include volume and issue numbers. In any case, in MLA style, volume numbers are not given. Instead, dates are provided. If magazines are published weekly or biweekly, the day is included along with the month, which is abbreviated. If the entire article does not appear on consecutive pages, give the first page number and a plus sign (+).

Foust, Dean, Michael Eidem, and Brian Bremner. "AFLAC: Its Ducks Are Not in a Row."

BusinessWeek 2 Feb. 2004: 52-53. Print.

Wilson, Chauncey E. "Usability and User Experience Design: The Next Decade."

Intercom 1 Jan. 2005: 6-9. Print.

18. Newspaper article: Entries for newspaper articles include the edition, when it is given (because different editions print different items), along with the date of publication and the section and page numbers. You should include the city of origin of a local newspaper within square brackets if it is not part of the title of the newspaper (for example, *Capital Times* [Madison]). You should also eliminate *The* at the beginning of the names of newspapers. When articles appear on discontinuous pages, give the first page number and a plus sign (+).

Fatsis, Stefan. "A More Modern Masters." *Wall Street Journal* 9 Apr. 2002: B1+. Print.

Title of Article

Authors

Phillips, Talinn, Candace Stewart, and Robert D. Stewart. "Geography Lessons, Bridge-Building, and Second Language Writers." *Writing Program Administration* 3.1/2 (2006): 83-100. Print.

Volume and Issue Numbers

Date of Publication

Page Range

Title of Journal

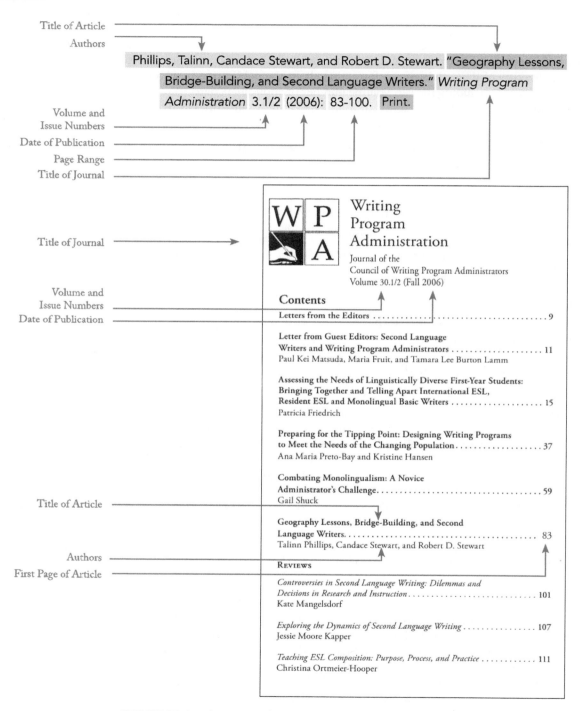

FIGURE 20.3   The Parts of a Works-Cited Entry for a Journal Article in MLA Style

19. Editorial: If an editorial is unsigned, use the form below. For signed editorials, begin the citation with the author's name.

"Moral Scoreboard." Editorial. *Arizona Republic* [Phoenix] 18 Feb. 2004: B10. Print.

20. Review: If there is no author for the review, alphabetize it by the title of the review. If the review also has no title, alphabetize by the title of what is being reviewed, even though your entry will begin with *Rev. of.* When citing a review, use the format appropriate for its place of publication.

Jablonski, Jeffrey. Rev. of *The New Careers: Individual Action and Economic Change,* by
Michael B. Arthur, Kerr Inkson, and Judith K. Pringle. *Technical Communication
Quarterly* 12 (2003): 230-34. Print.

21. Letter to the editor:

Rosati, Colette. Letter. *Arizona Republic* [Phoenix] 18 Feb. 2004: B10. Print.

Other Print Sources

22. Entry in a dictionary or reference work: In MLA style, entries in reference works are treated like entries in collections. If the author is known, begin with the author. Otherwise, start with the title of the entry. If the reference work is commonly known and regularly updated, you can simply give the edition and the date of publication.

"Express Mail." *Merriam-Webster's Collegiate Dictionary.* 11th ed. 2003. Print.

23. Government document: When the author of the document is not known, the agency is given as the author. Most publications from the U.S. federal government are published by the Government Printing Office (GPO). Give GPO as the publisher unless the title page indicates otherwise, as in the citation below.

United States. Dept. of Health and Human Services. National Institutes of Health.
*Toxicology and Carcinogenesis Studies of Resorcinal (CAS No. 108-46-3) in F344/N
Rats and B6C3F$_1$ Mice (Gavage Studies).* Research Triangle Park: National Insti-
tutes of Health, 1992. Print.

24. Pamphlet or brochure: Pamphlets and brochures are short documents and are usually held together by staples rather than a more formal binding. They are treated as books.

A Guide to Visiting the Lands of Many Nations & to the Lewis & Clark Bicentennial. St.
Louis: National Council of the Lewis & Clark Bicentennial, 2004. Print.

25. Published conference proceedings: The entire collection is treated as a book. Individual articles are treated as though they were in a collection by different authors.

> Buchanan, Elizabeth, and Nancy Morris. "Designing a Web-Based Program in Clinical Bioethics: Strategies and Procedures." *Proceedings of the 15th Annual Conference on Distance Teaching & Learning.* Madison: U of Wisconsin, 1999. 65-70. Print.

26. Unpublished doctoral dissertation:

> Edminster, Judith R. "The Diffusion of New Media Scholarship: Power, Innovation, and Resistance in Academe." Diss. U of South Florida, 2002. Print.

27. Letter: If the letter you are citing has been published, treat it as you would a work in an anthology, but also include the date.

> Hemingway, Ernest. "To Maxwell Perkins." 7 February 1936. *Ernest Hemingway: Selected Letters, 1917-1961.* Ed. Carlos Baker. New York: Scribner, 1981. 437-38. Print.

If the letter you are citing is a personal letter, start with the writer's name followed by "Letter to the author" and the date. For the medium, use "MS" for a handwritten letter and "TS" for a typed one.

> Morris, Patricia M. Letter to the author. 28 Dec. 2005. MS.

28. Map or chart:

> *San Francisco Bay.* Map. San Francisco: California State Automobile Association, 2004. Print.

29. Cartoon:

> Benson, Steve. Cartoon. *Arizona Republic* [Phoenix] 28 Dec. 2006: 17. Print.

30. Advertisement: Identify the product or company being advertised. Give the appropriate publication information for the medium where the ad appeared.

> Bristol-Myers Squibb. Advertisement. *Time.* 25 Dec. 2006: 81. Print.

ONLINE SOURCES

Because online sources change constantly, citing them is more complicated than citing print sources. In addition to the author's name (if known) and the title of the document and overall Web site, provide publication information (if known, such as the sponsoring organization and the date the site was last updated), the publication medium, and the date the document was accessed. Because URLs change often, they should be included at the end of citations only when readers might have trouble locating the document using author and title searches. When the document you are citing has a print as well as an electronic version, you may choose to provide publication information for both versions. See Figure 20.4 for guidelines on where to find the elements of a works-cited entry for an article accessed from an online database.

31. Basic professional or personal Web site:

American Medical Association. Home page. AMA. 2008. Web. 17 Feb. 2008.

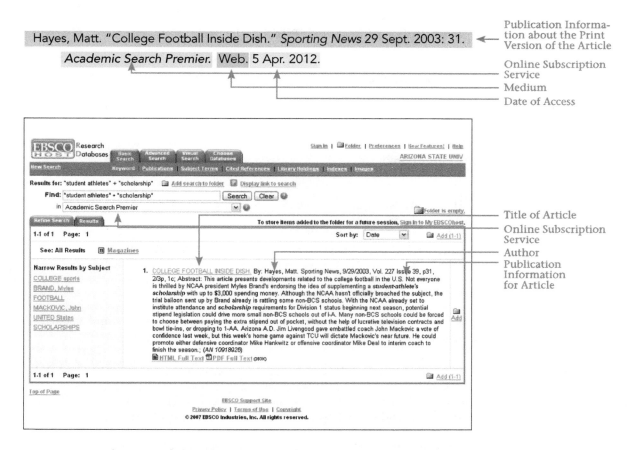

FIGURE 20.4 The Parts of a Works-Cited Entry for a Periodical Article Accessed from an Online Subscription Database

---

ELECTRONIC ENVIRONMENTS   **Using Microsoft Word to Develop Citations**

Within newer versions of Microsoft Word, you can build citations with the bibliographic information you've gathered about your sources. Select the "References" or "Document Elements" tab at the top, and then select the citation style you want to use—either MLA or APA. Choose "Insert Citation" (for Word 2010) or the tool icon and "Citation Source Manager." Make sure you choose the correct source type: book, article in a journal, Web site, or whatever is appropriate. From here you can enter the bibliographic information for your source by following the prompts. Each time you use a new source in the body of your project, add a new entry to the citations list, and Word will automatically track your sources. It is a good idea to review your project carefully before you submit it to ensure that every source that appears in the project has both an in-text citation and an entry in the works-cited (MLA) or reference (APA) page and that the format for each citation is correct.

---

32. Scholarly article retrieved from a database:

author   title of article

Johansen, Donald. "Microwave Propulsion Ionizer."

title of journal   vol./issue no., date, page range database

International Journal of Aerospace Innovations 3.2 (2011): 85-92. *EBSCOHost.*

medium date of access

Web. 28 April 2012.

33. Online book:

author   title of the online book   title of the Web site

Howells, William Dean. *Familiar Spanish Travels. Project Gutenberg.*

sponsoring agency   date site was updated   medium

Project Gutenberg Literacy Archive Foundation. 2008. Web.

date accessed

18 Feb. 2008. <http://www.gutenberg.nt>

URL included because "gutenberg.com" might be assumed and would lead the reader to a different site.

For books that you download to a digital device such as a Kindle or an iPad, MLA suggests that you use the guidelines for citing a book but replace the format type (Print) with the name of the digital file format, followed by the word "file." If you do not know the kind of file (PDF, for example), use "Digital file":

Slawenski, Kenneth. *J.D. Salinger: A Life.* New York: Random, 2011. n. pag.
Digital file.

34. Article from an online journal: When the online article is a digitized version of a print document, include the page numbers that you would find in print. However, if the document appears only in electronic form, page numbers may not exist. In that case, use *n. pg.* in your citation to indicate that no pagination was available.

> Salvo, Michael J. "Deafened to Their Demands: An Ethnographic Study of Accommo-
> dation." *Kairos* 7.1 (2002): n. pg. Web. 17 Feb. 2004.

35. Article from an online magazine:

> Cooper, Matthew, and Karen Tumulty. "Bring on the Cash!" *Time*. Time, 16 Feb. 2004.
> Web. 17 Feb. 2004.

36. Article from an online newspaper:

> Novovitch, Barbara. "It's Home Stupid Home, but the 'Clods' Can Read."
> *New York Times*. New York Times, 17 Feb. 2004. Web. 23 Feb. 2005.

37. Blog entry: Use the MLA format for general Web sites. Include the name of the author (bloggers often use pseudonyms); the name of the entry, enclosed in quotation marks; the name of the blog; the date of the entry (if available); the publication medium; and the date of access.

> Rice, J. "Network Academics." *Yellow Dog*. 30 Mar. 2007. Web. 31 Mar. 2007.

38. Wiki entry: Include the title of the entry, in quotation marks; the title of the wiki (italicized); the name of the sponsoring agency; the date the page was last updated; the publication medium; and the date you accessed the entry.

> "Rhetoric." *Wikipedia*. Wikimedia Foundation, 14 Nov. 2008. Web. 30 Nov. 2008.

39. Posting to an electronic forum such as a mailing list (listserv): This basic format is used for all online forums including Web-based postings.

> Peckham, Irvin. "Re: Update on AP and Dual Enrollment." *WPA-L*. 21 Sept. 2003. Web.
> 17 Feb. 2004.

40. E-mail message:

> Bernhardt, Stephen B. "Re: Congrats!" Message to B. Maid. 17 Feb. 2004. E-mail.

OTHER NONPRINT SOURCES

41. Television and radio programs: The basic elements for entries that cite radio and television programs include the title of the episode, the title of the program, or series, the name of the network, the call letters and the city of the local station, the broadcast date, and the medium of reception.

> "Dogs and More Dogs." Narr. John Lithgow. *Nova.* PBS. KAET, Phoenix, 3 Feb. 2004.
> Television.

> "Scientists Succeed in Cloning Human Embryo." Narr. Joe Palca. *All Things Consid-*
> *ered.* NPR. WGBH, Boston, 12 Feb. 2004. Radio.

42. Audio recording: A citation emphasizing a particular song would follow the format below. The citation ends with the medium accessed, such as *CD, LP,* or *MP3* file.

> Underwood, Carrie. "Blown Away." *Blown Away.* 19 Recordings Limited, 2012.
> MP3 file.

43. Film, DVD, or Blu-ray: In MLA style, the citation usually starts with the title and the director. The distributor, year of release, and medium are necessary. Other items, such as performers, are optional.

> *The Lord of the Rings: The Two Towers.* Dir. Peter Jackson. Perf. Elijah Wood
> and Ian McKellan. 2002. New Line Home Entertainment, 2003. DVD.

44. Nonperiodical publication on a CD-ROM:

> *The OWL Construction and Maintenance Guide.* Ed. James A. Inman and Clinton
> Gardner. Emmitsburg: IWCA, 2002. CD-ROM.

45. Personal, e-mail, or telephone interview: Indicate whether the interview was conducted in person, by e-mail, or by telephone following the name of the person you interviewed.

> Schwalm, D. Personal interview. 21 Feb. 2004.

46. Oral presentation:

> Russell, David R. "Teacher's Perception of Genre across the Curriculum: Making
> Classroom/Culture Connections Visible." Conf. on College Composition and
> Communication Convention. Atlanta Hilton, Atlanta. 26 Mar. 1999. Address.

47. Performance: If you are citing a play, an opera, a concert, or a ballet performance, start with the title, followed by the authors (*By*), and any other pertinent information (such as the director, identified as *Dir.*), the site where performed, the city, and the performance date; also note that it was a *Performance*.

> *The Norse Family.* By Jerry Jones. Dir. Walter Onger. Mesa Performing Arts Center, Mesa. 28 Dec. 2007. Performance.

48. Work of art:

> di Chirico, Giorgio. *The Philosopher's Conquest.* 1914. Oil on canvas. Joseph Winterbotham Collection. Art Institute of Chicago.

MLA Style: Sample Student Paper

Follow these guidelines if you are required to use MLA style:

- Note that a separate title page is not required. Instead, on the first page, put your name, your professor's name, the course number, and the date in the upper-left-hand corner, one inch from the top of the page, and follow with the title of your paper. The title should be centered, with major words capitalized (not articles and prepositions), and it should not be underlined or in a special typeface.
- Double-space the entire paper, including the information mentioned above, block quotations, and your list of works cited.
- Leave one-inch margins on all sides.
- Put page numbers in the upper-right-hand corner, one-half inch from the top. Just before each page number, put your last name.
- Indent the first line of paragraphs one-half inch from the left-hand margin.
- Begin your list of works cited on a new, consecutively numbered page. Include the title *Works Cited* one inch from the top. Center the title; do not use a special typeface for it.

The student paper that follows, "Money for Nothing" by Jessie Katz, is an example of a research project that uses MLA style.

1″

Jessie Katz

1″   Professor Wilson

English 105

April 16, 2012

Money for Nothing

For followers of college sports, February is a particularly exciting time of year. With the recent culmination of the football season in the bowl games and the anticipation of upcoming March Madness, all eyes seem glued to ESPN and the sports section of the newspaper as the drama of the season's games, rivalries, and players unfolds. In this charged atmosphere, the public turns its attention toward student-athletes and has ample occasion to contemplate the extraordinary lives that these young people lead. Indeed, some student-athletes apparently have it all: Aside from their national recognition and virtual stardom on and off of their campuses, these athletes also often receive special on-campus housing, the use of state-of-the-art training facilities, and, perhaps most notably, substantial scholarships from their schools.

1″

According to the National Collegiate Athletic Association (NCAA), colleges and universities award $1 billion in athletic scholarships annually to over 126,000 student-athletes (*Online*). NCAA defines athletic aid as "a grant, scholarship, tuition waiver, or other assistance from a college or university that is awarded on the basis of a student's athletic ability"; and a student-athlete is a member of the student body who receives athletic aid from his or her school sometime during his or her freshman year. Regardless of financial need or academic promise, athletic scholarships may cover tuition, fees, room and board, and books. Although nearly all Division I and Division II schools grant athletic scholarships, awarding this type of aid does little to benefit the academic prestige, community, or economic condition of colleges or universities. Giving scholarships based solely on athletic merit may in fact undermine the purpose of institutions of higher education, so colleges and universities need to reexamine the extraordinary amounts of money they currently spend on athletic aid to their students.

Like any social institution, colleges and universities exist to promote a certain set of goals. Even though mission statements differ from school to school, these organizations usually share three major objectives: academic scholarship through instruction

1″

Student's name.

Professor's name.

Course title.

Date.

Title centered; major words capitalized.

Shortened version of title of source enclosed in parentheses.

Thesis statement.

Katz   2

and research, service to the university's community, and economic development of the university and its surroundings. For instance, Arizona State University, one of the nation's premier research institutions and a member of the Pac-12, defines its current mission through the vision it calls "The New American University." The ASU Web site explains this vision

as follows:

> Arizona State University has developed a new model for the American research university, creating an institution that is committed to excellence, access and impact. ASU pursues research that contributes to the public good; and ASU assumes major responsibility for the economic, social and cultural vitality of the communities that surround it.

Universities, including ASU, promote their goals through their facilities, through their academic and community programs, and especially through their people, the large majority of whom are students. Students represent both a college's main source of income and its main product; and when a school awards a scholarship, it makes an investment in an individual who it feels will make a special contribution to its goals. However, granting athletes aid does not directly contribute to the three primary goals that most colleges and universities share.

Although they are part of institutions that society entrusts with the passage and creation of knowledge through scholarship and research, athletic departments often appear to disregard the academic success of student-athletes. Certainly not all student-athletes fit the "dumb jock" stereotype, but an alarming amount of data shows that these individuals fall behind their peers in the classroom. Academic underachievement in student-athletes starts at the recruitment level. To become a member of the NCAA and gain the privilege of practicing and playing sports and obtaining a sports scholarship at a Division I or Division II college, incoming freshmen must graduate from high school, complete at least fourteen core courses (including English, math, and physical and social sciences), have a minimum grade point average of 2.0, and achieve a minimum score of 820 on the SAT (*Online*). While these requirements appear reasonable, NCAA receives too many applicants and has a staff that is too small to carefully examine each potential student's high school record. In the most extreme cases of academic under-preparedness, student-athletes enter institutes of "higher" education without

Quotation longer than four lines indented 1 inch and double-spaced. Sentence that introduces it ends with colon. Page number not included because this is a Web source.

Katz   3

basic literacy and math skills. Since NCAA evaluates high school courses rather than college courses, after student-athletes are accepted into college, the regulation of student-athlete academic education becomes less centralized, falling to the universities' athletic departments, which may be motivated to keep student-athletes in the game and not on the academic chopping block. Instances abound in which advisors recommend lenient professors and classes with titles like Leisure and the Quality of Life, Sports Officiating, and Popular Music (Arizona State University). Surely, if and when academic education becomes subordinate to athletics, colleges and universities are counterproductive in funding their student-athletes'"scholarship."

One of the most disturbing facts concerning athletics in colleges and universities is that a substantial number of athletes are leaving these schools without a degree. In an effort to remedy the academic deficiencies prevalent in college sports, NCAA instituted the Academic Progress Rate (APR) program in 2004 (Bartter 1). Using a complex formula to assign each team an APR, NCAA supports teams with an APR of 925, the minimum value that predicts that the team will graduate at least half of its athletes, and higher. According to a recent study by the University of Central Florida, of the fifty-six Division I football teams selected to play in the 2006 Bowl games, twenty-three teams (including the previous national champion, University of Southern California) received an APR below 925, and twenty-seven teams had a graduation rate under 50%. For all Division I student-athletes, the U.S. Department of Education reports a 62% graduation rate, although the graduation rates for "the elite sports" (men's basketball and football) are considerably lower, with a basketball graduation rate of 44% and a football graduation rate of 54% (Wolverton). Admittedly, the total student-athlete graduation rate exceeds the graduation rate (60%) of non-athletes, but the success of many of these student-athletes may be bolstered by the financial support they receive. Consequently, a vast sum of the money that colleges give to their athletic students does not support the achievement of a degree, the most important tangible reward that a college or university can give a student. Indeed, unlike academic or music scholarships, which directly contribute to a college degree, athletic scholarships fund a pursuit unrelated, and at times even counterproductive, to what ASU's mission statement calls "fundamental fields of inquiry." Thus, granting athletic scholarships does not necessarily lead to academic returns for the university or the student-athlete.

Organization as author.

Source cited in parentheses, with page number.

Katz cites studies to support her thesis about athletic aid.

Katz   4

Despite the academic arguments against granting athletic scholarships, some institutions defend their awarding of financial aid based solely upon athletic performance with the argument that athletics contribute to the community service facet of a college's or university's stated mission. Certainly, a strong athletic program may benefit the community in a variety of healthy ways; a winning team engenders school spirit in its students and faculty, entices the citizens who live near the college to take an active interest in at least one aspect of the school, and earns state and national recognition and exposure, which may attract students and lead to increased enrollment. However, college athletics can be seen as having as many detrimental as positive effects on its community. In some instances, the same school spirit that fills the students with a sense of pride and place leads to very disreputable, unsportsmanlike conduct in the student body. In 2003, University of West Virginia students set over 100 fires and rioted in the streets after their football team defeated Virginia Tech (French 89). More recently, rioters set over forty fires and one person was shot after the University of Kentucky men's basketball team won the NCAA Championship in April 2012 (Kindelan). The athletes themselves also sometimes engage in activities that harm the communities; underage drinking and drug use occur in the athlete population as they do the general college population, and more serious events (such as allegations of rape against members of the University of Colorado football team in 2001 and the 2005 Baylor University incident in which one basketball player murdered his teammate) become highly publicized scandals. These events weaken considerably the positive impacts college athletics may have on schools' communities and undermine other community services, such as volunteer work, that students without any sort of scholarship perform. While athletics may benefit the community in many ways, they also have too many harmful effects on the community for colleges to justify the current levels of spending that many of them devote to athletic scholarships.

Perhaps the most common justification for granting student-athletes athletic scholarships is that college athletics is a major source of revenue for institutes of higher learning: through scholarships, athletes are allowed a portion of the money that they bring to their schools. This justification operates on the assumption that athletics do indeed attract capital to colleges and universities; yet an increasing amount of evidence shows that athletics departments actually cause a substantial deficit to the institutions that house them. The financial information from college athletics departments can be very misleading: in

Katz responds to counterargument about possible benefits of student athletics.

Katz   5

1994, NCAA reported that Division I-A athletics programs earned an average of about $13,632,000 and spent about $12,972,000, yielding an apparent profit of $660,000 (French 80). These numbers, though, did not account for the fact that some universities subsidized their athletic departments. If the direct transfers to athletics programs from their universities that year were subtracted from the average earnings, the result would reveal that these programs actually had a $174,000 deficit. In fact, some athletics departments had so little money that they could not even afford to fund their athletes' scholarships; instead, there is evidence of some universities dipping into the scholarship funds reserved for students with demonstrated financial need or academic merit (French 82).

Another misconception about athletic funding is that winning teams attract more monetary gifts from donors and alumni. A study by Cornell University management and economics professor Robert Frank, discussed in a 2004 *Sports Illustrated* article, demonstrates that "the presumed indirect benefits of sports, such as the spike in alumni giving and an enlarged applicant pool, are by all indications minimal." In fact, Frank discovered that "the revenues needed to compete have escalated to the point where the average big-time athletic program runs in the red. And when success brings a spike in donations, the money is routinely earmarked for the athletic program—not the general university fund" (qtd. in Fish). Therefore, even if a profit from student athletics is earned, universities usually cannot and do not use the money to advance their missions. Southern Methodist University President Gerald Turner confirms these conclusions: "I've been a university president now for about 20 years and I have never found any relationship between alumni giving to academic programs and the success of the athletic program" (qtd. in Fish). When colleges and universities award athletic scholarships, it may be less of a sound financial investment than boosters hope.

Without a doubt, athletics have an important entertainment role in a university setting. Yet, behind the Rose Bowl and March Madness, athletics programs are not as beneficial to their scholarly institutions as they may seem. It's time for colleges and universities to concentrate on their central missions—to promote academic scholarship, service to the university's community, and economic development of the university and its surroundings—instead of justifying the exorbitant expenditures of funds on programs that are more popular than they are useful to the school, the student, and the community at large.

Source cited in parentheses, with page number.

Information from authoritative source introduced by signal phrase within text.

Katz responds to two additional counterarguments; she responds to second counterargument by citing study and quoting expert.

Secondary source introduced in text, with *qtd. in* used in parenthetical citation.

Katz 6

Works Cited

Arizona State University. Home page. *Arizona State University.* 2012. Web. 3 Apr. 2012.

Bartter, Jessica. "Institute Study by Lapchick Looks at APR Rates and Graduation Rates for 2005–06 Bowl-Bound Teams." Devos Sport Business Management Program, College of Business Administration, University of Central Florida. 5 Dec. 2005. Web. 8 Apr. 2012.

Fish, Mike. "Separate Worlds: Studies Show Big-Time Athletics Don't Impact Academic Donations." *Sports Illustrated.* 14 Sept. 2004. Web. 8 Apr. 2012.

French, Peter A. *Ethics and College Sports: Ethics, Sports, and the University.* Lanham: Rowman, 2004. Print.

Kindelan, Katie. "Kentucky Students Riot after NCAA Championship Win." *ABCNews.com.* ABC News, 3 April 2012. Web. 8 April 2012.

The Online Resource for the National Collegiate Athletic Association. NCAA, 2005. Web. 8 Apr. 2012.

Wolverton, Brad. "Under New Formula, Graduation Rates Rise." *Chronicle of Higher Education* 52.21 (2006): A41. Web. 8 Apr. 2012.

New page, title centered; double space between title and first line of works-cited list.

Entries doublespaced, in alphabetical order.

First line of each entry at left margin; all other lines indented 1/2 inch.

Note that URLs are optional for Web sources.

APA Documentation Style

APA Style: In-Text Citation

In APA style, parenthetical in-text citations are used in conjunction with the list of references at the end of a paper to give readers the information they would need to locate the sources that you have quoted, paraphrased, or summarized. In-text citations include year of publication along with the author and page number. Suppose, for example, that you are quoting from page 282 of Deborah Tannen's *You Just Don't Understand: Woman and Men in Conversation,* published in 1990. In APA style, a parenthetical in-text citation would be "(Tannen, 1990, p. 282)." If you give the author's name within your sentence, however, the date appears in parentheses following the name. APA parenthetical citations have commas between the elements and "p." before the page number. Page numbers are needed only when you are citing a quotation or specific information.

The following are examples of how to cite different types of sources within your text using APA style.

A WORK WITH ONE AUTHOR

> Tony Horwitz (2012) describes the first reaction to rumors of an attack by those living near Harpers Ferry, Virginia, as both "swift and instinctive" (p. 173).

A WORK WITH MORE THAN ONE AUTHOR

For a source with up to five authors, use all the authors' last names in the first citation. If you give their names in parentheses, put an ampersand (&) between the last two names. After the first citation, use the first author's name followed by *et al.* for a work by three or more authors.

> Grafton, Most, and Settis (2010) write that "Chaucer's admiration of classical poetry, and the lessons he learned from it about irony, tragedy, history, fate, and love, made him a major conduit, and fashioner, of the classical tradition in England" (p. 193).

> Ever since the middle of the 20th century, nations have considered democracy as the only legitimate form of national government (Grafton, Most, & Settis, 2010, p. 256).

For a source with six or more authors, use *et al.* with every citation, including the first.

AN UNKNOWN AUTHOR

Use a shortened version of the title.

Employees of Google believe their corporate culture to be antithetical to that of Microsoft ("Google," 2006).

A GOVERNMENT AGENCY OR A CORPORATE AUTHOR

Give the complete name of most organizations every time you use them. After the first use, however, you can use an abbreviation for organizations with unwieldy names and well-known or easily understood abbreviations.

> The Federal Emergency Management Agency (FEMA, 2007) offers officials many suggestions in a new brochure. You can obtain a copy of FEMA's brochure at our main office.

A SECONDARY SOURCE

If you need to use a quotation from a secondary source, use *as cited in* to let your readers know that you are doing so.

> Aristotle noted that tiny animals can be found "in books, some of them similar to those found in clothes, others like tailless scorpions, very small indeed" (as cited in Greenblatt, 2011, p. 83).

AN ONLINE SOURCE

Cite in the same way that you would cite a print source. For a source with paragraph numbers, use *para.* or ¶. If you cannot find a date for the source, use the abbreviation *n.d.* (for "no date").

> According to Christopher Beam (2006), there are a number of methods that Internet service providers can use to block Web sites if a government orders them to.

A BLOCK QUOTATION

In APA style, block quotations are used for quotations of more than forty words and are indented one-half inch or five spaces, as in the following example:

> A political observer explains an analogy from the early days of Barack Obama's presidency:
>
>> Politics is not a meritocracy, and Obama realized no president was guaranteed credit or lucky bounces. But at times he couldn't help feeling, as he told one associate, a kinship with the protagonist in Ernest Hemingway's *The Old Man and the Sea*. He had, against tremendous odds, caught a big fish, but on the long voyage back to shore, his prized catch had been picked to pieces by sharks. (Corn, 2012, p. 15)

If the author's last name and year of publication are not included in the sentence that introduces the quotation, they should be provided in parentheses following the quotation along with the page number, as shown here.

APA Style: Constructing a References List

For a comparison of the MLA and APA styles for citing books and periodical articles, see page 558.

The section that follows includes model entries for different types of print and nonprint sources in APA style. Figure 20.5 provides you with a flowchart that will help you find the model entry that is closest to the source that you need to cite.

FIGURE 20.5
APA Style: A Flowchart for Determining the Model References Entry You Need

Is My Source a Complete Print Book or Part of a Print Book?

No	Yes, go to the next question below.	Go to this entry.
	Is it a book with only one author?	1
	Are you citing more than one book by this author?	2
	Is it a book with multiple authors?	3
	Is the author unknown or unnamed?	5
	Is the book by an organization of some kind?	4
	Does the book also have a translator?	10
	Is it a later publication or edition of the book?	6, 7
	Is it a multivolume work?	12
	Does the book have an editor or a translator?	8, 10
	Is the book an edited collection or anthology?	8, 9
	Is it a work in a collection or an anthology?	9
	Is it an introduction, a preface, a foreword, or an afterword?	11
	Is it a published interview?	13
	Is it an entry in a dictionary or reference work?	22

Is My Source from a Print Periodical Such as a Journal, a Magazine, or a Newspaper?

No	Yes, go to the next question below.	Go to this entry.
	Is it from a scholarly journal?	
	Do the journal's page numbers continue from one issue to the next?	14
	Does each issue start with page 1?	15
	Is it from a magazine?	16
	Is it a review?	19
	Is it from a newspaper?	17
	Is it an editorial?	18
	Is it a letter to the editor?	20
	Is it an article in a newsletter?	21

Is My Source a Print Source
but Not from a Journal, a Magazine, or a Newspaper?

No	Yes, go to the next question below.	Go to this entry.
	Is it an entry in a dictionary or reference work?	22
	Is it a government document?	23
	Is it an unpublished doctoral dissertation?	24
	Is it an academic report?	25

Is My Source a Nonprint Source from the Internet?

No	Yes, go to the next question below.	Go to this entry.
	Is it a professional or personal Web site?	26
	Is it an article?	
	Is it a scholarly article	27, 28
	Is it from an online magazine?	30
	Is it from an online newspaper?	31
	Is it an online book?	29
	Is it a posting to an electronic forum?	32
	Is it an e-mail message?	33
	Is it a blog entry?	34
	Is it an entry in a wiki?	35
	Is it a podcast?	36

Is My Source a Nonprint Source
That Is Not Published Online?

No	Yes, go to the next question below.	Go to this entry.
	Is it a television or radio program?	37
	Is it an audio recording?	38
	Is it a film, DVD, or Blu-ray?	39
	Is it an oral presentation?	40

Consult with Your Instructor about How to Cite Your Source.

PRINT DOCUMENTS
Books
The basic elements in an entry for a book are the author's name or authors' names, the date of publication, the title, and the publication information, consisting of the place of publication and the publisher. See Figure 20.6 on pages 584–85 for guidelines on where to find the elements of an entry in a list of references for an edited collection in APA style.

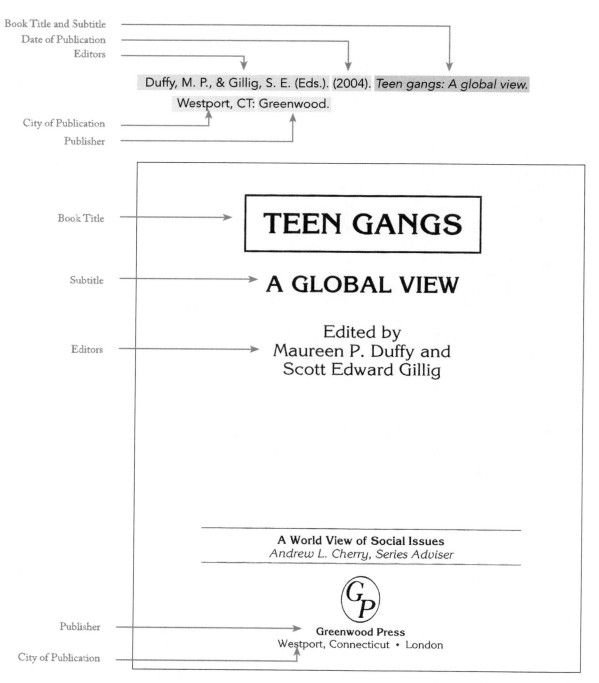

FIGURE 20.6 The Parts of a Reference Entry for an Edited Collection

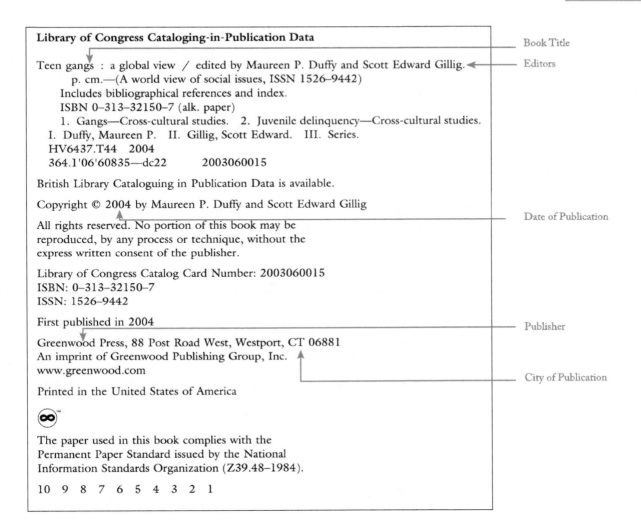

1. **Book with one author:** In APA style, the date of publication follows the author's name. The author's first and middle name are given as initials, and the title of the book is italicized. Only the first word of the title is capitalized, as well as any proper nouns and the first word following a colon.

                          date of
author   publication title   city   state publisher

Greenblatt, S. (2011). *The swerve.* New York, NY: Norton.

2. Two entries by the same author: The entries are listed in chronological order, with the earliest publication first. If more than one work was published in the same year, the works are ordered alphabetically based on the first letter of the title. Each work is given a lowercase letter after the date: for example, "(2004a)" for the first entry published in 2004 and "(2004b)" for the second entry. These letters would appear with the dates in the in-text citations.

> Greenblatt, S. (2004). *Will in the world: How Shakespeare became Shakespeare.* New
> York, NY: Norton.

> Greenblatt, S. (2011). *The swerve.* New York, NY: Norton.

3. Book with multiple authors: All authors' names are inverted. Use an ampersand to separate the last two entries. Give the names of all authors up to six; if there are more authors, follow the sixth name with *et al.*

> Bellah, R. N., Madsen, R., Sullivan, W. M., Swidler, A., & Tipton, S. M. (2007). *Habits of
> the heart: Individualism and commitment in American life* (3rd ed.). Berkeley,
> CA: University of California Press.

4. Book by a corporate entity or organization: When the publisher is the same as the author, use the word *Author* where the publisher's name is usually given.

> Adobe Systems Inc. (2001). *Adobe Acrobat 5.0: Getting started.* San Jose, CA: Author.

5. Book by an unknown author:

> *The Chicago manual of style: The essential guide for writers, editors, and publishers* (16th
> ed.). (2010). Chicago, IL: University of Chicago Press.

6. Republished book: The original date of publication must be included.

> Dickens, C. (1969). *Hard times.* (D. Craig, Ed.). Baltimore, MD: Penguin Books.
> (Original work published 1854)

7. Book in a later edition:

> Corbett, E. P. J. (1990). *Classical rhetoric for the modern student* (3rd ed.). New York, NY:
> Oxford University Press.

8. Edited collection:

> Inman, J. A., & Sewell, D. N. (Eds.). (2000). *Taking flight with owls: Examining electronic
> writing center work.* Mahwah, NJ: Erlbaum.

See also Figure 20.6 on pages 584–85.

9. Work in a collection or an anthology: In APA style, the page numbers come after the title and before the publication information.

> Anson, C. M., & Jewell, R. (2001). Shadows of the mountain. In E. E. Schell & P. L. Stock
>
> (Eds.), *Moving a mountain: Transforming the role of contingent faculty in compo-*
>
> *sition studies and higher education* (pp. 47–75). Urbana, IL: NCTE.

10. Translation:

> Larsson, S. (2010). *The girl who kicked the hornet's nest* (R. Keeland, Trans.). New York,
>
> NY: Knopf. (Original work published 2007)

11. Introduction, preface, foreword, or afterword:

> Campbell, T. C. (2008). Foreword. In C.B. Esselstyn, *Prevent and reverse heart disease*
>
> (pp. viii–ix). New York, NY: Avery.

12. A multivolume work published over more than one year:

> Campbell, J. (1959–1968). *The masks of god* (Vols. 1–4). New York, NY: Viking.

13. Published interview:

> Blair, K., & Takayoshi, P. (1999). Making the map: An interview with Gail Hawisher.
>
> [Interview with G. Hawisher] In K. Blair & P. Takayoshi (Eds.), *Feminist cyber-*
>
> *spaces: Mapping gendered academic spaces* (pp. 177–191). Stamford, CT:
>
> Ablex.

You should cite an interview published in a periodical as you would a periodical article (see nos. 14, 15, and 16). APA categorizes personal interviews as personal communications: Because such an interview cannot be recovered, there is no need to include an entry for it in a reference list, but the interview should be cited in the body of the text (see nos. 33 and 40).

PERIODICAL ARTICLES

The basic items in an entry for a periodical article are the author's name or authors' names, the date of publication in parentheses, the title of the article, and information about the publication in which the article appeared, including its title, volume and issue number (if applicable), and the page range for the article. See Figure 20.7 for guidelines.

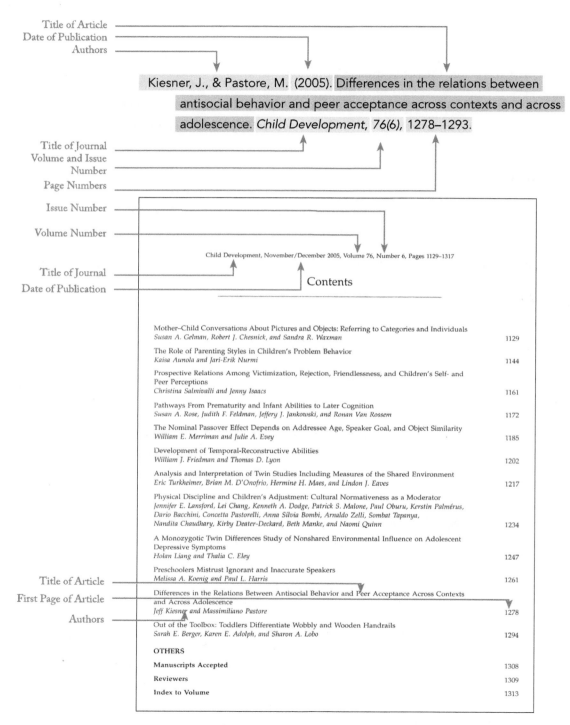

FIGURE 20.7 The Parts of a Reference Entry for a Journal Article

14. Article in a scholarly journal with continuous pagination: In APA style, the volume number is italicized. APA style uses full page numbers.

authors   date of publication   title

Thayer, A., & Kolko, B. E. (2004). Localization of digital games: The

title of periodical

process of blending for the global games market. *Technical*

volume no. and page range

Communication, 51, 477–488.

15. Article in a scholarly journal that is paginated by issue: When an article is from a journal that restarts the page numbers with each issue, the issue number follows the volume number in parentheses in APA style.

Peters, B. (2011). Lessons about writing to learn from a university–high school part-

nership. *Journal of the Council of Writing Program Administrators, 34*(2), 59–88.

16. Magazine article: Magazines may or may not include volume and issue numbers. In an entry in APA style, the volume number should be included, placed within commas between the name of the magazine and the page numbers of the article: "(*Scientifi c American, 290,* 54–61)." In the first example below, *BusinessWeek* is a magazine that does not use volume numbers.

Foust, D., Eidem, M., & Bremner, B. (2004, February 2). AFLAC: Its ducks are not in a

row. *BusinessWeek,* 52–53.

Wilson, C. E. (2005, January). Usability and user experience design: The next decade.

Intercom, 52, 6–9.

17. Newspaper article: When articles appear on discontinuous pages, as they often do, APA style requires you to list all the page numbers.

Fatsis, S. (2002, April 9). A more modern masters. *Wall Street Journal,* pp. B1, B4.

18. Editorial: If there is a title, it should precede "[Editorial]."

Moral scoreboard [Editorial]. (2004, February 18). *The Arizona Republic,* p. B10.

19. Review: If the review is titled, give the title in the usual position, preceding the bracketed information.

Jablonski, J. (2003). [Review of the book *The new careers: Individual action and*

economic change, by M. Arthur, K. Inkson, & J. K. Pringle]. *Technical Communi-*

cation Quarterly, 12, 230–234.

20. Letter to the editor:

> Rosati, C. (2004, February 18). Let's throw the book at Valley street racers [Letter to
> the editor]. *The Arizona Republic,* p. B10.

21. Newsletter article, no author:
Unsigned articles should be alphabetized in the list of references by the first word of the title. If there is a volume number, place it between the name of the publication and the page numbers, separated by commas. The following example from the newsletter of the Heard Museum of Native Cultures and Art has no volume number.

> Shared images: The jewelry of Yazzie Johnson and Gail Bird. (2007, January/
> February). *Earthsong,* 8.

Other Print Sources

22. Entry in a dictionary or reference work:
APA style uses page numbers even when the entries are alphabetical.

> Express Mail. (1993). In *Merriam-Webster's new collegiate dictionary* (p. 411).
> Springfield, MA: Merriam-Webster.

> Pfeiffer, R. H. (1974). Sumerian Poetry. In *Princeton Encyclopedia of Poetry
> and Poetics* (pp. 820–821). Princeton, NJ: Princeton University Press.

23. Government document:
Like MLA style, APA style lists the agency as the author of the report when the author is not known. If you list a subdepartment or agency, make certain that you also list the higher department if the subdepartment is not well known. If the publisher is not the Government Printing Office (GPO), list the highest known agency or department as the author. If the document has a specific publication number, list it after the title.

> National Institutes of Health. (1992). *Toxicology and carcinogenesis studies of
> Resorcinol (CAS No. 108-46-3) in F344/N rats and B6C3F$_1$ mice (Gavage Studies)*
> (NIH Publication No. 92-2858). Research Triangle Park, NC: Author.

24. Unpublished doctoral dissertation:

> Edminster, J. R. (2002). *The diffusion of new media scholarship: Power, innovation,
> and resistance in academe* (Unpublished doctoral dissertation). University of
> South Florida.

25. Academic report:

> Melnick, R., Welch, N., & Hart, B. (2005). *How Arizona compares: Real numbers and hot
> topics.* Tempe: Arizona State University, Morrison Institute for Public Policy.

ONLINE SOURCES

APA style requires including the Digital Object Identifier (DOI) for online sources, if one is available. Regulated by the International DOI Foundation (IDF), the DOI is a unique number that is registered with a specific agency that follows the standards of the IDF. It works similarly to the system that registers domain names on the Internet and helps people locate a specific reference, such as a journal article or an online book. If you were searching for an article on the topic of adolescent female gang behavior, you might find this article. You can see the DOI in the fourth line on the left.

Journal of Human Behavior in the Social Environment, 19:231–241, 2009
Copyright © Taylor & Francis Group, LLC
ISSN: 1091-1359 print/1540-3556 online
DOI: 10.1080/10911350802694584

**Spirituality as a Protective Factor Against
Female Gang Membership**

ELIZABETH S. MARSAL
Department of Criminal Justice, East Carolina University, Greenville, North Carolina

If there is no DOI, then include the home page URL using the format "Retrieved from http://www.xxxxx/" (with no period at the end).

26. Basic professional or personal Web site:

> American Medical Association. (2004). Home page. Retrieved from http://www
>
> .ama-assn.org/

27. Article from an online journal with a Digital Object Identifier (DOI): Include the issue number as well as the volume number; provide the DOI at the end of the entry.

> authors   date of publication   title of article
>
> Maylath, B., Grabill, J., & Gurak, L. (2010). Intellectual fit and programmatic power:
>
> Organizational profiles of four professional/technical/scientific communica-
>
> title of journal   volume and issue nos.   page range
>
> tion programs. *Technical Communication Quarterly, 19*(3), 262–280.
>
> DOI
>
> doi: 10.1080/10572252.2010.481535

28. Article from an online journal without a DOI: In APA style, the volume number is italicized.

> Salvo, M. J. (2002). Deafened to their demands: An ethnographic study of accommo-
>
> dation. *Kairos 7*(1). Retrieved from http://english.ttu.edu/ kairos/7.1/binder2.
>
> html?coverweb/salvo/ctx.html

Note: If you retrieved the article from an online database, include the URL of the home page for the database only if the article would be difficult to find otherwise (for example, "Retrieved from PsycARTICLES database: http: //psycnet.apa.org)."

29. Online book:

> Wolfe, T. (1998). *A man in full* [Kindle edition]. New York: Farrar, Straus,
>
> and Giroux. Kindle file.

APA suggests that you include in the reference list the author, date, title (with e-reader book type in square brackets if applicable); that you italicize the title but not the bracketed material, and source (DOI or URL, if available):

> Leonard, E. (2012). *Raylan*. [iBooks edition]. Retrieved from iBooks.

If you acquired the book through an online library (Google Books, ebrary, NetLibrary) and not on an e-reader device, omit the bracketed information from the reference.

30. Article from an online magazine:

> Cooper, M., & Tumulty, K. (2004, February 16). Bring on the cash! *Time.* Retrieved
>
> from http://www.time.com

31. Article from an online newspaper:

> Novovitch, B. (2004, February 17). It's home stupid home, but the "clods" can read.
>
> *New York Times.* Retrieved from http://www.nytimes.com

32. Posting to an electronic forum such as a mailing list (listserv): In APA style, list only electronic references that have been archived and are retrievable.

> Peckham, I. (2004, February 17). Update on AP and dual enrollment [Electronic
>
> mailing list message]. Retrieved from http://lists.asu.edu/cgi-bin/wa?A2=ind0
>
> 309&L=wpal&D=1&O=D&F=&S=&P=52156

33. E-mail message: In APA style, e-mail is cited only in the text as "personal communication," followed by the date of the e-mail.

34. Blog entry: Provide the name of the author (bloggers often use pseudonyms), date, title of entry, the words "Message posted to," name of blog, and the URL.

> Rice, J. (2007, March 30). Network academics [Web log post]. Retrieved from http://ydog.net/?page_id=345

35. Wiki entry:

> Rhetoric. (n.d.). Retrieved March 30, 2007, from http://en.wikipedia.org/wiki/Rhetoric

36. Podcast:

> Sharot, T. (Writer). (2012). *The optimism bias* [Video podcast]. Retrieved from http://www.ted.com

OTHER NONPRINT SOURCES

37. Television and radio programs: In APA style the names of the writers, directors, and producers are given as appropriate. Indicate whether the source is a television or radio broadcast in square brackets.

> Buckner, N., & Whittlesey, R. (Writers, Directors, Producers). (2004, February 3). Dogs and more dogs. *Nova* [Television broadcast]. Boston, MA, and Washington, DC: Public Broadcasting Service.

> Turpin, C. (Executive Producer). (2004, February 12). Scientists succeed in cloning human embryo. *All things considered* [Radio broadcast]. Washington, DC: National Public Radio.

38. Audio recording:

> Thompkins C., & Kear, J. (2012). Blown away [Recorded by C. Underwood]. On *Blown away* [CD]. Nashville, TN: Sony Nashville/Arista.

39. Film, DVD, or Blu-ray:

> Jackson, P. (Director). (2002). *The lord of the rings: The two towers* [DVD]. United States: New Line Home Entertainment.

40. Oral presentation: Because live lectures are not recoverable data, in APA style, they are cited parenthetically in the text but are not included in the list of references. However, when professional presentations are made from texts that can be recovered, they are cited.

> Russell, D. R. (1999, March). *Teacher's perception of genre across the curriculum:*
>
> *Making classroom/culture connections visible.* Paper presented at the
>
> Conference on College Composition and Communication Convention,
>
> Atlanta, GA.

APA Style: Sample Student Paper

The student paper that follows, "How Do Gangs Affect Adolescent Behavior?" by Aaron Zook, is an example of a paper that uses APA style.

If you write a paper using APA style, follow these guidelines:

- Include a separate title page. Center the title one-third of the way down the page, using capital and lowercase letters; do not use a special typeface for it. Give your name, the course name and number, and the date, all also centered and double spaced, on separate lines below the title. In the upper-right-hand corner, give the page number. In the upper-left-hand corner, type "Running head:" followed by a shortened version of the title in all capital letters. The words "Running head" should appear on the title page only; the shortened version of the title goes on all subsequent pages.

- On the second page of your paper, provide an abstract of the paper if your instructor requires one. An abstract is a brief (approximately 100–120 words) summary of your paper's contents. If you include an abstract, the paper itself begins on the third page. Repeat the title on the first page of your paper, centering it one inch from the top. Double-space to the first line of your text.

- Double-space the entire paper, including any block quotations and the items in your list of references.

- Leave one-inch margins on all sides.

- Place page numbers in the upper-right-hand corner after the running head, five spaces after the shortened version of the title.

- Indent paragraphs and block quotations one-half inch from the left margin.

- Note that some papers use headings to label sections of the text. If you use headings, center them and double-space above and below them.

- Put your list of references on a new page, with the title "References" centered at the top.

Running head: HOW DO GANGS AFFECT BEHAVIOR?   1

Running head is a shortened version of the title (preceded by "Running head:" on the first page only).

How Do Gangs Affect Adolescent Behavior?

Aaron Zook

Psychology 101

Professor Jones

March 23, 2010

Title is centered, one-third of the way down the page.

Name, title of course, name of professor, and date are centered and double-spaced on separate lines below the title.

↑ ½"

  1"

2

Title repeated on first page of paper, centered.

Double-space from title to first line of paper.

Information from sources cited with parenthetical references.

Quotation longer than forty words indented 1/2 inch or 5 spaces and double-spaced. Introductory sentence ends with a colon. Because no date is given in source, abbreviation *n.d.* is included.

How Do Gangs Affect Adolescent Behavior?

1"

Since the early 1920s, researchers have closely studied the relationship between street gangs and violent crime from a variety of perspectives: criminological, sociological, and psychological (Thabit, 2005). Whatever the underlying causes for gang membership, the results seem clear; members of street gangs admit to a far greater rate of serious crime, and to far more severe acts of violence (Penly Hall, Thornberry, & Lizotte, 2006) than non-gang members of the same age, race, and socioeconomic background. According to the Web site Safeyouth.org (n.d.), gang violence is certainly cause for concern:

> Gang members are responsible for much of the serious violence in the United States. . . . Teens that are gang members are much more likely than other teens to commit serious and violent crimes. For example, a survey in Denver found that while only 14% of teens were gang members, they were responsible for committing 89% of the serious violent crimes.

1"

Many researchers have therefore come to the conclusion that gangs necessarily cause violence and deviant behavior. As a matter of policy, then, it seems clear that the solution to a number of social ills is to break up, disrupt, or prevent the formation of gangs. Other programs seek to prevent young people from joining gangs through interventions of various types and levels of effectiveness. Most of these efforts take it as a given that gangs seriously distort behavior, even among individuals who already belong to "high-risk" demographic groups. Adolescents living in poverty or other disadvantaged circumstances; those attending violent and/or failing schools; members of criminalized peer groups; and children from violent and/or extremely dysfunctional households or demonstrating a predisposition toward antisocial behavior all seem to be at greater

Et al. used for first citation of work with six authors.

Zook presents synthesis of his findings.

risk for future gang membership, but a number of studies have shown that their own behaviors are considerably more violent while they belong to a gang than they were before or after membership (Gordon et al., 2004). After years of study, researchers still do not clearly understand how and why gangs exert such a powerful influence on behavior. A crucial answer might be found in the typical composition of a gang. Overwhelmingly, gangs are made up of adolescents and young adults. The median age of violent gang members has been estimated to be eighteen; members tend to join in their late teens, and contrary to popular fallacies and urban legends, youths generally leave a gang with

↕ 1"

few or no consequences within a year of joining (Thomas, 2005). Clearly, then, the gang problem can and should be understood in large part as a youth problem; researchers might come to a deeper understanding of the nature and impact of gangs by shifting some emphasis in their research from violence to adolescent adjustment behaviors.

The research community has by no means reached a consensus as to the precise definition of street gangs, however. The telltale sign that a group is a gang—one that most researchers, police organizations, the popular media, and gang members themselves agree on—is a tendency to commit violent acts (Katz & Jackson-Jacobs, 2004), but violence is not an adequate condition in itself. Why, for example, are Crips and Bloods considered gangs, but not Skinheads? Likewise, organized crime is now rarely considered "gang behavior," though early studies included these types of organizations. Yet all of these form distinct social groups and are involved in criminal behaviors (Thomas, 2005). One common distinction researchers draw is based on the motivation behind the group's violent activities. Does the group sell drugs or stolen merchandise? Do they operate according to an ideology or shared set of racial or cultural prejudices? Or are they primarily concerned with "turf," status, or violence for its own sake (U.S. Department of Education, n.d.)? Contemporary studies tend to maintain that only the latter group of motives typify "gangs" and have been particularly concerned with the seemingly random nature of the various criminal behaviors that many such gangs exhibit. The criminal acts seem to have largely symbolic value that is consistent with the way many street gangs are associated with the use of emblems, dress, and a shared name easily identified by all of their members (Katz & Jackson-Jacobs, 2004).

Experts in gang behavior have advanced numerous explanations for the most troubling examples of violent gang behavior: random drive-by shootings, seemingly unmotivated killings and aggravated assaults, car-jackings, and so on. Ritual initiations, turf wars, cycles of retribution between competing gangs, and intragang status are obvious motivators. Yet another explanation has involved the culpability of the media and the police in promoting gang imagery: The very definition of gangs as violent entities increases members' levels of violence. In other words, certain youths seek the rewards they think gang membership will afford them—status; protection; group identity; and entertainment, drugs, and sex (U.S. Department of Education, n.d.)—and are willing to engage in violent acts because "that's what a gang is." The image is reinforced by the

Opening paragraph sets up the issue.

First point: Difficulty of defining gangs.

Government agency as author.

HOW DO GANGS AFFECT BEHAVIOR?   4

news and popular media and by the folklore of the gang itself. It has also been argued that both gang members' own accounts of their activities and police statistics may be misleading. Because of the status violence confers on a perpetrator, a subject could conceivably exaggerate his or her criminal behavior in surveys and interviews as a means of bragging. Further, crime statistics reflect arrest and incarceration rates which, considering the general conspicuousness of gang members and police efforts to target these groups, could conceivably skew higher for gang offenders than for criminals who do not belong to gangs. A number of studies, less sensational in their findings and therefore less visible in the mainstream media, have found that most gang members spend the majority of their time simply "hanging out," albeit often within the context of drug or alcohol use (Katz & Jackson-Jacobs, 2004). In a sense, then, lacking any overarching objective such as profit or ideology, some gangs may see continued violence as a means of justifying their own existence and retaining members who would otherwise grow restless and leave.

If retention is indeed the motivation for violent gang behavior, then it seems unlikely that some special feature of gangs in their day-to-day operation enables violent extremes of behavior; rather, it is the symbolic value of the gang "family" that makes them sufficiently attractive to justify violence, the risk of death or imprisonment, and the common perception (however false) that one can never leave the gang. It seems likely that certain characteristics typical of adolescents—the desire to create a self-identity, establish a sense of belonging, and both derive status from and earn status within groups (Ausubel, 2002)—make them vulnerable to the allure of such symbolism. It also seems likely that, in addition to environmental and psychological factors such as peer pressure and/or facilitation (Gifford-Smith, Dodge, Dishion, & McCord, 2005), cultural factors also aggravate the problem of gang violence. That is to say, while many studies have rightly focused on how crumbling inner cities, poverty, and lack or loss of opportunity and hope affect a teen's predisposition toward gang affiliation, it might be worthwhile to examine how society itself provides gangs with false or mythical status that might add to their attraction.

Second point: Various explanations of gang behavior, leading to most satisfactory one.

Concludes with assertion that his arguments have led to: cultural factors contribute to gang violence.

HOW DO GANGS AFFECT BEHAVIOR? 5

References

Ausubel, D. P. (2002). *Theory and problems of adolescent development* (2nd ed.). Lincoln, NE: iUniverse.

Gifford-Smith, M., Dodge, K. A., Dishion, T. J., & McCord, J. (2005). Peer influence in children and adolescents: Crossing the bridge from developmental to intervention science. *Journal of Abnormal Child Psychology, 33*(3), 255–265.

Gordon, R. A., Lahey, B. B., Kawai, E., Loeber, R., Stouthamer-Loeber, M., & Farrington, D. P. (2004). Antisocial behavior and youth gang membership. *Criminology, 42*(1), 55–88. Abstract retrieved from Selection and Socialization database: http://onlinelibrary.wiley.com

Katz, J., & Jackson-Jacobs, C. (2004). The criminologists' gang. In C. Sumner (Ed.),
    . *The Blackwell companion to criminology.* Malden, MA: Blackwell Publishers.

National Youth Violence Prevention Center. (n.d.). *Youth gangs.* Retrieved from http://www.safeyouth.org/scripts/teens/gangs.asp

Penly Hall, G., Thornberry, T. P., & Lizotte, A. J. (2006). The gang facilitation effect and neighborhood risk: Do gangs have a stronger influence on delinquency in disadvantaged areas? In J. F. Short, Jr., & L. Hughes (Eds.), *Studying youth gangs.* Lanham, MD: Altamira Press.

Thabit, W. (2005). How did East New York become a ghetto? Retrieved from http://faculty.ncwc.edu/toconnor/301/301lect08.htm

Thomas, C. (2005). Serious delinquency and gang membership. *Psychiatric Times 22*(4). Retrieved from http://www.psychiatrictimes.com

U.S. Department of Education. (n.d.). *Youth gangs: Going beyond the myths to address a critical problem.* Retrieved from http://www.ed.gov/admins/lead/ safety/training/gangs/problem_pg3.html

New page, title centered; double-space between title and first line of reference list.

Entries doublespaced, in alphabetical order.

First line of each entry at left margin; all other lines indented 1/2 inch or 5 spaces.

Appendix A
Constructing a Writing Portfolio

Constructing a writing portfolio gives you the opportunity to select, display, and reflect on the work you have done in this course. Although there are many ways to construct a portfolio, this chapter offers you some common suggestions and guidelines that others have found useful. An important purpose for constructing the portfolio is to provide you with support for the claims that you will make about your writing in the course. In short, a portfolio helps you support this statement: "Here is what I have learned this semester, and here is the evidence that I have learned these writing strategies and conventions."

Your instructor will provide guidelines on how much evidence to include in the portfolio to support your claims about what you have learned. For some claims, a single example of your work will be sufficient evidence. In other cases, you may need to provide several examples. For instance, to demonstrate that you know how to adapt a message for a particular audience, you might need to show how you have done so for two or three different audiences.

What Is a Portfolio and Why Should I Construct One?

In the past, graphic artists and photographers were the only professionals who tended to keep portfolios of their work. These artists used portfolios to show potential clients their previous work and to give them a sense of what to expect in the future. More recently, many other professionals, such as technical or professional writers, have found that keeping a portfolio is helpful when they look for work.

Although no one will deny that the quality of the final product is important, from an educational perspective, how you arrived at that final product may be just as important as, or even more important than, the result you achieved. By looking at your process (the path you took to get to your endpoint) in a portfolio, your instructor can better assess your strengths and weaknesses as a writer.

When instructors or other readers look at a single piece of your writing, they may come away with a narrow view of your writing capabilities. They may see only a particular kind of writing, with its strengths and weaknesses. However, when readers look at a portfolio of your work, they gain a fuller picture of the writing you have accomplished.

Because the portfolio represents what you have learned throughout the course, the ideal time to read this appendix and to begin constructing your portfolio is during the first week of classes. Starting early will give you many opportunities to select and reflect on your work while that work is still fresh in your mind. Students who construct the most effective portfolios usually work on them a little each week.

Selecting Materials for Your Portfolio

As you decide what to include in your portfolio, ask yourself these questions:

- What have I learned about writing in each of the four areas of life—academic, professional, civic, and personal?
- What have I learned about writing for various purposes?
- What rhetorical skills and knowledge have I developed?
- What critical reading skills have I developed?
- What critical thinking skills have I developed?
- What have I learned about composing processes—invention, drafting, revising, and editing?
- What have I learned about working effectively with peers?
- What knowledge of conventions have I developed?
- What have I learned about strategies that will help me succeed as a writer?
- What have I learned about using technology?

As you respond to each of the questions listed above, consider a follow-up question: *What evidence will demonstrate that I have developed this set of skills or knowledge?* Think about all the work that you have done in the course. Among the print or electronic evidence—tangible evidence—available to you are the following:

- Invention work (listing, brainstorming, clustering, and freewriting)
- Research notes (from your library and online research, field research, and interviews)
- Reading notes (comments you made on the reading you did for the class)
- Drafts of papers
- Peers' written comments on your work
- Online discussions about your work
- Polished versions of your papers
- Reflections on your papers (that you write when you submit your papers)

Among the evidence that may not appear on paper or disk are the following:

- Discussions with peers about your writing
- Discussions with your instructor about your writing

You will, of course, need to transcribe evidence that exists only in your memory so that you can make it available to those who read your portfolio.

Reflecting on What You Have Written

As noted earlier, it is useful to reflect on your work regularly throughout the semester while that work is fresh in your mind. A week or a month later, you may not remember why you followed up on a peer's comments or how you might approach the topic differently if you were to write about it again. Remember that *reflective writing* asks you to do just what its name suggests: to think back on, to consider, to reflect on the work you did for the course. Consider answering the questions at the end of each chapter in Parts 2 and 3 of this book as a way to start that reflective process.

For more on journals, see pages 22–23.

There are several ways to keep track of your reflective writing. You may choose to keep a handwritten or electronic journal, or you may want to keep your own course blog where you regularly reflect on your course writing.

As you reflect on the work that you use as evidence in your portfolio, you might consider another question: *Why does this piece of evidence effectively demonstrate that I have developed a certain set of skills or knowledge?* Your response to that question should also appear in your portfolio because it illustrates that you are confident about what you have learned during the course.

As you reflect on your polished essays, you might wish to include a paragraph for each that begins, "If I had the opportunity to revise this paper further, I would . . . ." This kind of statement acknowledges the situation that exists in most courses: There is rarely enough time to revise as thoughtfully as you could even if the course were two semesters long.

Organizing Your Portfolio

There are many ways to organize your portfolio, and your instructor will let you know how he or she would like your portfolio to be arranged and organized. Some colleges and universities have specific portfolio requirements; if yours does, you will receive guidance on what you need to do.

Sometimes, your instructor will ask you to organize your portfolio in a *chronological* manner, starting with the first piece of writing you did for the class and ending with your final piece of writing. Other organizational schemes you may find especially useful include the following:

For an example from a writing portfolio organized by learning goals, see pages 605–7.

- **By learning goals:** This is an efficient and effective way to organize your portfolio. For example, the Writing Program Administrators Outcomes Statement (see page xl), which is prominent in this book, includes five categories of learning goals: (1) rhetorical knowledge; (2) critical thinking, reading, and writing; (3) processes; (4) knowledge of conventions; and (5) composing in electronic environments. If you use this scheme, you may wish to follow the order given here, or you may wish to reorganize the categories to reflect what you consider to be most important. Once you have decided on the order of the learning goals, those goals can become headings in your portfolio. Under each heading, then, you could respond to the three questions noted earlier:

  - What have I learned? How have I grown as a writer?

- What evidence demonstrates that I have learned this—that I have grown?
- Why is this evidence the most convincing evidence that I can choose?

- **By purpose:** If you use this organizational scheme, you could list the chapter titles from Parts 2 and 3 of this book as your headings—for example, "Writing to Explore," "Writing to Convince," "Writing to Propose Solutions," and so on. This pattern may allow you to focus on each purpose more fully, but it also may cause you to repeat statements about learning goals. That is, for each purpose, you might have to say, "Here's how I learned to adapt my message to an audience." If you do use this organizational pattern, you still can use the same questions:

  - What have I learned? How have I grown as a writer?
  - What evidence demonstrates that I have learned this—that I have grown?
  - Why is this evidence the most convincing evidence that I can choose?

Portfolio Formats

You may decide to submit—or your instructor may request that you submit— your portfolio in one of the following formats:

- **As a print document** in a three-ring binder.
- **As an electronic file,** either on a flash drive or CD. If you use this format, consider constructing a hypertext document so that readers can click on links to see other parts of your portfolio.
- **As a Web site.** This format enables you to provide links to other parts of your portfolio, as well as links to other Web sites or pages that you have found useful during the semester.

In the example shown in Figure A.1, note how student Eileen Holland has organized her electronic portfolio. As background for her work in her first-year writing course, she provided examples of her writing from elementary and secondary school. Because she was an avid reader who believed that reading helped her as a writer, she provided information about several of her favorite writers. Then she included materials to demonstrate that she learned skills and knowledge from the five areas of the Writing Program Administrators Outcomes Statement. Finally, she looked to the future by projecting what she hoped to learn in upcoming semesters.

A Portion of a Sample Portfolio

The portfolio excerpt that begins on page 605 comes from Chelsea Rundle, who constructed it in a second-semester writing course. Note how she used the Writing Program Administrators Outcomes Statement to organize her portfolio. Also note how she used evidence from her work to demonstrate what she had learned.

FIGURE A.1
Sample Portfolio
Entry

Electronic Portfolio
Introduction and Table of Contents
by Eileen Holland

My Writing in Elementary School

My Writing in High School

My Favorite Writers

Garrison Keillor

Jared Diamond

Sarah Vowell

Categories of Learning

Rhetorical Knowledge

Critical Thinking, Reading, and Writing

Processes

Knowledge of Conventions

Composing in Electronic Environments

My Future Goals for Learning to Write

Welcome to my writing portfolio for first-year composition. As my contents indicate, I've been interested in writing since elementary school because my teachers gave me fun writing projects and lots of encouragement. In high school, I was fortunate enough to work with teachers who offered me lots of constructive feedback; some of my friends did the same. I've also been inspired by writers such as Garrison Keillor, Jared Diamond, and Sarah Vowell.

In this portfolio I demonstrate how I have developed skills and knowledge in this course. In particular, I demonstrate how I have learned in five areas: (1) Rhetorical Knowledge; (2) Critical Thinking, Reading, and Writing; (3) Processes; (4) Knowledge of Conventions; and (5) Composing in Electronic Environments. In addition to describing what I have learned, I also offer evidence from my work this semester to prove that I have learned the kinds of knowledge and skills that we have studied.

When I finished high school, I thought that I knew all that I needed to know about writing. In this course, though, I have come to appreciate that learning to write is a never-ending journey. My teacher, who has been writing for more than five decades and teaching writing for almost three decades, told us that she's still learning to write. In class we talked about all sorts of people who keep learning to perform well in their fields until they retire— teachers, professional athletes, entertainers, engineers, painters, architects. People keep on learning.

PORTFOLIO

Chelsea Rundle

I cannot believe the semester is coming to a close already. Even though it has seemed quite short, I have learned a lot over the course of this semester. In English 102, I learned that a good paper topic is one that I am passionate about and is feasible. Picking topics that were particular to my major—applied biology—helped me explore different issues/trends in the field of biology and medical science through writing my English papers.

In my first paper, I explored the concept of personalized medicine by researching what others thought about it and then stepping back and forming my opinion on the topic. For the second paper, writing to convince, I addressed a topic I am very passionate about—CT scans causing radiation cancer. I was able to look at how these two topics affect one another because CT scans are an integral process in personalized medicine.

The topic for my evaluation was the biology program at ASU Tempe versus the biology program at another ASU campus. I picked this topic because I am planning on attending one campus for one more year, but I do not know what campus to attend after that. Even though in my evaluation I came to the conclusion that the other campus's biology program would be better for me—I am still not sure. You made the comment on one of my drafts that I should try taking a biology course at ASU Tempe. I may take your advice and try taking a course over there before making a final decision regarding which university to attend. Also, I am not certain what future career I want to enter into. It may be best for me to figure that out before picking which campus I want to attend.

For my proposing a solution paper, I chose a topic that I am passionate about but is not particular to my major. Instead, I chose a topic personal to me and those living in my neighborhood—a new parking regulation passed by the Home Owner's Association (HOA) that does not allow any vehicles to be parked on the street. I chose this topic because my sister will be getting her driver's license soon and I just bought a new truck, so my family will have too many vehicles to fit in our garage and driveway. You suggested that I go to the city council with my final paper, and I just might. The parking regulation has been a problem for a number of families in my neighborhood. If I get enough people to side with me and show the HOA why the regulation is a problem and what some possible solutions to the problem are, I have faith we can get the HOA to change their minds. We'll see.

While writing these four papers and revising them, I have expanded my writing knowledge and have learned how to strengthen my writing skills. I will demonstrate what I have learned in this portfolio. In the portfolio for writing goals and objectives, I used only examples from English 102 because it is the only class I took this semester in which I learned about writing.

RHETORICAL KNOWLEDGE

- Focus on a Purpose

In writing the first argument, I stayed focused on a purpose: persuading the audience to see the dangers of CT scans. To do this, I used a claim, support for my claim, and the refutation of counterarguments. In refuting counterarguments I addressed multiple viewpoints on the issue while showing the reader why my claim is correct. The following is a refutation of a counter-argument I used to strengthen the paper:

> Some argue that radiation cancer is not caused by CT scans, but can be caused by other factors. This is absolutely true, for radiation, or the release of energy, can be given off by a number of sources including household electrical appliances, heaters, the sun, and x-ray machines. For example, I recall my parents telling me that they were always warned as children not to stand too close to the microwave, or they would get cancer. This is hardly the case, for the type of radiation given off by electrical appliances and heaters isn't harmful enough to cause cancer. However, radiation cancer is caused by high exposure to the sun and x-ray machines. Therefore, as exposure to CT scans—a form of x-ray technology— increases, so does the risk of radiation cancer.

- Respond to the Needs of Different Audiences

When writing a paper particular to my major, I had to think about the needs of my audience. It is important to explain a topic and give background information at the beginning of the paper to avoid confusion. It is hard for readers to form an opinion from reading your paper if they don't understand the topic you are writing about. It is also important not to offend your audience, so the writer must determine how to use the three appeals—logos (logic), ethos (ethics), and pathos (emotions)—appropriately. Balancing logos, ethos, and pathos is a major challenge in writing an effective paper. Peer reviews helped me determine where more background information was needed.

To provide background information to the reader in a draft of my argument on the topic of CT scans, I wrote:

> The word <u>tomography</u> originates from the Greek word <u>tomos</u>, meaning "slice," and <u>graphia</u>, or "describing." CT scans, a form of tomography, have been used for years as the predominate method for medical imaging. The scans produce a three-dimensional image of an object's internal structure based on several x-ray images. Original uses of CT scans are to diagnose different cancers, guide biopsies and similar procedures, and to plan surgery or radiation treatment ("Computed").

Also regarding how to respond to the needs of audiences—I learned that it is crucial to maintain a negotiable stance while writing an argument. Arguments are rarely two-sided, so it is important to be open to all sides. If you form an opinion without getting all the facts and hearing other viewpoints, you can't honestly say your claim is correct. It is difficult to persuade your audience to see things from your perspective if you don't know all the perspectives yourself. . . .

Appendix B
Writing Effective Essay Examinations

In many of your college classes, you will be asked to take essay examinations—to sit and write (sometimes on a computer, more often by hand), for a specified period of time, about the material you have learned. Writing essay exams differs in several ways from writing academic papers that you might work on for several weeks. When you write an essay exam, you will find that the following is true:

- You usually have to rely on your memory.
- You don't have much time to figure out what you would like to say.
- You can't get feedback from your instructor and classmates.
- You usually do not have much time for revision.

It is no wonder, then, that some students worry about in-class essay examinations. Our purpose here is to help you overcome any possible fears about essay examinations by giving you some specific strategies to use before and during such tests.

Keep in mind that situations that are similar to essay exams may come along throughout your life. In your career or in a civic organization, for example, you may be asked to write quickly and without the luxury of invention work or peer feedback:

- As a small-business owner, you might have to draft and complete a cost estimate and quotation in a customer's home.
- As a member of a city council or town board, you may need to comment on a political issue at a town meeting or in response to a question from the media.
- If you write advertising copy or are a journalist, you will frequently have tight deadlines to contend with.

Think of college essay examinations as a way of preparing for life after college, when you often will have to write from memory in a short period of time.

To write an effective response to a question on an essay examination, you will need to do the following:

- Know and understand the information that the examination will cover.
- Be able to relate that information to other topics and ideas you have read about and discussed in class.
- Analyze and understand the question(s) that you are asked to address.
- Construct a thoughtful answer to the question(s), and get your ideas onto paper in the available time.

- Deal with any pre-exam stress issues that you might have. Much of what causes stress for any kind of examination occurs when students are not prepared for the exam, so just being ready can make a big difference in your anxiety level.
- Deal with the examination *scene*—whether you are writing by hand or on a computer, what distractions there might be (other students, noise), and so on.

Getting Ready: Information Gathering, Storage, and Retrieval

When you read and take notes for your college classes, remember that one day you probably will be tested on this information.

Chapter 2 provides useful strategies for reading effectively, and Chapter 4 offers strategies for writing about course material, so we suggest that you revisit those chapters with an eye to using them to help prepare you for essay examinations. Instructors don't expect students to remember everything covered in their classes, but they do expect them to recall and understand the main concepts and to relate those concepts to other ideas. As you read and listen in class, make note of the major concepts, and be sure you can explain them.

One reading strategy, for instance, requires you to annotate what you read, not only listing the main points but also jotting down any comments and questions you have about the text. This "talking back" to the text helps you remember what you've read and develop your own ideas and positions on the issues you read about—positions you may be asked to argue in an in-class essay examination.

For more on annotating, see Chapter 2, pages 17–18.

Considering Questions

As you read and listen to class lectures and participate in class discussions, consider the kinds of questions an instructor might ask you to write about. What are the big issues or ideas that have been covered in class or that you have encountered in your reading? As you think of possible questions, record them in your journal. Then set aside some time to write responses to those questions.

For example, in a humanities class where you are considering various periods in the world of art, it is quite possible that, for an in-class essay examination, your instructor will ask you to situate a group of specific artists in the historical context in which they lived and worked. In a political science class, you may be asked to write about how the specific political issues of the day influenced a particular political party or movement. In your history class, you may be asked to explain how the historical events that took place over a period of time led to the start of a war. It is important to recognize that you probably can make a good guess at what questions an instructor will ask on an essay examination, so it is worthwhile for you to consider what those questions might be—before the exam—and how you might answer them.

Analyzing Questions

In addition to thinking about and predicting what questions you might be asked, it is important to understand what the questions are asking you to do.

Because instructors know that students have only a limited time to respond to an essay examination, they generally will ask questions that have a narrow focus. For example, in a history class, a question for a major writing assignment might be worded like this:

Discuss the events that led up to the second Iraq war.

For an in-class examination, where students have only a brief time to respond, however, a question might be worded like this:

In no more than two pages, explain what was defined as Iraq's "no fly zone."

The following question is a writing prompt designed to elicit a brief response and is similar to prompts used on placement examinations—those tests that determine which writing class is appropriate for a student. How might you answer it?

Ernest Hemingway once commented, "As you get older, it is harder to have heroes, but it is sort of necessary." To what extent do you agree or disagree with his observation? Why? Support your opinion with specific examples.

What is this essay question asking you to *do?* If you have not studied Hemingway, this question might worry you, but consider this: The question is not about Hemingway; rather, it asks for your response to what he said about having heroes. Do you think that, in order to construct an effective essay, you might want to define what a hero is to you? That you might want to provide some examples of your own heroes? That when you answer the real question— whether you agree with Hemingway's comment—you will need to provide some specific examples to show what you mean?

When you see the test question(s) for your essay examination, ask yourself what the question(s) asks you to *do:*

- Does it ask you to *analyze* something—to explain how the parts make up the whole? Consider how you might answer this question:

For more on analysis, see Chapter 8.

   Analyze the use of the magic of flying in relation to the other illusions in the Harry Potter films.

- Does the question ask you to *evaluate* an idea or text or work of art? Consider how you might answer this question:

For more on evaluation, see Chapter 10.

   Of the short stories you read in English class this semester, explain which makes the most effective use of imagery.

- Does the exam question ask you to *show connections* between historical trends, or causal chains—to demonstrate that one event led to or caused other events? Here, of course, your answer will need to show clearly the connections that you see. How might you answer this question?

For more on cause and effect, see Chapter 11.

   How did the Gulf of Tonkin incident influence the start of the Vietnam War?

- Does the test ask you to *compare* one or more ideas or texts with others? Or does it ask you to *contrast* concepts or ideas or texts? If you are asked to compare things, then you will look for similarities between them; if you are asked to contrast, then you will look for (and provide examples of) differences. How might you answer the following question, from a political science class?

For more on comparison and contrast, see Chapter 13.

Briefly compare Canada's and Australia's reactions to the second Iraq war.

- Does the question ask you to *define* something? When you define something, you most often explain what you think it *is*, and then also set it against what it is *not*. Usually, questions that deal with definitions ask for more than just a dictionary definition.

- Does the question ask that you *discuss* an idea, a concept, or a text? In examination terms, "discuss" means to present the most important features of an idea or a concept and then analyze them. You will need to provide examples or other kinds of evidence to support your analysis. "Discuss" in an examination question also leaves your options fairly open—that is, you can discuss briefly or discuss in detail. In an essay *exam*, you can only discuss *briefly*, so consider only the main points you want to make and how you can support those specific points.

For more on definition, see Chapter 13.

- Does the question ask you to *illustrate* something—that is, to provide specific examples to explain the characteristics of the idea or concept?

- Does the examination ask you to *explain* an idea or concept? Think about how you might answer this question:

Explain the significance of rills on the lunar surface.

- Does the exam ask you to *critique* something (a work of art, a short story, a poem, an idea), outlining and explaining its strengths and weaknesses? Consider how you might answer this question:

Critique William Faulkner's use of time in "A Rose for Emily."

- Does the exam question ask that you *review* or *summarize* a particular philosophy or train of thought?

For more on rhetorical analysis, see pages 27–30.

- Does the exam ask you to *analyze* a topic (a text, a local agency, a business plan), to explain how the various aspects of that topic function and work together? Does it ask you to construct a *rhetorical analysis?*

If you are faced with a multiple-part question that seems difficult to answer, draw some lines between each section—in effect, break down the question into its component parts. For example, here is a multipart question:

Noting the recent changes in campus safety problems, argue that your campus needs more or less police protection, but without causing a siege or locked-in mentality for the student body.

Go through and mark each part of the question:

1. Noting the recent changes in campus safety problems
2. argue that your campus needs more or less police protection
3. but without causing a siege
4. or locked-in mentality for the student body

Part 1 asks that you outline what changes in campus safety issues have recently taken place.

Part 2 asks that you take a position on the amount of police protection your campus needs (if you argue for more protection, what does that increase mean: more police on campus? More police on foot patrol? Bicycle police? Should they be more heavily armed? Should police dogs be deployed on campus?).

Part 3 asks that you define what a "siege mentality" would be for the students. Part 4 of asks much the same: for a definition and explanation of what a "locked-in mentality" is.

Breaking down a complex question in this manner allows you to see and thus consider each part of the question, an analysis that helps ensure that you will answer all of its parts.

Constructing Thoughtful Answers

Once you understand exactly what the question is asking you, it is helpful to jot down your main ideas. Then think about what organizational method you might use.

Also think about whether it is a *short-* or *long-answer* essay exam. If you have an hour for the essay exam, for example, and there are ten questions, that gives you an average of six minutes to answer each question, a fairly good tipoff that you are working with a short-answer examination. For your answers to be effective, you will need to get right to the point and then state any supporting evidence as concisely as possible.

On the other hand, if you have ninety minutes to respond to one question on an exam, then you have time to brainstorm the ideas you might want to present, to construct a brief cluster diagram of how the parts of your answer relate to each other, and to do other invention work. And as you are writing the exam, you will have time to explain each aspect of your answer in greater detail than on a short-answer exam.

Often, the test question itself will give you a strong clue as to what kind of organization might be effective. For example, consider this sample question from a history class:

An understanding of the past is necessary for understanding the current situation.

Explain what you think the above statement means. Discuss the similarities between the 1964 presidential election, in which Lyndon Johnson soundly defeated Barry Goldwater, and the 2008 presidential election, in which Barack Obama soundly defeated John McCain. How does an understanding of past events help us to understand what happens in the present?

This is a three-part question, which means that a three-part answer might be the most efficient and effective strategy. If you break down the question into its parts, you have the following:

- *Explain* what the statement means. The first part of your answer should do just what the question asks, in your own words and from your own perspective: What do you think the statement means?

- *Discuss* the similarities, as the question asks you to do. What historical trends and events brought about Lyndon Johnson's election? What similar trends and events contributed to Barack Obama's election?

- *Discuss* how past events (in this case, the 1964 presidential election) help us understand a similar event that took place forty-four years later. Do these two events mean a similar election might happen again in 2052?

One type of organization that works well for essay examinations is what is commonly called the "classical scheme." This method of organizing ideas dates back at least to Aristotle, who noticed that effective speakers most often do the following:

1. State their position and what is important (what is "at stake" in the argument).
   a. State their first piece of evidence, always connecting it back to the main point
   b. State their second piece of evidence, connecting it back to the main point
   c. State the third piece of evidence . . .
   d. And so on

2. Briefly outline any objections to the main point; then explain why those objections are incorrect, or at least show how their position can accommodate the objection.

3. Summarize their position, restating their main points.

If you follow the classical scheme, you will do the following:

For more on the classical scheme, see Chapter 14.

- Construct a solid thesis statement, clearly indicating the main point that you want to make in your answer.

- Provide an effective and logical organizational pattern to follow.

- State your main point right at the start, forcing yourself to use supporting details that always relate back to that main idea. (If an idea or piece of supporting evidence does *not* help you accomplish what the test question asks you to do, then why is it there?)

- Acknowledge the other side of an issue or situation or idea, which tells your instructor that you are aware that there are other perspectives or approaches.

- Tie everything together at the end (which is what a conclusion should do).

Dealing with the Examination Scene

You probably have your favorite place to write, where it is quiet (or there is music playing), and where everything you need is at hand (computer, paper, pencil, pen, erasers, coffee). But you *rarely* will have such an ideal setting for an in-class examination—unless you construct it.

Because you usually know when an exam will take place, it's a good idea to prepare your test-taking environment as best you can, so the writing situation the examination presents is as normal and comfortable as possible. If you usually use a pencil to write, then make sure you have several sharpened pencils with you—or better yet, a good-quality mechanical pencil. If you are allowed to use notes as you write the exam, make sure your notes are clearly written and legible. Here are some other ways to prepare to construct an effective essay examination:

See Chapter 4, "Writing to Discover and to Learn," for more on study strategies.

- Know the material that you will be tested on, by using effective studying techniques (for example, recording and then listening to your notes; rewriting your in-class notes on your computer, to help impress them in your memory and also to make them available in readable form; working with others in study groups).

- Consider what questions you might be asked by constructing your own test questions. This activity forces you to look at the material from a different viewpoint (teacher rather than student), by asking, What would I like my students to know and understand about this material? What might be the best way for them to demonstrate that knowledge?

- *Before* taking the exam, think about how you will spend the time you are allotted. Surprisingly, few students really think about how they will spend the hour or ninety minutes or whatever time they will be given for the exam. If you have a plan going into the exam, then you will use your time more wisely. So think about how to use the time you will be allowed effectively, and then consider how much time you might spend on each of these tasks:

  - Understanding the question
  - Getting some ideas onto paper
  - Organizing those ideas
  - Actually writing the exam
  - Revising your response, once you have it on paper
  - Editing your work
  - Proofreading your work

Note whether some questions are worth more points than others; if so, then it makes sense to spend *more time* on the questions that are worth more. If you encounter a question that you cannot immediately answer, skip it and go on to other questions. That strategy gives you some time to think about it as you work on other answers.

 ## Terry Dolan Writes an Essay Examination

College student Terry Dolan received this prompt for a sixty-minute essay examination:

PROMPT

In his 2005 book *The World Is Flat,* Thomas Friedman talks of "ten forces that flattened the world." Name three of Friedman's ten forces, and explain how they helped to flatten the world.

TERRY DOLAN'S RESPONSE

In his book *The World Is Flat,* Thomas Friedman talks of ten forces that flattened the world. I will discuss how three of these forces—the fall of the Berlin Wall, Netscape going public, and open-sourcing—helped to flatten the twenty-first-century world.

On November 9, 1989, the Berlin Wall fell. While this was a major victory for the forces of democracy in East Berlin and East Germany, it also stood as a symbol for the eventual fall of communism in all of Europe. By opening up Eastern Europe, and eventually the old Soviet Union, to free market capitalism, the end of the Berlin Wall was Friedman's first "flattener." Friedman also talks about the IBM PC computer and how its introduction helped to facilitate the flattening process begun by the fall of the Berlin Wall. The computer with a modem helped to connect people in the old communist bloc with new computer and economic networks.

Friedman's second flattening force happened when the browser Netscape went public. Netscape was a major force because it really opened up the World Wide Web and the Internet for the general population. Before Netscape, the only way people had access to the Internet was in text-only environments. Although that type of access may have been interesting, it mainly attracted scientists and educators. Netscape let people use graphics, and eventually sound and video, online as well. One of the important advantages Netscape offered is that it could be used on any type of computer— PCs, Macs, or Unix boxes.

One important off-shoot of Netscape that helped flatten the world was the fact that when people began to send pictures, audio, and video files over the Internet, they needed more bandwidth. To accommodate this need, companies started laying more fiber optic cable. As a result, phone prices started dropping as well, enabling people to communicate more and faster.

Another flattener, according to Friedman, is the open-source movement. Unlike most software, you can download open-source software for free. Friedman explains that it works on the same model as scientific peer review. People participate in developing the software for the good of the group and the notoriety it gives them. The main open-source software that Friedman discusses is the Apache Web server. Friedman talks about how many of the main Internet Web sites run on Apache servers. Because there is no cost involved in buying the software, just about anyone who knows how can run a Web server.

An even more important example of open-source software is probably the Linux operating system. Linux is a kind of Unix, a powerful computer operating system. The advantage to Linux is that it's cheap (you can download it for free) and flexible (lots of computer people are constantly working to make it even better). The disadvantage to Linux is that most software is written to run on PCs. But more and more open-source software is being written to run on Linux boxes. You can now get Open Office and similar open-source programs that will let you do just about anything you could do with Microsoft software. All the open-source programs are free. You can also get Firefox, a web browser that runs on Linux. In other parts of the world, lots of computers run on Linux and use open-source software.

Finally, what I think is the most interesting point about all of Friedman's flatteners is that they're all about technology, mainly computer technology, and how that helps all of us connect to one another faster and better. Technology is what's making the world flat.

Selecting and using a particular "form" for your text involves making rhetorical choices. Before selecting any kind of format for your text, then, you first need to ask (and answer) the following questions:

- What do you want your writing to accomplish? Do you want to inform your reader, persuade your reader to do something, or evaluate a product, service, or creative work for your reader?

- What form will best serve your purpose?

- Who is your audience?

You already make these kinds of decisions about form all the time when you communicate with your friends, family members, and professors. For some communications (a letter to your great-aunt), a handwritten, personal letter will suffice; for others (asking a professor for a letter of recommendation to get into law school), a more formal business letter is a better choice.

In addition, you also select the size and kind of font to use as well as photographs and drawings, charts and graphs, and other visual aids; you decide whether to use headings in your document, whether bulleted or numbered lists are appropriate and useful, where a colored background or type is useful, and so on. These are all rhetorical choices that you as a writer make, whatever document you are constructing.

This appendix presents guidelines for designing ten different types of print or online documents, along with examples of each type.

Features of an Effective Business Letter

The audience for any piece of business writing will have specific expectations. The most obvious expectation is that you should address your colleagues more formally than you address your college classmates. As with any text, business letters (and memos—see p. 625) have real audiences and purposes, and the form that you use needs to fit your readers' concept of business correspondence:

- Use margins of at least one inch on all four sides of the letter.

- Use a standard 12-point font such as Times New Roman.

- Single-space addresses and paragraphs.

- If you use a block or modified block format (see Figure C.1), double-space between sections of the letter—return address of sender, date, name and address of person to whom the letter is being sent, salutation, paragraphs, and closing. If you use an indented format, you do not need to double-space between paragraphs.

- Use a colon after the salutation.
- Use formal, but not stilted, language.
- After the closing (usually "Sincerely"), use a comma.
- After the closing, include four blank lines for your signature; then type your name, and give your professional title, if applicable. If you are using your company's letterhead, then of course you do not need to duplicate the address, telephone numbers, and so on that are already printed on the letterhead.
- After your name and professional title, include a "cc:" (copy) line, an "Enc:" (enclosure) line, or both if necessary.

FIGURE C.1
Business Letter,
Block Format

Hanna Olsen	Return address of sender
1111 Lutefisk Lane	
Olso, WI 55555	Double-space between sections
October 1, 2011	Date
Kirsti Anderson, Director	Name and address of person to
Office of the Registrar	whom letter is being sent
413 Lefse Hall	
Oslo College	
Oslo, WI 55555	
Dear Ms. Andersen:	Salutation

I am writing to request that you adjust my tuition payment for this semester. Because of health problems, I have been forced to withdraw from two of my courses. I am requesting a partial tuition refund for those six credit hours.

Double-space between paragraphs

Three weeks after the semester began, I was diagnosed with mono-nucleosis, which has limited the number of hours that I can attend class and study. Fortunately, I am doing well in my other two courses, and I am confident that I will be able to carry a full course load next semester.

To document my illness, I have attached a note from the Campus Medical Center. If you need further evidence, I will be happy to provide it.

I look forward to hearing from you soon.

Sincerely,	Closing
	4 blank lines
Hanna Olsen	Signature
Hanna Olsen	Name
Enc: Note from Campus Medical Center	Enclosure line

- Because error-free letters give readers a positive impression, proofread your letter carefully and ask a friend or colleague to proofread it if possible. A second set of eyes is an effective insurance policy.

- Be sure to keep the electronic version of the letter. Back it up—just as you would for any important document.

Features of an Effective Letter of Application

Your purpose in writing a letter of application is just what you would expect it to be: You want your letter to get something for you—most often a job interview (and sometimes even the job itself).

- Use the features of the business-letter format described on pages 617–19.

- Use the exact job title from the job announcement to indicate the position for which you are applying. Businesses sometimes advertise for more than one position at a time, so it is crucial to get the job title right.

- Briefly summarize your qualifications for the job. Don't simply repeat what is on your résumé, which will be attached to your letter.

- If the job announcement includes "required qualifications" and "desired qualifications," you must discuss all of the required ones, and you should discuss as many of the desired ones as possible.

- Indicate how you can meet the needs of the hiring organization. Show that you are eager but not desperate.

- Subtly show that you have done your homework in learning as much as possible about the organization, the unit within the organization that you would be working for, and the job itself.

- Never misrepresent your skills, knowledge, or background. Honesty is the best approach.

Figure C.2 on page 620 is an example of a letter of application.

Features of an Effective Résumé

At first glance, writing a résumé might seem easy: Just list your work history and when you did it. But constructing an effective résumé involves a great deal of time and effort. To begin with, you need to consider carefully the audience to which you are addressing your résumé: Who will see your résumé? What information will they need, and what format should it be in? Should it be a paper résumé, or should it be in an electronic form? If you are adapting your résumé for a specific position, what does the job advertisement call for? You want to ensure that everything the advertisement asks for is included.

- You may—or may not—choose to include a concise career objective at the beginning of your résumé. Although such job objectives were common until recently, some experts now advise résumé writers not to include an objective because the objective is to acquire the job for which you are applying.

FIGURE C.2
Letter of
Application

Kirsti Brones
1234 Raaen Way
Modum, MN 55555

Return address of sender

Double-space between sections

July 5, 2011

Date

Anna Drolsum
Personnel Director
Super Computer Company, Inc.
2222 E. Cyberspace Dr.
Minneapolis, MN 55444

Name and address of person to
whom letter is being sent

Dear Ms. Drolsum:

Salutation

I am writing to apply for the sales representative position recently advertised in the *Minneapolis Star-Tribune*. The skills that I have developed in my
degree program support my strong interest in the position.

Double-space between paragraphs

In my recent internship with Excellent Computer Company, I had sales
responsibilities similar to those described in your advertisement and on
your Web site. Thus, I gained experience in maintaining sales accounts and
in making cold-calls to prospective corporate customers. Prior to my
internship, I learned how to handle customer concerns by working for
several years at the Customer Service desk of a Bull's-Eye Department
Store.

I am especially interested in working for Super Computer Company
because you have such a strong reputation for offering quality products
and being responsive to customers' needs.

I am eager to speak with you about the sales representative position. If you
have any questions about my enclosed résumé, please call me at
400-555-4371. Thank you for considering my application.

Sincerely,

Closing

Kirsti Brones

Signature

Kirsti Brones

Name

Enclosure

Enclosure line

- Include current contact information—name, mailing address, e-mail address,
  phone numbers.
- Use descriptive headings to label the sections of your résumé, such as "Education,"
  "Work Experience," "Skills," "Activities," "Awards," and "References." Include

activities if they demonstrate additional skills, such as leadership. Include awards that reveal qualities or achievements that are an asset to the job you are seeking.

- Do not include personal information such as age, race, ethnicity, marital status, sexual orientation, or health status because employers are not allowed to consider such information.

- If requested to do so, list your references. Before you list someone as a reference, make certain that he or she knows your work and feels comfortable recommending you for a job. As an alternative, you can add the line "References available upon request." If you post your résumé on a Web site, do not list your references.

- If you limit your résumé to a single page, hiring personnel can read it quickly. However, it is more important to include the information that will help you get a job—even if it takes several pages—so consider your audience and what they expect from you. In business, for example, one-page résumés are common; in colleges and universities, résumés are usually much longer and more detailed.

- Use good quality paper.

- A résumé must not have any errors, so be sure to proofread carefully. Ask friends to help with this task if possible. Do not rely solely on the spell-check function of your word-processing program.

- If you post your résumé on a Web site, keep in mind that readers will see it one screen at a time rather than one page at a time.

- Although it is easy to embellish an online résumé with ornate graphics, a simple online résumé is actually more effective.

- Because employers sometimes conduct Web searches for résumés, adding some key terms such as the word "résumé" itself to your online résumé will make it more likely that a search engine will detect your résumé.

Different Kinds of Résumés

The two most common kinds of résumés are the **chronological résumé** and the **functional résumé.** In a chronological résumé, you list all of the jobs you have held in the past in reverse chronological order with the most recent listed first. Your work history should appear just below your personal information. Figure C.3 on page 622 is an example of a chronological résumé. In a functional résumé, you make sure to highlight skills you possess or tasks you have accomplished in previous jobs. Another option is to combine the two formats by listing jobs chronologically and highlighting the tasks that you performed while employed in each job. Figure C.4 on page 623 is an example of a résumé that is both chronological and functional.

Electronic Résumés

As you enter today's employment market, you are likely to encounter employers who ask you to submit electronic résumés. Sometimes the electronic résumé can be nothing more than a digital copy (a *Word* document or a PDF) of your paper résumé. However, you might be asked to fill out a Web form that will serve as a résumé. When you are

FIGURE C.3
A Chronological
Résumé

Kirsti Brones   Name, centered and
bold font

1234 Raaen Way   Contact information,
Modum, MN 55555   centered
400-555-6981
kbrones@email.com

Work Experience   Heading, flush left and in bold
Double-space before and after headings

Marketing Intern, Excellent Computer Company, Anoka, MN, Spring 2010
Customer Service Representative, Bull's-Eye Department Store, Edina, MN,
2006–2009

Education

Bachelor of Science, Marketing, College of Business, University of Minnesota,
2010

Activities

President, Undergraduate Student Marketing Club, University of Minnesota,
2009–2010
Volunteer, Habitat for Humanity, 2008
Volunteer, Boys and Girls Club of America, Edina, MN, 2006–2008

References

Available upon request

submitting an electronic résumé of any kind, in all likelihood the first reader of your résumé will not be a human but a machine. When they read résumés, machines are programmed to search for predetermined keywords or phrases. That means that every résumé that contains the right keyword or phrase will go on to the next phase of screening—maybe by a human. Reading job ads closely will give you a good idea of what keywords or phrases might be important for the specific job you're applying for. While you already know the importance of proofreading a paper résumé, proofreading becomes even more important with electronic résumés. A human reader might forgive one small typo in a paper résumé. A machine can't forgive a typo because unless the words are all spelled correctly, they won't match the words the program is looking for. Keywords are highlighted in Figure C.4.

Features of an Effective E-mail Message

Especially in business environments, e-mail is everywhere. It has become the primary means of communication in many—if not most—businesses. To construct an effective e-mail, like any other kind of text, you need to consider the rhetorical situation, who your audience is, and what you want the e-mail to accomplish.

FIGURE C.4
A Mixed Chrono-
logical and
Functional Résumé

Kirsti Brones   Name, centered and
bold font

1234 Raaen Way   Contact information,
Modum, MN 55555   centered
400-555-6981

Work Experience   Heading, flush left and in bold
Double-space before and after headings

Marketing Intern, Excellent Computer Company, Anoka, MN, Spring 2010

➢ Facilitated focus groups
➢ Wrote questions for focus groups
➢ Wrote brochure copy
➢ Assisted with marketing research

Customer Service Representative, Bull's-Eye Department Store,
    Edina, MN, 2006–2009

➢ Helped solve problems for customers
➢ Responsible for inventory of returns

Education

Bachelor of Science, Marketing, College of Business,
    University of Minnesota, 2010

Activities

President, Undergraduate Student Marketing Club, University of Minnesota,
    2009–2010
Volunteer, Habitat for Humanity, 2008

➢ Coordinated volunteers
➢ Trained new volunteers in reading blueprints

Volunteer, Boys and Girls Club of America, Edina, MN, 2006–2008

References

Available upon request

In addition, because it is so easy to forward an e-mail (readers do not even need to cut and paste any of the text), it is important to understand that what you say to one person in an e-mail might be shared widely with people whom you did not intend to receive it.

- Use relatively short block paragraphs to make it easier for your readers to read the message. Single space, and include a blank line between paragraphs.
- Be very careful when using "reply to all" when you respond to an e-mail message, especially on listservs or online discussion forums.
- Before sending a "BCC" (blind copy) to people other than the primary recipients of your message, think carefully about the ethical implications of secretly sharing this message.

FIGURE C.5
E-mail Message

> **Date:** Thu, 24 May 2011 16:58:31 -0400
> **From:** O_DOOL@XYandZ.com
> **To:** needshybrid@cox.net
> **Subject:** Your new vehicle
>
> I am happy to tell you that your new Toyota Prius has arrived. We will have it prepared for you to pick up after 5:00 pm tomorrow evening.
>
> I think you'll find the colors you chose to your liking.
>
> Please respond to this e-mail to tell us when you'll pick up your new Prius. Could you also please make sure to bring a copy of your proof of insurance card? Our finance officer forgot to make a copy when she was doing your paperwork. We do need a copy for the files.
>
> Thanks for your business,
>
> Oscar Doolittle
> Sales Manager
> X, Y, & Z Toyota/Scion
> Yuma, AZ 85365
> (928) 555-4567

- Use a font that is easy to read on a screen, such as 10-point or 12-point Times New Roman or Arial.
- If you use an electronic signature for your e-mail, make certain that it includes relevant contact information. For business messages, use a signature that is suitable for business. Don't use a font that is too flashy, and if you do include a photograph or drawing, make sure it is not so large that downloading your message takes a long time.
- In business e-mail, it is best to not use emoticons such as smiley faces.
- If you intend to attach a file to the message, develop a system that helps you remember to attach the file. Also make certain that the file is free of viruses.

Figure C.5 is an example of an e-mail.

 ## Features of an Effective Memo

As with business letters, business memos have their own specific requirements as to format—and memos, too, always have a rhetorical purpose. Ask yourself the following questions when writing a memo:

- What do I want this memo to accomplish?
- Who is my audience? What will my readers already know about my topic? What additional information do I need to provide to accomplish my goals?
- What is the situation or context in which I'm writing this memo? How does that context affect what I write and how I write it?

FIGURE C.6
Memo

Date: March 29, 2012

   To: Information Technology Staff

From: Norman Jones, Assistant Director, Division of Information Technology

  RE: Latest Windows Migration

This July, all computers in the Division of Research and Development will be migrated to the new Windows operating system. The migration will be conducted over the course of the week of July 16.

Because we need to have the new Windows operating system installed and fully operational by the end of July, **all members of the information technology staff need to be on the job between July 16 and July 31.** For that reason, I cannot approve any requests for vacation time during that period.

I hope that this early notice affords you ample time to plan your summer vacations accordingly. I regret any inconvenience that this migration to a new operating system might cause.

Thank you for your good work.

cc: Linda Searcy, Director, Division of Information Technology

---

- If your office or organization has a memo template, use that format. If it does not, follow the generic format: Include a separate line for a "To" entry, a "From" entry, the date, and a "Regarding" or "RE" designation.

- For printed memos, use margins of at least one inch on all four sides.

- In the "RE" line, use a clear, concise subject heading.

- For printed memos that have legal significance, include your initials or legal signature, in ink.

- For memos that need to be shared with other people besides the primary recipient(s), add a "cc" (copy) line after the body of the memo.

- Use bold type sparingly for emphasis and to highlight any information that requires immediate attention.

In today's workplace, memos are usually attached to e-mail messages and are rarely distributed in print form. Figure C.6 is an example of a memo.

Threaded Discussion Groups and Listserv Postings

A number of publicly available Web sites such as *Yahoo!, MSN,* and *Google* offer online discussion groups (sometimes called **threaded discussions**). Organized by topic or interest area, these groups allow members to view and participate in written discussions over the Web. After a member posts a message about a particular topic, others may then post their responses. As the discussion proceeds, a Web page is automatically built around the discussion. Threaded discussions allow members to see all the postings in context on one Web page. This makes participating in and viewing the discussion easy.

A **Listserv** is another kind of online forum. Although the word *Listserv* technically should be capitalized because it is a registered trademark of a company called L-Soft International, Inc., the word is increasingly used as a common noun—in the way that "kleenex" is often used to mean "facial tissue," rather than as a brand name, Kleenex. A listserv distributes e-mail to the addresses of all people who have subscribed to that listserv. That is, when a subscriber sends a message to a listserv, the listserv automatically distributes it to all other subscribers. Listservs allow participants to transmit information to large numbers of people who share an interest or are involved in an organization, and they are an effective way to discuss important issues, share ideas, and make announcements. Figure C.7 is an example of a listserv posting.

FIGURE C.7
Listserv Posting

From: Duane Roen <Duane.Roen@asu.edu>

Subject: **Final Version of CWPA Conference Schedule: Thanks**

Date: May 25, 2012 9:26:10 AM MST

To: Writing Program Administration <WPA-L@ASU.EDU>

Reply-To: Writing Program Administration <WPA-L@asu.edu>

Dear Colleagues,

Dave Blakesley let us make some last-minute changes in the CWPA conference schedule before he begins printing the program. Thanks, Dave.

Here is the final (and we mean final) version of the CWPA conference schedule: http://wpacouncil.org/node/3813#attachments

I thank all the people who proposed such interesting presentations.

I also thank those who helped with the program. It's been a wonderfully collaborative effort!

Best,

Duane

Duane Roen

President, Council of Writing Program Administrators

Features of an Effective Threaded Discussion or Listserv Posting

- If you are posting a message as part of an ongoing discussion in a threaded discussion group or on a listserv, become familiar with previous postings on the topic so that you don't repeat what has already been written. Repetition may annoy other subscribers.

- Stay on the topic at hand unless it is appropriate to move to a new topic.

- If you disagree with someone's opinion on a topic, express your views clearly and politely. Do not engage in personal attacks (called flaming).

- Because server space costs money and online readers do not enjoy scrolling through prior messages, do not include in your posting the message to which you are responding. If you want to respond to a specific section of a previous posting, copy and paste the specific text instead, making sure to distinguish the text so that it is not confused with your own.

- Do not post personal messages ("thanks for that information, Joe") to the group or listserv, when that message is intended for just one person.

- Above all, be sure that you want to reply to the group or listserv as a whole rather than to an individual. Sometimes, people post a reply to a group or list that was intended for an individual. As you might imagine, such messages can be embarrassing.

- Keep your messages as brief as possible. Just as with an e-mail message, readers usually do not want to read a discussion posting that is longer than one screen of text.

Features of an Effective Brochure

As with a résumé, a brochure needs to accomplish something: to sell a product or service (or to get a reader interested in a product or service), perhaps, or to provide information (a voter's guide, for example).

- Include an informative and attention-getting headline.

- Include a visual element such as a photo or drawing if it grabs readers' attention and adds to the content of the brochure.

- If the brochure advertises an event, make certain that you include all relevant information—date, time, place, cost (if any), and a phone number interested parties can call or Web site address they can visit for further information.

- Your layout will depend on the number of folds that your brochure has. If you are using standard 8-1/2" x 11" paper, you may decide to have no fold, a bi-fold, or a tri-fold. A no-fold sheet fits well into a notebook. A tri-fold can fit into a shirt pocket.

FIGURE C.8
A Brochure for
an Art Show

Special Events and Activities

•Maryland Migratory Game Bird Design
Contest (Maryland Duck Stamp Contest)
Saturday, March 27th 12:00 noon

•Wildlife tram tour

• Adopt a Whooping Crane display

   All proceeds from the show support the
outreach and educational programs of the
Patuxent Research Refuge and research
activities at the Patuxent Wildlife Research
Center, America's premier wildlife research
institution.

*Join us at the
15th Annual Patuxent
Wildlife Art Show and Sale*

Artists' Reception
Friday, March 26th, 2004 6 p.m. -10 p.m.

Art Show and Sale
Saturday & Sunday, March 27th – 28th, 2004,
10 a.m. - 4:30 p.m.

   Over 50 nationally recognized artists will
display and sell wildlife art. Painters, sculptors,
master carvers, renowned photographers, and
superb artisans will be present.

   Spend a weekend surrounded by nature,
exquisite wildlife art, and interesting activities-
all taking place at the marvelous National
Wildlife Visitor Center which offers hiking
trails, wildlife and conservation exhibits, outdoor education, and guided tram tours.

   An Artists' Reception with the artists and the
Silent Auction will be held Friday evening from
6 p.m. - 9 p.m. Tickets to the Artists' Reception
will be $25.00 per person. *Admission to the Art
Show and Sale is free.*

- Consider the principles of proximity, contrast, alignment, and repetition. (See Chapter 18 for more on these design concepts.)
- If you use photos or graphics that are not your own, make certain that you have permission to display them publicly.

Figure C.8 is an example of a brochure.

Features of an Effective Poster

While posters often seem to be only large sheets of paper with a small amount of text and lots of illustrations and a colored background, they also have a rhetorical purpose: To convey a message to an audience. If you are preparing a poster, you need to answer questions such as these: What do you want your poster to do? Provide information? Show people how to get somewhere? Explain something?

- Include a headline that is informative and will grab viewers' attention.

- Include a visual element such as a photograph or drawing if it grabs viewers' attention and adds to the content of the poster.

- Because you will often need to reproduce a large quantity of posters, depending on the needs of your project, the quality, color, and size of the paper you use will affect your printing costs. At a certain point, you need to consider how much you are willing to spend in terms of your overall budget.

- Because using colored ink can also affect cost, keep your budget in mind when you determine whether or not your poster should be in color.

- Determine what size poster and what size font will be necessary for readers. Both will depend on the location of the poster and how close to the poster readers will be. Will they be whizzing by on their bikes, or will they be walking within a few feet of it?

- Consider the principles of proximity, contrast, alignment, and repetition described in Chapter 18.

- If you use photos or stock graphics, make certain that you have permission to display them publicly.

- If the poster advertises an event, make certain that you include all relevant information—date, time, place, cost (if any), and a phone number or Web site address where further information is available (if applicable).

FIGURE C.9
A Poster Advertising an Event

Figure C.9 is an example of an effective poster.

Features of an Effective Newsletter

Newsletters most often have a specific audience (usually employees or members of a club or organization of some kind). Those who produce newsletters for a group also have specific purposes. At our university, for example, we get newsletters from a number of places (often in electronic form), including the following:

- The university itself, including a "wellness newsletter," which tells of various workshops employees can attend to lose weight, stop smoking, and so on, as well as information on how to become better managers, learn new computer software, and other useful advice.

- The faculty senate, which lets us know about political issues on campus.
- Our department, letting us know about upcoming speakers, recent publications by our colleagues, and other news of interest.

For an effective newsletter, consider the following:

- It is very important to determine who your readers will be in order to select information that will be interesting and useful to those readers.
- Determine a purpose for the newsletter, and keep that purpose in mind as you decide what to include and what to exclude.
- Use headlines that clearly indicate the content of the stories that follow them.
- Consider the principles of proximity, contrast, alignment, and repetition. (See Chapter 18 for more on these design principles.)
- If you use photos or graphics that are not your own, make certain that you have permission to include them in your publication.

Figure C.10 is an example of an online newsletter.

FIGURE C.10
Part of a University
Newsletter

Features of Effective Web Sites

Do you have your own Web site (a collection of Web pages)? Would you like to? These days, more and more of us do have Web sites. For example, as a student you might develop a portfolio in which you display your work as a Web site. (See Appendix A.) As a member of an organization, you might develop a Web site that describes the activities of the organization. Or, like many people do these days, you might develop a Web site in which you tell your family's history.

As with any text, one primary consideration is audience—and for a Web site, that can mean just about anyone. Consider the following questions as you create your Web site:

- What do you want your Web site to do? To tell about you and who you are? About the work you do?

- What do you want to include on your Web site? Photos? Drawings?

When designing a Web site, you should keep several points in mind. First of all, you need to consider both the purpose of the site and its intended audience. You will design a personal Web site, intended to be viewed by your friends and family, very differently from a Web site that is intended to portray you as a professional. On your personal Web site you might display photographs of your family, your friends, your pets, or some of your favorite places. You might provide links to restaurants you enjoy or the Web sites of your favorite sports teams. On the other hand, on a professional Web site you might include your résumé as well as links to a professional organization to which you belong. Both sites, however, should provide those who visit them with a clear sense of how to navigate the site. You might have a navigation bar along the top or on the side, with buttons that link to different pages on the site, including the home page.

One other factor to keep in mind when designing a Web site is that although we call the parts of a Web site *Web pages,* we are really talking about screens. While paper pages are a uniform size, Web pages can vary in size depending on the size and resolution of the monitor on which they appear.

- Break text into smaller chunks, and write as concisely as possible. Give readers "breathers." Bulleted lists work especially well on the Web.

- Graphics can enhance the informational value and aesthetic appeal of Web pages, but they can also cause pages to download more slowly. Use graphics if they highlight, elaborate on, or can substitute for words on the screen.

- Try to design each page of your site so that readers can view the entire page with only a minimal amount of scrolling.

- To make pages usable to a wide audience, make them accessible to people with visual impairments. To determine if your site is accessible, you can consult *accessible.org* (http://www.accessible.org/bobby-approved.html). There are links on the site to further information on how to design your site so that it is more accessible.

- Each page on your Web site should have a design that is consistent with the other pages on your site. Although you have more flexibility on a personal Web

FIGURE C.11
The Web Site for
a Design School

site than with a professional site, you still want to give each page the same overall look and feel. A lack of consistency may make your viewers suspect that they have left your site for another.

- Organization and navigation work hand-in-hand on the Web. Organize material on the site so that the organizational principle is apparent to readers. Web designers frequently organize sites either sequentially or hierarchically. You might choose to organize the site sequentially, an organization similar to that of a numbered list. Or you might choose to organize hierarchically, where you begin with the most important or most general topic and then have your viewers "drill down" further into the site for the specific details.

- If you include links to external sites, periodically check to see if any links are "dead"—links to sites that are no longer active.

- Regularly examine the page to make certain that the information is current. Including a "last date updated" line helps to assure your viewers that you are keeping the site current.

Figure C.11 is an example of an effective home page for a design school's Web site.

Credits

TEXT CREDITS

CHAPTER 2

P. 18, Figure 2.1: Eric Bangeman, "The Ethics of 'Stealing' a WiFi Connection." Copyright © 2008 Condé Nast Publications. All rights reserved. Originally published in Ars Technica. Reprinted by permission. **P. 24:** Carlton Vogt, "Downloading Music: Harmful to the Artist, the Record Company, or Neither?," Ethics Matters column in *InfoWorld* and on www.infoworld.com. Reprinted by permission.

CHAPTER 3

P. 38 & 48: "Kill the Internet—and Other Anti-SOPA Myths" by Danny Goldberg. Reprinted with permission from the January 24, 2012 issue of *The Nation*. For subscription information, call 1-800-333-8536. Portions of each week's *Nation* magazine can be accessed at http://www.thenation.com. **P. 41:** "We Are the Media, and So Are You" by Jimmy Wales and Kat Walsh, *The Washington Post*, February 9, 2012. Reprinted by permission.

CHAPTER 5

P. 74: "A Priceless Lesson in Humility" by Felipe Morales. From *This I Believe: Life Lessons*, Edited by Dan Gediman with John Gregory and Mary Jo Gediman. Copyright © 2011 by This I Believe, Inc. All rights reserved. Reprinted with permission from John Wiley & Sons, Inc. **P. 83:** Tanya Barrientos's "Se Habla Espanol" [Copyright © 2004 by Tanya Barrientos] from BORDER-LINE PERSONALITIES Edited by MICHELLE HERRERA MULLIGAN and ROBYN MORENO. Compilation Copyright © 2004 by Michelle Herrera-Mulligan and Robyn Moreno. Reprinted by permission of HarperCollins Publishers. **P. 89:** Sherman Alexie, "Superman and Me," *Los Angeles Times Book Review*, April 19, 1998, p. 54. Copyright © 1998 Sherman Alexie. All rights reserved. Reprinted by permission.

CHAPTER 6

P. 121: Andrew Sullivan, excerpt from "Why I Blog," From *The Atlantic Magazine*. Copyright © 2012 by Andrew Sullivan. All Rights Reserved. Reprinted by permission of The Wylie Agency. **P. 127:** Owen Edwards, "The Tuskegee Airmen Plane's Last Flight," *Smithsonian Magazine*, November 2011, pp. 32, 34. http://www.smithsonianmag.com/arts-culture/The-Tuskegee-Airmen-Planes-Last-Flight.html?c=y&page=1. Copyright © 2011 Owen Edwards. Reprinted by permission of the author. **P. 131:** Kiva.org website screenshot. Copyright © 2005–2012 Kiva. All rights reserved. Reprinted by permission.

CHAPTER 7

P. 154: *The New York Times* website screenshot, Thursday, January 20, 2011. Copyright © 2011 The New York Times. All rights reserved. Used by permission and protected by the Copyright Laws of the United States. The printing, copying, redistribution, or retransmission of this Content without express written permission is prohibited. http://www.nytimes.com. **P. 165:** Carol Ezzell, "Clocking Cultures." *Scientific American*, September 2002, pp. 74-75. Reproduced with permission. Copyright © 2002 Scientific

American, Inc. All rights reserved. **P. 169:** Dan Fletcher, "A Brief History of Wikipedia," *Time.com*, August 18, 2009. (http://www.time.com/time/business/article/0,8599,1917002,00.html). Copyright © 2009, Time Inc. All rights reserved. Reprinted by permission.

CHAPTER 8

P. 196: "Fear Factor: Psychologists Help People Conquer Anxieties and Phobias," by Robin Gerrow. Reprinted by permission of The University of Texas at Austin. **P. 207:** James M. Lang, "Putting in the Hours," *The Chronicle of Higher Education*. May 16, 2003. Reprinted by permission of James M. Lang. **P. 211:** From *Quiet: The Power of Introverts in a World that Can't Stop Talking* by Susan Cain, copyright © 2012 by Susan Cain. Used by permission of Crown Publishers, a division of Random House, Inc. **P. 216:** Jesse Hassenger, "Irony as Disguise." Reprinted by permission of the author.

CHAPTER 9

P. 249: Marian Wright Edelman, "Still Hungry in America," *Huffington Post*, February 10, 2012 (http://www.huffingtonpost.com/marian-wright-edelman/hunger-in-america_b_1269450.html). Reprinted by permission of Children's Defense Fund. **P. 255:** Maureen Dowd, "Our Own Warrior Princess" from The New York Times, June 1, 2003 © 2003 The New York Times. All rights reserved. Used by permission and protected by the Copyright Laws of the United States. The printing, copying, redistribution, or retransmission of this Content without express written permission is prohibited. http://www.nytimes.com/2003/06/01/opinion/our-own-warrior-princess.html

CHAPTER 10

P. 291: Jonathan Liu, "The 5 Best Toys of All Time," *Wired.com*, January 31, 2011. (http://www.wired.com/geekdad/2011/01/the-5-best-toys-of-all-time/all/1). Copyright © 2012 Condé Nast. All rights reserved. Reprinted by permission. **P. 297:** Roger Ebert, "Review of Harry Potter and the Deathly Hallows, Part 2," Chicago Sun-Times, July 13, 2011. http://rogerebert.suntimes.com/apps/pbcs.dll/article?AID=/20110713/REVIEWS/110719994. Reprinted by permission of the Chicago Sun-Times. **P. 299:** Andrew O'Hehir, "'Harry Potter and the Deathly Hallows: Part 2': An Action-Packed Curtain Call," *Salon*, July 14, 2011. This article first appeared in Salon.com, at http://www.Salon.com. An online version remains in the *Salon* archives. Reprinted with permission.

CHAPTER 11

P. 338: Juan Williams, "The Ruling that Changed America." Reprinted with permission from *American School Board Journal*, April 2004. Copyright 2004 National School Boards Association. All rights reserved. **P. 343:** Neal Gabler, "How Urban Myths Reveal Society's Fears." *Los Angeles Times*, November 12, 1995. Reprinted by permission of the author.

CHAPTER 12

P. 372: Screenshot of accion.org website. Reprinted courtesy of Accion International. **P. 383:** Anya Kamenetz, "The Case for Girls," *Fast Company*,

November 17, 2011 (http://www.fastcompany.com/magazine/161/branding-for-girls-advertising-for-women). Reprinted by permission from *Fast Company*. **P. 388:** Virginia Heffernan, "Education Needs a Digital-Age Upgrade," from *The New York Times Online*, August 7, 2011 © 2011 The New York Times. All rights reserved. Used by permission and protected by the Copyright Laws of the United States. The printing, copying, redistribution, or retransmission of this Content without express written permission is prohibited. http://opinionator.blogs.nytimes.com/2011/08/07/education-needs-a-digital-age-upgrade/?emc=eta1. **P. 393:** Amy Baskin and Heather Fawcett, "Request for a Work Schedule Change." *More Than a Mom—Living a Full and Balanced Life When Your Child Has Special Needs*. www.morethanamom.net. Reprinted by permission of the authors.

CHAPTER 13

P. 425: Barbara Ehrenreich, from "A Step Back to the Workhouse." First published in *Ms. Magazine* November, 1987. Reprinted by permission of *Ms. Magazine*, © 1987. **P. 435:** "Viacom Sues YouTube for $1 Billion" by Seth Sutel, AP Business Writer. Used with permission of The Associated Press Copyright © 2009. All rights reserved. **P. 438:** "What is Good Bread?" is reprinted by permission of Ken Forkish, Ken's Artisan Bakery and Café. **P. 440:** Definition of "Mugwump" is reprinted by permission of Michael Quinion, *World Wide Words*. **P. 441:** Definition of "Luddite" from TechTargetNetwork is reprinted by permission from Tech Target Network. http://www.choosemyplate.gov/index.html

CHAPTER 14

P. 456: David Wolman, "Time to Cash Out: Why Paper Money Hurts the Economy." From *Wired.com*, 05/22/09, http://www.wired.com/culture/culturereviews/magazine/17-06/st_essay. Copyright © 2012 Condé Nast. All rights reserved. Reprinted by permission. **P. 460:** Jordan Weissman, "The Myth of Energy Independence: Why We Can't Drill Our Way to Oil Autonomy" *The Atlantic*, February 9, 2012. http://www.theatlantic.com/business/archive/2012/02/the-myth-of-energy-independence-why-we-cant-drill-our-way-to-oil-autonomy/252812/. Copyright © 2012 by The Atlantic Monthly Group. All Rights Reserved. Reprinted by permission. **P. 465:** Reprinted courtesy of *Sports Illustrated*: "Nothing but Nets" by Rick Reilly, May 1, 2006. Copyright 2006, Time Inc. All rights reserved.

CHAPTER 18

P. 497: ESOL Flyer from Fenway Neighborhood Service Center is reprinted by permission of Action for Boston Community Development, Inc. **P. 499, Figure 18.1:** Colorwheel is reprinted by permission of Newell Rubbermaid, Inc. **P. 500, Figure 18.3:** Reprinted by permission of Kim Peasley. **P. 504, Figure 18.4:** Pie chart showing composition of a slice of pizza is reprinted with permission of Mathematics Leagues, Inc. **P. 505, Figure 18.5:** Bar graph presenting the same data as the pie chart is reprinted with permission of Mathematics Leagues, Inc. **P. 508, Figure 18.7:** A Line Graph Illustrating the Relationship between Mileage and Value is reprinted by permission of Mathematics Leagues, Inc. **P. 509, Figure 18.8:** Universal Stain Color Selection Guide is reprinted by permission of Come To Buy, Inc. www.cometobuy.com. **P. 510, Figure 18.9:** Bigfoot Water Rocket Launcher Flowchart is reprinted by permission of Gary Ensmenger, President, Bigfoot Stilt Company. **P. 513, Figure 18.12:** Cartoon of a mammalian cell nucleus from "The Dynamics of Chromosome Organization and Gene Regulation" in the *Annual Review of Biochemistry*, 2003. 72:573–608. Copyright © 2003 by Annual Reviews, Inc. All rights reserved. Reprinted by permission. **P. 514, Figure 18.13:** Venn diagram on sustainable development is reprinted by permission of Manchester Development Education Project. See www.dep.org.uk. **P. 516, Figure 18.15:** Neanderthal Range Map is reprinted by permission

of Richard G. Klein. **P. 521, Figure 18.20:** Two maps of the U.S., one plain and one distorted, from "Diffusion-based methods for producing density-equalizing maps," Michael Gastner and Mark Newman, PNAS, May 18, 2004. Copyright © 2004 National Academy of Sciences, U. S. A. Reprinted with permission.

CHAPTER 19

P. 524: Definition of "adolescent" adapted and reproduced by permission from *The American Heritage® Medical Dictionary*. Copyright © 2007 Houghton Mifflin. **P. 525:** Search result for keywords, "male" and "gang" are reprinted by permission of EBSCO Publishing. **P. 526, Figure 19.1:** Search of the JStor Database Using the Search Term "adolescent gangs." Reprinted courtesy of JSTOR. JSTOR © 2012. All rights reserved. **P. 527, Figure 19.2:** Result of a Search using the Google Search engine and the keywords "Gang Behavior" + "Adolescent Female" © 2011 Google. **P. 528, Figure 19.3:** Result of a Search using the Google Search engine and the keywords "Gang Behavior" + "Adolescent Female" © 2011 Google. **P. 534, Figure 19.7:** Screenshot of Wikipedia entry for "Higher Education" is reprinted here under the creative commons license. http://creativecommons.org/licenses/by-sa/3.0/. **P. 535:** Blurb about authors Duffy and Gillig from the Greenwood Press online catalog is reproduced with permission of Greenwood Publishing Group, Inc., Westport, CT.

CHAPTER 20

P. 566, Figure 20.3: Journal table of contents is reprinted by permission of Council of Writing Program Administrators. **P. 569, Figure 20.4:** Copyright © EBSCO Publishing, Inc. Reprinted with permission. All rights reserved. **P. 575:** Source: Arizona State University, "A New American University." Arizona State University Homepage, Web. 3 April 2012. http://newamericanuniversity.asu.edu/about/#1. **P. 584, Figure 20.6:** Title & copyright pages from *Teen Gangs* by Maureen P. Duffy and Scott Edward Gillig. Copyright © 2004 by Maureen P. Duffy and Scott Edward Gillig. Copyright © 2004 by Greenwood Publishing Group, Inc. Reproduced with permission of ABC-CLIO, LLC, Santa Barbara, CA. **P. 588, Figure 20.7:** Journal table of contents page for *Child Development*, Nov/Dec 2005, Vol. 76, n. 6, Copyright © 2005 by Blackwell Publishing. Reproduced with permission of John Wiley & Sons Ltd.

APPENDIX C

Figure C9: Reprinted by permission of the City of Chicago.
Figure C10: Northern Arizona University Newsletter "Evolution of Staph Superbug traced between Humans and Food animals." http://www4.nau.edu/insidenau/bumps/2012/2_20_12/mrsa.html. Reprinted by permission of Northern Arizona University.
Figure C11: Reprinted by permission of the Chicago Portfolio School.

PHOTO CREDITS*

CHAPTER 1

Opener: © Nano Calvo/Alamy; **p.6** (left): © PhotoAlto/PunchStock RF; **p.6** (right): JGC/Jamie Grill/Getty Images RF

CHAPTER 2

Opener: Getty Images/Digital Division RF; **p.21:** Source: http://www.nasa.gov ; **p.28:** Photo by Simon Harsent, ad by BBH Singapore.

CHAPTER 3

Opener: Inti St. Clair/Getty Images RF; **p.38:** © Corbis; **p.41** (upper): Manuel Archain, Buenos Aires, http://www.manuelarchain.com; **p.41** (lower): Courtesy Gregory F. Maxwell.

CHAPTER 4
Opener: © Fancy Photography/Veer RF; **p.66:** © SuperStock/SuperStock.

CHAPTER 5
Opener: This I Believe Website Copyright ©2005–2012 by This I Believe, Inc. Used with permission; **p. 75:** Photodisc/Getty Images RF; **p.78:** LWA/Dan Tardif/Blend Images/Punchstock RF; **p.83:** DAVID CRUZ AL Dia Photos Latino USA/Newscom; **p.89:** Ulf Anderson/Getty Images; **p.90:** Hulton Archive/Getty Images.

CHAPTER 6
Opener: Source: NASA; **p.117:** © Bob Daemmrich/PhotoEdit; **p.121:** Peter Kramer/Getty Images; **p.121:** © Regine Edwards; **p.128** (upper): © Ray Pittman; **p.128** (lower): 20th Century Fox/LucasFilm Ltd/Partnership Pictures/The Kobal Collection; **pp. 131-132:** Courtesy Kiva; **p.142, 149** (lower) Hulton Archive/Stringer/Getty Images.

CHAPTER 7
Opener: Bloomberg via Getty Images; **p. 155:** Source: NASA; **p. 162:** © Bob Daemmrich/PhotoEdit; **p. 165:** Photo Courtesy of Carol Ezzell Webb; **p. 169** (upper): Courtesy Dan Fletcher; **p. 169** (lower): "Wikipedia" and the puzzle globe logo appearing in this book are registered trademarks of the Wikimedia Foundation. Used with permission; **p. 184** (left): Richard Newstead/Flickr/Getty Images; **p. 184** (center): Jeffrey Hamilton/Getty Images RF; **p. 184** (right): Robert Decelis Ltd/Digital Vision/Getty Images RF; **p. 184** lower: © Stockbyte/PunchStock RF; **p. 190:** © Stockbyte/PunchStock RF.

CHAPTER 8
Opener: © Stockbyte/Punchstock RF; **p. 203:** © The McGraw-Hill Companies/Lars Niki, photographer; **p. 207:** Courtesy of James Lang; **p. 211:** Courtesy Susan Cain. Photo by Aaron Fedor; **p. 216:** Courtesy Partnership for a Drug Free America.

CHAPTER 9
Opener: Courtesy of Mexican Tourism Board; **p. 245:** © Janine Wiedel Photolibrary/Alamy; **p. 249:** Jesse Grant/Stringer/Getty Images; **p. 255:** Fred R. Conrad/The New York Times/Redux; **p. 258:** Courtesy Allsup, Inc; **p. 268:** © Getty Images/Digital Vision RF.

CHAPTER 10
Opener: © New Line Cinema/Photofest; **p. 287:** © Luke Stettner/Getty Images; **p. 291** (upper): Courtesy Jonathan H. Liu; **p. 291** (lower): Purestock/Getty Images; **p. 297:** © Frank Trapper/Corbis; **p. 299:** Courtesy salon.com.

CHAPTER 11
Opener: © Lauri Kangas; **p. 334:** MM Design; **p. 338:** PRNewsFoto/SeniorNet/Newscom; **p. 343:** © AP/World Wide Photos; **p. 348** (upper): Courtesy Curosu Octavian Nicolae, deviantart.com, used with permission; **p. 348** (lower): Courtesy Curosu Octavian Nicolae deviantart.com, used with permission **p. 364:** with thanks to Louisa Burnham; **p. 365:** McKenney, Thomas Loraine and James Hall. History of the Indian Tribes of North America, with Biographical Sketches and Anecdotes, of the Principal Chiefs. Philadelphia: J. T. Bowen, 1848–1850.

CHAPTER 12
Page 380: © Najlah Feanny/Corbis; **p. 383:** Neilson Barnard/Stringer/Getty Images; **p. 386:** Courtesy AKQA; **p. 388:** JM11 WENN Photos/Newscom; **p. 393** (upper): Courtesy Amy Baskin, Jack Kesselman, photographer; **p. 393** (lower): Photo of Heather Fawcett, co-author of "Request for a Work Schedule Change", photo courtesy Heather Fawcett.

CHAPTER 13
Opener: Banana Stock/Jupiter Images RF; **p. 435:** Paramount/Photofest; **p. 439:** Jim Wehtje/Getty Images RF.

CHAPTER 14
Opener: Design Pics/Don Hammond/Getty Images; **p. 452:** © SuperStock/SuperStock; **p.456:** photo by Brett Patterson; **p. 458:** © Sijmen Hendriks; **p. 460:** Courtesy Jordan Weissmann; **p. 463:** © Roger Ressmeyer/CORBIS; **p. 465:** Courtesy Sports Illustrated; **p. 467:** Copyright © 2007 American Civil Liberties Union.

CHAPTER 15
Opener: Banana Stock/Jupiter Images RF.

CHAPTER 16
Opener: © Ocean/Corbis; **p. 480:** Kent Matthews/The Image Bank/Getty Images.

CHAPTER 17
Opener: The Bridgeman Art Library/Getty Images; **p. 494:** AP Photo/Newsweek.

CHAPTER 18
Opener: National Organization for Women Foundation; **p. 511** (left): Library of Congress, Prints and Photographs Division [LC-DIG-cwpb-04326]; **p. 511** (right): Royalty-Free/CORBIS; **p. 515:** New Line/Saul Zaentz/ Wing Nut/The Kobal Collection; **p. 518:** Courtesy of Feed the Children.

CHAPTER 19
Opener: © Anderson Ross/Getty Images RF; **p. 526:** Source: jstor.org; **p. 527:** © Google; **p. 528:** © Google; **p. 529** (upper): Oxford University Press; **p. 529** (lower): © The McGraw-Hill Companies, Inc./John Flournoy, photographer; **p. 530:** PRNewsFoto/Newsweek/AP Photos; **p. 531** (upper): PRNewsFoto/Business Traveler Magazine, Nathan Jalani/AP Photos; **p. 531** (middle): Reprinted by permission of FOREIGN AFFAIRS, July/August 2012. Copyright 2012 by the Council on Foreign Relations, Inc. www.ForeignAffairs.com; **p. 531** (lower): Courtesy Arizona Highways; **p. 532:** Source: © 2012 IRS; **p. 533:** Image Source/Getty Images RF.

CHAPTER 20
Opener: Pixland/AGE Fotostock RF.

*FRONT MATTER
Page xxvii: © Rubberball Productions RF; **p. xxix:** © Rubberball/Getty Images RF; **p. xxx:** © Digital Vision/Getty Images RF; **p. xxxii:** © Rubberball Productions RF.

Index

Guide to MLA Documentation Models in Chapter 20

Successful writers *adapt* to the circumstances they are writing for by understanding their audience and purpose and by establishing a voice that suits the context and follows the conventions of the genre in which they are writing.

The McGraw-Hill Guide will help you adapt to your writing circumstances by showing you how to set and achieve your writing goals and assess the effectiveness of your work.

SET clear writing goals

Questions that will help you *set* your goals:	Key points to know:
Why am I writing and for whom am I writing it?	Understanding your *Purpose, Audience,* and *Context* is a part of **rhetorical knowledge.**
Will I likely need sources to learn more about my topic?	Understanding how and when to use *sources* is an essential part of **critical thinking, reading, and writing.**
Am I writing a paper? A speech? An e-mail? A blog?	Understanding which *genre* to use for your project is just one part of knowing how to follow the **conventions** of any written project.
How do I get started?	Understanding how to work through **writing processes** will help you to achieve your writing goals.

ACHIEVE your writing goals

Questions that will help you *achieve* your goals:	Key points to know:
How formal should my voice or tone be for this project?	Establishing your *voice, tone, and point of view* is part of **rhetorical knowledge**.
What makes a particular kind of written work successful?	Learning the *qualities of an effective piece of writing* is an aspect of **critical thinking, reading, and writing.**
How do I go about organizing, drafting, and revising my work?	Composing consists of using a variety of **writing processes** that will help you assemble your project from *invention* and *research* all the way through *revision.*
What, if any, final touches should I make to my project before handing it in?	Following the **conventions** of writing means getting the details right: spelling, grammar, formatting, and documentation; all play a part in the success of the final product.

ASSESS the effectiveness of your work

Questions that will help you *assess* your goals:	Key points to know:
Have I achieved my purpose?	**Rhetorical knowledge**
Are all points supported clearly, accurately, and responsibly?	**Critical thinking, reading, and writing**
Did I revise thoroughly where needed?	**Writing processes**
Have I attended to all the details that my assignment requires?	**Conventions**

Guide to APA Documentation Models in Chapter 20

A
MOTHER LOSS
WORKBOOK

A MOTHER LOSS ❈ WORKBOOK ❈

Healing
Exercises
for
Daughters

Diane Hambrook, M.S.W., C.S.W.,
and Gail Eisenberg
with Herma M. Rosenthal

HarperPerennial
A Division of HarperCollins*Publishers*

HarperCollins books may be purchased for educational, business, or sales promotional use. For information please write: Special Markets Department, HarperCollins Publishers, Inc., 10 East 53rd Street, New York, NY 10022.

FIRST EDITION

Designed by Nancy Singer

ISBN 0-06-095222-9

97 98 99 00 01 ❖/RRD 10 9 8 7 6 5 4 3 2 1

TABLE OF CONTENTS

ACKNOWLEDGMENTS

This was a project with many parents. Our agent, Ellen Geiger at Curtis Brown, started it with the right combination, and our editor, Joëlle Delbourgo at HarperCollins, offered the unflagging enthusiasm that kept us going. Assistant editors Leigh Ann Sackrider and Tim Duggan and publicists Rose Carrano and Jessica Jonap extended helping hands to make us feel at home.

A special thanks goes to the volunteers at Motherless Daughters, Lori Brown, Naomi Helig, Dori Bernstein, Shema Rogoff, Karen Murray, and Janice Nase, who make sure we accomplish great things despite needing a bigger boat.

Our heartfelt gratitude to the women who were interviewed by phone or surveyed by mail, especially Patricia Murphy, who provided inspiring insights and anecdotes, and Shelly Cofield, whose unique perspective and uncanny memory helped fine tune the workbook.

Additionally, Diane would like to thank—

The first motherless daughter I ever met, Barbara H. Benson, and her husband, Bob Benson. Unfortunately, she understood. She took me under her wing and gave me more than I ever will be able to repay. My respect, love, and gratitude. Marguerite Stratton, C.S.W., helped me grow personally and professionally.

My sister Ellen J. Garrison, her husband, Harry, and children Bill, Michele, and Bob have been wonderfully supportive. My aunts Mary Ann Jankowski and Veronica Goetz, and cousins Veronica Andrews and Nancy Eck, answered the questions I had for my story.

I am blessed with outstanding role models in Mary Roviello, Betty Errante, Jean Schiraldi, Joan Imhof, Gayle Rawlings, Phina Hickey, Carol Hickey Remondino, Mary Ann Howell, Kathy Howell Deecken, Lorraine Brown, and Debbie Brown Lynch. To my other "sisters" for their love and laughter: Julie Benson Peluso, Lisa Benson Rosmarin, and Sandy Garrison Mendelsohn. My gratitude to their families as well.

For professional wisdom and guidance, Audrey Brockner, C.S.W.; Nancy Boyd-Webb, D.S.W.; Ralph LaBella; Barry Milberg; Richard H. Martin; Richard Cardillo; Ross Bertrand; Gary Laermer; William T. Sullivan; Rev. Philip J. Kelly; and Rev. Thomas Beck.

Along the way I received great support from Alice Scourby, Ph. D.; Robert Andrews, Ph.D.; Duffy Spencer, Ph.D.; Jane Weston Wilson; Patricia Gibbons; Suzanne Gabriel; Willie and Mary Powers Schembeck; Elizabeth Smith; Clara Evans; Kathleen Ross-Walker; Lynne Hughes; Patricia Tucker, C.S.W.; Julie Davidson; Rochelle Levine, Ph.D.; Larry Moore; Tim Finucane; George Tollefsen; Bernice Trojanowski; John Jankowski Jr. and his family; Carol Nash, and Gerry C. and Joseph W.

Among the many special people at Saint Vincent's Hospital are Sister Karen Helfenstein, S.C., F.A.C.H.E.; Gaetana M. Manuele, A.C.S.W.; Gail Monaco, Ph.D.; Barbara Horn, A.C.S.W.; Barbara Barrow Miller, A.C.S.W.; Larry Miller, C.S.W.; Stephane Lubicz, M.D.; Josh Torgovnick, M.D.; Michael Sheran, M.D.; Manny Revuelta, M.D.; Gayle Drummond, RN; Melissa Trindade, RN; Gabriel Torres, M.D.; Nicholas Gualtieri, M.D.; Sisters Eileen, Jorene, Teresita, and Pat; Maier Goldberg; Mauricio Valdes, M.D.; Anwar Shamim, M.D.; Holly Gilbert, M.D.; Andrew Gotzis, M.D.; Pam Call, M.D.; Oscar Klein, M.D.; and Juan Bailey, M.D.

Gail would like to thank—

My father, Mart, for breaking his silence and initiating conversation about my mother. Sincere appreciation to my stepmother Pat for enduring my angry years and the love and support she supplies my father. Thanks also to my stepbrothers and their families, who I think about often; and to my mother's childhood best friend, Mary Lou Pankole, who was there with answers when I was ready to ask.

To my aunt Diana, who offered an ear and a shoulder when my mother died, I extend a seventeen-year-old thank you. I wonder daily how things might have been different had I taken you up on your offer.

And special thanks to my uncle Bill, my mother's only sibling, who drove in the boxes of family photos. You, Lauren, and Michael are very important to me.

Loving appreciation to Leslie Herzik, for the hard time, good advice, and soft touches she provides; my friends Katchi Pritchet, Jo Moskow, Leslie Major, Paige Williams, Jane O'Reilly, Alan Drewsen, Daniel Thomas, John Dunn, Marisa Diaz-Granados, Márcia Tarter, Pam Sidman, Cordelia Bowe, Marlene Rachelle, Jen Slaybinck; and my employers (who I consider friends) for supporting this project and the organization. That's what friends are for. A special note to Kemllen . . . my ears and door are always open.

To Hope Edelman, I cannot say enough. I thank her for her courage to write *Motherless Daughters* and for the permission to finally grieve, for giving generously of her time, and for placing an ad in the *Village Voice* the same week that I happened to read it.

Finally, my greatest acknowledgment goes to my mother, Anne, who for so many years went without any.

And Herma would like to thank—

Reuben Tatz and Ileane Rudolph for opening first their hearts and then their home so this book could have a room of its own. They believed when I didn't. They still do. In a year in which both my parents died, my aunts Edwina Small and Josephine Ackerman reinforced our version of family values. I'm indebted to Karen Golden and Ilene Hochman for understanding the importance of ginger distance and Lauren and Rob Wik for meaning it when they asked if there was anything they could do. And a final thanks to my mother, Dorothy, whose most important contribution was love.

NOTES FROM THE AUTHORS

There are many things I can change about myself and my life, but I can never change the fact that I watched my mother die when I was twelve years old. I learned what cancer looks like and smells like and how people die from it. I learned how precious life is and saw how quickly it can go. The last time I saw my mother alive, she was curled up in a fetal position, in a coma. Walking into that hospital room in 1969 would change me forever. It changed who I was and who I would become. I had to start living without her, take care of myself, and show the world I was strong, had no problems, no pain. But I also had no sense of myself—except as empty.

When I was in college I volunteered for a suicide crisis hotline, and suddenly all of my life experiences fell into place. I discovered that helping someone made a difference to them and to me. There is a proverb that says, "When the student is ready, the teacher appears." I was ready, and I went back to school to get my master's degree in social work.

Dr. Patrick Del Zoppo taught my first bereavement counseling class. I was struck by his simple yet profound statement "Mourners need to tell their story and have someone bear witness to their experience." The seed for *A Mother Loss Workbook* was planted.

When the Motherless Daughters® Support Groups started in 1994, I began to hear the stories of how women felt growing up motherless. They talked about feeling empty, unloved, unimportant, guilty for not having done more, profoundly sad about never having gotten to know their mothers. They were confused and angry at their loss and the way it was handled by the adults in their lives. Many lacked self-esteem, convinced that others hold secrets lost to them when their mothers died.

A great deal of healing went on, and continues to go on, in those support groups, and I've had the honor to bear witness to it—to hear the stories, to feel the pain, and to share my own. I've met many wonderful, loving, supportive people on my road, and I'm thankful that I have. I've learned how to say yes to opportunities instead of "I can't do that because I don't have a mother." I've taken risks and grown. Most importantly, now I know that as a motherless daughter I am a survivor, not a victim. We all are. *A Mother Loss Workbook* is intended as a tool to help you discover and better understand yourself as a survivor.

The loss of my mother and the circumstances of her death irrevocably affected my life. Even as I write this twenty-eight years later, I want her back. I want to know what she thought, how she felt, who she was, and who I am because I am her daughter. I've tried but haven't gotten answers to many of these questions, so I must live with the yearning and with the void, a hole in my heart that will always be there. No one sees it but me, and the only people who know that it's there and understand it are other motherless daughters.

Columnist Russell Baker wrote in a *New York Times* article, "I am going to go back to where I belong, whenever I figure out where that is." Until very recently, this was the story of my life. I never felt I belonged anywhere, because no matter where I was, I didn't have a mother that I belonged to anymore. To all the motherless daughters out there, may this book bring you to a place where you can heal and blossom.

Diane Hambrook

It was early morning, May 19, 1980. My father knelt at my bedside and said, "Mama died." I was fourteen, an only child. On the outside I seemed to be handling it fine. I was a clown determined to make people smile, but more importantly, I made sure I was smiling. A smile represented happiness, not the shame, confusion, and isolation I felt. The sorrow was my secret; silence and denial, my friends. I resisted what little discussion took place about my mother, and before long there was none. The woman was forgotten, the questions left unasked, the answers left unspoken.

When I was twenty-two, a therapist broke my silence when she said, "Poor Gail. She doesn't have a mother." It was a slap in the face. I hated her. But it was the truth, this great part of my identity that I'd denied for eight years. The fact was, I didn't have a mother, and I did feel like poor Gail, abandoned and ashamed.

Slowly, my therapist and I began to talk about my mother's life and death, the particulars of our relationship. We'd revisit the past, the pain, all I felt or didn't feel after her death, and it would be done just between us and somehow still with a sense of secrecy. I would confront the issues . . . eventually.

Eventually became 1992. I saw an ad in a paper. It said something like "Writer seeking women who lost mothers during childhood and adolescence." I called and talked to a woman named Hope, who was writing a book, *Motherless Daughters*. She gave me a time and a place, and I then met Hope and her assistant, Adreme. Hope and Adreme. I was in a room telling my story to other motherless women who understood. The funny thing is, I'd always thought I was alone.

A Mother Loss Workbook is for the women who write to Motherless Daughters and say they feel defeated, why bother to change. They are women who refuse to fully live their lives without their mothers, who are ashamed of their loss and ask that we send information in unmarked envelopes. Women who still honor the silence. May you all gain insight, validation, and comfort, the courage to ask questions and to confront your mother's life and death.

It has taken seventeen years, every moment since my mother died, to put my experience of mother loss into perspective, into a framework I can manage. There wasn't a structure then, nothing to give me the courage to reunite with my past and my mourning, nothing that gave me the permission to grieve. There wasn't Hope Edelman's work, Motherless Daughters® Support Groups, or this workbook. There were no resources available to legitimize my feelings or provide a sense of unity. Now there are.

My story went public that night in 1992, and I continue to tell it in many ways. A bit here to that person, a paragraph there in a journal. We all need to tell our stories, if only to ourselves. Make this your year.

Gail Eisenberg

If nothing else, life is ironic. In the midst of working on *A Mother Loss Workbook,* my mother died. She had survived two types of cancer and diabetes only to be the victim of a bizarre car accident.

She was in a coma the last time I saw her, bruised, swollen, her breathing mechanically aided. My elderly father sat in the hospital helpless, in denial, refusing to believe the truth. She didn't know I was there. When the end came, I kissed her good-bye.

Then there were plans to be made. Funeral, burial, shiva, relatives to contact, planes to be met, papers to be signed, possessions to go through. The busy work of the bereaved. Through it all, through my sadness, through my grief, there was something else. In my mental preparations for a time I knew must come, I had assumed I would be an emotional wreck. I would simply fall apart over my mother's death. But that wasn't happening. Instead, I felt a profound sense of gratitude. I was grateful that I had lived so far into adulthood with a mother who loved me to the core of her being. Until I began collaborating on this book, I didn't know how much of a difference that would make.

For the next eight months, I worked on *A Mother Loss Workbook,* the presence of my own mother accompanying me in some unexplainable way. I hope that reading these pages comforts you as much as helping to write them did me.

Herma M. Rosenthal

BEGINNING

You don't heal from the loss of a loved one because time has passed, you heal because of what you do with the time.

—*Carol Crandall*

To tell you how to use this workbook would be like giving you instructions on how to grieve: impossible. The only thing we know for sure is that no two people will approach this work in the same way. If there's one thing you should remember as you begin this process, it is that you are not alone. With that knowledge, you've already begun to heal.

A Mother Loss Workbook is designed to let you tell the story you need to tell—your story. While it is an ideal supplement to personal therapy and support groups, it may be your *only* tool if you're just starting your journey or are hesitant to "go public." It is a safe place where no one will judge you and where the work that must be done can be done in your own time, at your own pace, and at any stage of mourning. If you are currently caring for a terminally ill mother, the workbook may be a therapeutic outlet for telling your story and documenting your feelings as they unfold.

To help you tell your tale, we've included numerous stories of other motherless women. You might find similar situations or share their conclusions, but it's unlikely that you will have taken the same road to get there. That's OK. The anecdotes are there to stimulate your thoughts, offer you inspiration, and assure you that you're not alone.

The workbook is divided into four parts and follows a chronological order. The first part covers life with Mom and the family; the second explores the circumstances and ramifications of her death; the next brings you to who you are today as a result of the loss; and finally, you approach a place of healing, where you work toward integrating the loss and taking charge of your future.

You don't have to work in sequential order. If your mother died when you were an infant, it may not make sense for you to start at a point before her death. This is not to say that there's nothing there, but it may be more advantageous for you to begin somewhere else. Skip around and get a feel for the workbook. Break its binding, dog-ear pages that evoke interest on first glance, use different-colored pens. Do whatever you have to do to make it your own. What works for you is the right way.

The exercises are used to elicit important information, to help you come to realizations and determine which questions need answers. They vary in their structure just as people vary in their approach and response to situations. We encourage you to come back to certain exercises, not only when you discover new information but also to note your progress. By all means build on the same exercise or return to issues that have special meaning to break new ground. Your story unfolds a little more each time you tell it. Try completing the exercises from another perspective— maybe an older sibling's or your own at a different developmental stage. Date each exercise so that you can see what develops over time.

"We do not write in order to be understood; we write in order to understand," C. Day-Lewis wrote. It is through your expression of the written word that your story takes shape. That's the purpose of the Safe Passages. Essentially, they are directed journal entries. Use them to reflect, inspect, sort out issues, arrange thoughts. Writing prods us to remember what we already know and to release emotions that may otherwise have no place to go.

"Writing is my way of unlocking what's in my head," Maria told us. "It's easier for me to write to sort things out than to talk. When I talk I go off on tangents. My mind races away. When I have the opportunity to sit down and write, I spend more time reflecting so that I cover everything I want to say."

Try to be specific. Details, details, details. If you don't fill up the space, that's fine. If you do, feel free to continue on the blank pages at the end of the book. Or you may want to document your passages on a home computer. Where you keep them is up to you. What's important is that you explore the issues. Read your work out loud to reinforce its message and validity.

Some of you may be more inclined to talk with someone you're close to rather than to sit down and write out exercises. Writing is a terrific tool, but it's more important to find your own comfort level. The discussion just might make it easier to get your thoughts down on paper later. Or, work through the exercises by talking with yourself. Use a tape recorder, if only for your initial thoughts.

Not all of what you write will be of equal importance or evoke the same reactions. Certain sentences or images are likely to pop out at you. They have a special meaning that only you can detect. We call these Key Passages. Each of these sentences could stimulate a journal entry in itself. By the end of the workbook, they'll tell an important story of their own. Come back and write about them any time you want. Determine the Key Passages out of all your entries, and continue narrowing the focus until you get down to the core. The core is what you eventually want to be working on. If you're considering therapy or a support group, these nuggets of truth can be a good starting place.

Record all of your Key Passages in the Part Breaks. These sections follow each major part of the workbook and serve as your file cabinet for information or questions. You'll be remembering old and uncovering new facts throughout the workbook. There'll be questions that arise, incidents that need clarification, people you've forgotten about, and amends galore. This is what the Part Break houses.

Don't censor yourself. People may have been doing that to you all your life. Let go. Be honest. Try to write the first thoughts that occur to you. Don't worry about spelling, punctuation, or grammar, just write the truth as specifically as you recall it. If something scary comes up, try to continue. Try to write through your resistance. This is where the intensity is. You may cry, you may laugh, but you will feel something—and that's good. If at any time you feel overwhelmed, skip the exercise or section and take a break. Trust your instincts on this one. Listen to yourself.

You might want to talk to someone about what you're going through.

Chapter 1 will help you develop a Safety Net for that purpose. Or you might want to consult a therapist or counselor or join a support group. Grief is different from clinical depression, and we strongly encourage you to seek professional help if you suspect that what you're experiencing goes beyond the kind, intensity, and duration of feelings we describe in this book.

One memory may flood you with others, necessitating a change in your priorities. You may discover that there are issues that demand your attention first. You have bigger, or at least other, fish to fry right now. Though these issues can be related to your loss, it may be more beneficial to deal with them first, then come back and focus on mother loss. Issues such as incest, abuse, and addiction are outside the scope of this workbook. We've compiled lists of national organizations and books that deal with those concerns, which can be found at the back of the workbook.

If you were too young to remember much about your mother, you may become frustrated. We tried to construct exercises applicable to loss at any age, but wherever necessary, ignore our time frame. We also intended the exercises to be easily understood and practical. For that reason, we have tried to avoid therapeutic jargon.

If you find that you are confused by one of the exercises or that it doesn't fit your situation, we assure you that it's not a reflection on you. Admittedly, we are not always able to accomplish our goals. You will probably have to adapt some exercises, but there may also be times when an exercise simply doesn't apply to you. Thinking no homework? Not to worry. There will be plenty of other work for you. But do try to seek answers from someone who remembers or holds information.

If you're the type motivated by telling people what you're about to undertake, get out there and scream it from the rooftops. It may be important for you to include in your declaration that you are not dwelling in the past—the grieving you're doing is something you were not able to do back then, something you must do now. Or you may choose not to tell anyone about your grief—at least for now. It's up to you. However, it's been our experience that there is healing in confiding and sharing your story. You don't have to make any decisions about this immediately. Keep it in the back of your mind as you work through the book. Your focus now should be on the commitment you're making to yourself and the action you're about to take.

Avoidance may be part of your process. It may take you hours to gear yourself up for an exercise. You may even look around one day and find your house the tidiest it's been in years. Be patient. Try to break the work down into bite-size pieces instead of seeing it as an overwhelming whole. Some of you may want to devise a schedule, while others would feel too confined by such a structure. If you are unsure, try both ways and then decide which is better. Consider organizing a time to discuss or complete the exercises with other motherless daughters you may know.

We encourage you to work honestly and thoroughly, yet only do what you are comfortable with at the time. Address issues as they need attention or when you're ready. You don't have to complete the exercises in one sitting. This is not a race or competition. It could very well be a life's work. Remember, the more you invest, the more you will get out of it. If you discover other approaches as you work, good for you.

We aren't going to kid you. Mourning is an unpredictable process. There are no quick fixes or miracle cures. You may feel better, stronger, or more precise in your recollections on some days than on others. You may even feel worse before you feel better. After all, you may have avoided feeling the pain of your losses for years, so feeling better is likely to occur gradually. We're never really done with grief. It sneaks up on us when we least expect it and stands us up when we do. With time and effort, our perspective on grief changes, as does its hold on us.

Finally, we have faith that *A Mother Loss Workbook* can be useful to those of you who are to some degree paralyzed by your loss, as well as solely defined by it, by helping you rediscover your talents, strengths, and resources. It is our hope that you take the issues, curiosities, truths, misconceptions, and answers you discover here beyond the scope of this book. Now you're ready to begin.

A NOTE OF EXPLANATION

The stories used in this book are based on surveys, letters, interviews, and focus groups with motherless women, who ranged in age from late teens to mid-seventies. In certain instances, we have edited their comments for reasons of space and comprehension, but wherever possible we have tried to retain their original language and syntax. To protect their anonymity, we have used multiple pseudonyms and changed identifying factors. We are indebted to them for their openness and generosity in sharing their stories.

REMEMBERING THE PAST

Life can only be understood backwards; but it must be lived forwards.
—*Søren Kierkegaard*

The first part of this workbook is devoted to recalling the past to gain insight for defining yourself and redefining your loss. Our memories provide history and continuity to our lives, linking the present with the past. We encourage you to get out the family photo album or go through the attic or basement where family mementos might be stored.

We begin by discussing the nature of grief, the different stages of mourning, and why it's important to address these issues, even if your mother's death seems like ancient history. The chapters then look back at your childhood, your mother's life, your relationship together, and the interactions of your family. These recollections are the first pieces of the puzzle, and they provide important information.

The exercises in these chapters are designed to activate your memory and stimulate you to review and reevaluate events from your past. We'll ask you to recall the facts and evoke images of yourself, your mother, and your family. If she died before you really got a chance to know her, we'll offer suggestions on how to get more information about her. We urge you to talk to people who knew you and her, to write about what you think and feel, and to dig deeper for answers and perhaps new questions.

1

GOOD GRIEF
Why Deal, Why Heal, Why Now?

> Grief is, by its nature, unmanageable. The most we can do is respect its might and then ride it, like some towering wave, until it dumps us back on the shore.
> —*Barbara Lazear Ascher*

Rita's Story: My mother died of colon cancer in 1934, when I was fourteen. It wasn't until 1976 that the pain about my mother got so intense. I was already a widow. It was then I started to write about her. I was sitting there writing two paragraphs, but the pain was so awful that I felt like a teenager again. From fourteen to seventy-six is sixty-two years of being a motherless daughter.

Bonnie's Story: My mother died from lung cancer when I was nineteen. Today, two years later, I finally realized my mother is really gone. At first it was a shock, and I denied it. I tried to keep myself very busy with school and working. After blaming everything else for my unhappiness and emptiness, I am realizing that this sadness is because of my mother's death.

THE PAST'S CLAIMS UPON THE PRESENT

Two months, two years, two decades, or more—the balm of time may heal the wound, but the scar never quite disappears. The death of a mother so early in her life—and too early in ours—changes us forever. It hovers over our shoulder and haunts who we are—our experiences, our emotions, our dreams. Yet how many of us have turned and looked directly at this shadow, acknowledging its presence in our lives? Though we may have gone through the motions of societal or religious rituals designed to help us come to terms with her dying and leaving, how many of us have truly grieved?

How could we? How could we know how deeply this loss would affect us? How could we know how much our lives would change? How could we know the awful ache we would feel on birthdays, holidays, days that take on meaning in our lives, and sometimes just on any day? As Fran says, "I think the big times I'll miss her are yet to come: getting married, having kids, things like that. Those are the biggies. That's when I'm going to wish that she were there."

In the days, months, and years after her death, who really wanted to hear about the hole in your heart? Mandy has recently begun to explore the aftereffects of her mother's death fifteen years ago. "I'm grieving in a time where the event happened, years ago," she explains. "People are like, why now? They don't understand this delayed grieving thing. It's like, you had your time, you had your six months that society gives you, and then you get a boot in the butt and go on with life. I skipped over mourning completely, and so did my whole family. But it's safe now. I'm out of my father's house, I have a job, a place to live, a life, and my mind is clearer. It's OK to be mad now."

DATE:_____

The last time I felt I should be over my mother's death was:

_____

_____

_____

What provoked that feeling was:

_____

Yes, we were supposed to have gotten over all of this. So we didn't speak about it and cried in silence. We tried to explain but couldn't get our message through. We tried to ignore the sadness or drown it in excesses. We mourned as best we could at the time. We continue to mourn today.

In *Grief Counseling and Grief Therapy,* psychologist J. William Worden writes, "There is a sense in which mourning can be finished and then there is a sense in which mourning is never finished." Worden cites a letter of Freud's to a friend, explaining that while "we know the acute stage of mourning will subside, we also know that we shall remain inconsolable and will never find a substitute."

FIVE MYTHS ABOUT MOURNING

1. Grief and mourning always decrease over time.
2. After the death of a loved one, it's healthier to put them out of your mind.
3. Mourning is over in a year.
4. You mourn the death but nothing else.
5. Grief is only psychological.

In skimming through this workbook, you've already acknowledged the importance of opening this chapter in your life. Remember, healing is a gradual process. Slowly we learn how to accept and accommodate loss, in our own time, in our own way, at our own pace. Since each of us—take Rita and Bonnie, for example—will be at different points along a very individual path, it's a good idea to figure out where you are on this journey without end but not without purpose. If you're nearer the beginning of this process, you're discovering how you've been affected by the loss of your mother. If you're further along, your focus may be on using your insights about the loss to reinvent your life.

To get a better sense of why you've picked up this book, check off any of the statements below that apply to you.

DATE:_____

_____ My mother died a long time ago, yet I still feel the pain of her loss.

_____ I've been working on these issues for a long time, and I think I've come as far as I can on my own.

_____ I don't think I will ever get over her loss, but I'm picking up this book on the chance that it will help me somehow.

_____ I have just started to realize how my mother's death has shaped my life and affected my development.

_____ I can't remember much about the events surrounding my mother's death.

_____ I want to find out more about my mother's life.

_____ I want to deal with issues surrounding mother loss, but I'm not sure how to go about it.

_____ I was too young to understand what death really meant.

_____ My family doesn't want to talk about my mother.

_____ I feel somehow I'm to blame for her leaving.

_____ I wasn't sorry she died.

_____ Someone I care about gave me this book.

_____ My therapist/counselor/support group facilitator suggested this workbook.

_____ I want to use this book as part of my work in a mother loss support group.

_____ I am afraid to deal with the overwhelming emotions I feel when I think about my mother.

_____ I feel as if some part of my development stopped when my mother died.

_____ I think other women know something about being a woman that I don't.

_____ I want to celebrate my mother and myself.

If you've checked off any of these sentences, this book can help you. It doesn't offer neat prescriptions. It offers information, insight, and a way to tell your story.

GRIEF REVEALED

"Don't give me grief" is an expression we've all heard. In fact, it may be what you're saying to yourself now: "It was hard enough then, why do I have to suffer through this again?" Though mourning is a lifelong process, the ability to understand and express our grief lessens the anxiety and uncertainty we feel. Adapting to a parent's death as children, adolescents, or even young adults often requires skills beyond our years and experience. Holding unresolved, unexpressed grief inside keeps feelings in a pressure cooker with the heat turned up. Clearly, ignoring them doesn't make them go away. They shape our identity, affect our behavior, and touch our relationships.

What exactly is grief? How does it show itself? Grief is a natural, profound reaction to death. Mourning is the process that allows us to let go of what was and learn to live with what is. It is a way of incorporating the death into our lives. For many of us, the mourning we did at the time our mothers died wasn't enough to accomplish that goal. (We'll discuss the reasons for incomplete mourning in later chapters.) We may live in a society dominated by a need for instant solutions, but grief doesn't care. *Follow these simple steps and you'll be fine* isn't its modus operandi. Grief doesn't share our passion for neatness.

Take a moment to think about how you define grief. Do you see it as something to be avoided at all costs or as painful but necessary? Define it in your own terms; for example, *Grief is an undertow that grabs you.*

DATE:_____

Grief is:

_____

_____

_____

What is your definition of mourning? _Mourning is a journey into the soul._

Mourning is:

_____

_____

_____

Your perceptions and expectations concerning grief and mourning reveal your readiness to do this work and your openness to growth. Theories hold that we go through different stages—denial, anger, bargaining, depression, acceptance—in the course of grieving. During the mourning process, we need to accomplish a set of tasks that allows us to come to grips with the loss. What we're doing as we work through these stages is accepting the reality of loss, experiencing the pain of loss, adjusting to a world without our mothers, and reinvesting our energies in other relationships.

That's the theoretical model. In reality, the progression is neither straightforward nor predictable. No step-by-step directions included. Each of us has her own fingerprint for grieving. Ordered starts and finishes have no place here; grief plots its own deliberate time and course. We may not go through all of the stages or pass through them sequentially. Then, just when we thought we had been there, done that, wham, something comes along to trigger the cycle and the emotions are off and running again.

Mary knows that feeling well. Her mother was pregnant with her when she was diagnosed with breast cancer and had died by the time Mary was four. That was forty-four years ago. Recently her father died, and she was unexpectedly devastated: "He was an eighty-year-old crotchety man, and we had a terrible relationship, so what was going on? I realized it was really old grief being touched and revisited. Every time I revisit grief, I visit it as an adult and as a four-year-old."

"We accept a loss in stages, quietly closing one door and moving on to the next," Hope Edelman wrote in her life-affirming book *Motherless Daughters*. "The loss of a mother is one of the most profound events that will occur in a woman's life, and like a loud sound in an empty house, it echoes on and on."

REACHING OUT

As you use this workbook, you may want to discuss the feelings it evokes, the issues you're working on, or the need for more information. If you're having a rough time, it's important to have people you can reach out to for support and encouragement. That's what we all want when we tackle hard tasks. It takes courage to ask for help. We want a compassionate listener, someone we feel safe sharing with, who we think will understand. This is your support system: the people who believe in, care for, and respect you. They should have the ability to challenge you without rancor or reproach and the sense to reassure you when needed. Is it your sister who made sure you didn't drop out of college? What about the husband who listens to everything, even the boring stuff? Is it a friend who cries at the same movies and laughs at the same goofy jokes? Or is it a therapist who helps you understand the seemingly inexplicable? Write down their names, addresses, and phone numbers and the qualities you value in them. Consider adding people as they come to mind. If you've been feeling isolated and have problems with issues of trust, your list might be pretty short. Try one small step—put down one name. You don't have to communicate now. Simply write the name and why you think he or she might be a compassionate listener. Even one name on a blank page can be very powerful.

┌───┐
│ SAFETY NET   │
│   │
│ **Name**   **Qualities**   **Phone/Address** │
│   │
│ _____   _____   _____ │
│   _____   _____ │
│ _____   _____   _____ │
│   _____   _____ │
│ _____   _____   _____ │
│   _____   _____ │
│ _____   _____   _____ │
│   _____   _____ │
│ _____   _____   _____ │
│   _____   _____ │
└───┘

If there are people on this list with whom you've never discussed being a motherless daughter, put a star next to their names. Consider what you would tell them about your mother's death.

SAFE PASSAGE: A JOURNAL WRITING EXERCISE

"It's funny," wrote June, whose mother had died in a car accident when she was three, "I've never cried thinking about my mother, but as I sit here and write this I can't stop. I hope this letter is read, so that maybe someone will understand."

Writing has the power to unveil what your conscious mind protects. For this Safe Passage, write about why you think this workbook will be helpful and what you hope to accomplish in it. In essence, why deal, why heal, why now? When you're finished, go back and reread what you've written. Put a star next to the sentence or sentences you think are the most significant, the ones that made you go "Aha!" At the end of Part I, there's a place for you to copy these Key Passages. As they build up, we think you'll see that you've reached some very important conclusions.

DATE:_____

_____

_____

_____

_____

_____

_____

_____

_____

_____

FINAL THOUGHTS

Grief hides in the places we don't want to look. The decision to walk toward our problems—not away from them—is a brave and difficult one. It's like starting on a new exercise plan. At times you gasp for air, your muscles get tired and the next day a little sore, but gradually you grow stronger. You've just had your first workout.

"The reason society says you must get on with it is because you remind them that it could happen to them too. That's why they turn away. It's that Death thing. Capital D. So you're left with this awful thing and nowhere to go. I think everyone owes it to themselves to be aware. You can't hide. Death is there. It's part of life. Somewhere, at some point, it's going to touch your family too."

—Susan, age twenty-six, whose mother died
when she was eleven

BEGINNING THE PICTURE
Who Was I?

To be a person is to have a story to tell.

—*Isak Dinesen*

❋ *Anne's Story: At thirteen, before my mom died, I thought I had it all together. I had my whole life planned out through retirement. I was going to graduate high school while I was in eleventh grade, then go on to flying school. My mom's graduation present would be flying lessons. By the time I was twenty, I would have a motorcycle, a truck, and a boat. At this point [nineteen], none of that stuff has happened.*

❋ *Lynda's Story: I heard scuffling in the kitchen, and when I went to see what was going on, I found my father holding my mother, limp from slitting her wrists. He asked me to get her some shoes, and I went into the closet and chose what I believed were her favorite pair. They were these sparkling silver high-heeled shoes from the seventies that she wore when she went dancing. Not exactly practical for someone losing blood, but what did I know? I was fourteen, and I wanted to make her happy.*

Tell us where you've been, and we'll tell you where you're going. Though the loss reverberates regardless of age, a toddler and a teenager deal with life—and death—in significantly different ways. Knowing who you were before your mother died is a prerequisite to figuring out who you are today—and why. If she died when you were still a baby, it's important to know what occurred during those formative years without her. We need reference points to signal what changed, note how far we've come, and mark what we hope to regain. We need to know more about that time in our lives—developmentally, emotionally, socially, within our family—to more clearly understand our reactions to a mother's death and subsequent losses. We need to go back to move forward.

Whether you were a child so young that mother is only a photograph, or a college student relishing being out from under her thumb, it's important to know where you were in the process of creating a self when she died. As we grow up, we add experiences and develop skills that transform us into fully integrated adults. Mothers play a crucial role in that complex emotional and cognitive process. Your developmental stage and the rites of passage you were undergoing provide clues about what maturational tasks were interrupted by your mother's death, which ones you had to accomplish without her, which you never accomplished, and what coping mechanisms you had at your disposal to respond to her death and your grief.

As you consider who you were, remember that we're not simply raw materials propelled through an assembly line, stopping at each work station to pick up essential parts. Some seven-year-olds act like forty-seven; not every teenager pierces her lip as an act of rebellion. We move at our own pace, affected by external influences as well as our own innate and very individual personalities. What kind of world did you grow up in? What got you really angry? What special moments stick out? What embarrassed you? The whole context is important in deciphering the reasons for your particular expressions of grief and helping make sense of your feelings.

Sara sums it up this way: "When I started to get in touch with my feelings, around age twenty-six, I went through a very intense period during which I really focused my life around the tasks of reconnecting with myself. I went back over my past, trying to retrieve every memory so I could reexperience it and feel the feelings I had been ignoring. Without the chance to finish telling my own personal narrative, I had never completed the tasks of inventing my own life."

The exercises in this chapter are designed to help you excavate memories buried in your childhood, particularly before your mother died. Composing an autobiography creates a self-portrait of the child you were. Try to recall specific events in your life before your mother died. If connected ideas, memories, or associations occur to you, write those down too. If this exercise arouses more extensive thoughts and images than we've left room for, use extra sheets of paper or the blank pages at the back of the workbook. Use this exercise as a reference for how you behaved, felt, and coped, what you were like, and what you want to recapture. Even if you were very young when your mother died, this can still be a valuable exercise, simply as a glimpse into your childhood.

DATE:_____

Title _____

I was born in _____ on _____ at _____.

I weighed _____ pounds, _____ ounces. People said I looked like

_____. My parents had ____ children, and I was the

_____. My nickname was _____ because

_____. I grew up mostly in

_____. I made friends _____, and

we would mostly_____. My best friend was

_____, and we talked about_____

a lot.

_____

_____ was important to me.

I was a _____ student, and I _____

_____.

My most/least favorite teacher/professor was _____,

and I remember him/her telling me _____

_____.

After school I liked to _____, but I

hated to _____. When I was alone, I would

often _____.

My favorite movie/TV show/book was _____,

and I remember feeling _____ after seeing it

(reading it) because _____.

I was _____ years old at the time.

_____ made me feel

secure. One of the things I would always say was _____

_____

As a child/adolescent/young adult, I was _____

_____.

I wanted to be a _____, and I thought that _____

_____.

The things I wanted in my life were_____

_____.

My biggest secret was _____

_____.

When I wanted something badly enough, I would _____

_____.

If I didn't get my way, I would _____

_____.

What always made me laugh was _____

_____.

When I was sad/unhappy/afraid/disappointed, I would _____

_____.

I felt as if I could talk to _____ because he/she made me

feel _____ when

he/she_____.

When I was excited/happy/proud, I would _____,

and he/she would _____. When I

_____, it was the

_____ in my life.

MEMORY BLANK

"I don't remember a lot of things from being in the third grade," Gena admits, "and my dad wouldn't know because he was at work. What were the things I liked to do? My favorite ice cream? What did I like to wear? Mothers remember those things." Do you have missing pieces and gaps in your memory too? Look back on your autobiography and consider what additional facts are important to you. Turn to the Memory Bank in Part Break I for a ledger to help you begin your information seeking. Piecing together your life requires detective work. You need something more than your own memory to rely on.

When Leslie was just four, her mother died from a blood clot. "I have no real memories of my mother," she says. "I feel like I was hatched. I don't have a history." What Leslie was old enough to understand was that something was missing in her life. The absence was palpable. "I first saw pictures of her when I was about thirty-six. I instinctively knew which ones were her."

True, childhood memories may be fuzzy, but we begin to form bonds of affection in infancy. Babies a few hours old can recognize their mother's smell. As we develop, the nature of our attachments, our ability to control emotions, and our view of illness, death, and loss change, but the constant throughout our push toward adulthood remains the need to feel safe and secure. Mothers are supposed to be there to provide that sense of well-being.

Within the first six months of life, infants show a strong preference for the person who has responded most to their signals. In most instances that's Mom. Beginning around six months, that attachment becomes increasingly intense and exclusive. While earlier you might have exhibited a marked response when anyone who was paying attention to you left, now it's primarily your mother's absence that draws cries of protest. By the age of two, the attachment between mother and child is so strong that even momentary separations can start the toddler crying, fussing, and fidgeting. If she doesn't return, the child begins to feel helpless, powerless, and even a sense of despair, from seeing no connection between her actions and the desired response.

A four-year-old, when told that her mother was now in God's house, immediately responded, "I'll just go in and break the window and get her out." In the eyes of toddlers and preschoolers, the world—real and imagined—has a literal meaning. You're straying from mother's apron strings, emboldened to explore what's beyond your own immediate environment. Yet that underlying need for safety and security remains. You look back over your shoulder to make sure she's there watching and encouraging your more daring escapades and explorations.

A mother's death isn't the only childhood loss or separation. A best friend may move, your parents may divorce, a pet may run away. It's the innocence lost when you find out that the tooth fairy is really your dad, or the separation anxiety when you're left with the baby-sitter. Your earlier losses may have set the pattern for future behavior as well as indicated how dependent you were on your mother or family. Remembering the impact of those experiences makes subsequent reactions more comprehensible.

SEPARATION AND LOSS

What other types of loss or separation can you recall prior to your mom dying? Check off the ones that apply to you, and add any of your own.

DATE:_____

_____ Going to school for the first time

_____ Going away to school

_____ Going away to camp

_____ Moving to a new neighborhood

_____ Having a friend move away

_____ Losing a first love

_____ Sleeping at a friend's or relative's for the first time

_____ Death of a pet

_____ Losing a tooth

_____ Losing an important possession

_____ Having an important possession stolen

_____ Loss of a dream

_____ Parents' separation

_____ Parents' divorce

_____ Death of an immediate family member

_____ Death of a close relative

_____ Death of a distant relative

_____ Loss of attention

_____ _____

_____ _____

    Pick a few of the most affecting experiences, and examine them in greater detail by answering the questions below.

How did I feel at the time?

_____

_____

_____

_____

_____

What was my understanding of separation, loss, and death?

_____

_____

_____

_____

How did I get that information?

_____

_____

_____

OFF TO SCHOOL

School brings greater responsibility and self-reliance, richer, more varied relationships with adults and children outside your family. We still seek a secure base from which to conquer new worlds, knowing we can return for that giant Band-Aid if we meet with a setback. We develop a heightened sense of shame, guilt, and concern for people we're close to. We begin to internalize rather than act out all our feelings. We come to understand how other people live, and as a result become more acutely aware of how our own home environment differs from others'.

Deirdre says she started school as "a naturally gregarious kid. I really wanted friends, but I had grown up in this rarefied household with parents twenty years older than everybody else's. They would play classical music and recite poetry, so I didn't know I was an egghead intellectual kid. I would come up to some other kid in third grade and say, 'What's your favorite string quartet?' and then wonder why I didn't have any friends." In response, Deirdre became more withdrawn. Her mother's death several years later exacerbated those early feelings of isolation.

Like most youngsters, Deirdre wanted to be popular and fit in at school. You may have craved more attention or just hipper clothes. Perhaps you wanted a better car to replace the one you were mortified about being picked up in, or maybe you wanted the all-American family. Though they can reveal lofty visions and goals, some longings reflect changes we wanted because what we had made us feel different and ashamed. The death of your mother may have reinforced feelings of shame already present, making you feel that somehow you didn't belong. Or perhaps it signaled the end of your dream, even if that dream was unrealistic. After all, how could you have the all-American family without a mother?

HEART'S DESIRE

What did you want before she died? If you know who had that quality or where you saw it, write that in too.

What I Wanted	**Who Had It**
Cool Mom	_My best friend Kathy_
Confidence	_Kids on the swim team_

Review your list. Why were those things important?

_____

_____

_____

_____

LEANING TOWARD ADULTHOOD

Tara was a rebellious fifteen-year-old during the Woodstock summer of '68: "I wanted to experiment with drugs and sex and liberation and all that the era stood for and, of course, separate from my parents. My mother was Victorian. She was waiting until I was twenty-one to tell me the facts of life. She was trying to control me (impossible). She died on December 15, 1969, never having connected with me as a woman."

Told to be home at 10, you deliberately come in at 10:30. Going through the fever of adolescence involves testing boundaries, renegotiating rules now seen as childish. Girls stop asking "Who am I?" and start asking "What must I do to please others?"

"Early adolescence is a time of physical and psychological change, self-absorption, preoccupation with peer approval and identity formation," writes Mary Pipher in *Reviving Ophelia*. "Calmness is replaced by anxiety. . . . Far below the surface, [teens] are struggling with the most basic of human questions: What is my place in the universe, what is my meaning?"

At a time when we most need an anchor, we reject parental advice, pursuing instead the acceptance and approval of our friends, the other inhabitants of this hostile, rebellious, and often painful world. The pressure to be cool suppresses who we are in favor of how we fit in. Behind the bravado lurks a desire to hold on to childhood attachments. Yes, we're embarrassed to be seen with our parents and endlessly scrutinize "unfair" restrictions, but, notes Pipher, "adolescents still have some of the magical thinking of childhood and believe their parents have the power to keep them safe and happy. They blame their parents for their misery, yet they make a point of not telling their parents how they think and feel."

Nancy was nineteen, thinking about career choices, when her mother died. "She worked very hard on me to make sure I got off my butt or wrote a résumé. I needed her for that motivation." In your late teens and early twenties, on the verge of adulthood, you're embarking on what you designate inwardly as your "real life," making important decisions about education, job and career, relationships, family, and living circumstances. This is the continuance of the lengthening excursions we take from the family base. For many women, it's a transitional period when a mother's blessing for the course chosen is still sought.

LIFE CURRENTS

A number of factors, both positive and negative—not just the loss of your mother—influenced your childhood development. Sometimes we tend to see everything in our lives as a direct result of her death. While that provides an easy answer, it's probably neither accurate nor helpful. Other factors that had a great impact on you can help put your mother's death in a broader perspective.

Below, make a list of the strongest factors in both categories. Keep in mind that some may have had both positive and negative effects. Put those in both columns. For instance, being the firstborn is a plus because initially you don't have to share attention with brothers and sisters, but later you may have to take on unwanted responsibilities.

DATE:_____

Positive Forces	Negative Forces
Growing up in a small town	*My high school math teacher Ms. Green, who hated me and made me feel stupid*
Being elected president of my class	*My mother's drinking problem*

Look over the items on your list and rank them from 1 to 3 in order of importance, with 1 being the most influential. Answer the following about those you rated as 1's.

The reasons these were positive:

_____

_____

_____

The reasons these were negative:

_____

_____

_____

REMEMBER WHEN

"The past is not stable: it does not return to the memory either with the same traits or in the same light," writes French philosopher Gaston Bachelard. We can't help but view the past through the prism of the present, so we match up our memories with the way we see the world today. Memory and imagination work in unison. For example, in looking back on your life before your mother died, your tendency is to paint those times with the knowledge of her subsequent death. It's like retouching a photo so that it conforms to your current perception.

Rosa, twenty-seven, whose mother died of a debilitating muscle disorder when Rosa was nineteen, divides her life into two categories, worlds apart: "There is BM, before with Mom, and AM, after without Mom." When Rosa looks back, she views, then judges her BM actions in light of the subsequent tragedy. Hers are not memories but recriminations and glorifications. The hard times become harder, the good times better, and her mistakes magnified to epic proportions.

REDEEMING VALUES

In reviewing your childhood, you may have said to yourself, "Boy, I'm happy I'm not like that any longer," or, "If only I could be like that again." Think about those youthful traits and qualities. Which are you better without? Which are you glad you still have? Which did you lose when your mother died? What do you want to recapture? (We'll refer to this exercise again in an upcoming chapter.)

DATE:_____

Glad to Be Rid Of	Glad That I Have	I Want to Recapture
Stubbornness	*Perseverance*	*Carefree attitude*

ROOM OF YOUR OWN

Your childhood personality shone through in any number of ways: how you dressed, what you owned, how you decorated your room. When your family couldn't afford something that was "in," did you come up with a way to get something comparable? Were you the one who always had an outrageous explanation for everything? We sometimes forget our early inventiveness, resourcefulness, and creativity. Remember the pink elephant wallpaper you insisted was perfect for your room and actually convinced your mother to buy? How did your imagination and ingenuity reveal itself?

I really, really wanted to get a set of cross-country skis, but my birthday had just passed and not a holiday was in sight. I saved money by collecting and recycling cans, selling lemonade, and telling people my goal in case they wanted to make a contribution.

DATE:_____

_____

_____

_____

_____

DREAM ON

Anne wanted to be a pilot. Erica thought she'd make a fantastic transla-tor. They might seem like impossible dreams today, but then they were vivid and alive. What did your inner voice say about your hopes and desires for the future? Those dreams speak to who you were and what you once wanted.

DATE:_____

My childhood/adolescent fantasies were:

_____

_____

_____

What happened to those dreams?

_____

_____

_____

Find a photo of yourself before your mother died. Paste it in the space provided. Describe, in as much detail as you can, the child, teen, or young adult you see. Do you see yourself as the Perfect Child, the Tomboy, Cool, Nerdy? How did other people describe you? How much attention did you pay to their opinions? When you're done, remember to pick out your Key Passage and save it in Part Break I.

DATE:_____

_____

_____

_____

_____

_____

_____

_____

_____

_____

FINAL THOUGHTS

We all carry inside us the child we once were. The personal history of that child, both the real and the imagined one, is contained in the adult we have become. Few if any of us escape from our formative years unscathed, but journeying back starts us on the road toward reclaiming our hopes and possibilities.

❋ 3 ❋

BEYOND MOTHERHOOD
Who Was She?

After [her] death I began to see her as she really had
been. . . . It was less like losing someone than discovering
someone.

—*Nancy Hale*

❋ *Brenda's Story: On the surface, she was happy and cheerful and fun.
Underneath, my mother did not have a voice. She didn't have the self-
esteem to believe she had intelligent opinions or that she could contradict
my dad or my grandmother, who had always been a very critical person.
My grandmother wanted everyone to smile and appear happy, and there
was never any room growing up in her family to express anything negative. It makes sense my mother would have married a man like my father.
It's like the only thing my mother did for herself was to kill herself. It was
the only action that said, "Here is my voice."*

❋ *Olivia's Story: My mother was a sculptress, and she died when I was
seven. Periodically when I clean the house, I clean her sculptures. I look at
them and think, What did she mean by making them? How did she come
up with that idea? Did it represent something in her life? I'm curious
about how she came up with those ideas.*

The difficult question for many women is "Who was that woman I
called mother?" Beyond her role as mother and apart from the woman

who exists in our imagination, can we paint a realistic portrait of a flesh-and-blood person? How we respond to loss depends in part on who it is we're grieving for. The woman whose loss you mourn may be as much a product of your own needs as it is a reflection of her true strengths and weaknesses.

Author Mary Pipher writes in *Reviving Ophelia* that "we think of our mothers in what Freud called the primary process, the thinking style of children. We have trouble growing up enough to see our mothers as people." For most of us, the woman and the mother are so intertwined that it's truly difficult to separate them. That's why we're asking you to go back to her early life and try to imagine the forces that shaped her identity.

In the previous chapter, you began your autobiography. Now it's time to be your mother's biographer. We'll delve into your relationship with your mother in the next chapter, but here the idea is to envision her outside the role of mother. We've concentrated on certain areas, but you may find others that can help you figure out who she was. For example, her religious beliefs or cultural background might be important. We urge you to take her biography in the direction that will provide you with the most insight into her personality and the way she conducted her life. Once again, try to recall specific events. If other memories, associations, or more extensive images occur to you, include those too.

DATE:_____

Title _____

My mother's name is _____. She was born on

_____ and died on _____. She was the daughter of

_____ and _____ and the sister of

_____.

I know the following about her childhood:_____

_____

_____

_____.

I know the following about her adolescence:_____

_____

_____

_____.

After she finished high school, she _____

_____, and then she

_____.

When she was _____, she met my father. They had a

_____ marriage. When she was a girl, she

wanted to _____ and _____.

She had the following hopes and dreams:_____

_____.

She was able to accomplish _____

_____, but she

never _____.

Some of the things she liked were _____

_____

_____.

She also loved to _____

_____

The people she was closest to were _____

_____.

My mother had _____ friends, and they would _____

_____. She hated it when _____

_____.

Her main philosophy about life and people was _____

_____

_____.

She frequently said_____

_____.

What made her happy was _____

_____.

She would get upset when _____

_____, and

then she would _____

_____.

Her biggest disappointment was _____

_____.

My mother considered herself a _____ person. I think

the thing she did best was _____

_____. I think she

would agree/disagree with this.

In examining your mother's life, more questions are likely to arise. Think about where you might get that information. Consider what else you want and need to know, and record those questions in the Memory Bank in Part Break I.

HALOS AND HORNS

A mother's early death removes the opportunity to make all the humanizing revisions that would eventuate naturally as you both aged. Robbed of real experiences, children are perfectly capable of concocting a new, improved version in which their mother is lovelier, smarter, and wittier.

Tina was eight when her mother died. In Tina's eyes, her mother was "a guardian angel. I never could look at her as a person, because I didn't know her as an adolescent or an adult. I worshipped her. I thought she was perfect." The romanticized, idealized woman that a child enshrines is never replaced by the multidimensional human being an adult perspective would provide. Imperfections vanish in a child's single-minded vision.

The woman Rae called mother was far from ideal.[1] An abusive alcoholic subject to black moods, she was more feared than revered. She died when Rae was four: "I remember smelling the alcohol and being very afraid of her. Even her mother said she was a horrible human being. But she had a couple of cousins I tried to get information out of, and they told me that when she wasn't drinking, she was a really nice person. She had a beautiful personality. Years later, when I went to nursing school, I started to understand what alcoholism was about. I thought she was

---

[1] It is beyond the scope of this workbook to deal with issues surrounding drug and alcohol addiction and psychological, physical, or sexual abuse. However, we strongly encourage women who are dealing with problems connected to these issues to seek additional help and to use this book in their work with a licensed therapist who has specialized training in these areas. In the Resources section at the end of this book, we have included a list of organizations to consult for information on these subjects.

nasty and mean, but I realized that it was the disease, not the person."

A mother who was abusive, had alcohol or drug problems, or who suffered from mental illness or a stigmatized disease like AIDS doesn't exactly fit the Mom-and-apple-pie fantasy. A deep-rooted hostility may color your ability to see who she really was. You may be angry at her, resentful about what you didn't have in a mother, perhaps ashamed or embarrassed by the one you did have, enraged by her abandoning you in life and in death, and mystified that you were attached to and even loved her. We're so caught up in the woman who let us down that she gets lost in our rage. Admitting her positive qualities means unlocking the hidden affection we've worked so long to repress.

As you try to rediscover your mother's life, you face the possibility that some of your revelations may contradict your invented version of who she was. This could be uncomfortable or disconcerting, illuminating, or simply informative. You may be torn between wanting to find out everything and leaving her memory in peace. Dismantling our shrines seems disloyal, while holding on to anger may be our way of keeping connections alive. Women who witnessed a mother's deterioration or long-term illness may find it hard to remember a woman of any vitality or to believe that despite physical frailties, she had other, perhaps less apparent, strengths. But despite any mixed feelings, the ability to reconcile ourselves to the truth and to forgive are essential to healing. You have lost a mother once to death. By uncovering her true story, you avoid losing her again.

Picture Perfect?

Photos can be extremely powerful and evocative. Find one of your mother and paste it in the space provided. If you don't have a photo, draw a picture. This exercise is designed not only to trigger your memory but to stimulate your desire to find out more about your mother.

Study the photo for a minute. If this weren't your mother, what would you think about her? Dig deep for qualities, good and bad, you think your mother possessed as a woman. They can be physical or temperamental, skills or shortcomings. They don't have to even out, but aim for some on both sides of the ledger. If you decide to do more research about your mother, make this an ongoing exercise.

DATE:_____

*Great sense of humor*_____

*Quick temper*_____

*Played the piano*_____

*Couldn't keep the house clean*___

Crinkly blue eyes _____

Too fat _____

_____

_____

_____

_____

_____

Look back at your list and put a check mark next to all the traits you really admire and a minus sign next to those you would have liked to change. Try to be selective, choosing the ones that are really important to you. Now put a star next to the descriptions that also fit you.

BACKGROUND CHECK

"My mother was an Italian Catholic growing up in the fifties," Lynda relates. "Her mother was extremely religious, so when my mother got pregnant when she was sixteen, it was not only a huge taboo at the time but also considered a sin for a good Catholic. She was kicked out of school. She was blindfolded when she had the baby and gave the infant, my unknown half-brother, up for adoption. She told me this when I was twelve and she was trying to explain why she was always so depressed. I didn't understand all that this meant then, but I know now what she must have been feeling: all the shame with society and the Church and all the guilt for giving up a child."

A mother's absence deprives us of knowledge about her and about ourselves. In her dwells the precursor to what we will be. The exploration of a mother's identity journeys back to when she was a child and continues through her young adulthood and on to her life with you. She was a woman defined by unique capacities and failings, attitudes and style, dreams achieved and neglected, a product of her times, her family, her education, and her beliefs.

Lynda's mother grew up in an extremely religious family at a time when the stigma of having a child out of wedlock was much greater than it is today. Those influences shaped her life, as the loss of our mothers shaped ours. A mother's death forces us to rely on static memories and images. Without knowledge, we feel detached from our past and wary about our future. That's the legacy motherless daughters seek to reclaim by collecting the details and piecing together the fragmented stories of a mother's life.

LIFE CURRENTS II

Make a list of the influences, both positive and negative, that most strongly affected your mother's life. Some may be double-edged. In Lynda's mother's life, for example, Catholicism may have provided her with a set of values and beliefs, but it also left her with tremendous guilt and shame, which contributed to her chronic depression.

DATE:_____

Positive Forces	**Negative Forces**
A strong family	*Had to drop out of school*
Loved her work as a teacher	*Abusive father*

Safe Passage: A Journal Writing Exercise

One woman sent us a copy of a letter she wrote to a mother she doesn't remember. In it she asks all the questions she has no answers for. For some questions, she may never find answers, but the letter voices her doubts, fears, and concerns. After reading these excerpts from Leslie's letter, compose your own. Since this is for your eyes only, ask anything. It may help you clarify what you want or need to know.

> Mother,
>
> This seems funny, writing to a woman I never knew. Who were you? What were you like? Did you love me? Did you love my father? I recently heard the two of you were very different. Were you ever sorry you married him? Did you want all of us kids? I noticed I was in a different picture frame from the other kids, so was I a surprise? Did you still want me?. . . If the truth were known, I could still use the tools you could have provided, tools to show me how to be a woman, a human, a Christian, a friend, a wife, a mother, or a lover. . . . You held all the answers to all my unanswered questions, and now I am trying to find a way to tap that information.
>
> Your daughter

_____

_____

_____

_____

_____

_____

_____

_____

_____

_____

FINAL THOUGHTS

Rachel is in the position many of us find ourselves in at one point or another: "In starting to find out information about my mother, I'm sort of biting my nails about what my family is going to say. Are they going to chew me out? My biggest fear is intruding. I'm afraid they'll turn around and say, 'Why do you want to do this now?' But I have every right to those memories and that information. She's my mother. I'm her daughter."

The work in this chapter is about memory and imagination, separation and connection. We hope it will help you reclaim your mother's past and reforge your links to it.

4

MOTHER AND CHILD
Who Were We?

Probably there is nothing in human nature more reso-
nant with charges than the flow of energy between two
biologically alike bodies, one of which has lain in amni-
otic bliss inside the other, one of which has labored to
give birth to the other.

—Adrienne Rich

*Lisa's Story: She was my one-hundred-percent support system, my cheer-
leader. I remember in eighth grade running for student council president,
and she helped me write my speeches and sell all my posters. She took me
shopping and taught me how to carry myself and always told me to believe
in myself. She was my entire support system, and when she died, I felt like
I had the rug pulled out from under me.*

*Eleanor's Story: The only time I remember when my mother gave me full
attention was when I had double pneumonia or scarlet fever and she sat
on the bed with me. Otherwise I can't conjure up any other time when we
were affectionate or close. It's pretty sad. What I wish I had from her was
more of her time, more personal time.*

Each relationship with a mother is unique, but we all sought the
basics: love, support, trust, respect, patience, companionship, food and

shelter, guidance and identity, security and protection. The maternal instinct may kick in with the birth of a child, but the complete package of mothering skills isn't necessarily standard issue. This chapter examines the mother-daughter relationship: what roles and functions she filled for you, what you learned from her, what she meant to you, what you wanted from her, and what you actually got. Whether she was a best friend or a distant presence, whether you were proud of her or embarrassed by her, these facts greatly affect how you mourned her then and mourn her now.

Many motherless women are yearning for either the great mother they had or the great mother they wanted. We tend to hold onto a mythical mother, in part out of loyalty, in part as a survival mechanism, in part to keep her alive. Do you miss her because she was loving, sensitive, and made you feel great about being her kid? Or do you miss her because you were hoping that she would show you the love and approval you wanted and needed before she died?

DUE UNTO ME

Think about how your mother acted toward you. Read the following list, and put an *M* next to the words that describe her and the way she related to you. Choose all the adjectives that apply, and add ones that might be missing.

DATE:_____

_ Loving	_ Smothering	_ Forgiving
_ Detached	_ Inconsistent	_ Erratic
_ Cold	_ Strict	_ Playful
_ Caring	_ Affectionate	_ Disapproving
_ Warm	_ Reproachful	_ Nurturing
_ Sharing	_ Unfair	_ Abusive
_ Supportive	_ Sacrificing	_ Good-humored

_ Controlling	_ Lax	_ Domineering
_ Angry	_ Anxious	_ Sympathetic
_ Overbearing	_ Nervous	_ Respectful
_ Annoying	_ Generous	_ Attentive
_ Nagging	_ Suspicious	_ Accommodating
_ Encouraging	_ Selfless	_ Mean
_ _____	_ _____	_ _____
_ _____	_ _____	_ _____
_ _____	_ _____	_ _____

This exercise might help you clarify feelings about your mother. The *M*'s may represent things you miss, things you still look for in relationships with friends, family, and lovers, and positive and negative behavior patterns in your own relationships. Now go back and put a *W* next to the words that represent how you wanted your mother to treat you. Again, add adjectives where necessary. If your mother died before you had real memories of her, just complete the second part of the exercise. These yearnings are the voice of the child asking for what she needed. It's the part of us still connected to the vulnerabilities of childhood that requires healing.

MOTHER OF OUR TIMES

Your first experience of love, nurturing, security, and tenderness is usually with your mother. A deep-seated attachment forms early, making her loss a shattering one, even if your time together was brief or troublesome. Your age and developmental requirements at the time of her death offer further insights into your interaction.

Ina was three when her mother died, and though she ransacks her brain for even the sketchiest memories, there's a void where a mother is supposed to be. Women whose mothers died when they were infants and toddlers often feel incredibly disconnected. Their mothers live only in borrowed stories and worn snapshots. Frequently, women who suffered early childhood loss have only vague sense memories—how she smelled, the touch of her hand, a look on her face. Natalie says her most vivid rec-ollection is of how she and her mother "would kiss rubbing noses like Eskimos. It's my favorite memory, but that's about all I remember."

SCENT OF A WOMAN

The senses can provide a route to your subconscious, allowing feelings or memories to surface that might not be available to the conscious mind. Using your sense memory, form as detailed a picture of you and your mother as possible. Set the scene, consider the mood, imagine the scents and sounds, what you're both doing, and how that feels. Not all your memories are pleasant ones, so don't be surprised if what comes to mind isn't a joyful event or a tender moment. When you have it clearly set in your mind, describe the scene. Why do you think you've conjured up those images? Facts may be sketchy, but each one adds another piece to the puzzle and another part to your story.

Here's what Gena, whose mother died when she was eight, pictures in her mind's eye: "I'm in the kitchen watching my mother with this huge aluminum or tin contraption making applesauce and apple pies. It's as though I'm watching the two of us standing at the kitchen table, and she's mashing them in a colander. It's the smells, the sound of the apples being smashed, and there's just this warm feeling of togetherness."

DATE:_____

_____

_____

_____

_____

_____

_____

_____

_____

_____

_____

At twenty-five, Lisa says she's first doing the growing up, the developing of an autonomous self, that she should have done at fifteen when her mother became ill: "I was nineteen when she died, but she got sick when I was fifteen, and that totally changed our relationship. I felt like developmentally things got stuck at that age. We didn't let our relationship develop naturally. It was almost like everything had to be good and positive. I'm starting to get the strength to be my own cheerleader, to tell myself I can do it and I'm worth it."

Candace echoes Lisa's story. She was twenty when her mother died from stomach cancer: "My mother made all my decisions. She was my confidence. I didn't really have it myself, and she was constantly reassuring me. The power of the relationship was so positive that it gave me a great deal of self-esteem. It's an area I still struggle with. I haven't found a way to do that for myself. I've been floundering ever since."

We all need guidance as we mature. What do you do when that direction is missing? "I became more independent and self-sufficient," Penelope asserts, like many motherless daughters. Equally undeniable is the feeling that some tasks were left undone. We grew up, but not quite in the same way as women who had a mother's guiding hand. And like Lisa and Candace, some women remain in a kind of developmental limbo, not exactly sure of how to proceed or in fear that moving on will sever that precious connection.

Many of us feel incomplete, as if we're missing some crucial piece of information that a mother was supposed to supply. Fran explains it this way: "It's always the what-if. What if she were alive? What would things be like if she were here? How would things be different? I was pretty resentful toward my dad because he was able to find a companion for himself and be happy again, where I was still missing someone to take over the role of a nurturing person."

WHAT IF . . .

This is a time for you to consider what you learned from your mother and your own what-ifs. Think about where you were in the maturational process when your mother became seriously ill or died. Ask yourself what developmental tasks, problems, and issues you faced. At six, Fran was mastering the skills needed to interact in school's larger social world, while at twenty, Candace turned to her mom for guidance in choosing what kind of education and career roads to take. The role a mother played at these pivotal stages in your life is important in gauging what has happened since her death.

DATE:_____

I learned these important life lessons from my mother:

I think I have my mother's voice. Not the sound of it but how she really always told people exactly what she thought or what needed to be said. She taught me to think for myself.

_____

_____

_____

_____

I needed my mother to:

I hadn't fully separated from my mother. I was just starting to be slightly rebellious, but we sort of squelched that from happening because everything had to be good and positive when she got sick. I needed her around so I could just be a normal teenage kid and not Pollyanna.

_____

_____

_____

_____

Take a look at your list. Did you find other role models or other ways of navigating through those stages, or do you find yourself no further along today? Concentrate on how things would be different if she were alive or had lived longer.

If my mother had lived longer:

I constantly think my life would have been a lot smoother. Had she been here, I think she would have supported me to go on with my writing. It would have happened earlier.

_____

_____

_____

_____

_____

_____

_____

_____

_____

"She was my best friend" were the words used by many women we inter-viewed, in particular those who were teenagers when their mothers died. Simple as it seems, the implications are broad: your mother was some-one you could trust, a confidante and a confidence builder. You made plans together and shared an uncommon bond. She made you feel spe-cial, knew everything about you, and loved you anyway.

Meg wrestles with a dilemma. She only wants to remember every-thing good about her mother, despite her father's efforts to convince her otherwise: "We didn't have a mother-daughter relationship. We had more of a best friend relationship. My world revolved around her. I would always say to my dad, 'I don't care what you say, Mom will always be perfect in my opinion.' I think he wanted to bring me back down to reality and show me that nobody could be perfect. Maybe I felt that if she was perfect, she might come back. A normal person, obviously their time would come, but a perfect person would be superhuman and couldn't die."

Canonizing a mother and ignoring the flaws in your relationship is a way of keeping her memory alive. It may be a consoling tribute, but it's not one that necessarily helps you accommodate her loss. You can wind up trying to prove something and be someone for a person who never existed. As Evelyn Bassoff writes in *Mothers and Daughters: Loving and Letting Go,* "One of the marks of a mature relationship occurs when the daughter no longer sees her mother as goddess, monster or fool, but rather as a human being." It's a hurdle of understanding many of us fail to clear or even attempt.

IN HER IMAGE

Ruth recalls, "She would take me on long, long walks in the winter and literally put her hands on me and say she was molding me. My sisters were too old; I was her baby. I guess she felt she had made mistakes with them." As our primary same-sex model, our mother is the pattern we're supposed to copy. Observing her, we learn much of the behavior associated with being female. We internalize what it means to be a woman by seeing in her what we might become. Paradoxically, she's also the person we most rebel against: "I would never want to be like her, she's so rigid, strict, uncool—," fill in the blanks. We're entwined in a delicate dance animated by conflicting needs for separation and closeness.

Pam remembers her mother telling her repeatedly, "You were created in my image. If I could have created a child in the womb, it would have been you." As daughters, we become extensions of our mothers. Because of our sameness, the boundaries between us are indistinct, our identities intertwined. At times, daughters are unable to see mothers as separate from themselves. This lack of detachment sometimes makes us so eager to please them that we fail to come to terms with our own limitations. As a consequence of this identification, many women feel they lose a part of themselves when a mother dies.

THE FEELING IS MUTUAL

The patterns of the mother-daughter bond inform our lives. By going back and reassessing this crucial relationship, we begin to understand the lessons it teaches. In Chapter 2, you placed your own life in context. You may find it useful information as you reconsider what role your mother played in your life and, equally significant, what you meant in hers.

DATE:_____

What my mother was to me:

*She was the person I feared.*_____

*She was my security.*_____

_____

_____

_____

What I was to my mother:

I was her second chance at motherhood. This time she would do it right.

I was a substitute sister.

A MOTHER'S WEAKNESS, A DAUGHTER'S STRENGTH

We attach a certain invincibility to our parents that's crushed by the onset of illness and/or prolonged deterioration. Gone is the all-powerful, all-sustaining woman. Emotionally or physically fragile, she may have been inattentive to our needs. Terry was six when her mother died after being ill for several years with breast cancer: "I knew that she was sick and that she couldn't play. I remember going to her bedroom every morning before kindergarten to say good morning because she couldn't get out of bed. She wasn't up to fix breakfast, she wasn't up when we got home. I remember crying outside the bathroom door when she was throwing up, not because I knew what was going on but because I knew how bad I felt when I threw up. I really couldn't understand why she was so sick all the time."

Indeed, parent-child roles are often reversed. She was supposed to take care of us. Instead we're taking care of her. "I became her partner," confides Hillary, who looked after an ailing mother for several years. "By this time she was receiving radiation. I would sit in the waiting room, and it was scary for a child to see people without noses, with serious kinds of cancer. After she saw the doctor, I would ask her, 'Did the doctor like how I changed your bandage? Did he say how professional it looked?' I was thinking I was her personal doctor at home." While the responsibilities of caretaking can lend a child a sense of importance and helpfulness, they're likely to be a staggering burden for a child who, despite all her effort, could not save her mother.

In the high-wire act of life, mothers are the safety net. As children and even as adolescents, we believe the world is a safe, secure place in which events proceed in a predictable, orderly fashion. A mother's role is to provide that sense of security and confidence for her children. Illness and death not only demolish that assumption, they take away the person you thought would keep the wolves at bay.

SAFE PASSAGE: A JOURNAL WRITING EXERCISE

Abigail was eight when her mother died: "My mother had promised me a little wallet that she had. I guess I must have played with it. But after her death, my grandmother and aunt took almost everything of hers out of our house. We came back, and there was nothing left of her. It was horrible. Then, one night six or seven years later, I heard a voice telling me to look in my father's portable closet. He thought I was nuts, but he searched in there anyway, and at the bottom of the closet, underneath all this stuff, was the wallet. It's been thirty years; I still have the wallet."

Sharon collects music boxes because they remind her of holiday times shared with her mother: "My mother loved Christmas. We had ornaments and music boxes all over the house. It's just a part of her that I keep with me." Cherished objects help us remember. Do you keep something that either belonged to your mother or is in some way symbolic of her? Perhaps there's something you wanted and never recovered. Lucy failed to get back her mother's wedding dress, insensitively given to a neighbor. Why is it an important memento for you? What does it represent?

DATE:_____

_____

_____

_____

_____

_____

_____

_____

_____

_____

FINAL THOUGHTS

"My mother would sit on the edge of my bed, and we would play a bedtime ritual we called Nother One," Gail recalls. "One of us would continuously and quickly say, 'Nother one,' while the other blew kisses. There wasn't much to the game, but it made us laugh, and it was ours."

Reminiscing about your mother and your life together may be painful. We encourage you to cherish your memories of her, relishing the good times and acknowledging the bad. You may find yourself crying because you miss the wonderful moments or because you regret the awful ones. We also hope you smile and even laugh.

5

THE FAMILY ALBUM

Who Were They?

> All happy families resemble one another; every unhappy
> family is unhappy in its own way.
>
> —*Leo Tolstoy*

※ *Sonya's Story: In high school, I always felt really normal. I had two parents who were together, and we lived in the suburbs, and we had a dog and a cat, and my parents had a boy and a girl. It was so fucking Ozzie and Harriet and not like it was always wonderful, but it just all felt so normal.*

※ *Mandy's Story: My family was very secretive, and they kept a lot of the yucky stuff away from the kids. They weren't very communicative. Things were kept behind closed doors. My parents were both extremely protective. They both came from bad backgrounds where their parents were fighting. There was a lot of violence and arguing. They didn't want to have that kind of environment for us, so they went overboard in protecting us.*

A DELICATE BALANCE

One question many of us have is "Why was it so hard for my family to share their grief?" We'll look at the impact of loss and how our families mourned in subsequent chapters, but the root of the answer lies in what our families were like before our mothers died.

Our expectation is that our family will give us shelter from the storm, yet as often as not the cause of the storm lies within the family. We look to our families for support, but even in the healthiest of families, it's terribly difficult to find solace when a death occurs. A mother's death throws a family off balance, deeply affecting not only each individual member but the functioning of the family as a whole. Examining the family dynamic reveals much about its ability to adapt to the changes a mother's death sets in motion.

The Family Genogram

A genogram is a useful tool for mapping out family structure and interaction. Like a family tree, it's a window that provides a view of our families across generations. However, a genogram not only shows how members are biologically and legally related but depicts patterns, problems, important events, and family characteristics. Think of it like the family medical history taken by your doctor, only this history also charts the lineage of emotional and behavioral attributes. Your red hair or brown eyes may not be the only things you inherit. Examining your family in a multigenerational context can help you recognize less apparent patterns that are part of your legacy. The genogram can reveal how shame, secrets, and your responses to adversity may be linked to learned behavior passed down through generations. It offers insight without blame.

To construct a genogram, first map the family structure, then record family information. We suggest you display at least three generations, but go back—or forward—as far as you would like. In the example we did, we used squares to represent males and circles to represent females. The horizontal and vertical lines show biological, legal, or emotional relationships. Within each person's circle or square, put their name, age, and if applicable, date of death. Customize your genogram by noting the data and patterns that are important to you: for example, religious beliefs, superstitions, professions, physical or emotional difficulties, significant events, family interactions, communication and behavioral patterns. Histories of grudges, long-held secrets, significant successes and failures all belong here. We've included some possibilities in our example, but these are only suggestions. Add any relevant details that sharpen your particular family portrait as they occur to you throughout the workbook.

GENOGRAM

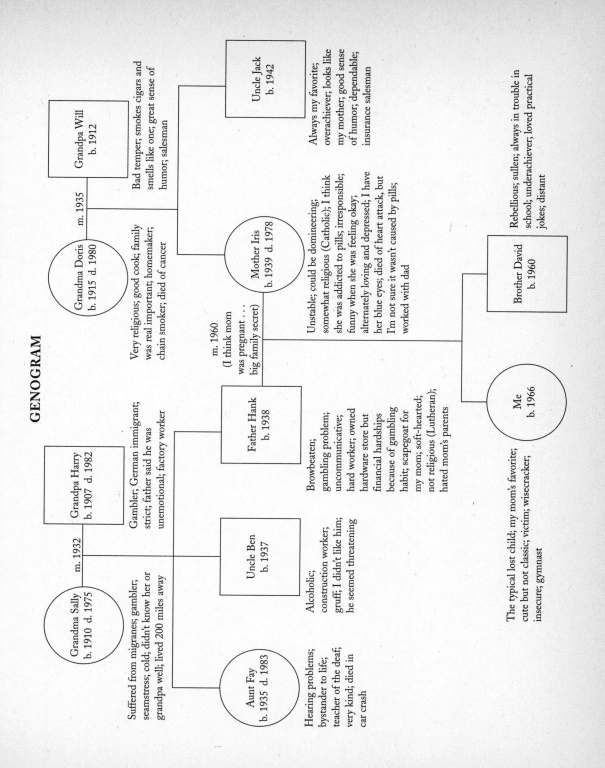

Grandma Sally
b. 1910 d. 1975

Grandpa Harry
b. 1907 d. 1982

m. 1932

Suffered from migranes; gambler; seamstress; cold; didn't know her or grandpa well; lived 200 miles away

Gambler; German immigrant; strict; father said he was unemotional; factory worker

Aunt Fay
b. 1935 d. 1983

Uncle Ben
b. 1937

Father Hank
b. 1938

Hearing problems; bystander to life; teacher of the deaf; very kind; died in car crash

Alcoholic; construction worker; gruff; I didn't like him; he seemed threatening

Browbeaten; gambling problem; uncommunicative; hard worker; owned hardware store but financial hardships because of gambling habit; scapegoat for my mom; soft-hearted; not religious (Lutheran); hated mom's parents

Grandma Doris
b. 1915 d. 1980

Grandpa Will
b. 1912

m. 1935

Very religious; good cook; family was real important; homemaker; chain smoker; died of cancer

Bad temper; smokes cigars and smells like one; great sense of humor; salesman

Mother Iris
b. 1939 d. 1978

Uncle Jack
b. 1942

Unstable; could be domineering; somewhat religious (Catholic); I think she was addicted to pills; irresponsible; funny when she was feeling okay; alternately loving and depressed; I have her blue eyes; died of heart attack, but I'm not sure it wasn't caused by pills; worked with dad

Always my favorite; overachiever; looks like my mother; good sense of humor; dependable; insurance salesman

m. 1960
(I think mom was pregnant . . . big family secret)

Brother David
b. 1960

Rebellious; sullen; always in trouble in school; underachiever; loved practical jokes; distant

Me
b. 1966

The typical lost child; my mom's favorite; cute but not classic; victim; wisecracker; insecure; gymnast

Me

A family's inability to deal with loss—even in previous generations—can affect your ability to cope today. A taboo passed on from past generations builds more fear and anxiety about an experience already painful enough. Go back to your genogram and see if you can detect patterns from generations past. Consider how they may have affected your immediate family.

Now turn back to the Separation and Loss exercise on page 20. Choose your most significant experience(s) with early loss or separation, and recall, if you can, what your family's response was.

DATE:_____

My family responded by:

_____

_____

_____

The way your family dealt with those experiences might have been a harbinger of future behavior. Were the messages passed on—directly or indirectly—cues to how to respond to the death of your mother? Are similar patterns of behavior noted in your genogram?

WATCH YOUR STEP

"I came from a household where you did what you were told," Beth says. "I didn't express any anger. Nobody in my family ever got angry. We were one of those families."

"Families vary in their ability to express and to tolerate feelings," J. William Worden explains in *Grief Counseling and Grief Therapy*. The patterns of communication in a family may be open or closed, direct or indirect, verbal or nonverbal, accepting or prohibitive of feelings, validating or rejecting. A close-knit family that communicates openly is apt to be able to pull together and bolster its members in a time of crisis. We aren't immunized from pain, but our experiences and emotional turmoil receive validation.

"Families that conspire to keep feelings down or at a distance may ultimately keep the individual from an adequate resolution of grief," Worden continues. Illness and death put a strain on any family. Add the trauma of death to an already dysfunctional family, and it's not hard to predict cataclysm. In a family characterized by conflict, hostility, chaos, or estrangement, long-term illness or death may be the final straw that breaks the clan apart.

INNER WORKINGS

It's important to assess your family dynamics realistically. Evaluate your family before your mother's death by exploring the characteristics that contribute to healthy and unhealthy functioning. Circle any description that applied to your family.

DATE:_____

Healthy	**Unhealthy**
Talks openly	Verbally abusive
Respects one another	Physically abusive
Has fun together	Has unachievable expectations
Can be honest with one another	Has difficulty resolving conflicts
Encouraging	Sets rigid limits
Shares good times and bad	Can't share negative feelings
Supports goals and desires	Discourages trying new things
Loves you unconditionally	Rejecting
Lets you act silly at times	Erratic and irrational
Marks your accomplishments	Gives you no credit

Healthy	Unhealthy
Can admit mistakes	Does not permit questioning
Can be trusted	Betrays trust
Respects the need for privacy	Has no respect for privacy
Is flexible enough to negotiate	Humiliates members
Listens to you	Nonnurturing
Can express feelings openly	Stifles feelings
Communicates openly	Secretive
Can express anger healthily	Unhealthy in expressing hostility
Makes decisions fairly	Makes arbitrary decisions
Assigns age-appropriate responsibilities	Overloads responsibilities
Shows appropriate affection	Physically removed
_____	_____
_____	_____

The results of this exercise might not be what you anticipated. Review what you've checked off and answer the following questions.

What does this exercise say about my family?

_____

_____

_____

_____

_____

How did my results differ from my expectations?

_____

_____

_____

FAMILY AFFAIRS

Given the emotional climate in Beth's family, it comes as no surprise to hear how they dealt with her mother's illness: "My mother had been sick for seven years, but it wasn't until I was twelve that I was told it was cancer. It was very much under wraps. Those are the years when children usually start forming their identity and start paying more attention to the outside world and what it thinks. Basically the lesson I learned was to ignore my own feelings. I didn't express anything or feel anything, because we were supposed to pretend that there was nothing wrong. Now I've come to believe that the secrecy was as much a problem as the actual death."

In troubled households, there's often a family equivalent of don't ask, don't tell. In *Vital Lies, Simple Truths*, psychologist Daniel Goleman cites the recollections of an adult child of an alcoholic: "In our family there were two very clear rules: the first was that there is nothing wrong here, and the second was, don't tell anyone." Families have a shared outlook that governs what and how issues are voiced. They construct a reality that defines the family's self-image. Anything that contradicts that collective definition is ignored or denied. In Beth's family, her mother's sickness challenged the notion that they were a normal, happy family, so nobody discussed it. But such silence increases feelings of shame. Surely it must be bad or wrong, you think, if you can't talk about it.

For many women, their mother's death and sometimes even the woman herself couldn't be discussed. This pattern of secrecy may have started before she died. Your family probably had at least one topic that was off limits. No one had to say, "That's not something we're going to talk about." You just knew it was a subject you shouldn't bring up, even though you didn't always know why.

KEEPING SECRETS

Healing requires breaking through walls of silence and telling the truth about what went on in your family. Revealing secrets can be frightening and feel like a betrayal, but it diminishes their power over you. Before you consider discussing these issues with your family, it may be easier and safer to do it here. Think about what was never or rarely discussed or only talked about in hushed tones within your immediate family. Revealing these family secrets, if only within the confines of this workbook, is the first step toward a more open discussion of your mother and her death.

DATE:_____

A family secret:

_____

_____

_____

The reason we didn't discuss it:

_____

_____

_____

I couldn't tell people because:

_____

_____

_____

CHARACTER PARTS

In most instances, mothers man the family nerve center. Generally, she's still the one charged with making sure everyone has three squares, mediating sibling squabbles, arranging family activities, keeping up holiday traditions, and a host of other responsibilities. A mother who suffers from prolonged physical and/or psychological illness isn't always able to fulfill those demands. A child's healthy development takes a backseat to caring for her mother. That's what happened in Wilma's case: "Prior to her illness when I was ten, we were a pretty typical family. Once she was diagnosed with cancer, our whole life changed. Our lives were ruled by the cancer. No matter how hard we tried, it was always there."

Cara remembers being six or seven and having to help her mother take care of the house: "I'd be upstairs cleaning, trying to be perfect. She would start to do things, and then she'd have to sit down and rest. It was very scary, and I didn't know what it meant."

Your reaction to family problems and stresses depends on a variety of factors—personality, age, family size, birth order, alliances, and parenting styles. Plus, we all have distinct roles within the family hierarchy: Breadwinner, Scapegoat, Martyr, Manipulator, Decision-maker, and the list goes on. That diversity explains why children brought up in the same household respond differently to a mother's death.

"After my mother died," says Sue Ann, who was eighteen when her mother committed suicide, "my aunt told me my mother had been a very different mother to me than my other sisters. I was the oldest, and she had no idea what to do with a child, and she would break into tears. When my middle sister was born, she was in her best emotional state. By the time my youngest sister was born, she was in a very bad way."

ROLE CALL

Roles, relationships, and alliances form the backbone of our families. Analyze how your family interacted. Here are questions you might want to consider.

Who made the rules in your family? How willing was he/she to listen to other family members' suggestions?

_____

_____

Were your parents partners or adversaries on family issues?

_____

_____

Who controlled the family finances?

_____

_____

If you had siblings, to whom were you closest? Why?

_____

_____

Whom were you most like? Why?

_____

_____

Who stuck up for you? Whom did you stick up for?

_____

_____

Who picked on you? Whom did you pick on?

_____

_____

Whom did you look up to? Why?

_____

_____

FAMILY FUNDAMENTALS

Danielle came from a tight-knit Greek family: "I didn't really hang out a lot outside, because the town I grew up in was primarily Irish and Italian, and we did a lot with the Greek Orthodox church. Our involvement with the church made us really close. It was an important part of our life, and it was where we turned when things got bad."

Religious, spiritual, or philosophical beliefs can help make sense of the world and its vicissitudes, offering a family comfort during painful times. Instilled faith and values are powerful resources when adversity forces us to question the reasons for our misfortune and we desperately reach for something steady to hold onto when all else seems shaky. On the other hand, when there's a stigma attached to a mother's death, as in the case of suicide, homicide, mental illness, physical abandonment, or substance abuse, some religious beliefs are so steeped in guilt and shame that they add to our burden by reinforcing those negative feelings within us.

LIFE CURRENTS III

Make a list of the factors that strongly influenced your family. Be sure to include both positive and negative ones. Also, add any relevant information or insights to your genogram.

DATE:_____

Positive Forces	**Negative Forces**
Involvement in community _activities_	_My mother's family was very_ _puritanical._
A warm extended family	_Financial difficulties_

Look over the items on your list and rank them from 1 to 3 in order of importance, with 1 being the most influential. Complete the following about those you rated as 1's.

These were positive because:

_____

_____

_____

_____

These were negative because:

_____

_____

_____

_____

_____

The message I got from my family was:

_____

_____

_____

_____

_____

SAFE PASSAGE: A JOURNAL WRITING EXERCISE

"I jog, and I often stop and run in place and watch the space of light that comes out of people's windows," Paula muses. "I know that represents life and a home and security and stability of some kind. Those lights remind me of when my house was like that. You know, Mom would be cooking dinner on a Sunday, and Dad would have the football buzz in the background. For me, that's very comforting. It meant the family was just doing its thing."

Family behavior tends to fall into predictable patterns. Certain events expose a family's inner workings; they reveal how it functions. Choose an experience, situation, or gathering that you think exemplifies—for better or worse—the way your family operated. It could be a holiday or just an everyday dinner. Think about what you really wanted to happen and how things usually turned out. How did each member of your family behave in this scenario? What were their roles? After you've written your story, you might want to ask other family members how they recall the same event. Maybe you can even ask them to do this exercise. Remember to find your Key Passage.

DATE:_____

_____

_____

_____

_____

_____

_____

_____

_____

_____

FINAL THOUGHTS

Family matters—the breaches and bonds, the distance and affection—define the landscape of your loss. Gather your memories, and try to ask the questions you need answered, if only of yourself. If at some later point you can also approach your family, do so with an open mind and, if possible, an open heart. As you gain new insights through these exercises, you may find yourself reconnecting with family history, realizing destructive patterns or recovering lost traditions.

When you're asking family members for information, don't be surprised if you come up against silence, ambivalence, or even hostility. Just because you're ready to start the conversation doesn't mean they are. Your work may open that locked door.

Part Break I

No matter where you are in the spiral of healing and no matter how slow your progress, your courage and persistence in coming this far deserve congratulations. This may have been a tough process, you may have a long way to go, but your commitment speaks volumes.

If you've skipped sections or exercises, don't be concerned. They'll be there the next time you open the book, and you can always come back to them. Or they may just not fit your needs or circumstances. By the same token, you might find repeating some exercises beneficial. If you're doing healing work in other therapeutic settings, you might want to use the exercises to jump-start a group discussion. Use your own creativity to adapt and expand the concepts put forth in the workbook.

Memory Bank

If information is missing or there are questions you need answered concerning you, your mother, family members, or specific events, document them here. A cousin, a family physician, or a childhood friend could very well hold the answers for you. This record will help you chart your course when you're ready to begin seeking information. These questions need to be asked and if possible answered honestly. They are essential to your story.

Ivy has finally reached the same conclusion: "I feel very sad that I can't share all of this with my family. I might try some letter writing because I'm more resilient to the no response now. I think it will be easier for me to look at it as their pain rather than a rejection of me. I always used to look at it as a rejection of me."

You may be hesitant because you fear resistance, the same old "You should be over this by now." You may feel ashamed that your loss still hurts. Consider what you risk if you ask. Weigh the consequences. Isn't asking the questions worth succumbing to tears in front of a sibling? This is not to say that you will be prepared to do this today. Nor is it to imply that it will be easy. It is, however, a necessary and helpful part of the process.

What I Need to Know	*Who* Might Have the Answer	*How* I Can Approach Them
Why I Resist	*When* I Will Try to Ask	*What Happened* When I Asked

What I Need to Know	*Who* Might Have the Answer	*How* I Can Approach Them
Why I Resist	*When* I Will Try to Ask	*What Happened* When I Asked

Are there other sources you need to consult—a photo album or a baby book, the house where your mother grew up, or a city agency? Take out old photos and see what they tell you about your family's traditions and rituals. Here's a place to keep your list of sources.

Source _____

Source _____

Source _____

Source _____

Source _____

Key Passages

If you haven't selected the Key Passages from your journal exercises, go back and reread your entries to see if something leaps out at you now. What seemed insignificant when you first sat down and wrote could trigger something momentous today: a surprising insight, a crystallizing phrase, a sentence repeated over and over, or a doodle in the margin. Seeing your thoughts strung together here, a pattern may emerge that sparks new observations and realizations, all of which may ultimately lead you down different—and perhaps deeper—paths of understanding.

Chapter 1

_____

_____

Chapter 2

_____

_____

Chapter 3

_____

_____

Chapter 4

_____

_____

Chapter 5

_____

_____

One more reminder: just because you've dealt with an issue in the context of this workbook doesn't mean you won't have problems with it anymore. Healing is a *process*. We move through it over and over and, with perseverance, learn and heal a little more each time. As a touchstone to assess where you've been, how you feel, and what you've accomplished in the first part of the workbook, reflect on the questions below.

How did I feel as I worked through these chapters?

How do I feel right now?

What surprised me about my responses or insights?

What was hardest to do?

What do I need to come back to?

What have I accomplished?

What can I do for myself right now?

PART BREAK I

PART II

TOUCHED BY LOSS

Once we appreciate the positive significance of the child's total dependency on the primal relationship, we cannot be surprised by the catastrophic effects that ensue when that relationship is disturbed or destroyed.

—*Erich Neumann*

In this part of the workbook, you're going to reflect on the circumstances surrounding your mother's death, the immediate impact of her loss, the short- and medium-term consequences of her death, and the changes in your life. You'll explore your feelings, both hidden and expressed, how you and your family mourned—or didn't, and the coping mechanisms you developed to deal with the tragedy. This work may bring up distressing, unsettling memories. If you're doing these exercises alone, try at least to inform someone who's part of your Safety Net, whether that's a spouse, a lover, a supportive friend, or a qualified counselor, so that you have somewhere to turn for a little help, encouragement, or an extra tissue.

The next three chapters will take you from the time of your mother's death through your own childhood, adolescence, or incipient adulthood. The goal of the exercises in Part II is not only to let you understand what happened but to help you see how the events that transpired, the losses and changes that occurred, contributed to your core beliefs and current behavior.

❊ 6 ❊

MOMENT OF IMPACT
When the World Came Tumbling Down

It is by going down into the abyss that we recover the treasure of life.

—*Joseph Campbell*

Recalling the day your mother died—even if it's in the forefront of your mind—isn't easy. You've probably spent years trying to suppress its emotional impact. Regardless of where you are in the mourning process, you can expect resistance when you think about that time. If you were too young to remember, it might be the day it really sank in that you didn't have a mother. It is the day your life changed forever.

Following are stories women have told us about their mothers' deaths. They are difficult, painful, and very powerful. Read theirs. Tell your own.

✳ *Nora's Story: My mother died the day before my high school graduation. My father woke us up in the middle of the night because she couldn't breathe. She was choking on her own bile, throwing it up. I weighed 110 pounds, and I literally picked up my mother who weighed 235 pounds. I was like the Incredible Hulk. My adrenaline must have been really pumping. I put her down on the floor and quickly changed the sheets. The bile was vile. I put her back in bed, but it happened again. That's when we called the hospital and everything broke down. The neighbors were all watching when they took her away. It was very embarrassing, this big woman coming down the steps, and it took three guys to carry her. We came back home from the hospital, but before long we got that call to go back. By then she was brain-dead, and we watched the final countdown, we watched everything. We were watching and waiting, and we had all these sick thoughts, like who's going to get the jewelry, does she have a will, how much longer,*

Date: _____

My Story:

_____

_____

_____

_____

_____

_____

_____

_____

_____

_____

_____

_____

_____

_____

_____

_____

what's going to happen, maybe she should pass away and be put out of her misery.

※ *Maggie's Story: We had no idea that anything was wrong. She was a jogger, and she used to run every day. I came home, and my dad had her on the floor and he was trying to do CPR, and he was trying to have me help him. I remember looking into her eyes, and then her eyes rolled back. The paramedics said she was dead when they got there, so I'm pretty sure that was the time she died. We found out later that her heart had never fully developed.*

※ *Gloria's Story: When my mother died, the feeling I got from the people around me was good riddance. I remember my grandmother saying, "Thank God I don't have to deal with that anymore." I never saw anybody cry, and I didn't cry. I didn't really understand what death was [Gloria was four], but later I realized that she wasn't going to come back and be abusive and I wouldn't have to hide from her under the bed.*

※ *Lucy's Story: I was eight when my father died. He was buried on my birthday, and my mother died two weeks later of liver cancer. She went into the hospital on the Fourth of July. I remember marching in the Independence Day parade, twirling down the street, and seeing her yellow and jaundiced. July 18 was her birthday, and they allowed me to go up to the room. I remember her needing the bedpan and my having to be ushered out. I said good-bye to her that day, and it was the last time I saw her. I was at a friend's house, and I saw my grandmother getting out of the car with my mother's bag, and I thought, Oh great, she's coming home. But my mother never got out. I started banging on the glass, saying, "I'm not doing this again."*

※ *Vicky's Story: A cement truck went right through a red light on the expressway service road. I don't know whether his brakes failed or he spaced out, but he drove right into Mom. She probably never knew what hit her. I hope that's the case. She was killed on impact.*

Rita's Story: Suddenly she's sleeping in my brother's room, and I saw bloody cloths soaking in the bathroom, and I wanted to know what it was. She didn't tell me. Nobody told me she was sick or anything. I was fourteen; what the heck did I know? She went into the hospital, but she never survived the operation. I didn't know what was going on. That morning my brother said we were going to the hospital. I was happy because I was doing something with my older brother. It was there I learned she was dead. Those years they didn't have funeral parlors. They brought her body home and put it on the floor where I slept. I watched from the door, and they wrapped her in a shroud and put her in the coffin. She wasn't embalmed. I stood scared to death. They opened the coffin and told me to look at her. And I looked at her. I was screaming with fear. There was a man— Mr. Greenberg—he was the only one with his arms around me. He was the only one there for me. Then my aunt told me not to go to the movies for a year, not to turn on the radio. I was to mourn.

For many of you, this was the first time you actually sat down and put your thoughts about that day on paper. Did you give up before you really got started? If you were unable to write your story, what stopped you? No one but you has to read this, and you're free to toss it in the trash, burn it, or launch it out to sea when you're done. You may be concerned or frustrated because you can't remember events in a logical order or because chunks of information are missing. Don't worry about whether it makes sense in its current form. Consider this a first draft to come back to as you continue through this workbook. Also, try reading it out loud. If you found you went off on tangents, maybe it's because you're avoiding the same things in your story that you're evading in real life.

Tragedy comes wrapped in different packages. Just ask the seventeen-year-old who saw a mother waste away from cancer, the ten-year-old whose legacy is the image of a mother leaping off a bridge, or the six-year-old who witnessed a mother's death in a traffic accident. In this chapter, we discuss your mother's cause of death, the circumstances surrounding it, how you found out, and what details you were told. These experiences deeply affect the feelings and attitudes you carry with you as an adult.

What's normal to feel when your mother dies? What should your immediate reaction have been? Sadness and sorrow? Shock, disbelief, confusion? Probably all of them. But you may also have reacted with anger, resentment, guilt, relief, shame, or a range of feelings you didn't want to acknowledge because they weren't what you thought you should feel. Perhaps you cried uncontrollably, and that was fine, at least for a little while. But what if you didn't? You may have sung her praises while at the same time hating her for leaving you. For most of us death was, and still may be, a forbidden subject, rarely if ever discussed. When it hit our lives, we weren't sure what to expect. Perhaps what you expected wasn't the way you responded after all. Here's the truth: normal reactions are varied, at times contradictory, and certainly unpredictable.

Now go back through your story, and with a different-colored pen, circle all of the emotions you felt, the words that describe your immediate reactions to her death. Are there a lot of circles? Do other feelings come to mind? If so, write them here.

DATE:_____

_____

_____

_____

Below are other women's reactions and the rationales for how they felt. Can you relate to any of these? Did you include them in your story? Check off any that apply to you. Why did you feel that way?

DATE:_____

____ Confusion: *I was too young to understand what was happening. Nobody told me the truth.*_____

_____

____ Fear/Anxiety: *Who will take care of me?*_____

_____

____ Guilt: *I wasn't at the hospital when she died. Our final words were angry.*_____

_____

____ Sadness: _____

_____

_____ Relief:_____

_____

_____ Withdrawal:_____

_____

_____ Shock/Disbelief:_____

_____

_____ Rage/Anger:_____

_____

_____ Shame:_____

_____

_____ Worthless:_____

_____

_____ Hopeless:_____

_____

_____ Helpless:_____

_____

_____ Betrayed/Resentful:_____

_____

_____ Vengeful:_____

_____

The facts and the feelings are equally crucial. It's important to know what happened and remember how you felt. It's natural to want to block out the painful memories associated with so traumatic an event, but writing is a way of discharging some of those feelings. "Only when [we]

Borders Books×Music×Cafe
Wayne, NJ
Books:973-785-0037/Music 973-785-0175
6131   0084/0002/02 000179   SALE
ITEM   TX RETAIL DISC SPEC EXTND
    MOTHER LOSS WORKBK
1 QP 4863057 1 15.00   15.00
    WHEN I AM OLD WOMAN I SHALL WE
1 CL 0562254 1 16.00 10% 14.40   14.40
                  SUBTOTAL   29.40
    6.000%   TAX1   1.77
2 Items   AMOUNT DUE   31.17
                  CASH   31.25
                  CHANGE DUE   .08
    07/02/98   08:19 PM
Thank you for shopping at Borders.

Opened videos, discs, and cassettes may
be exchanged for replacement copies of
            the original item only.

can acknowledge and express loss will we find comfort and healing even in the midst of lingering pain and loneliness," observes Earl A. Grollman in *Bereaved Children and Teens*. If you're still dealing with the phantoms of loss, in the long run it's easier to confront these demons. Running away hasn't made them disappear.

UNDERSTANDING DEATH

Many theorists believe that most of what holds true for a grieving adult is true for a child by the time she approaches the age of three. Grief is really about feelings. Despite differences in our ability to grasp the concept of death, we all feel. A child simply expresses those feelings in appropriately juvenile ways. How we comprehend death turns very much on what we're told. Our understanding undergoes a continuous reexamination as we mature, and our external manifestations of grief may change, but the intensity of grief and the impact of death are no less severe in children than in adults. Elaine, who was four when her mother died, analyzes it this way: "When the mother of a preschooler dies, part of the child dies with her. The ego isn't developed enough as a separate entity. I was very much aware of my dependence on my mother, though I only have about two memories of her."

Even a very young infant may exhibit signs of separation anxiety, crying for attention at needs unmet. An older infant or young toddler will show the onset of grief and mourning, behaving in ways that imply a protest over a mother's absence and an attempt to bring her back: crying and screaming and rejecting substitute care. When such a child realizes that her efforts are in vain, a period of despair and hopelessness may follow, evidenced by withdrawal and inactivity. In the view of psychiatrist John Bowlby, the child appears to be in a deep state of mourning.

In the magical thinking of a preschool child, a dead mother could return. After all, Sleeping Beauty was awakened by the kiss of a prince. Though a three-year-old may not truly understand, she can feel a mother's absence and sense the changes in the family and her emotional environment. Elaine says, "I cried because my brother Tim had cried. He was seven, I was four. A child of four doesn't understand the sense of permanence. It didn't register what it meant. Still, I knew all of my life that this was the major event and there was not going to be another event in my life that would be so pivotal."

As we mature, the finality and inevitability of death begin to sink in. We slowly comprehend our own vulnerability. That fragility is magnified when we see death as a physical end at a time when our own bodies are undergoing developmental changes. Beth, whose mother died when she was going through puberty, realizes that "part of wanting to be thin and not have a grown-up woman's body had to do with my mother having no ovaries, no pituitary—I don't know if she had a uterus or not—when she died. Associating sickness with female bodies doesn't quite lend itself to wanting to have one."

A mother's death during adolescence coincides with the period when confusing issues of ego stability and identity are paramount. We're trying to figure out who we are, how we fit in, and what we want to do when death interrupts the process. Our reactions reflect the emotional challenges we face at this critical juncture.

A CHILD'S VIEW OF DEATH		
Age	**General Understanding**	**Possible Reactions**
0–2	No cognitive understanding	Crankiness; feeding and sleep problems; bowel and bladder disturbances
3–5	May not understand permanence of loss	Fear of abandonment; guilt, anxiety, and anger; sleep disturbances; clinginess; withdrawal and attention problems; tantrums

Age	General Understanding	Possible Reactions
6–10	More likely to realize finality of death but not that it can happen to them; tendency to personify death	Often hostile reactions to deceased or idealization; bodily distress; may try to hide feelings
Adolescents	Know death is irreversible, final, and inevitable	Guilt, blame, shame, and anger; heightened anxiety over own death; mood swings

CIRCUMSTANTIAL EVIDENCE

The immediate blow of an unexpected loss or the painful preparations for a death foretold—either is untimely for a woman struck down in the prime of her life and traumatic for those left behind. But a sudden loss provokes different reactions than an anticipated one. The manner and circumstances of the death influence not only our own response but those of our family and society and, in turn, the support we receive.

Kelly's mother died in her sleep after pulling a muscle that day on the tennis court: "She'd never been sick, had no signs of illness. One day she was alive and healthy, and the next day she was dead." When death strikes without warning, it's an earthquake: no time to prepare, no time for good-byes, no time to set things straight. Shock, disbelief, and numbness set in. Any belief in the world as a safe place is shattered when catastrophe occurs before an alarm sounds. For a child, this terrifying event reaches a magnitude that's off the charts. How do you make sense of something so senseless? You're left feeling tremendously vulnerable, worried about your own existence and survival. Your concerns may have been hidden in the innocent questions a child asks: "Who's going to make my dinner?" "Do I have to stay with Grandma?" But the subtext was "What's going to happen to me?" "How am I going to get by?"

"Who will protect me?" "Will I die too?" Your striving to restore order and safety may not have been interpreted as a cry for help but rather misconstrued as a lack of understanding about death. With your pleas for reassurance ignored, your insecurity and helplessness were now compounded by feelings of worthlessness. What you take away from the experience is "I'm not important enough or significant enough to be cared about."

PLEAS/PLEASE

Elaine remembers being afraid of contracting the same disease as her mother: "I needed to be reassured that I wasn't going to get breast cancer just because my mother did." Do you remember what concerns you had? Could you ask for reassurance, or did you keep your needs hidden inside? If you were old enough to verbalize, what did you say? If not, how were you able to express yourself?

DATE:_____

My pleas were:

Tell me that you won't leave me too.

Show me that the world is still safe.

_____

_____

_____

I expressed my pleas by:

Clinging to my brother's leg

_____

If you felt as if your pleas were ignored or misunderstood back then, do you continue to keep similar needs to yourself today? Think about what they might be and how you express them.

THE BLAME GAME

We may feel guilt arising from unfinished business, contentious final interactions, a hostile wish, or the misguided belief that we should have been able to prevent a mother's death. Gladys reveals, "I thought I killed my mother. I wished her dead, and she died. I realize now that was what a lot of teenagers do, and no, I didn't kill her." A heated argument and an adolescent's rash yet familiar uttering of "I wish you were dead" carry a formidable burden of guilt when a mother's unexpected death eliminates the opportunity for resolution or forgiveness.

Mercedes ruefully recalls the last time she saw her mother alive: "I was going to sleep over at my best friend Claudia's. I don't really understand this, but I guess it was an eleven-year-old thing. My mother looked at me to give me a hug and a kiss, and for some reason, like I was too grown up to give my mother a kiss, I turned away. I have no idea why I didn't kiss her."

The suddenness lends disproportionate significance to what was happening at the time of death and discounts the balance of our relationship. We take on responsibility for the death, believing that if only we had done something different, she would be alive. Sue Ann, whose mother locked herself in the garage with the car motor turned on, will forever hear her sister's recriminating voice: "If only I had been home, I would have found her sooner, when she was still alive."

Blame and anger are the partners of guilt. Instances of sudden death greatly increase our need to blame. There's a sense of unreality as we ask, "How could this happen? I just spoke to her." It's not a far cry from "This is impossible" to "This was preventable." Someone or something must be condemned for allowing it to happen. We apportion the blame—to ourselves, our mothers, our fathers, God, or, in the case of an act of violence or negligence, the parties we deem responsible for causing the death. We may point a finger at the drunk driver who hit her, but we also rage at God for letting her die. The anger counteracts the feeling of utter helplessness that death elicits.

GUILT/REGRET

As in the last seconds of a basketball game, we remember the final moments most, emphasizing the would-haves, should-haves, and could-haves that might have saved us from defeat. We're quick to blame ourselves for missing the last shot, that last chance at victory, or criticize others for blowing the game. We forget that the game is more than just one shot.

Those last interactions with your mother are apt to produce similar feelings—guilt, blame, inadequacy, anger—and there are no do-overs. Time hasn't stood still, though you may find yourself frozen in those moments, replaying them over in your mind. What most of us fail to realize is the distinction between guilt—and the recriminations it generates—and regret. Regrets are what you wish you or someone else had done, what you could have done: "Why didn't I go to the hospital more?" "Why did I say those vicious last words?" When the *coulds* turn to *shoulds,* guilt arrives. Guilt stems from the belief that you did something wrong, that you should have done or felt something different.

For now, identify what caused you to feel guilt or regret. Write down anything that brought on these feelings, and put a *G* for guilt or *R* for regret next to the statement. Remember, 20/20 hindsight can make us more judgmental. Identifying what's at the root of your feelings starts to loosen their hold on you. (In Part IV, we'll return to this exercise and discuss what you can do to further alleviate some of these feelings.)

DATE:_____

I wasn't at the hospital when my mother died.

I'm angry with God for taking her.

_____

_____

_____

_____

_____

_____

_____

_____

DEATH FORETOLD

A chronic, lengthy, or deteriorating illness disrupts the natural rhythms of a family as hope and health decline. Knowing that your mother will die, you go through what's called anticipatory grief. In a sense, you begin your mourning before the actual death. You may be able to achieve some closure by righting wrongs, expressing your feelings, saying good-bye, and preparing for life without her. Unfortunately, your pain isn't lessened because you are forewarned. Instead life may become an emotional see-saw, as preparations for the inevitable alternate with feelings of denial propelled by a desperate belief that a miracle will happen. Separation and anxiety rise as your mother's health steadily sinks and death nears.

"I knew that Mommy was very, very, very, very sick, but somehow that did not ever translate into 'Yeah, but she could die,'" Toni relates. "Mount Everest can't be knocked over if a plane crashes into it." The death still comes as a shock for women who cannot bring themselves to believe that a mother's illness is really fatal.

Parents are supposed to be strong, powerful protectors, a role difficult to keep up for a mother suffering from the devastating effects and sometimes debilitating treatment of a disease. Over time, dealing with someone whose illness requires so much energy and attention saps your own resources. No wonder you might feel a burden lifted when she finally dies—and then pangs of guilt for breathing a sigh of relief.

Penny's mother knew that her cancer was fatal and started drawing her large extended family to her during those final months. "She wanted people around all the time," Penny recalls. "We must have had fifteen all-nighters with different people and faces and ordering pizza. There were times she didn't think she would make it through the morning, and then other times she'd say, 'We're all going to have eggs at 8:00 A.M.' She wasn't dramatic about saying good-bye, but she'd say, 'I'm going to give you the last hug,' and I'd be all touched. Then three hours later, she'd be saying it to someone else. She went on living for another several weeks."

Until We Meet Again

Was there some way your mother tried to say good-bye to you in her own way? It may not have been with words. Louisa's mother made sure an aunt took Louisa to her first Broadway show: "It was right before Christmas. I had never been to a Broadway play and would have been happy with any ticket, but she made sure I had front row seats for *Sweeney Todd.* It was the greatest experience. I remember coming home and describing it scene by scene and watching her listen to me. I think she knew that it was going to be her last holiday. We never acknowledged that she was going to die, but she was saying good-bye."

DATE:_____

My mother said good-bye by:

_____

_____

_____

If she didn't or couldn't say good-bye, how do you think she might have done it?

I would have liked her to say good-bye by:

_____

_____

_____

Awaiting a death over a long time places tremendous pressure on a family emotionally spent from anticipatory expressions of grief and sorrow. With no miracle in sight, impatience creeps in. As you watch someone suspended between life and death, you begin to hope the end will come sooner rather than later. "Impatience with the process of dying is not uncommon," Helen Fitzgerald writes in _The Mourning Handbook_. "Life with a dying loved one is like a roller-coaster ride, pushing you to the limits of your endurance."

STIGMA AND TRAUMA

It's been said that someone who commits suicide puts her psychological skeletons in the survivor's emotional closet. We're left not only with a terrible sense of loss but with an added weight of shame, fear, rejection, anger, and guilt. A self-imposed death often leaves you condemning yourself for your inability to stop it—particularly if it had been threatened or attempted before—and wondering why you weren't important enough to her to make her stay.

Usually depression or another mental illness or drug or alcohol abuse plagues the life of a mother who commits suicide. Perhaps you wished that she would finally do it so that you wouldn't have to deal with the repercussions of her troubled existence. You may have consoled yourself with the belief that she was delivered from her own suffering. But it's also hard to fight off feelings of self-recrimination.

Traumatic deaths—that is, deaths from accidents, disasters, and homicides as well as suicides—create unique issues for survivors. Since violence and mutilation can be involved, they are especially frightening. In *Living with Grief after Sudden Loss*, psychologist Therese Rando states that such a death "tends to leave mourners with relatively more intense emotional reactions, such as greater anger, ambivalence, guilt, helplessness, death anxiety, vulnerability, confusion, disorganization, and obsession with the deceased along with strong needs to make meaning of the death and to determine blame and affix responsibility." These reactions are also common in the case of multiple deaths or deaths that follow closely on each other. The combined emotional weight from concurrent crises makes it difficult to mourn the totality of the losses.

"My fifty-eight-year-old mother died while trapped in a brush fire," Missy confided. "I do not know how she died, so it has left me with a hell of a burden to sort through. It could have been a heart attack, a fire that somehow started after the heart attack, suicide, or even murder. All these are possible, but I will never know. Every day I deal with her death in a different way—the horror of an accidental tragedy, the sorrow of a natural death at a premature age, the anger of a suicide, the fury of a murder." Also fueling Missy's anger and uncertainty are disturbing concerns about whether her mother suffered physically or psychologically.

Out of Your Hands

Before you can transform feelings of helplessness and powerlessness, you need to comprehend what happened and be clear about what you and others were able to do. Here are some questions to ask yourself.

Date:_____

What was I able to do?

*I was able to control my tears.*_____

I was able to hold her hand.
_____
_____
_____

What was I unable to do?

I couldn't cure her cancer.
I wasn't strong enough to see her that sick.
_____
_____
_____

What were others unable to do?

The doctors couldn't save her.
She couldn't stop smoking.
_____
_____
_____

What made me feel as if I was doing something to help?

_____
_____
_____

What made me feel powerless?

_____
_____

_____

_____

Did I have realistic notions about who or what was responsible for her death?

_____

Did I have scapegoats that I blamed?

_____

Review your statements. Ask questions of your answers. Is there anything new you have come to realize while doing this exercise? If so, what is it?

I realize that:

_____

_____

_____

No News Is . . .

When Lee's aunt told her that her mother had died, it was as if she had been thrown off a cliff into rushing water. Before she had a chance to recover from the shock, her aunt said that Lee would have to stay with a neighbor while she and Lee's father made the funeral arrangements. The neighbor and her children were waiting, and from the way they treated Lee, it was clear that they knew: "They had heard about my mother before I did. Why didn't they tell me? Why didn't they tell me first? She was *my* mother."

There is no good way to hear about a loved one's illness or death. It's bound to be a shock even if you're prepared for it. But how we learn, what we're told, and from whom, affect our responses. Lee felt betrayed, angry, and confused. It was humiliating that others knew before she did.

Moreover, at a time when she most needed to be included, she was left out.

Mona was away at college when her mother died. A favorite uncle flew to her school to break the news: "All of a sudden, there's my uncle Don standing in the door. I gave him a hug, and he wouldn't let go. I said, 'Oh God, something's wrong,' and he said, 'Yeah, pal.' He was wonderful the way he handled it. He's a very compassionate person—his father died when he was ten—and I think he wanted to make sure I'd get home in the best possible way." Having someone to talk to and turn to didn't alter the essential tragedy of her mother's suicide, but the care that went into telling her imparted a reassuring message of concern.

Dawn, who was eight, has hazy recollections of being in the backseat of a car with her aunt: "She started to say something to me, not that my mother died, but something that made me more nervous, like I couldn't wait to get home. I wanted to push the car to make it go faster. When I got home, there were all these people. My brother called me into the bedroom, and we sat on my mother's bed, on the white bedspread. He said, 'Mom is with her mother now.' I didn't quite get what that meant, and I just sat there, and then my brother left. When I finally went into the living room, I remember feeling smaller than everyone, almost like I was invisible."

Ideally, you were told the truth in terms you could understand. Yet many women were left in the dark to draw their own conclusions from hushed conversations or half-truths. In the absence of sufficient information, fear and imagination take over. Comedian Rosie O'Donnell, whose mother died when she was ten, told *TV Guide* that she didn't learn the true cause until she was sixteen: "They told us she died of hepatitis. Figuring we were little and wouldn't know what that meant. I looked it up, I was in fifth grade, and it said a disease you got through dirty needles. I remember thinking, in a ten-year-old's rationalization and justification, that it was from sewing."

The motive may have been to shield you from a harsh reality. Instead it heightened your anxiety and confusion and undermined your trust in the people you depended upon most. Who do you turn to for support when no one will honestly tell you what's going on? And if no one tells you the truth, does it mean you're not worthy of hearing it? In the end, you may have been robbed of an important opportunity to help, reconcile differences, say good-bye, or express your love.

OBITUARY NOTICE

Brenda can't get the image out of her head: her mother hanging in the basement, wearing a red bathrobe, the clothesline around her neck. Perhaps it was you who discovered your mother's body. These are extremely distressing images, difficult to fathom, impossible to forget. Recalling a mother's death, no matter how many years ago it occurred, evokes an agonizing time in our lives. If you find this material sad, disturbing, overwhelming, you're not alone. If you need support, remember your Safety Net.

DATE: _____

How I found out:

_____

_____

_____

How I felt about the person who told me:

_____

_____

_____

What I did:

_____

_____

_____

What I thought:

_____

_____

_____

Whom I talked to:

_____

_____

_____

MORTAL CONCERNS

After her mother died, Gail carefully calculated how much longer she had to live. She researched life expectancies for women, broke it down into days, and figured out how many days she had lived and how many she had left: "I don't think my actions meant I feared death. Rather, I was suddenly more aware of it." Death comes into sharper focus when someone you're close to dies. The experience can raise awareness and fears for anyone. Place a check mark next to the concerns you felt at the time or ones that began to creep in as you got older.

DATE:_____

_____ My own death

_____ How long I might live

_____ That someone else I knew might die

_____ The way I might die

_____ That I might die in the same way my mother did

_____ The finality of death

_____ If there is life after death

_____ That I might go to hell

_____ What heaven is like

_____ What happens in general after death

_____ Bodily deterioration

_____ What would happen to my family

_____ Not existing anymore

_____ That I will be forgotten

_____ Not seeing my family and friends

_____ Other (please specify)_____

_____

_____

Safe Passage: A Journal Writing Exercise

Reread the story you wrote in the beginning of this chapter, and think about what you may have left out or glossed over. Go back through it, and at those points actually insert "what I meant to say is" and continue writing. Then ask yourself if there is something more you need to say. Sometimes, just when you think you've said it all, you realize you've only just begun. If new questions arise, document them in the Memory Bank in Part Break II. As you gain new information, come back and rewrite your story. Seek new insights and perspectives each time.

Date:_____

_____

_____

_____

_____

_____

_____

_____

_____

_____

_____

FINAL THOUGHTS

"It is the defining moment of my life," Rosie O'Donnell has said. A mother's death before we've grown to full adulthood is acutely painful because we're denied the closure that mitigates sorrow when a loved one dies at a more appropriate age. While experiences of grief are not comparable, we hope you've found some solace in the experiences of other women and catharsis in the telling of your own.

❖ 7 ❖

BUSINESS AS USUAL
How We Grieved

When a person is born we celebrate;
when they marry, we jubilate;
but when they die we act as if nothing happened.
—*Margaret Mead*

❖ *Marisa's Story: We didn't know she was dying. We didn't mourn. We didn't communicate about my mother, at least rarely, and not about her death. We were never asked how we were feeling. Some neighbors came in and helped with plans and getting rid of her clothes, but no one consulted us. It was all emotionally distant.*

❖ *Phoebe's Story: I went to pick out caskets in a large room full of caskets, like Macy's factory outlet for caskets. Then my sister made the black dress I wore. She had to sew me into it and cut me out of it three days later. I could hardly move in it, but I had nothing else to wear. One of my mother's best friends was sitting next to me and said, "It looks like she's going to sit up and open her big blue eyes and tell a joke." What a stupid thing to say in front of a child. It was an incredibly awful thing for a thirteen-year-old to hear at her mother's wake. For years and years afterward I had dreams about that, I think because part of me wanted that to happen so badly. The day after the funeral, everyone was supposed to go on as if nothing happened, to get over it, because we didn't want to deal with it. It was as if there was a huge gray cloud in the house, but no one talked about it, and I never asked any questions.*

YOU HAVEN'T GOT TIME FOR THE PAIN

Society tells you to get on with your life after a death, specifying some acceptable time frame for mourning and sadness. But grief doesn't know those boundaries. Sometimes the true impact of loss doesn't hit until friends and relations leave, the condolence cards are answered, and the house is back to "normal." Years after, a birthday, an impending marriage, a child's birth, or just nothing in particular triggers the pain of the loss, and we wonder why, so long after, the hurt still feels so close.

This chapter examines what happened during that prescribed period of bereavement and the subsequent weeks. That's when you were supposed to have put an end to your grief and obediently move on. From funeral rites to those first efforts to begin life without her, we'll see how you and your family began to deal with your mother's loss.

Only recently has the literature of loss begun to analyze and recognize the impact of a mother's untimely death. Now we know how truly devastating it is and therefore how important it is to be able to express, acknowledge, and receive validation for *all* of your feelings. The period of bereavement is a time to begin sorting out those feelings—uncomfortable, ambivalent, turbulent as they may be. It's a process that takes patience, love, understanding, and support. But for many of us, this period of mourning only accentuated our sadness, disorientation, and deep sense of loss.

COMPLICATING FACTORS

"After my mother died," Doreen recalls, "I was not allowed to mourn her loss. I was surrounded by a bunch of weak, psychotic adults. No one knew what to do with themselves, so no one knew what to do with me. I was told, 'You can't cry,' 'Don't cry,' 'Stop crying,' 'You have nothing to cry about,' 'Get over it,' 'You have to deal with it,' 'Your mother is dead, move on.'"

What kept you from expressing your grief and perhaps even threw you for another loop? For starters, life rarely presents the perfect scenario. And death, more than other aspects of life, tends to spin out of our control. Calamities seem to happen all at once. A wide variety of external circumstances can make the difficult process of grieving a more wrenching if not impossible one. Yes, this is a case of making bad matters worse. Coping most likely required a maturity beyond your years and your experience. Events may even have conspired to delay the process so that you seemed to be falling apart when it appeared that everyone else was getting it back together.

We've cited some of the factors listed in Helen Fitzgerald's *The Mourning Handbook* that may have complicated your mourning, but there are countless other possibilities. Check the ones that fit your circumstances, and add any others that affected you or forced you to put grief on the back burner.

_____ Multiple Deaths: Wendy's mother and young brother died in a traffic accident. One death is sufficiently devastating; dealing with a set of losses overloads your emotional circuits.

_____ Violent Death from Accident, Suicide, or Murder: These events are additionally weighted with overriding concerns about the possibility of your mother's suffering, guilt over your inability to prevent her death, and shame about the way it occurred. You may also have to deal with distractions from law enforcement and other official agencies.

_____ Questionable Deaths: Not knowing or being sure about the circumstances, as with Missy's mother, who died under ambiguous circumstances in a brush fire, can lead to intense anger and frustration.

_____ Discovering the Body: Sue Ann found her mother asphyxiated in the garage. Finding the body is shocking enough; having to break the news adds to the trauma.

_____ Witnessing the Death: While seeing a peaceful, tranquil death may be of some comfort, watching your mother die leaves a permanent imprint. That last impression may be all the more horrific if her death was under unusual or difficult circumstances.

_____ Hearing the News: Learning of your mother's death in a callous manner or getting confusing or dishonest information primes us for problematic mourning.

_____ Notoriety: Having a loved one die in a way that generates news coverage means putting a public face on private grief.

_____ A Body That's Not Presentable or No Body: Dealing with a badly damaged body may be particularly traumatic for a child or teen. Not being able to view or positively identify the remains can also produce lingering doubts.

_____ Secrets Discovered After Death: Bridget later discovered that the woman she had mourned as her mother was actually her grandmother. Even less startling facts that you find out after your mother's death may complicate mourning by causing you to reevaluate your relationship.

_____

_____

_____

DISCOMFORT ZONE

In many ways, we're a society uncomfortable with death, so geared toward being or seeming happy that we brush the unpleasant residue of death under the nearest rug. Our mourning rituals are often brief and superficial. Our natural inclination is to avoid pain. Defense mechanisms kick in, marshaling their forces to shield us from potential harm. Don't think about it, don't deal with it, move on. Only we can't leave grief behind; it's there lurking, demanding attention.

The overwhelming magnitude of your emotions may have caused an unconscious suppression of your feelings. In other words, you shut down, felt numb. An unexpected death can be so shattering that while you accept it intellectually, part of you denies that it occurred. How do you grieve for what couldn't have happened?

We passed judgment on our feelings and pronounced them unacceptable. As a daughter who saw her mother suffer through a prolonged illness that sapped family strength, you may have felt some relief when she died but feared expressing it. Perhaps you didn't know how to show you were angry at her for abandoning you or express the confusion you felt. Maybe you were ashamed of her when she was alive because she wasn't like other mothers or because she disappointed you. You're left choking down those feelings because, of course, you can't speak ill of the dead. And what could you do with the guilt? You believed you were to blame for her death, whether by hostile thoughts, words, or actions or by not being able to protect her from harm. The message blared, from our internal auditor or external sources: those feelings aren't appropriate now, closet them away. The ambivalence present in all human relationships was never allowed its say.

AGES OF GRIEF

Writing about how young children react to loss in *The Loss That Is Forever,* Maxine Harris observes that "the concepts and the very language of adult loss are inadequate to capture the panic, pain, terror and confusion of a grieving child." If you were very young when your mother died, you didn't possess the language or what Harris calls "the organizing text with which to process the loss." Children discern that their world order has been turned inside out, and they crave the reassurance that will put it right again.

Yet comforting a child whose world has just been blown to bits often confounds parents or guardians, especially when they are so caught up in their own grief that they fail to recognize how much the child needs them. Or, reading the child's message loud and clear, they may sidestep discussions as much to protect themselves as to shield the child from pain. Jill thinks that's why she and her siblings were given tranquilizers, which turned the week of official bereavement into a confusing haze.

> ### GUIDELINES FOR CHILDHOOD BEREAVEMENT
>
> 1. Give accurate, factual information appropriate to a child's age and cognitive functioning.
> 2. Allow children to express all of their feelings concerning illness and death.
> 3. Include children in family rituals such as the funeral.
> 4. Provide a stable environment, and tend to a child's needs in a secure, consistent manner.

Your family may not have recognized your anguish, fooled by the immature responses of a child whose grief seemed intermittent, by turns terribly upset and then cheerfully playing. Misconstruing your signals, they may have made little attempt to help you to understand what had happened and, if possible, why. If you seemed to be sailing through unscathed, why open Pandora's Box? So they kept the lid tightly shut, while fear and anxiety took root.

The truth dies in well-meaning efforts to cushion the impact of death. However pure the motive, lies deny the reality of illness, suffering, and loss. They contradict what you see with your eyes and experience in your heart. Instead of a loving embrace and an honest answer, you may have gotten a fuzzy fairy tale that made the confusion worse. A four-year-old told death is like sleeping not only thinks Mommy's going to awaken but believes it's her fault when that doesn't happen. Half-truths become the perfect breeding ground for feelings of guilt and helplessness.

HALF-TRUTHS

Sugar-coating and euphemisms, partial truths and misinformation—what's a kid to think? If you were spoon-fed a fiction or a watered-down version of the truth, your imagination may have filled in the blanks. Perhaps you developed your own scenario based on whispered conversations you were never supposed to overhear. A cliché may have meaning to an adult but can get lost in translation to a youngster. "OK, what is *passed away?*" asks Monica rhetorically. "It gave this idea that it was temporary. Dead isn't temporary."

For the next exercise, put a check mark next to the euphemisms, half-truths, or fairy tales that you heard when your mother died. Add others you heard to the list. On the right, explain how you interpreted them.

DATE:_____

I Heard	**I Thought**
_She is gone.	*She was lost and would be found.*
_She is sleeping.	*She could wake up.*
_She is with God.	*I hate God for taking my mother.*
_She is gone.	_____
_She is sleeping.	_____
_She is with God.	_____
_She was so good God wanted her.	_____
_She went away on a long journey.	_____
_She passed on/away.	_____
_She is no longer with us.	_____
_She's happier now.	_____
_She went to heaven.	_____
_It was her time to go.	_____
_____	_____
_____	_____
_____	_____

In the end, it's the truth, the whole truth, and nothing but the truth that facilitates healing. When and how did you finally find out or realize the whole truth?

_____

_____

My reaction was:

_____

_____

GROWING PAINS

The most consistent thing about a teenager's response to death may be that it reflects the turbulence of adolescence in general. Despite grasping the reality of death, teenagers tend to veer between quasi-adult and extremely juvenile behaviors. To demonstrate your maturity, you could have masked your real feelings or taken to heart a parent's admonition, "Be strong, your mother would have wanted it that way." But it was reassurance you really desired.

When you're going through puberty, heart-to-hearts with Dad aren't exactly the norm. To Jill, Dad was "the man who slept on the right side of the bed." Dealing with a teenage daughter was as uncomfortable for him as seeking his confidence was for her. Gail remembers her aunt, a woman left motherless at the age of sixteen, offering an ear, a shoulder to cry on, and a good idea of what the years to come would hold. At fourteen, Gail wasn't interested: "I convinced myself that I was OK. I didn't need her. Her what? Pity? Help? Hadn't I done just fine living with a depressed mother all those years? Wasn't I doing well in school, popular, athletic, involved? I was a soldier and declined her offer. I couldn't risk it. I was used to hiding my feelings, my hurt, my shame. Years later, when I began to realize the repercussions of my loss, I felt like an idiot for not talking to my aunt."

A teenager feels as though no one or maybe only her peers can understand her. You've cornered the market on emotions; no one has ever felt that way before. But a mother's death ranges beyond typical teenage conversation. Lipstick, boys, and death just don't fit neatly together. Lonely, isolated, without peers or adults to turn to, your feelings easily get denied, squelched, or acted out in behavior that reaches toward the extreme.

SIGNS OF DISTRESS

Clinging to a ratty old teddy bear relegated years ago to a shelf or feeling butterflies dive-bombing in your stomach may have been how your grief manifested itself. During the bereavement period, atypical behavior or physical symptoms are fairly common and mostly short-lived. Did you display any of the signs listed below? Circle the relevant ones, and add any others you remember.

DATE:_____

- Sleep disturbances

- Panic attacks

- Obsessive playing with toys

- Stomach problems

- Inability to concentrate

- Regressive or age-inappropriate behavior

- Weight gain or loss

- Excessive whining or sighing

- Rashes or allergic symptoms

- Symptoms similar to those of your mother

- Thumb-sucking

- Bed-wetting

- Problems talking to people

- Headaches

- Lack of energy

- Shortness of breath

- Tightness in your throat

- Fighting with siblings

- Racing heart

- Frenetic behavior

- _____

- _____

- _____

THE FAMILY BEREFT

Priscilla was eight when her mother died. She recalls, "We weren't allowed to go to the funeral. I wish we could have gone to say good-bye. There was no closing to it, there was no ending. The last time we saw my mother she was being rushed to the hospital. That was in June, and she died in December. My brother used to think she was still alive somewhere in the hospital. He lived with that for twenty years. Going to the funeral would have been important for us, to know that she was really gone, because you don't really know what *gone* is when you're little."

The funeral and burial services are important rites of passage in the life of a grieving family, allowing members to share in a crisis. At a time when you're apt to feel isolated and insecure, inclusion signifies that you belong. Taking part also helps children understand the finality of death and dispels the fantasies conjured up by fertile young imaginations, while offering an opportunity to bid farewell to a loved one. Such rituals can be comforting in providing a context for what has happened and a connection to a larger world.

But the services and mourning period can also be scary and confusing. Having never been told that her family was Catholic, Jill remembers the strange appearance of a priest. Phoebe was sent shopping for caskets. Miriam had to find a mother substitute to help her pick out something appropriate to wear to the funeral. Maria had a house full of strange people eating fruitcake, drinking, and even laughing.

Ideally, someone prepared you for what would take place, and you were allowed—if you wanted—to attend and perhaps participate. Unfortunately, many of us were either plunged unaware into these events or not given a chance to take part. Enid, who was ten when her mother died, remains angry that she was denied this experience: "My father forbade us from going to the cemetery. That is something I have never forgiven him for."

After the funeral, Priscilla and her siblings were separated and sent to different relatives: "That was very difficult because it was the time when we needed each other. When we came home, everything that was our mother's was gone. There was almost nothing left of her. I felt complete emptiness."

CLOSING CEREMONIES

Did you arrange them, attend them, or avoid them? Answer the following questions about the mourning rites, your participation, what you experienced, and what you saw others doing. This may have been a disturbing, disconcerting time, and thinking about it can awaken strong memories. Before you start, remember your Safety Net. It's there if you need added support.

DATE:_____

What were the circumstances that allowed you to attend or not attend a wake, funeral, burial, or other service?

_____

_____

If you were given a choice, why do you think you made the one you did?

_____

_____

If you attended against your wishes, how were you able to express that you didn't want to participate?

_____

_____

What was the rationale you were given for attending?

_____

_____

If you didn't attend, what did you do during the time others were taking part in the services?

_____

_____

Were you prepared for what would take place and what you might experience during these rituals? If so, how?

_____

_____

Who talked to you about it?_____

What preconceptions did you have about these rituals?

_____

_____

What are your most vivid memories of each service you attended?

_____

_____

Did anything bother you about what went on?

_____

_____

How did you react at each service you attended?

_____

_____

How do you feel about the way you behaved?

_____

_____

How did the adults act during any of the services?

_____

_____

Do you think they were trying to hide or be open about their emotions?

_____

_____

Were you encouraged to show your emotions or discouraged from it? How?

_____

_____

Was there anyone who tried to comfort you? In what ways?

_____

_____

Was it helpful? Why?

_____

_____

What was the worst part of this experience?

_____

_____

Do you think these rituals provided a sense of finality? Why or why not?

_____

_____

One of the painful chores following a mother's death is disposing of her belongings. If you were old enough, going through them with your family might have been a good time to share laughter and tears. You may have wanted to choose mementos. The jarring experience of returning to a house stripped of her mother intensified Priscilla's perception of a world in chaos. It was as if her mother had died a second time.

"My father 'helped' me grieve by leaving me alone five days after my mother's death to attend a conference," Vicki told *People* magazine. She was eleven at the time. "I determined that I wasn't supposed to mourn and allowed myself ten minutes of crying every Sunday night after I went to bed."

With the unfailing radar of children, we pick up cues for what's acceptable from a surviving parent, family members, or caretakers. If they aren't grieving, neither should we. A young child's constant questions about Mommy may be answered with reprimands in a family that doesn't want to be reminded.

For Didi, turning to her father produced cold comfort. His idea of mourning was quickly getting back to business as usual, as if the death had never occurred. The message was "Be brave, move on, and get with the program: permission to grieve not granted." Didi passed through her teens and into adulthood desperately trying to force the loss and what she believed were childish feelings into the past, surprised each time they didn't stay there.

Overwhelmed by their own grief, fathers may have found it impossible to take on the responsibilities of parenthood, let alone comfort and reassure you. Perhaps you were expected to be the strong one, left to fend for yourself or in the care of others. Some of us assumed our mother's roles, which included looking after inconsolable Dad. (We'll talk more about new roles in Chapter 8.) "Before my mother died," Toni recalls, "it was shield the kids. After she died, it was shield Daddy."

"I think I started to grieve almost immediately, but because nobody would talk with me, it got completely squelched," Mikki admits. "It was like, don't be emotional, hide your emotions. I did that for years."

You knew something was wrong, it just wasn't talked about. The loss itself became stigmatized, a story not to be told. "The act of *not* discussing or confiding the event may be more damaging than having experienced the event *per se*," writes psychologist James W. Pennebaker. Silence and secrecy denied you an opportunity to give voice to your grief with the people most affected by the loss—your family. They avoided discussions of your mother, at times making it seem as if she had never existed.

"This whole secrecy thing continues for me," says Carla. "We were very close for two weeks after Mom died, and nobody has ever talked about her death since. It's hard. I have a lot of shame about having these strange feelings, and nobody in my family wants to talk about it, and it's very painful for me. Sometimes I feel like I'm doing the work for the whole family."

When death is treated like dirty laundry not to be hung out in public, you deduce that silence is required, no matter how subtle the family code of secrecy. You may have felt awkward and embarrassed, even if your mother died from a "socially acceptable" cause like cancer or a car accident. If she committed suicide or died of a disease like AIDS, you shroud the death in a veil of shame. "My grandmother told our whole family that my mother died in a car accident," says Rosalyn, whose mother jumped off a bridge. Maybe you're ashamed because she died in a manner stigmatized by society, ashamed to have had her for a mother, ashamed because people may associate you with that stigma, ashamed because you're seen as different, and then ashamed that you have these feelings. You're in an impossible dilemma: how can you express your sorrow when the reason for that suffering must remain secret? You'll be pitied, ridiculed, and no one will understand, or so you think. Out of fear for your self-esteem and well-being, you safeguard your secret as if your life depends on it—and really believe it does.

In a perfect world, family, friends, and society would convey the messages loud and clear: CARING, REASSURANCE, ACKNOWLEDGMENT, VALIDATION. In the real world, those messages are mixed with FEAR, ANXIETY, SHAME, and GUILT—or at least that's how we perceived them. These signals and the way we interpreted them are good indicators of future self-perceptions, views, and behavior.

MIXED MESSAGES

The following exercise lists some of the messages you may have received and how you perceived them. Next to any message you received, write the initials of the person or persons who passed it on. Then match up the message with the conclusion(s) you drew from it. Note that each message could have led you to arrive at several conclusions. The ones we've listed are only possibilities. If your sister treated you coldly, you may have assumed that you weren't lovable, that emotions shouldn't be expressed, and that you had done something wrong. Remember, these are messages that came from external sources; they originated outside of you. They may have begun to fester inside, but they didn't begin there.

DATE:_____

Incoming Message	Outgoing Conclusion
___ Didn't discuss death	I don't count
___ Excluded me from funeral	I will be cared for
___ Told me half-truth	I am loved
___ Was cold	I'm unlovable
___ Displayed no affection toward me	I shouldn't express emotions
___ Was reassuring	I don't belong
___ Made me stay with relatives	I'm a burden
___ Explained everything to me	I'm to blame

Incoming Message	Outgoing Conclusion
___ Talked to me about my mom	I'm bad
___ Expressed pity	I have people who care about me
___ Said good things about my mom	I'm trusted
___ Said terrible things about my mom	I'm worthless
___ Showed compassion	I can't count on anyone
___ Was overprotective	I shouldn't be alive
___ Was physically demonstrative	I'm powerless
___ Told me the truth	I'm respected
___ Gave me the choice of whether to attend rites	I can't do anything right
___ Respected my feelings	I'm alone
___ Asked about my feelings	I have people to depend on
___ Yelled at me	I deserve to be abandoned
___ Ignored me	_____
_____	_____
_____	_____

SAFE PASSAGE: A JOURNAL WRITING EXERCISE

What would have been a proper farewell for your mother? Should it have been a Broadway tribute, a humorous roast, a picnic at her favorite spot? Maybe a giant family feast of her favorite foods? Something more traditional? A service you could attend this time and offer your own eulogy? Write about what you would like to have done or what you think she might have appreciated. Be honest, be imaginative, and be as daring as you'd like.

DATE:_____

_____

_____

_____

_____

_____

_____

_____

_____

_____

FINAL THOUGHTS

Psychologist Alice Miller writes, "It is not the traumas we suffer in childhood which make us emotionally ill but the inability to express the trauma." Death is as disturbing for children and teens as it is for adults. For many of us, there was a double whammy: not only did we have to deal with our mother's death but simultaneously we were forced to confront the terrible anxiety of the people who were supposed to be taking care of us and reconstructing our world. And so she was gone, and we were left on our own to mourn, without support, explanation, or understanding.

The full impact of loss doesn't hit all at once. You could never have anticipated all the moments you would miss her. Acknowledging your feelings will help you manage a lifetime of unexpected sorrow. Grief chooses its own time to creep up on you. As we grow older, we renegotiate our attachment and relationship with a mother who died. A Jewish proverb teaches us, "The only truly dead are those that have been forgotten."

8

TURNING POINTS
There'll Be Some Changes Made

There is something in the pang of change
More than the heart can bear
Unhappiness remembering happiness

—*Euripides*

※ *Greta's Story: I was living in shame because I was motherless. I couldn't figure out what the base of my pain was besides loss, confusion, missing her, and not learning a million things that a mother teaches a daughter. The shame was secrecy, the shame was silence, a wall of silence. Whenever I would try to find out information, my father would look down. He wouldn't look me in the eyes, and that's how you get validation, by someone looking you straight in the eyes. If they don't, it's like, what did I do wrong to not be worthy, to not deserve being looked at directly? I realize now these people came to me with shame, so then I had it, and it was a primary influence in my life, teaching me to shame myself. No one would tell the truth in my family. Secrets equal shame.*

※ *Molly's Story: I couldn't really believe she was gone for good. I used to call the house and listen to the phone ring. She had always been home but not anymore. Nobody answered. I kept thinking I would remember things to tell her, as if she was away on vacation. It just became a huge void, an emptiness.*

"A child must make his or her way in a changed world after catastrophe occurs," Maxine Harris tells us in *The Loss That Is Forever*. "The new world order is marked by *total discontinuity* with what went before. Everything feels different even though certain external realities—house, school, playmates—may look the same. While a child may have been naively aware of all the comforts and supports that lent a sense of security to childhood, he or she is all too aware of the *terrifying insecurity* that marks life after the catastrophe of early death intrudes."

Coping and change are the themes of this chapter as we look into the period of adjustment that follows loss and the formative years after your mother's death. What happens that first Christmas without her? How do you feel when everyone else has a mother to attend their recital and you don't? What do you think when her name is barely mentioned six months later? When a mother dies, you not only lose someone significant but the event ripples through the rest of your life, leading to other, or secondary, losses that profoundly influence you as well.

Section I of this chapter considers the internal or psychological ramifications: what you thought and felt about yourself, your outlook on life, and how you coped with these feelings and the loss itself. We'll also look at the repercussions from the way your family and society treated the loss. Section II deals with the concrete circumstances of your life: redefined relationships, changes in your home and lifestyle, and the adjustment to new roles.

Section I: Altered States

"At first," Betty says, "I'd wake up in the morning and two seconds after, it was 'Oh my God, my mother's dead.' After that it would hit me in the afternoon on my way to class. Finally, after a few months, it wasn't a shock anymore: it became a constant knowing."

Sorrow leaves its imprint. A mother's death seeps into your life, and you return to a familiar yet altered landscape bearing internal scars of loss. In Chapter 6, you were asked to recall your immediate, short-term reaction to her death, and in Chapter 7, you went back to the sanctioned mourning period to examine whether and how you and your family expressed grief. Here, your goal is to recognize the ways the loss began to take up residence, shaping your behavior and who you would become. As society was telling you to get on with it, the true measure of your mother's permanent loss was only dawning inside you. So yes, you started to get back to "normal," but normal had changed.

Slowly the shock recedes, the numbness subsides. Time heals neither totally nor instantaneously and only if you use it to mourn your loss. Acknowledging that mourning is never complete, recent studies suggest that the adjustment period for an anticipated death is two to four years and for sudden death, four to seven years. But mourning knows no certain progression, and since mothers are so entwined in the developmental process, issues of loss continue popping up. Misconceptions about what's correct to feel, for how long, and how intensely can confound the process, accentuating your sense of isolation and abnormality. You were expected to get back to the old routine, putting one foot in front of the other. No one told you that you would have to manage it on a tightrope.

ATTITUDE ADJUSTMENTS

Did your mother's death reinforce previous messages or stimulate new feelings? Betty believes her mother's suicide underscored an already impaired sense of self-value. The abandonment proved she wasn't worth loving: "I never had any self-esteem; I always felt worthless. I felt so validated by her death." Despite her popularity, Sheila admits, "I felt different and ashamed that I didn't have a mother. I began to have fears, worries in the middle of the night that I would be taken by God to die in my sleep."

Recall your own period of adjustment. (If your loss is very recent, you may be going through this now.) The statements below reflect some of the attitudes and emotions connected to a mother's death. They're typical of the tapes that ran constantly in our heads: "I don't deserve to be loved," "I'm afraid to trust anyone," "The world is too unpredictable." For some, this was a time when the wounds felt very fresh, while other women report that they didn't begin to experience the emotional aftermath of loss until much later. A few of these internal messages may seem like old friends; time hasn't dulled their impact. But if you've worked through any of them during your own healing, you know that they can become distant acquaintances. (If you did the Mixed Messages exercise on page 121, you can see the genesis of some of these beliefs.)

Roll the Tape

Part III will focus on who you are today, but for now think back on how you adjusted to a changed world. Which of the following statements pertain to you? Put a check mark in the space that best represents how often you said or felt similar things: 0 = never, 1 = seldom, 2 = sometimes, 3 = frequently, and 4 = all the time.

Date:_____

	0	1	2	3	4
Nobody understood how I felt	_	_	_	_	_
I felt self-conscious	_	_	_	_	_
I felt disconnected from people	_	_	_	_	_
I had to hide the real me	_	_	_	_	_
I didn't have any warmth or emotional support	_	_	_	_	_
I didn't deserve to be happy	_	_	_	_	_
I didn't deserve to be loved	_	_	_	_	_
I thought everything was my fault	_	_	_	_	_
I couldn't protect myself	_	_	_	_	_
I couldn't trust anyone	_	_	_	_	_
No one trusted me	_	_	_	_	_
I was anxious and scared	_	_	_	_	_

	0	1	2	3	4
I felt empty inside	–	–	–	–	–
I had difficulty expressing how I felt	–	–	–	–	–
I felt like an outsider	–	–	–	–	–
I had no one to rely on	–	–	–	–	–
I felt my world had collapsed	–	–	–	–	–
I had outbursts of rage	–	–	–	–	–
I found life overwhelming	–	–	–	–	–
I felt disloyal if I enjoyed myself	–	–	–	–	–
I felt abandoned and rejected	–	–	–	–	–
I believed life was unfair	–	–	–	–	–
I felt isolated and lonely	–	–	–	–	–
I was sad and depressed	–	–	–	–	–
I worried that people would die and leave me	–	–	–	–	–
I worried that more bad things would happen	–	–	–	–	–
I was numb to my feelings	–	–	–	–	–
I worried about getting sick	–	–	–	–	–

My strongest responses dealt with issues of:

_____

_____

The hardest statements for me to acknowledge were:

_____

_____

They were hard because:

_____

_____

_____

The motherless daughters we spoke to had the most difficulty around feelings of shame, anger, guilt, control, and self-esteem, and issues of secrecy and trust. They found themselves wondering who they were and whether they mattered and blaming themselves for any inadequacies.

SHAME ON YOU

In *Family Secrets*, John Bradshaw quotes the words of psychologist Sylvan Tompkins. "Death is unique in being a universal source of shame," Tompkins stated. This is especially true in a death-denying culture like ours. "Shame with a capital S," Gretchen agrees. "My biggest shame, apart from having just one parent who was malfunctioning, was an inner shame. I felt that I brought everything on myself. I carried it with me—ashamed that I didn't have a mother, that I had to ask someone else's parent to hem my pants. I was ashamed to be who I was because it wasn't who I would be if my mother had lived."

In *Shame: The Power of Caring*, Gershen Kaufman writes, "We yearn to feel that our lives are useful, that what we do and who we are do matter. Yet times come upon us when doubt creeps inside, as if an inner voice whispers despair. Suddenly we find ourselves questioning our very worth or adequacy. It may come in any number of ways: 'I can't relate to people.' 'I'm a failure.' 'Nobody could possibly love me.' 'I'm inadequate as a man/woman.' When we have begun to doubt ourselves, and in this way to question the very fabric of our lives, secretly we feel to blame; the deficiency lies within ourselves alone. Where we once stood secure in our personhood, now we feel a mounting inner anguish, a sickness of the soul, as Silvan Tompkins puts it. This is shame."

"Before she died I was fairly open," Olivia relates. "After she passed away, I was a lot more withdrawn. I used to think that people thought I was the world's biggest geek. I was like, why can't I be like other girls?" Motherless women find shame around every corner—from being different because you lack a mother; from a family that treats illness or death as a secret; from the stigma of death itself; from sitting in judgment on your own feelings, whatever they may be; from not being able to express those feelings; from thinking you should be able to move away from loss; from the sense of something missing in your life; from the insensitivity of a society that denies death; from friends who offer pity rather than understanding; from the incomprehensible anger at your mother for dying. You don't speak about these feelings because you're ashamed to have them. You cover them up, adding to the arsenal of secrecy and building a fortress based on shame.

DATE:_____

I felt ashamed that:

_____

_____

_____

GUILT AND RESPONSIBILITY

"I felt I didn't do enough, I wasn't good enough, I wasn't thin enough, I wasn't something enough, or she wouldn't have died," Lydia offers. The magical thinking of childhood decrees that bad things happen to bad people. A mother's desertion is just retribution for your behavior. "Oh, you'll be the death of me," a mother warns after you spill soda on the carpet again. Then she dies. So (a) you must be a terrible person, and (b) you're responsible for her death. Yes, it's rarely so clear-cut, but that's often the correlation you make as a child.

A hug and a kiss neglected or harsh words spat out from hormonal venom loom exceedingly large when a mother dies. Unable to accept the imperfections of any relationship, you hold yourself to an impossibly high standard. Judging yourself against that ideal ensures that you'll come up short. We're oh so quick to blame ourselves for what we might have done better.

Your mother's illness may have put your life on hold. It's certainly understandable to want to spend time with friends or take part in activities and hard not to feel resentful when you can't. You may have wanted all this to be over, as much to end her suffering as from your desire to be a normal kid. But then the tacit wish for her to finally die may seem cold and unfeeling instead of simply human. Guilt works overtime, convincing you that only a horrid, selfish person could harbor such thoughts.

Perhaps you even felt deep remorse for being alive, as if you were only living at the expense of her dying. Charlotte, who suffers from the same hereditary disease that killed her mother, asked herself, "Why am I alive? Why is my mother dead?" Implicit in the logic of survivor's guilt is the questioning of your own right to exist.

With guilt looking over your shoulder, you may have felt disloyal as you started to enjoy life again. As the sorrow became more intermittent, the self-recriminations crept in. You flogged yourself with questions about the adequacy of your feelings and fears that you might forget her if you began to try to live your own life fully. "How dare I laugh when she no longer can?" you asked, then wondered if you loved her enough.

DATE:_____

I felt guilty because:

_____

_____

_____

OUT OF CONTROL

Babies come into this world helpless and first learn mastery through a mother's response to their actions. As we mature, we begin to count on predictable feedback for our behavior. But we have no dominion over death. The inability to prevent a death gives rise to anger and feelings of helplessness. "In the loss of any important person," J. William Worden writes, "there is a tendency to regress, to feel helpless, to feel unable to exist without the person, and then to experience the anger that goes along with these feelings of anxiety."

After a death, the notion that the world is a safe, secure place vanishes. The idea that parents are invincible disappears. When these core beliefs crumble, you're apt to feel even more powerless, viewing the world as unpredictable and unreliable. What you need is open communication to express your fears and uncertainty, coupled with warmth, affection, and reassurances that someone is there to take care of you. Instead you may have gotten avoidance or minimizing of your pain. Lacking that steady stream of love and support, it's likely that you viewed your world as chaotic, your power over it, minimal. Without intervention, helplessness quickly turns to hopelessness. How can you have faith in a world that might shatter in an instant?

DATE:_____

I felt helpless/powerless because:

_____

_____

_____

I felt angry at:

_____

_____

_____

Trust and truth are important commodities in the healing process. When families deny the reality of illness, death, and the pain of loss, whether out of grief or self-protection, they compound the trauma. If you go along with the rules of that game, you enter a conspiracy of silence. Lobbying for the truth may bring you anger and rejection and sow seeds of self-doubt. Then you grow up in an atmosphere fraught with secrecy and denial, the hallmarks of shame, with a diminished sense of your own value. Unsure whether you can believe what you see, you start to question your own credibility. If information is withheld, it fosters the feeling that you can't be trusted. Your self-worth undermined, these issues of what and whom you can trust color your view of the world.

For many of us, our self-esteem was wrapped up in a mother's reflection. Candace observes: "The power of the relationship was so positive that it gave me a lot of esteem. We spoke every day when I was in college. I was lifted up by her response and the way she reacted. Just to talk to her was reassuring. When that wasn't there, I didn't have a way to get that from myself."

A mother's love is a powerful confidence builder. Such a stalwart booster isn't easily replaced. It's hard to overestimate her role in helping you create a self, even if only as a model to rebel against. Many women told us they felt that a part of them died along with their mothers. How, they asked, can you have a healthy sense of self when a slice of you is missing?

DATE:_____

I lacked self-esteem because:

_____

_____

_____

SURVIVAL TOOLS

Two aspirin and a bowl of chicken soup can help you get over a cold. How do you ward off emotional distress? Consciously or not, we all rely on coping mechanisms to get by, whether by denying discomfort exists or by fostering self-reliance. "My family shut themselves off, and I was suddenly faced with the fact that I was going to be alone unless I got out there and talked to people," Rebecca explains. "I became a lot more outgoing. I had to come out of my shell so I wouldn't be isolated."

Like sandbags against a flood, coping mechanisms defend us from the onslaught of overwhelming emotions. But though they provide a layer of protection, some are self-defeating or self-destructive in the final analysis, while others prove double-edged. For example, perhaps you taught yourself to be independent and then found it impossible to admit to your own needs.

TOOL SHED

Survival skills developed in childhood and adolescence are the precursors of those you cling to today. Chapter 9 focuses on the ones you continue to rely on and examines their useful and damaging aspects. Chapter 11 addresses healthier ways of coping. In this exercise, which we've adapted from Laura Davis's *The Courage to Heal Workbook*, circle the coping mechanisms you used to deal with the pain of living and growing up without a mother. The list reflects many common ones, but add any we neglected to mention.

DATE:_____

Adopted "why bother" attitude	Threw myself into school/activities	Denied problems existed
Became a perfectionist	Rationalized	Spaced out
Flew into rages easily	Became hypervigilant	Became more outgoing
Became introspective	Grew anxious/ fearful	Developed eating problems (anorexia, bulimia, overeating)

Tried to be smarter/ prettier/better	Took care of everyone else's needs	Ran away
Relied on self-protective humor	Engaged in excessive sexual activity	Abused drugs, alcohol, self
Had sleep problems	Became withdrawn	Engaged in other self-destructive behavior
Adopted "live for today" attitude	Became physically/ verbally abusive	Developed independence
Became perfect child	Grew more self-reliant	Fantasized
Minimized problems	Avoided intimacy	Saw everything in black-and-white terms
Withdrew into writing, drawing, or other creative activity	Became argumentative	Became distrustful/suspicious
Avoided conflict	Tried to control all situations	Withdrew faith in God
Became resourceful	Relied on faith in God	Regressed to earlier developmental stage
Grew vindictive	Became sick a lot	Matured quickly
Overidentified with grief	Became secretive	Became overdependent on friends
Grew disorganized	_____	_____

_____ _____ _____

_____ _____ _____

BACK TO BASICS

Each coping method fulfills an underlying need. By fantasizing, you could pretend everything was really OK. You didn't have to deal with reality, at least for the moment. Mikki says that she "walked around in a fog. I squelched my emotions by smoking a shitload of pot and having a lot of sex with my boyfriend. I'm sure I substituted sex for some kind of love." Renee's perfectionism satisfied a need to maintain control over her world. Identifying the fundamental reasons behind your earlier behavior leads to a deeper understanding of your behavior today, particularly when the survival tools of the child resurface as the entrenched patterns of the adult. In the space below, trace back the underlying reasons for the coping mechanisms you circled.

DATE:_____

Coping Mechanism: *I became the perfect child.*

Needs Met: *I was afraid if I did something wrong, my father would leave me too. I wanted him to give me love and affection, but I felt I wasn't really important in his life, so I had to keep proving it.*

Coping Mechanism:_____

_____

_____

Needs Met:_____

_____

_____

Coping Mechanism:_____

_____

_____

Needs Met:_____

_____

_____

Coping Mechanism:_____

_____

_____

Needs Met:_____

_____

_____

In hindsight, are there any survival tools you're ashamed of or regret? Did they involve short-lived behavior, like cutting school for a semester, or develop into more long-term patterns? For instance, did you take out your frustration by treating a sibling badly? Ask yourself why you chose those ways to cope. Why might you be able to forgive yourself now for that behavior?

_____ *I was only ten and didn't know how to express my anger in another way.*

_____ *I was angry with him because he couldn't protect my mother from dying.*

_____ *We were really strangers and had never learned how to communicate with each other.*

DATE:_____

Coping Mechanism:_____

I can begin to forgive myself because:

_____

_____

_____

Coping Mechanism:_____

I can begin to forgive myself because:

_____

_____

_____

Coping Mechanism:_____

I can begin to forgive myself because:

_____

_____

_____

   You may have found the reasons and rationales but still not be able to forgive yourself for some actions. Writing them down is a start. However, some of your behavior may have harmed someone else through misdirected rage or physical abuse.[1] Before you can ask yourself

---

[1]Although it is beyond the scope of this book to assist you in dealing with abusive behavior, if you're currently hurting others through verbal or physical abuse, or fear that you might, it's essential that you seek professional help. You may also need counseling to deal with the repercussions of past issues of abuse.

for forgiveness, you have to take responsibility for your actions. If these are ongoing behaviors, take steps to ensure that they won't be repeated, and make amends to those you've harmed. (We'll talk more of this in later chapters.) For these coping mechanisms, specify the steps you need to take before you can think about forgiveness.

Coping Mechanism: *Guilt-tripping my sister over my mother's death*

Before I can begin to forgive myself I must:

Acknowledge to myself that my reason for being angry at her was that I wanted to be away from all the pain that was going on during my mother's illness.

Admit that her being there wouldn't have saved my mom.

Apologize to her for being a jealous jerk.

Ask her forgiveness for treating her meanly.

Date:_____

Coping Mechanism:_____

Before I can begin to forgive myself I must:

_____

_____

_____

_____

_____

A mother helps mold the raw material of childhood or the not-quite-finished product of adolescence into an adult self. You count on her for guidance and support, to set boundaries, be a moderating influence, to act as mentor and model. When she dies, you're forced to deal with far too much far too early, challenged to complete creating a self without her. Developmentally, part of you may have raced ahead as you were asked to face enormous emotional difficulties and perhaps take on more responsibility. Necessary developmental tasks may have been interrupted or never entirely finished.

Beth describes it this way: "Basically the clock stopped after she died. I've felt stalled in a child's magical way of thinking, helpless, powerless." Inside the woman resides a child seeking to return to a point before the world came crashing down. A mother's early death can leave a daughter with ineffable yearnings and a nagging feeling that something within herself is missing. It impedes the messy progress through adolescence, when sexual, emotional, and ethical identities are being solidified, separation and individuation occur, and skill in dealing with the world advances. It cuts off the encouragement and endorsement a young woman in her twenties needs when she tests new wings.

Arrested development freezes a part of you at an earlier stage of maturity, where you were when your mother died. By not moving on, you maintain a connection to her. It's a way of negating her death. For some women, a kind of paralysis sets in. They remain suspended in limbo: it's too painful to go back to earlier times, but they're afraid to move forward because it implies severing the tie and accepting responsibility for their own lives. Lisa recalls that particular light bulb going off for her: "My therapist said, 'You refuse to live life without her.' And I had."

WHEN THE CLOCK STOPPED

In this exercise, think about how your mother's death affected your developmental progress. As in Beth's childhood, did the clock stop or stall at some stage? In what areas was your maturity sped up? Despite your chronological age, are there tasks of childhood or adolescence that remain incomplete?

DATE:_____

The clock stopped:

I never really separated from my mother, so I didn't know how to make decisions for myself.

_____

_____

The clock sped up:

I felt more competent than my friends because I was thirteen and basically taking care of my family.

_____

_____

SECTION II: THE NEW REALITY

"I was actually twelve when she died," Deirdre relates, "and my sisters are each a year and a half younger. My dad didn't know how to take the emotional reins of a difficult situation, and he would end up being one of the kids in any kind of altercation or problem. I would end up trying to be level-headed and reasonable. It turned out I was stronger than he was. That was really frightening because I was the person with one eye who's queen of the hill in the kingdom of the blind."

CHANGE OF LIFE

A mother's death precipitates changes, or secondary losses, in your home environment, family functioning, roles, relationships, and a host of other areas in your life. Changed circumstances can pose a whole new set of problems. "My dad put my cat to sleep when he sold the house," says Sally, "which I was very upset about. It seemed like another loss. Everything from the past was fragmenting. My mom died, my cat died, we sold the house, my dad was dating, everything was crazy. I just accepted the chaos. I wasn't going to fight it."

As a consequence of her mother's death, Charlotte, a top basketball recruit, was unable to take advantage of the college playing offers that came her way: "I had to deal with the further loss of a possible sports career. That was my life, and I couldn't play." For Joanne, it was the loss of extended family connections: "My grandparents were so offended because my father remarried so quickly that they never really talked to us again. My father kind of cut off the relationship with them. That was a real huge loss in my life. It hurt a lot and still infuriates me when I think about it." Rebecca says, "My home went from being a home to just a house. It was dead after that." To Jill, it was a loss of childhood: "I became so responsible. My sister said I went from eleven to forty-two."

These are losses that require their own grieving. They might be as tangible as moving away from your old house or far less concrete, like the loss of innocence. They might be financial or familial. In any case, these secondary losses also deserved compassion from those closest to you. At the time, perhaps, you didn't even understand that part of your sadness, anger, and pain grew out of these changes in your life. The awareness may have struck years later. Maybe you're first realizing it today.

Loss Leader

In this exercise, we ask you to name your losses, to acknowledge for yourself what others neglected to do. As a memory aid, look back at what you lost in the Separation and Loss exercise on page 20. Then think about the following questions: Was there something missing in my childhood or adolescence? Are there dreams, goals, or opportunities that I gave up? Were relationships affected? What other areas in my early life were touched by loss? (In Part IV, we'll offer suggestions about how to recapture some of what you lost and mourn what is gone forever.)

The changes/secondary losses I experienced were:

_____

_____

_____

_____

_____

How did you react to these changes—with resentment or resignation, anger or agitation? Review the major changes you just listed. Describe how—and why—you responded the way you did.

My reaction to loss was:

_____

_____

_____

_____

_____

At the time it may have been impossible to see any silver lining in your mother's death, but changes for the better may well have occurred. Priscilla told us, "I learned to be streetwise and use common-sense judgment to get by." Mikki said that death made her think about what she truly wanted from life. Lessons from the school of hard knocks are no less valuable. Out of this tragedy, were there any positive outcomes? Did you discover inner strengths, find helpful outside resources, develop new skills?

What I gained from this experience:

I can handle anything.

_____

_____

_____

AND THEN THERE WERE NONE

As you were attempting to deal with your mother's physical absence, what was happening to other signs of her? In some families, a mother becomes enshrined, her possessions left untouched long after her death. Walking into the Museum of Mom day after day may hamper adjustment to the fact that she's no longer there.

At the other extreme, Miriam returned from the funeral to find a spick-and-span house, cleaned of all traces of her mother. In Joanne's case, after six months, "It was like my mother never existed. My father got remarried, and they took everything of hers out of the house. They took the pictures of her away, which was a terrible way of dealing with the situation." What upset Geraldine was that her father waited until she was away at camp to make changes so that he wouldn't have to put up with any interference.

There are no set rules for these kinds of things, but it's the pattern that's most troubling: first she dies, then the signs that she ever lived disappear, and before long you barely talk about her. Here is a time line on which to chart what happened and when. Plot how long after she died these events occurred—three months, three years, whatever—and who was responsible for them.

DATE: _____

Within	1 mo.	3 mos.	6 mos.	1 yr.	2 yrs.	5 yrs.	10 yrs.
Mother's possessions are discarded	*Dad*						
Photos of Mother out of sight							
She's rarely discussed			*Stepmom*				
Conversation about her stops				*All*			
Stop acknowledging her on Mother's Day							
Stop celebrating her birthday							
Stop acknowledging anniversary of her death							
Diminished contact with her side of family							
No contact with her family							

Within	1 mo.	3 mos.	6 mos.	1 yr.	2 yrs.	5 yrs.	10 yrs.
Diminished contact with her friends							
No contact with her friends							
Fewer visits to cemetery							
Stop visiting the cemetery							

How much say did I have about what to keep?

_____

_____

What I concluded from the way these situations were handled:

_____

_____

How I would have liked them to be handled:

_____

_____

There might be a connection between these events and your behavior, like the fact that your grades took a nosedive when your dad sold your mom's porcelain collection. Check it out by looking at old report cards or talking to a former teacher. Finally, you may have to forgive, if only symbolically, the person who was responsible—yourself included—for permitting the various changes to occur and allowing your mother to disappear.

NEW ACCOMMODATIONS

When your mother dies, the family as it once was dies too. In a very real way, many of us lost not just one parent but two because our surviving parent was emotionally lost to us as well. The more dysfunctional your family was before she died—the more communication difficulties, the more secretive, the more unresolved issues of anger and guilt—the more likely it was to come apart without a mother to hold it together. Perhaps you all went off in your own directions or chose a scapegoat for displaced feelings of grief.

In Chapter 5, we asked you to evaluate the healthy and unhealthy characteristics of your family. Go back to the Inner Workings exercise on page 60, and consider how those traits came into play as your family tried to accommodate the loss. If your family was open and communicative, did it remain so after your mother died? Were you still able to express and receive acknowledgment for your feelings? If your family tended to be distant, did her death draw you farther apart or bring you any closer? Transfer the most important characteristics you checked off, and consider whether they helped or hindered your adjustment.

Characteristic: *Talks openly*

Even though it was really my mom who encouraged us to talk about things, the whole family pulled together to make sure we expressed how we were feeling. I could cry, get angry, or act immature, but I knew they understood, loved me, and were there for me.

Characteristic: *Makes arbitrary decisions*

Somehow it was assumed that my sister and I would take care of things. We never sat down and said, "OK, here's what we're going to do." Dad didn't consult us when he decided to remarry. It was simply his way or the highway. It made me feel like I didn't count.

DATE:_____

Characteristic: _____

_____

_____

_____

Characteristic: _____

_____

_____

_____

"The death of a family member disrupts the family's organization and requires new relational patterns to fulfill absent social role functions and restore missing emotional functions," psychologist Esther Shapiro notes. A family tries to reestablish stability by recasting a mother's numerous roles. But inappropriate roles and responsibilities within a family can be detrimental to both individual and family development and mourning.

Vanessa was eight when her mother died: "I was the oldest girl, and my father was from the old school. We had housekeepers, but basically I was in charge of taking care of everybody. I would have to baby-sit after school, do the cleaning, make sure dinner was ready. I was running the household at like nine or ten. It was frustrating because I didn't know how at that age. My brother and sister wouldn't listen or would forget to do something, and I would get yelled at because it wasn't done. My father would come home and talk to me like I was an adult, tell me his problems, bounce things off of me. I was supposed to be an adult at home, but when we went to visit people and I would sit with the adults, he'd tell me, 'Children are to be seen and not heard,' and to go play with the kids. I had nothing to say to other kids because I didn't hang out with any. My sister would curl up in my father's lap, and they would hug and cuddle, while I was supposed to be in the kitchen cleaning the dishes. Over the years, you just accept where you are in the family. It was how you fit in. I just became a loner. My father knew the best way to punish me was to send me *out* of my room."

Marisa was eleven when her mother died. She recollects a neighbor coming over and taking her teenage sister down to the washing machine to tell her that all the responsibility would now rest on her shoulders: "This was the seventies, and my sister was already smoking dope, doing acid, and she just dropped out. So I became responsible. I remember soaking dirty, stinky hankies in bleach and then ironing them. I don't know why I remember this, but someone told my sister she should do it, and she told me I should do it. To this day, if anything happens in my life, I immediately start cleaning."

Terry, who at six was the youngest when her mother died, saw life from another perspective. Wrapped in a cocoon of overprotection, she became the emotional outlet for her older siblings' grief. It was Terry who was clucked over and sent to therapy. "Poor little" became a permanent attachment to her name. At thirteen, Rhonda was also the youngest in her family: "I resented my older sisters' interference. They were always telling me what to do and what not to do. They would even order my father around. No suggestions, just commands. I hated it!"

Fewer people involved doesn't necessarily make the situation easier. Only children may feel even more isolated without a sibling going through the same experiences. They have less of an outlet for any anger and blame, so Dad receives the full frontal attack.

Enlisted

This exercise will help you to look at how your mother's familial and social roles and responsibilities were reassigned. On whose shoulders did most of the burden fall? Were the responsibilities age and role appropriate? What was the impact of these changes? Here's how it worked in Amanda's family: "My mom was really the one who kept in touch with people and made sure my grandparents were called, that so-and-so got a present when she got married, that the holiday cards went out." After her mother died, Amanda took on that responsibility as well as "making sure my little brother got to his appointments, his sports activities. I could have swept it all off to my dad, so I'm not sure why I did it. I think that I knew that my mom would have been upset if she knew how things were run."

In the box below, we've listed possible roles your family members played. In the charts that follow, next to the name of each person, write the role(s) he or she played. First do the exercise to reflect the situation when your mother was alive. Be sure to check off whether a role was assigned or voluntarily assumed. Also, customize the exercise to fit your family. For instance, if you need to, add categories or people or split up duties like cleaning. If your parents were divorced, note whether your responsibilities were different with each parent. Then redo the exercise to show how things changed.

Possible Roles: Cook, Housekeeper (cleaning chores), Family Financial Chief, Food Shopper, Peacekeeper, Rulemaker, Breadwinner, Family Chauffeur, Caretaker for Mom, Caretaker for Dad, Caretaker for Children, Protector, Martyr, Scapegoat, Ritual Maker (sees to vacations, holidays, celebrations), Maintainer of Family Connections, Pet Walker

DATE:_____

CHART A: ROLES WHEN MY MOM WAS ALIVE

Person (Name)	Roles	Assigned	Assumed
Mother	_____	_____	_____
_____	_____	_____	_____
	_____	_____	_____
	_____	_____	_____
Me	_____	_____	_____
_____	_____	_____	_____
	_____	_____	_____
Father	_____	_____	_____
_____	_____	_____	_____
	_____	_____	_____
Brother	_____	_____	_____
_____	_____	_____	_____
	_____	_____	_____
Brother	_____	_____	_____
_____	_____	_____	_____
	_____	_____	_____

Person (Name)	Roles	Assigned	Assumed	
Sister	_____	_____	_____	
_____	_____	_____	_____	
	_____	_____	_____	
Sister	_____	_____	_____	
_____	_____	_____	_____	
	_____	_____	_____	
Maternal grandmother	_____	_____	_____	
	_____	_____	_____	
_____	_____	_____	_____	
Maternal grandfather	_____	_____	_____	
	_____	_____	_____	
_____	_____	_____	_____	
Paternal grandmother	_____	_____	_____	
	_____	_____	_____	
_____	_____	_____	_____	
Paternal grandfather	_____	_____	_____	
	_____	_____	_____	
_____	_____	_____	_____	
Housekeeper/ Nanny	_____	_____	_____	
	_____	_____	_____	
_____	_____	_____	_____	

Person (Name)	Roles	Assigned	Assumed
Other	_____	_____	_____
_____	_____	_____	_____
	_____	_____	_____

CHART B: ROLES AFTER MY MOM DIED

Person (Name)	Roles	Assigned	Assumed
Me	_____	_____	_____
_____	_____	_____	_____
	_____	_____	_____
Father	_____	_____	_____
_____	_____	_____	_____
	_____	_____	_____
Brother	_____	_____	_____
_____	_____	_____	_____
	_____	_____	_____
Brother	_____	_____	_____
_____	_____	_____	_____
	_____	_____	_____
Sister	_____	_____	_____
_____	_____	_____	_____
	_____	_____	_____
Sister	_____	_____	_____
_____	_____	_____	_____
	_____	_____	_____

Person (Name)	Roles	Assigned	Assumed
Maternal grandmother	_____	_____	_____
	_____	_____	_____
_____	_____	_____	_____
Maternal grandfather	_____	_____	_____
	_____	_____	_____
_____	_____	_____	_____
Paternal grandmother	_____	_____	_____
	_____	_____	_____
_____	_____	_____	_____
Paternal grandfather	_____	_____	_____
	_____	_____	_____
_____	_____	_____	_____
Housekeeper/ Nanny	_____	_____	_____
	_____	_____	_____
_____	_____	_____	_____
Other	_____	_____	_____
	_____	_____	_____
_____	_____	_____	_____

Which areas and roles changed? Altered family dynamics may have caused new rifts and resentments. How many roles were assigned or simply assumed? Consider whether these responsibilities were age and peer level appropriate and distributed fairly. What purpose did they serve? Who benefited, and who felt left with the short end of the stick? (In Parts III and IV, we'll examine how these roles fit into your life today and suggest ways to resolve some of the issues that remain.)

Stepping into a mother's role is asking to be the bull's-eye in target practice. Lisa knows that firsthand: "I tried to fill my mother's shoes right away, and my brothers really resisted that. Nobody liked being home and around each other because my mother wasn't there. It made me crazy. I'd try and initiate all these things, but they just wouldn't happen. When I would get annoyed with them, they were like, who the hell are you to tell us?" Paula hated being thrust into the role of looking after her younger brother and showed it: "I was very cold. I'd do the basics. I would feed him, get this, potatoes, fish cakes, and peas every single night. To this day he won't eat them."

Another adult female relative, particularly a maternal aunt or grandmother, generally faces the fewest obstacles as a mother surrogate. The family connection eases the transition, provided that relatives don't resent these new responsibilities. At the age of eight, Lucy was left an orphan when her mother died and went to live with her grandmother: "I was very proud of what my grandmother did. She became my primary caretaker, and I've since learned that she had many, many offers from others to take care of me. But she thought I needed stability, to stay in one place and not be bounced around, given the circumstances."

Lucy's grandmother provided affection and a semblance of security, top priorities to be sure. Other areas proved harder. "My grandmother was sixty-four when I lived with her," Lucy says. "Obviously she had a daughter herself, but after all those years, you forget what you did with the first. It was very embarrassing to talk about things like bras or menstruation with her. I remember being in bed and telling her that my best friend had gotten a bra. I asked, 'Can I get one too?' I didn't wait for a response. I just dove into bed and pulled the covers up over my head."

THE OTHER WOMAN

The question of stepmothers draws passionate responses. Here are a few from women we interviewed and surveyed.

"It took a while for us to get used to another woman different than my mother," Lisa recalls. "I'll never forget the first time she didn't buy Kleenex. She bought Puffs or something. That killed me."

"My stepmother was plain nasty," Greta says, "cutting me like a knife, cutting me to my core, which is why I had no self-esteem. I was so mistreated. I'd come home from practice, and there'd be a plate of food left that would be cold. She didn't care. She would smash me in the head, knock me against the door frames. She locked me in my bedroom, so I took the door off its hinges. I refused to be caged."

"My stepmom and I had so much in common," Robyn observes, "from a love of antiques to the way we dressed. I didn't feel like she was trying to take my mother's place, and she made my father happy."

"I took out all my anger on my stepmother," Mary explains. "Part of it was me, part of it was that she would never measure up, no matter who she was. I was pissed because I didn't have what I wanted. She became my scapegoat."

Clearly not every stepmother is the proverbial wicked witch, but step-moms top motherless daughters' hit lists for having committed at least one cardinal sin: being the other woman, especially if the relationship followed quickly on the heels of a mother's death. Many men get involved hastily, partly out of emotional need, partly to lighten the load of parenthood. Daughters are likely to view the new woman as an enemy invader, competition for their father, a threat to the memory of their mother. And Cinderella sure didn't help. Stepmothers scarcely stand a chance if a fairy godmother—read: idealized mother—waits in the wings to grant every wish and fulfill every desire. The land mines are everywhere, and it's a rare woman who manages to avoid them all. Still, stepmothers sometimes sow the seeds of their own destruction through insensitivity, insecurity, inexperience, and occasionally outright abusiveness.

STEPMOTHERS' MISSTEPS

Too rapid involvement with a father/family that has experienced loss

Competing with the dead mother

Not respecting a family's feelings for the deceased

Favoring her own biological children

Turning stepchildren into servants

Jealousy of a daughter's relationship with her father

Taking out frustrations over difficult situations on the children

According to the women survyed by Hope Edelman in *Motherless Daughters,* nearly 60 percent of men remarry after their wife's death, and more than 75 percent do so within five years. It's hard not to associate the loss of your mother with the acquisition of your stepmother. In the Picture Perfect? exercise on page 38, we asked you to think objectively about the good and bad sides of your mother. If you had a stepmother—or someone who acted as if she was—try doing the same exercise for her, assessing the qualities she possessed as a woman. They can be physical and psychological, skills or shortcomings. They don't have to even out, but you should have some on both sides of the ledger.

DATE:_____

____ *Sense of style* _____

____ *Argumentative* _____

____ *Good housekeeper* _____

____ *Bossy* _____

____ *Athletic* _____

____ _____

____ _____

____ _____

____ _____

____ _____

Now think about how your stepmother acted toward you. Put an *S* next to the words that describe her and the way she related to you. Choose all the adjectives that apply, and add ones that might be missing.

_ Loving	_ Smothering	_ Forgiving
_ Detached	_ Inconsistent	_ Erratic
_ Cold	_ Strict	_ Playful
_ Caring	_ Affectionate	_ Disapproving
_ Warm	_ Reproachful	_ Nurturing
_ Sharing	_ Unfair	_ Abusive
_ Supportive	_ Sacrificing	_ Good-humored
_ Controlling	_ Lax	_ Domineering
_ Angry	_ Anxious	_ Sympathetic
_ Overbearing	_ Nervous	_ Respectful
_ Annoying	_ Generous	_ Attentive
_ Nagging	_ Suspicious	_ Accommodating
_ Encouraging	_ Selfless	_ Mean
_ _____	_ _____	_ _____
_ _____	_ _____	_ _____
_ _____	_ _____	_ _____

Compare this list with the one you completed about your mother in the Due Unto Me exercise on page 44 in Chapter 4. As you review the differences and similarities, think about whether your feelings are swayed by the ways she was like or unlike your mother. Did you accept or resent her because she tried to act like a mother or because she didn't? In what areas did your stepmother deserve a pat on the back? What did she do that earned her reproach?

DATE:_____

I accepted/resented my stepmother because:

_____

_____

_____

She deserves credit for:

_____

_____

_____

She merits criticism for:

_____

_____

_____

TRANSITIONAL STATES

Of course, sometimes it's Dad who takes on the lion's share of the responsibilities. Monica was only fifteen months old when her mother died, and her father didn't remarry until she was in the tenth grade: "It was just my father and I. We're very close and have a special relationship because of that. People are always saying, 'You lost your mom, but look at the relationship you have with your dad.'"

In learning to live without her, the challenges were in the ordinary as well as the extraordinary. At school, you were now the kid whose mother had died. Holidays commemorated your loss. Significant rites of passage, from menstruation to marriage to motherhood, were marked by her absence. Activities in which a mom's participation was expected began adding up.

Going back to school was generally excruciating. Uneasy classmates said nothing or offered clumsy condolences. "I do remember I had to go to school the next day," Enid relates. "That was my father's way. I was on the playground before school started, by the hopscotch board. I had a ton of friends in the fourth grade. I don't remember them being around me, but they probably were. What I do remember is this greaser, Dean Witherspoon—beautiful blue eyes and blond hair but such an ass. He came up to me and said, 'Hey kid, I heard your mother died.' I just looked at him in pain. I remember crying in class, being so embarrassed and thinking, What am I doing here? All this attention foisted on me. It was wretched. How messed up was my family to send me to school so soon after she died."

Feeling as if there was a sign on your back that read "Pity Me" made you want to duck into the nearest locker. "I never wanted that sympathy," says Brenda. She secretly wished that her mother's suicide would somehow be announced in a press release: "Suddenly everyone would know, and they would be like, 'Wow, she's so cool, she's so smart and strong and tough. You would never have imagined that kind of a crisis would have occurred in her life.'"

But for Lucy, pity was one way she could get the attention she craved: "I'd go to sleep-away camp, and people would get letters and things from their mothers. I remember being really upset and telling people my parents weren't alive. I told them, looking for that 'Oh my God' reaction. I needed attention, I needed people, and I used my parents' death to get it."

"When I got into second grade, everything was focused on Mom, Mom, Mom," says Monica of her motherless childhood. "In sixth or seventh grade, I was overwhelmed by the fact that mothers play a very different role than what parents play. In middle school, everybody knew how to do everything, like dances and lipstick. I really started to see myself as different and separate in that whole blossoming into womanhood deal."

Monica's dad tried to fill in: "He's so emotional, really just a big cheeseball. I told him when I got my period, and he went out and bought *Our Bodies, Ourselves* and twelve red roses and put them all over my room. Part of me was thankful and the other part sad and confused and just wanted to forget about the whole thing." At the onset of her period,

Gena remembers thinking, "How am I going to tell dad? He didn't know how to deal with two kids, let alone a growing teenage girl. Per usual, that evening he sat in his recliner with the newspaper opened, and I sat on the other side of the room. I said, 'I have something to tell you,' and he kept his nose in the newspaper. I quietly said that I got my period. He didn't move; he didn't flinch; he didn't take his eyes off the paper. I think he muttered something like 'Oh.'"

Most motherless women agree that growing up with a father teaching you the finer points of femininity and womanhood leaves a yawning gap in your education. Carrie says, "My father insisted that my hair be cut short so that it was easy to take care of. He didn't understand why I wanted pretty things and not just practical clothes." Vanessa notes, "I was raised from a male point of view. My father went so far as to teach us what he thought was the way to catch a man. He said we should always be interested in what the man was interested in. All him, him, him, and you end up losing yourself."

Even with loving guidance and nurturing from a surrogate or substitute mother, many daughters believe that only a birth mother holds the essential knowledge of womanhood. So we yearn for the secrets we think only our own mothers can teach us.

FEMININE MYSTIQUE

After your mother died, how did you learn about stuff like sex, clothes, makeup, those things we associate with being a woman? Father, stepmom, teacher, mom's best friend—was there someone or some source for any of this knowledge? What did you pick up and where? We've rounded up the likely suspects, but add any we've left out.

DATE:_____

____Teacher: I learned *the facts and just the facts of life.*_____

_____

____Father: I learned_____

_____

___Stepmom: I learned _____

_____

___Grandmother: I learned _____

_____

___Aunt: I learned _____

_____

___Family friend: I learned _____

_____

___Neighbor: I learned_____

_____

___Baby-sitter: I learned _____

_____

___Television: I learned _____

_____

___Magazines: I learned _____

_____

_____

_____

SAFE PASSAGE: A JOURNAL WRITING EXERCISE

Adjusting to life after your mother died involved a series of first times: the first play she wasn't there to applaud your performance, the first Thanksgiving without her turkey dressing, the first time your birthday—or hers—went by. Or, as in Monica's case, the first time you realized or understood the impact of not having a mother. One, if not several, of these events probably epitomizes, at least symbolically, what it meant to reach maturity without a mother. Write about that time, its significance in your life, what you missed, and how you felt.

DATE:_____

_____

_____

_____

_____

_____

_____

_____

_____

_____

FINAL THOUGHTS

The old saw about nothing being permanent except change might have seemed particularly appropriate as you worked through this chapter. Cataloging what you lost and what changed is like filling out the insurance report for a robbery—a necessary but arduous task.

Part Break II

We asked you to take a hard journey back and recall distressing events in your life. You deserve enormous credit for the tough, soul-searching work you've done. We hope the information and exercises in Part II have pushed the healing process along. If you're feeling a bit overworked at the moment, remember our exercise analogy. A strenuous workout may make your muscles sore, but it also makes them stronger.

Memory Bank

The last three chapters may have provoked additional questions. If there are more questions that need answers or if information is missing concerning you, your mother, family members, or specific events, document them here.

What I Need to Know	*Who* Might Have the Answer	*How* I Can Approach Them
Why I Resist	*When* I Will Try to Ask	*What Happened* When I Asked

What I Need to Know	*Who* Might Have the Answer	*How* I Can Approach Them
Why I Resist	*When* I Will Try to Ask	*What Happened* When I Asked

Are there other sources you need to consult? List them below.

Source _____

Source _____

Source _____

Key Passages

Be sure to go back and reread your Safe Passage entries to find your Key Passages. Then transfer them here.

Chapter 6

_____

_____

Chapter 7

_____

_____

Chapter 8

_____

_____

Finally, think about the effort you've put forth and the progress you've already made. As a touchstone to assess where you've been, how you feel, and what you've accomplished in the second part of the workbook, reflect on the questions below.

How did I feel as I worked through these chapters?

How do I feel right now?

What surprised me about my responses or insights?

What was hardest to do?

What do I need to come back to?

What have I accomplished?

What can I do for myself right now?

_____

_____

_____

_____

WHO AM I
NOW?

"Falling apart is curling up into a fetal position and staying in bed for a week," she said. "What you were doing is having the emotional response an individual has to the loss of someone they love. We cry to give voice to our pain."

"That's very poetic, Ms. Guerrero, but it doesn't make me feel any better."

"You are not going to feel any better for a long, long time, Ms. Gulden, and you know that far better than I do. But I refuse to believe that keeping your grief bottled up makes you feel better than crying."

"Like a five-year-old," I said, blowing my nose.

"The five-year-old who provides me with jokes never cries, Ms. Gulden. She does not understand what is happening. But you do."

—*Anna Quindlen in* One True Thing

The next two chapters deal with the here and now. Into the tapestry of the present is woven our past. We'll ask you to consider how loss has affected your outlook and your interactions with lovers, family, and friends. The first chapter will examine familiar demons from the past, like insecurity, anxiety, emptiness, and shame. You'll analyze the perceptions and beliefs you hold today and the defenses you maintain. We'll discuss how feeling unmothered influences how you define yourself as a woman, and why you continue to feel the pain of her loss. In the following chapter, you'll see how these beliefs and behaviors affect your closest relationships. The exercises are designed to help you see patterns repeated in your life, discern the reasons behind choices you've made—or put off making, and understand what's going on in the way you relate.

9

LIVING IN THE SHADOW OF LOSS

Who Have I Become?

It was as if I'd made a pact with my emotions not to feel, not to respond, but had forgotten to set a date at which the arrangement would end.

—*Leslie Epstein*

Mary's Story: I've spent so much of my energy just surviving. It's always such a struggle. It's been hard to ask for what I want because I already feel defeated. What I really want—my mother—I can't have. I live with a lot of anxiety. Worry and anxiety. I go to the doctor a lot, worry about hangnails, stay sicker than I should. It doesn't stop me from doing things, but any time some little thing happens, I catastrophize it.

Sara's Story: There are many themes in life today that I believe stem from being motherless. One issue is feeling unprotected. Since she died, I've had to fend for myself, so I try to avoid needing protection. I make decisions from a defensive position: the safe job instead of the fulfilling one. Every day I'm conscious of how few resources I have to fall back on. I'm always aware of experiencing life alone. I never got into the position of being ready to face the world without her. Now, even at thirty, I am overwhelmed by my own separateness.

In this chapter, we ask you to closely examine how your mother's death informs who you are today. It may be five years or twenty-five years after, but the loss and the feelings it generated continue to appear and reappear, a refrain that won't get out of your heart. Today we know how acutely a mother's early death shapes our adult development. We understand that silencing those feelings, whenever they occurred, didn't vanquish them. No matter how long ago it was, you may have a sense of never having fully matured past the age you were when she died, still yearn for something you think only she could provide, and have difficulty dealing with the milestones of your life that pass unmarked by a mother. These are the very reasons you picked up this book.

Section I of this chapter focuses on the emotional legacy of early loss and the belief systems and behavior patterns you've developed. Section II goes on to examine how the choices you've made were affected by your mother's premature death. Section III looks at issues of gender and femininity that stem from being unmothered. Finally, Section IV zeroes in on special times and life transitions that cause you to reexperience your loss and grief.

A multitude of factors have brought you to where you are today: your age and developmental needs at the time of your mother's death, your relationship, how she died, your family circumstances, what changes took place, and whether you received acknowledgment and validation for your feelings. The basics for any unhealed wounds can be found here.

SECTION I: WHY DOES IT STILL HURT?

"I don't take risks that could lead to rejection." "I'm so unsure of myself." "I understand how fragile life can be." "I control every part of my life that it's possible to control." "I have a fear of abandonment. I live in daily fear that my father or sisters will die and leave me." "Growing up without a mother has left me with a lack of trust in others and myself." "I'm totally self-sufficient, which is good . . . and not so good."

Again and again women have told us that regardless of how long ago their mothers died, the loss still resonates. Though your relationship with loss does change over time—you're not the same person at thirty-seven or fifty-seven that you were at seven or seventeen, because you experienced her death while in the midst of creating a self, it became a defining part of you and your core beliefs. Beyond the sadness and pain, the damage—whether from being abandoned, excluded, ignored, silenced, emotionally deprived, overprotected, disparaged, or overburdened—continues to affect who you are. Long after reason says it's useless, the yearning for what once was remains.

Rae describes it as "that void that's always there. I'm fifty years old now, and it has never changed. It's always 'I wish I had a mother.' I even still feel I wish someone could be my mother. I know it's not possible, but it's always there."

Roll the Tape Again

In the Roll the Tape exercise on page 128, we asked you to assess your emotional adjustment to your mother's death during those maturing years. Take your emotional temperature today to pinpoint where you continue to have problems. Initial difficulties in adjusting to your mother's death may have subsided over time, while new issues may have arisen, and still others deepened. Place a check mark in the space that best reflects how often you experience these feelings and attitudes right now: 0 = never, 1 = seldom, 2 = sometimes, 3 = frequently, and 4 = all the time. In the space labeled Growing Up, put the rating you chose the first time you did the exercise.

Date:_____

	0	1	2	3	4	Growing Up
Nobody understands how I feel	__	__	__	__	__	__
I feel self-conscious	__	__	__	__	__	__
I feel disconnected from people	__	__	__	__	__	__
I have to hide the real me	__	__	__	__	__	__

	0	1	2	3	4	Growing Up
I have no warmth or emotional support	—	—	—	—	—	—
I don't deserve to be happy	—	—	—	—	—	—
I don't deserve to be loved	—	—	—	—	—	—
I think everything is my fault	—	—	—	—	—	—
I can't protect myself	—	—	—	—	—	—
I can't trust anyone	—	—	—	—	—	—
No one trusts me	—	—	—	—	—	—
I'm anxious and scared	—	—	—	—	—	—
I feel empty inside	—	—	—	—	—	—
I have difficulty expressing how I feel	—	—	—	—	—	—
I feel like an outsider	—	—	—	—	—	—
I have no one to rely on	—	—	—	—	—	—
I feel my world is about to collapse	—	—	—	—	—	—
I have outbursts of anger	—	—	—	—	—	—
I find life overwhelming	—	—	—	—	—	—
I feel disloyal if I enjoy myself	—	—	—	—	—	—
I feel directionless	—	—	—	—	—	—
I believe life is unfair	—	—	—	—	—	—
I feel isolated and lonely	—	—	—	—	—	—
I am sad and depressed	—	—	—	—	—	—

	0	1	2	3	4	Growing Up
I worry people will die and leave me	—	—	—	—	—	—
I worry more bad things will happen	—	—	—	—	—	—
I'm numb to my feelings	—	—	—	—	—	—
I worry about getting sick	—	—	—	—	—	—

The biggest difference between my answers in Chapter 8 and now is:

I'm not as overwhelmed because I know that I can get through tough times.

_____

_____

_____

The areas I have the most difficulty with today are:

I still have problems trusting people.

_____

_____

_____

I've made strides in the following areas:

I don't let things build up and build up till I'm ready to bust.

_____

_____

_____

I've done this by:

If I've had a bad day, I come home and pound on the computer keyboard until I get through whatever's bothering me. I don't wait to confront things.

_____

_____

_____

PULLING UP THE ROOTS

Look back at the feelings you checked as having frequently or all the time. How are they related to your mother's death and its ramifications?

DATE:_____

My feelings of _____ are related to her death because:

_____

_____

_____

My feelings of_____ are related to her death because:

_____

_____

_____

My feelings of_____ are related to her death because:

_____

_____

_____

Sometimes we use our motherless condition as an excuse for our shortcomings. We think it's at the root of anything that goes sour in our lives. Blaming a problem on a mother's premature death may just be a way of avoiding responsibility or not dealing with personal demons. Or there may be other contributing factors. Maybe you saw the seeds of your feelings and beliefs planted when you worked through Part I of this book. Review the exercises in Part I, especially your genogram in Chapter 5, and see if you find any additional reasons for your current perceptions. Are other issues coming into play?

My feelings of shyness are unrelated to my mother's death because I was never really outgoing before she died. I've always had trouble in social situations. Her death just made it harder.

My feelings of _____ are unrelated to my mother's death because:

_____

_____

_____

My feelings of _____ are unrelated to my mother's death because:

_____

_____

_____

My feelings of _____ are unrelated to my mother's death because:

_____

_____

_____

Proof Positive

Out of adversity, the unanticipated emerges. The strengths you've developed may not always be as apparent as what you consider weaknesses. And recognizing them doesn't mean their acquisition was worth the price of a mother's death, nor should it minimize any suffering you've undergone. But acknowledging qualities that have helped you overcome obstacles thus far—and you have come a long way—will be useful as you continue the healing process.

From the list below, check off the qualities that apply to you, and be sure to add any relevant others.

Date:_____

_____I am resourceful.

_____I know how precious life is.

_____I live to the fullest.

_____I am compassionate and sensitive to others' problems and pains.

_____I am self-reliant.

_____I'm a person others can depend on.

_____I can handle a crisis.

_____I've lived through the worst, so I can get through anything.

_____I'm a real survivor.

_____I have courage.

_____I'm an independent spirit.

_____I value honesty.

_____I'm level-headed.

_____I'm achievement oriented.

_____

_____

Hearsay

Did you find it hard to identify your strengths? They do exist. You may be reluctant to recognize positive results coming from such a negative experience, but we urge you to keep returning to this exercise. Try recalling what other people have said about you.

DATE: _____

People have told me more than once that I'm:

_____

_____

When they told me, I believed/didn't believe them.

People have told me more than once that I'm:

_____

_____

When they told me, I believed/didn't believe them.

Tool Shed II

In the Tool Shed exercise on page 135, you indicated the survival skills you once relied on. Since then you've grown up, and the way you view and cope with the world may have changed. As an adult, what coping mechanisms do you continue to use, and what new ones have you developed? As before, circle the ones that apply to you, and add to the list if necessary.

Have a "why bother?" Rationalize attitude		Deny problems exist
Fly into rages easily	Act hypervigilant	Space out
Retreat into introspection	Act anxious/fearful	Lose myself in activities
Try to outdo others	Take care of everyone else's needs	Have eating problems (anorexia, bulimia, overeating)
Protect myself with humor	Engage in excessive sexual activity	Still behave in overly childish manner
Have sleep problems	Withdraw when difficulties arise	Abuse drugs, alcohol, self
Have a "live for today" attitude	Act physically/ verbally abusive	Engage in other self-destructive behavior
Must have things perfect	Act overly self-reliant	Act very independent
Minimize problems	Avoid intimacy	Fantasize
Use creative activity as an outlet	Engage frequently in excessive or outrageous behavior	See world in black-and-white terms
Avoid problems	Must control situations	Distrust people
Exhibit resourcefulness	Rely on faith in God	Lack faith in God
Overprotect others	Become overly concerned about health	Nurture others but not myself

Act vindictive	Regress to childish behavior	Overidentify with grief
Take life too seriously	Deal with matters in a disorganized fashion	Depend too much on friends
_____	_____	_____
_____	_____	_____

BACK TO BASICS II

The techniques you rely on have helped you survive, but they may be damaging in other respects. Review the coping behaviors you circled. What underlying needs are you trying to satisfy? Continue your honest introspection, and take this exercise one step further by indicating how your behavior is beneficial and/or damaging.

Coping Mechanism: _Excessive caretaking_

Needs Met: _It's my way of being appreciated. I can be the mother I never had. It's also comfortable because that's what I did after my mom died, and it gives me a sense of control._

It can be useful in the following ways:

I like looking after people and being appreciated.

It can be damaging in the following ways:

I tend to undercut my own needs and then feel as if no one pays attention to what I want.

DATE:_____

Coping Mechanism:_____

_____

_____

Needs Met:_____

_____

_____

It can be useful in the following ways:

_____

_____

It can be damaging in the following ways:

_____

_____

Coping Mechanism:_____

_____

_____

Needs Met:_____

_____

_____

It can be useful in the following ways:

_____

_____

It can be damaging in the following ways:

_____

_____

REPEATING THE PAST, REPEATING THE PAST, REPEATING THE PAST . . .

The beliefs about who we are, forged in part as a result of a mother's death, are central to our identity. This is precisely why we continue to hold on to them even when they're self-defeating. We set up our lives to reaffirm those core beliefs, putting ourselves in situations that confirm messages we received and internalized earlier. Childhood or adolescent patterns become the templates for what we think and do today. Beth saw her dying mother get the attention and nurturing she wanted and needed: "The lesson I learned when I was growing up was it's OK to be taken care of if you're sick. Today, I don't think I'm a hypochondriac, but health issues are a big thing for me."

We recreate and repeat the pain and suffering of childhood and adolescence. The child who kept her feelings hidden so that she wouldn't upset an anguished father has difficulty recognizing and getting her needs met as an adult. The teen who believes that her mother's death was an omen of a dark cloud over her life sees tragedy lurking around every corner.

The death of her mother when she was two led Marcia to think she was a magnet for tragedy. Bad things happened *to her*. Her woe-is-me outlook pervaded everything she did. "Why bother?" became her mantra. With the attitude that nothing good would come her way, she was assured that nothing would.

Amanda translated the shame she felt over a sick and dying mother into fears that people wouldn't like her because she was different. "I try hard to make sure everybody likes me and I don't offend anyone and keep my opinions to myself," she explains. Her people-pleasing strategy assures the tidy upkeep of her feelings of shame and worthlessness.

Why do we reinforce negative perceptions? In part, we're replicating what's familiar, the situations and experiences we found ourselves in as we were growing up. They may be painful, they may be self-defeating, they may rob us of our ability to fully enjoy life, but at least their outcome is predictable. Self-sabotaging patterns of thinking lead us to act and behave in ways that reinforce those beliefs. The negative messages we feed ourselves become a self-fulfilling prophecy.

SECTION II: WHOSE LIFE IS IT ANYWAY?

"For a long time," says Lisa, "I felt I had to develop in the shadow of my mother—what I thought she would want me to do. I used to beat myself up with that. She was so strong, and here I was paralyzed. I was so confused about how to develop autonomy, how to be myself. I didn't know what that meant. She would've killed me for having this 'poor me' attitude instead of gripping problems by the horns. I just didn't know how to do it, and then I would get down on myself even more and back through the cycle of 'She would never want me to be like this. She wouldn't like that.' I spent years beating myself up over it."

Mothers and daughters reflect one another as much in their differences as in their similarities. The unconscious process of identifying and differentiating from our mothers gives us both grounding and independence. The motherless daughter struggles more than other women to relinquish the need for a mother's approval. Though absent, our mothers continue to exert power over the decisions we make in our lives. "Detaching from a mother's posthumous control can be a long, arduous and painful journey, but it's often a necessary step in a daughter's mourning process," Hope Edelman writes in *Motherless Daughters*.

WORDS TO LIVE BY

"My mother told me to always speak my mind," Nicole reports. "I think that's something I try to do, to say what needs to be said." Marisa laughs when she recalls her mother's dating guide: "Don't do it in a car. Don't spend the night with him. Don't get pregnant." A mother's advice, overtly expressed or understood even if left unsaid, may still resonate with you today, influencing your beliefs and behavior. What were her words to live by?

MY MOTHER'S CREDO

Go to church every Sunday.

Marry a doctor.

Choose a profession you can fall back on.

_____

_____

_____

_____

_____

Review this roster of rules, and see if you can trace any of your attitudes, beliefs, or behavior back to her commandments. Think about whether you're obeying them or repudiating them and why. Is it blind faith? Do they still make sense? How do you feel when you break her rules?

DATE:_____

I continue to abide by my mother's rules about:

_____

_____

The reasons I abide by them are:

_____

_____

I don't think my mother was right about:

_____

_____

The reasons I disregard these rules are:

_____

_____

When I go against something she believed, I feel:

_____

_____

ALL OR NOTHING

Advice from a mother holds special authority. If it didn't come from her, we wonder whether to trust it. So we try to divine what she intended for us. For women who fear disconnecting, the thought of disappointing a mother, even one no longer alive, is apt to usher in guilt and self-reproach. You try to become the perfect daughter by living up to your mother's dream for you or living out her unrealized ones. Driven by a misplaced sense of obligation or deference, you sacrifice your own wants, needs, and ambitions to fulfill hers.

"I knew she was gone, but I was doing all these things to try and maintain a connection to her," Lydia says. "Being a dancer, that had something to do with what she wanted me to do. I spent a long time wondering what she would have wanted me to do. I mean I loved dancing and had a talent for it, but there was a lot of pathological stuff in trying to maintain that connection."

"I seem to be following in her footsteps," observes Olivia, who was seven when her mother died. "I eventually want to be a full-time artist and maybe pick up where she left off as one. Of course, my second goal is to be a mother because my mother never really got to be a mom through my teenage years."

Rosie O'Donnell admits that she's lived out her mother's fantasy by going into show business. It was a dream they shared. "I used to go to Broadway with her," O'Donnell said. "It was her passion for entertainment that started mine."

Motivating some women is the fear of becoming like their mothers, a fear that her worst traits will rub off. "I've worked very consciously to be different from her," says Ingrid, whose alcoholic mother succumbed to cancer when Ingrid was a teenager. "I never wanted to be controlled by a substance. I never wanted to be trapped, because for so many years I felt trapped with her. So I'm sober; she wasn't. I have an advanced degree; she only finished high school. I'm alive; she's dead."

Rae's caretakers didn't allay her fears that she'd turn into her abusive, alcoholic mother: "My family said I would probably turn out just like she was. They would say, 'You're just like your mother,' any time I did anything wrong. 'The apple doesn't fall far from the tree' and all that kind of stuff."

Living in total opposition to a mother, avoiding like the plague anything that smacks of her or might have met with her approval, has the hallmark of teenage rebellion unmoderated by time. Lacking the complete, humanizing cycle of a mother-daughter relationship, it's as if you only have two choices: to replicate her or be nothing like her. Anxious to avoid her fate, you deny those parts of yourself that bear any similarity to her. The apple may in fact not fall far from the tree—but it does roll.

MOTHER MAY I?

Go through the important areas in your life: professional, educational, spiritual, community, political, recreational, and social. (We'll discuss relationships at length in Chapter 10, so set that area aside for the time being.) Are you doing what you want to do? Is it what your mother would have chosen for you? Often we use a mother as a how-to guide for the shoulds or shouldn'ts of our lives.

"Lately," Amanda states, "I've been trying something that helps me a lot. I think of myself as the continuation of my mom, and it's like I've adopted a lot of her values, opinions, and ideas. It helps me make decisions I wouldn't have been able to make a year ago. Now I think about what I want and what her advice would be to come up with my own decisions."

Take inventory of your life, and consider whether she would put her stamp of approval on the choices you've made. How much does her opinion mean to you?

DATE:_____

Approve	Disapprove
I became a lawyer.	*I gave up playing the flute.*
_____	_____
_____	_____
_____	_____
_____	_____
_____	_____

Go back and mark with an *I* those decisions that you think were affected by your mother or her death. On a scale of 1 to 10, with 10 being the most influential and 1 the least, how do you rate her influence?

The choices you've made as well as your underlying motives can be very telling. It's important to realize whether you're following—or denying—your own bliss or hers. Is she your guide or your crutch? You may be sacrificing your own needs out of guilt or as a way to maintain an attachment.

TO DECIDE OR ABIDE

Every tough decision plunks Penny down in the midst of a conundrum: "What do I think she would want me to be doing?" What does she do? "I just freeze, and I don't do anything." The mother she counted on for counsel isn't around, and lacking confidence in her own ability, Penny opts for paralysis rather than take the "wrong" turn. Taking responsibility for those decisions would mean disconnecting from a mother's reach. Instead, her mother's good little girl doesn't have to grow up—and away—from Mom.

Many motherless daughters instead develop a take-charge, self-reliant character. Having learned to "take care of yourself because no one else will," you boldly climb the ladder of success. Yet accomplishment is often clouded by guilt for surpassing a mother's achievements. "Sometimes I feel loyalty means having the things she always wanted and never had," writes author Bookda Gheisar. "But when I am happy, I feel I am being disloyal by having more than she had." Starr, whose loss occurred at fourteen, believes that her lack of motherly guidance has granted her the freedom to "make it up as I go along without having to answer to anyone but myself." Madonna, whose mother died when she was five, expressed a similar notion. "Nothing in my life or career has been a path that anybody took," she told an interviewer.

Yet a vulnerability frequently accompanies the swagger. When paid a compliment, a motherless daughter is apt to respond, "Who, me?" Despite admiration expressed for your self-assured manner, you choose to believe your inadequacies are showing. Since the compliment didn't come from the source—Mother—it's discounted. We continue vainly to seek her approval.

Having had your share of instability, you may look for that missing control and certainty in a career. "Like a lot of motherless daughters, I have tended to become very independent," Elaine told us. "My financial independence has always been a source of pride, yet I still fear financial ruin, even though I'm financially secure. Security has always been a big topic for me; I'll take it over anything. It's why I ended up gravitating toward accounting as a field. Accounting consists of equations—debits and credits. An answer is right or it's wrong. It's predictable, unambiguous, and therefore very comforting."

We don't think it's sheer coincidence that so many motherless women wind up in the helping professions. Even our number cruncher Elaine admits, "I wanted to go into counseling and work with kids, but I didn't feel together enough to do it." It may be a way of setting the record straight—you couldn't help her, but maybe you can be of service to someone else. You're good at it because you've already dealt with really tough situations. You've learned that life is precious.

"Every field I ever got into," says Rae, "was one where I could help people. I don't know if it's something about being able to save somebody because I couldn't save her. I just know that when I'm with people who remind me of my mother, in the same condition she was in, I feel real good when I'm able to do something for them."

SECTION III: THE GENDER GAP

"I watched my roommate tonight," Gretchen relates. "She was walking around the apartment getting ready for a dinner party. It smelled of cooking, and she was so confident, well prepared. If I were to throw a dinner party you'd find me in the closet munching my nails. I'd be afraid the forks were on the wrong side of the plate. I don't even know how to cook. The party was for her mother's friends, and they all came over, and I'm sitting there with my thumb up my butt wondering what I'm supposed to do. Is my underwear showing? Is my skirt up over my head? Am I holding my drink right, do I put it on the table, do I bring it back to the sink? I'm just so awkward. And I can't help feeling that they're all judging me, looking at me funny because I'm doing something wrong. There's something I should know here. I was eleven when my mother died, and I was learning those things. After she died, that all disappeared. I would have known had my mother been there."

GIRL TALK

The secret handshake passed down from mother to daughter, the feeling that you're the only one in plain clothes at the costume party—however you describe it, you think you're missing a special ingredient that makes you a full-fledged woman. You maximize differences between yourself and other women while downplaying your similarities.

It may be true that many of our notions about womanhood come in one form or fashion from our mothers, but motherless daughters typically assign an almost magical power to this body of a mother's knowledge. That's why you may see yourself at a disadvantage, feeling unfeminine, unsure about exactly what feminine is, and assuming that it must consist of traits you lack. In reaction, you build a myth of womanhood based on stereotypical behaviors and appearances. Naturally this fabulous Barbie doll cum Martha Stewart is impossible to live up to. Congratulations, you've created the perfect climate for feelings of inferiority, embarrassment, and shame.

It's not wholly surprising that many women brought up primarily by men reach adulthood wondering whether their dads consulted Dr. Spock or Dr. Seuss. "I have one dress and I'm totally scared of it," relates Monica, now twenty, who was raised from infancy by her father. Realizing that some of your ideas about femininity come from a man's perspective can be helpful in working through feelings of inadequacy. Or as one woman put it, "Half the time I feel like I'm in drag."

"Right now I really feel confused," says nineteen-year-old Anne. "I think I have more male qualities than female qualities—like the way that I act and the hobbies I have. I'm more into cars than planting flowers, making dinner, and the family thing." A questioning of sexual identity may surface more frequently in unmothered women who, lacking a female role model, were taught by—and modeled their behavior after—a man.

Complicating it all, many motherless women long for a woman's nurturing and love. The desire to be mothered leaves some women perplexed about whether they're sexually attracted to women or simply seeking the emotional comfort a mother would have supplied. During adolescence, when issues of sexuality and gender identity are so paramount, this is a particularly sensitive area.

Monica maintains that "ever since the seventh grade, I've searched out women in my life to play a mother role for me. In my junior year in high school, I started to realize my serious interest in women. I understand genetic homosexuality, but I strongly believe that deep in my heart I'm gay because I never got that mother love."

The fact that you may want a soothing female touch or feel more comfortable around women does not necessarily mean you're gay. While the scientific community continues to debate the causes of sexual orientation, there's no evidence that a mother's death is a determining factor. If these remain troubling questions for you, consult a trained therapist to help sort them out.

"What's it like to be a woman?" Tara asks. "That's always been a tough one for me." Do you come up short when you compare yourself to other women, the way Gretchen does? Or like Priscilla, lament, "I never felt feminine feminine. Even on my wedding day. I didn't do anything extra to look special the way brides should." What essential knowledge and expertise do you think a mother passes on? Is it the art of putting on makeup, decorating a house, or knowing the proper gift to bring?

List the skills and know-how you believe daughters learn from mothers, how you learned them, and then decide whether you think you're up to snuff by grading yourself on an A to F scale.

DATE:_____

Mothers Teach Daughters How To	I Learned This From	My Grade Is
Take care of a family	*I'm not sure. I just always had to look after everyone in my family.*	*B+*
Cook	*I never really learned how.*	*D−*
_____	_____	_____
_____	_____	_____
_____	_____	_____
_____	_____	_____

Why do you think these are important things for women to know? How did you reach your definition of what makes a woman? Reconsider what really are *essential* skills for a woman, and put an *E* next to those. They may include skills you want to improve, while the rest may be nice to know but not crucial to your sense of well-being. For instance, Gretchen certainly isn't the only woman who hasn't the slightest idea how to cook. But if you wanted to learn, you could consult books, take a course, or read cooking magazines.

Now, how did you grade yourself in the essential areas? Did you pass or fail? Are they sources for feelings of inferiority? (In Chapter 11, we'll ask you to reality-test these flaws and suggest ways you can work toward changing them.)

SECTION IV: TIMES OF TRANSITION

"Whenever I move, I have really big loss issues," Joanne states. "When you move, you give up what your life is at that point and start fresh, and I find it very hard to make that transition. I start going through my loss all over again. It's good that I see there's a parallel. For the longest time I would get depressed every time we moved. Then I realized that I was reliving all my feelings of loss."

Sometimes it seems it's nothing at all that reactivates the hurt. In *One True Thing*, her novel about taking care of her dying mother, Anna Quindlen captures that haunting nature of loss perfectly.

> It's funny, isn't it, what will make your heart break? Your lover moves to London and falls in love with a news reader for the BBC and you feel fine and then one day you raise your umbrella slightly to cross Fifty-seventh Street and stare into the Burberry shop and begin to sob. Or your baby dies at birth and five years later, in an antique store, a small battered silver rattle with teeth marks in one end engraved with the name Emily lies on a square of velvet, and the sobs escape from the genie's bottle somewhere deep in your gut where they've lain low until then.
>
> Or the garbage bag breaks.

In numerous letters and interviews, women years removed from the actual event say they don't understand why, but with the passage of time, it's become more difficult to cope with a mother's death. Starr grapples with the apparent contradiction: "If time heals all wounds, how come her absence just makes my heart grow fonder?"

We're constantly renegotiating our relationship with loss. New losses trigger old. New experiences and situations arise to evoke a response of grief. Hillary found that with the recent death of her grandmother: "It hit me hard with my grandmother because it's the loss of my lineage. It's the last tie to my mother. She's the last one who could tell me stories about my mother when she was a child and about when I was a child. It brought back some of the pain of my mother's death."

Over time, we come to recognize the pervasive role mothers play throughout our lives. It may cross the mind of a ten-year-old, "Oh, she won't be there when I get married," but the potent reality only sinks in as the wedding day approaches. Her absence affects your present and future. And no one really takes her place. You establish different—not replacement—relationships.

A young child who doesn't cognitively understand grief can only let it in in small doses. It's too overwhelming. These suppressed, unvalidated feelings of childhood grief reignite in the adult when other losses occur. You're caught in an emotional time warp, experiencing the new grief as both an adult and a child.

"At times of subsequent loss—my father's death, my stepmother's death, the ending of a romance—the grief I experience always seems to me to be deeper than I thought was appropriate," Renee explains. "It's as if I'm still that four-year-old. Even though I understand the deeper layers of grief, even though I know to expect a rough ride, it still seems harder than it should be. I can anticipate the grief and pain, but I still find myself surprised. You expect the intensity of grief to subside over time, but sometimes it still carries a big wallop. The good news is that I do understand it better, so while the intensity is sometimes just as great as in the past, I usually regain my equilibrium much faster, and as I get older, fewer and fewer things trigger it."

Different milestones and transitions in your life may reactivate feelings of loss. Approaching fifty, Renee has gone through various periods when the death of her mother and its meaning has seemed more acute: "I never thought that I'd get out of my twenties and make it past the age she died. I was afraid to have a daughter and have her lose a mother like I did. My last couple of birthdays I've been pretty depressed as I've begun to accept that I won't be a mother. I didn't have a mother or a grandmother, so now I've lost out on three important relationships. Also, I realized that I equate my own birthdays with my mother because she was pregnant with me when she was diagnosed with cancer. I have all this angst tied up in these events."

"Until I passed the age that my mother was when she died," Madonna said, "I kept thinking, 'Here comes my death sentence.' Then once I passed it I breathed a sigh of relief."

MISSING MOMENTS

Some reminders reawaken painful emotions of grief, while others take on a wistful quality. There are times when you simply miss her—wish she could be there to share in the popping of corks or offer encouragement in tough situations. Every Thanksgiving you laugh about the time she forgot to turn on the oven to roast the turkey. Or an event may revive your anger at her for the slights of childhood. Mark off the times or transitions that act as trigger points for you. We've noted some that other women have told us about and left space for you to add whatever is appropriate in your life.

DATE:_____

_____ Surviving past the age she was when she died _____

_____ Living more years without her than with her _____

_____ Anniversary of her death _____

_____ Death of surviving parent _____

_____ Other subsequent death _____

_____ Mother's birthday _____

_____ My birthday _____

_____ Mother's Day _____

_____ Birth in family _____

_____ Parents' anniversary _____

_____ Holidays _____

_____ Wedding or engagement _____

_____ Family gathering/celebration _____

_____ Career or school accomplishment _____

_____ When people tell me I look/sound like my mother _____

_____ When I hear a song I associate with my mother _____

_____ When I look at old photos _____

_____ When I make a recipe I learned from my mother _____

_____ Times of stress or change _____

_____ Emotional setbacks _____

_____ Separations _____

_____ Divorce _____

_____ Illness _____

_____ Moving _____

_____ Approaching menopause _____

_____

_____

"At first I'd block all memories of my mother because thinking about her was too painful," Gail says. "Eventually I let myself think about her, but all I could do was cry. Now I can actually look back and smile." More than a year after his mother's death, Bill Clinton summed it up in a way that motherless women may identify with in their healing: "People grieve in different ways, but my advice is to—not to run away from it. . . . I have pictures of my mother everywhere, and there are still some Sunday nights I halfway pick up the phone to call her, but it isn't a source of pain to me. I miss her still, terribly, but she is now still a part of my life."

Go back through your reminders, and next to the ones you checked off or added, describe in a word or two how you feel at those times. With the passage of time, has your ability to cope with your feelings altered, as happened with Gail? We're not encouraging you to indulge in a morbid preoccupation. But sometimes it can be comforting to acknowledge your mother's presence and to learn that remembering her doesn't or won't always elicit pain and sadness.

When you reexperience the anguish, do you try to keep it private? It's been so long, you might think, isn't it time to be over this? But as you've discovered, there isn't a time limit for mourning. A mother is never banished from memories. When you keep your grief to yourself, you're likely to receive less acknowledgment and comfort, which leads you to feel more misunderstood, isolated, and hopeless. Understanding why and when these feelings arise may not vanquish painful ones, but you may find you're not leaving yourself as open to a sucker punch. (In Part IV, we'll help you come up with alternative ways to cope with grief revisited.)

Sure, death and funerals are anxiety-producing events for everyone, but as Renee suggested, they're apt to revive unhealed wounds for motherless daughters. Ellen Simon, a screenwriter and daughter of playwright Neil Simon, discovered this while writing about her husband's death, which was the basis for the movie *Moonlight and Valentino*. In the process of writing the film, she says she was also reexperiencing the trauma of her mother's death when she was sixteen. At that time, she recalls, "I had to be the strong one." She hadn't cried then, but the tears she was shedding now were for both her husband and her mother.

In *The Mourning Handbook*, Helen Fitzgerald asks, "What part of your early death experience do you bring with you to your adult life now whenever you experience a loss, death or even a major change in your life?" As you think about that question, consider what you've been able to gain from your experience of early loss. Can you speak more freely today about death, or is it still shrouded in silence and secrecy? Are there rituals you've created to help you through a new loss? (We'll discuss rituals more in Chapter 12.)

Gail recalls her grandmother's death, four years after her mother's: "I was eighteen and a freshman away at college. I used school as an excuse not to go to the funeral. Part of me thought I had already been to the funeral of all funerals, why go to this one? It's like once you've sat in the box seats, it's hard to sit in the bleachers. That's what I thought then. Now I know better."

Geraldine teaches children around the same age she was when her mother died. When they asked if she had a mother, she seized the opportunity to tell them what she wished she had been told: "This was the first time I ever shared with the kids that my mother died. I didn't want to scare them, being four-year-olds, but I wanted to be honest with them. I thought they could relate it somehow to other deaths they might have experienced, like a grandparent, which they did. They weren't frightened, and they asked, 'How did she die?' and then answered the question themselves, 'She was very, very sick.' They were fine, but I didn't know if *I* was going to make it through the conversation. When I was done, I knew the next time would be easier."

SAFE PASSAGE: A JOURNAL WRITING EXERCISE

Who do you think you are? Write about the characteristics that define you today in light of all you've been through. If you see yourself as a work in progress, tell what you've accomplished and what's left undone. Express as best you can your true identity, both what you love and what you despise.

DATE:_____

_____

_____

_____

_____

_____

_____

_____

_____

_____

Final Thoughts

In a letter written after the death of her mother, poet Edna St. Vincent Millay said, "the presence of that absence is everywhere." Most likely those words ring very true. You are the sum of all your experiences. Taking their full measure tells you where you are. It's up to you to determine where you're going. We may not know what the future holds, but we know who holds the future.

THEORIES OF RELATIVITY

How Do I Relate?

The family the soul wants is a felt network of relationship, an evocation of a certain kind of interconnection
that grounds, roots and nestles.

—*Thomas Moore*

※ *Bea's Story: I have big issues with feeling rejected and abandoned. That's
why I try and control and cling to my children. Anytime anyone leaves
me, even if it's for a positive reason, I feel it's because they don't want to be
with me. I know it's not healthy, but it's still hard for me to let go.*

※ *Audrey's Story: In my family, we were supposed to pretend that nothing
was wrong—my mother wasn't sick, she didn't die, our family wasn't
having a hard time. So I wasn't in touch with my own feelings, which
affects my relationships with people today. I was never real or honest with
myself or didn't know my own feelings, and it's made it a struggle to relate
to other people.*

TIES THAT BIND

This chapter shifts the focus to how your loss and what followed influence
how you relate to lovers, family, and friends today. So many of our relationships are held hostage to the past. Out of the core beliefs you devel-

oped from your mother's death arise many of the insecurities and destructive behavior patterns you bring to relationships today. Do you find yourself continuing to play a role thrust upon you during your mother's illness or after her death? Are you acting out the wounds of loss and abandonment in your significant relationships? How does her death color your expectations of others? You have already analyzed the factors that shaped your perceptions. Now consider your relationships in light of them.

SECTION I: LIFE WITH FATHER

"It's difficult for my dad and me to talk about her now," says Felice. "It's just different talking to a dad. They don't grasp and understand things the way a mother does." Felice and her father remain close, and although they can discuss many things, her mother's death isn't one of them.

Many fathers and daughters have warm, loving relationships. After a mother's death, the father may have provided a stable home environment, done his utmost to cushion his daughter from the pain of loss, and validated her feelings. But a significant number of the women we interviewed describe their relationships with their fathers as distant, troubled, or nonexistent—so much so that it seems fair to trace many current problems back to what happened between father and daughter before and after the death.

(Before continuing, you might want to reread relevant sections and exercises on family functioning in Chapters 5 and 8. We also suggest analyzing your genogram to see what it reveals, adding any pertinent information as it comes up.)

Lingering resentment at what your father did and didn't do frequently provides the subtext for how you interact today. You may still harbor tremendous anger at him for not sharing information about your mother's illness or death, for grieving not enough or too much, for not being able to see or understand your needs, for expecting you to take your mother's place, for overprotecting you, for not communicating, for being emotionally distant and unapproachable, for just not being there, for being helpless, for not knowing how to nurture you or teach you how to be a woman, for remarrying too soon.

The sounds of silence are what Sharon hears when she's with her dad. After Sharon's mother died, her father steadfastly avoided talking about her, his own feelings, or his children's grief. On the surface the strategy worked: the family picked up on Dad's cue and didn't talk about Mom or their loss. Today Sharon and her father are still unable to communicate about anything meaningful.

Benita describes her relationship with her father as a business deal—financially sound, emotionally bankrupt. "He tries to compensate for his lack of nurturing and support with money," she says. Amanda continues to make sure her father keeps up with family obligations like calling his own mother on Mother's Day: "I'm beginning to realize that people won't judge me by my father's actions. For a long time I felt I had to get in there and make things better." Nora says, "It pisses me off when my father says things like 'If your mother were alive, we'd be divorced by now.' I don't need to know that. I loved my mom, and I thought they had an incredible, loving relationship. I would prefer to remember them how they were when she died."

To help you analyze your relationship with your father, we've adapted some of the questions Susan Forward asked in her book *Toxic Parents*. Check the statements below that pertain to you and your dad.

DATE:_____

_____ My father treats me like a child.

_____ My father treats me more like a wife than a daughter.

_____ I base many of my decisions on what my father's reaction might be.

_____ I have a physical reaction (e.g., headache, stomach distress, allergies) when I have to spend time with my father.

_____ I find I'm anxious or upset when I have to spend time with my father.

_____ I'm very hesitant to express my opinions in front of my father.

_____ My father tries to make me feel guilty.

_____ My father tries to buy my affection.

_____ I feel responsible for my father's well-being.

_____ My father is unable to express his grief.

_____ My father continues to wallow in his pain.

_____ My father doesn't consider my feelings.

_____

_____

The statements you checked off may be connected to your mother's death, or they may simply be impediments to discussing problems honestly and directly.[1] A realistic view of this relationship can help you pinpoint the areas you need to work on. You may not be able to change your father, but you can alter your own perceptions and reactions.

The positive aspects of my relationship with my father are/were:

_____

_____

_____

The negative aspects of my relationship with my father are/were:

_____

_____

_____
[1] If there are issues of abuse or addiction connected to your father or in your family, we once again urge you to seek additional help in dealing with those issues. In the Resources section at the back of this book are agencies you can contact for information.

Message Center

In the Mixed Messages exercise on page 121, we asked you to connect the messages you received from significant people to your perceptions about yourself. Your dad's words or actions may still have the power to push your adult buttons. In this exercise, determine whether ongoing messages you receive reinforce those perceptions.

DATE:_____

Ongoing Messages	My Responses
He doesn't consult me about important family decisions.	*He doesn't think I can handle a difficult situation, and I feel worthless all over again.*
_____	_____
_____	_____
_____	_____

Now consider how issues and events related to your mother's death still color your relationship with your father. If you find yourself fighting the same battles over and over, can you trace the roots of arguments back to these past events? There may be specific incidents or patterns of behavior that continue to cause the friction you experience today.

The significant events or patterns from the past that affect my relationship with my father today are:

My dad withheld information about my mother's illness.

_____

_____

_____

_____

The ways they affect my relationship with him are:

I always think there's more to the story, so I spend more time cross-examining him than in conversation.

_____

_____

_____

_____

_____

Your father certainly may block discussions of a painful past, but sometimes it's your own queasiness about bringing up tough topics that's the impediment. Gaby realizes she's been the one avoiding the conversation: "I don't want to deal with the emotional exchange of talking about my mom because it makes me crazy to see my dad cry."

Ten years after the death, and craving more information about her mother, Starr called a meeting with her father: "We sat in his car and cried for three hours as I asked and he answered questions. Today he blows me kisses when we say good-bye on the phone and, at times, initiates conversation about my mom. It's a little startling to go from totally non-emotional to cute kisses."

Olivia, who's in her mid-twenties, and her father are locked in mutual dependency. She's ready to strike out on her own but afraid that if she moves out against his wishes, she'll lose him too. He's gotten used to Olivia taking on a wife's responsibilities, and though he might not admit it, fears the loss of his daughter. "I feel guilty the second I walk out the door," Olivia says. "It's this ongoing guilt thing when I leave him alone. My father, in his attempt to keep us close, is suffocating. I feel restrained here. I want to escape, but I can't." Liza is a successful thirty-five-year-old lawyer. The minute she walks into her father's house, she reverts to the bumbling ten-year-old she was when her mother died. To her father, she's still Daddy's little girl, too. Together, they keep the myth alive because it's their way of keeping a connection to someone they love.

Before you try to overcome the barriers that obstruct honest discussion with your father, it may help to define them.

Every time I say *anything about my mother,* he says *if she were still alive we'd be divorced by now.*

Every time he says *remember your mother on Mother's Day,* I *get angry and say I remember her all the time.*

DATE:_____

Every time I say/do _____ , he says/does _____

Every time he says/does _____ , I say/do _____.

Every time I say/do _____ , he says/does _____.

Every time he says/does _____ , I say/do _____.

He might be obstinate, the issues seemingly insurmountable, and your communication strained, but with work you may see movement—a little progress. Read your list again, and put an *O* next to those obstacles you believe you can overcome, if only in the smallest way. (We'll discuss communication again in Chapter 11.)

While a father may be guilty as charged, he's also simply human. Pulitzer Prize–winning playwright Neil Simon, whose wife, Joan, died of cancer leaving him with two young daughters, was asked if he regretted anything in his life. "What hurt me the most," he responded, "was not telling Nancy and Ellen about Joan being ill and waiting until it was too late for them to share those last weeks and months with Joan."

In His Shoes

Has analyzing your relationship with your father awakened dormant hostilities—he didn't do this, couldn't do that? Have you ever stopped to turn the tables? Write about the effect of the loss through his eyes. What were/are his fears? Has he been able to mourn or express himself? Does he have any interest in doing so or in helping you to? Could it be that his best way to mother you was to find someone else for the job? Try to be objective as you tell his side of the story.

DATE:_____

_____

_____

_____

_____

_____

_____

_____

_____

_____

_____

What do you think now that you've thought about how he feels? Compassion recognizes that we're all only human. Henry Wadsworth Longfellow wrote:

Believe me, every heart has its secret sorrows,
which the world knows not, and oftentimes we
call a man cold when he is only sad.

SECTION II: SIBLINGS AND THE FAMILY—NOT

"I automatically clicked into playing my mother's role, and I wasn't competent to do that," says Deirdre, who as a teenager took up the emotional reins of her family—a father and two sisters. "I think it damaged the sisterly part of our relationships today. I love them dearly, and I think they love me, but we have terrible difficulties relating. They fell together in what I characterized for years after as their runaway sense of entitlement to any little emotional quirk. The world had to stop for their sorrow. I called them griefheads and thought they were self-indulgent. Yet this is the most important sorrow anyone could have, and why should I have to be the strong one? Today they each have husbands to share their lives. When my dad was dying, my friends would call, and my sisters would resent that I was telling them about him. 'Why do they have to know our business?' my sister asked. Well, who the fuck am I supposed to talk to? Now I have to defend that I'm not emotionally promiscuous because I tell my friends about my life."

Sibling relationships often involve playing out past events in present terms. Death tests the strength of family bonds. Shared adversity should draw you closer, and in some families it did; siblings compensated, at least in part, for the absence of a mother's love and support. "We've all dealt with our mother's death in our own ways," Terry says. "One brother lives with my maternal grandmother as a way of being close to my mom. Another brother and sister are deep into their faith. And then there's one other brother, but I'm not sure how he deals with it. It will always be this tragedy in our lives. No matter what happens, we will remain close, despite not having our mother to hold us together."

But just as often the family realignment strains relationships, emphasizing their weaknesses. It magnifies sibling rivalry since now you are vying for the attention of only one parent. You become each other's targets for misplaced anger and grief. Brenda continues to damn her brother for an incident that happened a decade ago. "I hope my brother feels guilty," she says, recalling his fight with their mother shortly before she committed suicide. Her mother's note said, "It's nobody's fault." Not in Brenda's eyes.

Without a mother to pull a family together, many simply drift apart. "It seemed like she made her kids her life," Candace says. "She was always there when we got home from school. After she died, my dad was lost. The family just split apart. My dad and two brothers came to my graduation, and afterward I couldn't find them anywhere. I had to take pictures with my friend's family. They just left. That never would have happened if my mother was around."

RELATIVE ASSESSMENT

What's your current relationship with your siblings?

DATE:_____

The positive aspects of my relationship with *[name of sister or brother]* _____ are:

_____

_____

_____

The negative aspects of my relationship with *[name of sister or brother]* _____ are:

_____

_____

_____

The positive aspects of my relationship with *[name of sister or brother]* _____ are:

_____

_____

_____

The negative aspects of my relationship with *[name of sister or brother]* _____ are:

_____

_____

_____

Hierarchies are thrown out of whack when a child takes on the role of a parent. Inequities in roles and power change the balance between siblings, who under normal circumstances should be peers. Both sides are bitter. "My parents were divorced, and my father was unavailable," Nicole recalls. "My little sister resented me trying to be a mother, not her sister. I was twenty-one and about to move out to California, and I had to give that up. She took her anger out on me, and I did my best to make her feel guilty." It's hard, they find, to put years of hurt feelings behind them.

"Even though my brothers have no desire to help me through any of this," Lisa admits, "I feel this unbelievable burden or pressure to help them find happiness in their lives. They're so paralyzed. They haven't asked me for help. I just have this need to fix all of them."

TYPE CASTING

Whether problem child or problem solver, prodigy or dreamer, you and your siblings may continue to play or be cast in roles that were affected by your mother's death. Turn back to the Role Call exercise on page 64, and check your place in the family. Are the roles you and your siblings were thrust into ones you continue to play today? Who does what for whom in your family?

Fill in the chart on the next page by describing current roles in the family and how family members feel about them. In the first column, describe the roles. In the second column, give an example of how each role is manifested in the relationships within your family. For example, if you play a caretaker role, you might be the one who has to arrange family holidays.

Then reread your list and decide whether the roles you and your siblings play are by choice or habit. Place a *C* or an *H* by each role to indicate this. Would you characterize these roles as a source of comfort? Guilt? Pleasure? Resentment? Bitterness? Put that description in the third column. In the past, these roles may have satisfied perceived childhood needs. Today they may stifle continued growth and development.

Your siblings may not see the world the same way you do. Maureen says she tries to bring her family together; her youngest sister believes she's merely meddlesome. In the last column, describe how you think your siblings perceive the roles. You may discover that family conflicts arise from exaggerated, overdeveloped roles.

DATE:_____

My Current Role	What I Do	How I Feel	How Siblings Feel
Sister 1's Role	What She Does	How She Feels	How Siblings Feel
Sister 2's Role	What She Does	How She Feels	How Siblings Feel
Brother 1's Role	What He Does	How He Feels	How Siblings Feel
Brother 2's Role	What He Does	How He Feels	How Siblings Feel

RELATIVE STRANGERS

"Are you going through that again?" Lucy's brother responds when she asks him questions about their mother. "I had to work myself up to 'How did Mommy die?' We never discussed my mother other than in passing, like 'Oh, Mom loved chicken.'" In trying to break twenty years of silence with a resistant sibling, Lucy's opening up doors her brother would prefer remained shut. But her need to know outweighs her cold feet about approaching a sibling who would rather forget.

In the same way that the members of your family reacted differently to your mother's death, their present needs and ways of coping may differ from yours. Your inquiries could take them to places they would rather not go. As we've said before, we heal in our own way and time. It's hard to break down those walls.

Audrey discovered that: "I asked my sister if she was going to go to the cemetery when she was visiting her in-laws in Nevada, where my mother is buried, and she said no. She said she thought it was just cheap stimulus for feelings she has anyway. What I got from that was that she didn't want to talk about any of this. So we don't."

"My sister has a painting of my mother that she keeps turned to the wall in her closet," Joanne says. "Last year I asked her for it because she doesn't even look at it. I've dealt with a lot of my pain, and I'd like my children to see their grandmother. We had a huge fight about it. She won't even take a picture of it and send it to me. We've had a cold relationship ever since."

Working through this book means that you've acknowledged your issues and are taking steps to heal. What have your siblings done to cope with some of the same demons? Each of us reacts to grief in a different manner. A harsh judgment about the way your sibling deals with adversity may prevent you from getting to the heart of the matter—the consequences of your mother's death. Put yourself in their place now, and tell how they've dealt with loss and family dysfunction. Your insights may help you to better understand your siblings' perspectives, which will be important when and if you approach them in the future.

DATE:_____

My sister *[name]*_____ deals by:

_____

_____

_____

My brother *[name]*_____ deals by:

_____

_____

_____

My sister *[name]*_____ deals by:

_____

_____

_____

My brother *[name]*_____ deals by:

_____

_____

_____

Relationships are about giving and getting, not always—nor need they be—in equal proportion. Who in your family is making efforts to get answers, remember your mother, celebrate family milestones, or break through destructive patterns?

My nephew recently started to trace our family history because he just had a baby.

DATE:_____

_____

_____

What kind of reaction do they get?

It's opened the topic, and we can talk more easily to him since he's one generation removed and never knew my mother. He brings a clean slate.

_____

_____

For years Paula and her sister didn't talk about their mother's death or much else for that matter. Then their grandmother became ill: "Our relationship was on the level of 'Hi, how're you doing?' or we didn't talk for six months. My grandmother's illness is paving the way for our communication. My sister and I had a three-hour conversation about what had happened in our family. We threw all the garbage out and started over. We were quite honest, and we climbed to a different ground where we could reach out to each other. We'll always argue, but now we can listen instead of fighting constantly."

INNER WORKINGS II

Now we'd like you to reevaluate your family dynamics. In the Inner Workings exercise on page 60, we asked you to examine family interaction before your mother's death by exploring the characteristics that contribute to healthy and unhealthy functioning. Circle any description that applies to your family today.

DATE:_____

Healthy	**Unhealthy**
Talks openly	Verbally abusive
Respects one another	Physically abusive
Has fun together	Has unachievable expectations

Healthy	Unhealthy
Can be honest with one another	Has difficulty resolving conflicts
Encouraging	Sets rigid limits
Shares good times and bad	Can't share negative feelings
Supports goals and desires	Discourages trying new things
Loves you unconditionally	Rejecting
Lets you act silly at times	Erratic and irrational
Marks your accomplishments	Gives you no credit
Can admit mistakes	Does not permit questioning
Can be trusted	Betrays trust
Respects the need for privacy	Has no respect for privacy
Is flexible enough to negotiate	Humiliates members
Listens to you	Nonnurturing
Can express feelings openly	Stifles feelings
Communicates openly	Secretive
Can express anger healthily	Unhealthy in expressing hostility
Makes decisions fairly	Makes arbitrary decisions
Assigns age-appropriate responsibilities	Overloads responsibilities
Shows appropriate affection	Physically removed
_____	_____
_____	_____

In what ways were the responses similar to the first time you did this exercise? Do you see how your family dynamics influence your behavior and your relationships today? As you look back through this exercise, consider whether your family provides a base of support or a source of resistance. Are their names on your Safety Net list? Or did you—perhaps should you—choose others you're close to?

SECTION III: THE OTHER WOMEN

"For years I've had a problem with my stepmother," Ruth says. "She was an evil woman to me but not to my sisters. I think it was because I resemble my mother the most, and she's incapable of dealing with that. She recently sent back all this stuff I had given them when I was a girl, including crystal plates. When I opened the box, they were all broken. I told my sister, and she thought it strange because my stepmother is the best packer in the world. She can pack a box of cookies and not a single one gets broken."

Passions run high about stepmothers. The first question usually asked is "Do you like her?" If she came on the scene soon after your mother's death, or at least too soon for you, she was most likely cast as a villain before she had a chance to prove otherwise. Whether you were the nine-year-old who appreciated having someone there to sew on your Girl Scout patches or the rebellious teen who would have dismissed Mother Teresa, the new addition to your house was a constant reminder that things had changed. Your views may have been influenced as much by the circumstances of her arrival as by her personality. "I don't remember feeling sad about my mom until my dad remarried," observes Fran.

HEIR TO THE THRONE

You may be one of the lucky women who has a perfectly satisfactory relationship with her stepmother: close, warm, and leaving room for memories of your biological mother. If so, you probably don't need to do more than acknowledge what she's done to help you and your family.

But if you don't? Your views may have mellowed since she came on the scene. With 20/20 hindsight, many women come to accept that it was a difficult situation for everyone. Can you recall attempts to reach out or a show of compassion? If she had made it clearer that she wanted and saw you as a true daughter, would you have accepted the invitation? Or do you still see your stepmother as evil incarnate? Deservedly? Are the events of the past the problem in your relationship, or have new affronts been added to old? "To this day," says Emily, "my stepmother resents my father's sister and has a tantrum every time she has to see her." We've listed some of the reasons women continue to have difficulty with their stepmothers. Choose the ones that are generally true for you.

DATE:_____

True	False	My Stepmother...
___	___	Does not understand my feelings about my mother
___	___	Is overly critical
___	___	Competes with me for my dad's attention
___	___	Resents my mother and her family
___	___	Tries to erase all signs and memories of my mother
___	___	Doesn't treat me with respect
___	___	Is abusive
___	___	Interferes in family matters
___	___	Doesn't treat my father well
___	___	_____

You don't have to share a close relationship with a stepmother to realize that she may be of some benefit, if only indirectly, if only grudgingly, to your family. She may be a good companion for your father. Maybe she's the pressure valve for family tensions because you can release anger at her that you won't direct at your father or siblings.

DATE:_____

My stepmother's presence is/was helpful because:

_____

_____

_____

_____

_____

    Did you form relationships with other women who acted as surrogates for your mother? Consider the other women you look up to, even copy, and how they participate in your life as stand-ins for your mother. Tell when and why you turn to these women in your life.

I turn to _my aunt when I want to feel connected to my mother's family and to find out more about the resemblance between me and my mother._

I turn to_____

_____

_____

SECTION IV: INTIMATE STORIES

"As soon as I get into a relationship, I worry that the person is going to die," admits Ruth. "Even though I've been married for six years, I think I'm probably someone who's better off without a relationship because then I'm more capable of taking care of myself. I used to have these gory premonitions if Seth, my husband, was late. I'd picture him lying bleeding on the sidewalk with no one to help him. I never picture him having sex with another woman. Sex would be a relief. I can deal with that. Just please don't die."

Before we delve more deeply into the nature of your romantic ties, do you recognize yourself in the statements below? The ability to form fulfilling adult relationships depends on our feelings of security and self-worth. If these telltale signs of problems strike a familiar chord, then it's likely you're engaging in behavior that sabotages your relationships. Check off the statements that reflect what you believe or what you do in love relationships.

DATE:_____

_____ I'm afraid I'll be rejected or abandoned.

_____ I'm afraid people I care about will die.

_____ I leave people before they leave me.

_____ It's hard for me to let people love or help me.

_____ I frequently wind up taking care of people.

_____ I let other people control me.

_____ I worry about pleasing other people.

_____ I worry that people will find out I'm a fraud.

_____ I'm constantly seeking other people's approval.

_____ I go to great lengths to avoid any confrontation.

_____ I find it hard to trust people.

_____ I'm afraid to let people get close to me.

_____ I set up tests for people.

_____ I'm very needy in my relationships.

_____ _____

_____ _____

Obviously these struggles aren't the sole province of motherless daughters, but because so many of us grew up in an atmosphere colored by loss, an environment that may have been chaotic, unstable, or uncommunicative, they are traps we commonly fall into. As you continue through the rest of this chapter, consider how the statements you acknowledged hinder the development of closer, more satisfying relationships.

LOVE STRIFE

The inability to trust weaves through the relationships formed by motherless daughters. If we were abandoned by the most important person in our lives, the logic goes, how can we expect anyone else to stay with us, care for us, love us? Since it was all snatched away once, why can't it easily happen again? If we weren't told the truth about the circumstances of a mother's death, why should we believe anyone will tell us the truth now? What we've come to trust is that in some way, people will fail us.

"We've been together for sixteen years now, so I eventually started feeling like I could trust him," Bea says of her husband. "Not a hundred percent but a whole lot better than I've ever been able to trust someone else 'cause he's always proved himself to be there for me."

The deep need for love, affection, and nurturing exists side by side with the equally strong dread of being abandoned. Compound that with a lack of self-esteem, and you've got the prescription for problematic relationships. "I've only really had pathological relationships," says Brenda. "I'm always looking for a sense of self-worth based on what I'm getting from a guy. Does he love me, think I'm beautiful, think I'm smart? Is he going to build me up every time I'm feeling low? The test of love is that I could spill my guts and complain about everything that was wrong with me and he would still think I'm OK."

If you judge yourself unworthy of love, you work hard at proving your point by constantly testing the relationship, pushing with demands and outrageous behavior till it reaches the breaking point. When it ends, you feel justified. You were right, you're unlovable.

This questioning of self-worth may stem from feeling intrinsically defective for not having a mother. Our old friends shame, blame, and guilt undermine good relationships. Or you may repeatedly get involved with partners who criticize, treat you badly, or are unavailable. Once again the self-fulfilling prophecy comes true. Feeling bad is habitual; it's not pleasant, but it's certainly familiar.

Looking for the unconditional love you believe a mother supplies places a tremendous burden on an intimate relationship. The object of your affection can never measure up, nor can he or she ever replace a mother. The outcome is predictable: either the demands get so high that your partner leaves, or you get so irritated by not having your needs met—even if unexpressed—that you break it up.

In *The Seven Habits of Highly Successful People*, author Stephen R. Covey stresses the importance of forming relationships that are interdependent: "If I am emotionally interdependent, I derive a great sense of worth within myself, but I also recognize the need for love, for giving and receiving love from others." But motherless women tend to either revert to dependency or try not to rely on anyone.

Your core of need may be painted over with a coat of self-reliance that proclaims, "I'm a survivor, I'm independent, I don't need you." It's there to hide the screams of "I'm afraid to depend on anyone." Up go the barriers to intimacy. Exercising control remains the overriding goal. You choose someone equally aloof, who gives and asks for nothing, or you become involved with someone totally dependent upon you, assuring yourself that they won't leave because they need you too much.

"It's very hard for me to get it through my head that somebody else can be stronger than I am, that I can lean on someone," Deirdre says. "I have to fight hard not to implode and disconnect and retreat into myself. A lot of my relationships are lopsided that way. I don't really believe others have the strengths that I do. In some respect, I feel like I don't deserve any of their strength because after all I have more than my share."

At the other end of the spectrum is the woman seeking someone to take care of her the way a mother looks after her child. You look for partners who will foster your dependence. The attempt to fill the void you feel from a mother's death results in a tango of approach-avoidance. One woman describes it this way: "I back off from my relationships because I feel like I could swallow another person whole. That's how empty I feel."

Sometimes it's a desperate need for security that drives you into someone's arms. Gina says she married the first man who came along who offered any semblance of safety and protection: "I was just looking for some security because it had been so long since I had it. If there was a guy I liked well enough, he had to peel me off."

Do you mother your partner, trying to recreate the mother-daughter relationship in a romantic one? If you choose people you can look after rather than equals, you're probably confusing love and caretaking. You're trying to provide what you missed in the only way you know how to feel wanted and needed. You played mother in your family, so it's a role that fits like an old shoe. You either suffocate a lover or choose an emotional invalid as a partner in this exercise of excessive selflessness.

Uncertainty about how to proceed in intimate relationships can reinforce feelings of inadequacy about being a woman. "I have a certain naïveté about the dynamic of relationships because I never had a person to guide me on those sort of things," Hillary observes. "I didn't have a good example in my parents, and I think I pull back because of lack of knowledge. What I do is try and observe how my friends act and use some of those methods. It's embarrassing."

Augusta is still looking for her mother's approval on sexual matters: "Sexuality was really a taboo thing in our family. I remember this conversation I had with my mother when I was thirteen about making sure no one ever touches you. Now when I'm confronted with any sexual situation with guys I just freeze. I don't do anything. If she were alive and I was in a relationship and decided to sleep with someone, I would tell her. Even if she didn't approve, telling her would clear me. Now that she's not here and I can't tell her, I'm frozen."

Pattern Ending

True love never may run smooth, but it shouldn't be a demolition derby either. Do negative patterns recur in your intimate relationships? Are there things you do to sabotage a relationship or prevent it from even getting started? Is there something in the way you behave that almost guarantees you'll be hurt? Take a moment to review your love life—or its absence—and describe the patterns that emerge time and time again.

What happens in my relationships is:

_____

_____

_____

_____

_____

_____

_____

_____

"Almost everyone repeats negative patterns from childhood in self-defeating ways," explain psychologists Jeffrey E. Young and Janet S. Klosko in *Reinventing Your Life*. "This is the strange truth with which therapists contend. Somehow we manage to create, in adult life, conditions remarkably similar to those that were so destructive in childhood."

LOVING CONTRADICTIONS

What you say you want in a relationship and what you allow to develop don't necessarily coincide. Look at your intimate relationships, and you might come across these contradictions. If you're not involved with anyone, it may be that your fear outruns your desire. For this exercise, compare your theoretical wants with what actually happens.

What I Say I Want	**What I Actually Allow**
A close loving relationship	*I never really commit myself.*
_____	_____
_____	_____
_____	_____
_____	_____

SECTION IV: ON MOTHERHOOD

"I was talking to a woman whose mother died when she was eighteen, and we discussed something that neither of us had ever discussed with anyone else," Elaine recalls. "When our younger sisters were pregnant, we each had a hard time being around them or being there for them. It was tied to our ambivalence and fears about being mothers ourselves."

The decision to have children takes on added meaning for motherless daughters. Obviously myriad factors come under consideration before anyone embarks on parenthood, but it's likely that you view motherhood partly as a way of continuing your mother's legacy, connecting and identifying with her, and finishing a job she couldn't. And one question always lingers: "Will my children be lucky enough to grow up with a mother?" That uncertainty often persuades some women against motherhood.

"My mother's loss has created this issue for me," Maureen confides. "Should I have children? Should I not have children? It's the idea of leaving this child behind and having that child experience the same thing I experienced. That's some heavy shit to lay on a child. I remember asking Doug, 'If I died tomorrow, what would you tell this child about me?' He didn't know what to say. Are most people gonna know what to say?"

DATE:_____

The reasons I decided to have children:

_____

_____

_____

The reasons I decided not to have children:

_____

_____

_____

"When I think about whether or not I will have children, I feel like I'm letting her down," says Audrey, now in her early forties and still undecided about motherhood. "I saw her in that role and wanted to emulate her." Nicole concludes, "I guess I wanted to be a mother because I thought I would feel closer to my mother. When my son was born, I remember crying and feeling bad because those tears weren't of joy for my son, they were for my mother. I wanted my mother. But I would never not want to be a mother."

"It's a huge issue for me because all I ever wanted was a child," says Jill, whose husband remains unsure about having children. "I want it more and more the older I get. I have a couple of years left if I'm lucky, but my husband won't give me an answer. I think about it every period, every time I ovulate. I feel like I had my mother taken from me and now he's taking mothering away from me."

The perception that you lack essential maternal skills surfaces again when you consider parenthood. How do you know how to be a mother if you grew up without one? Nora put off having children because "I was afraid that I didn't know how to mother." Phyllis confronted that issue after her daughter's birth.[2] "When my daughter, Lana, was born, I began to question my ability to mother a daughter since I had been denied the full experience of being the daughter of a mother."

Partially raised in foster homes, Bea adopted a little boy. Her intense longing to have a family of her own because she grew up without one prevailed over any thoughts of failure: "I was so glad to have someone to belong to me. Maybe I was concerned subconsciously, but I loved him so much I knew I would do the right thing."

Daughters of loss often go through motherhood both preparing their children for and protecting them from the possibility that they might grow up without mothers too. "I'm very aware of making memories in case someone should slip away," Joan states. When Kim travels with her husband, she makes sure they take separate planes to ensure that they both don't die in a crash.

It's why Danielle chose not to return to her nursing work: "I'm afraid of leaving a legacy where all my kids remember is me leaving for eight to ten hours a day to go take care of other people. My kids are still young right now, and if I am to leave for some reason, I want them to remember that I did cook dinner every night, that we did sit together. My daughter Tonya is only a year and a half, and she knows that right after she's done eating she has to go to the stairs to go up and get her bath. The kids know this is the way we do things. If I was not to be here tomorrow, my son could tell people exactly what we do and why we do it. That's what's important to me—what my kids will remember—because that's what I remember—my mother being there happy to hear about my day."

From early exposure to loss comes a tendency to overprotect youngsters. "I hold on too tight to the kids," Vanessa concludes. "I love 'em to pieces, and the fear of losing them terrifies me. In thirteen years, I've never ever had a sitter; the kids are always with me. Letting them go into other people's cars, shopping—they always have to be in sight. I know I have to let them do things, but the fear of never seeing them again is so

---

[2]This is from a speech Phyllis delivered to her church congregation as part of a Mother's Day service. The longer text can be found on pages 277–279.

strong. I know in a way I'm hurting them. Half of me wants to let them go, and the other half wants to keep them so close."

Women exposed to sorrow and tragedy at an early age may encourage their children to give healthy expression to their fears, doubts, and concerns. Having had both her parents die at an early age, Lucy understands how her marital difficulties threaten her children's security. "I have a boy and a girl," she says, "and I try and be honest and sensitive to their needs and feelings because I never had anyone who was sensitive to mine. I've been going through a separation with my husband, and I look at them and think, Wow, that's how I felt when I was eight. I think it's good for them to feel, to get it all out and know they'll find support in me."

Phyllis's kids call her a wet blanket because she sees potential disaster lurking behind every situation. If your children were to characterize you as a parent, what do you think they would say?

DATE:_____

My son *[name]*_____would say:

_____

My daughter *[name]*_____would say:

_____

My son *[name]* _____would say:

_____

My daughter *[name]* _____would say:

_____

INNER WORKINGS III

Earlier in this chapter, we asked you to assess family dynamics with your father and siblings and to consider the characteristics that contribute to healthy and unhealthy functioning. Go back to Inner Workings II on page 215, and put a *T* next to any description that applies to the way you are raising your family today.

In comparing your birth family and your current family, you might see how lessons learned—both healthy and not—were used or rejected. For example, are silence and secrets part of the legacy, or is open communication encouraged? If you haven't added your current family to your genogram, do it now.

DATE:_____

The similarities between my birth family and the family I gave birth to are:

_____

_____

_____

The differences between my birth family and the family I gave birth to are:

_____

_____

_____

SECTION V: FRIENDS AND SOCIETY

"About a year and a half ago," Ingrid relates, "I ran into an old childhood friend and found out how many other people had lost a mother when we were in high school. The funny thing is no one ever discussed it."

In cultures where death is truly accepted and acknowledged, people are accustomed to speaking about and mourning the dead. In Mexico on the Day of the Dead, families make the favorite meals of deceased relatives. Here we're reluctant to confront what makes us uncomfortable, and mourning a death years after it occurred is likely to be greeted with cries of "Aren't you over that yet?" rather than understanding and validation. In fact, sometimes we measure friendships by whether or not a mother's death can be comfortably discussed.

Familiar refrains run through the friendships of motherless daughters: trust, secrecy, and fear of disappointment. For some, friends replace the family that let them down. "My friends have become much more important because my family was so disconnected after her death," says Hazel. "They've been my family." The risk lies in investing too much in friends, expecting them to understand something that is beyond their experience.

Ann Landers once offered this advice:

What not to say to mourners:
> Please don't tell me she's in a better place. She isn't here.
> Please don't ask me if I feel better. Bereavement isn't a condition that "clears up."
> Please don't tell me "at least you had her for x years." What year would you like your [mother] to die?
> Please just say you are sorry.
> Please just say you remember her, if you do.
> Please just let me talk if I want.
> Please let me cry when I must.

That doesn't stop the expectations about friendship from running high among motherless women. "At one point," Rae says, "I felt really dependent on other women, really needy, and then very ashamed of that neediness. Because of that, I find myself not opening up to them very much." Abandoned by one woman, we fear being abandoned by all. The discomfort we sense feeds the inadequacies we feel.

We extend a hand in friendship warily, disquieted by the possibility that a friend might not be there for us. "I choose my friends very carefully," says Nellie. "My coworkers say I'm a prickly porcupine, when I know inside I'm a marshmallow. I keep people at arm's length to avoid getting hurt."

Commonly, the way friends earlier in your life dealt with your mother's death sets the tone for future relationships. "It made me feel different than my friends, and I resented them for still having mothers," says Estelle. Frannie agrees that the scars of childhood have made it "harder for me to have close relationships." Still in her twenties, Augusta believes the issue of her mother's death six years ago continues to set her apart from her peers: "I had a friend who was incredible in college and was able to deal with me so well. A year ago we were arguing about something, and she said, 'I don't think you really want to get over your mother's death.' It hit really hard, and I kept thinking, Did she say that so I would pull away, or was it true? She's twenty-four and wants to go to happy hours, hang out, date, and this is just too heavy now. Why would somebody want to hear all of this stuff?"

Fearing the subject will put people off and make them—and us—uncomfortable, we don't know quite what to say. "Seth told me I have a pat answer when people ask about my mom," Ruth offers. "I have, like, three or four lines. 'My mother died when I was blah, blah, blah.' I get through it, and that's the end of it." Gaby adds, "Telling people the first time is such a pain in my ass. I hate dealing with that. Part of me wants to tell everybody, but then the other part is so frustrated because they don't already know."

Do you tell people your mother died? What do you say? To whom? How do you approach the subject?

DATE:_____

The circumstances under which I discuss my mother's death or my continuing grief with friends are:

_____

_____

_____

What I say is:

_____

_____

_____

When I do, it brings up feelings of:

_____

_____

_____

"I have always made friends more easily with men than with women," says Phyllis. "Often I sit in a room full of women feeling like a foreign creature." Phyllis has, like many women raised by a man, "problems owning the term *woman*." Such discomfort often comes off as coldness, and our camouflage of independence is mistaken for aloofness. We're more at home with the typically less emotional friendship of men.

GREAT EXPECTATIONS

Think about the people you allow yourself to be close to and the qualities you seek in a friend. Loyalty? Trust? Simply a good time? Someone you can talk to? Someone you don't have to talk to? These traits and what we're willing to invest in our friendships often reflect what we're trying to deal with—or avoid. They reveal what we think is important in ourselves.

DATE:_____

What I expect from a friend:

_____

_____

_____

What I bring to a friendship:

———————————————————————————

———————————————————————————

———————————————————————————

A seventeen-year-old wrote a letter wondering how she could help a friend whose mother had recently died. "I don't quite know how to deal with it," she wrote, "let alone what I can do to ease the pain for my friend. I know she needs me, but she doesn't give me any clue when I reach out to her. I keep thinking her mother will never see her daughter graduate from college, she won't be at her daughter's wedding, or holding her hand through her pregnancy, or even ever be a grandmother. This seems so completely unfair to me."

SAFE PASSAGE: A JOURNAL WRITING EXERCISE

In the quotation that opens this chapter, Thomas Moore speaks of "the family the soul wants." Family isn't only blood relations but the wider circle of meaningful people in your life. What constitutes the family your soul wants?

DATE:_____

———————————————————————————

———————————————————————————

———————————————————————————

———————————————————————————

———————————————————————————

———————————————————————————

———————————————————————————

_____

_____

_____

FINAL THOUGHTS

Our emotional connections tie us to joy and pain. They reveal the tug-of-war between our need for love and encouragement and the defensive behavior that prevents us from getting what we want. What's important to understand as you move toward reworking and building new relationships is that trust in yourself helps you to trust others.

Part Break III

Having gotten this far, you probably have a clearer understanding of how you became who you are today. While it's the nature of a self-help workbook to focus on issues and problems that need resolving, perhaps overemphasizing shortcomings, in the process we don't want to neglect the strength and resources you've developed. They're commendable and important. Acknowledge your spirit and the determination that this work affirms.

Giving Thanks

We hope the process of closely examining your relationships helped you discover the people who have tried to love you, be there for you, teach you about yourself and the world, and, even if inadvertently, serve as role models. They deserve thanks and acknowledgment. If you're embarrassed to do this in person—or think that they might be—look for other ways to accomplish the mission: search out the 45 record you know your sister would give her eye teeth for; offer to look after your brother's kids so that he can have a weekend getaway; or scribble a note to the local paper when you learn that the English teacher who took you under her wing is retiring.

Who I Need to Thank	*What* I Have to Acknowledge Them For	*How* I Can Do It

Who I Need to Thank	*What* I Have to Acknowledge Them For	*How* I Can Do It

Apology Accepted

You may have also come up with people to whom you owe an apology. This isn't an exercise in self-blame but a way of accepting your actions and trying to move on. You aren't apologizing for who you are but for actions that require "I'm sorry."

Who I Need to Apologize To	*What* I Have to Apologize For	*How* I Can Approach Them

Why I Resist	*When* I Will Try to Apologize	*What Happened* When I Did

Who I Need to Apologize To	*What* I Have to Apologize For	*How* I Can Approach Them
Why I Resist	*When* I Will Try to Apologize	*What Happened* When I Did

Memory Bank

Have you come up with more questions that cry out for answers? If so, document them here.

What I Need to Know	*Who* Might Have the Answer	*How* I Can Approach Them
Why I Resist	*When* I Will Try to Ask	*What Happened* When I Asked

Are there other sources you need to consult? List them below.

Source _____

Source _____

Source _____

Key Passages

If you haven't selected and recorded your Key Passages, go back to your Safe Passage Journal entries and enter them here.

Chapter 9

_____

_____

Chapter 10

_____

_____

The journey continues, but think about how far you've already traveled, the questions you've asked, and the soul-searching you've done. As a touchstone to assess where you've been, how you feel, and what you've accomplished in the third part of the workbook, simply reflect on the questions below.

How did I feel as I worked through these chapters?

How do I feel right now?

What surprised me about my responses or insights?

What was hardest to do?

What do I need to come back to?

What have I accomplished?

What can I do for myself right now?

_____

_____

_____

PART IV

WHO WILL I BE?

Try to strike that delicate balance between a yesterday that should be remembered and a tomorrow that must be created.

—*Earl A. Grollman*

We've asked you to take a good hard look at yourself and to acknowledge how your mother's death and your past history influence your life today. However, yesterdays are not necessarily indicative of tomorrows; they're merely signposts of where you've been. Who do you want to be, and what do you need to do to get there? The last part of this workbook is devoted to the ongoing journey to a future that recognizes the meaning of your loss, acknowledges that the pain may recur, but openly embraces the opportunity for growth, love, and a life fulfilled.

Yes, it takes stamina to smash through the barriers that result in stunted emotional growth, tainted relationships, and self-limiting behavior. More important, though, you must trust the indomitable spirit inside you to help in the work of healing and growing. Within you lies the answer; within you resides the strength. The healing process has already begun with the unfolding of your story. The courage to believe in yourself will ensure that it continues.

FUTURE CONDITIONAL
The Story Continues

> Destiny is not a matter of chance, it is a matter of choice;
> it is not a thing to be waited for, it is a thing to be achieved.
> —*William Jennings Bryan*

✷ *Janette's Story: I feel like the themes that get laid down early on in your life are more or less your themes. And as you write the variations, as you grow up and grow older, you want as much balance, as much interest, and as much variety as possible. But you also want to own up to what your themes are. I want to learn how to accept the loss, but I don't want to throw the baby out with the bath water. I have learned from my loss, and I want to use the strengths I have to enrich my life.*

✷ *Sonya's Story: Since I got through all those years of negative emotions, my life has been constantly changing. I think that we all have a core that doesn't change. All we can do is get rid of the bullshit, but first you have to realize what it is, and that takes all of my being. It's a life's work. Clarity is a new thing for me, and it keeps unfolding.*

THE HEART OF HEALING

Elaine told us a story about a six-year-old girl whose mother had died: "The girl drew a picture of her heart that was colored with varying degrees of shading. The outermost part of the heart was a very light shade of red. That was the part of her heart, the child explained, that had already healed. The part next to that, closer to the center, was a slightly darker shade of red. It was the part that was healing now but not fully healed. Closer still to the heart's center was an even darker shade of red. The young girl explained that this was the part of her heart that had not yet begun to heal, but she knew that it would in the future. The center of the heart was colored a very deep red. This was the part of her heart that would never heal."

The wisdom of a six-year-old captures the essence of much of this book. This exercise provides a clear illustration of your emotional state, how far you've come, and where you're going. Shade your heart the way the six-year-old did.

It's time to switch from what did happen—or at least what you think happened—to what *can* happen. From here on in, you decide how your story will continue. You supply the dream. "Most of us have the tendency to approach growth as a process of overcoming problems as opposed to a process of creating something we want," write David Gershon and Gail Straub in *Empowerment*. It's your job to figure out not only how to play the hand you've been dealt but how to shuffle those cards to create a reality full of possibility.

As a motherless woman, there's no denying you've been shaped by a traumatic event. You have to brave that storm. There's no easy way around it, you have to acknowledge and walk through it. But your mother's death shouldn't be an excuse for quitting on your dreams. Playing the victim isn't going to change the facts, nor is it productive. The story we strive to tell is not of victimization or denial but of triumph.

There's no magic potion that will take away pain or sadness. What we offer here are some suggestions for healing through forgiveness and acceptance, creating better coping skills for the next time the blues get you down, transforming self-limiting beliefs, and cherishing the abundance you have. By getting this far, you've done a lot of that already.

YOU CAN'T CHANGE THE FACTS, YOU CAN CHANGE THE FICTION

There are things you can change, and there are things you can't. You have to accept what you can't change and work on the rest. You can't bring your mother back. You can't relive your childhood. You can't be responsible for other people's behavior. You can be responsible for yourself, and you can take charge of your life from this point on.

Mikki came slowly to the realization that her life rested in her own hands: "I waited for my family to take care of me, and they didn't. Now I know that no one else can take my pain away. It's up to me. Acceptance is huge. For so long I denied the loss. It's learning that there's always going to be that soft brown spot in the apple."

DATE:_____

What I can't change:

_____

_____

_____

BAGGAGE CLAIM

"I did not know how heavy my baggage was until I stopped carrying it," someone once said. You pinpointed your baggage in the Roll the Tape Again exercise on page 173, when you rated the limiting attitudes and beliefs that plague you today as a result of your mother's death. Turn to that page, and add the numbers in the columns on the right. Think of those numbers as pounds. The total represents the emotional baggage you carry around.

The total baggage I carry is _____ pounds. Surprised?

Pack your suitcase by transferring the items you most want to work on, including the rating you assigned them, until the suitcase holds half your baggage. The load you carry should represent your priorities. You'll get to the rest of your baggage later—but not too much later. If you feel you're at a time in your life when you're ready to tackle your biggest issues, good for you. However, the most disruptive beliefs may not be the wisest ones to chip away at first. We are inspired most by results. The loss of a few pounds is often encouragement enough to continue a diet. So start with something manageable, and see how even small efforts can produce change.

lbs.
lbs.
lbs.
lbs.
lbs.
lbs.
lbs.
lbs.
lbs.

Total

If you've been carrying this baggage around for a long time, not to worry. It's never too late to change. Eleanor started working on her mother-loss issues two years ago when she was seventy-five: "There's still so much stuff, but I'm working through it. I began to write. I write my prayers. I write my gratitude. I bare myself." Billie knows the direction she needs to take: "I want to work on not feeling so sad. Somehow there's always a sadness that creeps in, even when I'm feeling happy or having a good day. I also don't like feeling distrustful of people. I think they really don't care about me, therefore I don't give much of myself to them. I would like to work on having these two areas change for me."

DO IT OR ELSE

Once you've identified areas you'd like to work on, it's time to make actual changes. "Understanding is one thing and action is another," advises Barbara Sher in *Wishcraft: How to Get What You Really Want.* You've gotten this far. What's it going to take for you to continue? How about the fact that you're not alone, that there are many other women working through the same loss issues? Consider the benefits change will bring in all aspects of your life. Think about the consequences of not changing.

DATE:_____

What price do I pay if I don't change?

_____

_____

_____

_____

_____

What do I stand to gain from change?

_____

_____

_____

_____

_____

Remember, insight comes quickly, but change comes slowly. The longer you wait to invest in yourself, the longer it will take to reap the dividends. Try to find the balance between being too hard on yourself because you're not seeing results fast enough and finding excuses to let yourself off the hook. Have compassion for yourself, but keep pushing.

CHECKLIST FOR CHANGE

Change takes more than wishful thinking. It takes perseverance. Backbone, if you will. We've provided some pledges for you to make to yourself before you begin the next phase of your journey. Resistance is natural. If changes were easy, you would have made them long ago. When you're having a tough time following through, consult these guidelines to put you back on course.

- I have been honest with myself in determining the problems I want to work on.

- I take responsibility for my life.

- I will allow myself to be vulnerable.

- I will start with one manageable task and build a sense of mastery.

- I will trust that I have the answers.

- I accept that I am imperfect.

- I will seek help—from a confidante or counselor—if I have trouble dealing with my problems.

- I am committed to actively confronting my problems.

- I am willing to forgive myself.

- I will consider forgiving others.

- I will try to find appropriate means to express my feelings.

- I will accept who I am.

- I believe my efforts will bring about change.

- I will acknowledge change, however small.

- _____

- _____

In Self-Defense

When you look in the mirror, what do you see? Is it an accurate reflection or one distorted by your perceptions and beliefs? It's likely that certain themes in this workbook have cropped up time and time again. Issues of trust, shame, self-esteem, control, abandonment, and guilt constitute the common legacy of motherless daughters. You've probably been reinforcing self-defeating views of yourself and the world for years. Do you continue putting yourself down with phrases like "I'm worthless" and then choose the facts to prove it? Stop to think. Have you convicted yourself without a fair trial? Try holding those beliefs up to more intense scrutiny, and present the arguments against them. On one side, write down what you think your negative qualities are, and on the other, try to disprove them.

DATE:_____

Statement	Rebuttal
I never learned how to be a mother.	_Mothering is about loving and caring, and I can provide that._
	I'm good with my nieces and nephews.
	There are books and classes that I can learn from.
	Having a mother isn't a prerequisite, because there are some women who grew up with mothers who have rotten kids.

_____   _____

_____   _____

_____   _____

_____   _____

_____   _____

_____   _____

_____   _____

_____   _____

_____

    Refuting assumptions lets you see yourself from another viewpoint. We all have flaws and imperfections, but yours may not be as glaring as you think. You just may be good enough. Or you may not have as far to go as you might think. As you whittle away at these issues, come back to this exercise and see what differences an altered perspective offers.

    This technique also works well when confronting the vestiges of guilt. Go back to the Guilt/Regret exercise you completed on page 92. Look over the statements you marked with a *G*. Do you still feel guilty about those situations? If so, transfer the *G*'s to this page and start the debate.

DATE:_____

Statement	Rebuttal
I shouldn't have fought with her.	*Teenagers tend to be rebellious.*
	Parents and children often fight.
	Fighting didn't cause her death.
	She would forgive me.
	She wouldn't want me to feel guilty.

_____   _____

                            _____

                            _____

                            _____

                            _____

_____   _____

                            _____

                            _____

                            _____

Guilt is a powerful emotion. If you still feel your guilt is justified, instead of having it eat away at you, look for constructive ways to diminish it. You may need to express your deep remorse through a letter, a ritual (we'll talk more of this in Chapter 12), or by making amends symbolically, like working on behalf of a charitable cause. For instance, if your mother died of breast cancer, you might want to devote time to an organization that fights this disease.

Face Value

If it's too hard to see beyond your beliefs, you need to call in an outside expert. In the Hearsay exercise on page 179, we asked you to recall what other people have said about your strengths. Now we suggest you actually ask them. Whether by letter, phone, or face to face, call on someone you love and trust. It might be someone you listed in your Safety Net. Ask that person to come to your defense. Tell them it's their job to describe your attributes as honestly and specifically as possible. "You're nice" or "You're a good friend" is too vague. You're after something like "You're a good friend *because* you're a compassionate listener, you're never judgmental, and you make me laugh at myself."

Your job is to listen carefully to what they have to say and think, Thank you, instead of, Who, me? Try not to play your negative tapes. Take their words at face value. Write down what they tell you in the space provided.

DATE: _____

WHAT PEOPLE SAY:

_____

_____

_____

_____

_____

If you don't feel comfortable enough to do this, consider it an assignment for the future. Enlisting others and asking for help are not signs of weakness but of strength and can only aid you in the healing process. Haven't you been alone with your loss long enough?

OPEN CHANNELS

Shakespeare advised us to "give sorrow words," and we have urged you—in the exercises and in your journal entries—to tell your story. The next step is telling others. Confiding helps sever shame's hold over us. Dale Larson writes in *The Helper's Journey,* "Our self-concealing behavior tends to influence our attitudes toward ourselves and we conclude that there is some part of ourselves that is in fact unlovable or else we would reveal it. The only way out of this vicious cycle is through disclosure to a caring and empathetic confidante."

Telling your story provides another path toward self-discovery and opens the door to validation and compassion. We have all felt inadequate, hopeless, as if we didn't belong. Hearing yourself speak breaks the ice and fosters intimacy in your relationships. Each disclosure brings the possibility of being more fully understood. It may be a battle at first, but finally it's a relief to just do it.

Obviously you don't need to share your life experience with anyone and everyone. You're looking for trust and support, not simply an ear. You may have already confided in family, friends, or lovers. You may want to share your story with a therapist, participate in group therapy, or seek the support of other motherless women.

"In our very open society," psychologist Maxine Harris explains, "there are only a few things we will not discuss easily with one another—unfortunately death is one of them. People feel awkward talking about their loss, especially if it was a long time ago. And others—even close friends—feel awkward listening. Don't let that awkwardness stop you. . . . Once you are out of the closet yourself, you will discover that there are others like you, others who can understand exactly how you feel because they've been there themselves." You do run the risk that there will be people who don't want to hear about what you're going through, who won't really understand, or who will try to comfort you with "I know just how you feel" when they have no idea. Moreover, someone going through her own crisis may not be anxious to hear about your grief. But there is a right time and the right person. Healing happens when you share your experiences.

START THE CONVERSATION

In *Family Secrets*, John Bradshaw writes about the price we pay for evading issues with our families: "The costs are paid in other relationships, usually in relationships with our current family members—spouses and children. The intensity we avoid with someone in our first family we bring to someone in our second—more often than not to our children."

"I need to talk to you" can be difficult to say. Silence, resentment, anger, stubbornness, shame, criticism, and intolerance—the dirty laundry has been piling up for years. It has prevented essential conversations. Waiting for someone else to broach the subject hasn't worked.

It's time to say what you need to say and ask the questions you need answered.

Your goal may be to feel comfortable enough to talk about your mother or to gain support for your belated grief work. You may need to express resentment or disappointment at how you were, and perhaps continue to be, treated. You may want to apologize for your own misdirected anger or for blaming others for events that were beyond their control. You may want to thank them for being there when you needed them. Part Break IV provides a place for you to record this information.

The pressure that you've worked hard at pushing down all these years may come out in a trickle or a torrent. The point is not to win an argument or to exact revenge but to find an appropriate means of expression. Carefully approach issues that push buttons. Work toward laughing at the things that irk you now or bothered you in the past. Try to compromise and find a new way of communicating to prevent the continuation of destructive patterns. Ask yourself where your world and needs intersect with those of others. Search for the common ground. Ideally, each of you comes to the table level-headed, though what you each have to say may be considerably different. You might begin by admitting that you haven't agreed in the past. The important thing is to start the conversation.

REFORMATTING YOUR FAMILY

Trying to change family interactions that have been frozen for years is a formidable task. "I've come to realize," Greta relates, "that my family is doing the best they can, they're just very limited. I was going to get approval, acceptance, understanding, compassion, direction, and guidance from people who couldn't give it. You can't get an orange in a hardware store."

Manage your expectations. Let go of the fantasy that one conversation will turn on the light. You may be tilting at windmills. If belittling and minimizing are family traits, anticipate them now. As an adult you can handle the situation better than you could as a child. Over the long haul, your relationships may progress, but be prepared for a painstakingly slow process. Or family members may remain stuck in one place. Take satisfaction in making the effort, and consider trying again later.

Sometimes you have to tiptoe up to your goal. That's fine. Choose what works for now. A face-to-face discussion may not be necessary or possible. A person you need to confront may no longer be alive. A phone call, a letter, words spoken into a tape recorder—the first move is up to you. The power is in the process.

OUT RAGE

After her father died, Mercedes was unsure whether she wanted to keep in touch with her stepmother, who had been a particularly spiteful woman: "For years I had problems with her. She was an immature woman, incapable of dealing with me. At the funeral we sat on different sides of the church." If there's someone you'd rather not have contact with, write them a letter anyway, for your own benefit. You don't have to send it, but you do need to release those feelings.

DATE:_____

The reasons I want to write them off:

_____

_____

_____

_____

_____

CALL WAITING

Analyzing the reasons you avoid essential discussions or procrastinate can pave the way toward action. When you know why you're reluctant to act, you can develop a game plan to overcome those obstacles.

DATE:_____

What's preventing me from starting the conversation?

_____

_____

_____

How I can work toward starting the conversation?

_____

_____

_____

    If you're not sure how to begin, try jump-starting the process by completing the following sentences as honestly as you can. Transfer your answers to Part Break IV.

    I was upset when you *married Lisa* because *I didn't want someone moving into our house and taking Mom's place. I hadn't even really accepted that Mom was dead, and here you were in love with somebody new.*

    I get angry *when you refuse to discuss Mom* because *it feels like you're denying part of me.*

To *[name or relationship]*_____: I was upset when you _____because

_____

_____

To *[name or relationship]*_____: I get angry when you _____because

_____

_____

To _[name or relationship]_____: I was hurt when you
_____because

_____

_____

To _[name or relationship]_____: I was glad that you
_____because

_____

_____

To _[name or relationship]_____: I need to tell you that

_____

_____

_____

To _[name or relationship]_____: I'm sorry that

_____

_____

_____

What do you think will happen during your heart-to-heart? Write out your fantasy as well as the worst-case scenario. Seeing the extremes might tone down unrealistic expectations and prepare you for all possibilities.

When I talk with _my dad,_ he will _start to cry, say he was a rat for remarrying so soon, and divorce my stepmother._

When I talk with _my dad,_ he will _scream at me and tell me again that he doesn't want to go to heaven because my mother might be there._

DATE:_____

When I talk with _____, he/she will_____

_____

_____

When I talk with _____, he/she will_____

_____

_____

FROM FORGIVING TO GIVING

Expressing your anger in some fashion directs you toward forgiveness. Let's clarify a few things. The idea of forgiveness is not to excuse someone's behavior but to accept that we are all imperfect and make mistakes. You won't necessarily become closer to your dad or sister or lover by forgiving them their trespasses. But forgiving a wrong robs it of the power to continue weighing you down. Barbara Lazear Ascher tells of reaching that conclusion: "That night I realized that the offender might not 'deserve' to be forgiven, but that we, the offended, deserve to forgive, to be free of the burden of bearing a grudge, the memory of harm. By not forgiving, we compound the inflicted pain. . . . We forgive not out of weakness but out of strength. To let go of anger takes courage."

OK, you still may not want to or be ready to forgive someone you believe caused irreparable damage. It's your decision. In Part Break IV, record the names of people you can forgive—now or in the future—and those you find yourself unable to, at least for now. Forgiving takes time. The words "I forgive you" may only pay lip service to their meaning. Expressing how you feel—whether to the object of your rage or on a mountaintop—releases a chunk of stored up anger and hurt.

The power of forgiveness extends to you. Forgive yourself for not being able to save your mother, for wishing she would die, for not grieving sooner. You were coping as best you could. You were a child, a teen, a young woman. You didn't possess the resources and skills you have today. Give yourself a break. You've struggled and made it through.

COPING WITH COPING

We've all found ways of dealing with the ups and downs life poses. The question asked earlier was "At what price?" The survival skills that may have protected you at an earlier stage in your life may no longer be worth holding onto. In Chapters 8 and 9, you evaluated your coping mechanisms. We asked you to consider not only the needs they met but their beneficial and damaging aspects. Some coping mechanisms do more harm than good. Now is the time to come up with alternative ways to meet those needs.[2]

You don't have to tackle all your destructive patterns at once or change a lifetime's behavior overnight. Remember, we rely on crutches to get by. The idea is to weed out and control the more self-destructive ones. Pick some first steps to take. Break behaviors down into bite-size pieces, and acknowledge small victories.

TAKING YOURSELF TO TASK

Select a coping mechanism that you would like to change from the Tool Shed exercise on page 135. List specific steps you could take, each a modest improvement on the last, that might lead to a better way of dealing with your needs. If you're having trouble figuring out how to accomplish any of those intermediary goals, break them down into smaller steps. Give yourself a realistic timetable. If you catch yourself procrastinating, remember what's at stake. En route to your eventual goal, reward yourself for making progress. Take credit for your triumphs.

As an example, we've chosen Sue Ann, who struggles with depen-

---

[2]If you're coping with problems of substance abuse, eating disorders, or involvement in abusive relationships, we urge you to seek professional guidance for these issues. The Resources section at the back of this book includes organizations that may be able to help get you started.

dency issues: "I've never learned to mother myself," she laments. "I've stayed in relationships and jobs way beyond the point that they were good for me and sometimes to the stage where they became destructive. I've nurtured a kind of deprivation regarding doing nice things for myself. It's hard for me to buy new clothes, get a massage, or do something special just for me. This inability to mother myself includes not knowing how to soothe myself in times of stress or anxiety."

Here's how Sue Ann might proceed in trying to alter her overdependency.

Coping mechanism I want to change: _Overdependency._

1. _Understand the origins of my behavior._

   a. Ask my sister about my mother's erratic behavior.

   b. Go back and read relevant chapters.

   c. Look over exercise answers.

2. _List the ways I depend on others._

   a. Review past relationships and ask myself what I got out of staying.

   b. Ask my husband for input.

3. _Note the circumstances when the behavior occurs._

4. _Try changing my response in one of those situations._

5. _Seek help from a professional or organization if necessary._

6. _Try changing responses in more situations._

   Result: See strengths within myself.

DATE:_____

Coping mechanism I want to change: _____

1. _____

   _____

2. _____

_____

3. _____

_____

4. _____

_____

5. _____

_____

Result: _____

GOAL ORIENTED

Do you have other, more concrete goals, like going after a promotion, moving out of your father's house, or finishing decorating your home? Do you keep postponing them or saying you're not up to the job? Or do you lurch from project to project without completing anything? If so, your inaction may be linked to (1) inertia because you're waiting for a mother's OK, (2) fear of growing up because it severs a connection to your mother, (3) discomfort at surpassing her accomplishments.

DATE:_____

What are goals I had but haven't accomplished?

_____

_____

_____

Why?

_____

_____

_____

What are projects I've started but haven't finished?

_____

_____

_____

Why?

_____

_____

_____

If you know what's holding you back, you've created the opportunity to move forward. Take a couple of goals or important projects and assign each one a completion date. Set it for next week or next year, but be sure to set one. You may need to change completion dates, the steps along the way, or the goal itself as windows of opportunity open or close; the dates and steps you choose are meant to help you keep on track, not set you up for failure. But if you keep putting things off and changing your completion dates, be sure to ask yourself why. Make sure the goals you list are your own, that you're not trying to live up to the expectations of others.

Choose a goal to start working on today. Then break it down into specific steps, each with its own completion date. Sometimes a goal seems so far away that you're not sure how to proceed. In that case, instead of starting at the bottom of what seems like an impossible mountain to scale, imagine that you've already reached the peak and are simply retracing your steps. For instance, if the goal is moving into your own apartment, start with having found the dream apartment and work from there.

My Goal	**Completion Date**
Move into my own affordable apartment with fireplace, exposed brick, southern exposure, skylights, huge windows, high ceilings, great water pressure, and quiet, fun neighbors.	*March 1, 1998*

My Goal	**Completion Date**
Start packing.	*February 17, 1998*
Schedule movers.	*February 16, 1998*
Sign a lease.	*February 15, 1998*
Find an apartment.	*January 15, 1998*
Investigate real-estate sections of newspapers.	*December 15, 1997*
Start schmoozing superintendents.	*November 15, 1997*
Tell friends my goal.	*November 1, 1997*
Start saving toward my apartment.	*Immediately*

DATE:_____

My Goal	**Completion Date**
_____	_____
_____	_____
_____	_____
_____	_____
_____	_____

My Goal	Completion Date
_____	_____
_____	_____
_____	_____
_____	_____
_____	_____

SAFE PASSAGE: A JOURNAL WRITING EXERCISE

"I would be happy if—" How many times have you said that? Forget the excuses—right or wrong, they'll hold you back. Toss out the fantasy of what might have been, and begin to construct the world of what can be. The conditions for your future rest in your hands. "I can be whoever I want to be because—" You fill in the blanks. Write about what you've accomplished, can achieve, and perhaps can reclaim from your past.

DATE:_____

_____

_____

_____

_____

_____

_____

_____

_____

_____

FINAL THOUGHTS

This is a great time to go back to the Part Breaks. If you haven't already begun key information gathering, take the initial plunge. If asking questions is too tough to start with, try going to sources like public records, baby books, photo collections, or official agencies.

The aim of this chapter is to spur you toward action. Since you can't climb a mountain in a single bound, take as many steps as you need to reach your ultimate goals. Mastering the small stuff builds the confidence to overcome bigger obstacles. It helps uncover the courage and determination you need to assume responsibility for your life. Call it the domino effect, ripples in the pond, whatever, but with each success, we rewrite our destiny.

DAYS OF RECKONING
Honor Thy Mother

In remembrance lies the secret of redemption.
—*The Baal Shem-Tov*

※ *Joanne's Story: I want to make sure that my mother is not forgotten—to mention her in conversation with my family, tell the babies how important she was to me. That's my mission, to keep her memory alive. That's how I feel about her. I feel that if she's forgotten, then we will have totally lost her.*

※ *Doris's Story: I honor her most by trying to be the daughter that she wanted and raised. Not by living or doing what she did but by being someone she would be proud of. I'm having a mass for the ten-year anniversary of her death, and I'm having her friends come. I want to videotape it for my children because it's going to be a lot of stories and fun. She was one of those people that everyone has a funny story about. It's the way I want to honor her because she was always happiest surrounded by family and friends.*

Even in her absence, your mother is a presence in your life. Earlier, we asked you to reconstruct the image of your mother, to review your relationship and to reassess how her loss has affected, and continues to affect, your life. This gives expression to your grief and accommodates the loss into your life. When you keep your mother's memory alive, you honor her and yourself. Completing this workbook won't dispel periodic longing and heartache. That's just not possible. What it can do is help you cherish her gifts and begin to heal the wounds of the past.

"A coworker is now taking care of her little brother because both of her parents are dead," says Robyn. "She asked me how she could help him. We had a long talk, and I told her not to shy away, not to make Mom a bad word. Let him talk and let him remember. Openly remember." This chapter focuses on integrating the loss into your life. In *Continuing Bonds,* the editors write, "We propose that rather than emphasize letting go, the emphasis should be on negotiating and renegotiating the meaning of loss over time. While the death is permanent and unchanging, the process is not. . . . People are changed by the experience; they do not get over it, and part of the change is a transformed but continuing relationship with the deceased. . . . Accommodation does not disregard past relationships, but incorporates them into a larger whole."

This runs contrary to what most of us either were told or believed. In the American model, you're supposed to let go of the past and disengage from the deceased. However, many other societies have long recognized a continuing relationship with the dead. In rural Japan, the dead remain an integral part of daily life. They're considered a respected presence that may offer more comfort and counsel in death than in life. "What is most striking about the Japanese way of death is that there is no stark, impenetrable wall to divide the living from the dead," the *New York Times* reported.

In the Mexican tradition of commemorating the Day of the Dead, families honor and celebrate the dead. They strew marigolds along the paths to houses so that the deceased can find their way home, prepare a favorite meal, and share a bread called *pan de los muertos.* Far from being a solemn occasion, it's joyous and festive.

We honor dead presidents on our money and fallen heroes on street signs, yet we neglect those we know and love. American culture offers little in the way of homage on an individual level. We remain a death-denying society. Our attempts to shield ourselves from its reality only isolate us from our feelings and from each other. No wonder we're confused about the persistence of grief.

> *"In the past, daily reminders of mortality kept the dead and thoughts of dying keenly in the minds of the living. Today many Americans prefer to keep death at a distance."*
>
> —*From* Memory and Mourning: American Expressions of Grief, *a 1996–98 touring exhibition exploring the history of the grieving process in America through historical artifacts*

Remembering and gathering information about your mother as part of a complex familial and social matrix, a woman with a history of her own, aids the mourning process. Accommodation requires coming to terms with the full human being you're mourning, identifying all of your losses, and constructively expressing the associated feelings.

DIALOGUE WITH THE DEAD

More than likely, you have unfinished business with your mother: good-byes left unsaid, emotions unexpressed, thanks left unspoken. What do you need to tell her? Is it love? Anger? Both? Praise or absolution? Is it about events from long ago or what you're up to now? Maybe it's what she means to you or that you finally understand. Be honest. Let your thoughts and emotions flow. Prohibitions about not speaking ill of the dead may have stopped you from expressing your feelings in the past, but it's no longer beneficial to keep them locked inside. Otherwise, how can you really begin to forgive your mother? Forgiving her for leaving and for her imperfections is one of the most important tasks ahead. This workbook is a safe place to say what's been left unsaid. Think of this as a continuing dialogue.

DATE:_____

What I need to tell my mother is:

For a long time I was pissed off that you were sick when I needed you to take care of me. I was pretty screwed up for a while, but I'm better now. I have a _wonderful husband, a great little girl, and even though I still miss you, I'm not so angry anymore._

_____

_____

_____

What I have to ask my mother is:

How did you know how to be a mother?

_____

_____

_____

Is there also something you believe she would like you to know?

My mother would want me to know that:

She loves me, forgives me my shortcomings, and she's sorry for any mistakes she made when we were together.

_____

_____

_____

Your mother bestowed talents and gifts that you carry on, pass down, share with family or the world. Olivia believes her artistic bent comes from her mother. What of your mother's legacy do you wish to acknowledge now? Don't discount anything because it seems silly or superficial: a recipe for meatloaf, the way you smile, a passion for chintz—they're all connections. They provide continuity and belonging, they link who we are to where we come from. "I don't want to lose my mom from my life," says Sheila, "and I guess I won't, because I'm her clone. She lives on a little bit through me."

What I want to acknowledge from my mother is:

_____

_____

_____

_____

RITING WRONGS

By marking events through satisfying rituals, we maintain a link to our past and redefine relationships. We've already examined certain rites and times of transition that hold particularly difficult or painful associations for motherless daughters: funeral-related rituals, holidays altered by a mother's loss, milestones experienced without her. By revisiting and reshaping our rituals, as well as creating new ones where necessary, we can better express our sorrow and our joy.

Rita related this story in the first issue of *daughterspeak*, the Motherless Daughters newsletter: "I am seventy-five years old. My mother died when I was fourteen and I have not wanted to visit her grave for the last fifty years. . . . Two weeks ago I went to my mother's grave. I took the fourteen-year-old to the cemetery to bury her mother in a new way, a loving way, and to mourn her leaving me. At the grave, I told her that I didn't want to be the fourteen-year-old anymore, to have the fear, confusion and the guilt. I just wanted to feel the love I have for her. I rested my head on her headstone and felt something shift in me."

If the services and activities surrounding your mother's death weren't a source of consolation, this may be a good place to start. Rituals exist not just to mark a death but to honor a life and facilitate the expression of grief. Rita was able to exorcise ghosts that had haunted her for more than half a century by going to the cemetery. A visit to the graveside can be cathartic, particularly if you weren't allowed to attend or participate as a child. Jill has found solace in "going to the cemetery more now. Last time I was there it was really wonderful. I just lay down under the big weeping willows, looked at the sky, and started to chat. I don't really know what I said, but I just talked and talked. It was the only time I had ever done that."

RITUAL REDUX

If you didn't attend the funeral, if it failed to address your needs or wasn't personally meaningful, redo the rites, if not literally, then symbolically. You might take a personal memento that belonged to your mother or a letter you wrote to her (see the Safe Passage at the end of this chapter) and bury it in a significant place. If your mother was cremated, you might burn the item or letter, then scatter or bury the ashes. Maybe you want to rewrite her epitaph. You can say a prayer, play her favorite song—whether it's a Sinatra tune or a Sousa march, light candles, or tell a story that always made you laugh. It's up to you to decide what will be meaningful and healing for you. You may have already come up with other ideas in your Safe Passage entry from Chapter 7.

One word of caution: This ritual may release strong emotions, and while we understand that some women may need this to be a very private activity, we strongly suggest that you let someone on your Safety Net list know what you're up to for support and comfort. Don't stifle your reactions; allow yourself to release the emotions.

You could plan a memorial service, like Doris, and enlist enlightened clergy to help you design the event. Determine what will best benefit you, keeping in mind that this isn't an exercise in wallowing. The idea is to free yourself from painful events of the past and to honor a life. Not everyone will benefit from these rituals, and you might collide with family members who think it maudlin. Respect their right to refuse participation, but don't let it stop you.

DATE:_____

Ritual I Want to Reshape	People I Want to Participate	What I Plan to Do
_____	_____	_____
_____	_____	_____
_____	_____	_____
_____	_____	_____
_____	_____	_____

HAPPY HOLIDAYS?

"When we were little, my mother would never, never turn on the Christmas tree lights until the first star on Christmas eve," Nicole recalls. "It drove my family crazy, but now my sisters and I will not turn those lights on until Christmas Eve. I feel really close to her when I do that because I know how important it was to her. The funny thing is that when she was alive, my sisters and I would dread it because everybody in the neighborhood had their lights on. Now it makes sense to us."

"Holidays were always hell on wheels," Mandy announces. "My mother died three days after Christmas. She loved Christmas, and it was everywhere in our house. She was very into holiday and family. After she died, Christmas fell off the deep end. All the holidays were dead. We did have one Christmas back in Vermont where we got to take out all the old packed-away ornaments. I hated decorating that tree. Some of the ornaments were smashed, all dusty and outdated. The healing part, though, was that my little niece had come along by then, and we bought new ornaments with her. We kept some of the old and got some new lights and a new star for the top of the tree. The old mixing with the new was a good thing. It's nice when someone can bring a new ritual in. The last two years I've had my own rituals. I got my own tree, bought my own ornaments. It started to feel more like Christmas. My father was hurt, but I think it was for the best."

For motherless women, holidays are rarely Kodak moments. More frequently, they bring on loneliness, isolation, fear, dread, and loathing. Since mothers often see to it that traditions are carried on, the holidays turn into stark reminders that she's no longer there. They're a pretty accurate reflection of the state of things. We'd like to believe that the rosy glow of holiday expectations will make problems and animosities disappear, but that's not usually the case. Instead, holidays tend to expose family tensions to a harsher light.

From the list below, check which statements apply to you and/or your family.

DATE:_____

_____ We tend to let holidays slip by.

_____ I usually face family holidays with dread.

_____ We do the same thing every year, but no one seems to enjoy it.

_____ My family resists changing the way we celebrate the holidays.

_____ I've stopped attending family holidays.

_____ The burden for planning or having a holiday gathering usually falls to the same people.

_____ We never discuss my mother at holiday times.

_____ We try to do what Mom used to do, but it somehow feels empty.

_____ I'm usually disappointed by family gatherings.

"Rituals assist in two major dimensions of human life—continuity and change," Evan Imber-Black and Janine Roberts remind us in *Rituals for Our Times*. In other words, rituals need to reflect the fact that times and lives change as well as preserve what remains meaningful. Think about which holidays you observe and which ones you've stopped celebrating because they've become too painful, too forced, or too unpleasant. Think about what you treasure in the ones you observe, what you'd like to toss out, what keeps the holidays from being celebratory, and how your family might react to changes. Also consider if there's something you would like to do to honor the memory of your mother during a holiday. Here are a few suggestions adapted from the New England Center for Loss and Transition *Grief Letter*.

- For Christmas, create a special ornament labeled with your mother's name and hang it on your tree.

- For Chanukah, recall a memory of your mother each night you light the candles.

- Share anecdotes and stories about your mother at a family gathering. If you start talking about her, others may feel comfortable enough to do the same.

- Make a donation in your mother's name at holiday time.

- Prepare one of your mother's specialties for a holiday.

HOME FOR THE HOLIDAYS

Lynda decided that this year Thanksgiving would be different. She made the following pledge to herself.

November 1997, Thanksgiving Day

The family hasn't been together for a holiday in a long time. I know the pitfalls . . . how—and why—we reinforce the worst in each other. It's hard for any of us to admit we're ever wrong, that we still hurt, and to get over the things we've done in the past. But this time I will ignore my father's criticism if he demeans my cooking efforts. I will do my best to intercept the same wobbly passes my siblings throw at one another with the understanding that I am only responsible for myself.

I am nervous about introducing a ritual at this gathering, but it's important to me. I want to read a letter of thanks dedicated to my mom. I need to acknowledge her presence in my life, especially around the holidays. Everyone coming to dinner knows about the letter, so it won't come as a surprise. I'm also using the plates that Mom always used for special occasions. They've been packed away, and I think it's time to not treat them as relics. I won't expect miracles, but perhaps enough time has passed that we can begin to feel like a family again.

Pick a holiday that's still several months away, and begin to plan. Whom could you enlist to help you? Whom do you want to include, and what might be important elements for you and for them? You may be starting a new tradition.

DATE:_____

The Holiday I Want to Celebrate	How I/We Celebrate Now	Traditions I Want to Keep
_____	_____	_____
_____	_____	_____
_____	_____	_____

What I Would Like to Change	I Plan to Do This By	I Need to Talk This Over With
_____	_____	_____
_____	_____	_____
_____	_____	_____

MOTHER'S DAYS

That Sunday in May. The almost inevitable grief attack, the feeling of being lost and out of place because it seems as if everyone else is celebrating. What to do? For women whose mothers are no longer living, Mother's Day can be a day to pull the covers over your head and hide. Or you can face it straight on and think about how to commemorate her life in an empowering way.

In 1997, motherless daughters in twenty-five cities throughout the United States and Canada came together to do just that on the second annual Motherless Daughters Day, held the Saturday before Mother's Day. In recognition of the continuing bond with their mothers and with each other, motherless daughters in each city joined hands in a Circle of Remembrance at the same time nationwide and acknowledged their mothers and themselves by name. Afterward, many wrote of the day's transformational power and of how grateful they were to finally be able to celebrate their mothers with women who truly understood.

As we continue to recognize the significance of early mother loss, local and national events of this type are certain to grow. Across the country, women are forming support groups, discussions of loss are springing up in civic and religious organizations, and there are on-line chat groups for the bereaved. But there are many ways to honor your mother at times that seem appropriate for you.

Here is an excerpt from a speech Phyllis gave at a Mother's Day service at her church.

On Mother's Day 1952, my mother died. I was seven years old. The impact on my young life was not realized by me until about thirty years later. As a result, Mother's Day every year has been a time of reflection, tears, and growth.

My reflections today are not about death but about role models in our church and their impact on my own mothering. When my two sons were born, I didn't question my ability to mother them and proceeded on the journey—struggling with my new role but not hurting.

When my daughter, Lana, was born, I began to question my ability to mother a daughter since I had been denied the full experience of being the daughter of a mother. From my early childhood, I have only sad memories of my mother, who was handicapped and in pain. I have only memories of confusion, abandonment, and hurt about her death.

How *do* I mother a daughter? How can I *own* the words *mother* and *woman*? What does it mean to be a role model for a daughter? Scary questions for me.

These questions were just below the surface when I joined [this] church. I came seeking religious education for the children and found religious and personal growth for myself—and wonderful role models.

I found strong women role models not only for myself but for my daughter. I listened intently as Bess Wilson described every interaction with her three daughters—seeking to find "the way" to be a mother of a daughter. I attended Death and Dying class and learned more; I taught Haunting House and grew more; I taught Growing Up Year and learned the value of milestones and communicating feelings.

I found women friends who helped me stretch and forced me to confront my fears and anxieties. I listened to their stories about their own mothers and learned more. I began to appreciate that not having a mother model was in some way liberating. I was free to pick and choose from a hundred women as role models—not locked into one definition!

Mothering for me has been a jigsaw puzzle. The birth of each baby definitely shaped the border of the puzzle. Then for the next years the puzzle grew as I searched for pieces that matched and felt right for ME. Pieces were found in books, some in classes, in experiences with other children and parents, in relatives, and some friends. The border was the easy part—finding the other 450 pieces has been the challenge.

Thank you to all of the women and men in our church for the pieces of themselves that they have shared.

My wish for all young women on this Mother's Day is that you will find many models for your personal growth.

My wish for all young mothers today is that you will look around and find pieces for *your* mother puzzle that fit for you.

I invite you to say the names of women who have been important in your life.

If there are dates or occasions that hold special meaning for you, how could you commemorate her on that day?

DATE:_____

On _____ I plan to:

_____

_____

On _____ I plan to:

_____

_____

MEMORIAL DAYS

Transitions or special occasions—a graduation, a wedding, a birth—are milestones you wish you could share with a mother. She can't be there, but many women have found wonderful, inventive ways of incorporating her into ceremonies at these important times.

Tricia sent a note explaining, "I recently got married, and as you will notice, in the wedding program I wrote a tribute to my mother. Words cannot possibly describe how much I missed her and what a tremendous yearning I had for her throughout the entire wedding planning and wedding day."

I would like to take a moment to remember my beautiful mother. As many of you already know, she looked forward to this day even more than words could describe. When I think about her I feel so lucky to have shared such a special relationship with her—a once in a lifetime relationship—the kind that only mothers and daughters can understand. I also feel fortunate to have had her in my life for as long as I did. She was my motivating force, "my biggest fan," and a very dear friend. Without her I couldn't possibly be the person I am today. I'm sure that when some of you look at me, talk to me, or just listen to me you think of her. I am in many ways her—she is a major part of me.

Today is the most important day of my life—so far. Although my mother cannot be here with me today, I truly believe that love has no boundaries. In my heart and in my soul she is with me. I can still hear her laugh, picture her smile, and feel the warmth of her hug. Today would have been one of the happiest days of her life. I only hope that with all of the support and guidance from my family and friends, this day is as beautiful as she would have made it. As always, she was my inspiration.

I love you, Mom.

Freelance writer Susan Shapiro told of having two weddings—one for herself and one planned by her mother, whose own mother had died when she was seven. After the second wedding, Susan found her mother staring at a picture of her dead mother. "It's the Hebrew date of her burial,' she whispered. We hugged and said good night. It was the first time I ever had a man stay with me in my pink childhood room. But I woke up at 3 A.M. and walked downstairs. The Scrabble board was set out, the yahrzeit candle flickering, as if she were playing with a ghost. I picked out letters, and we sat there silently for hours, eating and connecting words."

Healing through remembrance keeps us linked in an appropriate way. The AIDS quilt, for example, is a patchwork of lives lost but not forgotten. A tree planted in a mother's name is a living reminder that can grow for generations to come. One artist transformed the memory of her mother and the pain she endured into an illuminated manuscript. From Virginia Woolf to Madonna, creative people of all stripes have paid homage to a mother who never got to see them grow up. Their art is their eulogy through which they attempt to make sense of their feelings and experiences. In Missing Moments, we asked you to examine events that trigger reminders of your mother. At those joyous occasions and life transitions when thoughts of your mother are prominent, seize the opportunity to create your own connection.

OBJECTS OF AFFECTION

Videos, home movies, and photos of our mothers are usually treasured and evocative objects. If you don't already have one, you might consider putting together a video, photo album, or collage. You can construct a photo collage for your wall or a scrapbook that weaves together small bits and pieces of your mother's life. You can make one for yourself or give one as a family memento on an important occasion. Or get family and friends together and produce a tape of favorite stories and family lore. Although it may seem overly sentimental, even corny, when you're doing it, in years to come when you or your family drag out that album, video, or tape, you'll be glad you made the effort.

"I have my mother's baby pillow," Gaby says. "I can't go to sleep without it under my head." Gail prizes her mother's collection of 45 records. TV anchor Deborah Norville treasures her mother's old Kenmore sewing machine. Many women find solace in keeping such possessions. The objects aren't important in themselves, but they symbolically link you to your history and provide a sense of continuity. Is there something that holds that meaning for you? What does it represent for you?

The reason I treasure my mother's _____ is that:

_____

_____

_____

SPIRITUAL CONNECTION

"I guess I never really truly think she's gone," Maria explains. "Physically, yes. But there is some way, somehow, that she's always there. So there never really is a good-bye, it's just kind of a 'See you for now.' All of this has been a developmental process for me, and it's a matter of adapting to the change, adapting to each new situation without her. It doesn't get easier, but I'm always pretty strong. I know that somewhere her hand is going to push me in the right direction."

Rebecca believes her mother left her with "this calming core, a solid piece that I can go back to when things get crazy. That's what I said to her when I visited the cemetery a year ago: 'I don't think you realize that you gave me that, but it's the one thing I took that's gotten me through everything.'"

A significant number of women told us that their mothers continue to be a strong, almost palpable presence in their lives. Some, like Rebecca, point to a mother's deeply instilled philosophy of life, which has become a guiding influence. Others, like Maria, feel a more spiritual dimension to the relationship. Sheila believes her mother acts as a "guardian angel who looks out for me and helps me through life's journey." Tara contends that "a person who dies is with you. There's an invisible side of life that's present with everything that is concrete in life." We can't tell you what your relationship to your mother should be. Faith and spiritual belief are very individual matters. Our purpose is to help you live with loss, not in its shadow. Your loss may have touched your faith in some way or brought you spiritual insights. We hope that these beliefs offer comfort—not a hiding place—and aid your healing.

SAFE PASSAGE: A JOURNAL WRITING EXERCISE

In Chapter 3, we asked you to write a letter to your mother. We'd like you to do that again, only this time from a new perspective. Explain how you're going to deal with her loss and its meaning in your life from this point forward. And if you never got to say good-bye in the way you wanted, say it now. Tell her if there's something you're going to do to honor her memory, and let her know that you're all right.

DATE:_____

_____

_____

_____

_____

_____

_____

_____

_____

_____

_____

FINAL THOUGHTS

"As a society, we seem to have this notion that you can be engaged in grief too long, when, in reality, you never stop being engaged," explains Dr. Phyllis Silverman. "It's not a condition that you get over, like an illness or a germ that you can expunge. That's not how it works. To expect people to 'get over it' is inappropriate because it sets people up. If you've lost a loved one, you're going to feel it the rest of your life. The difference is that in the beginning, grief runs you. Later, you choose when to be sad, when to remember, and when to be enriched by those memories."

Gail thought this story neatly summed up the idea of integrating a loss: "I was playing with my four-year-old niece. She was sucking on an ice cube. The first time it fell out of her mouth, she cried. I picked it up, washed it off, and gave it back to her. She stopped crying and continued to suck on it, and it continued to melt in her mouth. It fell out again, and she cried again. One more time, I picked it up, wiped it off, and gave it back to her. We repeated this little ritual until finally the ice cube melted entirely in her mouth. She looked puzzled for a moment, smiled, then turned and walked away. The moral of the story: When the ice cube was apart from her she cried, but when she realized it was a part of her, integrated, she was content. That's the goal for motherless daughters."

CHANGING ROOM

Rewriting Your Destiny

The future belongs to those who believe in the beauty of
their dreams.

—*Eleanor Roosevelt*

You've come so far. You've endured the death of your mother, and you're here to tell the tale. Though the women whose stories appear throughout this book are at different points in their mourning, they are struggling, searching, surviving. They're thoughtfully scrutinizing their lives in order to create meaning out of loss. Take their stories to heart. Wherever you are on your journey, take this time to get your bearings. Use this space to record what you've learned, achieved, and hope to accomplish. Concentrate on the progress you've made, not the distance that lies ahead. The story you have to tell is the story you have to tell.

❋ *Selena's Story: I know how to live life more fully now. In fact, I asked my fiancé to marry me. Life is too short to wait for a guy to ask you.*

❋ *Ashley's Story: Before I reached out for support, my mom's death was an empty thing. Now that I know that there are all these people out there who've experienced the same loss, it doesn't seem so big anymore. It's weird—the thing that made my life so empty is making it full.*

❋ *Sheila's Story: Loss has affected me in so many ways. I'm closer to people. I treasure life and find so much beauty in this world. I meet people who are immediately attracted to me, drawn to me, because of what I give off. I was voted Most Inspirational— what can I say? What has taken place in the last six years since my mother died, it's amazing. Even after a huge loss, I still wake up every day blissed out to be Sheila. I wouldn't want to be anybody else.*

Date: _____

My Story:

_____
_____
_____
_____
_____
_____
_____
_____
_____
_____
_____
_____
_____
_____
_____
_____
_____
_____
_____

Charlotte's Story: The last thing my mother said to me was "Take your vitamins, and take care of yourself because no one else will." To be a motherless daughter is kind of like being your own mom—you have to love yourself unconditionally.

Joan's Story: I need to help myself, and I want to help others. When motherless daughters come together, we can feel whole, part of something beautiful, strong, and useful.

Nora's Story: There's nothing I can't conquer. Come on, I'm twenty-seven and I've lost two mothers. Life goes on. I'm learning that I have some say over my life. I don't always have to be a good kid. I can be a little selfish.

Clarissa's Story: For years I integrated my loss into my life by trying to be the best possible woman on all fronts: wife, mother, daughter, friend, student, organizer—everything my mother wasn't in my eyes. I didn't want to think too much about what or why I was reacting. More recently I have tried looking at life more realistically and humanely to to understand the pressures and circumstances that influence and pull people in different directions. We cannot escape or change our past, but we can accept it and use it as a base from which to build a more complete and satisfying existence.

Eva's Story: I used to think, Why me? Why us? and now I think, Why her? I think it's really bad that this happened, and I've thought, Why me? but it's worse that it happened to her. She's not alive, she didn't get to finish her life, but I can still live mine.

Jasmine's Story: I try to make the situation positive. "Where you find a rose, a thistle cannot grow." To me, being a motherless daughter means growing from the experience and living my life fully.

_____
_____
_____
_____
_____
_____
_____
_____
_____
_____
_____
_____
_____
_____

THE HOME STRETCH

The last chapter of this workbook deals with dreams and resilience, strength and accomplishment. Whether you've been carrying the weight of the world—the burden of caretaking, the millstone of secrecy, the conviction of guilt—for five years or fifteen, we hope you've begun to realize the benefits of confronting destructive patterns and of confiding, forgiving, apologizing, and expressing gratitude. Through these efforts you can rekindle the passion of your dreams.

This final chapter is only the beginning of a journey that continues with you as its guide. The course it takes is up to you. Continue to seek the power of your individual truth, gather pieces of your history—who you were, what your mother was like, and decide what you need to take with you as you travel forward. What must you work on to achieve your goals and dreams along the way?

There's no denying you've paid dearly for the lessons you've learned. But you have grown from grief, whether in a richer appreciation for life, deeper spirituality, or a more compassionate view of others' travails. We want you to put the human spirit to work to transform the limiting behaviors that developed in response to your loss and recognize your strengths.

STEADY AS SHE GOES

It's taken Lydia years to begin to see any light: "I'm not one of those women who just went out and conquered the world. I've struggled a lot, and I've not been independent. I'm still trying to make a life for myself. But because I suffered a lot at an early age, I do think I have some sort of wisdom."

"What does not destroy me makes me stronger," Nietzsche counseled. Easy for him to say. Such growth is usually a slow and difficult process. Inner strengths aren't always apparent. "Strength is silent," Greta believes. You're stronger than you think. Take time to look. It's there.

At times you're going to miss an opportunity to gain headway and you'll rely on old behaviors. There will be other chances, so give yourself credit for recognizing the problem. Slow and steady wins the race, but you must get back on the horse. Growth is an ongoing process. You're guaranteed to have your good days and bad, your moments of inspiration and despair, your certainty and your doubt. Be persistent, and don't let setbacks deter you. Continue to get your story down on paper and document your progress. New pieces unfold each time you tell it.

"I have a journal, and I write letters to my mom a lot and to my grandmother," says Maggie. "I'll write if I get really stressed out about my thoughts and don't have anyone to talk to. I usually feel better after I get all of my feelings out. I save everything I write, and I come back through to see what progress I've made in certain areas of my life. When I'm feeling low and like I'm not getting anywhere with the grief process, I'll go back and look at what I've written and realize that a year ago I wouldn't have been able to do what I've done today or say what I've said today."

ADJUSTING THE DIAL

What are the keys to enabling growth and celebrating life in the shadow of loss? You're already on your way. In the Checklist for Change on page 249, you've made promises to yourself. Consult them periodically.

Erasing the negative tapes you play in your head is a good place to start. The ones that tell you things like "I'm such a failure when it comes to things a woman is supposed to know" or "Bad things *always* happen to me" or "I'll *never* feel better." Watch out for these sweeping generalizations that stop you in your tracks. When you hear that whining, disrupt the pattern with a non sequitur, a joke, as off-the-wall an image as you can conjure up—the more exaggerated the better. Now that you've pressed the pause button, replace the tape with one that puts a new, positive spin on those reproachful thoughts. For instance, "*I'm such a failure when it comes to—*" OK, stop right there. Run interference with an outrageous image to create the break. All right, you've created the break. Now what could you say instead? How about "*I've made a few good female friends and I can learn from them.*" Wouldn't it be nice to become your own promoter occasionally?

Granted, the old messages are ingrained, so it will take some time to install the new ones. But the words you say to yourself are important. Talk the talk because what you say to yourself is what you become and make happen.

Enid lamented, "I'm forty, so I would say that if I still feel like I don't belong, that probably won't change. It's a horrible thought, but I suspect there's a lot of credence to it. I haven't thought about it for the future, but if I look back on the past forty years, why would there be any change? There's no indication." Enid's right: things may not change. What can change is you. Your beliefs and perceptions can change, and what you take away from experiences can change. Mistakes can be the best teachers if you learn from them. If plan A doesn't work, amend it, and try plan B. The past doesn't equal the future unless you keep thinking, believing, and doing the same old things. Whether you'll rise to the occasion and overcome adversity is really up to you. Gail is fond of saying, "Trust that the universe has ears, is willing to listen, and wants to help." You just have to do your part.

You can continue to allow the loss to paralyze you, or like Mikki, you can search for alternatives: "This sounds so clichéd, but once I realized that I had to learn how to accept and live without my mother, I developed this carpe diem attitude. You can live miserably, or you live in a positive way. I look at my brothers and how much pain they're in, and I say, 'I don't want to be like that.'"

"Think of your mind as a fertile piece of land," David Gershon and Gail Straub suggest in *Empowerment*. "Taking control of your thoughts and beliefs makes the difference between a garden that you cultivate and a patch of earth that's left to grow wild. Whether cultivated or neglected, something will grow. If you don't plant the seeds of something you want to cultivate then weeds will grow—and continue to produce more of the same."

AFFIRMATIVE ACTION

Look around. You have the tools to help you till that garden. Affirmations, meditations, and reflections are messages of hope with which to inspire yourself when life gets tough—pep talks for the soul. We suggest writing your own, but there's certainly a wealth of resources: poetry, the Bible, Frank Capra movies, Tracy Chapman songs. Take your pick, but tell yourself good things. Here are two from Carol Staudacher's *A Time to Grieve* that are particularly appropriate. There's room for you to add your own. Remember, writing them is only part of the drill. Reading the words (preferably out loud), internalizing them, believing, and acting on them makes them come true.

AFFIRMATION 1

I have within me all I need to get through this time in my life. Even though I can benefit tremendously by having others who can support me in compassionate, intelligent, and very practical ways, I—all by myself—have the necessary core of belief, courage, and know-how to work myself through my grief. I will agree to use, to my full capacity, my inner resources, never losing faith that they will sustain me. I have made it through challenging times before, and though this time may be the most challenging of all, I can and will do it again.

AFFIRMATION 2

I will not expect to heal by running away from conditions, reactions, and emotions that arise as a result of this death. I will not remain passive and assume things will get better. I will put forth effort to make progress through this grieving process. This will include recalling, feeling, sharing, and memorializing my loved one. Today I will do one of those things; tomorrow I will do another. And I will continue on, day after day, until I know in my heart and mind that I have confronted the most difficult part of this sorrow.

MY AFFIRMATION

DATE: _____

_____

_____

_____

_____

_____

```
┌──────────────────────────────────────────────────────┐
│                    MY AFFIRMATION                      │
│                                                        │
│   DATE: _____                               │
│                                                        │
│   _____ │
│                                                        │
│   _____ │
│                                                        │
│   _____ │
│                                                        │
│   _____ │
│                                                        │
│   _____ │
└──────────────────────────────────────────────────────┘
```

COUNTING YOUR BLESSINGS

If you walk around that garden, you'll see some flowers already there. They've been growing for a while. Just how have you come this far? This doesn't mean your life is without difficulty. Don't look at what's missing in your life but what's there. Take the time now to acknowledge all you have. For inspiration, we offer another of Carol Staudacher's affirmations.

I will realize that I may need to relearn my own happiness. I can access what I have salvaged from the devastation of loss and what I value most that is still with me. I will recognize that happiness is truly appreciating and desiring what I now have, the positive legacy of my relationship.

DATE:_____

What has kept me going?

____ *My daughter is my pride and joy.*

____ *My work has given me a sense of accomplishment.*

____ *My mother's example guides me in the right direction.*

_____

_____

_____

_____

_____

Model Behavior

Emulating a gardener with a green thumb can be helpful when cultivating your garden. You may want to seek out someone who has effectively come to terms with grief and whose attitude and accomplishments offer inspiration. A woman you admire in the office who exemplifies grace under pressure might be a candidate for a mentor. You could draw on the courage of a child or the kindness of a stranger. How have they designed their lives? What can you learn from their example?

Natalie discovered a role model on TV: "I saw a touching interview on _Nightline_ with a seventy-eight-year-old man dying of Lou Gehrig's disease. He was talking about his physical debilitation and impending death with calm detachment. But when he mentioned his mother, who had died when he was seven, he started to cry. Ted Koppel commented on his surprise at how cool this man could be about his own death, yet show such pain in connection with a loss that had occurred seventy years earlier. The man calmly explained that his tears were not of pain, they were just tears. He said he always felt sad when he thought about his mother, and he had no shame or embarrassment about those tears. He's my role model."

Perhaps some of the women's words in this workbook can serve as examples. Sheila has drawn meaning out of tragedy: "Being a motherless daughter is a nonstop journey. It's a title that I'm no longer ashamed to have, write, or speak. It's a part of my life, and it has shaped me into the person I am today. I really believe that there was a purpose for all of this."

Supermodels

Search around you for mentors. What is it about them that encourages you? Can you learn from merely observing and analyzing, or should you ask their advice?

DATE:_____

Who	Quality He/She Has	How I Can Learn
Support group leader	*Ability to be nonjudgmental*	*Listen to her analysis of situations*
_____	_____	_____
_____	_____	_____
_____	_____	_____

If your list isn't particularly inspiring, be prepared to look elsewhere. This workbook, as well as other literature on death, dying, and surviving life's tragedies, was written to bring understanding and encouragement to its readers. The bibliography and reading list at the end of this book offer more sources.

GIVING AT THE OFFICE

Support groups of motherless daughters can also be an invaluable resource.[1] Sharing your story, your grief, your pain, and your courage with other such women is a powerful experience. Not only do you open yourself to the understanding, compassion, and validation that other motherless women can provide, you bear witness to their stories. In helping others, you heal yourself.

As we've said, we don't think it's coincidence that a significant number of motherless daughters are engaged in helping professions and give at the office every day. Giving back by contributing to society or your community enriches your life as well as others' lives. It's a way of connecting to something bigger than yourself. Maybe you're a whiz with troubled kids, have the time to deliver meals to the homebound, or can put in hours with a community hotline. Find a cause you feel strongly about, and get involved. In the end you'll discover that not only is it better to give than to receive but it's downright healing.

There's one more thing you'll have to own. You don't need to go out and buy it; you've had it for years. You just need to look at it from a different perspective. It's the human spirit, which allows you to triumph over adversity, to recapture dreams and build a life, to try again. We are by nature regenerative, and the heart is a very resilient muscle.

Each and every one of you is a know-it-all. You know everything you need to know, even though access to this knowledge may have been obstructed. But if you're ready to take on the responsibility of knowing, you can reconnect to the wellspring of resilience inside you.

Where does it lie? The Redeeming Values exercise on page 27 shows the positive values you believe you once possessed. Those traits may be hibernating, but they can be reawakened. For example, you may not have youth's carefree attitude, but there may be times or situations when a glimmer of that feeling emerges—maybe when you're on vacation in Paris. Do you get that old sense of exhilaration when you land an important client? Do you revive your confidence when you ace a tennis serve? Do you feel serenity return when you see your child sleeping? Bring the memory to the foreground, and savor the sensation.

DATE:_____

I sometimes feel the way I did when:

I go for a beach vacation. The sea and salt air remind me of running on the beach when I was a kid. It's rejuvenating. Something about the ocean gets rid of the anxiety. I'm more willing to just let things happen and not try to control everything.

_____

_____

_____

_____

If you can recall, even fleetingly, times of well-being, vitality, or contentment, you're headed in the right direction. Under what circumstances are you able to recapture those feelings? You can't go on vacation every month, but how else could you increase those times? Would a soothing massage or a fire in your fireplace do the trick? What about a few hours stolen for serenity and reflection, either literally—at the creek deep in the woods where you took refuge as a child—or figuratively—by writing in your diary?

It took Gladys decades to figure out how to recover her own happiness. Now, she explains, "I take very good care of myself. It took me a long time to learn to do that. I'm in touch with my feelings, and I try to do something about them. I got rid of a load of people who caused me *agita*. I just don't want them in my life anymore. I take good care of my body, I exercise, I get the *Times* delivered and have cable TV. It costs money, and I spend it on myself."

If you're trying to rebuild confidence lost, think about something you're already proficient in and the satisfaction it brings you. Bring that state of mind to areas in which you feel less proficient. You weren't born knowing how to ride a bike. You learned step by step until you were more self-assured. You probably had your share of skinned knees, but with practice you learned to ride. We so often let the dark side scare us into paralysis. Try embracing the process and acknowledging forward progress with unabashed pride.

PARADISE LOST

Go back to the Room of Your Own exercise on page 27. Those stories are evidence of your resourcefulness and creativity. Do your childhood anecdotes reveal hidden strengths forgotten or dulled by disuse?

What my stories say about me:

I really, really wanted to get a set of cross-country skis, but my birthday had just passed and not a holiday was in sight. I saved money by collecting and recycling cans, selling lemonade, and telling people my goal in case they wanted to make a contribution.

I was determined, resourceful, and could talk my way into anything.

DATE:_____

_____

_____

_____

A child's sense of wonder and imagination is still within you; it just requires nurturing. "You don't get back your childhood, but you can get back some of the things that are you—like talents, gifts, and a sense of self," Arlene concedes.

As you begin to apply what you've learned so far, plug into your creative outlets. Artistic flair comes in different forms. Yours might take shape on an easel or in a notebook, in the kitchen or in the classroom. Use the Key Passages you've entered in the Part Breaks as the basis for a larger work. It doesn't have to get published or open on Broadway for you to benefit. The creative expression of who you are is the reward.

LIFE-AFTER-DEATH EXPERIENCE

With boundless futures ahead, the young answer effortlessly when asked, "Who do you want to be?" To an adult, however, these six words pose far more difficulty. So much seems to have gotten in the way; loss and disappointment have diminished expectations. The Dream On exercise on page 28 explores your dreams and fantasies. If necessary, turn back to refresh your memory.

Over time your hopes and dreams have certainly changed, and you've probably reinvented yourself several times over. But are there fantasies you still retain? What's stopping you from reaching for them? You may not become an astronaut, but you can learn to fly.

Dreams provide the raw material out of which we shape our lives. Sure there's a chance we'll fall short, but we grow by embarking on the journey. You may have been sidetracked, detoured, taken the wrong turn, but it's never too late to turn on your blinker and get back on the on-ramp.

PIECES OF DREAMS

Take three of your dreams, with no censoring or eliminating because they seem impossible. What could you do right now to move toward each one? Plan another step next week and more next month. Just start the engine. En route, your dreams may change, so be flexible enough to follow your instincts.

DATE:_____

Dream 1 _____

Steps:

Today I will _____

Next week I will _____

Next month I will _____

Dream 2 _____

Steps:

Today I will _____

Next week I will _____

Next month I will _____

Dream 3 _____

Steps:

Today I will _____

Next week I will _____

Next month I will _____

SOMETIMES YOU JUST GOTTA LAUGH

Both tears of pain and tears of joy serve as a release. Sometimes we laugh so hard we cry. Other times we cry so much we end up laughing. After each we feel better. No one gets through life without pain—it's the nature of the beast—though you may have had more than your share. The resilience of the human spirit is reflected in our capacity to laugh in the face of adversity and at ourselves, at life's bitter ironies and at our own shortcomings, not defensively but openly, generously, and unreservedly. Laughter *is* the best medicine. Sometimes what you truly need to do is seek out the things that will make you laugh, even if they bring a tear.

FINAL THOUGHTS

This workbook has been ambitious. We've asked you to reexperience the most wrenching moments of your life and to probe at situations and relationships that have eaten away at you. Surely it hasn't been easy, but as Rhonda reminded us, "If you want the rainbow, you have to put up with the rain." We hope that your mother's death has begun to have new meaning, that you've begun to see the world from a different point of view, that you know you are not alone, and that you can put your arms around your dreams. We promise: YOU CAN GET THERE FROM HERE. Trust in yourself, and harness the power within you.

Things are always changing, growing, evolving, and being transformed into something new, and so can you. When you work through the issues that have prevented you from being who you want to be, you discover the life you want. A life that has always been there—a life of your own.

> ## A FINAL AFFIRMATION
> *I must trust the process of grief and know that even though I may not think or feel that I am making any progress, healing is taking place within me. That healing is happening by degrees, and most of the time it is invisible, but as I review and express my reactions to death, I am being repaired. My heart and my mind are becoming accustomed to my loss, and I am learning to use my special resources to continue life in a changed way.*

Part Break IV

In the opening chapter of this book, we asked, "Why deal, why heal, why now?" As you reach the end of this workbook, perhaps you've found new answers to those questions. "That is what learning is," author Doris Lessing writes. "You suddenly understand something you knew all your life, but in a new way."

In one of our focus groups, Lucy revealed, "I found my feelings changed from day to day so drastically. I found myself thinking of different things, trying to remember. I found little things that I have. I had this perfume—Evening in Paris—that was my mother's. I would be upset. I didn't have answers. And then I thought of someone who used to baby-sit for me that I'm going to write a letter to. That's what I found myself doing, trying to find answers. I know that I don't really know my mother yet, or remember a lot, but now I can feel a closeness inside in just trying to remember." Consider what you've learned in the healing process. Writing what has been valuable will help motivate you to keep it up even after you close these pages.

DATE:_____

What has been valuable for me in doing this work?

_____

_____

_____

_____

The Best Approach

Start the conversation here with the people you've decided you must approach concerning your experience of mother loss.

Who I Need to Talk To	*What* I Need to Say	*How* I Can Approach Them
Why I Resist	*When* I Will Try to Talk to Them	*What Happened* When I Did

Is there anyone you need to forgive?

Who I Need to Forgive	*What* I Need to Forgive Him/Her For	*How* I Can Do This

Why I Resist	When I Will Try to Talk to Them	What Happened When I Did

While working through this part of the book, have you thought of other people you would like to acknowledge for being there for you?

Who I Need to Thank	What I Have to Acknowledge Them For	How I Can Do It

Who I Need to Thank	*What* I Have to Acknowledge Them For	*How* I Can Do It

Apology Accepted

Consider once again whether there's anyone you want to apologize to for something you said or did.

Who I Need to Apologize To	*What* I Have to Apologize For	*How* I Can Approach Them

Why I Resist	*When* I Will Try to Apologize	*What Happened* When I Did	

Lost Cause

"I'm going to let go of the car accident my parents died in," Yolanda has concluded. "I wanted to know what my parents died of, what actually caused the accident. Were they drinking? Maybe they were fighting. With all the accident reports I gathered and everything I found out, there's still no reason why."

As you continue to seek answers about your mother and her death, there will be times when you come up empty-handed. All your efforts and research may not bring you closer to the truth—not now, perhaps not ever. You will have to live with this uncertainty, and it may take time to adjust. You might have to make peace with not knowing or come to your own conclusions based on the information you do have. Draw satisfaction from being brave enough to seek out the truth and ask the questions.

Memory Bank

Gail received a reply from her aunt in response to a letter sent asking for information. Here's part of what it said. It shows what can happen when you ask.

Dear Gail,

Letter writing to a family member is not only appropriate, but a very effective way of being heard without fear of interruption, distraction, or rejection.

I can't make excuses for my husband, I can only tell you that months ago I gave him the names and addresses of his cousins; people to whom I write letters in Christmas cards every year, people whose faces I cannot even recall for the times we've actually met were so few, and they just got lost in the shuffle. The connection he feels toward those people in his life is minimal. That attitude, however, does not extend to his feelings toward you.

In your quest for inner peace and a sense of continuity in your life, you must add to that equation the sum total of others' motivations, conscious or subconscious, in maintaining their own equilibrium. In other words—don't try to figure out why Bob behaves as he does—if you need something, ask him! You'd be amazed how well persistence pays off.

I cannot speak for Bob, but since the letter was also addressed to me, I can speak for myself. I too, unfortunately, have considerable experience in the "delayed grief and healing process." Having lost my mother at the age of sixteen, and at the age of forty-five having just completed six years of therapy, I find that I will probably always be a bit impaired by the enormity of that loss.

You need to know that exploring the impact of your mother's death on you is paramount to moving on, but when a tragedy like that hits a family, no one is ever quite the same. I once read a quote by someone famous, I forget who, but it read: "Women live on their memories, men survive by forgetting and moving on." Well, thank God for women!!!

I know that casting about for reasons why someone has disappointed you is understandable. No one is seeking to punish you— we salute your efforts to fill the giant void left when you lost your mother.

Trust your instincts. Talk to Bob about your feelings. You'd be surprised how important you are to him. He doesn't want you to become another relative to whom his wife jots a card each Christmas.

Keep reaching, keep searching—it's amazing how much better the world looks when you don't have a gaping hole in your heart. We love you . . . we wish you good luck.

What questions do you still need to ask?

What I Need to Know	*Who* Might Have the Answer	*How* I Can Approach Them
Why I Resist	*When* I Will Try to Ask	*What Happened* When I Asked

Are there other sources you need to consult? List them below.

Source _____

Source _____

Source _____

Key Passages

After you've entered your final Key Passages, flip through the workbook and reread your statements. See if there are common threads or surprising results. Use them as a springboard for an entirely new Safe Passage.

Chapter 11

_____

_____

Chapter 12

_____

_____

Chapter 13

_____

_____

Date:_____

_____

_____

_____

_____

_____

_____

_____

_____

_____

_____

We sincerely hope the time, energy, and effort you've exerted has meant a few struggles lessened, fresh connections made, and hurt and anger diminished. As a touchstone to assess where you've been, how you feel, and what you've accomplished in the final part of the workbook, reflect on the questions below.

How did I feel as I worked through these chapters?

How do I feel right now?

What surprised me about my responses or insights?

What was hardest to do?

What do I need to come back to?

What have I accomplished?

What can I do for myself right now?

> *Be patient toward all that is unsolved in your heart and try to love the questions themselves. Do not seek answers that cannot be given you because you would not be able to live them, and the point is to live everything; live the questions now; perhaps you will gradually, without noticing it, live along some distant day into the answers.*
>
> —*Rainer Maria Rilke*

REFERENCE NOTES

Books/Journals/Pamphlets

Abrams, Jeremy. *Reclaiming the Inner Child.* Los Angeles: Jeremy Tarcher, 1990.

Altschul, Sara, ed. *Childhood Bereavement and Its Aftermath.* Madison, Conn.: International University Press, 1988.

Ascher, Barbara Lazear. *Landscape without Gravity.* Harrison, N.Y.: Delphinium Books, 1992.

Baker, John E., Mary Ann Sedney, and Esther Gross. "Psychological Tasks for Bereaved Children." *American Journal of Orthopsychiatry,* January 1992, pp. 105–116.

Bassoff, Evelyn. *Mothers and Daughers: Loving and Letting Go.* New York: NAL Dutton, 1988.

Bowlby, John. *Attachment.* Vol. 1, *Attachment and Loss.* New York: Basic Books, 1980.

———. *Loss, Sadness, and Depression.* Vol. 2, *Attachment and Loss.* New York: Basic Books, 1980.

———. *The Making and Breaking of Affectional Bonds.* London: Tavistock, 1979.

———. *A Secure Base.* New York: Basic Books, 1988.

———. *Separation Anxiety and Anger.* Vol. 3, *Attachment and Loss.* New York: Basic Books, 1980.

Bradshaw, John. *Family Secrets.* New York: Bantam, 1995.

———. *Homecoming.* New York: Bantam, 1992.

Brooks, Barbara, and Paula Siegel. *The Scared Child.* New York: John Wiley & Sons, 1996.

Covey, Steven R. *The Seven Habits of Highly Successful People.* New York: Simon & Schuster, 1989.

Crain, William. *Theories of Development.* 3rd ed. Englewood Cliffs, N.J.: Prentice Hall, 1992.

Davis, Laura. *The Courage to Heal Workbook.* New York: Harper & Row, 1990.

Del Zoppo, Patrick. *Passages in Teen Grief.* New York: Richmond Institute, 1993.

———. *Pastoral Bereavement Counseling.* New York: Rosemont, 1993.

———. *To Be Lifted Up: The Journey from Grief to Healing.* New York: Archdiocese of New York, 1989.

Doka, Kenneth J. *Disenfranchised Grief.* New York: Macmillan, 1989.

———. *Living with Life Threatening Illness.* New York: Macmillan, 1993.

Doka, Kenneth J., ed. *Children Mourning, Mourning Children.* Washington, D.C.: Hospice Foundation of America, 1995.

———. *Living with Grief after Sudden Loss.* Washington, D.C.: Hospice Foundation of America, 1996.

Dunne, Edward J., and others. *Suicide and Its Aftermath.* New York: W. W. Norton, 1987.

Edelman, Hope. *Motherless Daughters.* Reading, Mass.: Addison-Wesley, 1994.

Fitzgerald, Helen. *The Mourning Handbook.* New York: Simon & Schuster, 1994.

Forward, Susan. *Toxic Parents.* New York: Bantam, 1989.

Frankiel, Rita V., ed. *Essential Papers on Object Loss.* New York: New York University Press, 1994.

Friday, Nancy. *My Mother, My Self.* New York: Dell, 1977.

Furman, Erna. *A Child's Parent Dies.* New Haven: Yale University Press, 1974.

Gabbard, Glen O. *Psychodynamic Psychiatry in Clinical Practice: The DSM IV Edition.* Washington, D.C.: American Psychiatric Press, 1994.

Gaensbauer, Theo, and others. "Traumatic Loss in a One Year Old Girl," *Journal of the American Academy of Child and Adolescent Psychiatry* 34, no. 4 (1995).

Gershon, David, and Gail Straub. *Empowerment.* New York: Dell, 1989.

Gheisar, Bookda. *An Unfinished Story.* From *I Remember You: A Grief Journal,* Laynee Wild. San Francisco: HarperSanFrancisco, 1995.

Goldberg, Natalie. *Wild Mind.* New York: Bantam, 1990.

Goleman, Daniel. *Vital Lies, Simple Truths.* New York: Simon & Schuster, 1985.

Greene, Roberta R., and Paul H. Ephross. *Human Behavior Theory and Social Work Practice.* New York: Aldine De Gruyter, 1991.

Grollman, Earl A. *Bereaved Children and Teens.* Boston: Beacon Press, 1995.

———. *Explaining Death to Children.* Boston: Beacon Press, 1967.

Harris, Maxine. *The Loss That Is Forever.* New York: Dutton, 1995.

Imber-Black, Evan. *Secrets in Families and Family Therapy.* New York: W. W. Norton, 1993.

Imber-Black, Evan, and Janine Roberts. *Rituals for Our Times.* New York: Harper Perennial, 1993.

Jones, Constance. *R.I.P.: The Complete Book of Death and Dying.* New York: Harper Perennial, 1997.

Kaufman, Gershen. *Shame: The Power of Caring.* Rochester, Vt.: Schenkman Books, 1992.

Klass, Dennis, Phyllis Silverman, and Steven L. Nickman, eds. *Continuing Bonds.* Washington, D.C.: Taylor & Francis, 1996.

Kübler-Ross, Elizabeth. *Death: The Final Stage of Growth.* New York: Simon & Schuster, 1975.

Leman, Kevin, and Randy Carlson. *Unlocking the Secrets of Your Childhood Memories.* Nashville, Tenn.: Thomas Nelson, 1989.

McGoldrick, Monica, and Randy Gerson. *Genograms in Family Assessment.* New York: W. W. Norton, 1985.

Miller, Alice. *The Drama of the Gifted Child.* New York: Basic Books, 1981.

Miller, Patricia H., ed. *Theories of Development.* New York: W. H. Freeman, 1989.

Moffat, Mary Jane, ed. *In the Midst of Winter.* New York: Vintage, 1992.

Murray Parkes, Colin, and Joan Stevenson-Hinde, eds. *The Place of Attachment in Human Behavior.* New York: Basic Books, 1982.

O'Barr, Jean F., Deborah Pope, and Mary Wyer. *Ties That Bind.* Chicago: University of Chicago Press, 1990.

O'Toole, Donna. *Facing Change.* Burnsville, N.C.: Compassion Books, 1995.

Pennebaker, James W. "Traumatic Experience and Psychosomatic Disease," *Canadian Psychology 26,* 1985.

Pipher, Mary. *Reviving Ophelia.* New York: Grosset/Putnam, 1994.

Potter-Efron, Ronald and Patricia. *Letting Go of Shame.* San Francisco: HarperSanFrancisco, 1989.

Quindlen, Anna. *One True Thing.* New York: Random House, 1994.

Rando, Therese A. *Grief, Dying and Death.* Champaign, Ill.: Research Press, 1993.

———. "Complications in Mourning Traumatic Death." From *Living with Grief after Sudden Loss,* Kenneth J. Doka, ed. Washington, D.C.: Hospice Foundation of America, 1996.

———. *How to Go On Living When Someone You Love Dies.* New York: Bantam, 1991.

———. *Treatment of Complicated Mourning.* Champaign, Ill.: Research Press, 1993.

Schaefer, Dan, and Christine Lyons. *How Do We Tell the Children?* New York: Newmarket Press, 1993.

Seligman, Martin E. *Helplessness.* New York: W. H. Freeman, 1992.

Shapiro, Esther R. *Grief as a Family Process.* New York: Guilford Press, 1994.

Sher, Barbara. *Wishcraft: How to Get What You Really Want.* New York: Ballantine, 1993.

Silverman, Phyllis, and J. William Worden. "Children's Reactions in the Early Months after the Death of a Parent." *American Journal of Orthopsychiatry,* January 1992.

Solnit, Albert J., and others, eds. *The Psychoanalytic Study of the Child.* Vol. 49. New Haven: Yale University Press, 1994.

Sprang, Ginny, and John McNeil. *The Many Faces of Bereavement.* New York: Brunner Mazel, 1995.

Staudacher, Carol. *A Time to Grieve.* San Francisco: HarperSanFrancisco, 1994.

Walsh, Froma, and Monica McGoldrick. *Living beyond Loss.* New York: W. W. Norton, 1991.

Webb, Nancy Boyd, ed. *Helping Bereaved Children.* New York: Guilford Press, 1993.

Woititz, Janet G. *Healthy Parenting.* New York: Simon & Schuster, 1992.

Worden, J. William. *Grief Counseling and Grief Therapy.* New York: Springer, 1982.

Young, Jeffrey E., and Janet S. Klosko. *Reinventing Your Life.* New York: NAL Dutton, 1994.

Other Sources

Arlen, Susan. "People Aren't Goldfish." *Bereavement Magazine,* September 1993.

Ascher, Barbara Lazear. "How to Free Yourself from Anger." *Self,* February 1995.

———. "A Time to Grieve." *Self,* September 1994.

daughterspeak Newsletter Summer 1995.

Doka, Ken. "Transformative Grief—Loss as an Opportunity for Growth." New England Center for Loss and Transition *Grief Letter* 2, no. 1 (1996).

"How to Remember a Loved One at the Holidays." New England Center for Loss and Transition *Grief Letter* 1, no. 1 (1995).

Landers, Ann. *New York Daily News,* April 27, 1989.

"Letter to the Editor." *People,* August 24, 1994.

"Write of Passage." *People,* October 9, 1995.

Rando, Therese A. "Treating Guilt." New England Center for Loss and Transition *Grief Letter* 2, no. 2 (1996).

Silverman, Phyllis. Interview. New England Center for Loss and Transition *Grief Letter* 2, no. 2 (1996).

"The Bride Wore White—and Black." *New York Times Magazine,* September 29, 1996.

"Rosie . . . Really." *TV Guide,* June 15, 1996.

"Madonna's Moment." *Vogue,* October 1996.

Neil Simon appearance on the *Charlie Rose Show,* November 29, 1996.
Bill Clinton appearance on *Primetime Live,* October, 30, 1996.

Suggested Reading

Bass, Ellen, and Laura Davis. *The Courage to Heal: A Guide for Women Survivors of Child Sexual Abuse.* New York: Harper & Row, 1988.

Beattie, Melody. *Beyond Codependency.* San Francisco: Harper & Row, 1989.

Bode, Janet. *Death Is Hard to Live With.* New York: Delacorte Press, 1993.

Booth, Father Leo. *Spirituality and Recovery.* Deerfield Beach, Fla.: Health Communications, 1985.

Boston Women's Health Book Collective. *The New Our Bodies, Ourselves.* New York: Simon & Schuster, 1984.

Bradshaw, John. *Bradshaw On: The Family.* Deerfield Beach, Fla.: Health Communications, 1988.

———. *Creating Love.* New York: Bantam, 1992.

———. *Healing the Shame That Binds You.* Deerfield Beach, Fla.: Health Communications, 1988.

Campbell, David. *If You Don't Know Where You're Going, You'll Probably End Up Somewhere Else.* Valencia, Calif.: Tabor, 1974.

Covey, Steven R., Roger Merrill, and Rebecca R. Merrill. *First Things First.* New York: Simon & Schuster, 1994.

Dominguez, Joe, and Vicki Robin. *Your Money or Your Life.* New York: Penguin Books, 1992.

Dowling, Colette. *You Mean I Don't Have to Feel This Way?* New York: Charles Scribner's Sons, 1991.

Dyer, Wayne. *Real Magic: Creating Miracles in Everyday Life.* New York: HarperCollins, 1992.

Edelman, Hope. *Letters from Motherless Daughters.* New York: Delta, 1995.

Fitzgerald, Helen. *The Grieving Child.* New York: Simon & Schuster, 1992.

Frey, Diane, and C. Jesse Carlock. *Enhancing Self Esteem.* 2nd ed. Muncie, Ind.: Accelerated Development, 1989.

Gaylin, Willard. *Feelings.* New York: Harper & Row, 1979.

Goldberg, Natalie. *Writing Down the Bones.* Boston: Shambhala, 1986.

Graves, Sandra. *Expressions of Healing: Embracing the Process of Grief.* Hollywood, Calif.: Newcastle Publishing, 1994.

James, Muriel. *It's Never Too Late to Be Happy.* Reading, Mass.: Addison-Wesley, 1985.

Jampolsky, Gerald. *Love Is Letting Go of Fear.* Berkeley: Celestial Arts, 1979.

McFarland, Barbara, and Tyeis Baker-Baumann. *Feeding the Empty Heart: Adult Children and Compulsive Eating.* Center City, Minn.: Hazelden, 1988.

Moore, Thomas. *The Care of the Soul.* New York: Harper Perennial, 1992.

Novak, Philip. *The World's Wisdom.* New York: HarperCollins, 1994.

Oech, Roger von. *A Whack on the Side of the Head: How You Can Be More Creative.* New York: Warner Books, 1983.

O'Gorman, Patricia A., and Philip Oliver-Diaz. *Self-Parenting 12-Step Workbook: Windows to Your Inner Child.* Deerfield Beach, Fla.: Health Communications, 1990.

———. *12 Steps to Self-Parenting: For Adult Children of Alcoholics.* Deerfield Beach, Fla.: Health Communications, 1988.

Peale, Norman Vincent. *The Power of Positive Thinking.* New York: Fawcett Crest Books, 1952.

Pollard, John K., III. *Self Parenting: The Complete Guide to Your Inner Conversations.* Malibu, Calif.: Generic Human Studies, 1987.

Powell, John. *Why Am I Afraid to Tell You Who I Am?* Valencia, Calif.: Tabor, 1969.

Rinpoche, Sogyal. *The Tibetan Book of Living and Dying.* New York: HarperCollins, 1992.

Siegel, Bernie S. *Peace, Love and Healing.* New York: Harper & Row, 1989.

Sinetar, Marsha. *Do What You Love, the Money Will Follow.* New York: Dell, 1987.

Solly, Richard, and Roseann Lloyd. *Journey Notes.* New York: Harper/Hazelden, 1989.

Viorst, Judith. *Necessary Losses.* New York: Simon & Schuster, 1986.

Waitley, Denis. *The Psychology of Winning.* New York: Berkley, 1979.

RESOURCES

The Motherless Daughters Organization

Motherless Daughters[1]
Prince Street Station
P.O. Box 663
New York, NY 10012
212-614-8041

Motherless Daughters was founded in 1995 by five New York City women—Melissa Cook, Hope Edelman, Gail Eisenberg, Diane Hambrook, and Jane Weston Wilson—who had lost their mothers during childhood and adolescence. The organization was formed to provide support, community, and resources to women and girls who have experienced early mother loss. It is committed to bringing together motherless daughters, otherwise isolated, to encourage healing among them and to promote awareness about the long-lasting effects of such a loss. It publishes a newsletter, *daughterspeak,* three times a year.

For more information about the organization, the services it provides, and the cities that currently run Motherless Daughters® Support Groups, please send a standard-size self-addressed stamped envelope to the above address.

---

[1]We have found these organizations generally helpful. Inclusion on this list is not meant to imply their endorsement of this workbook.

Bereavement, Death and Dying

American Association of Suicidology
2459 South Ash Street
Denver, CO 80222
303-692-0985

American Suicide Foundation
1045 Park Avenue
New York, NY 10028
800-531-4477

Organizations above are survivor support groups for families and friends of a suicide.

Association for Death Education and Counseling
638 Prospect Avenue
Hartford, CT 06015
203-232-4825

Center for Loss and Transition
3735 Broken Bow Road
Ft. Collins, CO 80526

Organizations above offer published material on grieving and present educational workshops for the general public.

Dougy Center
3909 SE 52nd Avenue
Portland, OR 97286
503-775-5683

A center for grieving children and the people in their lives.

National Center for Death Education
Mt. Ida College
777 Dedham Street
Newton Center, MA 02159
617-969-7000

A resource center for bereavement and grief issues.

National Directory of Bereavement Support Groups and Services
ADM Publishing
P.O. Box 751155
Forest Hills, NY 11375-8755

A directory of bereavement support groups; Mary Wong, editor. Available in bookstores.

National Hospice Organization
1901 N. Moore Street, Suite 901
Arlington, VA 22209

Information on bereavement issues and services.

New England Center for Loss and Transition
P.O. Box 292
Guilford, CT 06437-0292
203-458-1734

An educational resource; publishes newsletter on issues of grief and bereavement.

Project on Death in America
Open Society
888 Seventh Avenue
New York, NY 10106
212-887-0150

An organization dedicated to educating and transforming the culture and experience of dying and bereavement in the United States.

On-Line

The Motherless Daughters Web Site
http://www.dfwnet.com

The Mother Loss Home Page provides a place to honor mothers.
http://www.win.bright.net/~cnelson/Motherloss.html

GriefNet is a virtual social service community with on-line support groups for grievers.
http://www.dspace.dial.pipex.com

Crisis, Grief and Healing is a site to post messages of grief and find links to relevant subjects and resources.
http://www.webhealing.com

Alcohol and Substance Abuse

Alcoholics Anonymous
General Services Office
475 Riverside Drive, 11th Floor
New York, NY 10115
212-870-3400

Alcohol and Drug Helpline
800-821-4357

Al-Anon
P.O. Box 862
Midtown Station
New York, NY 10018
800-356-9996

Alateen
P.O. Box 862
Midtown Station
New York, NY 10018
800-344-2666

Cocaine Helpline
800-Cocaine
Narcotics Anonymous
818-780-3951

National Clearinghouse for Alcohol and Drug Information
P.O. Box 2345
Rockville, MD 20847-2345
800-475-Hope

National Council on Alcohol and Drugs
800-475-Hope

Child Welfare

National Resource Center on Child Sexual Abuse
107 Lincoln Street
Huntsville, AL 35801
205-534-6868

A source of information on available resources.

Domestic Violence

Clearinghouse on Family Violence Information
P.O. Box 1182
Washington, DC 20013
703-385-7565

Domestic Violence Hotline
800-333-7233
National Family Violence Hotline
800-222-2000

All of the above are resource centers for information.

Eating Disorders

National Anorexic Aid Society
445 E. Granville Road
Worthington, OH 43085
614-436-1112

Resources and information on getting help for anorexia.

National Association of Anorexia Nervosa and Associated Disorders
Box 7
Highland Park, IL 60035
708-831-3438

Information, education, and resources on anorexia and other eating disorders.

National Eating Disorders Organization
Laureate Eating Disorders Program
6655 S. Yale Avenue
Tulsa, OK 74136
918-481-4044

Overeaters Anonymous
P.O. Box 44020
Rio Rancho, NM 87194
505-891-2664

A 12-step program for people who suffer from eating disorders.

Empowerment

Empowerment Newsletter
449A Route 28A
West Hurley, NY 12491
914-331-1312

A newsletter written by David Gershon and Gail Staub, authors of *Empowerment.*

Mental Health

Alliance of Information and Referral Systems
P.O. Box 3546
Joliet, IL 60434
815-744-6922

A professional association providing information and a referral service.

Anxiety Disorders Association of America
6100 Executive Boulevard, Suite 200
Rockville, MD 20852
301-231-9350

Information on professional treatment, support groups, and publications.

Council on Anxiety Disorders
P.O. Box 17011
Winston-Salem, NC 27116
919-722-7760

Education, advocacy, and support groups for people with anxiety disorders.

National Depressive and Manic Depressive Association
730 N. Franklin, Suite 501
Chicago, IL 60610
800-826-3632

Support and information for individuals with depressive illnesses and their families.

Obsessive-Compulsive Anonymous
P.O. Box 215
New Hyde Park, NY 11040
516-741-4901

12-step support groups for people with obsessive-compulsive disorder.

Parenting

Family Resource Coalition
200 S. Michigan Avenue, Suite 1520
Chicago, IL 60604-2404

Community support and resources to strengthen and empower families.

National Association of Mother's Centers
64 Division Avenue
Levittown, NY 11756
516-520-2929

An organization that supports and educates mothers.

National Organization of Single Mothers
P.O. Box 68
Midland, NC 28107
704-888-KIDS

Phone support, a pen-pal program, legal and psychological advice.

Sexual Abuse

National Resource Center on Child Sexual Abuse
107 Lincoln Street
Huntsville, AL 35801
205-534-6868
800-KIDS-006
800-227-5242

Resources and help for children who have been or are suspected of being abused.

Parents United International
615 15th Street
Modesto, CA 95354-2510
209-573-3446

Treatment for child sexual abuse; groups for victims, family members, and perpetrators.

Stepfamilies

Stepfamily Association of America
215 Centennial Mall, Suite 212
Lincoln, NE 68508-1814
800-735-0329

Helpful resources for members of step or blended families.